Wissenschaftliche Untersuchungen
zum Neuen Testament · 2. Reihe

Herausgeber / Editor
Jörg Frey (Zürich)

Mitherausgeber / Associate Editors
Friedrich Avemarie (Marburg)
Markus Bockmuehl (Oxford)
James A. Kelhoffer (Uppsala)
Hans-Josef Klauck (Chicago, IL)

316

Robert Matthew Calhoun

Paul's Definitions of the Gospel in Romans 1

Mohr Siebeck

ROBERT MATTHEW CALHOUN, born 1971; studied at University of Chicago, Humanities Division, Department of New Testament and Early Christian Literature; 2011 PhD.

ISBN 978-3-16-150949-0
ISSN 0340-9570 (Wissenschaftliche Untersuchungen zum Neuen Testament, 2. Reihe)

Die Deutsche Nationalbibliothek lists this publication in the Deutsche Nationalbibliographie; detailed bibliographic data are available on the Internet at *http://dnb.d-nb.de*.

© 2011 by Mohr Siebeck, Tübingen, Germany.

This book may not be reproduced, in whole or in part, in any form (beyond that permitted by copyright law) without the publisher's written permission. This applies particularly to reproductions, translations, microfilms and storage and processing in electronic systems.

The book was printed by Laupp & Göbel in Nehren on non-aging paper and bound by Buchbinderei Nädele in Nehren.

Printed in Germany.

In memoriam

Kiowa Tumok Garcia

December 28, 1971 – July 2, 2009

Preface and Acknowledgements

The present study, a revised version of my doctoral dissertation, investigates two passages in Paul's letter to the Romans, 1:2–4 and 16–17, in which he defines 'gospel' in distinct ways, using a complex array of methods. My thesis and arguments herein grow directly from the ancient philosophical and rhetorical theoretical sources. The decision to follow this path has two main consequences that require articulation here in the preface. First, I try to avoid bland citations, in other words, references in the text or footnotes to passages from ancient authors that give little information about what they are saying or why it matters. I therefore often give lengthy quotations of the Greek, Latin, or Hebrew texts, so that the reader may readily judge their relevance for my arguments. My translations tend toward the literal, sometimes at the expense of good English idiom, in order to render my interpretive decisions as clear as possible. The bibliography includes all of the editions from which I took the quotations, along with more idiomatic English translations, where available (some of the rhetorical theory remains untranslated in any modern language), for the reader's convenience. Second, my interactions with the vast body of modern secondary literature on Paul and his letter to the Romans are selective, illustrative, and by no means complete. The study deals foremost with Rom 1:2–4 and 16–17, how the ancient sources impact interpretation of those verses, and, at key points, how patristic readers help us to perceive useful connections between them. (In order to minimize bibliographic clutter, I normally cite the author's surname and the abbreviated title; one may find full references in the bibliography.)

Over the course of my study at the University of Chicago, I have accumulated many debts of gratitude that I am delighted now to pay. My committee and professors in the Department of New Testament and Early Christian Literature have exhibited extraordinary mentorship, patience, and generosity. Prof. Margaret M. Mitchell, my advisor, read the manuscript with a careful eye to the little and the big: the little in finding various errors and correcting problems with my translations, and the big in asking penetrating questions of my logic, and in applying her enormous erudition toward challenging my arguments. Prof. Elizabeth Asmis gave superb advice on the rhetorical and philosophical sources. Prof. Hans Dieter Betz, who retired many years ago, generously continued to read my work and share his vast expertise. Profs. Hans

Josef Klauck and David Martinez, who were present on several occasions upon which I presented portions of the dissertation, gave extremely helpful advice that has enriched the final product. Several friends and colleagues read parts of the manuscript and endured interminable hours of listening to me thinking out loud: Matthew C. Baldwin, Meira Z. Kensky, James A. Kelhoffer, Clare K. Rothschild, Janet E. Spittler, Trevor W. Thompson, and D. Dale Walker. It goes without saying that, with such a learned group of readers, any remaining faults are to be attributed solely to my stubborn refusal to heed their advice.

My study of early Christian literature began at Abilene Christian University under the tutelage of an excellent faculty. Three persons in particular were instrumental in stoking my curiosity and equipping me for future research: Profs. John T. Willis, Thomas C. Geer, Jr., and Jack Reese. I also thank three professors with whom I took numerous seminars at Chicago, and who have influenced me profoundly: Profs. Christopher A. Faraone of the Classics Department, and Adela Yarbro Collins and John J. Collins, now of Yale Divinity School.

The Christian Scholarship Foundation provided generous support for the academic years of 2002–2003 and 2003–2004. I thank the Foundation and its director, Prof. Carl R. Holladay of Emory University's Candler School of Theology.

My family and friends have been and remain a constant source of encouragement, without which I would have not been able to endure. This has been a labor of love; I know what love means because of them: my grandmother, Vera Nell Ellis; my mother Sandra Calhoun; my father and stepmother, Robert Lynn and Julie Calhoun; my siblings Andrew, Amanda, Daniel and Anna Grace; and a group of friends, too many to list, who helped me to maintain a precarious balance of sanity.

Finally, I thank Prof. Jörg Frey of Universität Zürich and Dr. Henning Ziebritzki of Mohr Siebeck for the honor of including my contribution in WUNT II, and Ms. Tanja Idler of Mohr Siebeck for her kind and thorough attention to detail in helping me to prepare the manuscript for publication.

I dedicate this project to the memory of a friend, Kiowa Tumok Garcia, who tragically took his own life on July 2, 2009.

Chicago
October, 2011

Table of Contents

Preface..VII

Table of Contents... IX

List of Abbreviations... XI

Chapter 1: Introduction.. 1

Chapter 2: The Features and Functions of Definition in Ancient Philosophy and Rhetoric..9

   2.1 Introduction..9
   2.2 The foundation: Plato's *Phaedrus*...10
   2.3 Rhetorical vs. philosophical definition 15
   2.4 Rhetorical definition in theory and practice...................................24
      2.4.1 Forensic oratory.. 24
      2.4.2 Deliberative oratory.. 29
      2.4.3 Epideictic oratory..33
   2.5 Conclusion... 38

Chapter 3: The Ancient Rhetorical Theorists on Brevity..........................39

   3.1 Introduction 39
   3.2 The utility of brevity 40
      3.2.1 Brevity as an ἀρετή of style 42
      3.2.2 Brevity in the opening sections of an oration...................... 49
      3.2.3 Brevity in epistolary style... 55
      3.2.4 Demetrius on the rhetorical impact of brevity..................... 59
   3.3 The methods of brevity 63
      3.3.1 The τεχναί and προγυμνάσματα on brevity of content and style................64
      3.3.2 Brevity as a rhetorical figure or trope................................... 67
      3.3.3 The figure of ἔλλειψις...71
      3.3.4 The figure or trope of συνεκδοχή..76
      3.3.5 The figure of ἀπὸ κοινοῦ..79
   3.4 Conclusion: brevity and Pauline exegesis......................................80

Chapter 4: The First Definition of the Gospel (1:2–4)............................. 85

   4.1 Introduction... 85
   4.2 The structure of the prescript (1:1–7).. 87
   4.3 The basic definition (1:2–3a)... 90

    4.4 The definition extended (1:3b–4) 91
        4.4.1 Is Rom 1:3b–4 a pre-Pauline formula? 92
        4.4.2 The mythological expanded epithet 106
        4.4.3 Mythological expanded epithets in the letters of Paul 119
        4.4.4 Analysis of 1:3b–4 123
    4.5 Conclusion 141

Chapter 5: The Second Definition of the Gospel (1:16–17) 143

    5.1 Introduction 143
    5.2 'Thanksgiving': the introduction continued (1:8–15) 144
    5.3 The basic definition (1:16) 147
        5.3.1 Divine power and salvation 149
        5.3.2 Faith and universalism 152
    5.4 Abbreviated proof (1:17) 156
        5.4.1 Δικαιοσύνη θεοῦ as divine justice 157
        5.4.2 Ἔλλειψις in ἐκ πίστεως εἰς πίστιν 169
        5.4.3 The quotation of Hab 2:4 187
    5.5 Conclusion 190

Chapter 6: Paul's Exegesis of His Definitions in Romans 193

    6.1 Introduction 193
    6.2 Rom 3:1–8 194
    6.3 Rom 3:21–31 197
    6.4 "The faithfulness of Jesus Christ" (3:22, 26)? 204
    6.5 Rom 9:1–10:21 212
    6.6 Conclusion 218

Chapter 7: Conclusion 219

Bibliography 223

Index of Ancient Sources 247

Index of Modern Authors 263

Index of Subjects 267

List of Abbreviations

The symbol * indicates that the abbreviation in question has a fuller citation in the bibliography of modern works; the symbol † indicates a fuller citation under the corpora of ancient works. The abbreviation conventions generally conform to those specified in Patrick Alexander, et al., editors, *The SBL Handbook of Style* (Peabody, Mass.: Hendrickson, 1999).

AB	Anchor Bible
ABD	Friedman, et al., *Anchor Bible Dictionary**
AET	Malherbe, *Ancient Epistolary Theorists*†
AJP	*American Journal of Philology*
Allen/Greenough	Greenough, et al., *Allen and Greenough's New Latin Grammar*
Althaus, *an die Römer*	Althaus, *Der Brief an die Römer* (NTD)*
ANRW	Temporini, Haase and Vogt, *Aufstieg und Niedergang der römischen Welt*
ANTC	Abingdon New Testament Commentaries
APAACS	American Philological Association, American Classical Studies
Barrett, *Romans*	Barrett, *A Commentary on the Epistle to the Romans* (HNTC)*
BDAG	Bauer, Danker, Arndt and Gingrich, *Greek-English Lexicon**
BDB	Brown, Driver and Briggs, *Hebrew and English Lexicon of the Old Testament**
BDF	Blass, Debrunner and Funk, *Greek Grammar**
BNP	Cancik and Schneider, *Brill's New Pauly**
BRS	Biblical Resource Series
Budé	Collection des universités de France, publiée sons le patronage de l'Association Guillaume Budé
CBET	Contributions to Biblical Exegesis and Theology
CBQ	*Catholic Biblical Quarterly*
CCS	Cambridge Classical Studies
CCSL	Corpus cristianorum: Series latina
C.H.	Nock and Festugière, *Corpus Hermeticum*†
CJ	*Classical Journal*
CQ	*Classical Quarterly*
Cranfield, *Romans*	Cranfield, *A Critical and Exegetical Commentary on the Epistle to the Romans* (ICC)*
CSEL	Corpus scriptorum ecclesiasticorum latinorum
CW	*Classical World*
DNP	Cancik and Schneider, *Der Neue Pauly**
Dodd, *Romans*	Dodd, *The Epistle of Paul to the Romans* (MNTC)*
Dunn, *Romans*	Dunn, *Romans* (WBC)*
EEC	Ferguson, *Encyclopedia of Early Christianity* (2nd ed.)*
EECh	Di Berardino, *Encyclopedia of the Early Church**
EKKNT	Evangelisch-katholischer Kommentar zum Neuen Testament

ESIC	Emory Studies in Early Christianity
EvT	*Evangelische Theologie*
ExpTim	*Expository Times*
FF	Foundations and Facets
Fitzmyer, *Romans*	Fitzmyer, *Romans* (AB)*
Furley/Bremer	Furley and Bremer, *Greek Hymns*†
García Martinez/ Tigchelaar	García Martinez and Tigchelaar, *Dead Sea Scrolls*†
GCS	Die griechisch-christlichen Schriftsteller der ersten [drei] Jahrhunderte
GKC	Gesenius, Kautzsch and Cowley, *Hebrew Grammar**
GRBS	*Greek, Roman and Byzantine Studies*
HB	*Hebrew Bible*
HNT	Handbuch zum Neuen Testament
HNTC	Harper's New Testament Commentaries
HSCP	*Harvard Studies in Classical Philology*
HTKNT	Herders theologischer Kommentar zum Neuen Testament
HUT	Hermeneutische Untersuchungen zur Theologie
ICC	International Critical Commentary
IDB	Buttrick, *Interpreter's Dictionary of the Bible*
JAC	*Jahrbuch für Antike und Christentum*
JBL	*Journal of Biblical Literature*
Jewett, *Romans*	Jewett, *Romans* (Hermeneia)*
JSNT	*Journal for the Study of the New Testament*
JSNTSup	*Journal for the Study of the New Testament* Supplement Series
JTS	*Journal of Theological Studies*
Käsemann, *Romans*	Käsemann, *Commentary on Romans**
Keck, *Romans*	Keck, *Romans* (ANTC)*
KEK	Kritisch-exegetischer Kommentar über das Neue Testament
Kirk/Raven	Kirk and Raven, *Presocratic Philosophers*†
KB	Koehler and Baumgartner, *Hebrew and Aramaic Lexicon*†
LAL	White, *Light from Ancient Letters*†
LCL	Loeb Classical Library
LEC	Library of Early Christianity
Lietzmann, *an die Römer*	Lietzmann, *Einführung in die Textgeschichte der Paulusbriefe; An die Römer* (HNT)*
LIMC	Ackerman and Gisler, *Lexicon iconographicum mythologiae classicae**
Lohse, *an die Römer*	Lohse, *Der Brief an die Römer* (KEK)*
Long/Sedley	Long and Sedley, *The Hellenistic Philosophers*†
LSJ	Liddell, Scott and Jones, *Greek-English Lexicon**
LXX	Septuagint
MNTC	Moffatt New Testament Commentary
MnemSup	*Mnemosyne* Supplement Series
Moo, *Romans*	Moo, *The Epistle to the Romans* (NICNT)
MS(S)	Manscript(s)
MT	Masoretic text
NAB	New American Bible
NEB	New English Bible
NIB	*New Interpreter's Bible*
NICNT	New International Commentary on the New Testament
NIV	New International Version

List of Abbreviations XIII

NovT	*Novum Testamentum*
NovTSup	*Novum Testamentum* Supplement Series
NRSV	New Revised Standard Version
NTAbh	Neutestamentliche Abhandlungen
NTD	Das Neue Testament Deutsch
NTS	*New Testament Studies*
NTTS	New Testament Tools and Studies
OCD	Hornblower and Spawforth, *Oxford Classical Dictionary* (3rd ed.)*
OCT	Oxford Classical Texts
OLD	Glare, *Oxford Latin Dictionary**
OTP	Charlesworth, *Old Testament Pseudepigrapha*†
PG	Migne, *Patrologia graeca**
PGL	Lampe, *Patristic Greek Lexicon**
PGM	Preisendanz and Henrichs, *Papyri graecae magicae*†
PKGK	Staab, *Pauluskommentare aus der griechischen Kirche*†
PVTG	Pseudepigrapha veteris testamenti graecae
RG	Spengel, *Rhetores graeci*†
RG-W	Walz, *Rhetores graeci*†
*RGG*⁴	Betz, ed., *Religion in Geschichte und Gegenwart* (4th ed.)*
RLM	Halm, *Rhetores latini minores*†
Sanday and Headlam, *Romans*	Sanday and Headlam, *A Critical and Exegetical Commentary on the Epistle to the Romans* (ICC)*
SBLDS	Society of Biblical Literature Dissertation Series
SBLRBS	Society of Biblical Literature Resources for Biblical Study
SBLSBS	Society of Biblical Literature Sources for Biblical Study
SBLTT	Society of Biblical Literature Texts and Translations
SBLWGRW	Society of Biblical Literature Writings from the Greco-Romans World
SD	Studies and Documents
Schlier, *Römerbrief*	Schlier, *Der Römerbrief* (HTKNT)*
Schmithals, *Römerbrief*	Schmithals, *Der Römerbrief**
Smyth	Smyth, *Greek Grammar**
SNT	Studien zum Neuen Testament
SNTSMS	Society for New Testament Studies Monograph Series
SBT	Studies in Biblical Theology
SGRR	Studies in Greek and Roman Religion
STAC	Studien und Texte zu Antike und Christentum
Stuhlmacher, *Romans*	Stuhlmacher, *Paul's Letter to the Romans**
SVF	Von Arnim, *Stoicorum veterum fragmenta*†
TAPA	*Transactions of the American Philological Association*
TDNT	Kittel and Friedrich, *Theological Dictionary of the New Testament**
Teubner	Biblioteca scriptorum graecorum et romanorum teubneriana
TDOT	*Theological Dictionary of the Old Testament**
TLG	Thesaurus linguae graecae
Totti	Totti, *Ausgewählte Texte der Isis- und Serapis-Religion*†
TSAJ	Texte und Studien zum Antiken Judentum
UUA	Uppsala Universitetsårskrift
VL	Vetus latina
Wilckens, *an die Römer*	Wilckens, *Der Brief an die Römer* (EKKNT)*
WUNT	Wissenschaftliche Untersuchungen zum Neuen Testament

Chapter 1

Introduction

In the seventeenth chapter of the book of Acts, the author poses an intriguing question: what if Paul, the great evangelist and hero of his narrative, were to have met and conversed with the eminent philosophers of his day? 'Luke' contrives a scenario wherein Paul has occasion to stop over in Athens while he awaits the arrival of his colleagues. Never one to waste an opportunity, Paul frequents the synagogues and street corners proclaiming the gospel. Meanwhile he notices with distress that Athens is κατείδωλος, "covered in idols." He also encounters other famous residents of the city, Stoic and Epicurean philosophers. Upon hearing his message, they describe him and it variously. He is a σπερμολόγος and a ξένων δαιμονίων καταγγελεύς, and the gospel a καινὴ διδαχή and ξενίζοντά τινα (17:18–20). They are obviously struggling to fit the square peg of the gospel into the round holes of phenomena more familiar to them. Surmising that Paul proclaims a foreign mystery cult, they ask: δυνάμεθα γνῶναι; βουλόμεθα οὖν γνῶναι τίνα θέλει ταῦτα εἶναι.

Luke humorously presents the philosophers as supercilious fad-chasers (17:21), but his characters in fact pose a serious question: if one were to ask the real Paul to elaborate what the gospel is in philosophical terms, how would he respond? The speech in Acts 17 lays out the gospel's origins in the action of a benevolent, if unknown, God "who made the world and all things in it" (ὁ ποιήσας τὸν κόσμον καὶ πάντα τὰ ἐν αὐτῷ, v. 24). He sketches the principles of philosophical piety which his audience would presumably likewise endorse, and then reaches the heart of the matter in vv. 30–31:

30 τοὺς μὲν οὖν χρόνους τῆς ἀγνοίας ὑπεριδὼν ὁ θεός, τὰ νῦν παραγγέλλει τοῖς ἀνθρώποις πάντας πανταχοῦ μετανοεῖν, 31 καθότι ἔστησεν ἡμέραν ἐν ᾗ μέλλει κρίνειν τὴν οἰκουμένην ἐν δικαιοσύνῃ ἐν ἀνδρὶ ᾧ ὥρισεν, πίστιν παρασχὼν πᾶσιν ἀναστήσας αὐτὸν ἐκ νεκρῶν.

30 Therefore God, after overlooking the times of ignorance, now commands humanity that all people everywhere must repent, 31 because he has fixed the day on which he is about to judge the universe with justice by a man whom he designated, furnishing proof to all by raising him from the dead.

Luke's Paul gives here a succinct summary of the gospel, a statement of the proclamation in a nutshell. He does not lay out the summary as a definition (the gospel is *a*, *b*, and *c*), but it could easily serve in lieu of a definition. He futhermore uses the verb ὁρίζειν which regularly occurs with the meaning "to define." Although the transition to vv. 30–31 may seem abrupt at first glance, it gathers previous parts of the speech through the concise repetition of key concepts.[1] His speech up to this point has dealt with the primordial past and the present, but now it looks ahead to the day of the judgment which God will execute with the assistance of Christ. In vv. 30–31, 'Paul' also abbreviates narrative elements of the gospel (Jesus' death, resurrection, and appointment) and eschatological ideas. If his audience were to have permitted him to continue his speech, he would presumably have unpacked this compression further,[2] but he collides with their skepticism regarding the possibility of resurrection (ἀνάστασις νεκρῶν, 17:32). Luke's Paul therefore gives in vv. 30–31 a concise and content-rich statement of the gospel's essence. As a part of the speech, the statement locates the gospel within a framework of philosophical piety, of worship properly rendered to a supramundane God, and merges this framework with the narrative of what God has done through Christ.

Luke's 'what-if' is in no way an idle question. It persists today in the continuing debates regarding the historical Paul's education and engagement with his Greco-Roman polytheistic environment. In spite of the protestations in his correspondence with the Corinthians to have little interest in the orator's elegances of style or the philosopher's lofty speculations and procedures (1 Cor 1:18–2:5), Paul's authentic letters recognizably draw from the vast fund of rhetorical techniques and philosophical methods of his day. He does not regard himself, of course, as foremost an orator or a philosopher. His identity as ἀπόστολος with a God-given responsibility to proclaim the gospel puts him in an altogether different category. He nonetheless wields the tools available to him to achieve his objectives, and he can 'switch hats' with bewildering suddenness. For example, in 1 Corinthians 15 he starts by reprising his role as an instructor in basic traditions (his readers' μυσταγωγός, as it were), then shifts to philosophical argumentation to defeat a proposition (ἀνάστασις νεκρῶν οὐκ ἔστιν) and to establish the kind of σῶμα that the resurrected dead will have,[3]

---

[1] Χρόνους in v. 30 recalls God's establishment of προστεταγμένους καιρούς in v. 26. Τῆς ἀγνοίας captures the blind groping after God in v. 27 (εἰ ἄρα γε ψηλαφήσειαν αὐτὸν καὶ εὕροιεν). With θεός 'Paul' concisely inserts his elaboration of the ἄγνωστος θεός in vv. 23–25, and with πάντας παντχοῦ the universalism of vv. 28–29, especially γένος οὖν ὑπάρχοντες θεοῦ. In v. 31, we find similar compressions: again, God's power to set times in ἔστησεν ἡμέραν; οἰκουμένη as the boundaries of human habitation (κατοικεῖν, κατοικίαν, v. 26); and the selection of a single person (ἐποίησέν τε ἐξ ἑνὸς πᾶν ἔθνος ἀνθρώπων) and his appointment (ὁρίσας, v. 26).

[2] Luke may provide a signal that Paul has more to say with τά in the phrase τὰ νῦν παραγγέλλει, which might mean: "he now commands the following things...." He is able to mention only the first because his audience interrupts him. On the other hand, τὰ νῦν may just mean "now" (so BDAG 681–82, s.v. νῦν, 2b).

[3] On philosophical argumentation in 1 Corinthians 15, see esp. Martin, *Corinthian Body*; Asher, *Polarity and Change*.

and along the way he discloses new "mysteries" as a prophet of the Parousia. He would not adopt these postures if he did not believe that they would work – in other words, that his addressees would regard the roles of transmitter of tradition, philosophical instructor, and prophet as both authoritative and familiar. Paul is clearly building upon the kinds of activities in which he was engaged when he was previously among the Corinthian Christians.

In the case of his letter to the Romans, he has no personal history with the majority of his audience. This does not mean, however, that the Roman Christians have no preconceptions of him. The fact that he goes back over territory which he covers in other contexts (particularly in Galatians and 1 Corinthians) strongly implies that he needs to do so, that the Roman Christians have heard about these arguments (or perhaps even read excerpts of them) from those who view him with suspicion or hostility.[4] His audience may thus have formed an unfavorable impression of him and his gospel. He must select his approach with great care if he will neutralize the residual negativity that may accompany his reputation, and make a new impression. The accomplishment of whatever goals he may have in writing to them – by no means a settled question among interpreters today – depends upon his audience's willingness to credit his authority as ἀπόστολος, to accept the validity of his previous evangelistic labors, and most of all to regard him as worth listening to.[5] He does not tell them of his call and commission (Gal 1:11–17), or of his accomplishments λόγῳ καὶ ἔργῳ, ἐν δυνάμει σημείων καὶ τεράτων, ἐν δυνάμει πνεύματος (Rom 15:18–19). Instead, he sends his letter as we have it before us.

Paul firmly indicates both the direction that the argument will go and the 'hat' that he elects to wear in the introductory sections of the letter. He appropriates therein a genre which properly has its home in Greco-Roman philosophy, but which enjoys widespread application in rhetorical contexts as well, namely *definition* (ὅρος). At the beginning and end of his introduction (προοίμιον), he offers two distinct definitions of the gospel. He folds the first (1:2–4) into the prescript. The second doubles as his thesis statement (πρόθεσις, 1:16–17), declaring in brief compass the entirety of the argument of Romans. In the present study I investigate these two definitions of the gospel: how Paul composes them, coordinates them, and deploys them in his argument. My thesis here has four components: (1) that vv. 2–4 and 16–17 comprise two coordinated definitions of τὸ εὐαγγέλιον, the former articulating *what it is* in terms of its content, and the latter *what it does* in terms of its function; (2) that Paul

---

[4] Romans 4 takes up the theme of Abraham's faith from Gal 3:6–18, and Romans 14–15 deal with the "weak" and the "strong," topics that he discusses in 1 Corinthians 8–9. Romans 2–3 also explain why the law cannot solve the problem of universal human culpability (cf. Gal 2:15–21). Also, the slander to which he refers in Rom 3:8 is more than rhetorical dressing: such portrayals of him and his gospel represent the kinds of things he expects the Romans to have heard.

[5] So also Stuhlmacher, "Apostle Paul's View of Righteousness," 76–77.

4   *Chapter 1: Introduction*

achieves the brevity necessary for definition with the rhetorical figures of συνεκδοχή (synecdoche), ἔλλειψις (omission), and ἀπὸ κοινοῦ (commonality); (3) that he deliberately invests vv. 16–17 with exploitable ambiguities in both the terminology and syntax; and (4) that his arguments proceed in part by 'exegeting the terms' of his essential and functional definitions, recombining their elements and maximizing the lexical meanings of their component terms along with their cognates toward a demonstration of how the gospel is God's δύναμις at work in the cosmos.

Scholars have occasionally noted that 1:2–4 and 16–17 are definitions,[6] although none has yet fully explored the implications that accompany this correct observation.[7] Ancient authors discuss definition at length, specifying what it is and what it should do, in both philosophical and rhetorical theoretical contexts. These discussions have direct bearing upon the composition of Paul's definitions of the gospel, so in chapter 2 I examine the theories of definition and study how orators use them in their speeches. One major conclu-

---

[6] E.g., Jewett (*Romans*, 99) calls 1:2–4 a "confessional definition of the gospel," but does not elaborate "definition" further. Similarly, vv. 16b and 17 each provide "a definition of the preceding contention about Paul not being ashamed of 'the gospel'" (ibid., 136). Again, Jewett leaves this point undeveloped. Stuhlmacher (*Romans*, 22) remarkably describes Rom "1:1ff." and 16–17 as a "twofold definition of the gospel"; see also idem, "Apostle Paul's View of Righteousness," 77–78. On Rom 1:16–17, Betz ("Christianity as Religion," 212–15) offers a short but incisive discussion of "the definition of the gospel." Note also that Betz approaches 12:1–2 as "two definitional statements," the first "of religion as voluntary self-sacrifice," and the second of "the apostle's concept of ethics" (ibid., 229–30; cf. idem, "Foundation of Christian Ethics"). Cf. Anderson (*Ancient Rhetorical Theory*, 216), who, on the basis of the ancient division of treatises into the categories of θέσις ("an argumentative treatment of the theme lacking the specifics of person and circumstances") and ὑπόθεσις ("an argumentative treatment of a specific case"), observes: "[I]t becomes clear that the theme of the letter to the Romans ... is much more reminiscent of a θέσις than a ὑπόθεσις. At that, it is much more reminiscent of a *philosophical* θέσις, than a rhetorical θέσις (which tended to deal with matters of public policy)."

[7] Scholars also rarely consider these two passages in light of each other. According to Bornkamm (*Paul*, 248–49), 1:3–4 "reproduces the Christology of the early (Jewish Christian) church," while 1:16–17 "is primitive Pauline and, unlike the purely Christological credo, is formulated in soteriological terms." "Both formulations," he continues, "are full and complete statements of the faith; they do not select from the gospel, the one the one thing and the other the other." Regarding the relationship between them, Bornkamm discounts the notion that "Paul quoted the traditional formula only in order to prove his orthodoxy." "The answer is not to be found in the (traditional) motif of Jesus as son of David ..., but rather in the honorific title 'Son of God'...." The soteriological event of the resurrection of Christ as God's *Son* plays out in what Christians are called to be: not "Christs" but "sons" and "heirs": "While these connections are not made explicit in Romans 1, as Paul understood it, 1:3 f. points forward to 1:16 f., and conversely, 1:16 f. points back to the credo as Paul reinterpreted it." Cf. also Fee (*Pauline Christology*, 240): "Verses 3–4 turn out to be one of the two places in the prooemium (1:1–17) where the gospel is given content." He contrasts vv. 3–4 and 16–17 based upon the christological emphasis of the former and the soteriological emphasis of the latter.

sion of this chapter is that definitions should be *brief*. In order to achieve the necessary brevity, authors have at their disposal another body of theoretical literature, which is devoted to techniques of condensing complex ideas into extremely concise statements. These tactics help authors to compress, and readers to decompress, definitions and other kinds of discourse that require brevity. Chapter 3 thus investigates methods of brevity, paying special attention to the rhetorical figures of ἔλλειψις, συνεκδοχή and ἀπὸ κοινοῦ, since Paul uses these figures to load his definitions of the gospel with implied content and multiple layers of meaning. In chapter 4, I analyze Rom 1:2–4, his first definition of the gospel, which declares *what it is*. It is that …

… 2 ὃ προεπηγγείλατο διὰ τῶν προφητῶν αὐτοῦ ἐν γραφαῖς ἁγίαις 3 περὶ τοῦ υἱοῦ αὐτοῦ τοῦ γενομένου ἐκ σπέρματος Δαυὶδ κατὰ σάρκα, 4 τοῦ ὁρισθέντος υἱοῦ θεοῦ ἐν δυνάμει κατὰ πνεῦμα ἁγιωσύνης ἐξ ἀναστάσεως νεκρῶν, Ἰησοῦ Χριστοῦ τοῦ κυρίου ἡμῶν.

… 2 which he [God] pre-proclaimed through his prophets in holy scriptures 3 concerning his Son, who was born from the seed of David according to the flesh, 4 who was appointed Son of God in power according to his spirit of holiness from his resurrection from the dead, Jesus Christ our Lord.

Research on these verses generally focuses upon their alleged inclusion of a 'pre-Pauline formula,' a hymnic or confessional fragment that scholars surmise Paul to have quoted or adapted. I argue instead that Paul composes them himself, using a literary form that often appears in hymns (the 'mythological expanded epithet'), thereby imparting to his first definition a hymnic flavor. With the rhetorical figure of συνεκδοχή, the definition gathers the entirety of scripture's testimony regarding Christ, and compresses the gospel's narrative content into a statement that describes him both temporally (his ἀρχή and τέλος) and anthropologically (his σάρξ and πνεῦμα). In chapter 5, I turn to Paul's careful composition of his second definition (1:16–17), which specifies the function of the gospel: "For I am not ashamed of the gospel, for it is God's power for salvation for everyone who believes, for both the Jew first and the Greek" (οὐ γὰρ ἐπαισχύνομαι τὸ εὐαγγέλιον, δύναμις γὰρ θεοῦ ἐστιν εἰς σωτηρίαν παντὶ τῷ πιστεύοντι, Ἰουδαίῳ τε πρῶτον καὶ Ἕλληνι). The definition also includes in v. 17 an abbreviated proof explaining how it can be God's δύναμις εἰς σωτηρίαν: "For God's justice is revealed in it from faith to faith, just as it has been written, 'The just one will live from faith'" (δικαιοσύνη γὰρ θεοῦ ἐν αὐτῷ ἀποκαλύπτεται ἐκ πίστεως εἰς πίστιν, καθὼς γέγραπται, «ὁ δὲ δίκαιος ἐκ πίστεως ζήσεται»). Paul designs vv. 16–17 as a statement of the gospel's cosmic function that makes sense in its context, that secures provisional endorsement from his addressees, and that invites the exposition which he will deliver in subsequent chapters. He futhermore takes full advantage of the ambiguities of meaning in some of the definition's key terms, particularly δύναμις, πίστις/πιστεύειν, and δικαιοσύνη. The ambiguity stands out especially in the difficult phrase ἐκ πίστεως εἰς πίστιν. Patristic readers of these verses often perceive Paul to have omitted some words (i.e., to have deployed the figure of ἔλλειψις), a helpful clue that I pursue at length. In chapter 6, I conclude the study with a brief examination of Paul's exegesis of the terms of the definition which he accomplishes by bringing forward their different meanings and recombining them to explore their implications.

Luke's 'what-if,' as projected in his narrative of Paul's visit to Athens, remains a product of his imagination, a hypothetical placement of Paul into a scenario where he delivers a speech to an audience of philosophers, adopts a persona as one of their peers, and explains the gospel in terms that they would recognize. In creating this scene, however, Luke builds upon a foundation laid by the apostle himself. Paul appropriates a philosophical mode of discourse in the opening sections of his letter to the Romans, wherein he also establishes his ἦθος and previews his themes and procedures. In setting forth his definitions of the gospel, he does not cast his addressees in the role of philosophers. But he certainly portrays them as more than capable of considering questions at a high intellectual level – as σοφοί, in other words, μεστοί ... ἀγαθωσύνης, πεπληρωμένοι πάσης [τῆς] γνώσεως, δυνάμενοι καὶ ἀλλήλους νουθετεῖν (15:14). It would be utterly incorrect to reduce Romans to a philosophical monograph. Yet it nonetheless partakes of some of the features of such texts. The investigation of how it does so in 1:1–17 and in its arguments that unpack elements of its two definitions of the gospel is my overall aim.

Any research into even the smallest aspect of Paul's letter to the Romans draws the student into protracted scholarly debates that, if he or she is not careful, can take over the project and distract from its proper objectives and scope. I must therefore operate on the basis of a set of assumptions: that the letter dates to the mid-to-late 50's C.E. and was probably written at Corinth;[8] that it is unitary and has survived without major interpolations that textual critics have failed to detect;[9] that its intended audience is the one that he spe-

---

[8] Such is the conclusion of the vast majority of scholars who have considered the question; see, e.g., Kümmel, *Introduction*, 311; Fitzmyer, *Romans*, 85–87; Jewett, *Romans*, 18–22; Dunn, *Romans*, xliii–iv.

[9] Contra O'Neill, *Paul's Letter to the Romans*, esp. his introduction, 11–22; also Walker, *Interpolations*. Schmithals' thesis that Romans is a composite letter has won little acceptance (see *Römerbrief*, 29 for his breakdown of the letter). The main dispute pertains to Romans 16, regarding which see Manson, "St. Paul's Letter to the Romans," who concludes: "We must then suppose that Paul prepared a letter (Rom. 1–15) and sent it to Rome. At the same time a copy was prepared to be sent to Ephesus. It may be assumed that this Ephesian copy would include the personalia of Rom. 15:14–33; for these, though primarily intended for the Roman church, nevertheless, contained information about Paul's plans which would be of interest to the Apostle's friends in Ephesus. ... Consequently all we have here in chapter 16 is an introduction to Phoebe, who may be regarded as the bearer of the letter to Ephesus; the greetings to Paul's friends in the province of Asia; and the exhortation of verses 17–20, which has points of contact with Paul's address to the Ephesian elders at Miletus [Acts 20:17–30]" (13). Many of Manson's points in this essay are persuasive, but I cannot understand why chapter 16, if it indeed went to Ephesus but not Rome, lacks its own epistolary prescript – in other

cifically identifies, Rome;[10] and that the ethnic composition of this audience is primarily Gentile.[11] I also presuppose that historical criticism remains the optimal method of investigating questions of the kind that I have set forth.[12] My application of the ancient sources regarding philosophy, rhetoric and epistolography toward an accurate understanding of Paul's compositional strategies is indeed a prominent feature of historical criticism as I practice it in this study.[13] I deliberately avoid the debates regarding the genre, internal structure,

---

words, why an editor would have wanted to obliterate a clear indication that Romans 16 belongs with the main letter but is addressed to Ephesus. When I weigh the plausibility of an excised prescript against the plausibility that he could have indeed known so many people at Rome (cf. ibid., 12–13), I incline toward the latter. See also Koester, *Introduction*, 2.143, and cf. the responses to Manson's thesis by Donfried, "Short Note"; Gamble, *Textual History*, 36–55; Wedderburn, *Reasons for Romans*, 12–18; Lampe, "The Roman Christians of Romans 16" and *From Paul to Valentinus*, 153–83.

[10] Contra Jervell, "Letter to Jerusalem."

[11] So, e.g., Munck, *Paul and the Salvation of Mankind*, 200–209; Nanos, *Mystery of Romans*, 75–84; Engberg-Pedersen, *Paul and the Stoics*, 185–86. Contra, e.g., Cranfield, *Romans*, 1.67–68; Campbell, *Rhetoric of Righteousness*, 14–19; Guerra, *Romans and the Apologetic Tradition*, 22–42; Watson, *Paul, Judaisim, and the Gentiles*, 163–91. See Rom 1:5–6 (ἐν πᾶσιν τοῖς ἔθνεσιν ... ἐν οἷς ἐστε καὶ ὑμεῖς κλητοί); 1:13 (ἵνα τινὰ καρπὸν σχῶ καὶ ἐν ὑμῖν καθὼς καὶ ἐν τοῖς λοιποῖς ἔθνεσιν); and 11:13 (ὑμῖν δὲ λέγω τοῖς ἔθνεσιν). In 7:1 (γινώσκουσιν γὰρ νόμον λαλῶ) Paul does not need to be implying that he addresses Jews or Jewish Christians *per se*, since in other contexts in which he indisputably addresses Gentiles (e.g., Galatians 3–4) he still presumes a high level of familiarity with the scriptures. The mixed ethnic composition of the Roman congregations is a central component of the hypothesis that Paul sends his letter in order to intervene in a conflict (see esp. Donfried, "Short Note" and "False Presuppositions"; Minear, *Obedience of Faith*; Watson, "Two Roman Congregations" and *Paul, Judaisim, and the Gentiles*, 163–91, and throughout the interpretation of Romans in subsequent chapters; Jewett, *Romans*, 46–74; and many others).

[12] Loudly trumpeted announcements of the demise of historical criticism by advocates of 'postmodernist' criticisms have evidently proven premature, as Aichele, Miscall and Walsh tacitly acknowledge in their recent article, "An Elephant in the Room." Historical critical research continues unabated across the broad spectrum of international scholarship on the New Testament and early Christian literature.

[13] All historically based rhetorical studies stand on the shoulders of Hans Dieter Betz and his 1979 Hermeneia commentary on Galatians, which reacquainted scholars with the ancient literature on this subject. Troy Martin has written a study, "Invention and Arrangement in Recent Pauline Rhetorical Studies" (presently unpublished), which exhaustively details this history of scholarship since 1979. The main complaints about Betz's and his followers' methodology pertain to the limitation of 'rhetorical criticism' to ancient sources, and the setting aside of contemporary rhetorical theory; Margaret M. Mitchell has written succint responses to such complaints (*Paul and the Rhetoric of Reconciliation*, 6–8, with references to the secondary literature; also "Rhetorical and New Literary Criticism," 620–26) which I can wholeheartedly endorse, so I will not address the matter further here. Others object from a different angle. Anderson (*Ancient Rhetorical Theory*, 249–57) concludes that one cannot properly apply ancient rhetorical genres and τάξις-theory to the analysis of Paul's letters, but he detects a rich usage of tropes and figures, which does not need to have derived from formal rhetorical education (which would somehow contaminate him, cf. ibid., 249–50), since "[t]he use of tropes and figures is ... common to all literate societies (254). My research here, in which I

and purpose(s) of the letter, beyond the carefully limited remarks on this topic I offer above and in chapter 7 below. My conclusions certainly have an impact upon answers to these difficult questions, but would require full studies of their own to argue well, instead of the incomplete treatments necessitated by the scope of the present project. I thus strive to maintain a tight focus on determinations of how Paul composes his definitions, what they mean and what he wants them to do in chapter 1, and how he deploys them elsewhere in his letter. These questions involve more than their share of intrusions into disputed areas of research (particularly on πίστις and δικαιοσύνη θεοῦ) even as they demand engagement with areas of ancient literature that may be unfamiliar to some interpreters of the New Testament. With these caveats in place, I now turn to the ancient sources on definition and on brevity.

---

interact at length with the ancient sources on style, should not be understood as supporting Anderson's or similar conclusions (see, e.g., Porter, "Theoretical Justification" and "Ancient Rhetorical Analysis," esp. the literature cited in the latter at 251, n. 2; cf. the review of Anderson's book by Mitchell, *CBQ* 60 [1998]: 356–58).

Chapter 2

The Features and Functions of Definition in Ancient Philosophy and Rhetoric

2.1 Introduction

In this first stage of my study, I introduce the ancient literature regarding what a definition (ὅρος, ὁρισμός, ὁρίζειν)[1] is, and the kinds of things that philosophers and orators thought it properly to do. Definition as we normally encounter it nowadays is a species of predicative statement (x is a, b, and c), recognized mainly through the context in which it appears. To take the most obvious example, if one were to receive a page of alphabetized words followed by short, enumerated statements, one would instantly know the page to come from a dictionary and the statements to be definitions of the words. In ordinary discourse, too, definition has a discernable tone and emphasis: with careful precision it specifies the meaning of a term so that it may serve as a conceptual anchor for working through a problem or for arguing a position.[2] As the questions under consideration become more complicated, the need for explicitly articulated definitions becomes more acute, and as a result they can become increasingly technical and dependent upon a broader knowledge of the subject. This spectrum of lesser or greater specificity and technicality likewise exists in ancient definitions, as well as in the theoretical texts that discuss them. Definition indeed belongs among the main tools of Greco-Roman philosophical investigation, so a great deal of thought went into establishing the principles which inform their composition and utilization. Some of these principles filter down into oratory and popular philosophy (by which I mean, texts on philosophical subjects directed to non-specialist audiences).

---

[1] Etymologically, ὅρος probably acquires the meaning "definition" in extension of its meanings "boundary" and "(de)limitation" (cf. the English word *horizon*). The sources use ὅρος and ὁρισμός without any discernable difference in valence; I typically use the former throughout as a convenience. See also the new volume edited by David Charles, *Definition in Greek Philosophy*, which appeared last year (2010).

[2] Definitions also provide a context for humor or pointed observations about human behavior, e.g., "Insanity is the repetition of a failed action with the expectation of a different outcome."

Sketching the outlines of these discussions as the background of Paul's definitions of the gospel is my objective in this chapter.

2.2 The foundation: Plato's *Phaedrus*

Theoretical discussions of definition begin in earnest in classical Athens.[3] Plato portrays Socrates and his interlocutors on numerous occasions erecting and then demolishing definitions as part of his method of ἔλεγχος.[4] Plato's treatment of the principles of ὅρος in the *Phaedrus* comes to exert wide influence over subsequent theory, so this text furnishes the logical place to begin.

The context is Socrates' first speech on love (ἔρως).[5] Earlier in the dialogue Phaedrus recites an oration by Lysias on this topic.[6] Socrates subjects this speech to rigorous criticism, and then accepts a challenge from Phaedrus

---

[3] Presocratic philosophers also occasionally use definitions or quasi-definitional statements. For example: "Anaximenes ... said that boundless air is the origin, the thing from which the things that are coming into existence, that have come into existence, and that will come into existence, the gods and divinities, [all] come into existence, and the remainder are from the offspring of this element," Ἀναξιμένης ... ἀέρα ἄπειρον ἔφη τὴν ἀρχὴν εἶναι, ἐξ οὗ τὰ γινόμενα καὶ τὰ γεγονότα καὶ τὰ ἐσόμενα καὶ θεοὺς καὶ θεῖα γινέσθαι, τὰ δὲ λοιπὰ ἐκ τῶν τούτου ἀπογόνων (Kirk/Raven 144, § 141). The passage goes on to identify the εἶδος of air, and to explain how it appears differently (i.e., as fire, wind, clouds, water, and earth) according to its density. Note the previous passage (ibid., § 140), describing the underlying nature, ἡ ὑποκειμένη φύσις (i.e., air) as οὐκ ἀόριστος but rather ὡρισμένη. Cf. also these technical descriptions of ψυχή, ἁρμονία and σῶμα: "They [Pythagoreans] say that it [the soul] is a kind of concord: for also [they say] that concord is the combination and synthesis of things which are opposed; and that the body is compounded from things opposed," ἁρμονίαν γάρ τινα αὐτὴν λέγουσι· καὶ γὰρ τὴν ἁρμονίαν κρᾶσιν καὶ σύνθεσιν ἐναντίων εἶναι καὶ τὸ σῶμα συγκεῖσθαι ἐξ ἐναντίων (Kirk/Raven 346, § 451, s.v. Philolaus). See further Kirk/Raven 362–64, § 476 (Anaxagoras on νοῦς); 442–43, § 603 (Diogenes of Apollonia on ἀήρ). As far as I know, no testimony survives regarding a Presocratic theoretical discussion on ὅρος; cf., however, Diogenes of Apollonia, whose treatise had the following opening lines: "It seems to me a necessity that the one who begins any speech render the beginning indisputable and the exposition plain and stately," λόγου παντὸς ἀρχόμενον δοκεῖ μοι χρεὼν εἶναι τὴν ἀρχὴν ἀναμφισβήτητον παρέχεσθαι, τὴν δὲ ἑρμηνείαν ἁπλῆν καὶ σεμνήν (Kirk/Raven 434, § 596). Plato evidently echoes this passage in the first speech on love in the *Phaedrus* discussed here.

[4] For an elaboration of this method and the place of definition within it, see Benson, "Priority of Definition."

[5] *Phaedr.* 237a–241d.

[6] The speech of Lysias appears at 230e–234c. The thesis (according to Phaedrus' summary) is that "favor is to be shown more to the man who is not in love than the one who is," λέγει γὰρ ὡς χαριστέον μὴ ἐρῶντι μᾶλλον ἢ ἐρῶντι (227c).

2.2 The foundation: Plato's Phaedrus

to deliver a speech more to his own liking.[7] His introduction (προοίμιον) explains why a definition of ἔρως should stand first in the order of business:

περὶ παντός, ὦ παῖ, μία ἀρχὴ τοῖς μέλλουσι καλῶς βουλεύεσθαι· εἰδέναι δεῖ περὶ οὗ ἂν ᾖ ἡ βουλή, ἢ παντὸς ἁμαρτάνειν ἀνάγκη. ... ἀλλ' ἐπειδὴ σοὶ καὶ ἐμοὶ ὁ λόγος πρόκειται πότερα ἐρῶντι ἢ μὴ μᾶλλον εἰς φιλίαν ἰτέον, περὶ ἔρωτος οἷόν τ' ἔστι καὶ ἣν ἔχει δύναμιν, ὁμολογίᾳ θέμενοι ὅρον, εἰς τοῦτο ἀποβλέποντες καὶ ἀναφέροντες τὴν σκέψιν ποιώμεθα, εἴτε ὠφελίαν εἴτε βλάβην παρέχει.

In every situation, my boy, there is one starting point for those who are about to deliberate something well: one must know whatever topic the deliberation may be about, or complete error necessarily occurs. ... But since there sits before you and me the subject of whether one should enter into friendship [εἰς φιλίαν] more with the one who loves [ἐρῶντι] than the one who does not, after assigning by agreement a definition regarding love – what sort of thing it is and what power it has – let us examine whether love causes benefit or injury by reviewing and referring to this. (*Phaedr.* 237c–d)

Several important points emerge out of Socrates' introductory statements here. First, a definition needs to declare *what something is* and *what function it has* (οἷόν τ' ἔστι καὶ ἣν ἔχει δύναμιν): such is his basic ὅρος τοῦ ὅρου. Second, it serves to *secure agreement* (ὁμολογία) between interlocutors on the terms of a deliberation (βουλή) toward the avoidance of error. One may "review and refer to" it throughout the inquiry (ἀποβλέποντες καὶ ἀναφέροντες) as something clearly articulated by the speaker and endorsed by the audience. Third, he identifies definition as a preliminary step, so he places his inquiry into the nature and function of ἔρως in the προοίμιον of his speech. Fourth, Socrates implicitly divides the investigative process into its constituent parts: the question, the definition of concepts within the question, the proposition, and the argument. Socrates and Phaedrus have before them questions to consider. Should one prefer a suitor who is in love, or one who is not? Does love produce benefit or harm? Answers to these questions – the formulation of propositions and their verification in argument – require an answer to a prior question: what is love? As Socrates looks back on his speech later in the dialogue, he identifies his method's two foundational tasks: first, "to bring into a single idea widely dispersed phenomena by viewing them together, in order that by defining each item regarding which one wants at that point to teach, one

---

[7] Socrates puts some distance between himself and the perspectives expressed in his speech with a narrative prelude (237b): "So once upon a time there was a very beautiful boy, rather a lad, and for him there were very many lovers. Now a certain one of these men was wily, who – although he loved him no less than anyone else – had convinced the boy that he was not in love. And one time as he was pleading with him, he was addressing this very point, that he ought to favor the one who is not in love instead of the one who is, and he was speaking as follows...." ἦν οὕτω δὴ παῖς, μᾶλλον δὲ μειρακίσκος, μάλα καλός· τούτῳ δὲ ἦσαν ἐρασταὶ πάνυ πολλοί. εἷς δέ τις αὐτῶν αἱμύλος ἦν, ὃς οὐδενὸς ἧττον ἐρῶν ἐπεπείκει τὸν παῖδα ὡς οὐκ ἐρῴη. καί ποτε αὐτὸν αἰτῶν ἔπειθεν τοῦτ' αὐτό, ὡς μὴ ἐρῶντι πρὸ τοῦ ἐρῶντος δέοι χαρίζεσθαι, ἔλεγέν τε ὧδε.

may make it clear" (εἰς μίαν τε ἰδέαν συνορῶντα ἄγειν τὰ πολλαχῇ διεσπαρμένα, ἵνα ἕκαστον ὁριζόμενος δῆλον ποιῇ περὶ οὗ ἂν ἀεὶ διδάσκειν ἐθέλῃ); and second, "to be able again to dissect things according to their kinds – according to the joints, where they have naturally occurred" (τὸ πάλιν κατ' εἴδη δύνασθαι διατέμνειν κατ' ἄρθρα ᾗ πέφυκε).[8] Definition thus works constructively, by "assembly" (συναγωγή), while dissection works analytically, by division (διαίρεσις) and classification (κατ' εἴδη).

A quick overview of the remainder of the προοίμιον of the speech will illustrate how these two tasks of assembly and division coordinate in practice. Socrates first identifies a self-evident feature: "Surely then it is clear to everyone that love is a kind of desire" (ὅτι μὲν οὖν δὴ ἐπιθυμία τις ὁ ἔρως, ἅπαντι δῆλον). "Desire" covers broader territory than "love" since all people (even οἱ μὴ ἐρῶντες) experience the former; the question rather hinges on who acts upon it. Socrates next explains two internal impulses, the innate desire for pleasures and an acquired opinion of what is best (ἡ μὲν ἔμφυτος οὖσα ἐπιθυμία ἡδονῶν, ἄλλη δὲ ἐπίκτητος δόξα, ἐφιεμένη τοῦ ἀρίστου).[9] He then elaborates the names which accompany these conditions:

δόξης μὲν οὖν ἐπὶ τὸ ἄριστον λόγῳ ἀγούσης καὶ κρατούσης τῷ κράτει σωφροσύνη ὄνομα· ἐπιθυμίας δὲ ἀλόγως ἑλκούσης ἐπὶ ἡδονὰς καὶ ἀρξάσης ἐν ἡμῖν τῇ ἀρχῇ ὕβρις ἐπωνομάσθη.

Indeed when the opinion guides by rationality to what is best and dominates, the name of this dominance is 'temperance.' But when desire irrationally draws us to pleasures and governs in us, the name 'hybris' is given to this governance. (*Phaedr.* 238a)

Socrates is implementing the procedure of διαίρεσις, dividing desire into two species, σωφροσύνη, in which it is dominated by rationality, and ὕβρις, in which it irrationally dominates. One may easily see where he is driving: ἔρως will become one of the sub-species of ὕβρις. Before taking this step, however, he elaborates other phenomena at the same taxonomic level:

ὕβρις δὲ δὴ πολυώνυμον – πολυμελὲς γὰρ καὶ πολυειδές – καὶ τούτων τῶν ἰδέων ἐκπρεπὴς ἣ ἂν τύχῃ γενομένη, τὴν αὑτῆς ἐπωνυμίαν ὀνομαζόμενον τὸν ἔχοντα παρέχεται, οὔτε τινὰ καλὴν οὔτ'

---

[8] *Phaedr.* 265d–e. The Stranger links διαίρεσις with διαλεκτικὴ ἐπιστήμη at *Soph.* 253d–e.

[9] *Phaedr.* 237d–e: "But we know that furthermore even the ones who do not love desire the beautiful. On what basis then shall we differentiate the one who loves from the one who does not? It is necessary moreover to perceive that in each of us there are two types that govern and guide, which we follow wherever they guide: one, the desire for pleasures which is innate, and the other, an acquired opinion which aims at what is best. Sometimes these are of a single mind in us, but there are occasions when they quarrel. And sometimes one dominates us, but at other times the other." ὅτι δ' αὖ καὶ μὴ ἐρῶντες ἐπιθυμοῦσι τῶν καλῶν, ἴσμεν. τῷ δὴ τὸν ἐρῶντά τε καὶ μὴ κρινοῦμεν; δεῖ αὖ νοῆσαι, ὅτι ἡμῶν ἐν ἑκάστῳ δύο τινέ ἐστον ἰδέα ἄρχοντε καὶ ἄγοντε, οἷν ἑπόμεθα ᾗ ἂν ἄγητον, ἡ μὲν ἔμφυτος οὖσα ἐπιθυμία ἡδονῶν, ἄλλη δὲ ἐπίκτητος δόξα, ἐφιεμένη τοῦ ἀρίστου. τούτω δὲ ἐν ἡμῖν τοτὲ μὲν ὁμονοεῖτον, ἔστι δὲ ὅτε στασιάζετον· καὶ τοτὲ μὲν ἡ ἑτέρα, ἄλλοτε δὲ ἡ ἑτέρα κρατεῖ.

ἐπαξίαν κεκτῆσθαι. περὶ μὲν γὰρ ἐδωδὴν κρατοῦσα τοῦ λόγου τε τοῦ ἀρίστου καὶ τῶν ἄλλων ἐπιθυμιῶν ἐπιθυμία γαστριμαργία τε καὶ τὸν ἔχοντα ταὐτὸν τοῦτο κεκλημένον παρέξεται· περὶ δ' αὖ μέθας τυραννεύσασα, τὸν κεκτημένον ταύτῃ ἄγουσα, δῆλον οὗ τεύξεται προσρήματος· καὶ τἆλλα δὴ τὰ τούτων ἀδελφὰ καὶ ἀδελφῶν ἐπιθυμιῶν ὀνόματα τῆς ἀεὶ δυναστευούσης ᾗ προσήκει καλεῖσθαι πρόδηλον.

But then hybris has many names, for it has many parts and forms. And of these forms, whichever one happens to become pre-eminent imparts its own moniker to the one who experiences it when he is called by name, with the result that he has acquired it as something neither beautiful nor worth mentioning. For, in the case of food, when desire for it dominates the best reasoning and the other desires, it becomes gluttony and it will impart this name [glutton] to the very one experiencing it when he is called. And again, in the case of strong wines, when desire plays the tyrant and guides the one who has acquired it, it is clear what sort of designation he will ultimately obtain. And indeed, with respect to the related names of these and related desires, when one perpetually dominates it is completely clear by which desire it is proper [for someone] to be called. (*Phaedr.* 238a–b)

Socrates characterizes the types of hybristic desire as forces which compel anyone in their grip toward the reception of the name which they themselves carry, reducing people to mere unflattering labels. The identification of these species and their undesirable results together form an argument by analogy which Socrates then brings to a conclusion in his final definition:

ἧς δ' ἕνεκα πάντα τὸ πρόσθεν εἴρηται, σχεδὸν μὲν ἤδη φανερόν, λεχθὲν δὲ ἢ μὴ λεχθὲν πάντως σαφέστερον· ἡ γὰρ ἄνευ λόγου δόξης ἐπὶ τὸ ὀρθὸν ὁρμώσης κρατήσασα ἐπιθυμία πρὸς ἡδονὴν ἀχθεῖσα κάλλους, καὶ ὑπὸ αὖ τῶν ἑαυτῆς συγγενῶν ἐπιθυμιῶν ἐπὶ σωμάτων κάλλος ἐρρωμένως ῥωσθεῖσα νικήσασα ἀγωγῇ, ἀπ' αὐτῆς τῆς ῥώμης ἐπωνυμίαν λαβοῦσα, ἔρως ἐκλήθη.

The reason that all the above has been said is already fairly evident, but something said is more clear than something not said in its entirety. For the desire that conquers without reason an opinion that goes for what is right, which was guided toward the pleasure of beauty, and which furthermore was vigorously strengthened by desires akin to itself toward the beauty of bodies, which conquers by guiding, which takes its moniker from this very force, was called love. (*Phaedr.* 238b–c)

Each clause of the definition gathers up and condenses concepts from the foregoing discussion: the doctrine of the two impulses (ἄνευ λόγου ἐπιθυμία, and δόξα ἐπὶ τὸ ὀρθὸν ὁρμῶσα); the dominance of desire over the reason (κρατήσασα, πρὸς ἡδονὴν ἀχθεῖσα κάλλους and νικήσασα ἀγωγῇ); and Socrates' interest in the transference of names (ἀπ' αὐτῆς τῆς ῥώμης ἐπωνυμίαν λαβοῦσα, supposing that ἔρως is derived from ῥώννυσθαι or ῥώεσθαι).[10] Both the definition and the discussion building up to it exhibit an obvious slant toward Socrates' proposition that one should prefer a suitor who is not in love. This bias clashes ironically with the claims made earlier about the necessity of ac-

---

[10] Dionysius of Halicarnassus complains of the lack of brevity in this definition, of Plato's "drawing out so large a roundabout statement when the subject is able to be encompassed in a few words," καὶ τοσαύτην ἐκμηκύνας περίφρασιν ὀλίγοις τοῖς ὀνόμασι δυναμένου περιληφθῆναι πράγματος (*Dem.* 7).

curate definitions, and paves the way for Socrates' retraction of the speech as impious and his replacement of it later in the dialogue. Explicit references to the definition scarcely appear in the rest of the speech; instead, it works – particularly in its negativity – as the foundation upon which Socrates makes his case. How could love so defined not lead to the conclusion that it causes harm to the beloved, and that the handsome παῖς should thus prefer an uninfatuated suitor? Socrates relentlessly accents the damages an infatuated lover bestows upon the beloved, and omits a case in favor of his proposition altogether – hence Phaedrus' protestation when he stops: "I thought [the speech] was only halfway through" (ᾤμην γε μεσοῦν αὐτόν).[11]

Whereas in other contexts Plato has Socrates use definition in a less playful manner, to place the definiendum on a taxonomic map of related phenomena developed through lengthy dialogue,[12] in the first speech on love in the

---

[11] *Phaedr.* 241d: "And yet I thought [the speech] was halfway through, and that it should speak equally regarding the one who is not in love, how it is necessary to show him more favor, stating moreover what good qualities he has. But why, Socrates, are you stopping now?" καίτοι ᾤμην γε μεσοῦν αὐτόν, καὶ ἐρεῖν τὰ ἴσα περὶ τοῦ μὴ ἐρῶντος, ὡς δεῖ ἐκείνῳ χαρίζεσθαι μᾶλλον, λέγων ὅσα αὖ ἔχει ἀγαθά· νῦν δὲ δή, ὦ Σώκρατες, τί ἀποπαύεις;

[12] E.g., Plato, *Soph.* 218b–c: "But you, in common with me, must now make an inquiry, beginning first (as it appears right to me) with the sophist, investigating and explaining with argument what sort of thing he is. For presently regarding this person you and I hold in common only the name, but the thing that we call upon [with the name] each of us may perhaps hold in our own minds privately. But it is always necessary that the matter itself have been agreed upon regarding every detail through arguments rather than the name alone without argument." κοινῇ δὲ μετ' ἐμοῦ σοι συσκεπτέον ἀρχομένῳ πρῶτον, ὡς ἐμοὶ φαίνεται, νῦν ἀπὸ τοῦ σοφιστοῦ, ζητοῦντι καὶ ἐμφανίζοντι λόγῳ τί ποτ' ἔστι. νῦν γὰρ δὴ σύ τε κἀγὼ τούτου πέρι τοὔνομα μόνον ἔχομεν κοινῇ, τὸ δὲ ἔργον ἐφ' ᾧ καλοῦμεν ἑκάτερος τάχ' ἂν ἰδίᾳ παρ' ἡμῖν αὐτοῖς ἔχοιμεν· δεῖ δὲ ἀεὶ παντὸς πέρι τὸ πρᾶγμα αὐτὸ μᾶλλον διὰ λόγων ἢ τοὔνομα μόνον συνωμολογῆσθαι χωρὶς λόγου. Definition as practiced by the Stranger in this dialogue first involves development of a taxonomic tree. A definition then moves from the top to the bottom of the tree, from the general to the specific, e.g. the art of fishing (221a–b): "Now then, regarding the fisherman's art both you and I have together agreed upon not only the name, but we have also sufficiently obtained the statement regarding its very function. For, of the art as a whole, half was the acquisitive part; and of the acquisitive half was the part that subdues others; and of the subduing part half was the hunting part; and of the hunting part half was the part that pursues animals; and of the pursuing part half was the part that pursues water creatures; and of the water-creature part the division below that was the fishing part as a whole; of the fishing part half was the striking part; and of the striking part, half was the part that uses fishhooks. Now of this part there is that part concerning the strike which draws [πληγὴ ἀνασπωμένη] upwards from below; the name, having taken its likeness from this very action, has now become 'the fisherman's art' [ἀσπαλιευτική], as it is known, which was sought by us." νῦν ἄρα τῆς ἀσπαλιευτικῆς πέρι σύ τε κἀγὼ συνωμολογήκαμεν οὐ μόνον τοὔνομα, ἀλλὰ καὶ τὸν λόγον περὶ αὐτὸ τοὔργον εἰλήφαμεν ἱκανῶς. συμπάσης γὰρ τέχνης τὸ μὲν ἥμισυ μέρος κτητικὸν ἦν, κτητικοῦ δὲ χειρωτικόν, χειρωτικοῦ δὲ θηρευτικόν, τοῦ δὲ θηρευτικοῦ ζῳοθηρικόν, ζῳοθηρικοῦ δὲ ἐνυγροθηρικόν, ἐνυγροθηρικοῦ δὲ τὸ κάτωθεν τμῆμα ὅλον ἁλιευτικόν, ἁλιευτικῆς δὲ πληκτικόν, πληκτικῆς δὲ ἀγκιστρευτικόν· τούτου δὲ τὸ περὶ τὴν κάτωθεν ἄνω πληγὴν ἀνασπωμένην, ἀπ' αὐτῆς τῆς πράξεως ἀφομοιωθὲν τοὔνομα, ἡ νῦν ἀσπαλιευτικὴ ζητηθεῖσα ἐπίκλην γέ-

Phaedrus he deploys it rhetorically, toward the demonstration of a proposition in a speech. The principle that he invokes – that a definition secures agreement between interlocutors by articulating what something is and what function it has – remains the same. Socrates implements the procedure of διαίρεσις, with each clause of his final definition gathering a step in his logic. The subsequent influence of Plato's definition of ὅρος and his model of its execution may in part derive from its oratorical setting: he has here conveniently packaged a philosophical method in a readily digestable form, even as he demonstrates its utility for the composition of speeches.[13]

2.3 Rhetorical vs. philosophical definition

Plato's interest in definitions generally, and his comments in the *Phaedrus* specifically, inaugurate philosophical debates on definition that extend through Aristotle (who strives to refine its application in logic and scientific research), to the Stoics and Epicureans, and beyond.

Excursus. Aristotle's ideas regarding definition are extremely complicated (not least because of how difficult it is to determine what 'being' means for him, in addition to the problem of the ambiguous phrase τὸ τί ἦν εἶναι, which interpreters normally render "essence"). His ideas furthermore have limited relevence for the present discussion, since the degree to which they

---

γονεν. The Stranger locates the sophist on the same taxonomic tree several times, producing numerous definitions (223b, 224c–e, 231b), in order to show that the sophist defies a single placement in the taxonomy. In reading this dialogue, one gradually perceives that Plato has the Stranger (and not Socrates!) engage in these *ad absurdum* procedures to illustrate both their necessity and their limitations – hence the attempt to apply them to the definition of 'being' later in the dialogue (247d–e), with only inconclusive results. Plato does not always use a taxonomic strategy of definition, however. (On this dialogue, see Brown, "Definition and Division," and Gill, "Division and Definition.") Later in the *Phaedrus* (245c–46a), Socrates briefly elaborates the immortality of the soul, first by defining the immortal as "that which is always in motion" (τὸ γὰρ ἀεικίνητον ἀθάνατον), and by contrasting it with "that which moves another thing and is moved by another thing" (τὸ δ' ἄλλο κινοῦν καὶ ὑπ' ἄλλου κινούμενον): "Indeed only that which moves itself, insofar as it does not leave itself behind, never stops moving, but this is also the wellspring and origin of motion for other things, which are moved," μόνον δὴ τὸ αὐτὸ κινοῦν, ἅτε οὐκ ἀπολεῖπον ἑαυτό, οὔποτε λήγει κινούμενον, ἀλλὰ καὶ τοῖς ἄλλοις ὅσα κινεῖται τοῦτο πηγὴ καὶ ἀρχὴ κινήσεως. He goes on to discuss ἀρχή, namely that it is ἀγένητον, and thus ἀθάνατος. He then ties these features back to the soul and its attributes. Plato thus has Socrates unpack the definition's component parts successively.

[13] On Plato's writings as stylistically exemplary, see Dionysius, *Dem.* 23: "Some see fit to declare that he explains subjects the most divinely of all philosophers and orators, and they direct us to use this man as the definition and standard of speeches which are at the same time pure and forceful," τινες ἀξιοῦσι πάντων αὐτὸν ἀποφαίνειν φιλοσόφων τε καὶ ῥητόρων ἑρμηνεῦσαι τὰ πράγματα δαιμονιώτατον παρακελεύονταί τε ἡμῖν ὅρῳ καὶ κανόνι χρῆσθαι καθαρῶν ἅμα καὶ ἰσχυρῶν λόγων τούτῳ τῷ ἀνδρί. Dionysius, for his part, expresses strong reservations regarding Plato's suitability as a stylistic model.

penetrate into rhetorical theory regarding definition is slight. He addresses definition in the *Topics* 1.4–5 and the *Posterior Analytics* 2.10, among several other places. In the the former he sets out the components of methods of argument (λόγος), and of deductive reasoning (συλλογισμός). He connects propositions (προτάσεις) to argument, and questions or problems (προβλήματα) to reasoning, then states that both "disclose a genus, a particularity, or something coincidental" (ἢ γένος ἢ ἴδιον ἢ συμβεβηκὸς δηλοῖ). He next places ὅρος under the heading of particularity as that which signifies what the essential nature of something is (τὸ μὲν τὸ τί ἦν εἶναι σημαῖνον), while retaining ἴδιον to refer to particularity that does not so signify (τὸ δ' οὐ σημαίνει). Four divisions thus result: definition, particularity, genus, and coincident. When Aristotle takes a detailed look at each, he reiterates his earlier definition of ὅρος (ἔστι δ' ὅρος μὲν λόγος ὁ τὸ τί ἦν εἶναι σημαίνων, 1.5, 101b39–102a40), then focuses on the relationship of "word" and "statement" ("But either a statement is given in place of a word, or a statement in place of a statement," ἀποδίδοται δὲ ἢ λόγος ἀντ' ὀνόματος ἢ λόγος ἀντὶ λόγου, 102a1–2) and on statements that are like definitions yet remain distinct from them (ὁρισμὸς λόγος, cf. on ὑπογραφή and ὑποτύπωσις below). He goes into greater detail in the *Posterior Analytics* about "essential nature" (*An. post.* 2.10, 93b29–94a14): (1) a definition is "a statement of *what* the word or some other noun-like statement signifies" (λόγος τοῦ τί σημαίνει τὸ ὄνομα ἢ λόγος ἕτερος ὀνοματώδης); (2) it is "a statement which clarifies *why* something is" (λόγος ὁ δηλῶν διὰ τί ἔστιν), frequently involving a demonstration of the *what* (ἔσται οἷον ἀπόδειξις τοῦ τί ἐστι); or (3) "definition of immediate essences [ἄμεσα] is the undemonstrated affirmation of *what* it is" (ὁ δὲ τῶν ἀμέσων ὁρισμὸς θέσις ἐστὶ τοῦ τί ἐστιν ἀναπόδεικτος). (By ἄμεσα Aristotle means attributes which do not have external causes – essential attributes in the strictest sense; *An. post.* 2.9, 93b22–24.) His first type of ὅρος must therefore involve attributes that result from outside causes and that are thus susceptible to demonstration: it is "the logical conclusion of a demonstration of what it is" (τῆς τοῦ τί ἐστιν ἀποδείξεως συμπέρασμα). Aristotle's inclusion of ἀπόδειξις in two of the three types of definition indicates that ὅρος can be the product of a preliminary investigative process which in turn facilitates the construction of valid προτάσεις and προβλήματα.[14]

The Stoics make ὅρος one of the two divisions of their dialectic, the "definitional species" (ὁρικὸν εἶδος) that coordinates with "the species dealing with canons and criteria" (τὸ περὶ κανόνων καὶ κριτηρίων [εἶδος]), Diogenes Laertius 7.41–42 = Long/Sedley 31A: "Now some say that the logical part is divided into two sciences, into the rhetorical and the dialectical. And some too divide [the dialectical] into the definitory species, and the species dealing with canons and criteria; but some strip away the definitory species. So then, they undertake the species dealing with canons and criteria for the purpose of discovering the truth; for with this they facilitate the differentiations of impressions. And the definitory species is likewise for the purpose of the recognition of truth, for things are apprehended through conceptions." τὸ δὲ λογικὸν μέρος φασὶν ἔνιοι εἰς δύο διαιρεῖσθαι ἐπιστήμας, εἰς ῥητορικὴν καὶ εἰς διαλεκτικήν. τινὲς δὲ καὶ εἰς τὸ ὁρικὸν εἶδος, τό ⟨τε⟩ περὶ κανόνων καὶ κριτηρίων· ἔνιοι δὲ τὸ ὁρικὸν περιαιροῦσι. τὸ μὲν οὖν περὶ κανόνων καὶ κριτηρίων παραλαμβάνουσι πρὸς τὸ τὴν ἀλήθειαν εὑρεῖν· ἐν [αὐτῷ]

---

[14] Cf. also *Metaph.* 7.4.12–13, 1030a17–23. For further discussion, see Deslauriers, "Plato and Aristotle on Division and Definition"; Bayer, "Classification and Explanation"; Ferejohn, "Definition and the Two Stages of Aristotelian Demonstration"; and the contributions by Chiba, Modrak, Charles and Lennox in Charles, *Definition in Greek Philosophy*, 203–355.

2.3 Rhetorical vs. philosophical definition

γὰρ τὰς τῶν φαντασιῶν διαφορὰς ἀπευθύνουσι. καὶ τὸ ὁρικὸν δὲ ὁμοίως πρὸς ἐπίγνωσιν τῆς ἀληθείας· διὰ γὰρ τῶν ἐννοιῶν τὰ πράγματα λαμβάνεται.[15]

Naturally the debates become increasingly abstruse, and were thus far out of reach for all but those who dedicated themselves to advanced philosophical study. But certain ideas about definition from the Hellenistic philosophers come to have a place beside Plato's basic insights. A passage of Cicero's *Orator* gathers many of these together in his advice on how to use definitions rhetorically:

> *Et quoniam in omnibus quae ratione docentur et via primum constituendum est quid quidque sit – nisi enim inter eos qui disceptant convenit quid sit illud quod ambigitur, nec recte disseri umquam nec ad exitum perveniri potest –, explicanda est saepe verbis mens nostra de quaque re atque involuta rei notitia definiendo aperienda est, si quidem est definitio oratio, quae quid sit id de quo agitur ostendit quam brevissime; .... Erit igitur haec facultas in eo quem volumus esse eloquentem, ut definire rem possit nec id faciat tam presse et anguste quam in illis eruditissimis disputationibus fieri solet, sed cum explanatius tum etiam uberius et ad commune iudicium popularemque intellegentiam accomodatius.*

> And since what each thing is should first be determined in all matters which are shown rationally and methodically (for unless there is agreement between those who debate regarding that which is uncertain, [the subject] cannot ever be examined correctly nor brought to a conclusion), our thinking should often be laid out verbally about each subject, and the enfolded conception of the subject should be opened up by definition, if indeed definition is a statement which discloses most concisely what the thing which is being deliberated about [actually] is. ... Therefore this skill will belong to the one whom we want to be eloquent: that he may be *able* to define the subject, and [yet] that he may *not* do it in as compressed and compact a manner as is customarily to be used in those most erudite debates, but not only more plainly but also more copiously, and more appropriately for common judgment and popular-level intelligence. (*Or.* 116–17)

These remarks appear in connection with Cicero's observations about the utility of philosophy for the orator. He has just advised careful study either of the logic of Aristotle or of Chrysippus.[16] We may note first Cicero's appropriation of the *Phaedrus*: a definition should secure agreement between the interlocutors or the discussion will not proceed "correctly" (*nec recte disseri ... potest*). He also cites an idea of the Stoics, that a definition should open up the enfolded conception (*involuta rei notitia definiendo aperienda est*): the definiendum has "folded" within it several component parts that a definition

---

[15] For further discussion of this passage, see Long, "Dialectic and the Stoic Sage," 85. For an illustration of the coordination of definition and division in Stoic thought, see Stobaeus, *Anth.* 2.88.8–90.6 = Long/Sedley 65A, a passage which defines πάθος and divides it into ἐπιθυμία, φόβος, λυπή, and ἡδονή. See also Crivelli, "The Stoics on Definition."

[16] *Or.* 115: "I am of the opinion that he who is drawn to the glory of eloquence is not to be generally ignorant of these subjects [i.e., dialectics], but either to be educated in that old instruction [of Aristotle] or that of Chrysippus," *ego eum censeo qui eloquentiae laude ducatur non esse earum rerum omnino rudem, sed vel illa antiqua vel hac Chrysippi disciplina institutum.*

"unfolds" (ἐξάπλωσις).[17] By the time of Cicero this has evidently become a commonplace. Cicero futhermore contrasts philosophical and rhetorical definition on the basis of their brevity.[18] While the orator should possess the ability to define as concisely as the philosophers, he should relax the taut style and strive for a plainness that adapts to the capabilities of the audience. Cicero does not say that rhetorical definitions should not be brief, only that they should be more discursive than those used in "erudite debates."[19] The contrast

---

[17] Stoic thinkers offer at least two definitions of ὅρος. Chrysippus gives the simplest, "the specification of a particularity" (ἰδίου ἀπόδοσις, Diogenes Laertius 7.60 = Long/Sedley 32C, SVF 2.226; cf. Sextus Empiricus, Pyr. 2.212). Antipater of Tarsus (ii B.C.E.) says a bit more discursively: "ὅρος is a statement borne out correspondingly according to analysis" (ὅρος δέ ἐστιν ... λόγος κατ' ἀνάλυσιν ἀπαρτιζόντως ἐκφερόμενος, Diogenes Laertius 7.60 = Long/Sedley 32C, SVF 2.226). Even though this definition is more discursive, it still makes little sense on its surface: the words ἀνάλυσις and ἀπαρτιζόντως have meanings that the definition, detached as it is from any exposition Antipater may have provided, does not make clear. A commentator on Aristotle's Topics, Alexander of Aphrodisias (ii–iii C.E.), helpfully elaborates these terms: "The ones who say that ὅρος is 'a statement borne out correspondingly according to analysis' – saying that 'analysis' is the unfolding of the definiendum, and summarily; and that 'correspondingly' is neither to exceed nor to lack [the necessary elements] – would be saying that ὅρος is no different than 'the specification of a particularity,'" οἱ δὲ λέγοντες ὅρον εἶναι λόγον κατὰ ἀνάλυσιν ἀπαρτιζόντως ἐκφερόμενον, ἀνάλυσιν μὲν λέγοντες τὴν ἐξάπλωσιν τοῦ ὁριστοῦ καὶ κεφαλαιωδῶς, ἀπαρτιζόντως δὲ τὸ μήτε ὑπερβάλλειν μήτε ἐνδεῖν, οὐδὲν ἂν λέγοιεν τὸν ὅρον διαφέρειν τῆς τοῦ ἰδίου ἀποδόσεως (In Arist. Top. 42.27–43.2 = Long/Sedley 32E). Chrysippus' and Antipater's definitions, Alexander concludes, amount to the same thing (a fault, in his estimation). His expansions of ἀνάλυσις and ἀπαρτιζόντως nevertheless unveil obscured details, namely that a ὅρος "unfolds" the definiendum (ἡ ἐξάπλωσις τοῦ ὁριστοῦ), it does so "summarily" (κεφαλαιωδῶς), and it does so completely, with no superfluities or omissions (τὸ μήτε ὑπερβάλλειν μήτε ἐνδεῖν). It seems probable that Alexander derives these expansions from Antipater's own elaboration of his definition.

[18] The doctrine that definitions should be brief perhaps originates with the Stoics. (E.g., Chrysippus' definition of ὅρος has only two words.) See further [Galen], Hist. phil. Kühn 19.236–37: "ὅρος is a concise statement leading us to knowledge of each subject; or, a statement which makes the proposed subject plain for us through a brief reminder; and, of definitions, some are essential, some conceptual," ὅρος δέ ἐστι λόγος σύντομος εἰς γνῶσιν ἡμᾶς ἄγων ἑκάστου πράγματος, ἢ λόγος διὰ βραχείας ὑπομνήσεως ἐμφανὲς ἡμῖν ἀπεργαζόμενος τὸ ὑποκείμενον πρᾶγμα· τῶν δὲ ὅρων οἱ μὲν εἰσὶν οὐσιώδεις, οἱ δὲ ἐννοηματικοί. [Athanasius], De definionibus 3, PG 28.533: "ὅρος is a concise indicative statement of the nature of a proposed subject," ὅρος ἐστὶ σύντομος δηλωτικὸς τῆς φύσεως τοῦ ὑποκειμένου πράγματος.

[19] Stoic definitions can exhibit extreme compaction of content and brevity of style even when they are relatively more discursive, for example the fourfold definition of ἐπιστήμη cited by Stobaeus (Anth. 2.73.16–74.3 = Long/Sedley 41H): "Knowledge is apprehension, secure and unchangeable by argument. And another knowledge is a system of such knowledges, e.g. the comprehensive rationality which exists in an excellent person. And another is a system of technical knowledges which has internal stability, as the virtues have. And another is the disposition which is receptive of impressions [and] which is unchangeable by argument, which, they say, is something latent in tension and power." εἶναι δὲ τὴν ἐπιστήμην κατάληψιν ἀσφαλῆ καὶ ἀμετάπτωτον ὑπὸ λόγου· ἑτέραν δὲ ἐπιστήμην σύστημα ἐξ ἐπιστημῶν τοιούτων,

of rhetorical and philosophical definition by means of their relative brevity captures the difference between logic and rhetoric, as silently expressed by Zeno – the former a fist, the latter an opening palm.[20]

In practice, then, philosophical and rhetorical definition are very similar, with the differences emerging from the force that their contextual usages impart to them. Both kinds of definition require brevity and have the function of acquiring agreement between interlocutors on the meaning of the definiendum. Philosophical definition, however, aims for completeness and scientific accuracy (the full coextension of definiendum and definition),[21] while rhetorical definition does not necessarily do so, instead serving the purpose of persuasion. The latter in some ways resembles what Stoic and Epicurean philosophers call ὑπογραφή or ὑποτύπωσις, "outline" or "sketch." According to Diogenes Laertius, the Stoics define ὑπογραφή as "a statement leading summarily into the subjects, or which has conveyed the force of definition more simply than definition" (ὑπογραφὴ δέ ἐστι λόγος τυπωδῶς εἰσάγων εἰς τὰ πράγματα, ἢ ὅρου ἁπλούστερον τὴν τοῦ ὅρου δύναμιν προσενηνεγμένος).[22] Epicurus

---

οἷον ἡ τῶν κατὰ μέρος λογικὴ ἐν τῷ σπουδαίῳ ὑπάρχουσα· ἄλλην δὲ σύστημα ἐξ ἐπιστημῶν τεχνικῶν ἐξ αὐτοῦ ἔχον τὸ βέβαιον, ὡς ἔχουσιν αἱ ἀρεταί· ἄλλην δὲ ἕξιν φαντασιῶν δεκτικὴν ἀμετάπτωτον ὑπὸ λόγου, ἥν τινά φασιν ἐν τόνῳ καὶ δυνάμει κεῖσθαι.

[20] Cicero, *Or.* 113; Sextus Empiricus, *Math.* 2.7 = Long/Sedley 31E.

[21] Cf. Cicero's short discussion of the elements of scientific definition at *Top.* 83: "Furthermore when it is asked what [something] is, one should unfold the concept – its particularity, its division, and its partition; for these are the things attributed to definition." *Cum autem quid sit quaeritur, notio explicanda est et proprietas et divisio et partitio. Haec enim sunt definitioni attributa.* The criterion of completeness is evident in the supplementation of Cleanthes' definition of τέχνη (Olympiodorus, *In Plat. Gorg.* 12.1; text per Long/Sedley 42A): "Cleanthes furthermore says: 'Skill is a disposition which achieves all things by method.' But this definition is incomplete, for nature is also a kind of disposition which does all things by method, for which reason Chrysippus, adding 'with the impressions,' said: 'Skill is a disposition which succeeds by method with the impressions.'" Κλεάνθης τοίνυν λέγει ὅτι «τέχνη ἐστὶν ἕξις ὁδῷ πάντα ἀνύουσα». ἀτελὴς δ' ἐστιν οὗτος ὁ ὅρος, καὶ γὰρ ἡ φύσις ἕξις τίς ἐστιν ὁδῷ πάντα ποιοῦσα· ὅθεν ὁ Χρύσιππος προσθεὶς τὸ «μετὰ φαντασιῶν» εἶπεν ὅτι «τέχνη ἐστὶν ἕξις ὁδῷ προιοῦσα μετὰ φαντασιῶν».

[22] Diogenes Laertius 7.60 = Long/Sedley 32C (following Sedley's emendation of ὅρος in the MSS to ὅρου). Cf. Galen, *Def. med.* Kühn 19.349 = *SVF* 2.227: "ὑπογραφή is a statement leading summarily into the clarified knowledge of the subject," ὑπογραφή ἐστι λόγος τυπωδῶς εἰσάγων εἰς τὴν δηλουμένην τοῦ πράγματος γνῶσιν. Also idem, *Diff. puls.* Kühn 8.708–9 = *SVF* 2.229: "Therefore let us begin again from conceptual definitions, which we say explain nothing more than those things which all people know ... which those who are skilled at terminology think fit to call not definitions, but both ὑπογραφαί and ὑποτυπώσεις," ἀρξώμεθα οὖν αὖθις ἀπὸ τῶν ἐννοηματικῶν ὅρων, οὓς οὐδὲν ἔφαμεν ἑρμηνεύειν πλέον ὧν ἅπαντες ἄνθρωποι γιγνώσκουσιν. ... οὓς οἱ δεινοὶ περὶ τὰς προηγορίας οὐδ' ὅρους ἀξιοῦσιν, ἀλλ' ὑπογραφάς τε καὶ ὑποτυπώσεις ὀνομάζειν. Stobaeus gives an example of a Stoic ὑπογραφή of ἐπιτήδευμα (*Anth.* 2.67.11–12 = Long/Sedley 26H): "They outline 'pursuit' in this manner: it is a road which leads through skill or [some] part [of skill] to things which are in accord with excellence," τό τε ἐπιτήδευμα τοῦτον ὑπογράφουσι τὸν τρόπον· ὁδὸν διὰ τέχνης ἢ μέρους ἄγουσαν ἐπὶ ⟨τὰ⟩ κατ'

and his school meanwhile reject ὅρος as a necessary preliminary step, probably because of their emphasis upon empiricism and induction,[23] although they endorse the use of such ὑπογραφαί. As Elizabeth Asmis explains,

> ... [a] definition was thought to "unfold" or "explicate" what a thing is, or, in other words, to display what is implicit in the ordinary concept of the thing. In contrast, an "outline" or "sketch" was said to be a description that brings to mind the ordinary, empirically acquired concept of a thing by stating certain prominent features that are obvious to everyone. Accordingly, whereas a definition was designed to replace an ordinary concept as a standard of investigation, an outline description was used to remind the investigator of the ordinary concept so that the ordinary concept might serve as a standard of investigation.[24]

Epicurus thereby strives to escape the logical trap of infinite regress that Sextus Empiricus points out (οὐδὲν ὁριζόμεθα διὰ τὴν εἰς ἄπειρον ἔκπτωσιν):[25] if in a ὑπογραφή one cleaves tightly only to obvious, indisputable attributes associated with the phenomenon in question, one avoids creating definitions comprised of elements which themselves require definitions *ad infinitum*. Nobody needs to define what everybody already knows, and if it requires more explication than a simple reminder it cannot serve as a useful foundation.[26] There-

---

ἀρετήν. This is an especially interesting sample. The passage earlier draws a contrast between sciences (ἐπιστῆμαι) and pursuits, the latter being the love of music, letters, horses and hunting: these train the mind and the body in a systematic fashion, but do not attain the level of research. The outline affirms their value in promoting ἀρετή. The thing that makes this statement a ὑπογραφή as opposed to a ὅρος is that it makes no effort to isolate the particularity which separates it from neighboring phenomena: it does not claim that a pursuit is the *only* thing which produces the stated results. Furthermore, the outline uses the ordinary meanings of words in order to speak both metaphorically (a pursuit is a *road* which leads to the achievement of *excellence*) and with philosophical precision (it is a *method* which leads to a life of *virtue*).

[23] Cicero, *Fin.* 1.22: "[Epicurus] abolishes definitions; he teaches nothing regarding dividing and partitioning; he does not transmit [instruction on] how an idea is proven and argued; he does not disclose [a method] by which fallacies are resolved and amibiguities rendered distinct; he places the criteria of things in the senses, by which, if in one instance something of the false is [determined to be] correct instead of the true, he regards every criterion of the true and the false to have been abolished...." *Tollit definitiones; nihil de dividendo ac partiendo docet; non quomodo efficiatur concludaturque ratio tradit, non qua via captiosa solvantur, ambigua distinguantur ostendit; iudicia rerum in sensibus ponit, quibus si semel aliquid falsi pro vero probatum sit, sublatum esse omne iudicium veri et falsi putat....*

[24] Asmis, *Epicurus' Scientific Method*, 43.

[25] Sextus Empiricus, *Pyr.* 2.207. The remark οὐδὲν ὁριζόμεθα διὰ τὴν εἰς ἄπειρον ἔκπτωσιν is part of his argument that one must define either everything or nothing. Ps.-Athenasius contrives an amusing solution to this problem (*De definitionibus* 3, PG 28.533): "The definition of definitions is the one which simultaneously defines all things and itself is defined by nothing: thus the only definition of definitions is God," ὅρος τῶν ὅρων ἐστὶν ὁ πάντα μὲν ὁρίζων, αὐτὸς δὲ ὑπ' οὐδενὸς ὁριζόμενος· ὥστε μόνος ὅρος τῶν ὅρων ἐστὶν ὁ θεός.

[26] On this point see Epicurus, *Herod.* 37–38 = Long/Sedley 17C, esp.: "For it is necessary that the first concept be perceived according to each [articulate] sound and to require nothing from demonstration, if we shall grasp the thing being investigated, or being made a matter of question and [subsequently] being believed, to which we shall refer," ἀνάγκη γὰρ τὸ πρῶτον

fore "the intrinsic clarity of a term is destroyed by definition."[27] We may now discern what Diogenes means in his definition of ὑπογραφή quoted above, that it conveys "the force of definition more simply than definition" (ἁπλούστερον τὴν τοῦ ὅρου δύναμιν προσενηνεγμένος). Ἁπλούστερον refers to a restriction in scope; a ὑπογραφή retains the formal features of a definition while limiting its claims to superficialities. It thus can serve as the starting point of an analysis toward the construction of a ὅρος, like Plato's description of ἔρως as a "kind of desire."

In spite of their similarities, however, rhetorical definitions are not ὑπογραφαί. Both obtain agreement between speaker and audience. But rhetorical definitions are not meant to call to mind the "empirically acquired concept of

---

ἐννόημα καθ' ἕκαστον φθόγγον βλέπεσθαι καὶ μηθὲν ἀποδείξεως προσδεῖσθαι, εἴπερ ἕξομεν τὸ ζητούμενον ἢ ἀπορούμενον καὶ δοξαζόμενον ἐφ' ὃ ἀνάξομεν. See also an anonymous commentator on Plato's *Theaetetus* (Long/Sedley 19F): "Epicurus says that names are clearer than definitions, and furthermore that it is silly if someone were to say 'Hello, rational mortal organism,' instead of 'Hello, Socrates,'" Ἐπίκου[ρ]ος τὰ ὀνόματά φησ[ι]ν σαφέστερα εἶναι τῶν ὅρων, καὶ μέντοι καὶ γελοῖον εἶναι εἴ τις ἀντὶ τοῦ εἰπεῖν «χαῖρε Σώκρατες» λέγοι «χαῖρε ζῷον λο[γ]ικὸν θνητόν».

[27] Asmis, *Epicurus' Scientific Method*, 39, esp. note 15. Diogenes Laertius gives a good example of an Epicurean ὑπογραφή at 10.33 = Long/Sedley 17E: "They mean 'preconception' as in 'apprehension,' or 'right opinion' or 'thought,' or 'a general idea held in store' – this is, memory – of something often externally perceived, for example: 'the human is such-and-such.' For at the moment that 'human' is uttered, immediately in accordance with preconception its type is also understood while the senses guide the way. Therefore the thing that primarily underlies any name is clear." τὴν δὲ πρόληψιν λέγουσιν οἱονεὶ κατάληψιν ἢ δόξαν ὀρθὴν ἢ ἔννοιαν ἢ καθολικὴν νόησιν ἐναποκειμένην, τουτέστι μνήμην, τοῦ πολλάκις ἔξωθεν φανέντος, οἷον τὸ «τοιοῦτόν ἐστιν ἄνθρωπος». ἅμα γὰρ τῷ ῥηθῆναι ἄνθρωπος εὐθὺς κατὰ πρόληψιν καὶ ὁ τύπος αὐτοῦ νοεῖται προηγουμένων τῶν αἰσθήσεων. παντὶ οὖν ὀνόματι τὸ πρώτως ὑποτεταγμένον ἐναργές ἐστι. Diogenes, in conformity with his Epicurean sources, omits the expected definition of preconception and offers instead a series of (undefined) words that explain the term from several angles, followed by an illustration of its function. Another good example occurs at Epicurus, *Menoec*. 123 = Long/Sedley 23B: "First, supposing that 'god' is an immortal and blessed organism (as the common notion of 'god' was outlined), attach to him nothing foreign to immortality or unsuitable to blessedness," πρῶτον μὲν τὸν θεὸν ζῷον ἄφθαρτον καὶ μακάριον νομίζων, ὡς ἡ κοινὴ τοῦ θεοῦ νόησις ὑπεγράφη, μηθὲν μήτε τῆς ἀφθαρσίας ἀλλότριον μήτε τῆς μακαριότητος ἀνοίκειον αὐτῷ πρόσαπτε. This ὑπογραφή specifies only two predicates to god, and says nothing of ἣν δύναμιν ἔχει. Contrast a Stoic definition of god (Diogenes Laertius 7.147 = Long/Sedley 54A): "But 'god' is an immortal organism; rational, perfect and intelligible in blessedness; not accepting of any evil thing; providential of the world and of things in the world. He is not, however, in human form. But he is indeed the craftsman of the entire universe and is just like a father of all things, both generally and the part of him which extends through all things, which is labeled with many names according to its functions." θεὸν δ' εἶναι ζῷον ἀθάνατον, λογικόν, τέλειον καὶ νοερὸν ἐν εὐδαιμονίᾳ, κακοῦ παντὸς ἀνεπίδεκτον, προνοητικὸν κόσμου τε καὶ τῶν ἐν κόσμῳ· μὴ εἶναι μέντοι ἀνθρωπόμορφον. εἶναι δὲ ⟨αὐ⟩τὸν μὴν δημιουργὸν τῶν ὅλων καὶ ὥσπερ πατέρα πάντων, κοινῶς τε καὶ τὸ μέρος αὐτοῦ τὸ διῆκον διὰ πάντων, ὃ πολλαῖς προσηγορίαις προσονομάζεται κατὰ τὰς δυνάμεις.

a thing" (Epicurus), nor do they serve as preliminary instruments of scientific analysis (the Stoics). Orators may, like Socrates in the *Phaedrus*, set forth arguments that support a definition, but they often simply posit definitions and deploy them as authoritative and true. Naturally the composition of rhetorical definitions demands a great deal of care, because they must both command acceptance from the audience and tendentiously support the objectives of the orations in which they appear. One may observe this dual concern in popular philosophical texts, too, as for example in the definitions of atheism and superstition that appear early in Plutarch's *De superstitione*:

ἡ μὲν ἀθεότης κρίσις οὖσα φαύλη τοῦ μηδὲν εἶναι μακάριον καὶ ἄφθαρτον εἰς ἀπάθειάν τινα δοκεῖ τῇ ἀπιστίᾳ τοῦ θείου περιφέρειν, καὶ τέλος ἐστὶν αὐτῇ τοῦ μὴ νομίζειν θεοὺς τὸ μὴ φοβεῖσθαι· τὴν δὲ δεισιδαιμονίαν μηνύει καὶ τοὔνομα δόξαν ἐμπαθῆ καὶ δέους ποιητικὴν ὑπόληψιν οὖσαν ἐκταπεινοῦντος καὶ συντρίβοντος τὸν ἄνθρωπον οἰόμενον μὲν εἶναι θεοὺς, εἶναι δὲ λυπηροὺς καὶ βλαβερούς.

On the one hand, atheism, which is the misjudgment that there is nothing blessed or incorruptible, seems to result in a certain emotional detachment by disbelief in the divine, and its goal of not esteeming the gods is not to fear them. On the other hand, even the name δεισιδαιμονία discloses it as that which is an emotional opinion and a notion productive of a terror which humiliates and shatters a person, since one supposes that there are gods, but that they are grievous and harmful. (*Superst.* 165b)

Plutarch loads his definitions with scornful language that facilitates his goal of discrediting atheism and superstition as factually incorrect and productive of harm. Given these statements as a foundation, how could one not agree that reasonable piety is the proper course? He furthermore makes no effort to locate ἀθεότης and δεισιδαιμονία on a taxonomic grid, to work out their place among related phenomena. He does not appeal to any kind of scientific inquiry. He simply states οἷόν τ' ἔστι and ἣν ἔχει δύναμιν and moves forward.

Regarding the formal features of definitions, they typically have a simple statement of "*x* is *a*, *b* and *c*,"[28] with a form of the verb εἶναι (most frequently ἐστίν, but also ἔστω, which underscores a stipulative intent).[29] They can also take the form of relative clauses and attributive participial phrases when they are embedded in other sentences, as in Plutarch's definition of ἀθεότης as κρί-

---

[28] I say "*a*, *b* and *c*" in order to reflect the penchant of definitions to have multiple clauses, as many of the examples quoted in the footnotes above amply attest.

[29] E.g., Aristotle, *Rhet.* 1.2.1, 1355b, "Let rhetoric then be the ability to perceive what is potentially persuasive in every situation," ἔστω δὴ ῥητορικὴ δύναμις περὶ ἕκαστον τοῦ θεωρῆσαι τὸ ἐνδεχόμενον πίθανον. Sometimes authors will present their definitions dialogically, for example Epictetus, *Diatr.* 1.22.9–10 = Long/Sedley 40T: "What then is it to be educated? To learn to fit the natural preconceptions with the things that exist in a particular state in a manner corresponding to nature, and further to distinguish that, of the things that exist, some are possible for us and others are not possible for us." τί οὖν ἐστι τὸ παιδεύεσθαι; μανθάνειν τὰς φυσικὰς προλήψεις ἐφαρμόζειν ταῖς ἐπὶ μέρους οὐσίαις καταλλήλως τῇ φύσει καὶ λοιπὸν διελεῖν, ὅτι τῶν ὄντων τὰ μέν ἐστιν ἐφ' ἡμῖν, τὰ δὲ οὐκ ἐφ' ἡμῖν.

σις οὖσα φαύλη τοῦ μηδὲν εἶναι μακάριον καὶ ἄφθαρτον. The anonymous author of a study *de Homero* uses a relative clause in this definition of a rhetorical figure: "κατάχρησις then, which transfers an expression from the thing properly signified to another thing which does not properly have that name, is found in the Poet whenever he says: 'golden chain'" (κατάχρησις μὲν δή, ἥπερ ἀπὸ τοῦ κυρίως δηλουμένου μεταφέρει τὴν φράσιν ἐφ' ἕτερον οὐκ ἔχον ὄνομα κύριον, ἔστι παρὰ τῷ ποιητῇ, ὅταν λέγῇ «σειρὴν χρυσείην»).[30] Here the definitional relative clause also has a finite verb, μεταφέρει, instead of a form of εἶναι. Finally, definitions can incorporate short explanatory riders and abbreviated proofs. Aristotle defines happiness (εὐδαιμονία) thus in the *Ars rhetorica*:

ἔστω δὴ εὐδαιμονία εὐπραξία μετ' ἀρετῆς, ἢ αὐτάρκεια ζωῆς, ἢ ὁ βίος ὁ μετὰ ἀσφαλείας ἥδιστος, ἢ εὐθηνία κτημάτων καὶ σωμάτων μετὰ δυνάμεως φυλακτικῆς τε καὶ πρακτικῆς τούτων· σχεδὸν γὰρ τούτων ἓν ἢ πλείω τὴν εὐδαιμονίαν ὁμολογοῦσιν εἶναι ἅπαντες.

Let happiness then be good conduct with virtue; or self-sufficiency of life; or the most pleasant mode of life with security; or the prosperity of possessions and bodies with the ability both to protect and to use them. For almost all people agree that happiness is one or more or these things. (*Rhet.* 1.5.5, 1360b)

He covers his bases here through the accumulation of multiple definitions in order that all may find one with which they can agree, as he explains (γάρ). These are not the product of his rigorous inquiry, but an anthology of popular ideas stated as ὅροι.[31]

Rhetorical definition thus resembles philosophical definition, and retains several of its features: brevity, its "unfolding" of the definiendum, and the goal of securing agreement. It does not necessarily strive for completeness

---

[30] [Plutarch], *De Hom.* 2.18. The author continues: "For σειρά [chain] properly is assigned to 'rope,'" σειρὰ γὰρ κυρίως ἐπὶ τοῦ σχοινίου τάσσεται. The illustration is from Homer, *Il.* 8.19.

[31] The Stoic definition of κόσμος as reported by Diogenes (7.137–8 = Long/Sedley 44F) also includes a proof with causal adverbial participial phrases: "He is himself the god of a kind who is uniquely [comprised] from all existence, who is immortal and unborn, since he is the Demiurge of regulative order by consuming all existence into himself at certain periods of time and giving birth again from himself," αὐτόν τε τὸν θεὸν τὸν ἐκ τῆς ἁπάσης οὐσίας ἰδίως ποιόν, ὃς δὴ ἄφθαρτός ἐστι καὶ ἀγένητος, δημιουργὸς ὢν τῆς διακοσμήσεως, κατὰ χρόνων ποιὰς περιόδους ἀναλίσκων εἰς ἑαυτὸν τὴν ἅπασαν οὐσίαν καὶ πάλιν ἐξ ἑαυτοῦ γεννῶν. Epictetus at one point uses a simile as part of a demonstration in definition (*Diatr.* 3.6.8): "When someone inquired, what is common sense? he said, 'Just as the 'hearing' that is only the differentiation of sounds would be said to be 'common,' but the differentiation of musical notes [would] no longer [be said to be] 'common' but 'technical,' so also there are things which the people who are not utterly twisted perceive in accordance with their common resources. Such a condition is called common sense." πυθομένου δέ τινος, τί ἐστιν ὁ κοινὸς νοῦς, ὥσπερ, φησίν, κοινή τις ἀκοὴ λέγοιτ' ἂν ἡ μόνον φωνῶν διακριτική, ἡ δὲ τῶν φθόγγων οὐκέτι κοινή, ἀλλὰ τεχνική, οὕτως ἐστί τινα, ἃ οἱ μὴ παντάπασιν διεστραμμένοι τῶν ἀνθρώπων κατὰ τὰς κοινὰς ἀφορμὰς ὁρῶσιν. ἡ τοιαύτη κατάστασις κοινὸς νοῦς καλεῖται.

and scientific accuracy, however, but instead serves the aim of persuasion in the case at hand.

2.4 Rhetorical definition in theory and practice

Now that I have identified the general features and functions of rhetorical definition and established how it differs from the philosophical, I shall turn to some examples of how orators use the former practically. I seek to expose the ways that they apply definition argumentatively in the three major rhetorical γένη. In forensic contests, it can have direct relevance for both the prosecution and defense. In deliberative and epideictic orations, it often surfaces when the speeches deal with philosophical topics at a popular level.

2.4.1 Forensic oratory

Definition has a special utility in connection with forensic oration, both in the process of invention (εὕρεσις) and in the execution of proofs (πίστεις). As a result, rhetorical theorists discuss forensic definition extensively. The instruction given on this topic has relevance beyond the courtrooms for two reasons: (1) it confirms that inculcation of the skill of constructing and deploying definitions was part of the rhetorical curriculum,[32] and (2) the rhetorical theorists

---

[32] Another factor elevates the position of ὅρος in the rhetorical curriculum: its inclusion among the rhetorical figures and tropes (cf. § 3.3.2 below). An especially detailed discussion appears at [Cicero], *Rhet. Her.* 4.25.35. The author first states the basic definition with a general illustration: "Definition is that which encompasses the particular properties of some subject briefly and completely, in this manner: 'The sovereignty of the republic is the thing of which the dignity and grandeur of the state consist,'" *definitio est, quae rei alicuius proprias amplectitur potestates breviter et absolute, hoc modo: «maiestas rei publicae est in qua continetur dignitas et amplitudo civitatis»*. The second illustration clearly arises in a judicial context: "Injuries are things which violate the life of a certain person either by assault of the body or by insult of the ear or by some other disgrace," *item: «iniuriae sunt, quae aut pulsatione corpus ⟨aut⟩ convicio auris aut aliqua turpitudine vitam cuiuspiam violant»*. The third illustration argues that an act represents not *diligentia*, but *avaritia*: "This is not your frugality, but avarice, because frugality is the intentional conservation of one's possessions, avarice the harmful desire for the possessions of others," *item: «non e⟨s⟩t ista diligentia, sed avaritia, ideo quod diligentia est accurata conservatio suorum, avaritia iniuriosa adpetitio ali⟨en⟩orum»*. The fourth argues similarly regarding *fortitudo* and *temeritas*: "This is not your fortitude, but temerity, because fortitude is the contempt of toil and peril with the deliberation of utility and the compensation of favorable [results]; temerity is the undertaking of perils with the gladiatorial endurance, without consideration of [any] sufferings [involved]," *item: «non est ista fortitudo, sed temeritas, propterea quod fortitudo est contemptio laboris et periculi cum ratione utilitatis et conpensatione commodorum, temeritas est cum inconsiderata dolorum perpessione gladiatoria periculorum susceptio»*. These two examples would befit either a deliberative setting, arguing against courses of action which have been proposed (*ista diligentia, ista fortitudo*) but not yet undertaken, or an epideictic setting, blaming someone for

2.4 Rhetorical definition in theory and practice

explicitly state that one should borrow forensic heuristic and evidentiary strategies, including definition, in one's deliberative and epideictic speeches.[33]

Aristotle explains the basic legal premise behind the utility of definition in forensic argumentation:

ἐπεὶ δ' ὁμολογοῦντες πολλάκις πεπραχέναι ἢ τὸ ἐπίγραμμα οὐχ ὁμολογοῦσιν ἢ περὶ ὃ τὸ ἐπίγραμμα, οἷον λαβεῖν μὲν ἀλλ' οὐ κλέψαι, καὶ πατάξαι πρότερον ἀλλ' οὐχ ὑβρίσαι, καὶ συγγενέσθαι ἀλλ' οὐ μοιχεῦσαι, ἢ κλέψαι ἀλλ' οὐχ ἱεροσυλῆσαι (οὐ γὰρ θεοῦ τι), ἢ ἐπεργάσασθαι μὲν ἀλλ' οὐ δημόσιαν, ἢ διειλέχθαι μὲν τοῖς πολεμίοις ἀλλ' οὐ προδοῦναι, διὰ ταῦτα δέοι ἂν καὶ περὶ τούτων διωρίσθαι, τί κλοπή, τί ὕβρις, τί μοιχεία, ὅπως ἐάν τε ὑπάρχειν ἐάν τε μὴ ὑπάρχειν βουλώμεθα δεικνύναι ἔχωμεν ἐμφανίζειν τὸ δίκαιον. ἔστι δὲ πάντα τὰ τοιαῦτα περὶ τοῦ ἄδικον εἶναι καὶ φαῦλον ἢ μὴ ἄδικον ἡ ἀμφισβήτησις· ἐν γὰρ τῇ προαιρέσει ἡ μοχθηρία καὶ τὸ ἀδικεῖν, τὰ δὲ τοιαῦτα τῶν ὀνομάτων προσσημαίνει τὴν προαίρεσιν, οἷον ὕβρις καὶ κλοπή.

But since people, often when they confess to having done something, do not confess either to the charge or to the matter to which the charge pertains – for example, to have indeed taken, but not to have stolen; and to have struck first but not to have committed criminal assault [ὑβρίσαι]; and to have 'been with' but not to have committed adultery; or to have stolen but not to have robbed a temple, for the item was not a god's; or indeed to have tilled land but not *public* land; or to have spoken with enemies but not to have betrayed – on account of these things it would be necessary that one supply definitions for oneself [διωρίσθαι] regarding them (what is theft, what is criminal assault, what is adultery) so that, if we want to show if it does or does not belong [to these categories],[34] we should be able to display the justice [of the act]. But in all such cases the dispute pertains [either] to the act being unjust and bad, or to not being unjust. For the depravity and the commission of injustice is in the *intent* [τῇ προαιρέσει], and such terms, for example criminal assault and theft, signify the intent. (*Rhet.* 1.13.9–10, 1373b–1374a)

The facts of the case and the legal categories to which they belong have a dynamic relationship; one may thus admit to an action but deny its criminality based upon the intent behind its commission.[35] Laws, both written and unwritten, against injustices supply the raw materials for the construction of defini-

---

the avarice or temerity of an act already committed. The latter differs from the second, forensic definition in that it impugns the addressee's moral character as opposed to prosecuting or defending against an accusation of criminality. After these illustrations, the author concludes: "Therefore this adornment is regarded as suitable, because it plainly and briefly lays out every function and property of any subject, so that it may not be seen as necessary to state it with more words, nor that it may be considered possible to state it more briefly," *haec ideo commoda putatur exornatio, quod omnem rei cuiuspiam vim et potestatem ita dilucide proponit et ⟨explicat⟩ breviter, ut neque pluribus verbis oportuisse dici videatur neque brevius potuisse dici putetur.*

[33] Cicero, *Inv.* 2.12; *Top.* 93–94; Quintilian, *Inst.* 3.6.81–82, 3.7.28.

[34] For this usage of ὑπάρχειν, see LSJ 1853–54, s.v. B.III.1.

[35] In classical Athens there evidently was a court dedicated to hearing such pleas, the δελφίνιον δικαστήριον, as Demosthenes (*Aristocr.* 74–75) describes it. This passage also interestingly states that the legislators "define clearly the circumstances under which it is permissable to kill," διορίζουσι σαφῶς ἐφ' οἷς ἐξεῖναι ἀποκτιννύναι (at *Lept.* 158 he names the legislator as Draco, ἔθηκεν ἐφ' οἷς ἐξεῖναι ἀποκτιννύναι). On this court see further Aristotle, *Ath. pol.* 57.3.

tions in one's speech, while the purely human factor of the presence (or absence) of προαίρεσις supplies a key standard for determining whether an action fits the definition.[36]

In Hellenistic rhetorical theory, definition becomes one of the στάσεις (*constitutiones, status*), the "issues" that serve as analytic tools in εὕρεσις.[37] Quintilian's overview indicates that numerous theorists had developed competing systems.[38] That of Hermagoras (ii B.C.E.) seems to have exerted the widest influence in the Greco-Roman period, as lucidly explained (and modified) by Quintilian and Cicero.[39] Στάσεις help one to identify the best method of attack or defense. Issues proceed from questions, which can either be general (θέσις) or attached to actual circumstances (ὑπόθεσις). Forensic contests between real litigants naturally fall into the latter category.[40] First, if the question pertains to the facts of the case (did X kill Y?), the στάσις is "conjecture" (στοχασμός, *coniectura*).[41] Second, if the question has to do with how to clas-

---

[36] Cf. [Aristotle], *Rhet. Alex.* 4.8–9, 1427a, giving advice regarding τὸ ἀπολογητικόν: "Define injustice, error and bad luck thus: make 'injustice' doing something bad *purposely* [ἐκ προνοίας], and say that it is necessary to take the greatest vengence on such acts; but one must say that 'error' is doing something harmful because of ignorance; and make 'bad luck' completing well nothing of what was intended, not because of oneself, but because of certain other people or because of luck. And say that acting unjustly is a particularity [ἴδιον] of evil people, but acting erroneously and suffering misfortune in one's actions are not only a particularity of oneself, but also a commonality [κοινόν] of both the jurors and of other human beings." ἀδικίαν δὲ καὶ ἁμάρτημα καὶ ἀτυχίαν ὧδε ὅρισαι· τὸ μὲν ἐκ προνοίας κακόν τι ποιεῖν ἀδικίαν τίθει, καὶ φάθι δεῖν τιμωρίαν ἐπὶ τοῖς τοιούτοις τὴν μεγίστην λαμβάνειν· τὸ δὲ δι' ἄγνοιαν βλαβερόν τι πράττειν ἁμαρτίαν εἶναι φατέον. τὸ δὲ μὴ δι' ἑαυτόν, ἀλλὰ δι' ἑτέρους τινὰς ἢ διὰ τύχην μηδὲν ἐπιτελεῖν τῶν βουλευθέντων καλῶς ἀτυχίαν τίθει, καὶ φάθι τὸ μὲν ἀδικεῖν εἶναι τῶν πονηρῶν ἀνθρώπων ἴδιον, τὸ δὲ ἐξαμαρτ(άν)ειν καὶ περὶ τὰς πράξεις ἀτυχεῖν οὐ μόνου εἶναι ἑαυτοῦ ἴδιον, ἀλλὰ καὶ κοινὸν καὶ τῶν δικαζόντων καὶ τῶν ἄλλων ἀνθρώπων. See also Antiphon, *Tetr.* 3.2.5: "But even the law according to which I am prosecuted absolves me. For it commands that *the one who plans* [to kill someone] is a murderer." ἀπολύει δέ με καὶ ὁ νόμος καθ' ὃν διώκομαι. τὸν γὰρ ἐπιβουλεύσαντα κελεύει φονέα εἶναι.

[37] For discussions of the origins and the complexities of *stasis*-theory, see Kennedy, *New History*, 97–101; Russell, *Greek Declamation*, 40–73; Heath, "Substructure of Stasis-Theory"; and the prolegomena of idem, *Hermogenes On Issues*, 1–27. Heath's translation and commentary in this last volume is an excellent resource for later *stasis*-theory. (I opt to present the system of Hermagoras according to Quintilian as the one most widely available to authors and audiences of Paul's generation.) Hermogenes introduces definition at *Stas.* 37 and discusses its divisions at 59–65. See also [Hermogenes], *Inv.* 3.14.

[38] *Inst.* 3.6.

[39] Quintilian does not describe his own system as a modification of Hermagoras', but his summary of the latter (*Inst.* 3.6.56–57) and his subsequent exposition make this sufficiently clear. I quote Cicero's definitions in the notes below.

[40] Quintilian, *Inst.* 3.5.5–9.

[41] Cicero, *Inv.* 1.10: "When the controversy is of fact, the *stasis* is named conjectural, since the case is strengthened with conjectures," *cum facti controversia est, quoniam coniecturis causa firmatur, constitutio coniecturalis appellatur.*

sify an admitted fact (X killed Y, but was it murder?), the στάσις is "definition" (ὅρος, *definitio*).[42] Third, if concomitant circumstances or other factors mitigate an admitted and classified fact (X murdered Y, but was it justified?), the στάσις is "quality" (ποιότης, κατὰ συμβεβηκός, *generalis, qualitas*).[43] Hermagoras proposes a fourth, "translation" (μετάληψις, *translatio*) that pleads the transference of the case to a different court.[44] Overall this theoretical framework deals with contests between litigants, but the theorists expressly state that it is equally essential for deliberative and epideictic orations: one can use στάσις-theory to analyze any question of a definite nature (i.e., that deals with concrete facts, whether real or hypothetical), or of an indefinite nature (general questions), that permits two or more competing positions, in order to isolate the best possible evidentiary tactics toward the desired result.

Cicero helpfully outlines the procedures of the definitional στάσις for both plaintiff and defendant in his *De inventione*.[45] He sketches out a case that pits the power of a tribune (*tribunicia potestas*) against that of a father (*patria potestas*). C. Flaminius proposes agrarian legislation designed to sow discord between the lower and upper classes. While he addresses the *concilium plebis*

---

[42] Cicero, *Inv.* 1.10: "When however [the controversy] is of name, the *stasis* is designated definitional, because the force of the term is to be defined with words," *cum autem nominis, quia vis vocabuli definienda verbis est, constitutio definitiva nominatur*. [Cicero], *Rhet. Her.* 1.11.19 places definition under the heading of "legal issue" (*legitima*) among sub-types that Hermagoras places under translation. The development of this στάσις may indirectly depend on Plato's *Euthyphro*, wherein the title character is prosecuting his father for φόνος (3e–4e), prompting his family's response that such prosecution is ἀνόσιον. Socrates and Euthyphro thus investigate the meanings of τὸ ὅσιον and τὸ ἀνόσιον. For analysis of this dialogue, see Cohen, "Socrates on the Definition of Piety"; Judson, "Carried Away in the *Euthyprho*."

[43] Cicero, *Inv.* 1.10: "But when moreover it is asked what kind of thing a subject is, the *stasis* is called generic, because the controversy is both regarding the meaning and the kind of situation " *cum vero, qualis res sit, quaeritur, quia et de vi et de genere negotii controversia est, constitutio generalis vocatur*. Hermagoras' divisions, according to Cicero (*Inv.* 1.12, cf. Quintilian, *Inst.* 3.6.56–57), are deliberative, demonstrative, *iuridicalis* (dealing with "the nature of the fair and the right," *aequi et recti natura*, 1.14) and *negotialis* ("in which it is considered what may be [the nature] of the law from public custom and equity," *in qua, quid iuris ex civili more et aequitate sit, consideratur*, ibid.). Cicero vigorously disputes the validity of the deliberative and demonstrative divisions.

[44] Quintilian, *Inst.* 3.6.60–61. Cicero, *Inv.* 1.10: "But when the case hangs on the fact either that the person does not appear to be the one who ought to bring the case, or not with [i.e., against] the one whom he ought, or not before which [judges], at which time, by which law, by which charge, by which penalty he ought, the stasis is called translative, because an action of transferrence or alteration [of venue] appears necessary," *at cum causa ex eo pendet, quia non aut is agere videtur, quem oportet, aut non cum eo, quicum oportet, aut non apud quos, quo tempora, qua lege, quo crimine, qua poena oportet, translativa dicitur constitutio, quia actio translationis et commutationis indigere videtur*.

[45] Heath (*Hermogenes On Issues*, 175–91) gives several more examples of definitional stasis with analysis according to the Hermogenean system.

his own father lays hands on him and hauls him from the rostrum, resulting in an accusation of lèse-majesté. Cicero sets forth the positions schematically:[46]

Complaint: "You committed lèse-majesté, because you pulled a tribune of the plebs from the rostrum," *maiestatem minuisti, quod tribunum plebis de templo deduxisti.*
Reply: "I did not commit lèse-majesté," *non minui maiestatem.*
Question: "Did he commit lèse-majesté?" *maiestatemne minuerit?*
Reasoning for the defense: "For I exercised the power which I had at the time over my son," *in filium enim quam habebam potestatem, ea sum usus.*
Rebuttal: "But surely the one who weakens the tribune's power – this is the *people's* power – with the father's power – this is a kind of *private* power – committed lèse-majesté," *at enim, qui patria potestate, hoc est privata quadam, tribuniciam potestatem, hoc est populi potestatem infirmat, minuit maiestatem.*
Point to be adjudicated: "Would the one who exercises the father's power against the tribune's power commit lèse-majesté?" *minuatne is maiestatem, qui in tribuniciam potestatem patria potestate utatur?*

Such an analysis of the problem into a quasi-dialogue between the plaintiff, defendant and the jury, culiminating in the identification of the point to be adjudicated (τὸ κρινόμενον, *iudicatio*) to which the litigants address their arguments,[47] constitutes the initial stage of εὕρεσις: through it one discovers the problem to be one of definition. Cicero then outlines the argumentative tactics of the prosecution as a series of steps.[48]

(1) The provision of a "brief, plain and generally credible definition" (*brevis et aperta et ex opinione hominum definitio*) of the key term.
(2) The confirmation of the accuracy of the definition.
(3) The assertion that the deed fits the definition.
(4) The appeal to the emotion of the jurors by exaggerating the heinousness of the crime.
(5) The refutation of the defendant's definition by showing that it does not conform to common usage, or that its acceptance is disadvantageous or dishonorable.[49]
(6) The affirmation of one's own definition with examples from parallel cases.

The defense follows a similar series of steps.[50]

(1) The provision of the definition.
(2) The confirmation of the definition.

---

[46] *Inv.* 2.52.

[47] *Inv.* 2.52: "It will be necessary to direct all arguments to this point to be adjudicated," *ad hanc iudicationem argumentationes omnes afferre oportebit.*

[48] *Inv.* 2.53–55.

[49] *Inv.* 2.54: "[The adversaries' definition] will also be disproved if the acceptance of this description is shown to be disgraceful or useless; and it will be shown, if [the definition] is conceded, what disadvantages may follow (this is, however, taken from the *partes* of honor and utility, about which we will offer explanation among the precepts of deliberation)," *item infirmabitur, si turpis aut inutilis esse* [*ostenditur*] *eius descriptionis adprobatio et, quae incommoda consecutura sint eo concesso, ostenditur – id autem ex honestas et ex utilitatis partibus sumetur, de quibus in deliberationis praeceptis exponemus.* This appeal to deliberative "precepts" in a forensic argumentive outline illustrates the easy transference of rhetorical strategies between γένη.

[50] *Inv.* 2.55–56.

(3) The separation of the act and the definition.
(4) The exaggeration of the deed's advantage and honor.
(5) The refutation of the plaintiff's definition by accusing him of "aiming not only to upend facts but also to pervert words" (*non res solum convertere, verum etiam verba commutare conari*), or by the use of other *communes loci* to arouse sympathy from the jury.

In conjunction with the first step Cicero gives two different definitions of lèse-majesté that illustrate the tendentious direction of rhetorical definition toward the orator's objective.[51] The plaintiff says: "To commit lèse-majesté is to diminish something about either the dignity, influence or power of the people, or those to whom the people gave power" (*maiestatem minuere est de dignitate aut amplitudine aut potestate populi aut eorum, quibus populus potestatem dedit, aliquid derogare*).[52] The defense counters by saying: "To commit lèse-majesté is to administer some business pertaining to the state when you do not have the power" (*maiestatem minuere est aliquid de re publica, cum potestatem non habeas, administrare*).[53] The plaintiff aims his definition at the point at issue, implicitly portraying any violence against a tribune as an offence against the people and their own *dignitas* and *potestas*. The defense blunts this by defining the term as the improper usurpation of *potestas*. In this situation, a father may exercise his right to discipline his adult son without any incursion into the dignity of the people; it remains purely a familial matter. However tendentious these definitions may be, neither litigant is excused from verifying its conformity with *opinio hominum*,[54] the primary standard by which the auditors judge it, in the second and subsequent steps of the argument. The litigants must "unfold" their definitions to demonstrate their accuracy prior to the crucial moment when each asks: "Does the definition accurately describe the act under consideration?"

2.4.2 Deliberative oratory

Deliberative speeches properly have their home in the public assembly (ἐκκλησία) in debates about state policy,[55] but the genre adapts well to the con-

---

[51] Cf. [Cicero], *Rhet. Her.* 2.12.17: "First, therefore, the meaning of the terms is assigned briefly and *toward utility*, in a manner befitting the case," *primum igitur vocabuli sententia breviter et ad utilitatem adcommodate causae describitur*.

[52] *Inv.* 2.53.

[53] *Inv.* 2.55.

[54] Such is the case unless the laws furnish part or all of the definitions of terms. Cf. Cicero, *De or.* 2.107, wherein Antonius discusses another trial for lèse-majesté: "I nevertheless was denying lèse-majéste by that man, on which term the entire case was hanging in view of the *lex Appuleia*," *tamen ab illo maiestatem minutam negebam, ex quo verbo lege Appuleia tota illa causa pendebat*. Antonius later declares that in a situation of definitional *stasis*, he does not construct actual definitions, since this strategy stikes him as puerile and unsuitable.

[55] Isocrates provides a couple of examples of how definition can factor into such speeches. In *De pace* 18 he says: "Thus I shall attempt to teach you regarding these matters through the entire speech, but first let's converse about peace, and consider why we might

sideration of philosophical questions at a popular level. Plato clearly marks Socrates' first oration on love as deliberative in its προοίμιον (βουλεύεσθαι, βουλή) and in the questions that he frames: should one prefer the suitor who is in the grip of ἔρως, or the one who is not? Does ἔρως cause benefit or harm? These questions broadly conform to the conventional wisdom that deliberative speeches weigh the advantages and disadvantages of particular courses of action.[56]

Another deliberative discourse that deals with abstractions similar to ἔρως is Dio Chrysostom's 14th oration περὶ δουλείας καὶ ἐλευθερίας. It begins like a speech, but it shifts toward dialogue mid-stream as Dio deploys diatribe as a means of moving his argument forward. After complaining that, while everyone knows that slavery is bad and freedom good, most people have no conception of what these terms mean and thus confuse the two (14.1–2), he proposes an investigation: "So come, let us consider if indeed most people know anything clear about freedom and slavery" (φέρε δὴ σκεψώμεθα εἰ ἄρα τι οἱ πολλοὶ ἐπίστανται περὶ ἐλευθερίας καὶ δουλείας σαφές, 14.3). He then quotes the ordinary definition of the former – "to be subject to nobody, but simply to do the things that seem good to oneself" (τὸ μηδενὸς ὑπήκοον, ἀλλὰ πράττειν ἁπλῶς τὰ δοκοῦντα ἑαυτῷ, 14.3) – and begins to test its veracity.[57] Already we

---

want it to be ours at this moment. For if we define these things well and sensibly, by keeping an eye on this proposition we shall deliberate better also regarding the other matters." ταῦτα μὲν οὖν διὰ παντὸς τοῦ λόγου πειρασόμεθα διδάσκειν ὑμᾶς. περὶ δὲ τῆς εἰρήνης πρῶτον διαλεχθῶμεν καὶ σκεψώμεθα τί ἂν ἐν τῷ παρόντι γενέσθαι βουληθεῖμεν ἡμῖν. ἢν γὰρ ταῦτα καλῶς ὁρισώμεθα καὶ νουνεχόντως, πρὸς ταύτην τὴν ὑπόθεσιν ἀποβλέποντες, ἄμεινον βουλευσόμεθα καὶ περὶ τῶν ἄλλων. In *Nic.* 9 he constructs a definition to exhort his reader: "First then we should consider what the function [ἔργον] of those who rule as kings is: for if we encompass well the meaning of the whole subject in summary terms, then by keeping an eye on it we will speak better also concerning its parts. I thus suppose that all would agree that it befits them [i.e., kings] to put a stop to a city that is in suffering, to protect one doing well, and to make a great one from a small one; for the other things which occur each and every day are to be taken care of for the sake of these things." πρῶτον μὲν οὖν σκεπτέον τί τῶν βασιλευόντων ἔργον ἐστίν· ἂν γὰρ ἐν κεφαλαίοις τὴν δύναμιν ὅλου τοῦ πράγματος καλῶς περιλάβωμεν, ἐνταῦθ' ἀποβλέποντες ἄμεινον καὶ περὶ τῶν μερῶν ἐροῦμεν. οἶμαι δὴ πάντας ἂν ὁμολογῆσαι προσήκειν αὐτοῖς πόλιν τε δυστυχοῦσαν παῦσαι καὶ καλῶς πράττουσαν διαφυλάξαι καὶ μεγάλην ἐκ μικρᾶς ποιῆσαι· τὰ γὰρ ἄλλα τὰ συμπίπτοντα κατὰ τὴν ἡμέραν ἑκάστην τούτων ἕνεκα πρακτέον ἐστί.

[56] As I say above, the deliberative γένος generally envisions a context of deliberating law or state policy, but the ancient sources also plainly state that the genre relates to the determination of what is *advantageous* (τὸ σύμφερον, Aristotle, *Rhet.* 1.3.5, 1358b; [Cicero], *Rhet. Her.* 3.2.3; cf. Quintilian, *Inst.* 3.8.1). Plato poses precisely this question. See further Mitchell, *Paul and the Rhetoric of Reconciliation*, 25–32.

[57] Cf. Epictetus' definition of ὁ ἐλεύθερός at *Diatr.* 4.1.1: "The free person is the one who lives as he wishes, whom it is possible neither to compel nor to hinder nor to constrain, whose impulses are unobstructed, desires achievable, aversions unstumbling," ἐλεύθερός ἐστιν ὁ ζῶν ὡς βούλεται, ὃν οὔτ' ἀναγκάσαι ἔστιν οὔτε κωλῦσαι οὔτε βιάσασθαι, οὗ αἱ ὁρμαὶ ἀνεμπόδιστοι, αἱ ὀρέξεις ἐπιτευκτικαί, αἱ ἐκκλίσεις ἀπερίπτωτοι.

encounter a significant difference between *Or.* 14 and our passage from the *Phaedrus.* Whereas Plato separates question, definition and proposition, Dio's question and proposition (which he has not yet disclosed) address the definition directly: is it correct or not? If it is not, what *is* the correct definition?

Dio uses a procedure that I shall call 'exegesis of the terms': the further ἐξάπλωσις of each of the definition's components in order to confirm or refute its validity.[58] He deconstructs the false definition of freedom initially by attacking its first term, τὸ μηδενὸς ὑπήκοον, with numerous examples of free people who submit to the control of others, and by relentlessly playing this term against the other, πράττειν ἁπλῶς τὰ δοκοῦντα ἑαυτῷ. Dio gives more credit to the tenacity of οἱ πολλοί as they cling to their mistaken idea of freedom, however, so he appoints for them a diatribal interlocutor at 14.11. Dio and his imaginary companion consider τὸ μηδενὸς ὑπήκοον from several more angles (acting to one's own advantage, the freedom to abuse others, the cases of captives of war or of pirates, and the case of the criminal in the power of a judge). Finally, the interlocutor, in a tacit admission of defeat, ventures a second definition that drops the first term and moves the second to the front: "But certainly it is right to declare, gathering [everything] together in a single statement, that he for whom it is possible to do what he wants is free, but he for whom it is not possible is a slave" (ἀλλὰ μὴν ἑνὶ λόγῳ συλλαβόντα χρὴ ἀποφήνασθαι ὡς ὅτῳ μὲν ἔξεστιν ὃ βούλεται πράττειν, ἐλεύθερός ἐστιν, ὅτῳ δὲ μὴ ἔξεστι, δοῦλος, 14.13). Dio immediately forces a qualification, however: free people may experience compulsion by circumstances, by laws,[59] and especially by public mores,[60] all of which override ὃ βούλεται. This concession renders the second term of the original definition null as well. Dio has finally cleared enough ground to start gathering his own elements toward the determination of the 'right' answer to the 'real' question: what are *true* freedom

---

[58] Cf. Varro, *Ling. lat.* 10.75, discussing his treatments of *analogia*: "I judge these things to be said more diligently than more clearly, but not more obscurely than are the definitions of the grammarians regarding a similar matter..., whose obscurities are so much less to be disapproved, since most definitions, when the matter is unfamiliar, are not easily studied on account of their extreme brevity, unless they are explicated point by point," *haec diligentius quam apertius dicta esse arbitror, sed non obscurius quam de re simili definitiones grammaticorum sunt..., quorum obscuritates eo minus reprehendendae, quod pleraeque definitiones re incognita propter summam brevitatem non facile perpiciuntur, nisi articulatim sunt explicata⟨e⟩.*

[59] 14.13: "Well then, it is in no way possible for others to do what they like, but if someone does [something] against the laws which are laid down, he will suffer punishment," οὐ τοίνυν οὐδὲ τοῖς ἄλλοις ἔξεστιν ἃ ἐθέλουσι ποιεῖν, ἀλλ' ἐάν τις παρὰ τοὺς νόμους τοὺς κειμένους πράττῃ, ζημιώσεται.

[60] 14.14: "Do you suppose that it is possible for you [to do] as much as has not been forbidden in writing by laws, but otherwise seems shameful and unnatural to people?" οἴει σοι ἐξεῖναι, ὅσα μὴ ἀπείρηται μὲν ὑπὸ τῶν νόμων ἐγγράφως, αἰσχρὰ δὲ ἄλλως δοκεῖ τοῖς ἀνθρώποις καὶ ἄτοπα.

and *true* slavery? The penalties that deter people from breaking laws or violating social taboos need to be known in order for them to operate effectively:

Οὐκοῦν οἱ φρόνιμοι ὅσα βούλονται πράττειν, ἔξεστιν αὐτοῖς· οἱ δὲ ἄφρονες ἃ βούλονται οὐκ ἐξὸν ἐπιχειροῦσι πράττειν· ὥστε ἀνάγκη τοὺς μὲν φρονίμους ἐλευθέρους τε εἶναι καὶ ἐξεῖναι αὐτοῖς ποιεῖν ὡς ἐθέλουσι, τοὺς δὲ ἀνοήτους δούλους τε εἶναι καὶ ἃ μὴ ἔξεστιν αὐτοῖς ταῦτα ποιεῖν;
Ἴσως.
Οὐκοῦν καὶ τὴν ἐλευθερίαν χρὴ λέγειν ἐπιστήμην τῶν ἐφειμένων καὶ τῶν κεκωλυμένων, τὴν δὲ δουλείαν ἄγνοιαν ὧν τε ἔξεστι καὶ ὧν μή.

Dio: Accordingly sensible people – it is possible for them to do as much as they want. But the senseless set out to do what they want – that being impossible.[61] So are the sensible necessarily free and is it possible for them to do as they will? And are the senseless slaves, and are they doing what is not possible for them?
Interl.: Perhaps.
Dio: Therefore it is necessary to say that freedom is knowledge of the permitted and the forbidden, and slavery is ignorance of what is possible and what is not. (14.17–18)

The logic seems to run as follows: (1) all people (from the greatest to the least) are constrained in their actions; (2) real penalties enforce these constraints; (3) the ability to recognize the constraints leads to the ability to act without penalty, while the inability results inevitably in punishment; (4) thus the former person is 'free' and the latter is a 'slave.' All of this depends upon the fundamental premise that slaves (deservingly?) experience punishment, an unexpressed defining particularity (ἴδιον). Now ἔξεστιν can mean a couple of different things here, "it is possible" (as I render it above), and "it is allowed" or "permitted" (as ἐπιστήμη τῶν ἐφειμένων might imply).[62] Something *impossible* and something *forbidden* are not necessarily the same: so which idea does Dio have in mind? He seems to want both meanings to be operative through the coordination of ἔξεστιν with ἐπιστήμη and ἄγνοια. The emphasis on law as an active deterrent upon the behavior of free people promotes the translation "it is permitted," but the *recognition* of the deterrents becomes for the φρόνιμος a matter of the *possible* and *impossible*. This recognition is unavailable to ὁ ἄφρων, causing the confusion that leads to his misery and enslavement.[63]

Dio's final definition and argument may not seem very persuasive to us, but the oration proves illuminating in two important ways. First, although he

---

[61] I intentionally preserve the awkward syntax in my translation here.

[62] See LSJ 592, s.v. ἔξεστι; BDAG 348–49, s.v.

[63] Dio continues his argument by saying that with these definitions it is possible for the Great King to be a slave, and the chained and abused to be free. The interlocutor remarks that it seems very odd (σφόδρα ἄτροπον) that this should be possible, so Dio concludes with illustrations that confirm it: the free women of Thrace bear tattoos all the way up and down the social ladder; the king of a foreign people rules from a tower that he can never leave; Cronus and Odysseus are no less kings by virtue of the former's chains and the latter's disguise as a beggar. In short, things are not always what they seem on their surfaces.

adopts a dialogical format and an overt philosophical tone, the oration remains just that – a presentation which he designs for the enjoyment and edification of a diverse audience, a deliberative speech dressed in philosophical costume. It hardly represents a substantive effort to probe the essence of ἐλευθερία and δουλεία. Dio instead urges his auditors to be φρόνιμοι, to act in a manner that avoids inciting punishment, by exploiting cultural attitudes about the shamefulness of slavery and the glory of freedom as an argumentative framework on the one hand and an emotional goad on the other. Anyone of any social standing or educational level can take his exhortation to heart. Second, Dio uses methods common in philosophical inquiry, and is self-consciously following the model of Plato's definitional dialogues. He sets out to demolish the popular definition of freedom by refuting its first term with counter-examples, then its second by pointing to legal and social constraints on what a free person can do. The wreckage of the second term then supplies the building blocks for his own definition: the knowledge of constraints results in the freedom to act unpunished. Dio does not, however, employ the procedure of διαίρεσις here (beyond the division of humanity into "slaves" and "free"), which he may have judged to be unsuitable for his audience. The oration de-mystifies the philosophical method of definition for a popular audience toward the promotion of their power to improve their own lots in life.

2.4.3 Epideictic oratory

The province of epideictic oratory is praise and blame, frequently (but not always) for the purpose of displaying the speaker's rhetorical prowess. When the subject is a human being, carefully formulated definitions of the sort we have examined above rarely if ever come into play. But one may regard an epideictic speech as broadly definitional, since it strives to capture a person's nature by outlining his or her parentage, rearing, and deeds with a view to defending the thesis that such a person deserves accolade or reproach.[64] Epideictic speeches also address the virtues of inanimate objects or abstractions.[65] For

---

[64] On these topics as features of ἐγκώμιον, see Burgess, *Epideictic Literature*, 199–26, and the sources cited there.

[65] See Burgess, *Epideictic Literature*, 157–66, on παράδοξον ἐγκώμιον. These kinds of speeches must be very old, since Aristotle refers to them in passing (*Rhet.* 1.9.2, 1366a): "But since it happens that (either without seriousness or with seriousness) someone often praises not only a person or a god but also lifeless things and any possible one of the other animals...," ἐπεὶ δὲ συμβαίνει καὶ χωρὶς σπουδῆς καὶ μετὰ σπουδῆς ἐπαινεῖν πολλάκις οὐ μόνον ἄνθρωπον ἢ θεὸν ἀλλὰ καὶ ἄψυχα καὶ τῶν ἄλλων ζῴων τὸ τυχόν.... See also Quintilian, *Inst.* 3.7.6, 26–28; Menander Rhetor, *Epid.* 1.332. Burgess remarks (*Epideictic Literature*, 165): "The oration assigned to Lysias in Plato's *Phaedrus* (231–34B) may be classed as a παράδοξον ἐγκώμιον." In a way, he is right: as in declamation in later rhetoric, which could take the *form* of a forensic or deliberative speech (*controversia, suasoria*) but retain the *function* of epideictic display, Lysias does not present a real deliberation (i.e., he is not attempting

34 Chapter 2: The Features and Functions of Definition

example, why does law (ὁ νόμος) deserve praise? Because it is "a ruler of life, a universal administrator of states, a just guideline for cases, with which each person must set his own way of life straight; otherwise it will be crooked and worthless" (ἔστι δὲ ὁ νόμος τοῦ βίου μὲν ἡγεμών, τῶν πόλεων δὲ ἐπιστάτης κοινός, τῶν δὲ πραγμάτων κανὼν δίκαιος, πρὸς ὃν ἕκαστον ἀπευθύνειν δεῖ τὸν αὑτοῦ τρόπον· εἰ δὲ μή, σκόλιος ἔσται καὶ πονηρός).[66] And why does custom (τὸ ἔθος) deserve praise? Because it is "the common judgment of those who use it, and an unwritten law of a people or state, and voluntarily just, pleasing to all for these same reasons, and a discovery of no one person, but of life and time" (ἔστι δὲ τὸ ἔθος γνώμη μὲν τῶν χρωμένων κοινή, νόμος δὲ ἄγραφος ἔθνους ἢ πόλεως, δίκαιον δὲ ἑκούσιον, κατὰ ταὐτὰ πᾶσιν ἀρέσκον, εὕρημα δὲ ἀνθρώπων οὐδενός, ἀλλὰ βίου καὶ χρόνου).[67]

The oration from which the latter quotation comes, Dio's 76th, illustrates how definition and argument can relate in epideictic argument. The speech has a very simple structure. The definition of τὸ ἔθος functions as both the thesis statement (πρόθεσις) and introduction (προοίμιον). The proofs (πίστεις) are a series of self-contained comparisons (συγκρίσεις) of τὸ ἔθος and ὁ νόμος, giving the speech a sententious flavor. The oration lacks a conclusion (ἐπίλογος). *Or.* 76 may perhaps be an outline for a longer speech which would include the ordinary structural elements: Dio would select from the συγκρίσεις, and amplify them with illustrations and other arguments. But, as it stands, it conforms to Aristotle's observation that the most basic components of a speech are the πρόθεσις and the πίστεις.[68] Dio's first series of συγκρίσεις exegete the definition's terms in reverse order (χιασμός).

---

to seduce Phaedrus) but intends his speech for entertainment and instruction, like Socrates' later speech on the same themes.

[66] Dio Chrysostom, *Or.* 75.1. In this speech Dio offers several more definitions in which he makes no attempt at brevity. He instead praises by piling on clauses. For example, he declares that law benefits the gods as well as humans, "for which reason, I suppose, it has reasonably been called 'the king of humans and gods,' since it ends violence, overpowers insolence, corrects ignorance, punishes evil, helps all who petition it in private and public, aids the wronged, and discloses the proper course to those who are confused about something," ὅθεν οἶμαι καὶ βασιλεὺς εἰκότως ἀνθρώπων καὶ θεῶν κέκληται, τὴν μὲν βίαν καταλύων, τὴν δὲ ὕβριν καθαιρῶν, τὴν δὲ ἄνοιαν σωφρονίζων, τὴν δὲ κακίαν κολάζων, ἰδίᾳ δὲ καὶ κοινῇ πάντας τοὺς δεομένους ὠφελῶν, τοῖς μὲν ἀδικουμένοις βοηθῶν, τοῖς δὲ ἀπορουμένοις περί τινος μηνύων τὸ δέον (75.2). It is also "an assistant of old age, a teacher of youth, a co-worker of poverty, a protector of wealth, an ally to peace and an enemy to war," οὗτος ἐπίκουρος γήρως, διδάσκαλος νεότητος, πενίας συνεργός, φύλαξ πλούτου, τῇ μὲν εἰρήνῃ σύμμαχος, τῷ δὲ πολέμῳ ἐνάντιος (75.9).

[67] Dio Chrysostom, *Or.* 76.1.

[68] *Rhet.* 3.13.1, 1414a (see § 3.2.2 below).

(5) εὕρημα δὲ ἀνθρώπων οὐδένος, ἀλλὰ βίου καὶ χρόνου
76.1 τῶν μὲν οὖν ἄλλων νόμων ἕκαστος ἅπαξ δοκιμασθεὶς ἔλαβε τὴν ἰσχύν· τὸ δὲ ἔθος ἀεὶ δοκιμάζεται.
76.1 Therefore each of the other laws, once approved, has obtained its force; but custom is always being approved.

(4) κατὰ ταὐτὰ πᾶσιν ἀρέσκον
καὶ νόμος μὲν οὐδεὶς ῥαδίως ὑπὸ πάντων κριθήσεται· ταῖς γὰρ τῶν πλειόνων δόξαις κυροῦται· ἔθος δὲ οὐκ ἐνῆν γενέσθαι μὴ προδεχθὲν ὑπὸ πάντων.
And no single law will easily be judged acceptable by all, for it is ratified by the opinions of the majority; but custom cannot exist when it is not accepted by all.

(3) δίκαιον δὲ ἑκούσιον
κἀκεῖνος ἀπειλῶν καὶ βιαζόμενος μένει κύριος, ὑπὸ δὲ τῶν ἐθῶν πειθόμενοι καὶ καλὰ καὶ συμφέροντα κρίνομεν αὐτά. 76.2 διὸ μοι δοκεῖ τις ἂν προσεικάσαι τὸν μὲν ἔγγραφον νόμον τῇ δυνάμει τῆς τυραννίδος· φόβῳ γὰρ ἕκαστον καὶ μετὰ προστάγματος διαπράττεται· τὸ δὲ ἔθος μᾶλλον τῇ φιλανθρωπίᾳ τῆς βασιλείας. βουλόμενοι γὰρ αὐτῷ πάντες καὶ δίχα ἀνάγκης ἕπονται.
And that [law] remains the master by making threats and by forcing; but being persuaded by customs we judge them to be both good and beneficial. 76.2 Therefore it seems to me that someone might liken the written law to the power of tyranny, for it is brought into effect by fear and with command; but custom is more [like] the benevolence of kingship, for all people follow it willingly and apart from compulsion.[69]

(2) νόμος δὲ ἄγραφος ἔθνους ἢ πόλεως
καὶ νόμους μὲν ἴσμεν πολλοὺς ἀνῃρημένους ὑπὸ τῶν θέντων αὐτούς, ὡς πονηρούς· ἔθος δὲ οὐκ ἂν οὐδεὶς ῥᾳδίως δείξειε λελυμένον. καὶ μὴν τῷ παντὶ ῥᾷόν ἐστιν ἀνελεῖν ὅ τι βούλει τῶν ἐγγράφων ἢ τῶν ἐθῶν. 76.3 τὰ μὲν γὰρ ἂν ἀπαλείψῃς ἅπαξ, ἡμέρᾳ μιᾷ λέλυται· συνήθειαν δὲ πόλεως οὐκ ἔστιν ἐν πάνυ πολλῷ καταλῦσαι χρόνῳ. κἀκεῖνον μὲν ἐν σανίσιν ἢ στήλαις φυλάττονται· τῶν δὲ ἕκαστον ἐν ταῖς ἡμετέραις ψυχαῖς.
And we know about many laws which have been abolished as evil by those who set them; but nobody would easily identify a dissolved custom. And surely in every case it is easier to abolish whichever of the written laws one wishes than [any] of the customs. 76.3 For if you erase the former once, in a single day it has been dissolved; but it is not possible to destroy a town's custom [even] with very much time. And, regarding the former, they are preserved on tablets or stelae; but each one of [the customs are preserved] on our souls.

With this strategy Dio has confirmed each of his definition's terms except for the first, γνώμη μὲν τῶν χρωμένων κοινή, which effectively governs the others. The definition "unfolds" τὸ ἔθος, and the first series of proofs "unfold" it further, part by part. Custom, Dio shows, merits admiration because it exerts its strength at precisely the points where law is weak. Dio's procedure of exeget-

---

[69] Dio's remarks here hold immense interest for interpreters of Paul, who characterizes νόμος as a παιδαγωγός (Gal 3:23–39), and as the one of τὰ στοιχεῖα τοῦ κόσμου under which ἤμεθα δεδουλωμένοι (Gal 4:3). Cf. also Dio, Or. 76.4: "But in general one would say that the laws make a commonwealth of slaves, but customs on the contrary make one of free people. For the former cause punishments to their bodies; but when a custom is transgressed, it has turned out that the penalty is shame." καθόλου δὲ τοὺς μὲν νόμους φαίη τις ἂν ποιεῖν δούλων πολιτείαν, τὰ δὲ ἔθη τοὐναντίον ἐλευθέρων. ἐκεῖνοι μὲν γὰρ ποιοῦσιν εἰς τὰ σώματα κολάσεις· παραβαινομένου δὲ ἔθους τὴν ζημίαν εἶναι συμβέβηκεν αἰσχύνην.

ing the terms of his definitions, seen here and in *Or.* 14 discussed above, will ultimately prove vital for a comprehension of what Paul is doing in Romans.

The prose hymn, a type of ἐγκώμιον about or addressed to a divinity, is another context in which definitions can come into play, especially when the author praises the god as a personified force that operates within nature.[70] For both theory and practice Plato again supplies authoritative models.[71] In the *Symposium*, Agathon's speech (194e–97e) begins with a statement of the optimal method of praising Eros:

ἐγὼ δὲ δὴ βούλομαι πρῶτον μὲν εἰπεῖν ὡς χρή με εἰπεῖν, ἔπειτα εἰπεῖν. δοκοῦσι γάρ μοι πάντες οἱ πρόσθεν εἰρηκότες οὐ τὸν θεὸν ἐγκωμιάζειν, ἀλλὰ τοὺς ἀνθρώπους εὐδαιμονίζειν τῶν ἀγαθῶν ὧν ὁ θεὸς αὐτοῖς αἴτιος· ὁποῖος δέ τις αὐτὸς ὢν ταῦτα ἐδωρήσατο, οὐδεὶς εἴρηκεν. εἷς δὲ τρόπος ὀρθὸς παντὸς ἐπαίνου περὶ παντός, λόγῳ διελθεῖν οἷος οἵων αἴτιος ὢν τυγχάνει περὶ οὗ ἂν ὁ λόγος ᾖ. οὕτω δὴ τὸν Ἔρωτα καὶ ἡμᾶς δίκαιον ἐπαινέσαι πρῶτον αὐτὸν οἷός ἐστιν, ἔπειτα τὰς δόσεις.

Now I want first to say how I should speak, then to speak. For all those who have spoken earlier seem to me not to praise the god, but to pronounce humans happy for the good things of which, in their opinion, the god is the cause. But nobody has stated what sort of being gave these things, who he *is*. But there is one right way of praising any person about whom one is speaking, to go through in the speech what sort of person happens to be the cause of what sort of things: so then, it is right that we praise Eros first for what sort of person he is, then for his gifts. (*Symp.* 194e–95a)

The final sentence clearly recalls the instruction in the *Phaedrus* that a ὅρος should state οἷόν τ' ἔστι καὶ ἣν ἔχει δύναμιν, only here the prose hymn itself, in its entirety, praises αὐτὸν οἷός ἐστιν, ἔπειτα τὰς δόσεις.[72] Agathon next declares

---

[70] Cf. Menander Rhetor, *Epid.* 1.333: "Natural [hymns] are the sort which the followers of Parmenides and Empedocles devised, explaining what the nature of Apollo is, what [the nature] of Zeus is. And many [hymns] of Orpheus are of this fashion." φυσικοὶ δὲ οἵους οἱ περὶ Παρμενίδην καὶ Ἐμπεδοκλέα ἐποίησαν, τίς ἡ τοῦ Ἀπόλλωνος φύσις, τίς ἡ τοῦ Διός, παρατιθέμενοι. καὶ οἱ πολλοὶ τῶν Ὀρφέως τούτου τοῦ τρόπου.

[71] On Plato as offering a stylistic model of prose hymns, see Menander Rhetor, *Epid.* 1.334.

[72] Although Agathon criticizes his predecessors' speeches for their failure in this area, Phaedrus and Eryximachus proceed with precisely such a definitional τρόπος. The former concludes his speech by declaring that "of the gods Eros is the oldest, most honorable and most powerful for the acquisition of virtue and happiness for humans, both living and dead," Ἔρωτα θεῶν καὶ πρεσβύτατον καὶ τιμιώτατον καὶ κυριώτατον εἶναι εἰς ἀρετῆς καὶ εὐδαιμονίας κτῆσιν ἀνθρώποις καὶ ζῶσι καὶ τελευτήσασιν (180b). The latter, in response to Pausanias' division of love into higher and lower forms, says: "But I seem to myself to have observed from medicine, our craft, that it [love/Eros] exists not only for the souls of humans toward beautiful people, but exists both toward many other things and in [these] others, both the bodies of all creatures and the things which grow in the earth, and practically in all things that exist – how the god, great and marvellous and all-encompassing as he is, extends both throughout human and divine affairs," ὅτι δὲ οὐ μόνον ἐστὶν ἐπὶ ταῖς ψυχαῖς τῶν ἀνθρώπων πρὸς τοὺς καλοὺς ἀλλὰ καὶ πρὸς ἄλλα πολλὰ καὶ ἐν τοῖς ἄλλοις, τοῖς τε σώμασι τῶν πάντων ζῴων καὶ τοῖς ἐν τῇ γῇ φυομένοις καὶ ὡς ἔπος εἰπεῖν ἐν πᾶσι τοῖς οὖσι, καθεωρακέναι μοι δοκῶ ἐκ τῆς ἰατρικῆς, τῆς ἡμετέρας τέχνης, ὡς μέγας καὶ θαυμαστὸς καὶ ἐπὶ πᾶν ὁ θεὸς τείνει καὶ κατ' ἀνθρώπινα καὶ κατὰ

the πρόθεσις of his speech as an incomplete definition: "Therefore I say (if it is right and blameless to say so), that although all the gods are happy, Eros is the happiest of them, since he is the most beautiful and the best" (φημὶ οὖν ἐγὼ πάντων θεῶν εὐδαιμόνων ὄντων Ἔρωτα, εἰ θέμις καὶ ἀνεμέσητον εἰπεῖν, εὐδαιμονέστατον εἶναι αὐτῶν, κάλλιστον ὄντα καὶ ἄριστον).[73] This rhetorical definition locates Eros among his own kind (the gods) according to the feature that defines them (happiness), then identifies the two outstanding characteristics that set him apart from his peers (beauty and excellence). The rest of the speech elaborates these two characteristics. Under the heading of beauty, Agathon describes him as youthful (νέος), delicate (ἁπλός) and having pliant or soft form (ὑγρὸς τὸ εἶδος). His excellence is manifest in his justice (δικαιοσύνη), prudence (σωφροσύνη), courage (ἀνδρεία), and wisdom (σοφία). Agathon here inverts the process that we find in the *Phaedrus*. The definition there is a product of a preliminary inquiry, starting from a generality (love is a kind of desire) toward a taxonomy, gradually yielding a specific statement. The definition then serves as a foundation for a separate inquiry. Agathon instead posits his definition, and spends the remainder of the speech unfolding its constituent parts. Agathon furthermore proceeds as if his thesis (that Eros deserves praise as the most beautiful and excellent of the gods) admits contro-

---

θεῖα πράγματα (186a–b). These definitions treat ἔρως simultaneously as a force at work in the cosmos and as a divinity. The degree to which Plato presents these speakers as ascribing a real personality to Eros is unclear, but the logic proceeds on the basis that love *qua* Eros deserves worship because of its/his essence and power. See also Quintilian, *Inst.* 3.7.7–9, esp.: "But generally we shall first extol the greatness of their very nature, then the power of each and the inventions which they gave as something useful to humanity," *verum in deis generaliter primum maiestatem ipsius eorum naturae venerabimur, deinde proprie vim cuiusque et inventa quae utile aliquid hominibus attulerint.* Cf. Aelius Aristides, *Or.* 45.15 εἰς Σάραπιν: "Let it be for the priests and orators of the Egyptians both to speak and to know who the god is and what nature he has. But before us is set [the subject] of how great and of what sort of benefits for humans he is the cause. If we praise him adquately as we now speak, it is also possible that at the same time his nature too will be spotted through these same things. For if we articulate what he signifies and freely gives, we have perhaps articulated also 'who he is' and 'what nature he has.'" ὅστις μὲν δὴ καὶ ἥντινα τὴν φύσιν ἔχων ἐστὶν ὁ θεὸς ἱερεῦσί τε καὶ λογίοις Αἰγυπτίων παρείσθω λέγειν τε καὶ εἰδέναι, ὅσων δὲ καὶ οἵων ἀγαθῶν αἴτιος ἀνθρώποις δείκνυται, ἀρκούντως τ' ἂν ἐγκωμιάζοιμεν ὡς ἐν τῷ παρόντι λέγοντες καὶ ἅμα καὶ τὴν φύσιν αὐτοῦ διὰ τῶν αὐτῶν τούτων ἔξεστιν ἐπισκοπεῖσθαι. ἂν γὰρ ἃ δύναταί τε καὶ διαδίδωσιν εἴπωμεν, καὶ τὸ ὅστις ἐστὶ καὶ ἥντινα ἔχει τὴν φύσιν σχεδὸν εἰρήκαμεν.

[73] *Symp.* 195a. Cf. Aelius Aristides, *Or.* 43.7 εἰς Δία, whose πρόθεσις for this speech does not have the form of a definition, but retains its force: "Zeus made all things, and all things which exist are the works of Zeus: rivers and land; sea and sky; things which are between these and things which are above them; gods and humans and things which have soul; things which come into sight and things which are necessary to apprehend with thought." Ζεὺς τὰ πάντα ἐποίησεν καὶ Διός ἐστιν ἔργα ὅσα ἐστὶ πάντα, καὶ ποταμοὶ καὶ γῆ καὶ θάλαττα καὶ οὐρανὸς καὶ ὅσα τούτων μεταξὺ [ἄνω] καὶ ὅσα ὑπὲρ ταῦτα, καὶ θεοὶ καὶ ἄνθρωποι καὶ ὅσα ψυχὴν ἔχει καὶ ὅσα εἰς ὄψιν ἀφικνεῖται καὶ ὅσα δεῖ νοήσει λαβεῖν.

versy. That Eros deserves praise none of his listeners would deny, since they offer their own hymnic speeches; but that he deserves praise for the reasons which Agathon specifies requires a demonstration. Thus, the praise is in the proof. This fact is probably a consequence of the πρόθεσις taking the form of a definition, as well as of the hymn's presentation as an oration instead a poem.

2.5 Conclusion

Several conclusions have emerged from my examination of definition and its argumentative applications. First, Plato articulates the influential principle that a definition does two things: it states what something is, and what it does. He also remarks on its function: it secures ὁμολογία between interlocutors. These points become commonplaces in subsequent theoretical discussions of ὅρος. Second, in rhetorical contexts the stipulative role of definition moves to the front. This may involve a preliminary investigation of the definiendum (as in the προοίμιον of Socrates' first speech on love in the *Phaedrus*). Definition may also be the focus of the entire oration. In both cases the philosophical methods of taxonomy and dialectics can have a prominent place in order to test or demonstrate a definition's validity. But often a speaker will simply posit a definition, relying on its general plausibility or taking it over from some other source. Third, definitions are useful in all three major rhetorical γένη. Forensic speeches deploy them to dispute or confirm the criminality of admitted facts and the applicability of relevant laws. Deliberations of advantage can turn on the definitions of conceptions buried within the question under consideration. Praise can proceed definitionally, particularly when one lauds a divinity as a personified force, or an abstraction (like law or custom) for the benefits that they provide. When deliberative and epideictic speeches deal with philosophical topics, the utility of definition naturally increases. In this way rhetorical definition retains its philosophical character: placing it in the προοίμιον would send a strong signal to the audience to expect a (popular) philosophical discourse. Fourth, definition should "unfold" the definiendum concisely. It requires density of content and brevity of style, so next we turn to the methods which rhetorical theorists devised for loading statements with meaning while maintaining economy in diction.

Chapter 3

The Ancient Rhetorical Theorists on Brevity

3.1 Introduction

I demonstrated in the previous chapter that ancient thinkers regard brevity as a distinctive feature of definition.[1] In order to achieve the goal of instilling their definitions with a maximum of content with a minimum of wording, authors possessed a substantial fund of methods from the rhetorical theory on style (λέξις). The ability to speak and write concisely was indeed a prominent aim of the rhetorical curriculum. Definition is only one of many contexts in which brevity is regarded as suitable, so it arises at several points in the extant theoretical sources. Interpreters of the New Testament have occasionally alighted upon these sources in conjunction with their research: Luke Timothy Johnson on taciturnity in James, Margaret M. Mitchell on rhetorical shorthand in 1 and 2 Corinthians, Ronald F. Hock and Edward N. O'Neil on the χρεία, and Loveday Alexander on literary and scientific prefaces in conjunction with the introductions of Luke and Acts.[2] The present study demands a thorough comprehension of the ancient literature on this subject: the general admiration of brevity, its utility in types of discourse that Paul uses, and the methods of compressing content and wording, especially the figures of ἔλλειψις (omission), συνεκδοχή (synecdoche) and ἀπὸ κοινοῦ (commonality). When authors deploy tactics of brevity, they must proceed with the reasonable expectation that their audiences will detect these tactics and interpret accordingly. A review of the sources on brevity will furnish us with access to the shared knowledge of Paul and his audiences in this area, and will equip us with instruments to analyze his writings at the level of their composition, that is, at the intersection of their objectives, organization and style.

---

[1] Βραχυλογία, βραχύτης and συντομία, along with their cognates and *brevitas* in Latin, have virtually equivalent meanings in the context of discussions of style. For the sake of consistency, I ordinarily render βραχυλογία and βραχύτης as "brevity" and συντομία as "conciseness" in my translations.

[2] Johnson, "Taciturnity"; Mitchell, "Rhetorical Shorthand"; Hock and O'Neil, *Chreia in Ancient Rhetoric*, 1.23–24; Alexander, *Preface to Luke's Gospel*, 92–93, esp. n. 50. See also the list of theological abbreviations in Galatians compiled by Betz (*Galatians*, 27–28).

3.2 The utility of brevity

Brevity enjoys high esteem in the Greco-Roman world as an indicator of wisdom, self-control and oratorical mastery. I begin with Plato's testimony about brevity among the sophists in classical Athens, and then I examine the texts that number it among the virtues of style (ἀρεταὶ τῆς λέξεως) and that specify its utility for the opening sections of an oration and for letters.

At a couple of points in his dialogues, Plato reveals that the sophists prided themselves on the ability to say the same thing at length (μακρολογία) and in brief (βραχυλογία), implying the existence of established methods of doing both. Gorgias, for example, when Socrates begs him to curtail the long-winded replies to his questions, boasts: "No one could say the same things in briefer statements than mine" (μηδένα ἂν ἐν βραχυτέροις ἐμοῦ τὰ αὐτὰ εἰπεῖν). Socrates affirms his present interest in βραχυλογία ("of verbosity there is need some other time," μακρολογίας δὲ [δεῖ] εἰσαῦθις), then Gorgias repeats his boast: "You will say that you have heard nobody briefer in speech" (οὐδενὸς φήσεις βραχυλογωτέρου ἀκοῦσαι).[3] Gorgias was evidently well-known for making these kinds of claims, perhaps in advertising himself to prospective students. He possesses and can impart the useful skills of βραχυλογία and μακρολογία.[4] This exchange furthermore yields a strong impression that these words have already at this early point become stylistic technical terms. But they are equally valued; at some points one wants to be concise, at others verbose. In the *Phaedrus*, Plato discloses that Gorgias and Tisias "invented conciseness and boundless lengths of speeches concerning all things" (συντομίαν τε λόγων καὶ ἄπειρα μήκη περὶ πάντων ἀνηῦρον),[5] among other rhetorical inventions.[6] Obviously they did not create brevity *per se*. Rather, they invented

---

[3] *Gorg.* 449b–c.

[4] Βραχυλογία and μακρολογία become something of a running joke throughout the rest of the *Gorgias*; see, e.g., 449d (νὴ τὴν Ἥραν, ὦ Γοργία, ἄγαμαί γε τὰς ἀποκρίσεις, ὅτι ἀποκρίνῃ ὡς οἷόν τε διὰ βραχυτάτων), 461d–e, 465e, 519e. Cf. Socrates' conversation with Protagoras, where the former insists that the latter display his rhetorical skill by speaking τῇ βραχυλογίᾳ (*Prot.* 333c–335c). The teachability of these skills also comes up in this context: "But I said, 'Indeed I have heard that you yourself are able both to teach another regarding the same things, and, if you wish, to speak at length, such that speech never fails you, and again to speak in brief, such that nobody speaks in briefer statements than you," ἀκήκοα γοῦν, ἦν δ' ἐγώ, ὅτι σὺ οἷός τ' εἶ καὶ αὐτὸς καὶ ἄλλον διδάξαι περὶ τῶν αὐτῶν καὶ μακρὰ λέγειν, ἐὰν βούλῃ, οὕτως ὥστε τὸν λόγον μηδέποτε ἐπιλιπεῖν, καὶ αὖ βραχέα οὕτως ὥστε μηδένα σοῦ ἐν βραχυτέροις εἰπεῖν (334e).

[5] There may be an instance of παρονομασία (word-play) here: if the accent on μήκη moves to the ultima, it means "bleating."

[6] *Phaedr.* 267a–b: "And shall we allow Tisias and Gorgias to slumber, who saw probabilities as to be valued more than truths; and who furthermore, because of their force of eloquence, make small things appear great and great things appear small, and new things old and

3.2 The utility of brevity

the teachable methods of compressing and extending one's utterances. Plato mainly wishes to portray the sophists as vain and silly with his characterizations of their claims and educational methods, but in so doing he establishes the desirability of both βραχυλογία and μακρολογία for certain notable figures and their students.[7]

In classical Athens a body of rhetorical theory that addresses brevity and verbosity thus emerges in the classrooms and lecture-halls of the sophists. The ancient Spartans, if their widely attested reputation for 'laconic' speech holds any truth, forego μακρολογία altogether and direct their efforts solely to the cultivation of βραχυλογία. Plutarch credits this reputation (of which he wholeheartedly approves) to the intentional design of Lycurgus, and to the educational practices that he established.[8] Lycurgus himself supplies an excellent model of βραχυλογία.[9] Now Plutarch asserts an ethical objective in the

---

the opposite things new; who invented conciseness and boundless lengths of speeches concerning all things? Now one time when Prodicus heard these things from me, he laughed and said that he alone had invented the art of what speeches one needs – that one needs speeches neither of long nor short, but of moderate lengths." Τεισίαν δὲ Γοργίαν τε ἐάσομεν εὕδειν, οἳ πρὸ τῶν ἀληθῶν τὰ εἰκότα εἶδον ὡς τιμητέα μᾶλλον, τά τε αὖ σμικρὰ μεγάλα καὶ τὰ μεγάλα σμικρὰ φαίνεσθαι ποιοῦσιν διὰ ῥώμην λόγου, καινά τε ἀρχαίως τά τ' ἐναντία καινῶς, συντομίαν τε λόγων καὶ ἄπειρα μήκη περὶ πάντων ἀνηῦρον; ταῦτα δὲ ἀκούων ποτέ μου Πρόδικος ἐγέλασεν, καὶ μόνος αὐτὸς ηὑρηκέναι ἔφη ὧν δεῖ λόγων τέχνην· δεῖν δὲ οὔτε μακρῶν οὔτε βραχέων, ἀλλὰ μετρίων.

[7] Aristotle confirms and perpetuates the equal interest in brevity and verbosity at *Rhet.* 3.6.1, 1407b; see § 3.3.1 below.

[8] *Lyc.* 19.1–5: "Now [the Spartans] used to teach their boys to use speech which has bitterness mixed with charm, and much reflection from brief diction. For Lycurgus (as it has been said) caused his iron currency to have little worth from much weight; but in contrast he equipped the currency of speech from frugal and slight diction toward great and abundant thought, crafting the boys by much silence to be apophthegmatic and disciplined with their answers. For as the seed of intemperate men in their sexual unions is for the most part sterile and unfruitful, so the lack of self-control in speaking makes one's speech empty and vapid. ... And I notice also that Spartan speech seems to be brief, above all when it aims at the subjects and grips the meaning of what is heard." ἐδίδασκον δὲ τοὺς παῖδας καὶ λόγῳ χρῆσθαι πικρίαν ἔχοντι μεμειγμένην χάριτι καὶ πολλὴν ἀπὸ βραχείας λέξεως ἀναθεώρησιν. τὸ μὲν γὰρ σιδηροῦν νόμισμα μικρὰν ἔχειν ἐποίησεν ἀπὸ πολλοῦ σταθμοῦ δύναμιν ὁ Λυκοῦργος, ὡς εἴρηται, τὸ δὲ τοῦ λόγου νόμισμα τοὐναντίον ἀπ' εὐτελοῦς καὶ ὀλίγης λέξεως εἰς πολλὴν καὶ περιττὴν κατεσκεύασε διάνοιαν, τῇ πολλῇ σιωπῇ τοὺς παῖδας ἀποφθεγματικοὺς καὶ πεπαιδευμένους πρὸς τὰς ἀποκρίσεις μηχανώμενος. ὡς γὰρ τὸ σπέρμα τῶν πρὸς τὰς συνουσίας ἀκολάστων ἄγονον ὡς τὰ πολλὰ καὶ ἄκαρπόν ἐστιν, οὕτως ἡ πρὸς τὸ λαλεῖν ἀκρασία κενὸν τὸν λόγον ποιεῖ καὶ ἀνόητον. ... ἐγὼ δὲ καὶ τὸν λόγον ὁρῶ τὸν Λακωνικὸν βραχὺν μὲν εἶναι δοκοῦντα, μάλιστα δὲ τῶν πραγμάτων ἐφικνούμενον, καὶ τῆς διανοίας ἁπτόμενον τῶν ἀκροωμένων.

[9] Stobaeus (*Anth.* 3.35.9) preserves the following pithy remark: "To the one who said, 'Why do the Spartans practice brief speech?' Lycurgus said, 'Because it is close to being silent,'" Λυκοῦργος πρὸς τὸν εἰπόντα «διὰ τί Λακεδαιμόνιοι τὴν βραχυλογίαν ἀσκοῦσιν;» εἶπεν «ὅτι ἐγγύς ἐστι τοῦ σιγᾶν». Cf. [Plutarch], *Reg. imp. apophth.* 16, 193d, "To the Spartans who were accusing the Thebans of many great offenses, [Epameinondas] said: 'Well these [The-

great importance that the Spartans attach to brevity, namely the avoidance of ἀκρασία. Lycurgus was thus "preparing the boys by much silence to be apophthegmatic and disciplined in their answers" (τῇ πολλῇ σιωπῇ τοὺς παῖδας ἀποφθεγματικοὺς καὶ πεπαιδευμένους πρὸς τὰς ἀποκρίσεις μηχανώμενος). Plutarch's information about Lycurgus' prioritizing of taciturnity in the Spartan educational curriculum could be pure fantasy. Alternatively, it may reflect a historical inference of his own, that only systematic instruction could cause such a dominant cultural trait. Whether true or not, his testimony affirms the value of brevity in general discourse both in classical Sparta and in the estimation of later generations who look back at its culture of verbal economy with admiration.

3.2.1 Brevity as an ἀρετή of style

Two developments in Hellenistic rhetorical theory converge to entrench further the independent value of brevity and to elevate its position in the educational curriculum. First, philososphers and rhetorical theorists begin to codify lists of stylistic "virtues" or "excellences" (ἀρεταί).[10] The discussion in the available literature begins with Aristotle, but it extends back further, since he responds to earlier theorists on the subject.[11] He divides λέξις into three broad categories corresponding to the rhetorical γένη, "deliberative" (δημηγορική), "demonstrative" (ἐπιδεικτική) and "forensic" (δικανική).[12] He then says:

τὸ δὲ προσδιαιρεῖσθαι τὴν λέξιν, ὅτι ἡδεῖαν δεῖ καὶ μεγαλοπρεπῆ, περίεργον· τί γὰρ μᾶλλον ἢ σώφρονα καὶ ἐλευθέριον καὶ εἴ τις ἄλλη ἤθους ἀρετή; τὸ γὰρ ἡδεῖαν εἶναι ποιήσει δηλονότι τὰ εἰρημένα, εἴπερ ὀρθῶς ὥρισται ἡ ἀρετὴ τῆς λέξεως· τίνος γὰρ ἕνεκα δεῖ σαφῆ καὶ μὴ ταπεινὴν εἶναι ἀλλὰ πρέπουσαν; ἄν τε γὰρ ἀδολεσχῇ, οὐ σαφής, οὐδὲ ἂν σύντομος, ἀλλὰ δῆλον ὅτι τὸ μέσον

---

bans] put a stop to you speaking briefly!'" πρὸς δὲ τοὺς Σπαρτιάτας πολλὰ καὶ μεγάλα τῶν Θηβαίων κατηγοροῦντας, «οὗτοι μέντοι» εἶπεν «ὑμᾶς βραχυλογοῦντας ἔπαυσαν». Plutarch cites several examples of Lycurgus' brevity in *Lyc.* 19 as well as some instances from other Spartans (note especially the jokes). See also ps.-Plutarch's compilation of *Apophthegmata Laconica*.

[10] For discussions of stylistic ἀρεταί, see Solmsen, "Aristotelian Tradition," 43–44, 181–86; Bonner, *Literary Treatises*, 15–24; Russell, *Criticism in Antiquity*, 135–37; and van Wyk Cronjé, *Dionysius*, 137–41. I use "virtue" as a translation of ἀρετή throughout with a full awareness of its ethical associations, because the ancient theorists made this association self-consciously: as just mentioned, Plutarch sees the Spartans' training in speech to result in self-control, and Aristotle explicitly links ἤθους ἀρετή and ἡ ἀρετὴ τῆς λέξεως (see below).

[11] Cf. Plato, *Phaedr.* 234e: "And should the oration [of Lysias] be praised by me and you both, precisely because the author has said the things that he should, but not only for that, also because they are clear and terse, and that each of the statements has been rounded to a nicety?" καὶ ταύτῃ δεῖ ὑπ' ἐμοῦ τε καὶ σοῦ τὸν λόγον ἐπαινεθῆναι, ὡς τὰ δέοντα εἰρηκότος τοῦ ποιητοῦ, ἀλλ' οὐκ ἐκείνῃ μόνον, ὅτι σαφῆ καὶ στρογγύλα, καὶ ἀκριβῶς ἕκαστα τῶν ὀνομάτων ἀποτετόρνευται;

[12] On this division, see also *Rhet.* 3.12.1–3, 1413b.

ἁρμόττει. καὶ τὸ ἡδεῖαν τὰ εἰρημένα ποιήσει, ἂν εὖ μιχθῇ, τὸ εἰωθὸς καὶ ⟨τὸ⟩ ξενικόν, καὶ ὁ ῥυθμός, καὶ τὸ πιθανὸν ἐκ τοῦ πρέποντος.

Now to subdivide style further – because it is necessary [to distinguish] the pleasurable and the grand – is superfluous. For why are these more [necessary] than moderation and liberality and any other virtue of character? For if the virtue of style has in fact been defined correctly, clearly the things which have been discussed [i.e., in the foregoing sections of book 3] will make [one's style] pleasurable. For why should it be clear and not humble, but suitable? Because if one babbles, and if one is not concise, one is not clear. Obviously the mean is appropriate. The things which have been discussed will make [one's style] pleasurable – customary usage and foreign, and rhythm, and persuasiveness that derives from propriety – if they are mixed well. (*Rhet.* 3.12.6, 1414a)

Style should thus flow from what is appropriate for the specific venues in which one will speak. Pleasurability and grandeur are by-products, but should never become goals in themselves. Aristotle does not isolate συντομία as a virtue here. Instead, he subordinates it and all other qualities to σαφήνεια, clarity.[13] His successor Theophrastus adds three more ἀρεταί (Hellenism, propriety and ornament) according to the testimony of Cicero.[14] The Stoics, however, promote συντομία to the status of a virtue, as we learn from Diogenes' overview of their doctrines in his biography of Zeno:[15]

ἀρεταὶ δὲ λόγου εἰσὶ πέντε· Ἑλληνισμός, σαφήνεια, συντομία, πρέπον, κατασκευή. Ἑλληνισμὸς μὲν οὖν ἐστι φράσις ἀδιάπτωτος ἐν τῇ τεχνικῇ καὶ μὴ εἰκαίᾳ συνηθείᾳ· σαφήνεια δέ ἐστι λέξις γνωρίμως παριστᾶσα τὸ νοούμενον· συντομία δέ ἐστι λέξις αὐτὰ τὰ ἀναγκαῖα περιέχουσα πρὸς δήλωσιν τοῦ πράγματος· πρέπον δέ ἐστι λέξις οἰκεία τῷ πράγματι· κατασκευὴ δέ ⟨ἐστι⟩ λέξις

---

[13] Cf. his discussion of σαφήνεια in *Rhet.* 3.2.1–5, 1404b, esp. the opening remark: "Therefore let these things which have been considered stand, and let the virtue of style be defined as being clear. (For the speech is a proof: if it does not communicate plainly, will not achieve its own function.) And [let style be defined] neither as humble nor beyond dignity, but rather as appropriate; for poetic [style] is perhaps not humble, but it is not suitable for a speech" (3.2.1). ἔστω οὖν ἐκεῖνα τεθεωρημένα, καὶ ὡρίσθω λέξεως ἀρετὴ σαφῆ εἶναι (σημεῖον γάρ τε ὁ λόγος, ἐὰν μὴ δηλοῖ οὐ ποιήσει τὸ ἑαυτοῦ ἔργον), καὶ μήτε ταπεινὴν μήτε ὑπὲρ τὸ ἀξίωμα, ἀλλὰ πρέπουσαν· ἡ γὰρ ποιητικὴ ἴσως οὐ ταπεινή, ἀλλ' οὐ πρέπουσα λόγῳ. Hendrickson rightly states (at "Peripatetic Mean," 133, n. 2): "In this connection emphasis should be laid on the fact that Aristotle does not speak of 'virtues' of style as is customary in later rhetoric, (for him its excellence is a unit – ἡ ἀρετή) ...." Aristotle mentions, however, several terms that later become classed as virtues: Hellenism (ἑλληνίζειν) in 3.5.1–6, 1407a–b, συντομία in 3.6, 1407b–1408a (quoted in § 3.3.1 below); propriety (πρέπον) in 3.7.1–5, 1408a; character (ἠθικὴ λέξις) in 3.7.6–7, 1408a; and the right amount of rhythm in 3.8, 1408b–1409a.

[14] *Or.* 79: "The diction will also be pure Latin; it will be spoken clearly and plainly; that which is appropriate will be sought. One thing will be absent [from the list so far] which Theophrastus ennumerates as fourth among virtues of style: that is, ornament [applied] pleasantly and abundantly." *Sermo purus erit et Latinus, dilucide planeque dicetur, quid deceat circumspicietur; unum aberit, quod quartum numerat Theophrastus in orationis laudibus: ornatum illud, suave et adfluens.* For further discussion of Theophrastus' development of the stylistic virtues, see Kennedy, *New History,* 84–87.

[15] For Diogenes' characterization of Zeno as βραχυλόγος, see 7.16–18.

ἐκπεφυγυῖα τὸν ἰδιωτισμόν. ὁ δὲ βαρβαρισμὸς ἐκ τῶν κακιῶν λέξις ἐστὶ παρὰ τὸ ἔθος τῶν εὐδαιμονούντων Ἑλλήνων, σολοικισμὸς δέ ἐστι λόγος ἀκαταλλήλως συντεταγμένος.

There are five virtues of style: Hellenism, clarity, conciseness, propriety, ornament. Hellenism, then, is faultless expression in skillful and not casual habit; clarity is style which intelligibly presents that which is meant; conciseness is style which encompasses only the very necessities for disclosure of the subject; propriety is style suitable for the subject; ornament is style which has avoided vulgarity. Barbarism is style that, because of its faults, is beyond the custom of prosperous Greeks, and solecism is speech which has been arranged ungrammatically. (7.59)

The Stoics' addition of συντομία to Theophrastus' list must have proven controversial. Although some later theorists include it among the general virtues of style, others pointedly omit it (while often still admitting its importance for some portions of an oration).[16] The inclusion of συντομία and βραχυλογία among the general stylistic virtues nevertheless persists well into late antiquity.[17]

The second important Hellenistic development is the formation of a canon of authors (primarily the major Athenian orators) whose works become rhetorical models. The critical essays of Dionysius of Halicarnassus, who expends considerable energy on assessing the strengths and weaknesses of canonical authors, show well how the canon and the ἀρεταί converge at a practi-

---

[16] See, e.g., Quintilian, *Inst.* 1.5.1, naming three (correctness, clarity and ornament, with propriety falling under the last). Cicero at one point denies brevity a place among the cardinal stylistic virtues (*Brut.* 50: "Indeed brevity is occasionally a merit in a certain part of delivering a speech, [but] in general eloquence it does not have merit," *brevitas autem laus est interdum in aliqua parte dicendi, in universa eloquentia laudem non habet*), but at another point he affirms it in a discussion of two styles, one of "simple words" (more conversational) and the other of "conjoined words" (more formal), *simplicia* and *coniuncta verba* (*Part. or.* 19: "But there are these five commonalities, excellences as it were, of simple and conjoined words: clarity, brevity, plausibility, luster, pleasure," *communia autem simplicium coniunctorumque haec sunt quinque quasi lumina, dilucidum breve probabile inlustre suave*). See further *De or.* 2.83, where his Antonius says: "Now indeed when they command that the narration have verisimilitude, and be clear and brief, they admonish us rightly; when they regard these to be properties more of narration than of oratory as a whole, they assuredly seem to me to err," *iam vero narrationem quod iubent veri similem esse et apertam et brevem, recte nos admonent; quod haec narrationis magis putant esse propria quam totius orationis, valde mihi videntur errare.*

[17] E.g., Aelius Herodian (ii C.E., per *BNP* 6.260–262, s.v.), *Soloec.* p. 308 (τοῦ λόγου ἀρεταὶ μὲν ἕξ, ἑλληνισμός, σαφήνεια, συντομία, κυριολογία, εὐσυνθεσία, εὐπρέπεια); [Aelius Aristides] (ii C.E., per Kennedy, *Later Greek Rhetoric*, 75), *Rhet.* 1.1 (αἵτινες [i.e., εἴδη καὶ ἀρεταὶ] τοιαίδε καὶ τοσαίδε εἰσί, σεμνότης, βαρύτης, περιβολή, ἀξιοπιστία, σφοδρότης, ἔμφασις, δεινότης, ἐπιμέλεια, γλυκύτης, σαφήνεια καὶ καθαρότης, βραχύτης καὶ συντομία, κόλασις); Anonymous, *Proleg. RG-W* 6.36 (ἑρμηνείας δὲ ἀρεταὶ τέσσαρες, ἑλληνισμός, σαφήνεια, συντομία, πιθανότης). Robert N. Gaines ("Qualities of Rhetorical Expression") has reconstructed six virtues for Philodemus by filling in lacunae in περὶ ῥητορικῆς book 4 with parts of περὶ ποιημάτων book 5: Ἑλληνιστικὴ ἑρμηνεία, ἀσάφεια/σαφηνεῖα, ἔμφασις, συντομία, εὐπρέπεια, κατασκευή/κόμψεια.

cal level. He has a two-tiered organization of primary and secondary virtues that he claims to have inherited from previous theorists.[18] His "necessary" tier includes purity, clarity and conciseness, and his "supplementary" tier sublimity, elegance, solemnity and grandeur.[19] His architecture of ἀρεταί and the

---

[18] *Thuc.* 22: "It has been said by many before that of the so-called virtues there are those which are necessary and ought to be present in all speeches, and there are those which are supplementary, and, when the first are in place, then they obtain their own force. I should thus say nothing now concerning them nor from which premises and precepts each of these virtues is born, because there are many. For these matters also have met with most exact treatment [elsewhere]." καὶ ὅτι τῶν καλουμένων ἀρετῶν αἳ μέν εἰσιν ἀναγκαῖαι καὶ ἐν ἅπασιν ὀφείλουσι παρεῖναι τοῖς λόγοις, αἳ δ' ἐπίθετοι καὶ ὅταν ὑποστῶσιν αἱ πρῶται, τότε τὴν ἑαυτῶν ἰσχὺν λαμβάνουσιν, εἴρηται πολλοῖς πρότερον. ὥστε οὐδὲν δεῖ περὶ αὐτῶν ἐμὲ νυνὶ λέγειν οὐδ' ἐξ ὧν θεωρημάτων τε καὶ παραγγελμάτων τούτων τῶν ἀρετῶν ἑκάστη γίνεται, πολλῶν ὄντων· καὶ γὰρ ταῦτα τῆς ἀκριβεστάτης τέτευχεν ἐξεργασίας. See also Bonner, *Literary Treatises*, 18–21; Russell, *Criticism in Antiquity*, 137.

[19] His analysis of οἱ πρὸ Θουκυδίδου γενόμενοι συγγραφεῖς includes the following observations regarding their λέξις (*Thuc.* 23): "Indeed the style of all of them has the necessary virtues, for it is sufficiently pure, clear and concise, with each [style] preserving the distinctive imprint [χαρακτῆρα] of the dialect. But, in terms of the supplementary virtues, from which the power of an orator becomes especially obvious, [their style] neither has them all, nor has them approaching a height [of excellence], but it has few [of these virtues] and in brief. I am referring to sublimity, elegance, solemnity and grandeur. Neither [does their style have] tension nor gravity nor emotion which arouses the mind, nor vigorous and energetic spirit, from which there is what is called forcefulness." τὰς μὲν οὖν ἀναγκαίας ἀρετὰς ἡ λέξις αὐτῶν πάντων ἔχει (καὶ γὰρ καθαρὰ καὶ σαφὴς καὶ σύντομός ἐστιν ἀποχρώντως, σῴζουσα τὸν ἴδιον ἑκάστη τῆς διαλέκτου χαρακτῆρα)· τὰς δ' ἐπιθέτους, ἐξ ὧν μάλιστα διάδηλος ἡ τοῦ ῥήτορος γίνεται δύναμις, οὔτε ἁπάσας οὔτε εἰς ἄκρον ἠκούσας, ἀλλ' ὀλίγας καὶ ἐπὶ βραχύ, ὕψος λέγω καὶ καλλιρημοσύνην καὶ σεμνολογίαν καὶ μεγαλοπρέπειαν· οὐδὲ δὴ τόνον οὐδὲ βάρος οὐδὲ πάθος διεγεῖρον τὸν νοῦν οὐδὲ τὸ ἐρρωμένον καὶ ἐναγώνιον πνεῦμα, ἐξ ὧν ἡ καλουμένη γίνεται δεινότης. Dionysius elaborates these tiers further in context of a comparison of Thucydides and Herodotus in *Pomp.* 3.17–20. Omitting his evaluative comments regarding Herodotus and Thucydides where possible, the text regarding the supplementary virtues reads: "After these vividness has been placed first of the supplementary virtues. ... After this virtue is joined the imitation of characters and emotions. ... After these are the virtues which display greatness and admirability of ornament. ... And the virtues which encompass strength and tension and similar properties of expression follow these. ... Herodotus, better than Thucydides by far, introduces pleasure, persuasiveness, delight, and the similarly related virtues. And Herodotus has striven for a natural [style] of expression of words, Thucydides vehemence. The most dominant of all the virtues in speeches remains propriety." ἐνάργεια μετὰ ταῦτα τέτακται πρώτη μὲν τῶν ἐπιθέτων ἀρετῶν· ... μετὰ ταύτην συνίσταται τὴν ἀρετὴν [τῶν] ἠθῶν τε καὶ παθῶν μίμησις· ... μετὰ ταῦτα αἱ τὸ μέγα καὶ θαυμαστὸν ἐκφαίνουσαι τῆς κατασκευῆς ἀρεταί· ... ἕπονται ταύταις αἱ τὴν ἰσχὺν καὶ τὸν τόνον καὶ τὰς ὁμοιοτρόπους δυνάμεις τῆς φράσεως ἀρεταὶ περιέχουσαι· ... ἡδονὴν δὲ καὶ πειθὼ καὶ τέρψιν καὶ τὰς ὁμοιωγενεῖς ἀρετὰς εἰσφέρεται μακρῷ Θουκυδίδου κρείττονας Ἡρόδοτος. τῆς ⟨δὲ⟩ φράσεως [τῶν ὀνομάτων] τὸ μὲν κατὰ φύσιν Ἡρόδοτος ἐζήλωκε, τὸ δὲ δεινὸν Θουκυδίδης. ⟨λείπει⟩ πασῶν ἐν λόγοις ἀρετῶν ἡ κυριωτάτη τὸ πρέπον. The sentence that contrasts the natural style of Herodotus with the vehemence of Thucydides does not seem to be identifying more virtues as much as explaining why each author is stronger or

others to which he refers have foremost an educational purpose. His application of virtue-theory to the canon is no mere scholastic exercise in classification; instead, it enhances imitation of the exemplars by pinpointing where one may find excellent instances of (and combinations of) the primary and secondary virtues, so that one may then learn how to do it as well. Dionysius praises Lysias and Isaeus as admirable exemplars of brevity,[20] while criticizing Isocrates for his failure in this area.[21] Brevity also remains a quality worth mentioning in later discussions of canonical authors.[22] The position of brevity

---

weaker in particular supplementary virtues before back-tracking to add another necessary item. Propriety thus appears to be a belated addition to the primary list.

Eventually, in the wake of Hermogenes' work περὶ ἰδεῶν, theories of stylistic ἀρεταί decline. (His system lacks συντομία or βραχυλογία, and instead includes brevity under the heading of γοργότης, "vigor"; see Hermogenes, Id. 2.1). For further discussion of this development, see Rutherford, Canons of Style, chapter 1, 8–21; Russell, Criticism in Antiquity, 137–43.

[20] For example, Dionysius commends Lysias' ability to balance clarity (σαφήνεια) and brevity in Lys. 4: "Furthermore there is the disclosing of [his] thoughts briefly with [disclosing them] clearly, since it is naturally a difficult matter to bring both these things together and to blend them in a moderate way," καὶ μὴν τό γε βραχέως ἐκφέρειν τὰ νοήματα μετὰ τοῦ σαφῶς, χαλεποῦ πράγματος ὄντος φύσει τοῦ συναγαγεῖν ἄμφω ταῦτα καὶ κεράσαι μετρίως. Dionysius concludes in Lys. 5: "So also the brevity of Lysias is to be imitated; for it could not be found in a more moderate fashion in any other rhetor," μιμητέον δὴ καὶ βραχύτητα τὴν Λυσίου· μετριωτέρα γὰρ οὐκ ἂν εὑρεθείη παρ' ἑτέρῳ ῥήτορι. He approves of Isaeus similarly in Is. 3: "The style of Isaeus, no less than of Lysias, is on the one hand pure, accurate, clear, authoritative [or, "ordinary"], vivid and concise; and on the other hand in addition to these [traits, it is] both persuasive and fitting to the subject matters, both terse and suitable for a forensic speech," καθαρὰ μὲν καὶ ἀκριβὴς καὶ σαφὴς κυρία τε καὶ ἐναργὴς καὶ σύντομος, πρὸς δὲ τούτοις πιθανή τε καὶ πρέπουσα τοῖς ὑποκειμένοις στρογγύλη τε καὶ δικανικὴ οὐκ ἧττόν ἐστιν ἡ Ἰσαίου λέξις τῆς Λυσίου. Cf. Dio Chrysostom, Or. 18.11.

[21] Isoc. 2: "But it [i.e., Isocrates' λέξις] is not terse and welded together and appropriate for forensic contests, like that [of Lysias], but it is especially top-heavy and richly poured forth, nor is it so concise, but meager and slower than is moderate," στρογγύλη δὲ οὐκ ἔστιν, ὥσπερ ἐκείνη, καὶ συγκεκροτημένη καὶ πρὸς ἀγῶνας δικανικοὺς εὔθετος, ὑπτία δέ ἐστι μᾶλλον καὶ κεχυμένη πλουσίως, οὐδὲ δὴ σύντομος οὕτως, ἀλλὰ καὶ κατασκελὴς καὶ βραδυτέρα τοῦ μετρίου. Cf. also ibid. 3, where Dionysius attributes Isocrates' lack of brevity to overuse of periods and σχήματα, and 11, which summarizes the comparison of the λέξις of Isocrates and Lysias.

[22] Philostratus, for example, says regarding Critias' stylistic quality (ἡ ἰδέα τοῦ λόγου): "I observe also that the man uses βραχυλογία competently," ὁρῶ τὸν ἄνδρα καὶ βραχυλογοῦντα ἱκανῶς (Vit. soph. 16.503). Regarding Isaeus, see ibid. 20.514 ("An invention of Isaeus was explaining briefly – both this and the compression of every premise into a brief [utterance]," καὶ τὸ βραχέως ἑρμηνεύειν, τοῦτό τε καὶ πᾶσαν ὑπόθεσιν συνελεῖν ἐς βραχὺ Ἰσαίου εὕρημα). Regarding Apollonius, see Vit. Apoll. 4.33 (giving counsel to the Spartans on what to write to the emperor in response to an insulting letter, ὧδε ἐβραχυλόγησε – in other words, teaching the Spartans how to be laconic!).

in the high tier of stylistic ἀρεταί thus underscores its significance in practical rhetorical instruction.[23]

Beyond the emergence of virtue-theory and the selection of a canon of exemplary authors, a third, somewhat later, development deals specifically with συντομία apart from the other virtues: its division into the subcategories of style or language (λέξις), and of content (πράγματα) or thought (γνώμη). Dionysius and Demetrius, the author of *De elocutione*,[24] do not seem aware of

---

[23] Just how much this is so becomes clear in Dionysius' spirited reply to those who fault Demosthenes for his occasional use of πλεονασμός (redundancy or prolixity) in *Dem*. 58: "Now with respect to this further matter, there are some who label it as a characteristic and others as a fault of the rhetor; I am speaking of the occasional clarification of the same subject with many words." Some examples of πλεονασμός from Demosthenes' speeches follow. "Certainly those who declare it to be a particularity of the style of Demosthenes have a point. For the man uses it advantageously, just as he uses a clipped and brief style more frequently and more appropriately than all. But those who hold it in the order of a fault accuse him unnecessarily, since they have not examined the reasons why he customarily draws out his language [πλεονάζειν] on occasion. Rather, they who quibble about this seem to demand brevity all the time, which, as I said, he displays more often and more appropriately than anyone. But of the other virtues they demand none, because they do not yet see that the rhetor must aim for clarity, vividness, amplification and rhythm in the composition of the words; but, above all these things, he must aim to make his style emotional as well as ethical and vehement, in which traits lies the largest part of persuasion. Now brevity is not most powerfully able to accomplish each of these virtues, rather πλεονασμός of some words, which Demosthenes too makes use of." ἤδη δέ που κἀκεῖνό τινες οἱ μὲν ὡς χαρακτηρικὸν οἱ δ' ὡς ἁμάρτημα τοῦ ῥήτορος ἐσημειώσαντο, λέγω δὲ τὸ πολλοῖς ὀνόμασι τὸ αὐτὸ πρᾶγμα δηλοῦν ἐνίοτε δή. ... ὅσοι μὲν οὖν ἰδίωμα τοῦ χαρακτῆρος αὐτὸ ἀποφαίνουσι τοῦ Δημοσθένους, ὀρθῶς λέγουσι· κέχρηται γὰρ αὐτῷ χρησίμως ὁ ἀνήρ, ὥσπερ καὶ τῇ τμητικῇ [καὶ τῇ] βραχυλογίᾳ πάντων γε μᾶλλον καὶ εὐκαιρότερον. ὅσοι δ' ἐν ἁμαρτήματος αὐτὸ μοίρᾳ φέρουσι, τὰς αἰτίας οὐκ ἐξητακότες, δι' ἃς εἰώθει πλεονάζειν ἐνίοτε ἐν τοῖς ὀνόμασιν, οὐ δεόντως αὐτοῦ κατηγοροῦσιν, ἀλλ' ἐοίκασιν οἱ τοῦτο συκοφαντοῦντες τὴν βραχυλογίαν ἐκ παντὸς ἀπαιτεῖν, ἥν, ὅπερ εἶπον, παντὸς μᾶλλον καὶ εὐκαιρότερον παρέχεται, τῶν δὲ ἄλλων ἀρετῶν οὐδεμίαν, οὐκέτι συνορῶντες ὅτι καὶ τῆς σαφηνείας δεῖ στοχάζεσθαι τὸν ῥήτορα καὶ τῆς ἐναργείας καὶ τῆς αὐξήσεως καὶ τῆς περὶ τὴν σύνθεσιν τῶν ὀνομάτων εὐρυθμίας, ὑπὲρ ἅπαντα δὲ ταῦτα τοῦ παθητικήν τε καὶ ἠθικὴν καὶ ἐναγώνιον ποιεῖν τὴν λέξιν, ἐν οἷς ἐστιν ἡ πλείστη τοῦ πιθανοῦ μοῖρα. τούτων δὲ τῶν ἀρετῶν ἑκάστην οὐχ ἡ βραχυλογία κράτιστα δύναται ποιεῖν, ἀλλὰ καὶ ὁ πλεονασμὸς ἐνίων ὀνομάτων, ᾧ καὶ ὁ Δημοσθένης κέχρηται. Critics of Demosthenes' style had made what Dionysius determines to be a crucial error by moving βραχυλογία ahead of all the other stylistic virtues, which causes them to overlook Demothenes' mastery in choosing the style most appropriate for persuading his audience at any given time. Dionysius' vigorous defense indicates with perfect clarity the ancients' high opinion of βραχυλογία: he never denies its stylistic merit, and in fact he asserts that Demosthenes employs it "more often and more appropriately" (μᾶλλον καὶ εὐκαιρότερον) than anyone else. But its high value should never lead one to fault an author's πλεονάζειν when he has sufficient reasons to prefer it instead. On this passage see further Wooten, "Dionysius," 576–88.

[24] Cf., however, Demetrius' remarks on the style of letters (*Eloc*. 228, quoted more fully below): τὸ δὲ μέγεθος συνεστάλθω τῆς ἐπιστολῆς, ὥσπερ καὶ ἡ λέξις. (In using the name 'Demetrius' here and elsewhere in the present study I do not mean to imply a position on the dis-

this division, although the remarks of Cicero and others on brevity in the διήγησις of a speech presuppose it, as we shall see in a moment. An *Ars rhetorica* falsely attributed to Aelius Aristides conveys the general principle:

βραχύτης δὲ καὶ συν⟨τομ⟩ία γίνεται κατὰ γνώμην ⟨καὶ⟩ κατὰ λέξιν. κατὰ μὲν γνώμην οὕτως, ὅταν τοῖς ἀναγκαίοις εὐθὺς συμπλέκηται τῶν πραγμάτων, καὶ ὅταν τις μὴ πᾶσιν ὡς προηγουμένοις χρῆται, ἀλλὰ τοῖς μὲν ⟨ὡς⟩ προηγουμένοις, τοῖς δὲ μὴ οὕτω. κατὰ λέξιν δὲ γίνεται βραχύτης καὶ συντομία, ὅταν τις μὴ ταῖς περιφραστικαῖς τῶν λέξεων, ἀλλὰ ταῖς εὐθείαις χρῆται, ⟨καὶ⟩ ὅταν μὴ ἐπαγωνίζηται τῇ λέξει τὰ ἰσοδυναμοῦντα παρατιθείς, ἀλλὰ δηλώσας τὸ πρᾶγμα τῇ σημαινούσῃ λέξει εὐθὺς ἀπαλλαγῇ καὶ ἐν ὀλίγῳ, καὶ ὅταν τις μὴ φιλοτιμῆται πρὸς τὴν λέξιν, ἀλλὰ [καὶ] πρὸς τὰ πράγματα ἀποβλέπῃ.

Now brevity and conciseness occur in thought and in style. [They occur] in thought in this way: whenever [the thought] is directly woven into the necessary elements of the subjects; and whenever one does not treat all the facts as principal, but some as principal and others as not so. And brevity and conciseness occur in style, whenever one does not use periphrastic forms of statements, but straightforward ones; and whenever one does not lay stress upon the style by appending statements of equivalent meaning, but, after disclosing the subject with declarative language and in small compass, one immediately moves forward; and whenever one is not overambitious with the style, but pays close attention to the subjects. (*Rhet.* 1.136–37)

One may apply this principle (anachronistically) to earlier theorists. Plato's Socrates asks Gorgias for a reduction in the length of his responses by bringing only those subjects which are most immediately relevant to the front (βραχύτης κατὰ γνώμην). Gorgias' boasts, however, imply that he can fit everything that he would have said into a much smaller package (βραχύτης κατὰ λέξιν). Spartan taciturnity focuses, as Plutarch says, on βραχεῖα λέξις. Dionysius generally has λέξις in mind in his comments as well. Whoever first articulated this division surely did so in order to facilitate instruction, since particular methods of verbal compression are subsumed under each: the selection and organization of subjects under "thought," and the selection and economization of words under "style." This division of brevity into style and subject informs much of the theory discussed in the rest of the present chapter.

Therefore, to gather the insights gleaned so far, βραχυλογία enters the rhetorical technical vocabulary and curriculum with the sophists in Athens, as the counterpart of μακρολογία. It soon takes on a life of its own, however, as an ideal feature of general discourse – an adoption of the Spartan perspective on the subject, perhaps. The Stoics' and Dionysius' promotion of συντομία to a virtue, and the latter's extensive application of it as a standard for assessing the stylistic achievements of canonical authors, reflect the emerging prominence of brevity and confirm its continuing vitality in rhetorical education.

---

puted question of the text's date and the veracity of its ascription to Demetrius of Phaleron or to some other later Demetrius; see Innes' introduction to the LCL edition, at 312–21; Kennedy, *New History*, 68–90; Russell, *Criticism in Antiquity*, 40.)

3.2.2 Brevity in the opening sections of an oration

We obtain a sense of the contexts in which ancient instructors honed the skill of brevity among their students in the discussions of its suitability for three parts of an oration: the introduction (προοίμιον), the proposition (πρόθεσις), and the narrative (διήγησις). Their advice is clearest and strongest for the διήγησις, so I shall begin with it, and then double back to cover the προοίμιον and πρόθεσις.

According to Quintilian, no less an authority than Isocrates teaches that a *narratio* should be "clear, brief [and] verisimilar" (*esse lucidam brevem veri similem*).[25] Aristotle vigorously disputes this view, calling the notion that a narrative should be "quick" absurd (νῦν δὲ γελοίως τὴν διήγησίν φασι δεῖν εἶναι ταχεῖαν), and declaring that moderation must guide the orator: "to say as much as will clarify the subject" (τὸ λέγειν ὅσα δηλώσει τὸ πρᾶγμα).[26] Aristotle's position ultimately fails to win the day, since a consensus solidifies that a διήγησις should exhibit σαφήνεια, συντομία and πιθανότης, as the *Rhetorica ad Alexandrum*,[27] Cicero,[28] the *Rhetorica ad Herennium*,[29] and Quintilian all

---

[25] *Inst.* 4.2.31–33: "Most writers, and especially those who are after Isocrates, propose that it [i.e., *narratio*] is to be clear, brief [and] verisimilar. ... The division is likewise pleasing to us, although even Aristotle disagrees in one part with Isocrates, mocking the precept of brevity, as if it is necessary that exposition is long or short, and that it is not allowed to take a median course. [The disciples] of Theodorus too leave behind only the last part, because it is not always useful to explain either briefly or clearly." *Eam plerique scriptores maximeque qui sunt ab Isocrate volunt esse lucidam brevem veri similem. ... Eadem nobis placet divisio, quamquam et Aristoteles ab Isocrate parte in una dissenserit, praeceptum brevitatis inridens tamquam necesse sit longam esse aut brevem expositionem nec liceat ire per medium, Theodorei quoque solam relinquant ultimam partem, quia nec breviter utique nec dilucide semper sit utile exponere.*

[26] *Rhet.* 3.16.4, 1416b–17a: "But nowadays they ridiculously say that the narrative must be quick. ... For one must not narrate at length, just as one must neither make the introduction [προοιμιάζεσθαι] nor expound proofs at length. For here the ideal is neither speaking quickly nor concisely but moderately; but this means saying as much as will clarify the subject, or as much as will cause someone to accept that something has happened or that someone has been damaged or has acted unjustly, or that matters are so great as one wishes." νῦν δὲ γελοίως τὴν διήγησίν φασι δεῖν εἶναι ταχεῖαν. ... δεῖ γὰρ μὴ μακρῶς διηγεῖσθαι ὥσπερ οὐδὲ προοιμιάζεσθαι μακρῶς, οὐδὲ τὰς πίστεις λέγειν. οὐδὲ γὰρ ἐνταῦθά ἐστι τὸ εὖ [ἢ] τὸ ταχὺ ἢ τὸ συντόμως, ἀλλὰ τὸ μετρίως· τοῦτο δ᾿ ἐστὶ τὸ λέγειν ὅσα δηλώσει τὸ πρᾶγμα, ἢ ὅσα ποιήσει ὑπολαβεῖν γεγονέναι ἢ βεβλαφέναι ἢ ἠδικηκέναι, ἢ τηλικαῦτα ἡλίκα βούλει.

[27] [Aristotle], *Rhet. Alex.* 30.4–5, 1438a: "But whenever we ourselves in speaking publicly are going through one of the events which have occurred, or we are clarifying present events, or we are predicting future events, it is necessary to do each of these clearly, briefly, and not without credibility: clearly, so that the hearers may understand the subjects under discussion; concisely, in order that they may remember what was said; credibly, so that they may not reject our explanations before we confirm the argument with proofs and legal arguments." ὅταν δὲ αὐτοὶ δημηγοροῦντες τῶν παρεληλυθότων τι διεξίωμεν ἢ {καὶ} τὰ παρόντα δηλῶμεν ἢ τὰ μέλλοντα προλέγωμεν, δεῖ τούτων ἕκαστον ποιεῖν σαφῶς καὶ βράχεως καὶ μὴ ἀπί-

agree.³⁰ The preliminary rhetorical exercises (προγυμνάσματα)³¹ counsel likewise in their instruction for the διήγησις or διήγημα, describing σαφήνεια, συντομία and πιθανότης as ἀρεταί.³² Theon defines συντομία in this connection as "speech which indicates the most vital elements of the subjects, neither adding something unnecessary nor excluding something necessary in accordance with the subjects and style" (λόγος τὰ καιριώτατα τῶν πραγμάτων σημαίνων, μήτε προστιθεὶς τὸ μὴ ἀναγκαῖον μήτε ἀφαιρῶν τὸ ἀναγκαῖον κατὰ τὰ

στως, σαφῶς μέν, ὅπως καταμάθωσι τὰ λεγόμενα πράγματα, συντόμως δέ, ἵνα μνημονεύσωσι τὰ ῥηθέντα, πιστῶς δέ, ὅπως μὴ πρὸ τοῦ ταῖς πίστεσι καὶ ταῖς δικαιολογίαις βεβαιῶσαι τὸν λόγον ἡμᾶς τὰς ἐξηγήσεις ἡμῶν οἱ ἀκούοντες ἀποδοκιμάσωσιν. Πράγματα, in the context of theoretical discussions of διήγησις, clearly refer to the "events" being narrated; I retain the translation "subjects," however, to underscore the continuity of the theory on brevity κατὰ πράγματα in narrative with that of brevity in general.

²⁸ *Part. or.* 31–32: "For it is necessary that we narrate clearly and plausibly, but we also add pleasantness. Therefore in order to narrate clearly we will return to those same precepts of explaining and illustrating which were discussed above, among which brevity is the one that is most often praised in narrative." *Nam ut dilucide probabiliterque narremus, necessarium est, sed adsumimus etiam suavitatem. Ergo ad dilucide narrandum eadem illa superiora explicandi et inlustrandi praecepta repetemus, in quibus sit brevitas ea quae saepissime in narratione laudatur, de qua supra dictum est.* See also *De or.* 2.80, 83; *Inv.* 1.28.

²⁹ [Cicero], *Rhet. Her.* 1.8.14: "It is appropriate that the narrative have three features: that it is brief, that is is clear, [and] that it is verisimilar," *tres res convenit habere narrationem: ut brevis, ut dilucida, ut veri similis sit.* The author dedicates the rest of this section to tactics of achieving brevity.

³⁰ See n. 25 above. Other supporters include Rufus (ii C.E.?, see Kennedy *Later Greek Rhetoric*, 27–28), *Rhet.* 17, who further defines συντομία as "whenever we go through only necessary things, neither beginning too far away nor stopping on the smallest matters," συντομία δὲ ὅταν αὐτὰ μόνα τὰ ἀναγκαῖα διεξίωμεν μήτε πόρρω ἀρχόμενοι μήτ' ἐπὶ μακρότατα παυόμενοι (19), and Anonymous Seguerianus (v C.E. per *BNP* 1.714, s.v.; ii–iii C.E. per Dilts and Kennedy, *Two Greek Rhetorical Treatises*, xiii), *Rhet.* 63.

³¹ On προγυμνάσματα, see Marrou, *History*, 194–205; Bonner, *Education*, 250–76; Kennedy, *New History*, 202–8; idem, *Progymnasmata*, ix–xvi (with bibliography); Aune, *Westminster Dictionary*, s.v., 375–78.

³² Theon (i C.E. per *BNP* 14.499–500, s.v. 6; Kennedy, *Progymnasmata*, 1–3), after listing the three traditional virtues, writes (*Prog.* 5, *RG* 2.79): "Therefore, if it is possible, it is especially necessary that the narrative have all the virtues; but if it should be unworkable for conciseness not to be somehow contrary to clarity and persuasiveness, the more urgent thing is to be aimed for," διὸ μάλιστα μέν, εἰ δυνατόν ἐστιν, ἁπάσας τὰς ἀρετὰς ἔχειν δεῖ τὴν διήγησιν· ἐὰν δὲ τοῦτο ἀμήχανον εἴη, τὸ μὴ ἐνάντιαν εἶναί πως τὴν συντομίαν τῇ τε σαφηνείᾳ καὶ τῇ πιθανότητι, τοῦ κατεπείγοντος μᾶλλον στοχαστέον. Theon thus acknowledges that different circumstances require different balances of these virtues. See also Aphthonius (iv–v C.E. per *BNP* 1.836–37, s.v.; Kennedy, *Progymnasmata*, 89–90), *Prog.* 2, *RG* 2.22 (ἀρεταὶ δὲ διηγήματος τέσσαρες, σαφήνεια, συντομία, πιθανότης καὶ ὁ τῶν ὀνομάτων ἑλληνισμός); Nicolaus (v C.E. per *BNP* 9.728–29, s.v. 4a; Kennedy, *Progymnasmata*, 129–31), *Prog.* 2 (affirming the usual three, but denying ἡδονή and μεγαλοπρέπεια); ps.-Hermogenes (ii–iii C.E. per *BNP* 6.234–35, s.v. 7) has a section περὶ διηγήματος (*Prog.* 2, *RG* 2.4), but does not mention ἀρεταί therein. Cf. [Cicero], *Rhet. Her.* 1.13.

πράγματα καὶ τὴν λέξιν).[33] He then crosses into the territory of methods of brief composition in his advice regarding conciseness ἐκ τῶν πραγμάτων on the one hand and ἐκ τῆς λέξεως on the other – following the division described above.[34] Theon echoes an earlier discussion of the proper style of a narrative, that of the *Rhetorica ad Alexandrum*: "And [we will explain] concisely if we take away *from the subjects and words* the things which are not necessary to be stated, leaving behind only those things which, if taken away, will render the utterance obscure" (συντόμως δέ, ἐὰν ἀπὸ τῶν πραγμάτων καὶ τῶν ὀνομάτων περιαιρῶμεν τὰ μὴ ἀναγκαῖα ῥηθῆναι, ταῦτα μόνα καταλείποντες, ὧν ἀφαιρεθέντων ἀσαφὴς ἔσται ὁ λόγος).[35] It seems probable that the division of methods of brevity into subject and style initially occurs in the theoretical context of the διήγησις.

Although the sources do not refer to brevity specifically as an ἀρετή for the προοίμιον and the πρόθεσις (or for any other part of an oration except the διήγησις),[36] some still identify it as tactically suitable for them. This topic intersects with complicated questions regarding the development of τάξις-theory and of ideas regarding the purposes of each section. The debate goes back at least to Aristotle,[37] who says that a speech requires only two parts, πρόθεσις and πίστις,[38] and has at a maximum four: προοίμιον, πρόθεσις, πίστις and ἐπίλογος.[39] Curiously, he does not supply as full an elaboration regarding the

---

[33] *Prog.* 5 (*RG* 2.83).

[34] I return to this passage to treat it in greater detail in § 3.3.1.

[35] *Rhet. Alex.* 30.8, 1438a.

[36] Cf., however, [Hermogenes], *Prog.* 10.49, ἀρεταὶ δὲ ἐκφράσεως μάλιστα μὲν σαφήνεια καὶ ἐνάργεια.

[37] See *Rhet.* 3.16, 1416b–17b. Cf. Lausberg, *Handbook*, 136–37, § 289 on the πρόθεσις as part of the διήγησις; see Aune, *Westminster Dictionary*, 175–76 ("Exordium"), 380 ("Prooimion"), and especially 62–64 on "Arrangement," an article which includes a comparative table of various ancient τάξις-schemes (cf. Lausberg, *Handbook*, 122–23).

[38] *Rhet.* 3.13.1, 1414a: "Now there are two parts of a speech: for it is necessary to state the subject concerning which [one is speaking], and to demonstrate it. ... One of these is the πρόθεσις, and the other is the πίστις." ἔστι δὲ τοῦ λόγου δύο μέρη· ἀναγκαῖον γὰρ τό τε πρᾶγμα εἰπεῖν περὶ οὗ, καὶ τοῦτ᾽ ἀποδεῖξαι. ... τούτων δὲ τὸ μὲν πρόθεσίς ἐστι τὸ δὲ πίστις. Aristotle then mocks those who have proliferated the parts of the speech unnecessarily, declaring that a διήγησις properly appears only in forensic speeches. Also, Anonymous Seguerianus (*Rhet.* 113–31) has an overview of the continuing debate as to whether one should use διηγήσεις in all situations; similarly for the προοίμιον he writes (21): "It is to be understood that often προοίμια should be avoided, for one should not always use a προοίμιον" (ἰστέον ὅτι πολλάκις δεῖ παραιτεῖσθαι τὰ προοίμια· οὐ γὰρ ἀεὶ προοιμιαστέον), for example when a subject lacks pathos, when more pathos will further excite an already agitated audience, when one has an audience of relatives, or when time is short. The sections which follow (26–36) record the debates among theorists on the necessity of προοίμια.

[39] *Rhet.* 3.13.4, 1414b: "The necessary parts, then, are πρόθεσις and πίστις. These are furthermore proper to it, but at the most [a speech will have] a προοίμιον, a πρόθεσις, a πίστις

πρόθεσις as he does for the other three parts, substituting an exposition of the διήγησις instead.[40] Subsequent theorists sometimes connect the objective of a πρόθεσις (to state the premise which one sets out to prove) with the προοίμιον. A προοίμιον properly aims for three things: the audience's favorable opinion, attention, and receptivity.[41] A preview of the speech and an articulation of one's objectives serve the goal of securing receptivity.[42] A πρόθεσις thus has a role to play in this context, as Dionysius indicates in connection with the speeches of Lysias: it normally (but not always) marks the point of transition

---

[and] an ἐπίλογος." ἀναγκαῖα ἄρα μόρια πρόθεσις καὶ πίστις. ἴδια μὲν οὖν ταῦτα, τὰ δὲ πλεῖστα προοίμιον πρόθεσις πίστις ἐπίλογος.

[40] Quintilian, probably following Aristotle, says that in forensic speeches a simple *propositio* can replace a *narratio* outlining the points to be proven or disproven, when the background facts are not in doubt (*Inst.* 4.2.4–8).

[41] E.g., [Aristotle], *Rhet. Alex.* 29.1, 1436a: "Now a προοίμιον, speaking generally, is [1] a preparation of the hearers and a clarification of the subject in summary fashion for those who do not know it, in order that they may understand what the speech is about and follow the argument; [2] for urging them to pay attention; and [3] insofar as it is possible for a speech, for making them favorable to us," ἔστι δὲ προοίμιον καθόλου μὲν εἰπεῖν ἀκροατῶν παρασκευὴ καὶ τοῦ πράγματος ἐν κεφαλαίῳ μὴ εἰδόσι δήλωσις, ἵνα γινώσκωσι, περὶ ὧν ὁ λόγος παρακαλουθῶσί τε τῇ ὑποθέσει, καὶ ἐπὶ ⟨τὸ⟩ προσέχειν παρακαλέσαι καὶ καθ' ὅσον τῷ λόγῳ δυνατὸν εὔνους ἡμῖν αὐτοὺς ποιῆσαι. The author then gives a couple of examples of τὸ φράζειν ἐν κεφαλαίῳ τὸ πρᾶγμα: "I stood up in order to advise that we should go to war on behalf of the Syracusians; I stood up in order to show that we should not help the Syracusians," ἀνέστην συμβουλεύσων, ὡς χρὴ πολεμεῖν ἡμᾶς ὑπὲρ Συρακουσίων· ἀνέστην ἀποφανούμενος, ὡς οὐ χρὴ βοηθεῖν ἡμᾶς Συρακουσίοις (29.2, 1436b). See further 35.1–4, 1440b (regarding epideictic προοίμια) and 36.1–16, 1441b–42a (regarding judicial); cf. Cicero, *Inv.* 1.20. Aristotle similarly writes (*Rhet.* 3.14.6, 1415a): "[A προοίμιον] in prologues and epics is the plan of the speech, in order that [the auditors] may know ahead of time what the speech may be about and that the purpose may not be left dangling. For that which is undefined is confusing. Therefore the one who gave the beginning, as it were, into [the hearer's] hand, causes the one who holds on to it tightly to follow the speech." ἐν δὲ προλόγοις καὶ ἔπεσι δεῖγμά ἐστιν τοῦ λόγου, ἵνα προειδῶσι περὶ οὗ [ᾖ] ὁ λόγος καὶ μὴ κρέμηται ἡ διάνοια· τὸ γὰρ ἀόριστον πλανᾷ· ὁ δοὺς οὖν ὥσπερ εἰς τὴν χεῖρα τὴν ἀρχὴν ποιεῖ ἐχόμενον ἀκολουθεῖν τῷ λόγῳ. Note also Longinus (iii C.E. per *BNP* 7.808–11, s.v. 1; Kennedy, *Later Greek Rhetoric*, 3–4), *Rhet.* fr. 48.132 (the προοίμιον is ἡ παρασκευὴ καὶ θεραπεία τῶν ἀκροωμένων); and Anonymous Seguerianus, *Rhet.* 9 (σκόπος δὲ τοῦ προοιμίου τὸ τοιόνδε παρασκευάσθαι τὸ ἀκροητήν· τέλος δὲ τὸ προσοχὴν καὶ εὐμάθειαν καὶ εὔνοιαν ἀπεργάσασθαι).

[42] Cicero, *Inv.* 1.23. Aristotle, *Rhet.* 3.14.6, 1415a: "Indeed the most necessary function of the προοίμιον – and this is its particularity – is to clarify what is the goal on behalf of which the speech [is given]. Therefore if the subject is clear and minor, one should not use a προοίμιον." τὸ μὲν οὖν ἀναγκαιότατον ἔργον τοῦ προοιμίου καὶ ἴδιον τοῦτο, δηλῶσαι τί ἐστιν τὸ τέλος οὗ ἕνεκα ὁ λόγος (διόπερ ἂν δῆλον ᾖ καὶ μικρὸν τὸ πρᾶγμα, οὐ χρηστέον προοιμίῳ). Cf. Longinus, *Rhet.* fr. 48.124–25: ἐὰν δὲ ὑπὲρ μικρῶν καὶ φαύλων ὁ λόγος ᾖ, μικρὸν ἔστω τὸ προοίμιον.

from the introduction to the body of the speech in Lysias' orations.[43] If, however, a theorist recommends a τάξις-scheme that has more than four parts, the πρόθεσις does not typically belong with the introduction, rather between the διήγησις and the πίστις. Anonymous Seguerianus, for example, assumes that the πρόθεσις properly sits after the διήγησις, as a means of redirecting the audience's attention and as a transitional device. But, like Dionysius, he does not approach this matter dogmatically, since one may also put it before the διήγησις or replace the προοίμιον with it.[44]

Regarding brevity in προοίμια, some theorists caution against boring or confusing one's audience with undue long-windedness.[45] Dionysius gives the

---

[43] *Lys.* 17: "But after concisely and simply including these things with useful thoughts, suitable maxims, and measured arguments, he presses on to the πρόθεσις, through which, after foretelling the things which are about to be said in the demonstrations and preparing the hearer to be receptive to the pending speech, he establishes the narrative. And for him the πρόθεσις is commonly the boundary between the two of these forms [i.e., προοίμιον and διήγησις], but once in a while he began with this [the προοίμιον] alone. And sometimes he entered [the speech] without an introduction, taking the narrative as a starting-point." ταῦτα δὲ συντόμως καὶ ἀφελῶς διανοίαις τε χρησταῖς καὶ γνώμαις εὐκαίροις καὶ ἐνθυμήμασι μετρίοις περιλαβὼν ἐπὶ τὴν πρόθεσιν ἐπείγεται, δι' ἧς τὰ μέλλοντα ἐν ταῖς ἀποδείξεσι λέγεσθαι προειπὼν καὶ τὸν ἀκροατὴν παρασκευάσας εὐμαθῆ πρὸς τὸν μέλλοντα λόγον ἐπὶ τὴν διήγησιν καθίσταται· καὶ ἔστι μεθόριον αὐτῷ ἑκατέρας τῶν ἰδεῶν ὡς τὰ πολλὰ ἡ πρόθεσις, ἤδη δέ ποτε καὶ ἀπὸ μόνης ταύτης ἤρξατο. καὶ ἀπροοιμιάστως ποτὲ εἰσέβαλε τὴν διήγησιν ἀρχὴν λαβών.

[44] *Rhet.* 161–66: "The πρόθεσις is an exposition of the point under dispute, as it were, the aim and articulation of the pending demonstration. Now the πρόθεσις is taken up first in order to make the hearers more attentive, for by knowing the πρόθεσις toward which one is making the arguments, they will become more attentive; second, in order that the transition from the narrative to the proofs becomes obvious to all; third, for the sake of amplification ... It is also taken up for the sake of diminution.... And then, he says, [a πρόθεσις] that directs the hearer's attention has the place of an introduction. The πρόθεσις is also placed before the narratives...." πρόθεσίς ἐστιν ἔκθεσις τοῦ ζητουμένου ὥσπερ εἰ σκοπὸς καὶ ἐπαγγελία τῆς μελλούσης κατασκευῆς. λαμβάνεται δὲ [γὰρ] ἡ πρόθεσις πρῶτον μὲν ⟨ἕνεκεν⟩ τοῦ προσεχεστέρους ποιῆσαι τοὺς ἀκροατάς· εἰδότες γὰρ τὴν πρόθεσιν ἐφ' ἣν ποιεῖται τοὺς λόγους, προσεκτικώτεροι γίνονται· δεύτερον δὲ ἕνεκεν τοῦ τὴν μετάβασιν τὴν ἐπὶ τὰς πίστεις ἐκ τοῦ διηγήματος πᾶσι φανερὰν γενέσθαι· τρίτον αὐξήσεως ἕνεκεν· ... λαμβάνεται δὲ καὶ μειώσεως ἕνεκεν.... τότε δέ, φησί, προοιμίου τάξιν ἔχει τὸν ἀκροατὴν ἐπιστρέφουσα. τίθεται πρόθεσις καὶ πρὸ τῶν διηγήσεων....

[45] Cicero, *Inv.* 1.26; Quintilian, *Inst.* 4.1.62. Longinus (*Rhet.* fr. 48.141–47) writes regarding the cooperation of the προοίμιον and the διήγησις: "But also concerning the διήγησις it is to be said that you should state the disclosure of the events both with many and the least amount [of words]: if the subjects are many, with many [words], but if the subjects are few, with the least amount [of words]. For you will additionally instruct by proceeding into the propositions and various διηγήσεις in their turns, identifying in the προοίμια what you are about to prove and to narrate section by section. For if you say all these together all at once, you will both confuse and be confused." ἀλλὰ καὶ περὶ διηγήσεως λεκτέον, ὅτι καὶ διὰ πλειόνων καὶ ἐλαχίστων εἴποις ἂν τὴν δήλωσιν τῶν πραγμάτων, ἂν μὲν ᾖ πολλὰ πράγματα, διὰ πολλῶν, ἂν δὲ ὀλίγα, δι' ἐλαχίστων. ἐπεκδιδάξεις γὰρ εἰς προτάσεις ἄγων καὶ πολλὰς διηγήσεις τὰς

firmest counsel in his citation of a set of "rules" (οἱ κανόνες οἱ τῶν τέχνων) that one should "speak in a compressed way" in προοίμια:

καὶ μὴν εἴς γε τὸ εὐμαθεῖς τοὺς ἀκοατὰς ποιῆσαι κελεύουσι συστρέψαντας εἰπεῖν τὸ πρᾶγμα, ἵνα μὴ ἀγνοῶσι τὴν ὑπόθεσιν οἱ δικασταί, καὶ οἷά περ ᾖ τὰ μέλλοντα λέγεσθαι, τοιοῦτο καὶ τὸ προοίμιον ὑποτίθεσθαι ἀπ' ἀρχῆς καὶ δεῖγμα τοῦ πράγματος ποιουμένους κατευθὺ ἀπ' ἐνθυμημάτων πειρᾶσθαι ἄρχεσθαι.

And further they [οἱ κανόνες] urge us to make the hearers receptive [1] by declaring the subject in a compressed way, in order that the jurors may not be ignorant of the hypothesis; [2] and by giving a preview of the topics by laying out the προοίμιον in such a manner from the start, [3] and by striving to begin with an immediate demonstration of the subject from the arguments. (*Lys.* 24)

Συστρέφειν does not necessarily refer to concise style, but to the compression of the full scope of one's speech into the introduction in order to facilitate the audience's comprehension – συντομία ἐκ τῶν πραγμάτων, in other words. Dionysius' remarks hearken back to the *Rhetorica ad Alexandrum* which identifies stating ἐν κεφαλαίῳ τὸ πρᾶγμα as an element of acquiring an audience's receptivity within the introduction.[46] Such summaries in προοίμια have both the form and objectives of a πρόθεσις, to relay in brief compass the proposition and plan of one's speech.[47]

ἐπὶ μέρους, κατ' εἶδος ὀνομάζων ἐν τοῖς προοιμίοις ὃ μέλλεις ἀποδεικνύειν καὶ διηγεῖσθαι. εἰ γὰρ πάντα ἅμα ἀθρόως ἐρεῖς, ταράξεις τε καὶ ταραχθήσῃ.

[46] See note 41 above. Cf. Aristotle, *Rhet.* 3.14.8, 1415b: if one has a smart audience, "there is no need for a προοίμιον, except as far as stating the matter summarily, in order that like a body [the speech] may have a head," οὐθὲν δεῖ προοιμίου, ἀλλ' ἢ ὅσον τὸ πρᾶγμα εἰπεῖν κεφαλαιωδῶς, ἵνα ἔχῃ ὥσπερ σῶμα κεφαλήν. See also Anonymous Seguerianus, *Rhet.* 10–11: "For by knowing what the speeches are about the hearers will become more receptive. Now pre-exposition [προέκθεσις], reminder and division cause receptivity. Pre-exposition is whenever the things which someone is about to say are set out ahead of time as in a summary." εἰδότες γὰρ οἱ ἀκούοντες περὶ ὧν οἱ λόγοι, εὐμαθέστεροι γενήσονται. εὐμάθειαν δὲ ποιεῖ προέκθεσις, ἀνανέωσις, μερισμός. προέκθεσις μέν ἐστιν ὅταν ἃ μέλλει τις λέγειν ὡς ἐν κεφαλαίῳ προεκθῆται. The author apparently uses προέκθεσις to distinguish between a πρόθεσις in the introduction and that which ordinarily sits between the narrative and the proofs.

[47] Quintilian gives more specific direction regarding brevity in the crafting of summary statements in the introduction (*Inst.* 4.1.34–35): "Without a doubt, this attentiveness itself also furnishes receptivity, but this too, if we will have briefly and distinctly [*breviter et dilucide*] disclosed a summary of the matter concerning which he [i.e., the judge] is obliged to investigate.... For the method of this condition [i.e., attentiveness] is that [the summary statement] be more like a proposition than an exposition, and that the speaker show not in what way everything was done, but what he is intending to speak about." *Docilem sine dubio et haec ipsa praestat attentio, sed et illud, si breviter et dilucide summam rei de qua cognoscere debeat indicarimus...: nam is eius rei modus est ut propositioni similior sit quam expositioni, nec quo modo quidque sit actum sed de quibus dicturus sit orator ostendat.* Quintilian here discloses his presupposition that a *propositio* (= πρόθεσις) exhibits *brevitas* (which, like a χρεία, is short by definition), and that a brief and distinct summary furthers the goal of obtaining receptivity from one's audience.

3.2 The utility of brevity

The opening sections of an oration, especially the διήγησις, but also the προοίμιον and πρόθεσις, are thus appropriate contexts for the utilization of methods of brevity. This conclusion underscores further the importance of brevity in rhetorical instruction: learning to compose an oration would necessarily involve learning to compose with conciseness in content and style.

3.2.3 Brevity in epistolary style

Brevity additionally holds a prominent position in theory regarding proper epistolary style.[48] Demetrius, our earliest extant theorist on this subject, propounds four positive stylistic types, each with its negative analogue: the grand (μεγαλοπρέπης) with the cold (ψυχρός), the elegant (γλαφυρός) with the affected (κακόζηλος), the plain (ἰσχνός) with the dry (ξηρός), and the forceful (δεινός) with the uncharming (ἄχαρις).[49] He offers his observations regarding letters (*Eloc.* 223–35) in connection with plain style, immediately before he addresses the dry. On the topic of brevity, he writes:

τὸ δὲ μέγεθος συνεστάλθω τῆς ἐπιστολῆς, ὥσπερ καὶ ἡ λέξις. αἱ δὲ ἄγαν μακραί, καὶ προσέτι κατὰ τὴν ἑρμηνείαν ὀγκωδέστεραι, οὐ μὰ τὴν ἀλήθειαν ἐπιστολαὶ γένοιτο ἄν, ἀλλὰ συγγράμματα, τὸ χαίρειν ἔχοντα προσγεγραμμένον, καθάπερ τοῦ Πλάτωνος πολλαὶ καὶ ἡ Θουκυδίδου. ... εἰ γάρ τις ἐν ἐπιστολῇ σοφίσματα γράφοι καὶ φυσιολογίας, γράφει μέν, οὐ μὴν ἐπιστολὴν γράφει. φιλοφρόνησις γάρ τις βούλεται εἶναι ἡ ἐπιστολὴ σύντομος, καὶ περὶ ἁπλοῦ πράγματος ἔκθεσις καὶ ἐν ὀνόμασιν ἁπλοῖς.

But let the size of the letter be compressed, as also its style. Letters that are excessively long, and more bloated in their style besides, would surely not in truth be letters, but monographs which have the greeting inscribed at the top, just like many letters of Plato and the letter of Thucydides. ... For if someone should write sophisms and discourses on nature in a letter, indeed he writes, yet he is not writing a letter. For the letter, as a certain expression of friendly regard, wants to be concise, and an exposition regarding a simple subject and in simple words. (*Eloc.* 228, 231)

---

[48] The earliest sources on epistolary theory primarily address the style of the letter between friends (and social equals), e.g. Demetrius, *Eloc.* 224–25 (see also the letters of Cicero and Seneca quoted in *AET* 21–29): "For the letter should be somewhat more ornamented than a dialogue; for the dialogue imitates someone speaking off the cuff, but the letter is written and sent in a certain sense as a gift. Who at any rate would converse with a friend like Aristotle does when writing to Antipater on behalf of the fugitive old man: 'If this man who has gone into exile travels to all lands, so as not to come back, it is clear that no one is jealous of those who want to descend to Hades' [home]'? For the person who converses thus is more like someone delivering an epideictic oration, not someone talking." δεῖ γὰρ ὑποκατεσκευάσθαι πως μᾶλλον τοῦ διαλόγου τὴν ἐπιστολήν· ὁ μὲν γὰρ μιμεῖται αὐτοσχεδιάζοντα, ἡ δὲ γράφεται καὶ δῶρον πέμπεται τρόπον τινά. τίς γοῦν οὕτως ἂν διαλεχθείη πρὸς φίλον ὥσπερ ὁ Ἀριστοτέλης πρὸς Ἀντίπατρον ὑπὲρ τοῦ φυγάδος γράφων τοῦ γέροντός φησιν· «εἰ δὲ πρὸς ἁπάσας οἴχεται τὰς φυγὰς οὗτος, ὥστε μὴ κατάγειν, δῆλον ὡς τοῖς γε εἰς Ἅιδου κατελθεῖν βουλομένοις οὐδεὶς φθόνος»· ὁ γὰρ οὕτως διαλεγόμενος ἐπιδεικνυμένῳ ἔοικεν μᾶλλον, οὐ λαλοῦντι.

[49] For discussion of this and other stylistic schemes, see chapter 9 of Russell, *Criticism in Antiquity*; Hendrickson, "Peripatetic Mean," and idem, "Origin and Meaning."

He concludes in 235: "But on the whole let the letter be mixed in style from these two stylistic types, the graceful and the plain" (καθόλου δὲ μεμίχθω ἡ ἐπιστολὴ κατὰ τὴν ἑρμηνείαν ἐκ δυοῖν χαρακτήροιν τούτοιν, τοῦ τε χαρίεντος καὶ τοῦ ἰσχνοῦ). Demetrius underscores τὸ πρέπον (propriety) as a guiding principle: in order to be friendly, a letter requires a tone that balances conversation and formal oration on the one hand,[50] and that is restrained in length, style and subject on the other – hence its nature as an amalgam of the plain and graceful styles. Other authors likewise perceive brevity as characteristic of epistolary style. Plutarch, for example, lauds Brutus for his letters' ἀποφθεγματικὴ καὶ Λακονικὴ βραχυλογία,[51] and Ammonius cites Aristotle's epistolary "correctness" (including συντομία).[52] Later theorists begin to stress moderation of brevity, however, with an implicit division into subject-matter and style. For the latter, one must not sacrifice σαφήνεια in pursuit of συν-

---

[50] Demetrius reinforces this point in *Eloc.* 229 on syntax: "And surely let a letter be more relaxed in syntax; for to use periods is silly, as if one is writing not a letter but a forensic speech. And to use periods is not only silly, it is not friendly (for surely it is said so according to the proverb 'let figs be figs') to use these things in letters." καὶ τῇ συντάξει μέντοι λελύσθω μᾶλλον· γελοῖον γὰρ περιοδεύειν, ὥσπερ οὐκ ἐπιστολὴν ἀλλὰ δίκην γράφοντα· καὶ οὐδὲ γελοῖον μόνον ἀλλ' οὐδὲ φιλικόν (τὸ γὰρ δὴ κατὰ τὴν παροιμίαν «τὰ σῦκα σῦκα» λεγόμενον) ἐπιστολαῖς ταῦτα ἐπιτηδεύειν. Cf. Quintilian's comparison of *oratio* with *sermo* and *epistula* in his discussion of *compositio* (*Inst.* 9.4.19): "Therefore, first of all, some oratory is bound and interwoven, other oratory is loose, as in conversation and letters except when they handle something beyond their own nature, for instance regarding philosophy, regarding the state and similar topics," *est igitur ante omnia oratio alia vincta atque contexta, soluta alia, qualis in sermone et epistulis, nisi cum aliquid supra naturam suam tractant, ut de philosophia, de re publica similibusque.* Cf. also the remarks of Julius Victor (*Rhet.* 27, *AET* 62; iv C.E. per *BNP* 6.1088–89, s.v. IV.24) on the official letter (as opposed to the personal: *in familiaribus litteris primo brevitas observanda*): "In this type weightiness of ideas, clarity of words, and conspicuous performances of figures of abbreviation are required, together with all oratorical precepts besides, with only one exception, that we remove something from the greatest wealth [of language] and that a more intimate style unfold the oratory," *in hoc genere et sententiarum pondera et verborum lumina et figurarum insignia conpendii opera requiruntur atque omnia denique oratoria praecepta, una modo exceptione, ut aliquid de summis copiis detrahamus et orationem proprius sermo explicet.*

[51] See below for this text.

[52] Quoted by Rose at 411 in his edition of Aristotle's fragments: "In [his] letters he appears perfectly correct with respect to his epistolary style, which should be concise, clear and free of all harsh connection and expression," ἐν δὲ ταῖς ἐπιστολαῖς φαίνεται κατωρθωκὼς τὸν ἐπιστολιμαῖον χαρακτῆρα, ὃν καὶ σύντομον εἶναι δεῖ καὶ σαφῆ καὶ ἀπηλλαγμένον πάσης περισκελοῦς συνδέσεώς τε καὶ φράσεως. Demetrius, who otherwise has critical things to say about Aristotle's epistles, nonetheless notes (*Eloc.* 230): "It is necessary to acknowledge that not only [is there an epistolary] style, but also certain epistolary subjects. At any rate Aristotle, who seems to have attained most successfully the same epistolary style, says: 'I am not writing about this to you, for it is not suitable for a letter.'" εἰδέναι δὲ χρή, ὅτι οὐχ ἑρμηνεία μόνον ἀλλὰ καὶ πράγματά τινα ἐπιστολικά ἐστιν. Ἀριστοτέλης γοῦν ὃς μάλιστα ἐπιτετευχέναι δοκεῖ τοῦ [αὐτοῦ] ἐπιστολικοῦ, «τοῦτο δὲ οὐ γράφω σοί» φησίν· «οὐ γὰρ ἦν ἐπιστολικόν».

τομία,⁵³ and for the former necessity must determine the size of the composition.⁵⁴ On these points, the advice seems tailored to ensure that one avoids the tactics of full-blown rhetorical display: Atticism, periods, rich ornamentation – in short, ostentatious elegance.⁵⁵ One should cut all such things out and strive for charming simplicity. Brevity thus remains a feature of the *style* even as the *length* of the letter becomes less of a concern.

The Greek epistles of Brutus powerfully illustrate the ancient perception of letters as ideally concise. This corpus and the cover letter affixed to it by the editor of its second edition, a 'Mithridates,'⁵⁶ have rarely received attention from scholars. But just as Dionysius identifies certain orators as exemplary for the purposes of imitation, these letters – whether Brutus wrote them or not – appear in Philostratus' and Photius' lists of epistolary models.⁵⁷ Plu-

---

⁵³ E.g., Philostratus, *Epist.* (*AET* 42): "Clarity is a good governor of all speech, but especially of the letter," σαφήνεια δὲ ἀγαθὴ μὲν ἡγεμὼν ἅπαντος λόγου, μάλιστα δὲ ἐπιστολῆς. Also [Libanius], *Epist.* 49 (*AET* 72): "… likewise it is [the duty] of an eloquent person – but of only the one who aims at moderation with correctness of diction and who makes what is said entirely clear – neither to speak foolishly beyond that which is proper, nor to welcome βραχυλογία because of perplexity and [thus] to conceal the clarity of one's letters," … οὕτως οὔτε τὸ πέρα τοῦ προσήκοντος ληρεῖν οὔτε τὸ βραχυλογίαν ἀσπάζεσθαι δι' ἀπορίαν καὶ τὸ σαφὲς ἐπικρύπτειν τῶν ἐπιστάλσεων ἀνδρός ἐστι λογίου, ἀλλὰ μόνου τοῦ μετ' εὐφραδείας τῆς συμμετρίας στοχαζομένου καὶ τὸ λεγόμενον καλῶς σαφηνίζοντος.

⁵⁴ So Gregory of Nazianzus, *Ep.* 51.2 (*AET* 58): "Now need [as a determining factor] is the measure of letters: one must neither write longer where the subjects are not many, nor write shorter where [the subjects] are many," ἔστι δὲ μέτρον τῶν ἐπιστολῶν, ἡ χρεία· καὶ οὔτε μακρότερα γραπτέον, οὗ μὴ πολλὰ τὰ πράγματα, οὔτε μικρολογητέον, ἔνθα πολλά. See also [Libanius], *Epist.* 50 (*AET* 72): "Indeed the length of the letter is to be as much as is in accordance with the subjects, and not always is it a good thing to disparage the size as a fault; rather one should even extend some letters as need requires on occasion," τὸ μὲν οὖν μέγεθος τῆς ἐπιστολῆς ὡς πρὸς τὰ πράγματα, καὶ οὐ πάντως τὸ πλῆθος καθάπερ κακίαν ἀτιμάζειν καλόν, ἀλλὰ δεῖ καί τινας ἐπιστολὰς ἀπομηκύνειν ἐν καιρῷ πρὸς τὴν ἀπαιτοῦσαν χρείαν.

⁵⁵ See Demetrius, *Eloc.* 229 (quoted in n. 50), and Philostratus (*AET* 42): "I agree with polishing off a period in the briefer of letters, in order that at least by this the brevity (by being wholly confined) may bloom into another resonance, but it is necessary to excise periods from letters that proceed to [great] length, for this is more agonistic [i.e., forensic] than is suited to a letter, unless somehow at the end of letters one wants either to gather the things which have been said before or to close up the meaning in all [that has been said]." κύκλον δὲ ἀποτορνεύειν ἐν μὲν ταῖς βραχυτέραις τῶν ἐπιστολῶν ξυγχωρῶ, ἵνα τούτῳ γοῦν ἡ βραχυλογία ὡραίζοιτο ἐς ἄλλην ἠχὼ πᾶσα στενὴ οὖσα, τῶν δὲ ἐς μῆκος προηγμένων ἐπιστολῶν ἐξαιρεῖν χρὴ κύκλους, ἀγωνιστικώτερον γὰρ ἢ κατὰ ἐπιστολὴν τοῦτο, πλὴν εἰ μή που ἐπὶ τελευτῆς τῶν ἐπεσταλμένων ἢ ξυλλαβεῖν δέοι τὰ προειρημένα ἢ ξυγκλεῖσαι τὸ ἐπὶ πᾶσι νόημα.

⁵⁶ Mithridates claims to have composed plausible responses to Brutus' letters, and he furthermore includes a description of his methods (paralleling Thucydides 1.21.1–4 and Lucian, *Hist. conscr.* 58 for speeches in historical texts); cf. Theon, *Prog.* 10; Nicolaus, *Prog.* 10; and Malherbe's discussion of "Letter Writing in the Schools," *AET* 6–7. See further my essay, "The *Letter* of Mithridates."

⁵⁷ Philostratus, *Epist.* (*AET* 42): "After the ancients, [the following persons] seem to me to observe best the epistolary style of discourse: of philosophers, the Tyanan [Apollonius] and

tarch confirms both this admiration and the existence of the letters in the first century C.E. in more or less the same form as we have them now.[58] The letters (all but one addressed to cities) are extremely concise, each having no more

---

Dio; of generals, Brutus or whomever Brutus used for the purpose of writing letters; of kings, divine Marcus in the things he wrote in letters, for in addition to him being distinguished in speech the steadfastness of his character has also been stamped on his letters; of rhetors, Herodes the Athenian wrote letters best, but by over-Atticizing and over-speaking he often falls from the style which is suitable for letters." τὸν ἐπιστολικὸν χαρακτῆρα τοῦ λόγου μετὰ τοὺς παλαιοὺς ἄριστά μοι δοκοῦσι διεσκέφθαι φιλοσόφων μὲν ὁ Τυαννεὺς καὶ Δίων, στρατηγῶν δὲ Βροῦτος ἢ ὅτῳ Βροῦτος ἐς τὸ ἐπιστέλλειν ἐχρῆτο, βασιλέων δὲ ὁ θεσπέσιος Μάρκος ἐν οἷς ἐπέστελλεν αὐτός, πρὸς γὰρ τῷ κεκριμένῳ τοῦ λόγου καὶ τὸ ἑδραῖον τοῦ ἤθους ἐντετύπωτο τοῖς γράμμασι, ῥητόρων δὲ ἄριστα μὲν Ἡρώδης ὁ Ἀθηναῖος ἐπέστελλεν, ὑπεραττικίζων δὲ καὶ ὑπερλαλῶν ἐκπίπτει πολλαχοῦ τοῦ πρέποντος ἐπιστολῇ χαρατῆρος. Photius (ix C.E.), Ep. 206.10–16, Ἀμφιλοχίῳ μητροπολίτῃ Κυζίκου: "So with what letters should one be familiar, and with what [letters] shall we assemble the exercise by fitting [it] to the style that became known to us through [their] art? There is indeed another boundless multitude, but in order that the course of exercise may not be long for you, you have, I suppose, the letters attributed to Phalaris, the Acragantian tyrant; and those which Brutus, the general of the Romans, inscribes; and Libanius, the sage among kings and the sophist in most [of his letters]." τίσιν οὖν ἐπιστολαῖς ὁμιλητέον καὶ τίσι τὸν ἐπιγνωσθέντα ἡμῖν διὰ τῆς τέχνης χαρακτῆρα ἐφαρμόζοντες τὴν γυμνασίαν συλλεξόμεθα; ἔστιν μὲν καὶ ἄλλο πλῆθος ἄπειρον· ἔχεις δ', ἵνα μηδὲ μακρὸν ᾖ σοι τὸ τῆς γυμνασίας στάδιον, τὰς εἰς Φάλαριν ἐκεῖνον οἶμαι τὸν Ἀκραγαντίνον τύραννον ἀναφερομένας ἐπιστολάς καὶ αἷς Βροῦτος ὁ Ῥωμαίων στρατηγὸς ἐπιγράφεται καὶ τὸν ἐν βασιλεῦσι φιλόσοφον καὶ τὸν σοφιστὴν ἐν ταῖς πλείσταις Λιβάνιον. Cf. Demetrius' comments on Aristotle at Eloc. 223, 225, 230, 233–34; also Quintilian, Inst. 10.1.107 on the letters of Demosthenes and Cicero.

[58] Brut. 2.5–8: "In Latin Brutus was indeed competently trained for expositions and trials, but in Greek he is sometimes distinguished when he pursues apophthegmatic and Spartan brevity in his letters. For example, when he had already set out for battle, he writes to the Pergamenes: 'I hear that you have given supplies to Dolobella. If you gave them voluntarily, confess to acting unjustly; but if involuntarily, prove it by giving them voluntarily to me' [Ep. 1]. Again, to the Samians: 'Your counsels are contemptuous, your compliances are late. What do you intend as a result of these?' [Ep. 69]. And another: 'The Xanthians, by ignoring my philanthropy, have had their homeland as a tomb for their folly, but the Patareans, by entrusting themselves to me, lose nothing of their freedom as they manage each their own affairs. Hence it is possible for you too to choose either the decision of the Patareans or the fate of the Xanthians.' [Ep. 25]. Such indeed is the type of his distinguished letters." Ῥωμαϊστὶ μὲν οὖν ἤσκητο πρὸς τὰς ⟨δι⟩εξόδους καὶ τοὺς ἀγῶνας ἱκανῶς ὁ βροῦτος, Ἑλληνιστὶ δὲ τὴν ἀποφθεγματικὴν καὶ Λακωνικὴν ἐπιτηδεύων βραχολογίαν ἐν ταῖς ἐπιστολαῖς ἐνιαχοῦ παράσημός ἐστιν. οἷον ἤδη καθεστηκὼς εἰς τὸν πόλεμον γράφει Περγαμηνοῖς· «ἀκούω ὑμᾶς Δολοβέλλᾳ δεδωκέναι χρήματα· ἃ εἰ μὲν ἑκόντες ἔδοτε, ὁμολογεῖτε ἀδικεῖν· εἰ δ' ἄκοντες, ἀποδείξατε τῷ ἐμοὶ ἑκόντες δοῦναι.» πάλιν Σαμίοις· «αἱ βουλαὶ ὑμῶν ὀλίγωροι, αἱ ὑπουργίαι βραδεῖαι. τί τούτων τέλος ἐννοεῖσθε;» καὶ [περὶ Παταρέων] ἑτέραν· «Ξάνθιοι τὴν ἐμὴν εὐεργεσίαν ὑπεριδόντες τάφον ἀπονοίας ἐσχήκασι τὴν πατρίδα, Παταρεῖς δὲ πιστεύσαντες ἑαυτοὺς ἐμοὶ οὐδὲν ἐλλείπουσι διοικοῦντες τὰ καθ' ἕκαστα τῆς ἐλευθερίας. ἐξὸν οὖν καὶ ὑμῖν ἢ τὴν Παταρέων κρίσιν ἢ τὴν Ξανθίων τύχην ἑλέσθαι.» τὸ μὲν οὖν τῶν παρασήμων γένος ἐπιστολίων τοιοῦτόν ἐστιν.

than a few sentences.[59] Plutarch, however, approves of their ἀποφθεγματικὴ καὶ Λακωνικὴ βραχυλογία, in other words, their terse style.[60] Mithridates begins his cover letter for the Brutan corpus with a similar sentiment:

τὰς Βρούτου ἐθαύμασα πολλάκις ἐπιστολάς, οὐ μόνον δεινότητος καὶ συντομίας χάριν, ἀλλὰ καὶ ὡς ἡγεμονικοῦ φρονήματος ἐχούσας χαρακτῆρα· ἐοίκασι γὰρ οὐδὲν νομίζειν καλόν, εἰ μὴ καὶ μεγαλοψυχίας ἔχοιτο.

I have often admired the letters of Brutus, not only on account of [their] forcefulness and conciseness, but also for possessing the style of a leader's mind. For they seem to make use of nothing elegant unless it might adhere to greatness of soul. (*Letter* 1–2)

He states here why he republishes the corpus with his own additions: he is enhancing its utility as a textbook of epistolary style in the areas of δεινότης, συντομία, and ἦθος (the transparency of authorial voice, in Brutus' case, as a ἡγεμών). Most letters will not, of course, exhibit the level of brevity and forcefulness that Brutus manages, but his mastery of these virtues ensures the corpus' status as required reading for anyone who seeks excellence in epistolary composition.[61]

Brevity is therefore a defining feature of epistolary style, but letters should be as long as their scope and objectives demand. The theorists thereby accommodate their instruction more thoroughly to the various contexts in which letters were useful beyond correspondence between friends – an effort furthermore visible in the proliferation of epistolary types during the same period.

3.2.4 Demetrius on the rhetorical impact of brevity

Only one ancient theorist gives a detailed discussion of the rhetorical impact of brevity: Demetrius, the author of *De elocutione*. He does not approach βραχυλογία, βραχύτης and συντομία as figures or tropes,[62] but as stylistic modes that aid the achievement of several of his major categories of style. He treats brevity in letters as an element of the plain style (ἰσχνός), as we saw in § 3.2.2

---

[59] The longest is *Ep.* 55, Βροῦτος Τραλλιανοῖς. The one to an individual is also the shortest, *Ep.* 19: Βροῦτος Δαμᾶ. ὅπλων καὶ χρημάτων χρεία. ἢ πέμπε ἢ ἀποφαίνου.

[60] See n. 58 above. Cf. *Suda*, s.v. B § 561: "Brutus, a general of the Romans, wrote *Letters* and an epitome of the books of Polybius the historian. He is admired for the form, this is to say style, of his letters," Βροῦτος, στρατηγὸς Ῥωμαίων, ἔγραψεν Ἐπιστολὰς καὶ τῶν Πολυβίου τοῦ ἱστορικοῦ Βίβλων ἐπιτομήν. θαυμάζεται δὲ εἰς τὴν τῶν ἐπιστολῶν ἰδέαν, ἤγουν χαρακτῆρα.

[61] This high esteem lasts as late as the tenth century (per the testimony of the *Suda*, see above) and beyond, given that the manuscripts date from the tenth to the fifteenth centuries (per Torraca, *Marco Giunio Bruto Epistole Greche*, xxxiii–xlv).

[62] He is aware of figures and tropes, however, and uses them at points in his treatise. I discuss one instance of this in chapter 5 below (ἀναδίπλωσις, the repetition of words for emphasis, in the phrase ἐκ πίστεως εἰς πίστιν in Rom 1:17).

above. He also names it as a "primary charm" of the elegant style (γλαφυρός), since the alacrity one obtains from συντομία steps up the pace, while lengthening converts one's utterance into a "bare narrative" (διήγημα ψιλόν).[63]

Demetrius' most extensive observations relate to δεινότης, forcefulness. Βραχύτης and δεινότης appear together early in his essay, in his sections on sentence structure, as part of his advice on how to write clauses (κῶλα) with appropriate content and length:

τῶν δὲ μικρῶν κώλων κἂν δεινότητι χρῆσίς ἐστι· δεινότερον γὰρ τὸ ἐν ὀλίγῳ πολὺ ἐμφαινόμενον καὶ σφοδρότερον, διὸ καὶ οἱ Λάκωνες βραχυλόγοι ὑπὸ δεινότητος· καὶ τὸ μὲν ἐπιτάσσειν σύντομον καὶ βραχύ, καὶ πᾶς δεσπότης δούλῳ μονοσύλλαβος, τὸ δὲ ἱκετεύειν μακρὸν καὶ τὸ ὀδύρεσθαι. ⟨καὶ γὰρ⟩ αἱ Λιταὶ καθ᾽ Ὅμηρον καὶ χωλαὶ καὶ ῥυσαὶ ὑπὸ βραδυτῆτος, τουτέστιν ὑπὸ μακρολογίας, καὶ οἱ γέροντες μακρολόγοι διὰ τὴν ἀσθένειαν. παράδειγμα δὲ βραχείας συνθέσεως τὸ «Λακεδαιμόνιοι Φιλίππῳ· Διονύσιος ἐν Κορίνθῳ». πολὺ γὰρ δεινότερον φαίνεται ῥηθὲν οὕτω βραχέως, ἢ εἴπερ αὐτὸ μακρῶς ἐκτείναντες εἶπον, ὅτι ὁ Διονύσιός ποτε μέγας ὢν τύραννος ὥσπερ σὺ ὅμως νῦν ἰδιωτεύων οἰκεῖ Κόρινθον. οὐ γὰρ ἔτι διὰ πολλῶν ῥηθὲν ἐπιπλήξει ἐῴκει ἀλλὰ διηγήματι, καὶ μᾶλλόν τινι διδάσκοντι, οὐκ ἐκφοβοῦντι· οὕτως ἐκτεινόμενον ἐκλύεται τοῦ λόγου τὸ θυμικὸν καὶ σφοδρόν. ὥσπερ ⟨γὰρ⟩ τὰ θηρία συστρέψαντα ἑαυτὰ μάχεται, τοιαύτη τις ἂν εἴη συστροφὴ καὶ λόγου καθάπερ ἐσπειραμένου πρὸς δεινότητα. ἡ δὲ τοιαύτη βραχύτης κατὰ τὴν σύνθεσιν κόμμα ὀνομάζεται. ὁρίζονται δ᾽ αὐτὸ ὧδε, κόμμα ἐστὶν τὸ κώλου ἔλαττον, οἷον τὸ προειρημένον, τό [τε] «Διονύσιος ἐν Κορίνθῳ», καὶ τὸ «γνῶθι σεαυτόν», καὶ τὸ «ἕπου θεῷ» τὰ τῶν σοφῶν. ἔστι γὰρ καὶ ἀποφθεγματικὸν ἡ βραχύτης καὶ γνωμολογικόν, καὶ σοφώτερον τὸ ἐν ὀλίγῳ πολλὴν διάνοιαν ἠθροῖσθαι, καθάπερ ἐν τοῖς σπέρμασιν δένδρων ὅλων δυνάμεις· εἰ δ᾽ ἐκτείνοιτό τις τὴν γνώμην ἐν μακροῖς, διδασκαλία γίνεταί τις καὶ ῥητορεία ἀντὶ γνώμης.

Short clauses are useful for forcefulness also, for the clause which indicates much with little is more forceful and more intense, for which reason also the Spartans are brief [βραχυλόγοι] by virtue of [their] forcefulness. And commanding is concise and brief [σύντομον καὶ βραχύ], and every master is monosyllabic with his slave, but supplicating and grieving are long. For also Homer's *Litai* are both lame and desiccated by reason of a plodding pace – this is to say verbosity – and old men are verbose because of weakness. Now an example of brief composition is: "The Spartans to Philip: Dionysius is in Corinth." For by being said so briefly it seems

---

[63] *Eloc.* 137: "Straightaway, therefore, the primary charm comes from συντομία, whenever the same statement by being lengthened becomes graceless, but by swiftness becomes graceful, as in Xenophon [*Anab.* 3.1.31]: '"In reality nothing of Greece has a share in that man, since I saw him as if he were a Lydian who had pierced both his ears," and he had [them] thus.' For the line 'and he had [them] thus' tacked on the end affects charm by [its] conciseness. But if it was lengthened with more words, 'he said these things truly, for he clearly had himself pierced,' it would become bare narrative instead of charm." εὐθὺς οὖν πρώτη ἐστὶ χάρις ἡ ἐκ συντομίας, ὅταν τὸ αὐτὸ μηκυνόμενον ἄχαρι γένηται, ὑπὸ δὲ τάχους χάριεν, ὥσπερ παρὰ Ξενοφῶντι, «τῷ ὄντι τούτῳ οὐδὲν μέτεστι τῆς Ἑλλάδος, ἐπεὶ ἐγὼ αὐτὸν εἶδον ὡσπερεὶ Λυδὸν ἀμφότερα τὰ ὦτα τετρυπημένον· καὶ εἶχεν οὕτως». τὸ γὰρ ἐπιλεγόμενον τὸ «εἶχεν οὕτως» ὑπὸ τῆς συντομίας τὴν χάριν ποιεῖ, εἰ δὲ ἐμηκύνθη διὰ πλειόνων, ὅτι «ἔλεγεν ταῦτα ἀληθῆ, σαφῶς γὰρ ἐτετρύπητο», διήγημα ἂν ψιλὸν ἐγένετο ἀντὶ χάριτος. "Lengthening" here thus seems to mean lengthening one's exposition, hence the danger of creating a "bare narrative." Demetrius thus conforms to the trend of restricting συντομία brevity in content not style.

much more forceful than if they had extended it at length, saying: "Dionysius, although he was once a great tyrant like you, nevertheless now lives in Corinth as a commoner." For when it is said in many words it does not seem like a rebuke but a narrative, and more like someone teaching, not inspiring fear. By being extended thus it relaxes the fervor and intensity of the utterance. For just as wild animals attack after gathering themselves into a pack, so should be the gathering up of the speech too, as if it were coiled, for the purpose of forcefulness. Now such βραχύτης in composition is called a phrase, and it is defined as follows: a phrase is shorter than a clause, such as the previously mentioned "Dionysius in Corinth," and the sayings of the wise, "know yourself," and "follow God." For βραχύτης is apophthegmatic and gnomic, and to have collected much thought in little [wording] is wiser, just as the potentialities of whole trees exist in the seeds. But if someone extends a maxim at length, it becomes a kind of teaching and an oration instead of a maxim. (*Eloc.* 7–9)

Demetrius offers three important observations in this passage. First, brevity produces forcefulness because of its formal resemblance to commands (τὸ ἐπιτάσσειν), which become more terse as the gap in social status increases. Βραχύτης thus borrows its authoritative character from the communicative conventions of a culture that used language to reinforce its strict social status hierarchies. Demetrius says later in a recapitulation of this section: "Brevity is more forceful and commanding, but to speak at length befits supplication and request" (δεινότερον γὰρ τὸ βραχὺ καὶ ἐπιτακτικόν, τὸ μακρηγορεῖν δὲ τῷ ἱκετεύειν πρέπει καὶ αἰτεῖν).[64] One lengthens speech as one speaks up or across the social ladder, and shortens it when speaking down. Other authors associate forcefulness and brevity for similar reasons. Mithridates, too, praises the letters of Brutus for their συντομία and δεινότης. And Plutarch justifies Phocion's "commanding, austere and unsweetened brevity" (προστακτικὴν τινα καὶ αὐ-

---

[64] The text of *Eloc.* 241–43 reads: "Now throughout one's composition this style should occur first if it has phrases instead of clauses. For length loosens intensity, but displaying much in little is more forceful. An example is the statement of the Spartans to Philip: 'Dionysius in Corinth.' But if they had extended it: 'Dionysius, after falling from [his] rule, lives in poverty as one teaching elementary school in Corinth,' it would have been nearly a narrative instead of a reproach. And in other [statements] Spartans were naturally in the habit of speaking briefly [ἐβραχυλόγουν]. For brevity is more forceful and commanding, but to speak at length befits supplication and entreaty. Therefore also symbols have forcefulness, because they resemble instances of βραχυλογία. For it is also necessary to infer most things from something said briefly, as from symbols, hence also saying allegorically 'From the ground the cicadas will sing to you' [Aristotle, *Rhet.* 2.21.8, 3.11.6] is more forceful than if it was simply said, 'Your trees will be chopped down.'" κατὰ δὲ τὴν σύνθεσιν ὁ χαρακτὴρ οὗτος γίνοιτ' ἂν πρῶτον μὲν εἰ κόμματα ἔχοι ἀντὶ κώλων· τὸ γὰρ μῆκος ἐκλύει τὴν σφοδρότητα, τὸ δὲ ἐν ὀλίγῳ πολὺ ἐμφαινόμενον δεινότερον· παράδειγμα τὸ Λακεδαιμονίων πρὸς Φίλιππον, «Διονύσιος ἐν Κορίνθῳ»· εἰ δὲ ἐξέτειναν αὐτό· «Διονύσιος ἐκπεσὼν τῆς ἀρχῆς πτωχεύει ἐν Κορίνθῳ διδάσκων γράμματα», διήγημα σχεδὸν ἂν ἦν μᾶλλον ἀντὶ λοιδορίας. κἂν τοῖς ἄλλοις δὲ φύσει ἐβραχυλόγουν οἱ Λάκωνες· δεινότερον γὰρ τὸ βραχὺ καὶ ἐπιτακτικόν, τὸ μακρηγορεῖν δὲ τῷ ἱκετεύειν πρέπει καὶ αἰτεῖν. διὸ καὶ τὰ σύμβολα ἔχει δεινότητας, ὅτι ἐμφερῆ ταῖς βραχυλογίαις· καὶ γὰρ ἐκ τοῦ βραχέως ῥηθέντος ὑπονοῆσαι τὰ πλεῖστα δεῖ, καθάπερ ἐκ τῶν συμβόλων· οὕτως καὶ τὸ «χαμόθεν οἱ τέττιγες ὑμῖν ᾄσονται» δεινότερον ἀλληγορικῶς ῥηθὲν ἢ εἴπερ ἁπλῶς ἐρρήθη, «τὰ δένδρα ὑμῶν ἐκκοπήσεται».

στηράν καὶ ἀνήδυντον ... βραχυλογίαν) by underscoring his statements' dense saturation of thought.⁶⁵

Second, Demetrius illustrates his point with a famous instance of Spartan brevity, a five-word diplomatic letter to Philip of Macedon. The prescript, Λακεδαιμόνιοι Φιλίππῳ, stands devoid of any honorifics or gestures of respect from the officials of one state to those of another. The content, Διονύσιος ἐν Κορίνθῳ, reminds the addressee of the fate of Dionysius, the former tyrant of Syracuse.⁶⁶ Demetrius notes that this letter's compactness facilitates the explicit "rebuke" of Philip and implicit threat of the reversal of fortune that inevitably awaits those who pursue tyranny. The citation of this example helps to explain the esteem which Brutus' letters enjoy: they communicate threats in extremely concise yet frighteningly evocative language.⁶⁷ In *Eloc.* 243 Demetrius furthermore points out that σύμβολα have a forcefulness similar to instances of βραχυλογία, and cites a threat: "From the ground the cicadas will sing to you."

Third, and perhaps most importantly, Demetrius says that through its forcefulness brevity imparts an aura of wisdom to an utterance, for "to have collected much thought in a little [wording] is wiser" (σοφώτερον τὸ ἐν ὀλίγῳ πολλὴν διάνοιαν ἠθροῖσθαι). This idea constitutes the most widely attested and firmly asserted rhetorical effect of brevity. Diodorus Siculus (9.26.3) observes that the Seven Sages lived in an era "when brevity was esteemed in the judgment of the educated" (παρὰ δὲ τοῖς πεπαιδευμένοις τῆς βραχυλογίας ... ζηλουμένης), in order to explain why King Croesus was so annoyed by the responses of the Sages to his displays of wealth. Instead of effusions of admiration, he received crisply phrased criticism. Plutarch concludes his overview of Spartan brevity by saying: "In fact their kind of apophthegmata was such that someone not wrongly says that to be a Spartan is more to love wisdom than to love exercise" (τὸ μὲν οὖν τῶν ἀποφθεγμάτων εἶδος ἦν τοιοῦτον ὥστε καὶ λέγειν τινὰς οὐκ ἀτόπως ὅτι μᾶλλόν ἐστι τὸ φιλοσοφεῖν ἢ τὸ φιλογυμναστεῖν λα-

---

⁶⁵ Plutarch, *Phoc.* 5.1–6: "And likewise Phocion's speech was also somehow salutary for useful ideas and helpful insights, although it had a certain commanding, austere and unsweetened brevity. For just as Zeno used to say that a philosopher must display his style by saturating [it] in thought, so Phocion's speech had the most thought in the sparest style. ... For as the value of a coin has the greatest power in the briefest weight, so the forcefulness of [his] speech seemed to signify many things from few." ὁμοίως δέ πως τοῦ Φωκίωνος καὶ ὁ λόγος ἦν ἐπὶ χρηστοῖς ἐνθυμήμασι καὶ διανοήμασι σωτήριος, προστακτικὴν τινα καὶ αὐστηρὰν καὶ ἀνήδυντον ἔχων βραχυλογίαν. ὡς γὰρ ὁ Ζήνων ἔλεγεν ὅτι δεῖ τὸν φιλόσοφον εἰς νοῦν ἀποβάπτοντα προφέρεσθαι τὴν λέξιν, οὕτως ὁ Φωκίωνος λόγος πλεῖστον ἐν ἐλαχίστῃ λέξει νοῦν εἶχε. ... ὡς γὰρ ἡ τοῦ νομίσματος ἀξία πλείστην ἐν ὄγκῳ βραχυτάτῳ δύναμιν ἔχει, οὕτω λόγου δεινότης [ἐ]-δόκει πολλὰ σημαίνειν ἀπ' ὀλίγων.

⁶⁶ This is Dionysius II (born 396 B.C.E.), removed from his position in 344; see *BNP* 4.474–75, s.v.

⁶⁷ See particularly the examples cited by Plutarch in n. 58 above.

κωνίζειν).⁶⁸ The "someone" to whom Plutarch refers is none other than Plato, in a passage wherein he attributes the Delphic maxims γνῶθι σαῦτον and μηδὲν ἄγαν to the Spartans, since "a certain Laconic brevity was this, the ancients' form of philosophy" (οὗτος ὁ τρόπος ἦν τῶν παλαιῶν τῆς φιλοσοφίας, βραχυλογία τις Λακωνική).⁶⁹ In this context the doctrine that definitions should be concise makes perfect sense, because it is primarily a philosophical literary genre. Formulating a definition with the brevity of a maxim elevates its impression of authority, because it would then bear a formal resemblance to γνῶμαι and ἀποφθέγματα.

Several points have emerged from our survey of the sources. Brevity enters the rhetorical curriculum among the sophists in Athens, and that its prominence solidifies considerably through its inclusion among the general virtues of style. Theorists also specify its utility for the opening sections of an oration, thereby revealing the contexts in which students applied themselves to mastery of it, a point further confirmed by the προγυμνάσματα. Letters too require brevity of style, and represent another context of instruction. Demetrius calls attention to the forcefulness and the impression of wisdom that brevity imparts; the former by virtue of its similarity to the way one addresses inferiors, and the latter by the condensation of much thought in few words. Definition is therefore by no means the only, or even the most common, kind of discourse that demands brevity. Its broad utility ensures the thorough dissemination of the methods associated with it among the educated in the ancient world. It is to these methods that we presently turn.

3.3 The methods of brevity

If one determines that brevity is admirable and useful in a wide variety of contexts, how then can one achieve it? The division of brevity into style and content provides a foundational level of practical instruction, so I shall discuss it first. I then turn to rhetorical figures and tropes of brevity, with an emphasis

---

⁶⁸ Plutarch, *Lyc.* 20.6.
⁶⁹ Plato, *Prot.* 343b. See also Plutarch, *Garr.* 17, 510e–11d, esp. 511a: "And the brief speakers among the ancients too are admired," θαυμάζονται δὲ καὶ τῶν παλαιῶν οἱ βραχυλόγοι. He goes on to cite the Delphic maxims whose authors "... admired gravity and plainness of style, encompassing a [carefully] wrought idea in brief. And is not the god himself fond of conciseness, and brief in [his] oracles, and is he not called *Loxias* because he flees idle chatter more than obscurity?" ... θαυμάσαντες τῆς λέξεως τὸ εὔογκον καὶ τὸ λιτόν, ἐν βραχεῖ σφυρήλατον νοῦν περιεχούσης. αὐτὸς δ' ὁ θεὸς οὐ φιλοσύντομός ἐστι καὶ βραχυλόγος ἐν τοῖς χρησμοῖς, καὶ Λοξίας καλεῖται διὰ τὸ φεύγειν τὴν ἀδολεσχίαν μᾶλλον ἢ τὴν ἀσάφειαν; (Cf. idem, *Pyth. orac.* 29, 408e–9a). Cf. Trypho¹, *Trop.* 2.9 (quoted in § 4 below, and, regarding this author, see n. 84).

upon the three that will prove most important to the interpretation of Rom 1:2–4 and 16–17.

3.3.1 The τεχναί and προγυμνάσματα on brevity of content and style

The earlier rhetorical τεχναί know nothing of the division of the methods of brevity into the sub-categories of content and style. Their instruction generally addresses the latter. Aristotle, for instance, explains how to achieve συντομία or ὄγκος τῆς λέξεως:

εἰς ὄγκον δὲ τῆς λέξεως συμβάλλεται τάδε, τὸ λόγῳ χρῆσθαι ἀντ' ὀνόματος, οἷον μὴ κύκλον, ἀλλ' ἐπίπεδον τὸ ἐκ τοῦ μέσου ἴσον· εἰς δὲ συντομίαν τὸ ἐναντίον, ἀντὶ τοῦ λόγου ὄνομα.

The following things contribute to bulkiness of style: to use a phrase instead of a word, for example, not "'a circle" but "a plane equal [in distance] from its center." But the opposite contributes to conciseness, to use a word instead of a phrase." (*Rhet.* 3.6.1, 1407b.)[70]

Aristotle then says that a discussion of anything "shameful" or "inappropriate" provides opportunites for both ὄγκος τῆς λέξεως and συντομία: if the αἰσχρόν exists in the λόγος, use the ὄνομα instead, and if it exists in the ὄνομα, use the λόγος. One can further accomplish ὄγκος with metaphors, plural forms where one would expect singulars, repetitions of the article in attributive constructions (for example, τῆς γυναικὸς τῆς ἡμετέρας; and, for συντομία, the opposite: τῆς ἡμετέρας γυναικός), and negative descriptions (e.g., τὸ ἄχορδον καὶ τὸ ἄλυρον μέλος, "the song without strings or lyre"). Aristotle spotlights particular moments in a composition where extension or compression would serve some other rhetorical goal, with a distinct emphasis on style. But already in the *Rhetorica ad Alexandrum* we begin to see the separation of methods of συντομία ἐκ τῶν πραγμάτων and ἐκ τῆς λέξεως. The author devotes a portion of his instruction to explaining how μηκύνειν τοὺς λόγους, βραχυλογεῖν and μέσως λέγειν. Regarding the second, he says:

Βραχυλογεῖν δὲ βουλόμενον ⟨δεῖ⟩ ὅλον τὸ πρᾶγμα ἑνὶ ὀνόματι περιλαμβάνειν, καὶ τούτῳ ὃ ἂν ὑπάρχῃ βραχύτατον τῷ πράγματι· χρὴ δὲ καὶ ⟨τοὺς⟩ συνδέσμους ὀλίγους ποιεῖν, τὰ πλεῖστα δὲ ζευγνύναι {ὀνομάζειν μὲν οὕτω, τῇ δὲ λέξει εἰς δύο χρῆσθαι} καὶ παλιλογίαν τὴν σύντομον ἐκ τῶν μερῶν ἀφαιρεῖν, ἐν δὲ ταῖς τελευταῖς μόνον παλιλογεῖν. καὶ τοῦτον μὲν τὸν τρόπον βραχεῖς τοὺς λόγους ποιήσομεν.

The one who wishes to speak briefly must encompass the whole subject in a single word – and with whichever happens to be the briefest for the subject. And it is also necessary to compose with few conjunctions, and indeed to conjoin the most words [into single clauses]. Use words in this manner, and use one phrase for two. And excise the concise recapitulation

---

[70] Interpreters and translators often take ὄγκος to mean "loftiness" or "majesty," e.g., LSJ 1197, s.v., II.3, and Russell, *Criticism in Antiquity*, 135: "dignity"; but Aristotle's contrast of this term with συντομία in no way implies that the latter is *inferior* – as a translation of ὄγκος with "majesty" might imply – only *shorter*. A more proper translation of ὄγκος is something more descriptive and less evaluative, such as "bulkiness," LSJ s.v., I.1, "bulk, size, mass."

3.3 The methods of brevity

from the parts [of the speech], but recapitulate only in the final stages. And in this way you will make your speeches brief. ([Aristotle], *Rhet. Alex.* 22.5, 1434b)

The first part of the author's advice deals with language, and the second with the elimination of a structural feature of the speech, the παλιλογία that commonly concludes each μέρος.[71] The author addresses brevity further in conjunction with the ἀρεταί διηγήσεως: "[We will demonstrate] concisely if we excise *from the subjects and words* that which is not necessary to be said" (συντόμως δέ, ἐὰν ἀπὸ τῶν πραγμάτων καὶ τῶν ὀνομάτων περιαιρῶμεν τὰ μὴ ἀναγκαῖα ῥηθῆναι).[72] One therefore achieves brevity best by sticking to the essentials.

When the division between πράγματα and λέξις becomes entrenched, the theorists begin to identify many more methods specific to each. Theon's statements on διήγημα indicate the kind of basic instruction given on this topic. First he defines συντομία: "For conciseness is speech which indicates only the most important of the subjects, while neither adding anything unnecessary or omitting something necessary in accordance with the subjects and the style" (ἔστι γὰρ ἡ συντομία λόγος τὰ καιρώτατα τῶν πραγμάτων σημαίνων, μήτε προστιθεὶς τὸ μὴ ἀναγκαῖον μήτε ἀφαιρῶν τὸ ἀναγκαῖον κατὰ τὰ πράγματα καὶ τὴν λέξιν).[73] Regarding πράγματα (which, in the context of διηγήματα, also refers to "events"), he urges one to restrict oneself to the most relevant facts and to avoid digressions.[74] Quintilian says similarly that one should select the facts with a view to persuading the judge, omit anything irrelevant,

---

[71] The former holds special relevance for the present study, since I shall later argue that Paul implements this sort of instruction in his definitions of the gospel: he collapses narratives and whole sections of his argument into particular words, and loads his statements with multiple layers of meaning.

[72] [Aristotle], *Rhet. Alex.* 30.8, 1438a.

[73] *Prog.* 5, *RG* 2.83.

[74] *Prog.* 5, *RG* 2.83: "[Conciseness occurs] therefore from the subjects whenever we neither gather many subjects together at the same time, nor throw them all together with other things, but we pass over as many as seem to be understood [from the context]; whenever we neither begin from [too] far back, nor waste the speech on things brought in extraneously, as do those who customarily narrate beyond the subjects. For these things would probably be suitable for history: to lengthen [the narrative] and to begin from far back and to work over any of the things which seem to be secondary. But when someone is telling the narrative toward the summary of the entire subject which he proposed, he ought to pay attention to only those things contributing to it when one takes them up in the narrative." ἐκ μὲν οὖν τῶν πραγμάτων, ὅταν μήτε συλλαμβάνωμεν ἅμα [τὰ] πολλὰ πράγματα, μήθ' ἑτέροις ἐπεμβάλλωμεν, παραλείπωμέν τε ὅσα συνυπακούεσθαι δοκεῖ, μήτε πόρρωθεν ἀρχώμεθα, μήτε εἰς τὰ παρέλκοντα τὸν λόγον καταναλίσκωμεν, ὡς οἱ μετὰ τὰ πράγματα εἰωθότες διηγεῖσθαι. ταῦτα γὰρ ἂν ἴσως ἱστορίᾳ πρέποι, τό τε μηκύνειν καὶ τὸ πόρρωθεν ἄρχεσθαι καὶ ἐπεξεργάζεσθαί τινα τῶν παρέργων εἶναι δοκούντων. διήγησιν δὲ λέγων τις πρὸς τὸ κεφάλαιον τοῦ ὅλου πράγματος, ὃ προύθετο, ἀποβλέπειν ὀφείλει τὰ εἰς τοῦτο συντελοῦντα μόνα ἐν τῇ διηγήσει παραλαμβάνων.

and scale back anything else unless doing so would endanger the case.[75] For conciseness in style, Theon's tactics cover (1) the elimination of pleonastic synonyms; (2) the replacement of florid or metaphorical phrases with simple, direct wording; (3) the omission of anything which the audience can infer from the context; and (4) the selection of shorter words where possible.[76] Taken together, these items seem like a more developed version of Aristotle's advice on ὄγκος and συντομία. One may immediately grasp the goal of such counsel: simplicity and staccato delivery would contribute to the overall credibility of a διήγησις of relevant facts. He concludes with a warning of the risk of vulgarity (ἰδιωτισμός) and obscurity (ἀσάφεια) inherent in the pursuit of stylistic συντομία. Συντομία ἐκ τῶν πραγμάτων therefore limits the *size* of the διήγησις through the careful selection of included elements, and συντομία ἐκ τῆς λέξεως limits the *style* through the excision of superfluous language and the selection of shorter words where possible.

Theon's προγυμνάσματα elsewhere indicate that the classical Athenian sophists' educational strategies toward the abilities of μακρολογεῖν and βραχυλογεῖν continue to thrive, although he labels them differently, as "compression and expansion," συστέλλειν καὶ ἐπεκτείνειν. This exercise has utility for more than narrative:[77] "we extend by lengthening the characterizations in the μῦθος,

---

[75] *Inst.* 4.2.40: "The narrative will be brief first of all if we will begin to set out the matter at the place from where it is relevant to the judge; next if we will say nothing beyond the case, then also if we will have excised all things by which, once they have been removed, a detraction occurs neither to the trial nor to [our own] advantage," *brevis erit narratio ante omnia si inde coeperimus rem exponere unde ad iudicem pertinet, deinde si nihil extra causam dixerimus, tum etiam si reciderimus omnia quibus sublatis neque cognitioni quicquam neque utilitati detrahatur.* Cf. ibid. 4.2.48–50.

[76] *Prog.* 5, *RG* 2.84: "Now among things pertaining to style, one must also take care not to use synonyms. For words that have the same force make the speech needlessly longer, as in the case of Demosthenes in the second of the Olynthiacs: 'It in every way resembles a certain godlike and divine kindness.' [One must moreover take care] not to use a phrase in the place of a word, for example 'he departed life' instead of 'he died,' and things like these. Furthermore, for the one who wishes to report concisely, things which are understood [from the context] are to be stripped away entirely, and also simple words are to be used rather than compounds, and shorter words rather than longer whenever they mean the same thing. However, one must take care lest one fall unintentionally into vulgarity or obscurity by a desire for conciseness." ἐν δὲ τοῖς κατὰ τὴν λέξιν παρατηρητέον καὶ τὸ μήτε συνωνύμοις χρῆσθαι· τὰ γὰρ τὴν αὐτὴν ἔχοντα δύναμιν ὀνόματα μακρότερον ποιεῖ τὸν λόγον οὐδὲν δέον, ὡς παρὰ Δημοσθένει ἐν τῷ Ὀλυνθιακῶν δευτέρῳ· «δαιμονίᾳ τινὶ καὶ θείᾳ παντάπασιν ἔοικεν εὐεργεσίᾳ»· μήτε λόγον ἀντὶ ὀνόματος ποιεῖν, οἷον ἀντὶ τοῦ ἀπέθανεν ἐξέλιπε τὸν βίον, καὶ ὅσα τούτοις ὅμοια. ἔτι δὲ καὶ τὰ συνυπακουόμενα πάντως συμπεριαιρετέον τῷ συντόμως ἀπαγγέλλειν βουλομένῳ, χρηστέον δὲ καὶ τοῖς ἁπλοῖς ὀνόμασι μᾶλλον ἢ τοῖς συνθέτοις, καὶ τοῖς βραχυτέροις μᾶλλον ἢ τοῖς μακροτέροις, ὅταν τὸ αὐτὸ σημαίνωσιν· εὐλαβητέον δὲ ὅμως μὴ λάθῃ τις ἐπιθυμίᾳ συντομίας εἰς ἰδιωτισμὸν ἢ ἀσάφειαν ἐκπεσών.

[77] Theon in his instruction regarding διήγημα (*Prog.* 5, *RG* 2.85–86) refers back to his section on fables for tactics of συστολή τε καὶ ἐπέκτασις.

and by describing vividly a river or something of the like; we compress by doing the opposite" (ἐπεκτείνομεν δὲ τὰς ἐν τῷ μύθῳ προσωποποιΐας μηκύνοντες, καὶ ποταμὸν ἤ τι τῶν τοιούτων ἐκφράζοντες· τὸ ἐναντίον δὲ ποιοῦντες συστέλλομεν).[78] Similarly, "we extend the χρεία whenever we lengthen the questions and answers in it, and if a certain action or emotion occurs therein, we lengthen that too; and we compress by doing the opposite" (ἐπεκτείνομεν δὲ τὴν χρείαν, ἐπειδὰν τὰς ἐν αὐτῇ ἐρωτήσεις τε καὶ ἀποκρίσεις, καὶ εἰ πρᾶξίς τις ἢ πάθος ἐνυπάρχῃ, μηκύνωμεν· συστέλλομεν δὲ τὸ ἐναντίον ποιοῦντες).[79] This exercise sharpens the skill of συντομία ἐκ τῶν πραγμάτων, hence its connection with the characteristically short discourse types (διήγημα, χρεία, μῦθος).[80] The curriculum thus reinforces the skills of compression and expansion in a variety of contexts.

3.3.2 Brevity as a rhetorical figure or trope

The ancient sources disagree about the precise distinctions between figures (σχήματα) and tropes (τροπαί, τρόποι).[81] Taken as a group, their overall purposes are on the one hand compositional, to help authors to dress their compositions with adornments that advance their aims, and on the other hand analytic (like the ἀρεταί of style), to help readers to study and imitate the canonical exemplars. Theoretical literature specifically devoted to figures and tropes

---

[78] *Prog.* 4 (*RG* 2.75). See also [Hermogenes], *Prog.* 1.13–15 (with examples), s.v. μῦθος.

[79] *Prog.* 3 (*RG* 2.103–4).

[80] According to Theon (*Prog.* 3, *RG* 2.96), "A χρεία is a concise declaration or action that pointedly refers to a certain defined person, or thing analogous to a person," χρεία ἐστὶ σύντομος ἀπόφασις ἢ πρᾶξις μετ' εὐστοχίας ἀναφερομένη εἴς τι ὡρισμένον πρόσωπον ἢ ἀναλογοῦν προσώπῳ. On the χρεία see further the introduction of and the texts collected in Hock and O'Neil, *Chreia in Ancient Rhetoric*.

[81] Cf. the definitions in [Plutarch], *De Hom.* 2.15: "The turning aside of words is called τρόπος, but the turning aside of composition [i.e., syntax] is called σχῆμα, and the forms of these are written up in systematic treatment," καὶ ἡ μὲν τῶν λέξεων ἐκτροπὴ καλεῖται τρόπος, καὶ ἡ δὲ τῆς συνθέσεως σχῆμα (καὶ ἔστι τὰ εἴδη τούτων ἐν τῇ τεχνηλογίᾳ ἀνεγεγραμμένα). (By τεχνολογία in the singular, the author seems to mean the long discussion that follows.) According to Phoebammon (*RG* 3.44; v–vi C.E. per LSJ xxxii), Caecilius (i B.C.E. per *BNP* 2.885, s.v., III.5) defines σχῆμα as "a turning to something of thought and of style which is not natural," σχῆμά ἐστι τροπὴ εἰς τὸ μὴ κατὰ φύσιν τὸ τῆς διανοίας καὶ τῆς λέξεως. Cf. Quintilian, *Inst.* 8.6.1–3, 9.1.1–21, esp. 4. The organizational schemes of figures often group them into those "of thought" and "of style/diction." The theory on this subject is very difficult to sort out; according to Russell (*Criticism in Antiquity*, 144–45) the Stoics probably developed the basic system of tropes (numbering eight, including συνεκδοχή); he adds: "The distinction between the 'tropes' and the 'figures' is probably also Stoic. It is that a 'trope' is a deviation from nature (*phusis*) in the use of an individual word, while a 'figure' is a similar deviation in the arrangement of words or the cast of thought. Naturally, these distinctions were hard to maintain in practice; and the ancient treatises on these subjects … present an extraordinary and frustrating confusion of terminology" (145). See also Kennedy, *New History*, 228–29.

begins to appear in the Hellenistic period,[82] in the form of monographs detailing lists of items, with definitions and illustrations from canonical authors (especially Homer and Demosthenes) for each item. The extant monographs date from the second century C.E. through late antiquity and beyond.[83] They borrow from each other extensively, although no one leaps out as the obvious source of any of the others. The questions of their textual relationships and transmission histories cannot detain us here.[84] It suffices to stress their strong conservative imprint: definitions and illustrations often recur in multiple texts with minor variations. In spite of the overall conservatism, however, theories of figures and tropes continually evolve toward greater variety and specificity, as illustrated by the division of brevity as a figure into a constellation of figures and tropes that achieve it, including ἀποσιώπησις,[85] ἀσύνδετον,[86] ζεῦγμα,[87]

---

[82] Russell, *Criticism in Antiquity*, 145–46: "The doctrine of the figures – both 'of speech' and 'of thought' – was ... a Hellenistic product. The definitive systemizations were made in the first centuries BC by two men: Gorgias, who taught Cicero's son at Athens in 44 BC and later declaimed at Rome in the hearing of the elder Seneca; and Caecilius of Caleacte, better known as the opponent attacked in *On Sublimity*." The treatises of the early authors on figures and tropes have not survived, so we cannot know for certain whether they had the same list-format that we find in the *artes* and the monographs, or a more discursive format, resembling, say, the critical essays of Dionysius or the monograph *De elocutione* of Demetrius. Nonetheless, the arrangement of the material in lists in later texts implies that the early discussions had a similar form.

[83] The dates of most of the individual texts cannot be determined with certainty since they naturally give little information internally to pin them down (the ones using illustrations from Christian texts being the exception – these cannot date much earlier than the third century). Their attributions to well-known authors also merit doubt, as West ("Tryphon *De Tropis*," 231) points out in connection with the tracts *de tropis*, but applying just as well to those *de figuris*: "The ascriptions of the extant works are of doubtful authority. It is evident that few if any of them are original compositions, but rather revisions and rearrangments of traditional material; and a celebrated grammarian's name might easily have found itself attached to a summary (or prolix) Byzantine text of which his own work was a distant ancestor. The history of scholia gives a warning example of how a grammatical text may suffer in transmission."

[84] West has already started the project for the relationships of the monographs on tropes ("Tryphon *De Tropis*," 230–33, and cf. the lemma at 235). The author of interest to him is Trypho, an Alexandrian grammarian of the first century B.C.E. (*OCD* 1557). He believes that the tract attributed to Trypho and the one attributed to Gregory of Corinth in *RG* may both ultimately derive from one actually written by the real Trypho. Following West, I separate the two from one another by 'Trypho^I' (i.e., Spengel's 'Trypho'), and 'Trypho^{II}' (i.e., 'Gregory'). I cite the text of the latter according to West's edition.

[85] Alexander Rhetor, *Fig.* 1.16 (*RG* 3.22; ii C.E. per *BNP* 1.480, s.v. 25): "Ἀποσιώπησις is speech that heightens something passed over in silence, or that leaves aside something that is known, or that falls silent at something shameful," ἀποσιώπησίς ἐστι λόγος ἐπιτείνων τὸ παρασιωπώμενον, ἢ παραλείπων τὸ γινωσκόμενον, ἢ σιωπῶν τὸ αἰσχρόν. See also [Cicero], *Rhet. Her.* 4.54.67; Quintilian, *Inst.* 9.2.54–57; Phoebammon, *Fig.* 2.1 (*RG* 3.50); Tiberius Rhetor, *Fig.* 10 (*RG* 3.62).

[86] Phoebammon, *Fig.* 1.2 (*RG* 3.45–46): "Ἀσύνδετον is an expression in which the connecting connectives [*sic*] are left out, as if someone should say about someone else: 'I found him, I spoke, I persuaded,'" ἀσύνδετόν ἐστι φράσις, ἐν ᾗ παραλείπονται οἱ συνδέοντες σύνδε-

3.3 The methods of brevity

and the three which I single out for detailed scrutiny below, ἔλλειψις, συνεκδοχή and ἀπὸ κοινοῦ.[88]

Brevity becomes numbered among the rhetorical figures by the time of Cicero. After listing various figures of verbal expansion in *De oratore* book 3, he writes: "And the opposite to this is often 'rapid review' [*percursio*, ἐπιτροχασμός] and 'emphasis' [*significatio*, ἔμφασις] toward the [auditors'] comprehension of more than you will have said, and clearly terse 'brevity'" (*et huic contraria saepe percursio est et plus ad intellegendum, quam dixeris significatio; et distincte concisa brevitas*).[89] Cicero's comments here lack defini-

---

σμοι, ὡς εἴ τις εἴποι περί τινος, εὗρον αὐτόν, ἐλάλησα, ἔπεισα. See also Alexander Rhetor, *Fig.* 2.12 (*RG* 3.23–33), Tiberius Rhetor, *Fig.* 40 (*RG* 3.77–78); iii–iv c.e. per *BNP* 14.656, s.v. I.1); Zonaeus, *Fig.* 2.19 (*RG* 3.169).

[87] I discuss this figure below in connection with ἀπὸ κοινοῦ.

[88] The remarks of Anonymous Seguerianus, *Rhet.* 75–78 on brevity in a διήγησις illustrate the close association of many of these figures under the heading of συντομία. In 69–74, he advises the deletion of synonyms, epithets and perphrases before turning to specific figures: "And that which is called ἔλλειψις produces conciseness, for example, 'You love him and he you,' for 'loves' is omitted. And τὸ ἐπεζευγμένον also produces conciseness, whenever you apply a single complementary term to two or three words or subjects, for example, 'They showed kindness to the Rhodians who were allies; and the Byzantines, relatives; and the Tenedians, who had made themselves evenly matched; and many other allies.' And ἀσύνδετον also cultivates the appearance of conciseness, e.g., 'But when the ships had been stolen, Cherronese was being savaged,' and the following. And you will produce conciseness also when you speak with the appearance of omission [κατ᾽ ἔμφασιν παραλείψεως = συνεκδοχή?], like Demosthenes: 'For when Philip seized Olynthus,' for through 'seized' [the author] disclosed many things." καὶ ἡ λεγομένη δὲ ἔλλειψις συντομίαν ἐργάζεται, οἷον «σὺ τοῦτον φιλεῖς καὶ οὗτος σέ»· λείπει γὰρ τὸ φιλεῖ. ἐργάζεται δὲ συντομίαν καὶ τὸ ἐπεζευγμένον, ὅταν δύο ἢ καὶ τρισὶν ὀνόμασιν ἢ πράγμασι μίαν ἐπάγῃς λέξιν συμπληρωτικήν, οἷον «Ῥοδίους μὲν συμμάχους ὄντας, Βυζαντίους δὲ συγγενεῖς, Τενεδίους δὲ πεποιημένους ἰσοπαλίαν, πλείους δὲ ἄλλους συμμάχους εὐεργέτησαν». πολεῖ δὲ καὶ τὸ ἀσύνδετον δόξαν συντομίας, οἷον «ἀλλ᾽ ἐπειδὴ τὰ πλοῖα σεσύληται, Χερρόνησος ἐπορθεῖτο», καὶ τὰ ἑξῆς. ποιήσεις δὲ συντομίαν καὶ ὅτε κατ᾽ ἔμφασιν παραλείψεως λέγεις, ὡς ὁ Δημοσθένης· «ἐπειδὴ γὰρ εἷλεν Ὄλυνθον Φίλιππος»· διὰ γὰρ τοῦ εἷλεν πολλὰ ἐδήλωσεν.

[89] *De or.* 3.202. Note the edition of Kumaniecki *ad loc.* in the critical apparatus regarding *percursio*: some manuscripts read *praecisio* = ἀποσιώπησις. Regarding ἐπιτροχασμός, Alexander Rhetor (*Fig.* 1.17, *RG* 3.22) writes: "Ἐπιτροχασμός is a figure related to συναθροι-σμός [assembly] and ἐπιμονή [delay], but differs from these because it gathers more temporally separated events and is said [all at once] for plausibility, as this passage of Demosthenes has it: 'But he went to the Hellespont, he earlier came to Ambracia, he holds Elis, the great city in the Peloponessus, and lately he plotted against the Megarians' [*3 Philip.* 27]," ἐπιτροχασμός ἐστι προσκείμενον σχῆμα τῷ τε συναθροισμῷ καὶ τῇ ἐπιμονῇ, διαφέρει δὲ ἐκείνων, ὅτι τὰ πολὺ διεστηκότα συνάγει καὶ ἀξιοπιστίας ἕνεκα λέγεται, ὡς ἔχει τὸ Δημοσθενικόν, «ἀλλ᾽ ἐφ᾽ Ἑλλήσποντον οἴχεται, πρότερον ἧκεν ἐπ᾽ Ἀμβρικίαν, Ἦλιν ἔχει τηλικαύτην πόλιν ἐν Πελοποννήσῳ, Μεγάροις ἐπεβούλευσε πρώην». Cf. also Phoebammon, *Fig.* 2.1 (*RG* 3.50): "And ἐπιτροχασμός is the naming of events which proceeds by a single recounting, without the narrative concerning them, so that someone might recount when accusing somebody that many wicked things have been done, by saying about them 'this and that have been done by you,' but not by say-

tions and illustrations; his presupposition that his readers know what he means discloses the general availability of knowledge regarding figures, including *brevitas*. The author of the *Rhetorica ad Herennium* likewise associates *significatio* and *brevitas*. He defines *significatio* as "the thing which leaves more to surmise than is given in a statement" (*significatio est res, quae plus in suspicione relinquit, quam positum in oratione*).[90] After treating the sub-types of the figure (including ἀποσιώπησις, *abscisio*) he says: "Certainly it allows the auditor himself to surmise something by tacit speeech" (*sinit enim quiddam tacito ⟨orat⟩ore ipsum auditorem suspicari*).[91] He then defines and illustrates *brevitas*:

> *Brevitas est res ipsis tantummodo verbis necessariis expedita, hoc modo: «Lemnum praeteriens cepit, inde Thasi praesidium reliquit, post urbem Viminacium sustilit, inde pulsus in Hellespontum statim potitur Abydi». Item: «Modo consul quo⟨n⟩dam, is deinde primus era⟨t⟩ civitatis; tum proficiscitur in Asiam; deinde hostis ⟨et exul⟩ est dictus; post imperator, et postremo factus est consul». Habet paucis conprehensa brevitas multarum rerum expeditionem. Quare adhibenda saepe est, cum aut res non egent longae orationis aut tempus non sinet commorari.*

> *Brevitas* is a subject explained only with the necessary words, in this manner: "While passing Lemnus he took it, then left behind the camp on Thasus, afterwards ruined the city Viminacium, then, after a strike against the Hellespont, he at once obtains Abydus." Likewise: "Once recently consul, the he was first man of the state, next he departed to Asia, then he was declared an enemy and exile, afterwards imperator, and finally he was made consul." *Brevitas* encompasses the unfolding of many subjects with few [words] which is comprehended [by the audience]. For this reason it should often be used when either the subject does not have need of a long speech or time does not permit one to linger. ([Cicero], *Rhet. Her.* 4.54.68)

These illustrations link *brevitas* with narrative, a brevity ἐκ τῶν πραγμάτων that also wastes no words. Συντομία as an ἀρετὴ διηγήσεως is clearly exerting some influence on the theory of *brevitas* as a figure. *Significatio*, in contrast, appears to deal primarily with style, through insinuation and the dependence upon the auditors to infer whatever one leaves unstated. Trypho[1], the only theorist writing in Greek who has both συντομία and βραχύτης as independent figures, connects the former to διήγησις:

> συντομία ἐστὶ φράσις αὐτὰ τὰ ἀναγκαῖα τοῦ δηλουμένου ἔχουσα, οἷον «κεῖται Πάτροκλος· νέκυος δὲ δὴ ἀμφιμάχονται | γυμνοῦ· ἀτὰρ τά γε τεύχε' ἔχει κορυθαίολος Ἕκτωρ»· καὶ «σφαῖραν ἔπειτ' ἔρριψε μετ' ἀμφίπολον βασίλεια, | ἀμφιπόλου μὲν ἅμαρτε, βαθείῃ δ' ἔμπεσε δίνῃ· | αἱ δ' ἐπὶ μακρὸν ἄϋσαν· ὁ δ' ἔγρετο δῖος Ὀδυσσεύς».

---

ing *how* they have been done," ἐπιτροχασμὸς δὲ ὀνομασία πραγμάτων κατὰ μόνην ἀπαρίθμησιν γινομένη, ἄνευ τῆς περὶ αὐτῶν διηγήσεως, ὡς ἵνα αἰτιώμενός τινα ὡς πολλὰ κακὰ πεποιηκότα ἀπαριθμήσηται αὐτὰ λέγων, τόδε καὶ τόδε πέπρακταί σοι μὴ τὸ πῶς δὲ πέπρακται λέγων. See Lausberg, *Handbook*, 142–43, § 299 for more references.

[90] [Cicero], *Rhet. Her.* 4.53.67.

[91] Ibid. Quintilian does not give separate treatment of βραχυλογία, only referring to it only in passing (*Inst.* 9.3.50, 99).

Συντομία is an expression having the very necessities of that which is being disclosed, for example: "Patroclus lies there and now they wage war around his naked corpse. But gleaming-helmed Hector has his armor" [Homer, *Il.* 18.20–21]. And: "Then the king's daughter threw the ball with a handmaiden; she missed the handmaiden but it fell in a deep whirlpool; and they cried out loudly and bright Odysseus arose" [*Od.* 6.115–17]. (*Trop.* 2.8, *RG* 3.202)

The illustrations disclose the context of συντομία as conciseness in narration more clearly than the definition, which clearly recalls Theon's definition of it in connection with διήγησις as "speech which indicates the most vital elements of the subjects" (λόγος τὰ καιριώτατα τῶν πραγμάτων σημαίνων). Βραχύτης meanwhile pertains to style:

βραχύτης ἐστὶ φράσις πλέον τι τοῦ ἀκουομένου νοούμενον ἔχουσα, οἷά ἐστι τὰ Δελφικὰ ἀποφθέγματα, «γνῶθι σαυτόν»· «χρόνου φείδου»· «μηδὲν ἄγαν». βραχύτητα δὲ ἔχει καὶ τὸ «Λακεδαιμόνιοι Φιλίππῳ, Διονύσιος ἐν Κορίνθῳ»· βούλονται γὰρ εἰπεῖν, μὴ ὑψαύχει ἀφορῶν εἰς Διονύσιον τανῦν γράμματα ἐν Κορίνθῳ διδάσκοντα, ὃς πρότερον ἐτυράννει.

Βραχύτης is an expression having something more than what is heard. Such are the Delphic maxims "know yourself," "use time sparingly," "nothing in excess."[92] This also has βραχύτης: "The Spartans to Philip: Dionysius is in Corinth." For they want to say: "Don't be arrogant when you look at Dionysius, who previously ruled as a tyrant, but now teaches primary school in Corinth." (*Trop.* 2.9, *RG* 3.202)

This division of brevity into content (συντομία) and style (βραχύτης) in this theorist's remarks again reflects discussions about the suitability of brevity occurring in other provinces of rhetorical theory.

The above definitions of *brevitas*, συντομία, and βραχύτης are general in a way that invites further development. In the earlier Latin theorists, *brevitas* appears alongside other related figures like *significatio* and ἀποσιώπησις. Trypho[I] attempts to accommodate the existing division of συντομία ἐκ τῶν πραγμάτων and ἐκ τῆς λέξεως by relabeling them as συντομία and βραχύτης. An interesting consistency in the definitions emerges in the way they describe brevity in terms of the presence of only "necessary" wording, not in terms of omission. The latter acquires its own name, ἔλλειψις.

3.3.3 The figure of ἔλλειψις

Ἔλλειψις does not ordinarily appear in the *artes rhetoricae* as a figure.[93] Indeed the first available definition of ἔλλειψις (as a σχῆμα and not as a stylistic

---

[92] Cf. Rutilius Lupus (i B.C.E. per *BNP* 12.797, s.v. II.6), *Fig.* 2.8: "*Brachylogia*. This is customarily to be used when an orator surpasses the expectation of the auditor with the brevity of a maxim." *Brachylogia. Hoc fieri solet, cum orator brevitate sententiae praecedit auditoris exspectationem.*

[93] For modern discussions of ἔλλειψις, see also Lausberg, *Handbook*, 307–8, §§ 690–91; Smyth 677–78, § 3022, and cf. his comments on βραχυλογία, 674–77, §§ 3017–18; BDF 253–56, §§ 479–83; Anderson, *Glossary*, 41 (cf. 30 on βραχυλογία; 112–13 on συντομία); Rowe, "Style," 135; Nagy, "Ellipsis in Homer."

fault), that of Alexander Rhetor in the 2nd century C.E., bears a partial resemblance to the definitions of *significatio* in the *ad Herennium* and of βραχύτης in the *De Tropis* of Tripho[1]:

ἔλλειψις δὲ γίνεται, ὅταν ὀνόματα πολλὰ περιηρημένα χρὴ ὀνομαστὶ μὴ κειμένων, ὅτε δέ τι νοεῖται πλέον, ὡς ὁ Δημοσθένης, «εἴ τις ἐπακολουθῶν ἐπὶ τὸ μνῆμα διεξίοι, εἰ τὸ καὶ τὸ ἐποίησεν, οὐκ ἂν ἀπέθανεν· ἐμβρόντητε, εἶτα νῦν λέγεις;» νοεῖται γὰρ τὸ φαίη ἄν τις πρὸς αὐτὸν ἢ εἴποι. καὶ πάλιν, «μέλει δ' οὐδενὶ οὐδὲ μέμνηται», καὶ γὰρ ἐνταῦθα ἐλλείπει τὸ οὐδείς· πάθους δὲ ἔμφασιν ἔχει τὸ σχῆμα.

Ἔλλειψις occurs when, in a situation where many words have been removed,[94] there is a need of things not explicitly present, and when something more is understood. For example Demosthenes [writes]: "If someone goes along, following to the tomb [...]:[95] 'If he had done this-or-that, he would not have died!' – so, you idiot, are you now saying this?" [*Cor.* 243], for "he would say to him" or "he would speak" is understood. And again: "But it is a concern for nobody, nor has [...] remembered [it]" [*Fals. leg.* 136]. For here also he leaves out "anybody." Now the figure [of ἔλλειψις] has the impression of emotion. (*Fig.* 2.13, *RG* 3.33)

Like a statement *quae plus in suspicione relinquit*, or πλέον τι τοῦ ἀκουομένου νοούμενον ἔχουσα, according to Alexander ἔλλειψις occurs where τι νοεῖται πλέον, although he more emphatically accents the omission of required wording (χρὴ ὀνομαστὶ μὴ κειμένων). Phoebammon's entry similarly refers to both omission and inference: "ἔλλειψις is the omission of wording which is understood from the context" (ἔλλειψις δέ ἐστι παράλειψις λέξεως νοουμένης ἐκ τῆς συμφράσεως).[96] In spite of the fact that Tripho[1] applies it differently than

---

[94] This phrase is somewhat difficult to translate. I am taking ὀνόματα πολλὰ περιηρημένα as an adverbial accusative absolute (Smyth 461–62, § 2076). Alexander might have omitted ὦσιν, thereby illustrating the figure: "ἔλλειψις is whenever there [are] many words which have been removed; there is a need of things not explicitly present...."

[95] I use square brackets enclosing an ellipse, [...], to signify in my translations the ἔλλειψις discussed by the theorists.

[96] Phoebammon, *Fig.* 2 (*RG* 3.46), s.v. περὶ ἐνδείας, "regarding deficiency." He continues: "... such that we might say: 'He [...] master of the matter, he [...] the one who convinces others, he [...] the one who commands.' For 'is' has been omitted in these [clauses]." ὡς ἵνα εἴπωμεν, αὐτὸς κύριος τοῦ πράγματος, αὐτὸς ὁ πείθων τοὺς ἄλλους, αὐτὸς ὁ κελεύων· παραλέλειπται γὰρ ἐν τούτοις τὸ ἐστί. Cf. the definitions of Zonaeus, *Fig.* 2.10 (*RG* 3.167): "Ἔλλειψις is whenever some part of an utterance has been removed for the sake of conciseness," ἔλλειψίς ἐστιν, ὅταν ᾖ περιηρημένον μέρος λόγου τι συντομίας ἕνεκα, and "ἔλλειψις is diction not borne out to the fullest extent," ἔλλειψίς ἐστι λέξις οὐ κατὰ τὸ πλῆρες ἐκφερομένη. The latter pertains to dropping letters from words (probably adapting Tripho[1]'s entry). Note also the definition of [Plutarch], *De Hom.* 2.39: "And the things said above are either figured according to πλεονασμός or according to some sort of adjustment [of language]. But others are figured according to a lack of wording. Among these is the one which is called ἔλλειψις, whenever, without some wording being expressly stated, the sense is made evident from what had been said before." καὶ τὰ μὲν προειρημένα ἤτοι κατὰ πλεονασμὸν ἢ κατά τινα ποιὰν πλάσιν σχηματίζεται, ἄλλα δὲ κατὰ ἔνδειαν λέξεως, ὧν ἐστιν ἡ καλουμένη ἔλλειψις, ὅταν καὶ ἄνευ τοῦ ῥηθῆναί τινα λέξιν ἐκ τῶν προειρημένων ἡ διάνοια φαίνεται.

those who follow him (he refers to omitting letters, not words),[97] his definition supplies perhaps the earliest attestation of a frequently repeated formula: "ἔλλειψις is wording not carried out to the fullest extent" (ἔλλειψις [δέ] ἐστι λέξις [or φράσις, or λόγος] μὴ κατὰ τὸ πλῆρες ἐκφερομένη [or ἐξενηνεγμένη]).[98]

Ἔλλειψις thus requires of a reader or auditor two interpretive moves: first, the recognition of the absence of language from an utterance; and second, the utilization of the context to supply what is missing in order to complete the sense. The two samples quoted by Alexander illustrate these moves well: in both cases Demosthenes has clearly omitted necessary words, prompting the auditor to fill the gaps as they hear the sentence. Tiberius Rhetor invokes the same passage from *Cor.* 243:

---

[97] Trypho[I], *Trop.* 1.13 (*RG* 3.198): "Ἔλλειψις is wording not borne out to the fullest extent; it happens at the beginning, at the middle [and] at the end, e.g., the removal of initial letters, the forshortening [of words], and breaking off [at the end of words]. At the beginning, e.g., λείβειν εἴβειν ['to libate']; at the middle, e.g., μονώνυχας μώνυχας ['animals with uncloven hoofs']; and at the end, e.g., δῶμα δῶ ['house']." Ἔλλειψίς ἐστι λέξις οὐ κατὰ τὸ πλῆρες ἐξενηνεγμένη, γίνεται δὲ κατ' ἀρχήν, κατὰ μέσον, κατὰ τέλος, οἷον ἀφαίρεσις, συγκοπὴ καὶ ἀποκοπή. κατ' ἀρχὴν μέν, οἷον λείβειν εἴβειν, κατὰ μέσον, οἷον μονώνυχας μώνυχας, κατὰ δὲ τὸ τέλος, δῶμα δῶ. See also [Plutarch], *De Hom.* 2.9: "And [Homer] uses the customary ἔλλειψις of the Dorians for brevity, saying δῶ [but meaning] δῶμα," καὶ Δωριέων μὲν τῇ συνήθει τῆς βραχυλογίας ἐλλείψει κέχρηται, τὸ δῶμα λέγων δῶ.

[98] Trypho[II], *Trop.* 13: "Ἔλλειψις is an expression which is not borne out to the fullest extent, but which leaves out one or more words, such as 'smiting with both [...].' For [the text] leaves out 'hands.' Likewise: '... in a clear [...], which space was seen [to be] clear of corpses' [Homer, *Il.* 8.489–91, 10.194–200]. ⟨For it leaves out 'area.' And:⟩ 'But if the greathearted Athenians shall give [you] the prize, fittingly in accordance with feeling, [...] so that it will be an equivalent' [*Il.* 1.135-36]. For it leaves out 'it would be fine.' For the thought was suspended. Some call this trope προσυπακουόμενον ['filling in something unexpressed']." Ἔλλειψίς ἐστι φράσις οὐ κατὰ τὸ πλῆρες ἐκφερομένη, ἀλλὰ μιᾷ λέξει ἢ πλείοσιν ἐλλείπουσα· οἷον «κόπτων ἀμφοτέρῃσιν», ἐλλείπει γὰρ ταῖς χερσίν. ὁμοίως «ἐν καθαρῷ, ὅθι δὴ νεκύων διεφαίνετο χῶρος». ⟨ἐλλείπει γὰρ τὸ τόπῳ. καὶ⟩ «ἀλλ' εἰ μὲν δώσουσι γέρας μεγάθυμοι Ἀχαιοί, | ἄρσαντες κατὰ θυμόν, ὅπως ἀντάξιον ἔσται». ἐλλείπει γὰρ τὸ καλῶς ἂν ἔχοι· ἀπεκρέματο γὰρ ἡ διάνοια. ἔνιοι δὲ τὸν τρόπον τοῦτον προσυπακουόμενον καλοῦσιν. Anonymous, *Trop.* 12 (*RG* 3.211): "Now ἔλλειψις is wording which is not borne out to the fullest extent, but which allows [one] to infer that which follows e.g., '[...] good to hope in the Lord.' For 'it is' is elliptically inferred, and the day of resurrection, and so forth." Ἔλλειψις δέ ἐστι λόγος μὴ κατὰ τὸ πλῆρες ἐκφερόμενος, παρέχων δὲ νοεῖν τὸ ἑπόμενον, ὡς τὸ ἀγαθὸν ἐλπίζειν ἐπὶ κύριον· τὸ γὰρ ἐστὶν ἐλλειπτικῶς νοεῖται, καὶ ἀναστάσεως ἡμέρα καὶ τὰ τοιαῦτα. Georgius Choeroboscus, *Trop.* 15 (*RG* 3.252; ix C.E. per *BNP* 3.241–42, s.v.): "Ἔλλειψις is an expression which is not borne out to the fullest extent, but which allows us to infer that which follows, as whenever someone who is weeping and wailing says: 'I was striking my chest with both [...],' it is clear that [he means] 'hands,' or as in the Poet: 'smiting with both [...],' this is to say 'hands.'" Ἔλλειψίς ἐστι λόγος ὁ μὴ κατὰ τὸ πλῆρες ἐκφερόμενος, παρέχων δὲ ἡμῖν νοεῖν τὸ ἑπόμενον, ὡς ὅταν τις πενθῶν καὶ ὀδυρόμενος εἴπῃ, τὸ στῆθός μου ἔτυπτον ἀμφοτέραις, δηλονότι χερσίν, ἢ ὡς παρὰ τῷ ποιητῇ «κόπτων ἀμφοτέραις» τουτέστι χερσίν.

ἔλλειψις δέ ἐστιν ὅταν ὁ λέγων ἐλλείπῃ λέξιν ἣν παρ' αὑτοῦ ἔδει προσθεῖναι τῷ νοήματι, οἷον «θέαμα δεινὸν καὶ ἐλεεινόν»· ἐλλείπει γὰρ τὸ ἐστί. κἀκεῖνο δὲ ἔλλειψις· «πρῶτον μέν, ὦ Ἀθηναῖοι, τοῖς θεοῖς εὔχομαι πᾶσι καὶ πάσαις»· ἐλλείπει γὰρ ταῖς θεαῖς. καὶ πάλιν, «ὥσπερ ἄν τις ἰατρὸς ἀσθενοῦσι μὲν τοῖς κάμνουσιν εἰσιὼν μὴ λέγοι μηδὲ δεικνύοι δι' ὧν ἀποφεύξονται τὴν νόσον, ἐπειδὰν δὲ τελευτήσειέ τις αὐτῶν καὶ τὰ νομιζόμενα ἐπ' αὐτῷ φέροιτο, ἀκολουθῶν ἐπὶ τὸ μνῆμα διεξίοι, εἰ τὸ καὶ τὸ ἐποίησεν ἄνθρωπος, οὐκ ἂν ἀπέθανεν. ἐμβρόντητε, εἶτα νῦν λέγεις;» καὶ πάλιν, «εἶπον τοίνυν ὡς μὲν ὑπαρχόντων Θηβαίων Φιλίππῳ λίαν θορυβουμένων»· ἐλλείπει γὰρ τὸ φίλων καὶ συμμάχων.

Ἔλλειψις is whenever the speaker leaves out wording which one must add oneself to the thought, for example, "[...] a dire and piteous spectacle" (*Fals. leg.* 65). For he leaves out "it is." And this also is ἔλλειψις: "First of all, Athenians, I pray to all the gods and to all [...]" [*Cor.* 1; cf. *Ep.* 1.1]. For he leaves out "the goddesses." And again: "[It's] as if some doctor, coming in, does not speak to those suffering illnesses, nor indicate through what means they will escape the disease, but when one of them dies and the funeral rites are conducted for him, he [the doctor] goes along, following to the tomb [...]: 'If the man had done this-or-that, he would not have died' – so, you idiot, are you now saying this?" [*Cor.* 243]. And again, "I said furthermore, 'As when the Thebans, who were [...] to Philip, were very distressed...'" [*Cor.* 174]. For he left out "friends and allies." (*Fig.* 42, *RG* 3.78–79)

Based on these illustrations one can see that the figure encompasses virtually the omission of any wording, from the obvious (forms of εἶναι or words dropped because of parallel structure) to a wide variety of less obvious items, including any of the parts of speech and even whole phrases.[99] Alexander's observation regarding the rhetorical impact of ἔλλειψις holds further interest: it "has the impression of emotion" (πάθους ἔμφασιν ἔχει), probably because intense feeling causes hasty or broken speech. Aquila Romanus similarly stresses the dynamism that a quicker pace imparts to an utterance (*ut ipsa celeritate commotior esset enuntiatio*).[100]

---

[99] Cocondrius (*Trop.* 27, *RG* 3.242; of Byzantine date, per *BNP* 3.496, s.v.) focuses on the omission of prepositions: "Ἔλλειψις is an expression which leaves out some part of speech: 'Aetolians, protecting themselves [...] lovely Calydon' [Homer, *Il.* 9.531], instead of "*around* Calydon." And: 'Until he chased him [...] the fruit-bearing plain' [*Il.* 21.602], instead of "*through* the plain." And: 'Angered in mood [...] the well-girded woman' [*Il.* 1.429], instead of '*about* the woman.'" Ἔλλειψίς ἐστι φράσις μέρει λόγου τινὶ ἐλλείπουσα, «Αἰτωλοὶ μὲν ἀμυνόμενοι Καλυδῶνος ἐραννῆς», ἀντὶ τοῦ περὶ Καλυδῶνος· καὶ «ἕως τὸν πεδίοιο διώκετο πυροφόροιο», ἀντὶ τοῦ διὰ πεδίου· καὶ «χωόμενος κατὰ θυμὸν ἐϋζώνοιο γυναικός» ἀντὶ τοῦ περὶ γυναικός.

[100] *Fig.* 46 (*RLM* 37; iii c.e. per *BNP* 1.929, s.v. 5): "Ἔλλειψις, i.e., *detractio*, is a figure opposite to the one above [i.e., πλεονασμός, discussed in the previous entry]. An utterance is enhanced when we remove any word from its expression, in this manner: 'I do indeed forgive that person who repels death from himself by the death of an enemy. Moreover the judges, who cast votes on that man's behalf, also seem [...] to me; for I hear that there were many [such votes].' Here all this appears to be lacking: 'Moreover the judges also seem to me *to have determined* (or, *to have forgiven*) *the same thing.*' But because it was understood, it was left out, so that the declaration might be more dynamic by its own alacrity." ἔλλειψις, *id est detractio, contraria superiori figura. Ornatur oratio, cum verbum aliquod detrahimus a sua significatione, hoc modo:* «Et illi quidem, qui a se mortem morte inimici reppulit ignosco.

3.3 The methods of brevity

The ancient sources unfortunately supply little direct assistance toward articulating the precise difference between ἔλλειψις and βραχυλογία. Herbert Weir Smyth wrestles with this problem. He defines βραχυλογία thus:

> Brachylogia ... is a concise form of expression by which an element is not repeated or is omitted when its repetition or use would make the thought or the grammatical construction complete. The suppressed element must be supplied from some corresponding word in the context, in which case it often appears with some change of form or construction; or it must be taken from the connection of the thought.[101]

Ἔλλειψις, meanwhile, "is the suppression of a word or of several words of minor importance to the logical expression of the thought, but necessary to the construction."[102] As for the differences between the two, he admits:

> *Brachylogy* and *ellipse* cannot always be distinguished sharply. In ellipse the suppressed word is not to be supplied from a corresponding word in the context; and, in general, ellipse is less artificial and less dependent on the momentary and arbitrary will of the speaker or writer.[103]

The sources do not, however, support this distinction based on whether the omitted language has or lacks some corresponding element in the context; in fact, they approach ἔλλειψις as the omission of *any* language that the reader must supply.[104] Βραχυλογία, βραχύτης and συντομία have more inclusive usages by virtue of their longer history as stylistic technical terms. And while βραχυλογία *et alia* and ἔλλειψις both depend on the auditor to infer more than is actually stated, the definitions and illustrations of the former stress the *presence* of only the necessary wording or subject matters. This might or might not entail omission. In contrast, the definitions and illustrations of ἔλλειψις emphasize the *absence* of wording. In sum, one may accomplish βραχυλογία through ἔλλειψις, but not the other way around; logically, the latter figure is a species of the former.

Videntur autem mihi et iudices, qui sententias pro illo tulerunt: nam multas fuisse audio». Hic apparet totum illud denesse: «videntur autem mihi et iudices idem senisse» vel «ignovisse». Sed quia intellegebatur, id detractum est, ut ipsa celeritate commotior esset enuntiatio. Cf. [Plutarch], *De Hom.* 2.39: "The result of this figure [of ἔλλειψις] is rapidity," ἔργον δὲ τοῦ σχήματος τάχος.

[101] Smyth 674–75, § 3017.

[102] Ibid., 677–78, § 3022. He continues: "Ellipse gives brevity, force, and liveliness; it is usually readily to be supplied, often unconscious, and appears especially in common phrases, constructions and expressions of popular speech ...."

[103] Ibid., 675, § 3017.

[104] Cf. BDF 253–54, § 480: "By ellipsis in the strict sense is understood a case in which a term neither is present nor can be supplied from some related term. The following can be omitted from this category: whatever is obvious from the structure of the sentence, like the copula ...; the subject if it is very general ('thing' or 'men') or is required by the assertion ...; the substantive if it is made sufficiently evident by an attributive ...; or the article with certain attributive genitives.... Such ellipses are conventional and partially corresponding usages are found in other languages." Some of these omitted items from this "strict" definition collide with the illustrations in the definitions quoted above.

3.3.4 The figure or trope of συνεκδοχή

As sometimes occurs in the developing technical vocabulary of rhetorical figures, συνεκδοχή either initially did not have the meaning that it eventually acquired, or it had more than one usage from the very start.[105] The term first appears in Quintilian, who uses it in two distinct ways. In book 9, where he classes it among the figures of speech that achieve *detractio*, "subtraction,"[106] he defines it as "when some omitted word is sufficiently understood from the others" (*cum subtractum verbum aliquod satis ex ceteris intellegitur*). His examples indicate that he perceives it to be virtually synonymous with ἔλλειψις:

... *ut Caelius in Antonium:* «*stupere gaudio Graecus*»: *simul enim auditur* «*coepit*»; *Cicero ad Brutum:* «*Sermo nullus scilicet nisi de te: quid enim potius? Tum Flavius, Cras, inquit, tabellarii, et ego ibidem has inter cenam exaravi*». *Cui similia sunt illa meo quidem iudicio, in quibus verba decenter pudoris gratia subtrahuntur:* «*novimus et qui te, transversa tuentibus hircis,* | *et quo, sed faciles Nymphae risere, sacello*».

... such as Caelius against Antonius: "The Greek [...] to be stunned with delight." For "he began" is at once heard. [Also] Cicero to Brutus: "Obviously no conversation [...] except about you: for what [...] better? Then Flavius says: '[...] tomorrow by messenger,' and at that moment during dinner I wrote these [...]." Whereby indeed in my judgment the following cases are similar, in which words are properly removed for the sake of modesty: "We're aware of who you are, as the he-goats are looking askance, and at which chapel – but the Nymphs are ready to break out in giggles' [Virgil, *Ecl.* 3.8–9]." (*Inst.* 9.3.58–59)[107]

Both the definition and the examples recall those on ἔλλειψις examined above. Quintilian's earlier discussion, however, under the heading of tropes in book 8, matches what other theorists have to say about συνεκδοχή:

... *haec variare sermonem potest, ut ex uno plura intellegamus, parte totum, specie genus, praecedentibus sequentia, vel omnia haec contra. Liberior poetis quam oratoribus, nam prorsa, ut* «*mucronem*» *pro gladio et* «*tectum*» *pro domo recipiet, ita non* «*puppem*» *pro navi nec* «*abietem*» *pro tabellis, et rursus, ut pro gladio* «*ferrum*», *ita non pro equo* «*quadrupedem*».

This [trope, συνεκδοχή] is able to vary one's speech, so that we understand a plurality of things from one, the whole from the part, the genus from the species, the results from the pre-

---

[105] For modern discussions of the figure, see Aune, *Westminster Dictionary*, 453–54, s.v. "Synecdoche"; Smyth 683, § 3047; Lausberg, *Handbook*, 260–62, §§572–77.

[106] *Inst.* 9.3.58: "The figures which are made through subtraction primarily pursue the charm of brevity and novelty," *at quae detractionem fiunt figurae, brevitatis novitatisque maxime gratiam petunt*. Other figures of subtraction include the deletion of conjunctions; ἐπεζευγμένον (i.e., ζεῦγμα) where a verb stated once functions in multiple clauses, or where singulars and plurals or the genders join together (*sed haec adeo sunt vulgaria ut sibi artem figurarum adserere non possint*, 9.3.64); and the combination of constructions. Quintilian's use of the Greek term συνεκδοχή instead of a Latin equivalent (cf. *Rhet. Her.* 4.33.44–45, cited below, *intellectio*) naturally implies that he is building upon an older tradition, and may in fact be taking his different meanings of the term from distinct traditional strands and placing them separately into his system of tropes and figures.

[107] Quintilian goes on to dispute whether this properly is an instance of ἀποσιώπησις.

ceding events, or all these in reverse. It is more free for poets than orators [i.e., it can be more freely used by them], for it is prosaic that one exchange "edge" for sword and "shelter" for house, but not "poop deck" for ship nor "fir wood" for tablets; and once more "iron" for sword, but not "four-legger" for horse. (*Inst.* 8.6.19–20)

He next points out that variations between singular and plural are a common form of συνεκδοχή, and then explains how as a figure of speech it differs from the trope:

Quidam synecdochen vocant et cum id in contextu sermonis quod tacetur accipimus: verbum enim ex verbis intellegi, quod inter vitia ellipsis vocatur: «Arcades ad portas ruere». Mihi hanc figuram esse magis placet, illic ergo reddetur.

Some call it *synecdoche* also when we understand in the context of an utterance that which is left unstated, for instance a word is to be comprehended from the [other] words, which is called *ellipsis* among the [stylistic] vices: "The Arcadians [...] to hasten to the gates" [Virgil, *Aen.* 11.142]. It seems much better to me that this is a figure, so it will be returned to there. (*Inst.* 8.6.21–22)

For Quintilian, συνεκδοχή thus encompasses what eventually becomes ἔλλειψις, but he splits the latter away as the faulty manifestation of the former (*quod inter vitia ellipsis vocatur*).[108] A definition very similar to his tropic version recurs in the monographs on figures and tropes, as in that of Trypho[1]:

συνεκδοχή ἐστι φράσις οὐ κατὰ τὸ πλῆρες ἐξενηνεγμένη, προσδεομένη δέ τινος ἔξωθεν ἀκολουθίας. τῶν δὲ συνεκδοχῶν εἰσι διαφοραὶ πλείους· αἱ μὲν γὰρ ἀπὸ μέρους τὸ ὅλον δηλοῦσιν, ὡς ἀργυρόπεζα Θέτις καὶ λευκώλενος Ἥρη· ἢ ἀπὸ τοῦ ὅλου τὸ μέρος, οἷον χάλκεον ἔγχος· οὐ γὰρ ὅλον, ἀλλὰ μέρος· καὶ βόας αὔας τὰς βύρσας· ἢ ἀπὸ τῆς ὕλης τὸ ἀποτέλεσμα, οἷον «χρυσὸν δ' αὐτὸς ἔδυνε περὶ χροΐ», ἀντὶ τοῦ χρυσέην πανοπλίαν. ἢ ἀπὸ τοῦ προηγουμένου τὸ ἀκόλουθον, οἷον «πολλὰς δ' ἰφθίμους ψυχάς»: ἢ ἀπὸ τοῦ ἀκολούθου τὸ προηγούμενον, οἷον· «ἑζόμενοι λεύκαινον ὕδωρ ξεστῇς ἐλάτῃσι».

Συνεκδοχή is expression which is not carried out to the fullest extent, but which requires something that follows logically from outside. There are many variations of συνεκδοχαί: for they indicate the whole from the part, like "silver-footed" Thetis and "white-armed" Hera. Or they indicate the part from the whole, for example "bronze" as a sword (for it is not the whole but the part) and "withered cattle" as hides. Or they indicate the finished product from its constituent substance, for example "But he put the gold around his body" [Homer, *Il.* 8.43], instead of "golden armor." Or they indicate result from the antecedent, for example "while sitting [they rowed] the whitening water with polished oars" [*Od.* 12.172]. (*Trop.* 7, *RG* 3.195–96)

---

[108] Note in addition *Inst.* 8.3.50: "Ἔλλειψις ought also to be shunned, when something in an utterance is missing by which it would be more complete, although it is a vice of obscure, rather than unornamented, speech. But this also, when it is done judiciously, is customarily said to be a figure." *Vitari ⟨debet⟩ et* ἔλλειψις, *cum sermoni deest aliquid, quo minus plenus sit, quamquam id obscurae potius quam inornatae orationis est vitium. Sed hoc quoque, cum a prudentibus fit, schema dici solet.* Cf. Aristotle's discussion of the contribution ἔλλειψις makes toward fallacy in *Rhet.* 2.24.3, 1401b; 2.24.7, 1401b; and 2.24.29, 1401b–2a. Also, Theon, *Prog.* 12 (*RG* 2.129) on its contribution to ἀσάφεια in νόμος.

Trypho[I] uses the same language in his definition of συνεκδοχή that others use for ἔλλειψις,[109] while his illustrations presuppose a meaning like that of the *Rhetorica ad Herennium* for *intellectio*: "*Intellectio* is when a whole thing is understood from a small part or the part from the whole" (*intellectio est cum res tota parva de parte cognoscitur aut de toto pars*).[110]

It might seem that this figure does not properly belong with other figures of brevity, since it would not bring about a reduction of language in every case. But the theorists maintain precisely this association. Returning for a moment to Quintilian's analysis, one passing remark deserves additional emphasis: *ut ex uno plura intellegamus*.[111] This notion, which Trypho[I] substantially echoes (προσδεομένη δέ τινος ἔξωθεν ἀκολουθίας), is the basis of the classification of συνεκδοχή among other figures of brevity: it enables an utterance to imply much more than it actually says, and it relies on upon the reader's ability to follow the leap from part to whole, whole to part and so forth. Margaret M. Mitchell's labeling of συνεκδοχή as "rhetorical shorthand" is very

---

[109] Cf. Anonymous, *Trop.* 7 (*RG* 3.209–10), συνεκδοχή ἐστι φράσις ἢ λέξις οὐ κατὰ τὸ πλῆρες ἐκφερομένη, προσδεομένη δέ τινος ἔξωθεν, with *twelve* listed variations (apparently merging several sources); Trypho[II], *Trop.* 7, συνεκδοχή ἐστι φράσις οὐ κατὰ τὸ πλῆρες ἐκφερομένη, προσδεομένη δέ τινος ἔξωθεν διανοίας. The illustrations in [Plutarch], *De Hom.* 2.22 recur in the monographs, but the definition is unique: "Another trope is so-called συνεκδοχή, which represents from what is properly signified some other things under the same category; and this trope is likewise variegated." ἄλλος τρόπος ⟨ἐστὶν⟩ ἡ συνεκδοχὴ λεγομένη, ἀπὸ τοῦ κυρίως σημαινομένου ἕτερόν τι τῶν ὑπὸ τὸ αὐτὸ γένος ὄντων παριστᾶσα. καὶ ἔστιν ὁμοίως καὶ ὁ τρόπος οὗτος ποικίλος.

[110] [Cicero], *Rhet. Her.* 4.33.44–45. The author gives illustrations for the whole from the part, the part from the whole, the plural from the singular and the singular from the plural. Note also Cocondrius, *Trop.* 12 (*RG* 3.236–37): "συνεκδοχή is a word or an expression which displays the whole meaning from the part, or the part through the whole. Now συνεκδοχαί occur according to four modes. For it is either the whole from the part, or the part from the whole, or the proper name from the epithet, or the proper name from the attribute." συνεκδοχή ἐστι λέξις ἢ φράσις ἀπὸ μέρους ὅλην διάνοιαν ἐμφαίνουσα, ἢ διὰ τοῦ παντὸς τὸ μέρος, γίνονται δὲ αἱ συνεκδοχαὶ κατὰ τρόπους τέσσαρας· ἢ γὰρ ἀπὸ μέρους τὸ ὅλον, ἢ ἀπὸ ὅλου τὸ μέρος, ἢ ἀπὸ ἐπωνύμου τὸ κύριον, ἢ ἀπὸ τοῦ παρεπομένου τὸ κύριον.

[111] Cf. [Aelius Aristides], *Rhet.* 2.98: "Now in plain speech also words should not be brought forward for only one subject, but also to signify two and three [subjects], for example since 'to depart' has many meanings, all these are to be considered: for it encompasses in it 'near' and 'far' and 'by land' and 'by sea,' and 'to have problems' and 'to cause problems,' and there are actually a myriad things which it signifies." δεῖ δὲ καὶ τὸ ὀνόματα ἐν τῷ ἀφελεῖ λόγῳ μὴ καθ' ἑνὸς μόνον πράγματος προάγεσθαι, ἀλλὰ καὶ δύο καὶ τρία σημαίνειν, οἷον ἐπειδὴ τό [τε] «ἀπεῖναι» εἴδη πλείω ἔχει τινά, πάντα ταῦτα ἐπισκεπτέον· περιέχει γὰρ ἐν αὐτῷ καὶ τὸ πλησίον καὶ τὸ πόρρω καὶ ἐν γῇ καὶ ἐν θαλάσσῃ, καὶ πράγματα ἔχειν καὶ παρέχειν, καὶ ὅλως μυρία ἐστίν, ἃ σημαίνει.

apt,[112] especially in its ability to evoke narratives by reference to a distinctive part.

3.3.5 The rhetorical figure of ἀπὸ κοινοῦ

The final figure requiring separate treatment is ἀπὸ κοινοῦ, which involves the re-use of a syntatical element. Phoebammon defines and illustrates the figure thus:

ἀπὸ κοινοῦ δέ ἐστι λέξις ἅπαξ λεγομένη, πολλάκις δὲ νοουμένη καὶ συντασσομένη, ὡς ἵνα τις εἴπῃ, ἀπελθὼν ᾔτησα τοὺς ἄνδρας, μάλιστα δὲ τόνδε καὶ τόνδε. ἀπὸ κοινοῦ γὰρ συντάσσεται ἐνταῦθα τὸ ᾔτησα.

Ἀπὸ κοινοῦ is language said once, but which is understood and used in the syntax several times, so that someone may say: "After going out I asked the men, especially that one and that one." For "I asked" is used in the syntax here from the common element [ἀπὸ κοινοῦ]. (*Fig.* 1.2, *RG* 3.46)

The definition of Lesbonax differs slightly from Phoebammon's, but his illustrations reveal that he shares the same basic conception:

ἀπὸ κοινοῦ ἐστι λέξις ἅπαξ μὲν λεγομένη, πολλάκις δὲ νοουμένη καὶ ἔξωθεν λαμβανομένη, οἷον «ἀπελθὼν ᾔτησα τοὺς ἄνδρας, μάλιστα δὲ Χαρίδημον καὶ Ἵππαρχον», καὶ Ὅμηρος «ἐλίσσετο πάντας Ἀχαιούς, Ἀτρεΐδα δὲ μάλιστα». ἀπὸ κοινοῦ γὰρ ἐπ' ἐκείνου μὲν τὸ ᾔτησα, ἐπὶ τούτου δὲ τὸ ἐλίσσετο.

Ἀπὸ κοινοῦ is wording which is said once but is understood and is taken from outside several times, for example: "After going out, I asked the men, but especially Charidemus and Hipparchus." And Homer: "He was begging all the Achaeans, but especially the sons of Atreus" (*Il.* 1.15). For "I asked" is ἀπὸ κοινοῦ in the former, and "he was begging" in the latter.[113] (*Fig.* 31B, Blank 207)

The illustrations envision a situation wherein a syntactical element in one clause is distributed to other clauses. Ἀπὸ κοινοῦ can thus closely resemble the figure of ζεῦγμα, except that the definitions of the latter stress the "yoking together" of multiple clauses as a particularity of the figure.[114] The definitions

---

[112] She argues in her article "Rhetorical Shorthand" that τὸ εὐαγγέλιον functions as an instance of βραχυλογία for narratives such as 1 Cor 15:1–11, and she notes the many ways that Paul employs elements of τὸ εὐαγγέλιον synecdochically in 1 and 2 Corinthians. I discuss her article further in the conclusion (§ 3.4) below.

[113] Lesbonax's dates are "uncertain (perhaps before the end of the 2nd cent. AD)," per *BNP* 7.428, s.v. Cf. [Aelius Herodian], *Fig.*, *RG* 3.94: "Ἀπὸ κοινοῦ is the connection of words in a thought, which creates a partnership from a single word for the completion [of the thought] to the greatest possible extent, for example: 'He was begging all the Achaeans, but especially the two sons of Atreus, leaders of the peoples' [Homer, *Il.* 1.15–16]," ἀπὸ κοινοῦ μέν ἐστι λόγων συνέχεια ἐν διανοίᾳ κοινωνοῦσα ὡς ἐπὶ τὸ πλεῖστον ἑνὸς ῥήματος εἰς συντέλειαν, οἷον «καὶ ἐλίσσετο πάντας Ἀχαιούς, | Ἀτρεΐδα δὲ μάλιστα δύο κοσμήτορε λαῶν».

[114] E.g., Zonaeus, *Fig.* 2.14, *RG* 3.168: "Ζεῦγμα is whenever one word binds together different clauses, sitting either after them or before them, for example: '... imitating the word of

quoted above permit greater latitude than the illustrations convey, however. For example, Tiberius Rhetor gives no definition, but his example involves a change in the form of the element "understood several times":

τὸ δὲ ἀπὸ κοινοῦ οὕτως· «καὶ τῷ μὲν Εὐβαίῳ τῷ τὸν Βοιωτὸν ἀποκτείναντι πολλὴν συγγνώμην ἔχω· δοκοῦσι δέ μοι καὶ τῶν δικασάντων τότε πολλοί». ἀπὸ κοινοῦ συγγνώμην ἔχειν. εὐειδὲς τὸ σχῆμα.

The [figure] ἀπὸ κοινοῦ is thus: "I have much leniency for Euaeon, who murdered the Boetian; for many of those sitting in judgment at that time seem to me [...]" (Demosthenes, *Mid.* 74–75). The ἀπὸ κοινοῦ is "to have leniency." The figure is beautiful. (*Fig.* 37, *RG* 3.76)

The definitions of ἀπὸ κοινοῦ furthermore can include multiple syntactical usage *within the same clause*, although none of the illustrations show it. This variation would involve, for instance, a noun which could construe both syntactically and logically with a finite verb and participle. Prepositional phrases could likewise construe with more than one of the verbs, nouns or adjectives in their clauses. An author would thereby avoid repetition, and would impart multiple layers of meaning to a single clause. I shall argue in the next two chapters that Paul deploys ἀπὸ κοινοῦ in precisely this manner in both of his definitions of the gospel in Romans 1.

3.4 Conclusion; brevity and Pauline exegesis

I have shown several things in the survey above. (1) The ability to communicate concisely enjoyed wide, perhaps even universal, admiration among authors in the ancient world, such that some theorists promote it to the status of a cardinal virtue of style. (2) Brevity was determined to be useful when one wishes to increase the force of an utterance (an ancient equivalent of italic type, so to speak) or to create the impression of wisdom – hence its utility for definitions, which accrue an extra aura of accuracy and authority through their similarity to maxims. (3) Brevity has special utility for the early sections of an oration, especially the διήγησις, and for the composition of letters. (4) The substantial amount of theory dedicated to brevity unambiguously reveals that educators dedicated considerable energy toward the cultivation of the skill. And (5) theorists come to divide methods of brevity into that of content (ἐκ τῶν πραγμάτων) and of style (ἐκ τῆς λέξεως). Tactics specific to each emerge,

---

some people, but the deed of others, but the meekness of others, but the quietness of others, but the risks of others, but the greater number [of aspects] of others, but the entirety [of aspects] of others.' For 'imitating' yokes together [ζεύγυσι] the clauses." ζεῦγμά ἐστιν, ὅταν διάφορα κῶλα μία συνδῇ λέξις ἢ μετ' αὐτὰ τεθεῖσα ἢ πρὸ αὐτῶν, οἷον «τῶν μὲν τὸν λόγον, τῶν δὲ τὴν πρᾶξιν, τῶν δὲ τὸ πρᾷον, τῶν δὲ τὸ ἥσυχον, τῶν δὲ τοὺς κινδύνους, τῶν δὲ τὰ πλείω, τῶν δὲ τὰ πάντα μιμησάμενος». τὸ γὰρ μιμησάμενος ζεύγνυσι τὰ κῶλα. See also Alexander Rhetor, *Fig.* 2.17 (*RG* 3.35), and cf. Lausberg, *Handbook*, 309–15, §§ 692–708.

particularly rhetorical figures and tropes that economize language and evoke more than what one actually states.

This investigation will prove helpful in several respects both for the interpretation of Paul generally and for my analysis of his definitions of the gospel in Romans 1. The suitability of brevity in the composition of letters should put readers of Paul on constant alert for evidence of it, at the levels both of content and of style. Within his letters, he also constructs προοίμια (i.e., prescripts and thanksgiving sections), προθέσεις and διηγήσεις that call forth the established strategies of brevity.[115] Paul's διήγησις in Galatians, for example, very capably illustrates συντομία ἐκ τῶν πραγμάτων. He maintains a tight focus on the point he intends it to make (1:12, οὐδὲ γὰρ ἐγὼ παρὰ ἀνθρώπου παρέλαβον αὐτὸ οὔτε ἐδιδάχθην ἀλλὰ δι' ἀποκαλύψεως Ἰησοῦ Χριστοῦ). He sketches the years prior to his call in a single sentence (1:13–14), omits details of what he was doing in Arabia, Syria and Cilicia (1:17, 21) and during the fourteen years before he goes up to confer with οἱ δοκοῦντες (2:1–2). His account of this meeting singles out his triumph over those who would change his gospel, culminating in the division of evangelistic labor (2:9–10). The brisk pace of the narration furthermore contrasts noticeably with the few instances of μακρολογία (the attributive participial phrases in 1:15, the vivid description of his opponents in 2:4–5, and the expansion of his one-sentence summary of his dispute with Peter in 2:15–21 that doubles as the πρόθεσις of the letter).[116] These all serve his aim of presenting himself as his addressees' advocate for their freedom and as *their* apostle, as well as amplifying the narrative's pathos. The expression οἱ δοκοῦντες, which appears in 2:2, deserves special mention as an instance of ἔλλειψις, since it omits the expected εἶναι with a predicate. What precisely do these persons, to whom Paul privately presents τὸ εὐαγγέλιον ὃ κηρύσσω ἐν τοῖς ἔθνεσιν, seem to be? He later expands his own ἔλλειψις in 2:6 (ἀπὸ δὲ τῶν δοκούντων εἶναί τι, – ὁποῖοί ποτε ἦσαν οὐδέν μοι διαφέρει· πρόσωπον [ὁ] θεὸς ἀνθρώπου οὐ λαμβάνει – ἐμοὶ γὰρ οἱ δοκοῦντες οὐδὲν προσανέθεντο), and again in 2:9, where he adds names and the title of "pillars" (Ἰάκωβος καὶ Κηφᾶς καὶ Ἰωάννης, οἱ δοκοῦντες στῦλοι εἶναι, δεξιὰς ἔδωκαν ἐμοὶ καὶ Βαρναβᾷ κοινωνίας). The initial omission in 2:2 creates a blank space which Paul can himself fill with descriptions that simultaneously acknowledge and diminish the importance of the "pillars": they are partners, but not supervisors; they and Paul are coevals with clearly defined territories within which to work.

---

[115] This principle works in reverse as well: given that Paul and his addressees share an expectation that letters exhibit βραχυλογία, instances of μακρολογία stand out dramatically and one should interpret them with this in mind.

[116] See the analysis of Betz, *Galatians*, 18–19.

82 Chapter 3: The Ancient Rhetorical Theorists on Brevity

My research in this chapter also facilitates the application of technical vocabulary to the interpretation of Paul's letters. In learning to read, write and speak, he acquired the skill of βραχυλογία, including the figures and tropes associated with it. Our improved comprehension of ancient strategies of brevity will not only aid accurate analysis of the γένος and τάξις of his letters, but will also help to resolve interpretive problems in particular verses through analysis of the style. Margaret M. Mitchell has already demonstrated this in her article, "Rhetorical Shorthand in Pauline Argumentation: The Functions of 'the Gospel' in the Corinthian Correspondence." She documents several instances of βραχύτης (as a figure), συνεκδοχή, and μεταφορά in the ways that Paul uses τὸ εὐαγγέλιον argumentatively.[117] The word εὐαγγέλιον itself, she observes, "serves as a 'superabbreviation' of the whole, functioning as a title which both characterizes its full contents and interprets its meaning for the reader."[118] It can do this for semantic reasons,

... because the very term "good news" ... points outside of itself to the content and story which must have been told (at least once) for the referent to be clear to the audience. The way that Paul uses the phrase absolutely, that is, without any qualifier (as in about half of Pauline usages), shows that he assumes that the audience knows well to what he refers. Yet even the qualified uses of the phrase, such as τὸ εὐαγγέλιον τοῦ θεοῦ or τὸ εὐαγγέλιον τοῦ Χριστοῦ, rely as much upon the hearers' acquaintance with the narrative events to which they refer.[119]

Paul's strategies of brevity build directly upon the referential character of τὸ εὐαγγέλιον. He can assume that his Corinthian readers will comprehend what he is doing with them, because he knows that they know the full content and soteriological significance of the gospel: he delivered it to them, as it was delivered to him (1 Cor 11:23, 15:3). He has made no such delivery to the Roman Christians, and yet he still assumes their detailed knowledge of the gospel's narrative and their ability to understand his tactics of brevity in relation to it, as I shall demonstrate in the next two chapters.

A recent article by Todd A. Wilson furnishes a convenient example of the consequences of not using the ancient categories and theoretical discussions about brevity as a basis for one's own. He sets out to illuminate the "theological abbreviation" of ὑπὸ νόμον in Galatians.[120] The sources that discuss συνεκδοχή should underpin his category of "theological abbreviation," but curiously they do not.[121] This failure becomes starkly obvious in his "reliable criteria with which to discern the use of shorthand":

---

[117] She discusses the ancient sources at "Rhetorical Shorthand," 66–69.
[118] Ibid., 64.
[119] Ibid., 65.
[120] Wilson, "'Under Law' in Galatians."
[121] This happens in spite of the fact that he cites Mitchell's essay on "Rhetorical Shorthand" ("'Under Law' in Galatians," 366, n. 11).

3.4 Conclusion; brevity and Pauline exegesis 83

First, a shorthand expression obviously must be *shorter* ... than its longhand equivalent. Secondly, a shorthand expression must have some *discernible verbal connection* to its longhand equivalent. For if there is no verbal link between the two expressions, there would be no way to detect whether the particular expression was serving as shorthand for another, as opposed to any other expression that happens to refer to the same thing. Thirdly, a shorthand expression must have the *same referent* as its longhand equivalent. One can safely assume that a particular expression is shorthand for another expression only when both expressions refer to the same thing. This is not, of course, to deny slight differences in connotation between the two expressions as a result of the various associations that may arise from differences in form; only that an expression cannot be shorthand for another expression without possessing the same referent.[122]

These criteria seem sufficiently reasonable on their surface, but would Paul or any other ancient author have agreed with them? Would the criteria align with their understanding of any of the figures associated with βραχυλογία? Regarding the second criterion, Mitchell correctly analyzes ὁ λόγος τοῦ σταυροῦ in 1 Cor 1:18 as an instance of συνεκδοχή, the figure that most closely resembles which Wilson describes:[123] the word εὐαγγέλιον is itself, as noted above, a "superabbreviation" of such narratives – and yet no "discernible verbal connection" between ὁ λόγος τοῦ σταυροῦ and τὸ εὐαγγέλιον exists. 'Rhetorical shorthand' can prove more flexible than Wilson allows. The "slight differences in connotation" furthermore supply the primary incentive for using συνεκδοχή in the first place, creating problems for Wilson's third criterion. Just because ὁ λόγος τοῦ σταυροῦ gathers and compresses Paul's proclamation,[124] it does not follow that he is making *full use* of *all* of the soteriologically and theologically interpreted narratives and exegetical traditions buried within τὸ εὐαγγέλιον at that particular moment. An abbreviation and its "longhand" expression thus have a more complicated relationship than simply one of equivalence. Finally, Wilson seems to tailor these criteria to facilitate his argument that "under law" in Galatians abbreviates "under the curse of the law" (a precise expression which Paul does not use) in all of the passages where it

---

[122] "'Under Law' in Galatians," 364–65, italics original.

[123] Mitchell, "Rhetorical Shorthand," 70–71: "The idea here is not that Paul preached to the Corinthians a gospel without resurrection ..., but rather that the whole of the gospel can be alluded to by reference to one of its parts. The choice of which part depends in each case on Paul's particular argument. Here, where Paul seeks to combat Corinthian self-aggrandizement, he turns to the gospel and its preaching as the standard for Christian life and in so doing elevates the foolish, utterly defeated-looking crucifixion to set the 'worldly standards' (which the Corinthians are emulating) on their heads."

[124] The phrase ὁ λόγος τοῦ σταυροῦ can do this not because it is entirely coextensive with or transparent of the events and concepts to which it refers, nor because it overshadows them in importance in Paul's point of view, but because it works like a handle or hook by which he picks up a fuller account of Jesus' death, burial and resurrection. In this context it works particularly well, since in addition to capturing much more than Paul actually says, it directs attention to the thing that makes τὸ κήρυγμα look like μωρία to the Greeks and a σκάνδαλον to the Jews.

appears. In a manner parallel to εὐαγγέλιον, νόμος superabbreviates a vast body of literature, as well as certain exegetical conclusions that speak to its relevance for Paul and his readers. Ὑπὸ νόμον in Galatians refers broadly to being under the law's power or authority; the law enforces this power with a curse, as Paul says. Naturally, whenever he mentions the law subsequently in the letter, his earlier points remain operative and contextually relevant. When Paul talks about the law as pedagogue (3:23–4:7), or being under the law's authority as servitude (4:21–5:1; cf. 5:18), he is adding further expansions of ὑπὸ νόμου that move well beyond a flat equation of law and curse. Furthermore, Paul has already referred to νόμος a few times prior to 3:10, in the expression ἐξ ἔργων νόμου (2:16, 3:1–5). Would these previous usages not color his application of νόμος in relation to the curse and in later usages of the word? Wilson's failure to conform his criteria to the rhetorical theory on συνεκδοχή therefore proves fatal to his argument. Engagement with the ancient theory would have insulated him from these problems, and enabled him to deal better with the rhetorically complex manner that Paul deploys νόμος synecdochically in the argument of Galatians.

Flexibility will characterize Paul's application of συνεκδοχή, ἔλλειψις and ἀπὸ κοινοῦ in his carefully composed statements of the essence and function of the gospel. One will recall that the theorists discussed above frequently warn against the fault of obscurity when an author strives to be brief. Paul evidently regards this risk as an opportunity – as a feature, not a flaw, of βραχυλογία. His definitions, particularly the second, ride the line between ambiguity and obscurity. This fact results from his desire to maximize the semantic ranges of his definition's component terms, in other words, to take advantage of the ambiguities inherent in the words themselves and in their syntactical positions, as I shall show in the following chapters.

Chapter 4

The First Definition of the Gospel (1:2–4)

4.1 Introduction

The analyses of definition and of brevity in the above chapters help to open fresh avenues of investigation into Rom 1:2–4 and 16–17. First, do these two passages recognizably conform to the principles of definition as articulated in the ancient philosophical and rhetorical sources? Both are predicative statements: the latter has ἐστίν (δύναμις γὰρ θεοῦ ἐστιν) and the former is a relative clause (ὃ προεπηγγείλατο) with two coordinated attributive participial phrases (τοῦ υἱοῦ, τοῦ γενομένου ... τοῦ ὁρισθέντος), following common methods of embedding definitions in other statements. Their placement at either end of the introductory sections of Romans recalls Plato's advice that an inquiry should start with the definition of terms within the question. Paul's appropriation in 1:2–4 of traditional themes which are otherwise unattested in his letters suggests that the passage has a stipulative function, stating ideas about the definiendum which he and his readers share, and which enjoy general support.[1] Both passages immediately strike the reader as extraordinarily dense in style and content. Their brevity contributes to a solemnity of tone, and implies a high level of care applied to their composition, as befits definition. Paul does not locate the gospel within a taxonomy of related phenomena, identifying completely the particularities that distinguish it from its neighbors, as is characteristic of philosophical definition. He does, however, identify the classes to which the gospel belongs, namely God's promises or pre-proclamations (ὃ προεπηγγείλατο) in vv. 2–4 and God's powers or abilities (δύναμις θεοῦ) in vv. 16–17.[2] If these observations accumulate into a provisional conclusion that 1:2–4 and 16–17 are indeed Paul's definitions of the gospel, other, more complicated questions emerge. How does Paul deploy strategies of brevity in order to load them with unstated wording and content? Does he intend to give *complete* definitions of the gospel? And why does he give *two* very different

---

[1] Several interpreters have surmised a similar role for 1:2–4, e.g., Dodd, *Romans*, 4–5; Barrett, *Romans*, 18–19; Käsemann, *Romans*, 13; Stuhlmacher, *Romans*, 19; Schlier, *Römerbrief*, 23; Cranfield, *Romans*, 1.57; Jervis, *Purpose of Romans*, 158.

[2] Taxonomy is, in any case, less common in rhetorical and popular philosophical definition than in strict philosophical definition.

definitions? Does he mean for the latter to replace the former, or do they somehow work in tandem?

I devote this chapter and the next to wrestling with these questions. Paul sets out to create definitions with tremendous flexibility and pregnancy of meaning. His primary method of brevity involves taking full advantage of the ambiguities inherent in the component terms of the definitions. The figures of ἔλλειψις, συνεκδοχή and ἀπὸ κοινοῦ facilitate and enhance this maximization of plural meanings. The rhetorical theorists' words of caution against obscurity implicitly acknowledge the utility of deliberate ambiguity when one strives for βραχυλογία. Scholars who research Paul's letters have a tendency to regard certain words as theological technical terms, and they furthermore have a comprehensible desire to ascertain what these terms *mean for Paul*, in distinction to or in continuity with their usages in early Christianity's Second Temple Jewish and Greco-Roman environments. The interminable debates regarding what Paul 'means' by πίστις and πιστεύειν, and by δικαιοσύνη (θεοῦ) and δικαιοῦν, persist in part because Paul consciously exploits their polysemy.[3] He does not furnish for them clear, complete definitions intended to serve as conceptual anchors in his arguments. Even his definitions of the gospel serve no such purpose; he does not offer full ἐξαπλώσεις of all τὰ ἴδια which distinguish the gospel from other members of its class, in order to argue for or against a proposition that somehow depends upon the meaning of τὸ εὐαγγέλιον, as would be proper in philosophical inquiry. Paul achieves whatever completeness he attempts through evocation, through what he does *not* say directly but which he sufficiently implies. An important corollary of all this is that the component terms of his definitions carry their most inclusive meanings. Paul can thereby bring forward specific usages without diminishing others at certain points in his argument. Ultimately it will become clear that the two definitions work together, the former stating the gospel's *essence* and the latter its *function*. They therefore conform to the principle outlined in Plato's *Phaedrus* that a definition should declare οἷόν τ' ἔστι and ἣν ἔχει δύναμιν of the definiendum.

The present chapter deals with the first definition, the statement of οἷόν τ' ἔστι. I first analyze the structure of the prescript of Romans at the levels of syntax and style in order to determine how vv. 2–4 fit within it (4.2). I next turn my attention to vv. 2–3a, the first part of the definition, the relative clause

---

[3] Some scholars have drawn attention to this possibility in connection with their arguments that πίστις Χριστοῦ means "Christ's fidelity," e.g., Johnson, "Romans 3:21–26," 81 ("Paul can use *pistis* and its cognates in more than one sense; and Paul can indicate the same reality by more than one word"). See also Hays, *Faith of Jesus Christ*, xxxiv, 227–28, and cf. Sanders, *Paul and Palestinian Judaism*, 490–95. Downing ("Ambiguity, Ancient Semantics, and Faith") helpfully explains from the sources how Paul's maximization of some of his key words (e.g., πίστις) depends upon ancient ideas of meaning and how language conveys it.

that governs the other two parts (4.3). I then examine vv. 3b–4 (4.4), a project that involves four components. The vast majority of scholarship dedicated to 1:3b–4 accepts and builds upon the premise that Paul is quoting or redacting a christological formula that he has inherited from tradition, and that the Roman Christians may themselves know and use. In my judgment, this hypothesis adequately explains neither 1:3b–4 as we have it in the text nor its similarities with other christological statements which scholars likewise surmise to be pre-Pauline. I thus scrutinize the arguments put forward in favor of this hypothesis toward a firm rejection of it (4.4.1), and then seek to replace it with a better hypothesis, namely that Paul uses a common religious-literary form, the 'mythological expanded epithet,' which has ample precedents in both Greco-Roman and Hellenistic Jewish literature, and which characteristically uses συνεκδοχή to evoke narratives associated with a god (4.4.2). I then identify several other instances of this form in Paul's letters (4.4.3), highlighting its flexibility both in composition and function. Next, I analyze how Paul deploys the form in combination with ἀντίθεσις in order to enfold the entirety of the Son into his first definition of the gospel (4.4.4). The two participial phrases address two axes of the Son's life, the temporal (his ἀρχή and τέλος in what he was born and what he was appointed to be) and the anthropological (his σάρξ and πνεῦμα). My interpretation underscores Paul's sophisticated implementation of strategies of brevity, which calls upon members his audience to supply from their own knowledge what he does not say.

4.2 The structure of the prescript (1:1–7)

Vv. 1–7 of the first chapter of Romans represent the longest and most complex prescript of Paul's letters. The following outline of the prescript serves as the basis for my analysis:[4]

I. Superscription, vv. 1–6.
   A. Self-identification of the sender, Παῦλος, v. 1.
   B. Titles.
      1. δοῦλος Χριστοῦ Ἰησοῦ.
      2. κλητός.
      3. ἀπόστολος.[5]

---

[4] Cf. the outline of Jewett, *Romans*, 99. My analysis resembles his in many respects. The main differences relate to his perception of a confessional formula in vv. 3–4, his description of v. 5 as Paul's statement of "apostolic credentials" (but note ἡμῶν and ἐλάβομεν in vv. 4–5, which seem to include the addressees), and his inclusion of v. 6 in the "address" (which technically begins in v. 7). For a detailed comparison of the prescript of Romans with other Pauline prescripts, see Jervis, *Purpose of Romans*, 69–85.

[5] Items 2 and 3 could belong together as a single item, κλητὸς ἀπόστολος; so Origen, *Comm. Rom.* 1.4 (2); Fitzmyer, *Romans*, 228; Cranfield, *Romans,* 1.51–52; Jewett, *Romans*,

        4. ἀφωρισμένος εἰς εὐαγγέλιον θεοῦ.
    C. Definition of εὐαγγέλιον in three parts, vv. 2–4.
        1. First part, vv. 2–3a, the basic definition.
            a. Pre-proclamation/promise: ὃ προεπηγγείλατο.
            b. Three prepositional qualifiers.
                (1) διὰ τῶν προφητῶν αὐτοῦ.
                (2) ἐν γραφαῖς ἁγίαις.
                (3) περὶ τοῦ υἱοῦ αὐτοῦ.
        2. Second part, v. 3b, the first expansion of περὶ τοῦ υἱοῦ αὐτοῦ, addressing origin and flesh.
            a. Attributive participle: τοῦ γενομένου.
            b. Two prepositional qualifiers.
                (1) ἐκ σπέρματος Δαυὶδ (expressing implied predicate, υἱοῦ Δαυὶδ).
                (2) κατὰ σάρκα.
        3. Third part, v. 4, the second expansion of περὶ τοῦ υἱοῦ αὐτοῦ, addressing end and spirit.
            a. Attributive participle and predicate: τοῦ ὁρισθέντος υἱοῦ θεοῦ.
            b. Three prepositional qualifiers.
                (1) ἐν δυνάμει.
                (2) κατὰ πνεῦμα ἁγιωσύνης.
                (3) ἐξ ἀναστάσεως νεκρῶν.
            c. Apposite proper noun with further epithets: Ἰησοῦ Χριστοῦ τοῦ κυρίου ἡμῶν.
    D. Relative clause supplementing the definition, v. 5–6.
        1. Basic clause: δι' οὗ ἐλάβομεν χάριν καὶ ἀποστολήν.
        2. Three prepositional qualifiers.
            a. εἰς ὑπακοὴν πίστεως.

101; Moo, *Romans*, 40–42; Jervis, *Purpose of Romans*, 72–73. Keck (*Romans*, 40) astutely observes: "In claiming that he is a 'called apostle' he is not saying that he is 'called an apostle' (by others) or that he is 'called to be an apostle' (as translations have it), as if invited to that status; rather, he is saying that 'call' is the means by which he became an apostle. This 'call' is neither an invitation nor a summons but God's sovereign action, God's deliberate choice...." I give κλητός its own entry in the outline in part to emphasize the strength of the idea of 'call' as Keck aptly describes it, although I recognize that the four titles overlap and are mutually supportive, and that κλητὸς ἀπόστολος logically belong together. Cf. the remarks of Eusebius of Emesa (*PKGK* 46): "Now some wonder in vain whether the appellative 'called' is to be added to the preceding [word], in order that it might be 'called slave,' or to the following, as 'called apostle,' although the thought is unbefitting in neither case, inasmuch as all are 'called,' and have been called commonly to this faith and grace, and have been elevated according to election into the apostolic order. Therefore in either case he is 'called' both as 'slave' and as 'apostle.'" διαποροῦσι δέ τινες μάτην, πότερον τῷ ἡγουμένῳ προσθετέον τὸ «κλητὸς» πρόσρημα ἵνα εἴη «δοῦλος, κλητός», ἢ τῷ ἑπομένῳ ὡς «ἀπόστολος κλητός», κατ' οὐδέτερον ἀπᾳδούσης τῆς ἐννοίας, ἅτε δὴ κλητῶν ὄντων ἁπάντων καὶ κοινῶς τῶν εἰς τὴν πίστιν καὶ τὴν χάριν ταύτην κεκλημένων καὶ τῶν κατ' ἐκλογὴν εἰς τὴν ἀποστολικὴν τάξιν ἀνηγμένων. καθ' ἕτερον τοίνυν «κλητὸς» καὶ ὡς «δοῦλος» καὶ ὡς «ἀπόστολος». The position of the adjective seems to be driving both the remarks of Eusebius (n.b., ἀπόστολος κλητός) and the commentators to whom he responds: since κλητός follows δοῦλος, it must belong with it; Eusebius replies that it syntactically and logically belongs both with δοῦλος and ἀπόστολος.

  b. ἐν πᾶσιν τοῖς ἔθνεσιν.
  c. ὑπὲρ τοῦ ὀνόματος αὐτοῦ.
 3. Relative clause expanding 2.c: ἐν οἷς ἐστε καὶ ὑμεῖς κλητοὶ Ἰησοῦ Χριστοῦ.
II. Adscription, v. 7a.
 A. Identification of recipients: πᾶσιν τοῖς οὖσιν ἐν Ῥώμῃ ἀγαπητοῖς θεοῦ.
 B. Honorific adjectives: κλητοῖς ἁγίοις.
III. Greeting, v. 7b: χάρις ὑμῖν καὶ εἰρήνη ἀπὸ θεοῦ πατρὸς ἡμῶν καὶ κυρίου Ἰησοῦ Χριστοῦ.

As is typical, the prescript breaks into three major parts, superscription (I), adscription (II) and greeting (III). The adscription and greeting are fairly standard in length for Paul, but the superscription includes two complex relative clauses elaborating two of his titles, ἀπόστολος and ἀφωρισμένος εἰς εὐαγγέλιον θεοῦ, in reverse sequence. There is also consistency in the way he arranges the clauses. Several begin with a <u>verb</u>, followed by <u>predicates</u> and/or two or three <u>prepositional phrases</u>:

... ὃ <u>προεπηγγείλατο</u> | <u>διὰ τῶν προφητῶν αὐτοῦ</u> | <u>ἐν γραφαῖς ἁγίαις</u> | <u>περὶ τοῦ υἱοῦ αὐτοῦ</u>
τοῦ <u>γενομένου</u> | <u>ἐκ σπέρματος Δαυὶδ</u> | <u>κατὰ σάρκα</u>,
τοῦ <u>ὁρισθέντος</u> υἱοῦ θεοῦ | <u>ἐν δυνάμει</u> | <u>κατὰ πνεῦμα ἁγιωσύνης</u> | <u>ἐξ ἀναστάσεως νεκρῶν</u>,
Ἰησοῦ Χριστοῦ τοῦ κυρίου ἡμῶν,
δι' οὗ <u>ἐλάβομεν</u> <u>χάριν καὶ ἀποστολὴν</u> | <u>εἰς ὑπακοὴν πίστεως</u> | <u>ἐν πᾶσιν τοῖς ἔθνεσιν</u> | <u>ὑπὲρ τοῦ ὀνόματος αὐτοῦ</u>,
ἐν οἷς ἐστε καὶ ὑμεῖς κλητοὶ Ἰησοῦ Χριστοῦ ....

Paul marks the conclusion of each part with an aberration from the pattern, Ἰησοῦ Χριστοῦ τοῦ κυρίου ἡμῶν in v. 4 and ἐν οἷς ἐστε καὶ ὑμεῖς κλητοὶ Ἰησοῦ Χριστοῦ in v. 6. The syntactical uniformity further strengthens the impression that Paul composes the entire prescript, including vv. 3–4.

Paul commonly aims for a grand style in his prescripts, and Rom 1:1–7 is no exception. On each side of his definition, the prescript exhibits μακρολογία: he addresses his readers and describes himself with honorifics,[6] and he generously applies epithets to God in v. 7 and to Jesus in vv. 1, 4 and 6–7 – a lavish use of language that will extend into the thanksgiving section. Paul also takes care in vv. 1–7 to unite himself and the gospel that he proclaims, and extraordinarily concludes his superscript by referring to his readers. He already anticipates this move in v. 5 with ἐλάβομεν, which refers both to himself and his

---

[6] The recognition that Paul is pursuing a grand style helps to explain something that scholars have wrestled with in the past, namely why he does not address his readers collectively as an ἐκκλησία, as he does with other Christian communities (e.g., Klein, "Paul's Purpose"). Does he not regard the Roman Christians as a legitimate church? It seems sufficiently clear that he does. The phrase πᾶσιν τοῖς οὖσιν ἐν Ῥώμῃ ἀγαπητοῖς θεοῦ is a phrase equivalent to ἐκκλησία, which Paul constructs as part of his overall stylistic aim of praising God and his readers (and, indirectly, himself) with such instances of μακρολογία. Note also that he describes his addressees in Philippi with comparable μακρολογία in Phil 1:1: πᾶσιν τοῖς ἁγίοις ἐν Χριστῷ Ἰησοῦ τοῖς οὖσιν ἐν Φιλίπποις σὺν ἐπισκόποις καὶ διακόνοις.

apostolic colleagues on the one hand, and his addressees as partners in proclaiming the gospel "among the Gentiles, among whom you in Rome are the called of Jesus Christ," on the other. He will continue this presentation of partnership in the 'thanksgiving' (1:8–15), and will finally resume it in 15:14–33, where he frames his petitions for assistance.

4.3 The basic definition (1:2–3a)

Paul's first definition of the gospel has three main structural components, the basic definition in vv. 2–3a, and two expansions of περὶ τοῦ υἱοῦ αὐτοῦ in vv. 3b–4.[7] In all three parts he uses his terms' pluralities of meaning and συνεκδοχή as methods of loading the verses with content. He initially defines the gospel as that "which [God] pre-proclaimed [promised] beforehand through his prophets in the holy scriptures regarding his Son" (ὃ προεπηγγείλατο διὰ τῶν προφητῶν αὐτοῦ ἐν γραφαῖς ἁγίαις περὶ τοῦ υἱοῦ αὐτοῦ). Several questions arise from this basic definition. First, προεπαγγέλλεσθαι can mean either "to proclaim ahead of time," or "to promise beforehand."[8] Both meanings are active in the present context, the former because Paul is unfolding the gospel (εὐαγγέλιον) which he proclaims (εὐαγγελίζεσθαι) in continuity with what God himself proclaims (προεπαγγελίζεθαι) through the prophets, and the latter because he characterizes God as someone who follows through with his promises. Second, διὰ τῶν προφητῶν αὐτοῦ and ἐν γραφαῖς ἁγίαις may seem redundant (an instance of the figure πλεονασμός), but they are not. Paul carefully separates the source of the definiendum (God), its human medium of initial delivery (the prophets), and its medium of preservation and universal dissemination (the scriptures). These distinctions become relevant in conjunction

---

[7] Contra Cranfield, *Romans*, 1.57: "It is very much better to place a comma at the end of v. 2 and take vv. 3–4 as an attribute of εὐαγγέλιον than to understand them as a continuation of the relative clause; for this punctuation yields a better balanced sentence and avoids one unbroken string of three relative clauses, the second depending on the first and the third on the second, which connecting vv. 3–4 to v. 2 involves."

[8] For the lexicographical data, see LSJ 1478, s.v.; BDAG 868, s.v. (listing only the meaning "promise before(hand), previously"; Schniewind and Friedrich, "ἐπαγγέλλω ... προεπαγγέλλομαι," *TDNT* 2.586. Commentators commonly assume one meaning without even mentioning the possibility of the other (an exception is Schlier, *Römerbrief*, 22). For "promise beforehand" or something similar, see Dodd, *Romans*, 4; Barrett, *Romans*, 18; Cranfield, *Romans*, 1.55–56; Fitzmyer, *Romans*, 233; Moo, *Romans*, 44; Wilckens, *an die Römer*, 1.63–64; Lohse, *an die Römer*, 63–64; and Käsemann, *Romans*, 9, who adds this insightful observation: "Thus the Scriptures have more than a historical context because as ἐπαγγελία they participate in the εὐαγγέλιον. The dialectical relation between promise and gospel is theologically relevant. For Paul ... ἐπαγγελία is a prototype of the gospel even as the law is its antithesis." For "proclaim beforehand," see Jewett, *Romans*, 103.

with Paul's claim to be κλητὸς ἀπόστολος ἀφωρισμένος εἰς εὐαγγέλιον θεοῦ. He is likening himself to a προφήτης, although with more subtlety than he displays in Gal 1:15–16. What the prophets proclaimed in the past, he proclaims in the present; the message for Israel in their scriptures is what he received a direct commission to carry to the world. He thereby further stresses the unity (if not identity) of himself and the gospel, and the continuity of himself and the prophets. Third, we have here an instance of συνεκδοχή wherein the whole of the scriptures stands in for the parts that pre-proclaim the gospel. Paul does not need to quote or even allude to these scriptures. He can presuppose this knowledge among his readers, so he omits any specific references and proceeds directly to the two events that represent the most important fulfillments: the birth of Jesus as a descendant of David, and his designation as υἱὸς θεοῦ. His selection of the whole for the part effectively declares that *all* of scripture, *all* of the prophets in concert preach the gospel ahead of its full manifestation in Christ. He thus summons to mind particular passages of messianically interpreted oracles, while simultaneously stressing the unitary testimony of scripture.

4.4 The definition extended (1:3b–4)

So far, Paul has defined the gospel as that which God promised and pre-proclaimed concerning his Son. He thus addresses its past (even its pre-existence, so to speak) in the prophetic oracles preserved in the scriptures. With the two attributive participial phrases in vv. 3b–4, the focus turns to the fulfillment actualized in the origin and end, and the flesh and spirit, of the Son. I shall argue that Paul enfolds the entirety of the nature and the story of the Son into his first definition of the gospel. His main tools for achieving this enfolding include (1) a religious-literary form that characteristically uses συνεκδοχή of narratives in conjunction with a divine name ('mythological expanded epithet'), (2) rhetorical ἀντίθεσις, and (3) his audience's ability to infer what he leaves unstated. Rom 1:3b–4 has attracted the interest of scholars primarily because they surmise Paul to be quoting a primitive christological formula which represents less his own perspectives than those of other early Christians.[9] Interpreters have thus expended considerable energy on the sepa-

---

[9] Johannes Weiss (*Das Urchristentum*, 89; ET *Earliest Christianity*, 123) first suggested this in 1917. See also Bultmann, *Theology*, 1.49–50; Dodd, *Apostolic Preaching*, 14; Bornkamm, *Paul*, 248; Hengel, *Son of God*, 59–66; Wedderburn, *Reasons for Romans*, 93–96; Schweizer, "Röm 1,3f."; Linnemann, "Tradition"; Schneider, "Κατὰ Πνεῦμα Ἁγιωσύνης"; Dunn, "Jesus – Flesh and Spirit"; de Jonge, "Jesus, Son of David," esp. 101–3; Strecker, *Theology*, 66–69; Hurtado, *Lord Jesus Christ*, 107, 133; Barrett, *Romans*, 18–21; Dodd, *Romans*, 4–5; Käsemann, *Romans*, 10–13; Fitzmyer, *Romans*, 229–30; Schlier, *Römerbrief*, 23–27; Wilckens, *an die Römer*, 1.56–61; Lohse, *an die Römer*, 63–67; Jewett, "Redaction and Use";

ration of the redactional elements from the 'original' formula, which Paul allegedly adds in order to bring it into closer line with his own christological perspectives. This hypothesis has become so deeply entrenched that I must refute it in some detail prior to setting forth my own arguments in support of the interpretation of vv. 3b–4 which I outline above.

4.4.1 Is Rom 1:3b–4 a pre-Pauline formula?

Robert Jewett has assembled a list of "observations" regarding 1:3b–4, which "have led researchers to the conclusion that Paul is citing traditional material."[10] The list extends to twelve items, covering peculiarities of syntax, style, vocabulary and theology. Taken together, the items appear to make an impressive case.[11] When one scrutinizes each item more carefully, however, the case begins to weaken, and eventually becomes unsustainable. Jewett's list of observations furnishes a convenient architecture, so I shall work through his items sequentially. I do not dispute the cogency of many of his observations *per se*; the verses indeed present many peculiarities that require explanation. Instead, I aim to refute the logical leap that he makes from the observations to the conclusion that vv. 3b–4 are pre-Pauline.

Before assessing these observations, I may point to a couple of preliminary problems for the consensus, first and foremost the description of vv. 3b–4 as 'traditional material.' What does this label mean? 'Traditional material' could, in principle, cover a wide range of phenomena: ideas, ritual actions, oral and written narratives, and corpora of authoritative texts (primarily the Septuagint) along with shared interpretive strategies that facilitate their appropriation. Different standards of evidence apply depending upon what kind of traditional material one is investigating. Traditional ideas, for example, can manifest themselves across the full spectrum of early Christian literature. One may thus confirm their existence, determine their outlines, and trace their evolution with little regard for exact duplication of wording and syntax. Baptism and eucharist are traditions inherited from the earliest Christians. Paul can assume that the former is practiced in the Roman churches, and that his audience would credit his description of it as a ritual of participation in Christ's death and burial (6:1–11). We nonetheless know very little about these rites,

---

and many others. A few scholars have expressed dissent, however: Delling, *Worship*, 80; Polythress, "Is Romans 1³⁻⁴," 180–83; Scott, *Adoption*, 223–44 (his is the most extensive rebuttal to date); Fridrichsen, *Apostle Paul*, 10; and Stowers, *Rereading of Romans*, 216. Cf. Cranfield, *Romans*, 1.57, and Moo, *Romans*, 45–46.

[10] Jewett, "Redaction and Use," 100, and see idem, *Romans*, 97–98 for a slightly revised and updated version.

[11] "It is widely recognized that some of these observations carry more weight than others. Nevertheless the impression made by these details is that Romans 1 contains 'a kind of potted creed,' to use the expression that A. M. Hunter in 1940. Even those commentators who stress the predominance of Pauline language in these lines acknowledge that traditional confessional materials are being used" (Jewett, "Redaction and Use," 102).

how they were actually conducted, because the sources do not support detailed reconstructions. Also, one may correlate Paul's strategies of interpreting scripture with those employed at Qumran, by Philo, and by later Rabbinic sources. These, too, are 'traditional,' and fortunately susceptible to confirmation as such. In his list of observations, Jewett presupposes something more precise than 'traditional material' implies, however, namely a traditional *text* that exists independently of Paul, and that other early Christians know and use in worship or other activities of the community. Such a text would require relatively stable wording in order to qualify as a traditional *formula*, particularly if one intends to peel away the layers of redaction and recover its original wording, as Jewett and many others do.[12] The limitations of the available evidence intrude at this point. How can one reliably surmise that one is looking at such a formula? Do the adduced 'observations' properly carry the weight of criteria? Does the hypothesis of the quotation of a pre-Pauline formula best account for the more cogent of the 'observations,' or can one offer a simpler and less speculative solution?

The possible uses for which early Christians would have composed such formulas presents another tangled set of difficulties. Several form-critical studies have sought to clarify the extent and shape of the 'traditional material' in the New Testament by sorting the apparently formulaic passages into various genres – kerygmatic, confessional, acclamatory, liturgical, and didactic – with their corresponding original *Sitze im Leben*.[13] Naturally some disagreements occur regarding the categories to which individual passages belong, but many scholars wisely avoid pushing their generic classifications too hard, since they recognize that, when one gets down to specific cases, a formula's initial purpose and context would not prevent its appropriation into other contexts from the very moment of its creation. It thus becomes very difficult to pin down which is the primary and which are the subsequent settings.[14] For

---

[12] In addition to Jewett's article and commentary (n. 10), see, e.g., Barrett, *Romans*, 18–21; Bultmann, *Theology*, 1.49; Fitzmyer, *Romans*, 229–30; Strecker, *Theology*, 67–68.

[13] The form-critical studies which I consulted include the following: Cullmann, *Earliest Christian Confessions*, 41; Neufeld, *Earliest Christian Confessions*; Hahn, *Titles of Jesus*, 246–51; Kramer, *Christ*; Wengst, *Christologische Formeln*, 112–17. For discussions of form-critical criteria see Dahl, "Form-Critical Observations," 30–36; Stauffer, *New Testament Theology*, part 3 "The Creeds of the Primitive Church" (233–57), and "Twelve Criteria of Creedal Formulae in the New Testament" (338–39); Barth, "Traditions in Ephesians," 9–10; de Jonge, *Christology*, 25–26; and Richards, *Paul and First-Century Letter Writing*, 97–99.

[14] See, e.g., the cautious remarks of de Jonge (*Christology*, 23–26) and Dahl ("Form-Critical Observations," 30), and esp. Cullmann's discussion (*Earliest Christian Confessions*, 18, and all of ch. 2) regarding the multiple, simultaneous causes of the formation of confessions (baptism and catechumenism, regular worship, exorcism, persecution, and polemic against heretics). Rather strangely, however, Cullmann dismisses the tripartite formulas (i.e., those which have articles for Father, Son and Holy Spirit) from his discussion, since "[t]he trinitarian declarations in the New Testament (especially 2 Cor. 13:13) have rather a liturgical character and are not confessions of faith" (36, n. 1). Actually, 2 Cor 13:13 is a benediction

example, christological statements of Jesus' identity and significance have obvious applications for routine worship, for preaching both to 'insiders' and 'outsiders,' for the rite of baptism,[15] and for the instruction of new believers. Such a formula might have emerged in connection with any one of these contexts, but would be useful in all of them.[16] It thus seems questionable to force particular texts into rigid generic and situational categories which are still in the process of emerging at this early period.[17]

(cf. 1 Thess 5:28; Phil 4:23; Gal 6:18; 1 Cor 16:23–24; Rom 15:33, 16:20) which could have had a confessional foundation or an eventual utility for the creation of new confessions, according to the principles outlined by Cullman in ch. 2. Cf. Neufeld's multiple origins for κύριος Ἰησοῦς (*Earliest Christian Confessions*, 60–67).

[15] The confession of the eunuch in Acts 8:37 (attested in a 'Western' variant), πιστεύω τὸν υἱὸν τοῦ θεοῦ τὸν Ἰησοῦν Χριστόν, would be a plausible instance of a confessional formula in a baptismal context. Metzger notes that, even though the first MS in which it appears dates to the sixth century (E), it apparently dates as far back as the second century, "for Irenaeus quotes part of it (*Against Heresies*, III.xiii.8)" (*Textual Commentary*, 315). See also Cullman, *Earliest Christian Confessions*, 19–20, and cf. the recent contribution by Hellholm on baptismal formulas, "Impact of the Situational Contexts."

[16] Another prominent form-critical strategy that appears in connection with pre-Pauline traditions joins particular messianic titles, christologies and confessions with the outlooks of the various factions within early Christianity, e.g., Bousset's *Kyrios Christos*, wherein he connects υἱὸς τοῦ ἀνθρώπου and Jewish notions of Messiah with the "Palestinian Christian community," and κύριος (as "lord of the community") and the title Χριστός (as a virtual proper name) with the "Gentile Christian community."

[17] Polythress ("Is Romans 1[3–4]," 182) makes a similar point: "Does not this view [that Rom 1:3–4 is a fixed confession] push back into apostolic times a rigidity of formulation characteristic only of the second and later centuries? New Testament 'creeds' show tantalizing similarities to one another but seldom verbal identity – just what one would expect in a situation of fluidity." The places where Paul unambiguously refers to previous traditions will further illustrate some of the difficulties inherent in the attempt to recover pre-Pauline traditions and their original *Sitze im Leben*. Many scholars suppose much of the wording of the παράδοσις in 1 Cor 11:23–26 to have come from the liturgy of the Lord's banquet: Paul is speaking back to the Corinthians words which they say on a regular basis (see, e.g., Jeremias, *Eucharistic Words*, 101–5, and ch. 3, 106–37, "The Influence of Worship on the Transmission of the Eucharistic Texts"; Conzelmann, *1 Corinthians*, 196–202; Bornkamm, "Lord's Supper and Church in Paul," 123–60). The only words which Paul claims come from someone else, however, are those which he attributes to Jesus, opening up other possibilities. The text as we have it could be Paul's own condensation of a longer narrative, perhaps a precursor of the Synoptic passion accounts. His passing references to parts of the story which he does not elaborate, for example the events surrounding Jesus' betrayal in 11:23, point in that direction. A condensed, formulaic version of this part of a passion account would certainly fit very well with a ritual reenactment of Jesus' last supper. But it seems no less probable that the narrative, even if it had not yet become part of a written text, was part of the basic oral instruction transmitted by Paul to the Corinthians at their initial conversion. It could just as plausibly have functioned within Paul's evangelistic proclamation of what Jesus did and how he did it. None of these options cancels out the others. A similar set of possibilities arises in connection with 1 Cor 15:3–8, a thumbnail sketch of what Paul calls τὸ εὐαγγέλιον ὃ εὐηγγελισάμην ὑμῖν (on the pre-Pauline character of this passage, see Conzelmann, *1 Corinthians*, 248–60; Strecker, *Theology*, 74–78). This passage contains within it a narrative or, more pre-

4.4 The definition extended (1:3b–4) 95

These preliminary points bear directly upon the first four of Jewett's 'observations,' which deal with syntax and style: (1) the participial phrases introduced by τοῦ γενομένου and τοῦ ὁρισθέντος "are typical for confessional materials elsewhere in the New Testament"; (2) "the position of the participles at the beginning of the subordinate clauses has been taken as an indication of the citation of traditional material"; (3) the extensive parallelism "has indicated to a wide range of researchers the presence of careful, solemn composition typical for liturgical use"; (4) "the lack of articles with many of the nouns has been suggested as a feature of traditional material."[18] In many respects, these observations are indisputable. The participles indeed stand first in their phrases, which have carefully arranged parallel elements. Rom 1:2–4 has

---

cisely, a narrative summary: Christ died, he was buried, he was raised, and he appeared to a variety of people – with the majority of Paul's attention going to the appearances. This formulaic summary of the gospel could have originated, as some argue, in early Christian proclamation (so, e.g., Dodd, *Apostolic Preaching*, 10–11; Kramer, *Christ*, 63–67). Paul's remark in v. 11 about "what we preach" and "what you believed" supports this argument. But it could also have had an apologetic origin, in view of the list of witnesses which early Christians may have crafted in response to skepticism about the resurrection. A liturgical or didactic *Sitz im Leben* could likewise account for the formation of these verses. Or maybe Paul is condensing one part of a longer narrative, perhaps the same one to which he refers in 1 Corinthians 11. He seems to presume an awareness of a more complete account into which he weaves his own experience of the risen Christ. The fact that he relates these passages to παραδόσεις does not automatically signal that he cites particular formulas word-for-word; he might be setting forth his own summaries to highlight the traditional elements which best serve his immediate objectives.

[18] "Redaction and Use," 100–1. Cf. the criteria for 'hymnic' material supplied by Martin (*Carmen Christi*, 12–13): "a certain rhythmical lilt ascertainable when the passage is read aloud, a correspondence between words and phrases which are placed in the sentences in an obviously carefully selected position, not always *ad sensum*; the use of *parallelismus membrorum*...; and traces of rudimentary meter and the employment of rhetorical devices such as *homoioteleuton*, alliteration and *chiasmus*." He later adds a few more (18–19): "the presence of introductory formulas (as in Eph. v. 14; I Tim. iii. 16); the use of rhythmical style and unusual vocabulary...; the presence of theological concepts (especially Christological doctrines) which are expressed in language which is exalted and liturgical; and the setting of certain passages in a cultic *milieu*...." For Jewett's item 1, cf. Stauffer's eleventh criterion, "Creedal formulae often favor participles and relative clauses" (*New Testament Theology*, 339), and Barth's fourth criterion, "Frequent third person singular aorists, esp. participles; relative, final and/or consecutive clauses; infinitives and other descriptions of purpose or result" ("Traditions," 10). For Jewett's items 3 and 4, cf. Stauffer's sixth and seventh criteria: "Creedal formulae often strike us by their simple and clear syntax. They avoid particles, conjunctions and complicated constructions, and prefer parataxis to hypotaxis. Their thought proceeds by thesis rather than by argument...." And: "Creedal formulae often stand out by reason of their monumental stylistic construction. They favor an antithetic or anaphoral style..." (*New Testament Theology*, 339). Cf. also Barth: "Divisibility of the textual unit into lines of almost identical syllable numbers, beats, and length; correspondence of the substance of cola-pairs, equally the traditional Semitic syn- or antithetical, specifying climactic *parallelismus membrorum*"; and, "Brevity achieved by the use of anarthrous abstract nouns – sometimes coupled with repetitions and pleonasms in the form of synonyms or genitive apposition" ("Traditions," 10).

eleven anarthrous nouns; the omission of articles contributes to economical diction.[19] And yet, Jewett's first four items jump from observation to conclusion without sufficient justification. How does one determine what is *typical for confessional materials* or *typical for liturgical use*, given how little we know for certain about early Christian worship? How does one obtain a reliable body of comparative data? Paul does not clearly mark as 'confession' or 'hymn' any of passages commonly cited as comparanda, such that they comprise firm evidence of the use and position of attributive participles, or of antithesis, or of omission of articles, in texts composed for such purposes. Only multiple attestation can confirm that a formula exists independently of Paul, permitting in turn a general supposition of its potential ritual function. For example, we are able to speak with relative certainty in the case of several short formulas, namely κύριος Ἰησοῦς,[20] εἷς θεός,[21] and αββα ὁ πατήρ.[22] While it may

---

[19] The instances are ἐν γραφαῖς ἁγίαις, ἐκ σπέρματος Δαυίδ (two articles omitted); κατὰ σάρκα; υἱοῦ θεοῦ (one omission; υἱοῦ is in the predicate position); ἐν δυνάμει; κατὰ πνεῦμα ἁγιωσύνης (two); and ἐξ ἀναστάσεως νεκρῶν (two). The omissions here do not present substantial deviations from acceptable grammar. Many reasons exist for a noun to be anarthrous where one might expect it to have the article; Smyth lists several, including "when a word is sufficiently definite by itself," and "very often ... in phrases containing a preposition." Especially importantly Smyth observes: "The generic article is frequently omitted, especially with abstracts ..., without appreciable difference in meaning. Its presence or absence is often determined by the need of distinguishing subject from predicate ..., by the rhythm of the sentence, etc." (288–89, §§ 1126–30). In Rom 1:3–4, we have five prepositonal phrases, three abstract nouns (δύναμις, ἁγιωσύνη, ἀνάστασις), and at least one term which seems sufficiently definite (υἱὸς θεοῦ) even if it were not a predicate.

[20] See 1 Cor 12:3, διὸ γνωρίζω ὑμῖν ὅτι οὐδεὶς ἐν πνεύματι θεοῦ λαλῶν λέγει, ἀνάθεμα Ἰησοῦς, καὶ οὐδεὶς δύναται εἰπεῖν, κύριος Ἰησοῦς, εἰ μὴ ἐν πνεύματι ἁγίῳ; Rom 10:9–10, ὅτι ἐὰν ὁμολογήσῃς ἐν τῷ στόματί σου κύριον Ἰησοῦν καὶ πιστεύσῃς ἐν τῇ καρδίᾳ σου ὅτι ὁ θεὸς αὐτὸν ἤγειρεν ἐκ νεκρῶν, σωθήσῃ· καρδίᾳ γὰρ πιστεύεται εἰς δικαιοσύνην, στόματι δὲ ὁμολογεῖται εἰς σωτηρίαν. On this formula as a possible rejoinder to κύριος Καῖσαρ, see Bousset, *Kyrios Christos*, 138–41; Cullmann, *Earliest Christian Confessions*, 27–30; Neufeld, *Earliest Christian Confessions*, 42–44; Kramer, *Christ*, 65–107.

[21] The "God is one" or "one God" motif appears in a variety of contexts, and in combination with other singularities, e.g., Gal 3:20, ὁ δὲ μεσίτης ἑνὸς οὐκ ἔστιν, ὁ δὲ θεὸς εἷς ἐστιν; Eph 4:4–6, ἓν σῶμα καὶ ἓν πνεῦμα, καθὼς καὶ ἐκλήθητε ἐν μιᾷ ἐλπίδι τῆς κλήσεως ὑμῶν· εἷς κύριος, μία πίστις, ἓν βάπτισμα, εἷς θεὸς καὶ πατὴρ πάντων, ὁ ἐπὶ πάντων καὶ διὰ πάντων καὶ ἐν πᾶσιν; 1 Tim 2:5–6, εἷς γὰρ θεός, εἷς καὶ μεσίτης θεοῦ καὶ ἀνθρώπων, ἄνθρωπος Χριστὸς Ἰησοῦς, ὁ δοὺς ἑαυτὸν ἀντίλυτρον ὑπὲρ πάντων, τὸ μαρτύριον καιροῖς ἰδίοις. Cf. 1 Cor 8:6. See also Neufeld, *Earliest Christian Confessions*, 44–45; Versnel, *Inconsistencies in Greek and Roman Religion*, vol. 1, *Ter Unus: Isis, Dionysos, Hermes: Three Studies in Henotheism*; Guerra, *Romans and the Apologetic Tradition*, 74–101, with special emphasis on the formula's application in Jewish apologetics.

[22] See Rom 8:15–16, οὐ γὰρ ἐλάβετε πνεῦμα δουλείας πάλιν εἰς φόβον ἀλλὰ ἐλάβετε πνεῦμα υἱοθεσίας ἐν ᾧ κράζομεν, αββα ὁ πατήρ. αὐτὸ τὸ πνεῦμα συμμαρτυρεῖ τῷ πνεύματι ἡμῶν ὅτι ἐσμὲν τέκνα θεοῦ; Gal 4:6, ὅτι δέ ἐστε υἱοί, ἐξαπέστειλεν ὁ θεὸς τὸ πνεῦμα τοῦ υἱοῦ αὐτοῦ εἰς τὰς καρδίας ἡμῶν κρᾶζον, αββα ὁ πατήρ.

seem reasonable that a brief slogan like κύριος Ἰησοῦς would eventually develop into longer, more descriptive formulas that exhibit certain commonalities of content and form, the comparanda exhibit small yet meaningful variations that complicate recovery of the original wording, for example:

Rom 4:24–25, ... τοῖς πιστεύουσιν ἐπὶ τὸν ἐγείραντα Ἰησοῦν τὸν κύριον ἡμῶν ἐκ νεκρῶν, ὃς παρεδόθη διὰ τὰ παραπτώματα ἡμῶν καὶ ἠγέρθη διὰ τὴν δικαίωσιν ἡμῶν.[23]

Rom 8:11, εἰ δὲ τὸ πνεῦμα τοῦ ἐγείραντος τὸν Ἰησοῦν ἐκ νεκρῶν οἰκεῖ ἐν ὑμῖν, ὁ ἐγείρας Χριστὸν ἐκ νεκρῶν ζῳοποιήσει καὶ τὰ θνητὰ σώματα ὑμῶν διὰ τοῦ ἐνοικοῦντος αὐτοῦ πνεύματος ἐν ὑμῖν.

Gal 1:1, Παῦλος ἀπόστολος οὐκ ἀπ᾽ ἀνθρώπων οὐδὲ δι᾽ ἀνθρώπου ἀλλὰ διὰ Ἰησοῦ Χριστοῦ καὶ θεοῦ πατρὸς τοῦ ἐγείραντος αὐτὸν ἐκ νεκρῶν ....[24]

1 Thess 1:10, ... καὶ ἀναμένειν τὸν υἱὸν αὐτοῦ ἐκ τῶν οὐρανῶν, ὃν ἤγειρεν ἐκ [τῶν] νεκρῶν, Ἰησοῦν τὸν ῥυόμενον ἡμᾶς ἐκ τῆς ὀργῆς τῆς ἐρχομένης.[25]

These statements have God as their subject, and a general similarity both in sequence and vocabulary. At the same time, fluctuations occur in small details, in the presence or absence of definite articles, and in the phrasing of the second element of the sequence, Jesus' name and titles. Such fluctuations are not at all insignificant for a creed or a hymn, wherein rhythm and uniform diction aid memorization and communal recitation. The further expansions with relative clauses or attributive participial phrases in Rom 4:24–25, 8:11 and 1 Thess 1:10 pull the basic statement in distinct directions according Paul's objectives, rendering each instance contextually unique. The similarities and the differences promote the idea not that these four passages have a confessional fragment as their foundation, but that they reflect Paul's own linguistic habits in combination with a religious-literary form. However, evidence of the utilization of a *form* does not inevitably mean that a text is a traditional *formula*, a point to which I will return below. A deeper problem lies in the circular nature of the argument, the verification of one hypothesis with another. How does one know that passage *x* is a pre-Pauline formula? Because passages *y* and *z* are, and *x* looks like them. But how does one know that *y* is a formula? Because *x* and *z* are, and *y* looks like them; and so forth.

---

[23] Parts or all of vv. 24–25 are pre-Pauline according to Käsemann, *Romans*, 128–29; Fitzmyer, *Romans*, 389–90; Moo, *Romans* 288; Barrett (*Romans*, 100; the διά-phrases are "an attempt at rhetorical antithesis in a creedal formula"). Jewett (*Romans* 342–43) regards the verses as Paul's composition.

[24] This passage is pre-Pauline according to Betz, *Galatians*, 39, 41–42; Martyn, *Galatians*, 84–85, 88–90, 95–97. A more developed version of this "handing over" and its purposes/results appears in Rom 3:24–26, another pre-Pauline formula according to the analysis of some interpreters (e.g., Fitzmyer, *Romans*, 342–43, 347–54; Käsemann, *Romans*, 95–101).

[25] See Kramer, *Christ*, 123–25. Cf. Malherbe, *Letters to the Thessalonians*, 121: "The designation of Jesus as God's Son and that he would come from the heavens suggests to some scholars that we here have to do with a pre-Pauline formulation.... But this theory remains speculative and is not particularly helpful."

98 Chapter 4: The First Definition of the Gospel (1:2–4)

In order to for Jewett's first two items to have evidentiary merit, it is also necessary to show how the presence and position of the participles in Rom 1:3b–4 and other pre-Pauline formulas represent a significant departure from Paul's normal prose style.[26] Participles are indeed a common, although not universal, feature of the other supposed formulas. In Rom 1:3b–4, they stand in the attributive position: περὶ τοῦ υἱοῦ αὐτοῦ τοῦ γενομένου ... τοῦ ὁρισθέντος. Similar constructions occur, for example, in 1 Thess 1:9 (Ἰησοῦν τὸν ῥυόμενον ἡμᾶς ἐκ τῆς ὀργῆς τῆς ἐρχόμενος), Gal 1:3–4 (ἀπὸ ... Ἰησοῦ Χριστοῦ τοῦ δόντος ἑαυτὸν ὑπὲρ τῶν ἁμαρτιῶν), and Rom 8:34 (Χριστὸς [Ἰησοῦς] ὁ ἀποθανών, μᾶλλον δὲ ἐγερθείς). If the participles in these and other passages are to confirm that Rom 1:3b–4 are pre-Pauline, they must contrast with Paul's diction in such a way that they stand out from the contexts in which they appear. One such participle followed by a prepositional phrase appears right before Rom 1:3–4, ἀφωρισμένος εἰς εὐαγγέλιον θεοῦ in verse 1. I have already pointed out above the consistencies in the organization of the clauses in the prescript of Romans. Paul's prescript and 'thanksgiving' sections otherwise commonly feature attributive participles alongside adjectives, relative clauses, and apposite nouns, as, for example, in 1 Cor 1:1–9 (1:2, τῇ ἐκκλησίᾳ τοῦ θεοῦ τῇ οὔσῃ ἐν Κορίνθῳ, ἡγιασμένοις ἐν Χριστῷ Ἰησοῦ, κλητοῖς ἁγίοις, σὺν πᾶσιν τοῖς ἐπικαλουμένοις τὸ ὄνομα τοῦ κυρίου ἡμῶν Ἰησοῦ Χριστοῦ ἐν παντὶ τόπῳ, and 4, ἐπὶ τῇ χάριτι τοῦ θεοῦ τῇ δοθείσῃ ὑμῖν ἐν Χριστῷ Ἰησοῦ). The prescripts of Romans and 1 Corinthians are hardly unique in their use of such attributive participles;[27] and similar constructions appear in other contexts as well.[28] When Paul

---

[26] Cf. Polythress, "Is Roman 1³⁻⁴," 180: "Though the participles and parallelism of vv. 3–4 suggest formulaic origin, they do not demonstrate it. ... The participial construction is simply the most natural way for things to be expressed in the syntactic context of Ro 1²."

[27] The prescript and 'thanksgiving' of 2 Corinthians offer several instances: 1:1, τῇ ἐκκλησίᾳ τοῦ θεοῦ τῇ οὔσῃ ἐν Κορίνθῳ σὺν τοῖς ἁγίοις πᾶσιν τοῖς οὖσιν ἐν ὅλῃ τῇ Ἀχαΐᾳ; 1:3–4, εὐλογητὸς ὁ θεὸς καὶ πατὴρ τοῦ κυρίου ἡμῶν Ἰησοῦ Χριστοῦ, ὁ πατὴρ τῶν οἰκτιρμῶν καὶ θεὸς πάσης παρακλήσεως, ὁ παρακαλῶν ἡμᾶς ἐπὶ πάσῃ τῇ θλίψει ἡμῶν; 1:8, ὑπὲρ τῆς θλίψεως ἡμῶν τῆς γενομένης ἐν τῇ Ἀσίᾳ; 1:9, ἵνα μὴ πεποιθότες ὦμεν ἐφ' ἑαυτοῖς ἀλλ' ἐπὶ τῷ θεῷ τῷ ἐγείροντι τοὺς νεκρούς. See also Phil 1:2, πᾶσιν τοῖς ἁγίοις ἐν Χριστῷ Ἰησοῦ τοῖς οὖσιν ἐν Φιλίπποις σὺν ἐπισκόποις καὶ διακόνοις; Rom 1:7, πᾶσιν τοῖς οὖσιν ἐν Ῥώμῃ ἀγαπητοῖς θεοῦ; and 1 Thess 1:4, ἀδελφοὶ ἠγαπημένοι ὑπὸ [τοῦ] θεοῦ.

[28] E.g., 1 Thess 2:12, τοῦ θεοῦ τοῦ καλοῦντος ὑμᾶς εἰς τὴν ἑαυτοῦ βασιλείαν καὶ δόξαν; 2:14, τῶν ἐκκλησιῶν τοῦ θεοῦ τῶν οὐσῶν ἐν τῇ Ἰουδαίᾳ ἐν Χριστῷ Ἰησοῦ; 4:5, τὰ ἔθνη τὰ μὴ εἰδότα τὸν θεόν; 4:8, τὸν θεὸν τὸν [καὶ] διδόντα τὸ πνεῦμα αὐτοῦ τὸ ἅγιον εἰς ὑμᾶς; 4:13, οἱ λοιποὶ οἱ μὴ ἔχοντες ἐλπίδα; Gal 3:17, διαθήκην προκεκυρωμένην ὑπὸ τοῦ θεοῦ; Phil 4:7, ἡ εἰρήνη τοῦ θεοῦ ἡ ὑπερέχουσα πάντα νοῦν; Rom 2:3, ὦ ἄνθρωπε ὁ κρίνων τοὺς τὰ τοιαῦτα πράσσοντας καὶ ποιῶν αὐτά; 3:5, ὁ θεὸς ὁ ἐπιφέρων τὴν ὀργήν; 3:21, νυνὶ δὲ χωρὶς νόμου δικαιοσύνη θεοῦ πεφανέρωται μαρτυρουμένη ὑπὸ τοῦ νόμου καὶ τῶν προφητῶν; 4:17, θεοῦ τοῦ ζῳοποιοῦντος τοὺς νεκροὺς καὶ καλοῦντος τὰ μὴ ὄντα ὡς ὄντα. There are also some examples with the objects, prepositional phrases and other modifiers in various places, e.g., 1 Cor 2:6, τῶν ἀρχόν-

narrates his past relationship with the "pillars" in Gal 1:10–2:14, attributive participles appear several times, in 1:11 regarding the gospel (τὸ εὐαγγέλιον τὸ εὐαγγελισθὲν ὑπ' ἐμοῦ), in 1:15 regarding God (ὁ θεὸς ὁ ἀφορίσας με ἐκ κοιλίας μητρός μου καὶ καλέσας διὰ τῆς χάριτος αὐτοῦ), and in 2:9 regarding grace (καὶ γνόντες τὴν χάριν τὴν δοθεῖσάν μοι).[29] We also have adjectival participles functioning as substantives in this section, in 1:23 regarding Paul (ὁ διώκων ἡμᾶς ποτε), in 2:6 regarding the "pillars" (οἱ δοκοῦντες), and in 2:8 regarding God (ὁ ἐνεργήσας). Some of these examples also show the weakness of Jewett's second item, since the objects, prepositional phrases, and adverbs in 1:11, 1:15, and 1:23 *follow* the participles. A construction which is so characteristic of Paul's prose, especially in contexts parallel to Rom 1:1–7, cannot be singled out as proof that he cites a traditional formula in vv. 3b–4. A different kind of hypothesis is needed, one that accounts for the similarities and differences in the participial phrases and relative clauses of the alleged formulas on the one hand, and their general consistency with Paul's prose style on the other.

The next group of observations listed by Jewett relates to peculiarities of vocabulary: (5) "the presence of non-Pauline terms like ὁρισθέντος and πνεῦμα ἁγιωσύνης lends itself to a theory of citation"; (6) "the expression ἐξ ἀναστάσεως νεκρῶν is used elsewhere in the Pauline letters to refer to the resurrection of the dead in a general sense in contrast to the use here in reference to Christ's resurrection"; and (7) "the terms σάρξ and πνεῦμα are used in an uncharacteristic way as compared with Pauline letters where they have an anthropological focus and a more clearly antithetical intent."[30] The criterion of "non-Pauline" vocabulary seems like an excellent tool for discerning both traditional material and interpolations, although it does have some limits. Paul obviously does not exhaust his entire vocabulary in his extant letters, so one should exercise restraint in asserting that he *cannot*, or *would not*, utilize certain words in certain ways. Ἀφορίζειν occurs in v. 1 as well as in Gal 1:15 and 2:12; if he knows the compound form, it seems reasonable that he could use

---

των τοῦ αἰῶνος τούτου τῶν καταργου-μένων; 2 Cor 1:19, ὁ τοῦ θεοῦ γὰρ υἱὸς Ἰησοῦς Χριστὸς ὁ ἐν ὑμῖν δι' ἡμῶν κηρυχθείς; Rom 1:18, ἀνθρώπων τῶν τὴν ἀλήθειαν ἐν ἀδικίᾳ κατεχόντων.

[29] See also 1 Cor 3:10, κατὰ τὴν χάριν τοῦ θεοῦ τὴν δοθεῖσάν μου; 15:10, ἡ χάρις αὐτοῦ ἡ εἰς ἐμέ, ἡ χάρις τοῦ θεοῦ [ἡ] σὺν ἐμοί.

[30] "Redaction and Use," 101. Cf. Stauffer's fourth criterion: "The creedal formula often exhibits a different linguistic usage, terminology or style from its context…" (*New Testament Theology*, 339). See also Käsemann, *Commentary*, 10–11, in response to those who would strike the elements of σάρξ and πνεῦμα from the original formula: "The antithesis in v. 4 makes good sense. That this contrast of flesh and spirit cannot be ascribed to Paul alone can be seen, for example, from John 6:63. Furthermore, it is not formulated in a specifically Pauline way here. Finally, its orientation is christological rather than (as in Paul) anthropological. In good OT and Jewish fashion σάρξ refers here to the weak and corruptible flesh, not the flesh entangled in sin as in 8:3" (11).

the simple form. Ἁγιωσύνη appears in 1 Thess 3:13,[31] and numerous cognates occur in many other passages, including twice in the immediate context of Rom 1:3b–4. Also, πνεῦμα ἁγιωσύνης may at first glance look like an unusual locution for πνεῦμα ἅγιον. Paul elsewhere adds genitive forms of other abstract nouns to πνεῦμα, however, as in Rom 8:2 (ὁ νόμος τοῦ πνεύματος τῆς ζωῆς ἐν Χριστῷ Ἰησοῦ), 8:15 (οὐ γὰρ ἐλάβετε πνεῦμα δουλείας ... ἀλλὰ ἐλάβετε πνεῦμα υἱοθεσίας), and 1 Cor 4:21 (ἐν ἀγάπῃ πνεύματί τε πραΰτητος). The first two instances could refer to the Holy Spirit, but the third clearly does not. As for ἐξ ἀναστάσεως νεκρῶν, it does not need to refer *only* to the general resurrection of the dead based upon the other contexts in which the phrase appears.[32] Finally, σάρξ appears in connection with Christ's physical descent in Rom 9:5 (ὧν οἱ πατέρες καὶ ἐξ ὧν ὁ Χριστὸς τὸ κατὰ σάρκα), and its coordination in 1:3–4 with πνεῦμα does not inevitably force it to carry a strongly negative tone.[33] The case from vocabulary thus does not prove as persuasive as it may initially appear.

---

[31] Note the proximity of ἁγιωσύνη and ἅγιοι in 1 Thess 3:13, εἰς τὸ στηρίξαι ὑμῶν τὰς καρδίας ἀμέμπτους ἐν ἁγιωσύνῃ ἔμπροσθεν τοῦ θεοῦ καὶ πατρὸς ἡμῶν ἐν τῇ παρουσίᾳ τοῦ κυρίου ἡμῶν Ἰησοῦ μετὰ πάντων τῶν ἁγίων αὐτοῦ, [ἀμήν], and cf. ἁγιασμός in 4:3–4, 7.

[32] In 1 Cor 15:12–19, the prepositional phrase ἐκ νεκρῶν in connection with a form of ἐγείρειν parallels the expression ἀνάστασις νεκρῶν, as shown by vv. 12–13 where Paul discusses the possibility of resurrection, covering *both* the general expectation of Christians *and* the specific event of Christ's resurrection. The conditional clauses broadly equate ἐγείρεσθαι ἐκ νεκρῶν with ἀνάστασις νεκρῶν. Paul never uses ἡ Χριστοῦ ἀνάστασις ἡ ἐκ νεκρῶν or something similar, but in 1 Corinthians 15 this fact probably results from his desire to hammer home by the repetition of finite verbs that *Christ has indeed been raised*, and *if he has not been raised*, the Corinthians' faith has no point whatsoever. Furthermore we do not have in this passage or elsewhere in Paul's letters a nominal form of the verb ἐγείρειν. He also generally prefers ἐγείρειν to ἀνιστάναι, which he uses to refer to resurrection only twice (1 Thess 4:14, 16). The noun ἀνάστασις and the verb ἐγείρειν are thus typical for him while ἔγερσις and ἀνιστάναι are not, so a phrase like ἐξ ἀναστάσεως νεκρῶν where Christ's resurrection is in view coheres with Paul's customary usage.

[33] When Paul pits σάρξ and πνεῦμα against one another in the context of discussions of ethics and anthropology, "flesh" can convey a strongly negative connotation and "spirit" a strongly positive one (e.g., Rom 7:5–6, 8:3–4). But σάρξ by itself can carry a more neutral note in connection with physical relationship, as in Paul's reference in Rom 9:3 to οἱ ἀδελφοί μου οἱ συγγενεῖς μου κατὰ σάρκα or in 11:14 where he talks of "provoking my flesh to jealousy," παραζηλοῦν μου τὴν σάρκα – a passage wherein Paul goes on to extol the merits of the Israelites. The assertion that the contrast of flesh (in a neutral sense) and spirit in Rom 1:3b–4 is an impossible or even unlikely usage for Paul (as Dunn argues in his essay "Jesus – Flesh and Spirit") thus deserves skepticism. Vv. 3b–4 are furthermore not dealing with ethical matters, nor with the condition of ordinary humanity. They instead summarize christological ideas as they pertain to the humanity of Christ. Cf. also Rom 4:1 (τί οὖν ἐροῦμεν εὑρηκέναι Ἀβραὰμ τὸν προπάτορα ἡμῶν κατὰ σάρκα;); 15:27 (εἰ γὰρ τοῖς πνευματικοῖς αὐτῶν ἐκοινώνησαν τὰ ἔθνη, ὀφείλουσιν καὶ ἐν τοῖς σαρκικοῖς λειτουργῆσαι αὐτοῖς); 1 Cor 15:39 (οὐ πᾶσα σὰρξ ἡ αὐτὴ σάρξ ἀλλὰ ἄλλη μὲν ἀνθρώπων, ἄλλη δὲ σὰρξ κτηνῶν, ἄλλη δὲ σὰρξ πτηνῶν, ἄλλη

The next set of Jewett's observations deal with disjunctions between vv. 3b–4 and Pauline theology in general: (8) "disparities with Pauline theology as visible elsewhere in the letters are quite striking," in particular the reference to Jesus' Davidic heritage and tension with passages like 2 Cor 5:16; (9) "the lack of a reference to the cross or to Jesus' death seems very distant from Paul's usual emphasis, summarized in 1 Cor 2:2"; and (10) "the unmistakably adoptionist tone of this confession is entirely lacking in other [c]hristological utterances of Paul, who typically stresses pre-existence."[34] I may quickly dispense with point 9. Σταυρός and σταυροῦν not only fail to appear in vv. 3–4, they appear nowhere in Romans, and ἐξ ἀναστάσεως νεκρῶν concisely and sufficiently implies Jesus' death and burial, since they are logically prior events. While I agree that the mention of Jesus' Davidic heritage seems "non-Pauline,"[35] I would call attention to the way the text phrases this point, ἐκ σπέρματος Δαυίδ. Paul sometimes expresses physical descent in precisely this manner, ordinarily in connection with Abraham, as in Rom 11:1 (καὶ γὰρ ἐγὼ Ἰσραηλίτης εἰμί, ἐκ σπέρματος Ἀβραάμ), or 2 Cor 11:2 (σπέρμα Ἀβραάμ εἰσιν; κἀγώ). On the basis of τοῦ ὁρισθέντος υἱοῦ θεοῦ, one would expect not "born from the seed of David" but the "born the *son* of David." Other early Christian authors freely call Jesus the son of David,[36] and it is hard to imagine why an early christological formula – especially if it is confessional – would prefer

---

δὲ ἰχθύων); and Phil 1:21–22 (ἐμοὶ γὰρ τὸ ζῆν Χριστὸς καὶ τὸ ἀποθανεῖν κέρδος. εἰ δὲ τὸ ζῆν ἐν σαρκί, τοῦτό μοι καρπὸς ἔργου, καὶ τί αἱρήσομαι οὐ γνωρίζω).

[34] "Redaction and Use," 101–2.

[35] Polythress ("Is Romans 1[3–4]," 181) refers to Paul's citation of Isa 11:10 in Rom 15:12, καὶ πάλιν Ἡσαΐας λέγει, «ἔσται ἡ ῥίζα τοῦ Ἰεσσαὶ καὶ ὁ ἀνιστάμενος ἄρχειν ἐθνῶν, ἐπ' αὐτῷ ἔθνη ἐλπιοῦσιν». Scott (*Adoption*, 233) adds Gal 3:16 on the basis of its putative connection with 2 Sam 7:12. See also Whitsett's essay "Son of God" for elaboration of what he believes to be the scriptural foundation of Rom 1:3 in Paul's theology, i.e., a "conflation" of Isa 11:10 and 2 Sam 7:12–14. Although these passages probably lie somewhere behind the notion of a Davidic Messiah, and although the parallels between 2 Sam 7:12–14 and Rom 1:3b–4 may initially seem impressive (καὶ ἀναστήσω τὸ σπέρμα σου μετὰ σέ ... ἐγὼ ἔσομαι αὐτῷ εἰς πατέρα, καὶ αὐτὸς ἔσται μοι εἰς υἱόν), one should approach Whitsett's claims with caution, since Paul offers in Rom 1:2–4 an *assertion* of Jesus' Davidic lineage and an *assumption* of its significance without articulating the latter's scriptural basis. Paul cites Isa 11:10 in Rom 15:12 (in a series addressing τὰ ἔθνη), but gives no explicit hook (e.g., καθὼς γέγραπται) to 2 Sam 7:12–14. The specific texts *for Paul* that form the foundation of his assertion in Rom 1:3b thus remain an area of (more-or-less informed) speculation.

[36] E.g., Matt 1:1; Mark 12:35–37 (note the critical tone, however) *par.* Matt 22:41–46, Luke 20:41–44; Luke 1:32. The phrase ἐκ σπέρματος Δαυίδ shows up in other christological statements, e.g., 2 Tim 2:8, μνημόνευε Ἰησοῦν Χριστὸν ἐγηγερμένον ἐκ νεκρῶν, ἐκ σπέρματος Δαυίδ, κατὰ τὸ εὐαγγέλιόν μου; John 7:42 οὐχ ἡ γραφὴ εἶπεν ὅτι ἐκ τοῦ σπέρματος Δαυίδ καὶ ἀπὸ Βηθλέεμ τῆς κώμης ὅπου ἦν Δαυίδ ἔρχεται ὁ Χριστός; The former passage has some strong affinities with Rom 1:3–4, but the wording is different enough to prevent one from thinking that both passages stem from the same source. Cf. also Acts 13:23 (τούτου ὁ θεὸς ἀπὸ τοῦ σπέρματος κατ' ἐπαγγελίαν ἤγαγεν τῷ Ἰσραὴλ σωτῆρα Ἰησοῦν).

γενομένου ἐκ σπέρματος Δαυίδ to γενομένου υἱοῦ Δαυίδ when the parallel structure calls for the latter. In other words, ἐκ σπέρματος Δαυίδ at least has the possibility of Pauline provenance based on instances of ἐκ σπέρματος Ἀβραάμ,[37] while the christological title υἱὸς Δαυίδ which would better fit a confession is avoided. The inconsistent parallelism could result from Paul's redaction, but it would be simpler to perceive instead his selection and arrangement of traditional themes. Jesus' descent from David fulfills the promises mentioned in v. 2; the greater portion of emphasis falls, however, on Jesus' status as υἱὸς θεοῦ, in a manner which generally coheres with Paul's christological perspectives.[38] Rom 1:4 indeed seems inconsistent with Paul's notion of a pre-

---

[37] Cf. also Gal 4:4–5, ὅτε δὲ ἦλθεν τὸ πλήρωμα τοῦ χρόνου, ἐξαπέστειλεν ὁ θεὸς τὸν υἱὸν αὐτοῦ, γενόμενον ἐκ γυναικός, γενόμενον ὑπὸ νόμον, ἵνα τοὺς ὑπὸ νόμον ἐξαγοράσῃ, ἵνα τὴν υἱοθεσίαν ἀπολάβωμεν. Some have argued that these verses depend on a pre-Pauline formula, for example Betz (*Galatians*, 205–8), who points out that the second participial phrase, γενόμενον ὑπὸ νόμου, has immediate relevance for the context, while the first seems out of place: "This christology emphasizes Christ's existence as a human being, in particular his being a Jew. As a parallel to 'born from a woman' the phrase 'put under the law' must have originally had a positive meaning, in contrast to the Pauline context, where it is viewed negatively" (207). I agree that traditional material underpins these statements, but, as with Rom 1:3–4, I believe it better to perceive not a formula as their origin but general premises which Paul works into his argument. "Born from a woman" and "born under law" (the law being one of the enslaving στοιχεῖα mentioned in Gal 4:3) have a crucial relationship in Christ's case: he came as the Son of God, human, and Jewish, all with the objective of redeeming both Jews and Gentiles from the enslavement imposed by the law, and then replacing it with υἱοθεσία; therefore, his Gentile addressees should not accept re-enslavement. This point reflects Paul's priorities at the levels of argument and composition in Galatians. Underneath there lies tradition (Jesus was a human and a Jew sent to save his people), but the whole gist of vv. 4–5 seems too well-integrated into Paul's argument for them to have existed independently as a formula which one can recover from his wording. Cf. Kramer, *Christ*, 112–15, and the response of Scott, *Adoption*, 169–71.

[38] Alternatively, one might say that the datum of Jesus' descent from David as a freestanding christological theme does not hold much weight for Paul. But as part of a more comprehensive constellation of ways that Jesus fulfills prophetic promises, it has a significant christological function. In any case, I doubt that Paul is self-consciously repudiating or refuting a "national Jewish messianic expectation" by his avoidance of υἱὸς Δαυίδ (see, e.g., Wengst, *Christologische Formeln*, 115; Schmithals, *Römerbrief*, 50), since, at the end of the day, "born from the seed of David" and "born the son of David" amount to the same thing in tone and substance. Paul cannot invoke Jesus' Davidic heritage alongside the theme of fulfilled prophecy without bringing Jewish messianic expectations along with it. Rom 1:3 indeed stands in tension with 2 Cor 5:16–17, where Paul says: ὥστε ἡμεῖς ἀπὸ τοῦ νῦν οὐδένα οἴδαμεν κατὰ σάρκα· εἰ καὶ ἐγνώκαμεν κατὰ σάρκα Χριστόν, ἀλλὰ νῦν οὐκέτι γινώσκομεν. ὥστε εἴ τις ἐν Χριστῷ, καινὴ κτίσις· τὰ ἀρχαῖα παρῆλθεν, ἰδοὺ γέγονεν καινά. He does not with these words contradict what we find in Rom 1:3–4, although he does give some insight into his general disinterest about Jesus's earthly life. But one can scarcely say that he has *no* interest in such matters, because in 1 Cor 11:23–26 he presumes among his readers a wider knowledge about the events surrounding Jesus' final days – a knowledge which he claims to have "handed

4.4 The definition extended (1:3b–4)

existent Christ (as surmised from Phil 2:5–11), since he appears to say that Jesus becomes υἱὸς θεοῦ only *after* the resurrection, a christological position later known as adoptionism.[39] The apparent adoptionism presents significant problems for the synthesis of a coherent Pauline christology, and perhaps encourages scholars to argue that he is quoting an old formula – something which he can keep at arm's length from his own christology because it is not really his, or something he cites in deference to its antiquity but which is quite primitive in comparison with his own more developed ideas.[40] But one cannot so easily drive a wedge between Paul's christology and the views expressed in the alleged formula. If he quotes it, he gives sufficient reason to think that he endorses it.[41] He evidently does not discern any disagreement between Christ "having been designated" or "appointed" and his pre-existence.[42] Attributing

---

over" to them. His point in 2 Cor 5:16 is simply that what anyone *was* no longer matters, just like what Jesus *was* κατὰ σάρκα pales in comparison to what he *is*.

[39] See M. Simonetti, "Adoptianists," *EECh* 1.11; Winrich A. Löhr, "Adoptianismus," *RGG*⁴ 1.123; Lionel R. Wickham, "Adoptionism," *EEC* 1.20.

[40] One may observe such tendencies at work in the comments of Käsemann, *Romans*, 13 ("... [I]t should be remembered that what Paul takes from the formula as the decisive thing for him ... is only the title 'Son of God,' which for Paul belongs to the preexistent one"), and in the way the 'theologies of the NT' position their discussions of Rom 1:3b–4, usually under the rubric of "the christology of the early church" (or some such), and separated from "the theology of Paul," e.g., Bultmann, *Theology*, 1.49–50 (under "the kerygma of the earliest church" and "Jesus' meaning to the faith of the early church," as opposed to the "theology of Paul"); Kramer, *Christ*, 108–11 (under "pre-Pauline material" as opposed to "Pauline material"); Strecker, *Theology*, 66–69 (placing vv. 3–4 under "redemption and liberation – the theology of Paul," but in a preliminary section: "history-of-religions presuppositions – prepauline elements in Pauline theology"). See also the remarks of Dodd (*Romans*, 5): "The present statement ... falls short of what Paul would regard as an adequate doctrine of the Person of Christ. ... The statement is pre-theological."

[41] So also Scott (*Adoption*, 234–36; cf. Moo, *Romans*, 45–46, n. 31), although I disagree with him that Acts 13:33 provides "independent, historical evidence that Paul did indeed confirm the Christology contained in Rom 1:4," since I doubt the value of Acts as a consistently reliable witness of the historical Paul. If one approaches Acts 13:33 with a proper historical skepticism, it can provide at most attestation of the currency of adoptionist ideas in the early church and *one form* of the logic adduced to support it, namely, that Jesus' resurrection constitutes the moment at which God made him his Son in fulfillment of Ps 2:7. This verse possibly lies somewhere buried within Rom 1:3–4, but the text as we have it does not make this clear in a discernable fashion (contra Whitsett, "Son of God," 676–77; see n. 35 above and n. 103 below).

[42] Some have sought to soften the conflict with Paul's assertions of Christ's pre-existence by qualifying the degree of adoptionism represented in 1:4, for example, Polythress, "Is Romans 1³⁻⁴," 181: "'Constituted Son of God' is not so much as reference to Christ's deity (though that is assumed by Paul) as to the transformation of his humanity. It is better, then, to say that the passage speaks of enthronement, not adoption." He goes on to say that "'adoptionist' language was used to put all the emphasis on the significance of the resurrection, without regard one way or the other for Christ's deity prior to the resurrection." See also Barrett, *Romans*, 20 ("The first attempts at Christological thought were made not in essential but

the origin of vv. 3b–4 to a traditional formula does not make this problem vanish – unless, of course, one wants to argue that someone other than Paul added them to the prescript.[43] Since he does not perceive the problem, he does not feel the need to work it out systematically.

Jewett's final two observations have very little evidentiary value. The second-to-last addresses a probability based on what Paul does elsewhere: (11) "Paul introduces this material in Rom 1:1–2 as a summary of the 'gospel' he had been preaching, which leads one to expect the citation of traditional material, as in 1 Cor 15:1–4."[44] Jewett seemingly regards εὐαγγέλιον as an indicator of the citation of a formula. There is, however, at least one passage in Paul's writings, not far from Rom 1:3b–4, where Paul gives a highly condensed, even formulaic, summary of εὐαγγέλιον, and where his own composition does not stand in doubt: Rom 1:16–17, the thesis statement of Romans.

---

in functional terms"); Hahn, *Christological Titles*, 248; Cranfield, *Romans*, 1.58; Dunn, *Romans*, 1.15 (adoptionism is "anachronistic").

[43] O'Neill (*Paul's Letter to the Romans*, 26–28), for example, eliminates vv. 3–4 by arguing that an interpolator added them, because: (1) Paul makes no more use of the ideas expressed therein later in his letter, (2) "this section completely overloads the salutation and makes it a grammatical monstrosity, which no one writer would have perpetrated," and (3) a single manuscript, G^p, omits them (ibid., 26). Instead, O'Neill avers, vv. 3–4 started out as a marginal note that eventually crept into the text. According to the reproduction of G^p by Reinhardt (*Codex Boernerianus*, ad loc.), the MS has the opening line of Romans, Παυλος δουλος ιυ χυ κλητος αποστολος), followed by a substantial gap which would easily accommodate 1:1b–5a, then picks up with 5b a little less than halfway down the page with εν πασιν εθνεσιν υπερ του ονοματος αυτου etc. MS G^p has several such gaps, as does the related Codex Augiensis (F^p) (see Hatch, "On the Relationship of Codex Augiensis and Codex Boernerianus"; for the following observations, I consulted Scrivner, *Exact Transcript of Codex Augiensis*). Unfortunately F^p cannot help us with Rom 1:1b–5a, since it is missing 1:1–3:19, but note the gap in G^p at 2:16–25, where blank space is left on half of one page and about one-third of the next, and the parallel lacunae *and spaces* left in both MSS for 1 Cor 3:8–16 and 6:7–14. In the case of the latter passage, both MSS conclude v. 7 with the addition of και ου επι αγιων, and begin v. 15 with the same mistake, η ουκ ουδατε instead of η ουκ οιδατε (the scribe of G^p was perhaps at first forgetting to leave a space, stopping once he wrote ουκ οιδατε after v. 6). All of this provides a different explanation of what the gap in G^p where Rom 1:1b–5a belongs might be: such spaces seem to indicate missing or damaged leaves in the exemplar(s) of F^p and G^p, not a more accurate preservation of Paul's original text. The first page of Romans in an ancestor of these two MSS must have been damaged for these verses, so the scribes left space for the passage to be filled in from another MS. The text-critical basis of O'Neill's argument thus falls apart, unless he would wish to argue for the interpolation or inadvertant marginal insertion of 1 Cor 3:8–16 and 6:7–14 on a similar basis.

[44] "Redaction and Use," 102. Cf. Stauffer's first criterion: "Often the most reliable guide is the language of the immediate context: the creedal formulae or their constitutive elements are inserted and introduced by such words as 'deliver,' 'believe' or 'confess' ..." (*New Testament Theology*, 338); εὐαγγέλιον would thus presumably be one of the words which signal insertions. For an illuminating discussion of the relationship of 'tradition' and 'gospel' in German scholarship prior to 1975, see Schütz, *Paul and the Anatomy of Apostolic Authority*, 35–83.

The final observation relates to the ease with which vv. 3–4 may be deleted: (12) a "smooth transition" would result from the deletion of the parallel participial phrases: "... the gospel about his son, ... Jesus Christ our Lord, through whom we received grace and apostleship...."[45] James Scott correctly points out in response that "*any* nonrestrictive participial clause" can be removed without "disturbing the flow of thought" in a Greek sentence.[46] A "smooth transition" would likewise result from the deletion of the relative clauses in vv. 5–6, or any of the adjectives and appositional nouns which Paul sprinkles liberally throughout the prescript. In fact, the deletion of the entirety of vv. 2–6 would leave a completely smooth, albeit impoverished, prescript to his letter. The removability of vv. 3b–4 is evenly matched by the removability of any other part of the prescript except for the basic epistolary salutation, Παῦλος τοῖς οὖσιν ἐν Ῥώμῃ χάρις καὶ εἰρήνη.

Jewett's observations, therefore, even when they accurately describe the many peculiar features of Rom 1:3b–4 and other passages which resemble it, fail as tools for the discovery and classification of formulas quoted or redacted by Paul. The case from syntax and style suffers from the inability to collect valid comparanda, and does not take Paul's own stylistic habits into adequate consideration. The case from vocabulary overstates differences from his normal usages, and involves unwarranted speculation regarding the size of his working vocabulary and regarding words that he could not or would not use. The case from theology may seem impressive, but the presence of christological perspectives which are unique in Paul's letters at most affirms the manipulation of traditional ideas, not quotation. None of Jewett's observations, taken individually or all together, *necessarily* point to Paul's appropriation of a traditional formula in Rom 1:3b–4. They do, however, help to sharpen perception of the phenomena which any competing hypothesis must explain, namely: (1) the syntactical and stylistic regularities that indeed exist between vv. 3b–4 and other predicative statements attached to God or Christ; (2) the differences between these statements that make them unique formulations in their contexts; (3) the topical regularities (Jesus' death and resurrection, for instance), and the similarities in methods of setting these topics forth; and (4) the nature of the sources that underpin the statements. I shall argue that Paul composes vv. 3b–4 and many similar statements himself, using a hymnic form, the 'mythological expanded epithet,' which deploys συνεκδοχή as a method of concisely summarizing mythological narratives associated with a divinity. This form occurs in Greco-Roman hymns and prayers, as well as in many prophetic passages of the Septuagint. These two literary streams influence Paul's utilization of the form and the ways that his audiences would hear it. This hypothesis provides simpler, less speculative explanations of the phe-

---

[45] "Redaction and Use," 102.
[46] *Adoption*, 229.

nomena listed above than recourse to the theory that Paul quotes or redacts a formula. In the following sections, I shall first identify the literary precedents; next, I examine instances of the form in Paul's letters in order to confirm his awareness of it, and to reveal consistencies in the ways that he uses it; and finally, I analyze vv. 3b–4 as an instance of the form in order to show the special role that it plays in his first definition of the gospel.

4.4.2 The mythological expanded epithet

"Epithet" (ἐπίθετον), a common phenomenon in the religious literatures of the ancient world, refers to an apposite noun, adjective or short phrase either attached to or standing in for a divine name. Functionally, it praises the divinity by expounding his or her identity with the specification of a distinguishing attribute.[47] It is thus a kind of συνεκδοχή, since it describes a whole god or goddess by means of a readily identifiable part.[48]

Excursus 1. My definition here emphasizes epithet *in religious literature* (hymns, prayers, prophetic texts, etc.). Epic poetry, most influentially the *Iliad* and *Odyssey*, also uses epithet extensively to add dynamism and poetic texture to the narrative.[49] The illustrative power of epithet in both epic poetry and religious literature promotes its usage in rhetorical contexts as well, so it receives some attention in the theoretical sources in connection with style. Aristotle approaches it as a category of noun or adjective that has both benefits and risks for the stylistic virtue of σαφήνεια. On the benefits he says (*Rhet.* 3.2.14, 1405b): "And in epithets one may compose additions [ἐπιθέσεις] from something ugly or shameful (for example, 'the matricide'), and from something better (for example, 'the father's avenger'). And Simonides, when the person who won [a race] with mules was paying him a small fee, he did not wish to compose a poem since he scorned writing poetry for mules. But when the person paid a sufficient fee, he wrote, 'Greetings, daughters of horses with feet like the storm,' although they too were the daughters of asses." καὶ ἐν τοῖς ἐπιθέτοις ἔστι μὲν τὰς ἐπιθέσεις ποιεῖσθαι ἀπὸ φαύλου ἢ αἰσχροῦ, οἷον ὁ μητροφόντης, ἔστι δ' ἀπὸ τοῦ βελτίονος, οἷον ὁ πατρὸς ἀμύντωρ· καὶ ὁ Σιμωνίδης, ὅτε μὲν ἐδίδου μισθὸς ὀλίγον αὐτῷ ὁ νικήσας τοῖς ὀρεῦσιν, οὐκ ἤθελε ποιεῖν, ὡς δυσχεραίνων

---

[47] For discussion of the signifiance of names in classical Greek hymns and prayers, see Pulleyn, "Power of Names"; cf. also Furley/Bremer 1.52: "[T]he precise naming of the god addressed was important both from the point of view of politeness and courtesy, so as not to offend a sensitive power, and from the point of view of establishing the precise channels along which one wished divine succor to flow. The composers of Greek hymns often used more names than one to address and identify a god; their motive may have been partly to avoid the sin of omission, and partly to demonstrate technical proficiency to the divine and human listeners."

[48] Mitchell (*Heavenly Trumpet*, 72) stresses the synecdochic character of epithets, describing them as "portraits in shorthand," and calling attention to the definition of ἀντονομασία given by Trypho[1] (*Trop.* 2.17, *RG* 3.204) which explicitly links this figure with συνεκδοχή: "Some people subordinate ἔλλειψις and ἀντονομασία to συνεκδοχή," ἔνιοι δὲ τὴν ἔλλειψιν καὶ τὴν ἀντονομασίαν ὑποτάττουσι τῇ συνεκδοχῇ.

[49] See H. J. Rose and Simon Hornblower, "Epithets, Divine: Greek," *OCD* 548–49; Vivante, *Epithets in Homer*, esp. 151–59 on definitions; Dee, *Epitheta Deorum apud Homerum*, esp. xviii–xix on "descriptive clauses"; on more general problems related to the definitions of 'prayer' and 'hymn,' see Pulleyn, *Prayer in Greek Religion*, 39–55.

4.4 The definition extended (1:3b–4) 107

εἰς ἡμιόνους ποιεῖν, ἐπεὶ δ᾽ ἱκανὸν ἔδωκεν, ἐποίησε «χαίρετ᾽ ἀελλοπόδων θύγατρες ἵππων»· καίτοι καὶ τῶν ὄνων θυγατέρες ἦσαν. On the risks, he names the overuse of epithets as the third cause of the stylistic fault of frigidity (τὰ ψυχρά, *Rhet.* 3.3.3., 1406a): "Thirdly, there is in epithets the use of those that are long, ill-suited or densely packed together. For in poetry it is suitable to say 'white milk,' but such things in a speech are less suitable, and, if they are excessive, they expose [one] and render it obvious that it is poetry. And yet it is necessary to use them, for they transform the ordinary and render the style exotic. But one ought to aim for the mean, since it causes fault worse than speaking without a plan. For the latter is not good, but the former is terrible. Hence [the epithets] of Alcidamas seem frigid. For he uses epithets (which [for him] are so densely packed, excessive and obvious) not as seasonings but as the food [itself]." Several examples follow, then Aristotle concludes: "Therefore those that speak poetically [to such an extent] produce absurdity and frigidity by their lack of decorum, and obscurity because of their prolixity. For whenever one overloads someone who knows [already what one is talking about], one dissolves the clarity by overshadowing it." τρίτον δ᾽ ἐν τοῖς ἐπιθέτοις τὸ ἢ μακροῖς ἢ ἀκαίροις ἢ πυκνοῖς χρῆσθαι· ἐν μὲν γὰρ ποιήσει πρέπει «γάλα λευκὸν» εἰπεῖν, ἐν δὲ λόγῳ τὰ μὲν ἀπρεπέστερα· τὰ δέ, ἂν ᾖ κατακορῆ, ἐξελέγχει καὶ ποιεῖ φανερὸν ὅτι ποίησις ἐστίν· ἐπεὶ δεῖ γε χρῆσθαι αὐτοῖς (ἐξαλλάττει γὰρ τὸ εἰωθός, καὶ ξενικὴν ποιεῖ τὴν λέξιν), ἀλλὰ δεῖ στοχάζεσθαι τοῦ μετρίου, ἐπεὶ μεῖζον ποιεῖ κακὸν τοῦ εἰκῇ λέγειν· ἡ μὲν γὰρ οὐκ ἔχει τὸ εὖ, ἡ δὲ τὸ κακῶς. διὸ τὰ Ἀλκιδάμαντος ψυχρὰ φαίνεται· οὐ γὰρ ἡδύσματι χρῆται ἀλλ᾽ ὡς ἐδέσματι τοῖς ἐπιθέτοις ⟨τοῖς⟩ οὕτω πυκνοῖς καὶ μείζοσι καὶ ἐπιδήλοις. ... διὸ ποιητικῶς λέγοντες τῇ ἀπρεπείᾳ τὸ γελοῖον καὶ τὸ ψυχρὸν ἐμποιοῦσι, καὶ τὸ ἀσαφὲς διὰ τὴν ἀδολεσχίαν· ὅταν γὰρ γιγνώσκοντι ἐπεμβάλλῃ, διαλύει τὸ σαφὲς τῷ ἐπισκοτεῖν. Eventually ἐπίθετον becomes classed as a figure or trope, either under that name or under that of ἀντονομασία. Quintilian (*Inst.* 8.6.43) notes: "But there are people to whom this [i.e., epithet] does not seem altogether a trope, because it alters nothing, nor is it always [a trope], but [only] when that which was appended [*id quod est adpositum*] – if you were to separate it from its referent – means something separately, and causes an *antonomasia*. For if you say 'he who overthrew Numantia and Carthage,' it is *antonomasia*; if you attached 'Scipio,' it is epithet [*adpositum*]." *Sunt autem quibus non videatur hic omnino tropos quia nihil vertat, nec est semper, sed cum id quod est adpositum, si a proprio diviseris, per se significat et facit antonomasian. Nam si dicas «ille qui Numantiam et Carthaginem evertit», antonomasia est, si adieceris «Scipio» adpositum.* The distinction thus depends on the presence (in epithet) or absence (in antonomasia) of the proper name (note esp. the relative clause Quintilian uses as an illustration, *illi qui Numantiam et Carthaginem evertit*). Others knew of no such distinction, e.g. [Plutarch], *De Hom.* 2.24: "Ἀντονομασία, language which signifies a particular word through epithets or tokens, is also another trope, as in this: 'But the son of Peleus again addressed the son of Atreus with mischievous words,' for it indicates both Achilles and Agamemnon through these words. And again, 'Cheer up, Tritogeneia, beloved child,' and in other passages, 'Unshorn Apollo.' For the one indicates Athena and the other Apollo." ἔστι καὶ ἄλλος τρόπος ἡ ἀντονομασία, λέξις δι᾽ ἐπιθέτων ἢ συσσήμων ὄνομα ἴδιον σημαίνουσα, ὡς ἐν τούτῳ· «Πηλεΐδης δ᾽ ἐξαῦτις ἀταρτηροῖς ἐπέεσσιν | Ἀτρεΐδην προσέειπε»· δηλοῖ γὰρ διὰ τούτων τόν τε Ἀχιλλέα καὶ τὸν Ἀγαμέμνονα. καὶ πάλιν «θάρσει, Τριτογένεια, φίλον τέκος», καὶ ἐν ἄλλοις «Φοῖβος ἀκερσεκόμης»· τὸ μὲν γὰρ τὴν Ἀθηνᾶν τὸ δὲ τὸν Ἀπόλλωνα δηλοῖ.

I am coining the term 'expanded epithet' to refer to a class of relative clause or attributive participial phrase, which has the same general character and function of simple epithet, but which has a greater descriptive flexibility than simple epithet by virtue of its increased length. Expanded epithets in Greek hymns often specify divine attributes, spheres of authority, habitual behaviors and preferred haunts.

Excursus 2. For example, the invocation of a paean from an inscription at Delphi (2nd century B.C.E.) reads: "Listen, fair-armed daughters of loud-thundering | Zeus whose appointed place is deeply-wooded Mt. Helicon, | come here to praise in song your brother Phoibos | of the golden hair, who ascends the twin-peaked seat | of this Parnassian rock and with the famous Delphic women | visits the abundant waters of Kastalia's spring, | making for his lofty mantic seat in Delphi," κεκλυθ' Ἑλι]κῶνα βαθύδενδρον αἶ λάχετε Διό]ς | ἐ[ρι]βρόμου θύγατρες εὐώλ[ενοι,] μόλετε, συνόμ- | -αιμον ἵνα Φοῖβον ὠιδα[ῖ]σι μέλψητε χρυσεοκόμαν, | ὃς ἀνὰ δικόρυνβα Παρνασσίδος τᾶσδε πετέρας ἔδραν' ἄμ | [ἀ]γακλυταῖς Δελφίσιν Κασταλίδος εὐύδρου | νάματ' ἐπινίσεται Δελφὸν ἀνὰ [πρ]ῶνα μαν- | -τεῖον ἐφέπων πάγον (text and translation per Furley/Bremer § 2.6.1, lines 1–7, 1.135–36, 2.85–86). This portion of the hymn has two relative clauses that elaborate the Muses on the one hand, and Apollo on the other, both focusing on the gods' habits and habitations. The following hymn to Hestia, "found in 1903 at the Athenian temple-treasury in Delphi" according to Furley and Bremer (1.117), also mentions the home and habits of the goddess (4th century B.C.E.): "Holy Queen of Sanctity, | we hymn you, Hestia, whose abiding realm | is Olympus and the middle point of earth | and the Delphic laurel tree. ... We salute you, daughter of Kronos | and Rhea, who alone brings firelight | to the sacred altars of the gods." [Ἱ]ερὰν ἱερῶν ἄνασσαν | Ἑστίαν [ὑ]μνήσομεν, ἃ καὶ Ὄλυμπο[ν] | καὶ μυ[χὸν γ]αίας μεσόμφαλον αἰεὶ | Πυθίαν [τε δ]άφναν κατέχουσα. ... χαῖρε Κρόνου θύγατερ | καὶ Ῥέας, μούνα πυ[ρὶ φλ]έ[γ]ουσα | βωμοὺς ἀθανάτων ἐριτίμους (text and translation per Furley/Bremer § 2.3, lines 1–4, 11–13, 1.116, 2.38). The attributive participial phrases have precisely the same function as the relative clauses in the other hymn, to identify Hestia's habitation as what she forever holds and what she characteristically does. Further instances from the Furley/Bremer volume include §1.1 (1.68–69, 2.1–2), esp. lines 1–4: "Io! most mighty youth, I salute you, son of Kronos, almighty splendour, who stand as leader of the company of gods!" (Ἰὼ μέγιστε κοῦρε | χαῖρέ μοι, Κρόνειε | παγκρατὲς γάνος, βέβακες | δαιμόνων ἀγώμενος); § 2.6.2 (1.137–38, 2.92–94), line 3: "Muses of Pieria, who inhabit Helikon's snow-covered crags" (Πιερίδες, αἳ νιφοβόλους πέτρας ναίεθ' [Ἑλι]κωνίδ[ας]), and lines 21–22: "So you who hold the seat of divination, come to sacred Mt. Parnassus, beloved of the god (ἀλ[λὰ χρησμ]ωιδὸν ὃς ἔχεις τρίποδα, βαῖν' ἐπὶ θεοστιβ[έα | τάνδε Π]αρνα[σ]σίαν δειράδα φιλένθεον); § 4.5 (a petition attributed to Anakreon by Dio Chysostom, 1.176, 2.125–26), lines 1–6: "Lord, with whom conqueror Eros and the blue-eyed Nymphs and radiant Aphrodite like to cavort, you who haunt preciptious mountain tops, I beseech you..." (ὦναξ, ὧι δαμάλης Ἔρως | καὶ Νύμφαι κυανώπιδες | πορφυρῆ τ' Ἀφροδίτη συμπαίζουσιν, ἐπιστρέφεαι | δ' ὑψηλὰς ὀρέων κορυφάς, | γουνοῦμαί σε ...). Note also Hesiod, fr. 310: "Of the Muses, who cause a man to be very wise [and] to speak divinely," Μουσάων, αἵ τ' ἄνδρα πολυφραδέοντα τιθεῖσι θέσπιον αὐδήεντα; *Op.* 1–2, "Come, Muses from Pieria, who make fame with song, speak of Zeus as you hymn your own father," Μοῦσαι Πιερίηθεν ἀοιδῇσι κλείουσαι | δεῦτε, Δι' ἐννέπετε, σφέτερον πατέρ' ὑμνείουσαι (cf. 8, "Zeus high-thunderer, who inhabits the loftiest home," Ζεὺς ὑψιβρεμέτης, ὃς ὑπέρτατα δώματα ναίει); *Theog.* 1–4: "Let us begin to sing of the Heliconian Muses, who hold the great and sacred mountain of Helicon, who dance on tender feet around the purple well and the altar of the mighty son of Cronos," Μουσάων Ἑλικωνιάδων ἀρχώμεθ' ἀείδειν, | αἵ θ' Ἑλικῶνος ἔχουσιν ὄρος μέγα τε ζάθεόν τε | καί τε περὶ κρήνην ἰοειδέα πόσσ' ἁπαλοῖσιν | ὀρχεῦνται καὶ βωμὸν ἐρισθενέος Κρονίωνος; Homeric *Hymn* 3 *to Apollo* 334–36: "Heed me now, Gaea and broad Uranus above, and Titans, gods who live under the earth around great Tartarus, from whom [were born] both men and gods" (κέκλυτε νῦν μοι, Γαῖα καὶ Οὐρανὸς εὐρὺς ὕπερθεν | Τιτῆνές τε θεοί, τοὶ ὑπὸ χθονὶ ναιετάουσιν | Τάρταρον ἀμφὶ μέγαν, τῶν ἐξ ἄνδρες τε θεοί τε); Cleanthes, *Hymn to Zeus* 1–2: "Most-honored of the immortals, many-named, forever all-powerful Zeus, originator of nature, who steers all things with law" (κύδιστ' ἀθανάτων, πολυώνυμε, παγκρατὲς αἰεί, | Ζεῦ, φύσεως ἀρχηγέ, νόμου μέτα πάντα κυβερνῶν). Also *Orph. Hymn* 25 (to Proteus): "I invoke Proteus, who holds the keys of the sea, first-born, who revealed the origins of all nature, who changes sacred substance to polymorphous forms" (Πρωτέα κικλήσκω, πόντου κληῖδας ἔχοντα, | πρωτογενῆ, πάσης φύσεως ἀρχὰς ὃς ἔφηνεν | ὕλην ἀλλάσσων ἱερὴν ἰδέαις πολυμόρφοις).

'Mythological expanded epithet' differs from other members of its class on account of the peculiar manner in which it takes advantage of the synecdochic dimension of epithets in general: it illustrates a divinity's character by capturing the entirety of a myth by reference to a distinctive part. Such myths surely inform other kinds of expanded epithets, insofar as they explain how, for example, a god or goddess came to have a particular sphere of authority or preferred habitation. But mythological expanded epithet focuses primarily on the myth,[50] and requires the hearers to draw any additional relevant inferences from it themselves. This phenomonenon possesses special importance for a comprehension of how Paul composes Rom 1:3b–4. Two broad streams mediate this form to Paul and other early Christians: (1) Greek hymns and prayers; and (2) the Septuagint, particularly the rich use of the form in prophetic texts. I shall presently examine some samples from both streams to ascertain how συνεκδοχή operates within mythological expanded epithets.

The collection of Homeric hymns may initially seem remote from any manifestation of the form in early Christian texts. They reflect broader Greek hymnic customs,[51] however, that remain in place long after their composition.

---

[50] Some scholars of the NT (e.g., Hays, *Faith of Jesus Christ*, 15–18) reject the term 'myth' as imprecise and misleading. The word indeed has been used for many purposes and with many resonances in theology, exegesis of the NT, and Classical scholarship (for the last, see the survey in Graf, *Greek Mythology*, 9–56). I use it here in a literary sense, i.e., to refer to narratives about gods and heroes, with no commitment to any specific notion of their social function or attachment to rituals, but with the general assertion that its tradents regarded the narratives as having relevance for human life and as meriting preservation and retelling. In this sense, the narrative aspects of the gospel fall into the category of 'myth.'

[51] Classical scholars have noted that hymns and prayers commonly have a tripartite structure, invocation (identifying the addressee by name and with epithets), argument (announcing the credentials of the person praying, expounding the special abilities of the god(dess) or briefly narrating a myth), and petition. For further discussion of hymnic structural features, see Bremer, "Greek Hymns," the introduction of Furley/Bremer vol. 1, "The Nature of Greek Hymns" and "Form and Composition," and Gordley, *Colossian Hymn*, 127–33. Note also Race's list of "elements usually encountered in hymns," including relative clauses ("Relativstil") and participial clauses ("Partizipialstil") (*Style and Rhetoric*, 85–86; cf. his analyses of Pindar's composition of several odes in ibid. ch. 4, "Style and Rhetoric in Opening Hymns"). Also informative is Race's observation regarding two broad categories of hymns, the rhapsodic and the cultic (ibid., 102–3): "Rhapsodic (or epic) hymns are represented chiefly by the collection of thirty-three Homeric Hymns and by the later imitations of Kallimachos and Theokritos. The main intention of rhapsodic hymns is to sing *about* the god; they are characteristically more impersonal than cultic hymns, describe the god in the third person ("Er-Stil"), and are more concerned with relating the god's attributes and achievements than with obtaining any specific request. ... Cultic hymns, in contrast, are decidedly more personal; they address the god in the second person ("Du-Stil"), often are concerned with a spe-

Some of them exert durable literary influence over the composition of later hymns.[52] They also illustrate how one may wield mythological expanded epithets both to invoke the god or goddess and to evoke the narratives which comprise the central portions of the compositions. For example, the invocation of the *Hymn 2 to Demeter* (1–3) reads:

Δήμητρ᾽ ἠΰκομον, σεμνὴν θεὸν ἄρχομ᾽ ἀείδειν,
αὐτὴν ἠδὲ θύγατρα τανίσφυρον, ἣν Ἀιδωνεύς
ἥρπαξεν, δῶκεν δὲ βαρύκτυπος εὐρύοπα Ζεύς....

I begin to sing of long-haired Demeter, revered goddess:
her and her slender-ankled daughter, whom Hades
seized, but whom loud-thundering, wide-eyed Zeus gave away....

The poet then tells at length the story that he has summarily outlined in the two relative clauses. The clauses in fact mark the parameters of the story which the poet will tell, specifying its beginning in the seizure of Persephone and its conclusion in the intervention of Zeus. *Hymn 4 to Hermes* likewise deploys a mythological expanded epithet in combination with a list of regular epithets as foreshadowing (13–16):

καὶ τότ᾽ ἐγείνατο παῖδα πολύτροπον, αἱμυλομήτην,
ληϊστῆρ᾽, ἐλατῆρα βοῶν, ἡγήτορ᾽ ὀνείρων,
νυκτὸς ὀπωπητῆρα, πυληδόκον, ὃς τάχ᾽ ἔμελλεν
ἀμφανέειν κλυτὰ ἔργα μετ᾽ ἀθανάτοισι θεοῖσιν·

And then she [Maia] bore a many-shaped child: extremely clever,
a thief, a cattle-rustler, a chieftain of dreams,
a spy of the night, a gate-watcher, who shortly was about
to display glorious deeds among the immortal gods.

By the time the poet arrives at the final relative clause, he has already indicated the "glorious deeds" that Hermes would soon be doing in the hymn's narrative with the epithets that he lists (ληιστῆρα, ἐλατῆρα βοῶν).

The Greek magical papyri contain many similar hymns with such mythological abbreviations. The texts present several instances of the conventional type of Greek hymn that may in a few cases derive from temple inscriptions, public festivals or possibly even the rites of mystery cults.[53] Others (particu-

---

cific situation, and emphasize the request. Every element in a cultic hymn is part of a rhetorical strategy whose purpose is to dispose the god favorably toward the request...."

[52] The hymns in the collection were evidently composed and performed as preludes to the rhapsodic performance of other poems (e.g., Homeric epic); see William D. Furley, "Homeric Hymns," *BNP* 6.444–47; Furley/Bremer 1.41–43; Foley, *Homeric Hymn to Demeter*, 151–53. On the influence of the hymns on Callimachus, see Dihle, *History of Greek Literature*, 257–59; Furley/Bremer 1.45–47.

[53] See the hymnic extracts of spells compiled in the second volume Preisendanz's and Henrichs' edition of the PGM, pp. 237–66, e.g., Hymn 2, lines 2–4 ("Pan, who divided the world by {your own} divine spirit; and you Meliouchos, who created all things, appeared first from the firstborn, from the violent water," Πάν, ὁ διαστήσας τὸν κόσμον {τῷ σεαυτῷ} πνεύ-

larly those in prose) are the compositions of the magicians themselves,[54] either specifically for the spells in which they presently stand or taken from other spells and tailored for their new contexts. All of these instances are rich in traditional Greek and Egyptian religious imagery and motifs. But unlike the performed and published hymns of the civic cults, the hymns and prayers in the magical papyri generally have only the addressed gods as their intended audience, so in many cases they reflect the customs of the private petitions of ordinary individuals stretching back well before the spells' late antique dates.[55] Any time a magician addresses a god, the expanded epithet pattern plays a role alongside simple epithets and secret names (*voces magicae*) that ideally render the god amenable to the petition.[56] Sometimes a magician in-

---

ματι θε⟨ί⟩ῳ. | πρῶτος δ' ἐξεφάνης ἐκ πρωτογόνου, Μελιοῦχε, | ὕδατος ⟨ἐκ⟩ βιαίου ὁ τὰ πάντα κτίσσας). For discussions of appropriations from mystery cults, see Betz, "Fragments of a Catabasis Ritual"; idem, "Magic and Mystery," esp. 219–27 (on mystery cult terminology in the papyri).

[54] The creation and sustenance of the cosmos is a pervasive theme, e.g. PGM IV.1146–58 (στήλη ἀπόκρυφος): "I praise you, the god of gods, who prepared the world [*voces magicae*], who furnished the abyss with the unseen foundation of [every] place [*v.m.*], who divided sky and earth, and who sheltered the sky with eternal golden wings [*v.m.*], but who strengthened the earth with eternal foundations...," αἰνῶ σε, ὁ θεὸς τῶν θεῶν, ὁ τὸν κόσμον καταρτισάμενος [*v.m.*], ὁ τὴν ἄβυσσον θησαυρίσας ἀοράτῳ θέσεως ἐδράσματι [*v.m.*], ὁ διαστήσας οὐρανὸν καὶ γῆν καὶ τὸν μὲν οὐρανὸν πτέρυξιν χρυσείαις αἰωνίαις σκεπάσας [*v.m.*], τὴν δὲ γῆν ἑδράσμασιν αἰωνίοις στηρίσας. Cf. these epithets that refer to the sustenance of the cosmos in the opening of a θεαγωγὸς λόγος (PGM IV.987–97): "I invoke you, the greatest god, Lord Horus Harpocrates [*v.m.*], who enlightens all things and who shines through the whole world by your own power, god of gods, benefactor [*v.m.*], who manages night and day [*v.m.*], who holds the reins and who steers the rudder, who binds the dragon, holy Agathos Daimon, whose name is [*v.m.*], whom the rising and setting [stars] hymn as you rise and set," ἐπικαλοῦμαί σε, τὸν μέγιστον θεόν, δυνάστην Ὧρον Ἁρποκράτην [*v.m.*]· τὸν τὰ πάντα φωτίζοντα καὶ διαυγάζοντα τῇ ἰδίᾳ δυνάμει τὸν σύμπαντα κόσμον, θεὲ θεῶν, εὐεργέτα [*v.m.*]· ὁ διέπων νύκτα καὶ ἡμέραν [*v.m.*]· ἡνιοχῶν καὶ κυβερνῶν οἴακα, κατέχων δράκοντα, Ἀγαθὸν ἱερὸν Δαίμονα, ᾧ ὄνομα [*v.m.*], ὃν ἀνατολαὶ καὶ δύσεις ὑμνοῦσι ἀνατέλλονα καὶ δύνοντα. Also PGM I.30–32: "Come to me holy Orion, who reclines in the north, who causes the streams of the Nile to roll on, and who mingles them with the sea, and who alters the seed to life like a man's in copulation," ἧκέ μοι, ὁ ἅγιος Ὠρίω[ν, ὁ ἀνακ]είμενος ἐν τῷ βορείῳ, ἐπικυλινδούμενος [τὰ τοῦ Νε]ίλου ῥεύματα καὶ ἐπιμιγνύων τῇ θαλάττῃ καὶ ἀλλ[οιῶν ζω]ῇ καθώσπερ ἀνδρὸς ἐπὶ τῆς συνουσίας τὴν σποράν.

[55] On this point see especially Graf, "Prayer," passim; on Greek customs of prayer more generally, see Pulleyn, *Prayer in Greek Religion*. Cf. Race, *Style and Rhetoric*, 103: "When cultic hymns are very brief and the request predominates, they become indistinguishable from prayers." He adds in a footnote: "The distinction between cultic hymns and prayers mainly involves a question of emphasis," i.e., if the focus is on the petition, it is a prayer, while "cultic hymns have more elaborate invocations; sometimes there is not even a request...."

[56] "In several instances, the papyri state that these names were secret, that the god enjoys being called by them and helps out of joy: it was the gods themselves who had revealed them. The magician behaves not very differently from the initiate of a mystery cult: both claim a special relationship with their respective gods, based on revealed knowledge – this can ex-

troduces himself – either to underscore the unique relationship between himself and the deity, or to masquerade as another god[57] – using ἐγώ εἰμι statements supplemented with mythological expanded epithets.[58] The ubiquity of mythological expanded epithets in pagan petitionary contexts ensures the familiarity of Paul's Gentile readers with the form. As converts from Greco-Roman polytheism, they would have formerly participated in the public festi-

---

plain why parts of mystery rituals were taken over into the prayers of the magical papyri" (Graf, "Prayer," 192).

[57] These statements often appear in the central section of the hymn, the argument, in order to present the petitioner's credentials. See, e.g., PGM IV.185–87, wherein the magician addresses Typhon: "I am the one who, with you, scoured the entire world and who searched out great Osiris, whom I presented to you as a prisoner. I am the one who fought the gods with you." ἐγώ εἰμι ὁ σύν σοι τὴν ὅλην οἰκουμένην ἀνασκαλεύσας καὶ ἐξευρὼν τὸν μέγαν Ὄσιριν, ὅν σοι δέσμιον προσήνεγκα. ἐγώ εἰμι ὁ σύν σοι συμμαχήσας τοῖς θεοῖς.

[58] The ἐγώ εἰμι statements in the PGM resemble what one finds in the 'Isis aretalogies,' lists of statements in the first person by the goddess that their authors published in the temple-precincts of Asia Minor and Egypt (for a succinct overview of the aretalogies, see Gordley, *Colossian Hymn*, 147–55). Isis speaks in short declaratives, as in the opening lines of an aretalogy attested in multiple inscriptions (Totti 1a): "3 I, Isis, am the tyrant of every land; and I was taught by Hermes and I discovered letters, both the sacred and the ordinary, with Hermes, in order that all things might not be written in the same letters. 4 I enacted laws for humans, and I legislated what no one is able to change. 5 I am the oldest daughter of Cronus. 6 I am the wife and sister of Osiris the king. 7 I am the one who discovered fruit for humans. 8 I am the mother of Horus the king. 9 I am the one who commands by means of the Dog Star. 10 I am the goddess who is invoked in the presence of women." 3 Ἴσις ἐγώ εἰμι ἡ τύραννος πάσης χώρας· καὶ ἐπαιδεύθην ὑπὸ Ἑρμοῦ καὶ γράμματα εὗρον μετὰ Ἑρμοῦ, τά τε ἱερὰ καὶ τὰ δημόσια, ἵνα μὴ τοῖς αὐτοῖς πάντα γράφηται. 4 ἐγὼ νόμους ἀνθρώποις ἐθέμην, καὶ ἐνομοθέτησα ἃ οὐθεὶς δύναται μεταθεῖναι. 5 ἐγώ εἰμι Κρόνου θυγατὴρ πρεσβυτάτη. 6 ἐγώ εἰμι γυνὴ καὶ ἀδελφὴ Ὀσίριδος βασιλέως. 7 ἐγώ εἰμι ἡ καρπὸν ἀνθρώποις εὑροῦσα. 8 ἐγώ εἰμι μήτηρ Ὥρου βασιλέως. 9 ἐγώ εἰμι ἡ ἐν τῷ τοῦ Κυνὸς ἄστρῳ ἐπιτέλλουσα. 10 ἐγώ εἰμι ἡ παρὰ γυναιξὶ θεὸς καλουμένη. The expanded epithets (7, 9, 10) here are not sitting alongside one-word epithets as is typical in the Greek hymns discussed above; instead we have complete sentences that directly assert her virtues and deeds. One can detect a small yet significant increase in emphasis over the statements that lack the pattern, especially items 7 and 10: I *and no other* am the one who civilized humanity with the gift of grain; I *and no other* am the deity of women *par excellence*. The aretalogies may have functioned as promotional texts – literary theophanies, as it were – for the cult of Isis. In addition to stressing her cosmogonic roles (Totti 1a.12–14), and to portraying her as the primary civilizing agent through her dispensation of laws and her discovery of important technologies (1a passim), the aretalogies position her within the more familiar framework of the Greek pantheon (1a.3, 5), they mention her power over the sea (1a.15, 39, 43, 49, 53–54), human relationships and childbirth (1a.17–18, 27), and εἱμαρμένη (1a.55–56). These advertisements would attract petitioners to her temple who wish her to intervene in these areas. Many of the declarations abbreviate mythological narratives, for example about her birth and her education with Hermes, but also about her part in the origin of the cosmos and how she came to invent so many important things. The aretalogies' authors may thus have designed her brief statements as bait to attract the curious and to draw them toward initiation and a closer alliance with the goddess.

vals of the civic cults, listened to the hymns offered in praise, and even used expanded epithets in their own devotions.

The other major tributary stream toward the utilization of the expanded epithet pattern in Paul's letters flows from the Hebrew Bible through the Septuagint. The Psalmists use the pattern only rarely, in contrast with its popularity in Greek hymns and prayers.[59] But it often appears in legal contexts, communicating God's assertion of his right to command, as in the opening of the decalogue (Exod 20:2, cf. Deut 5:6): "I am the Lord your God, who led you out from the land of Egypt, from the house of slavery" (ἐγώ εἰμι κύριος ὁ θεός σου, ὅστις ἐξήγαγόν σε [אֲשֶׁר הוֹצֵאתִיךָ] ἐκ γῆς Αἰγύπτου ἐξ οἴκου δουλείας).[60] Prophets similarly introduce their oracles with "thus says the Lord who...," as in Isaiah 43 and 44:

43:1 καὶ νῦν οὕτως λέγει κύριος ὁ θεὸς ὁ ποιήσας σε [בֹּרַאֲךָ], Ιακωβ, ὁ πλάσας σε [וְיֹצֶרְךָ], Ισραηλ .... 14 οὕτως λέγει κύριος ὁ θεὸς ὁ λυτρούμενος ὑμᾶς [גֹּאַלְכֶם] ὁ ἅγιος Ισραηλ.... 15 ἐγώ κύριος ὁ θεὸς ὁ ἅγιος ὑμῶν ὁ καταδείξας [בּוֹרֵא] Ισραηλ βασιλέα ὑμῶν. 16 οὕτως λέγει κύριος ὁ διδοὺς [הַנּוֹתֵן] ὁδὸν ἐν θαλάσσῃ καὶ ἐν ὕδατι ἰσχυρῷ τρίβον 17 ὁ ἐξαγαγών [הַמּוֹצִיא] ἅρματα καὶ ἵππον καὶ ὄχλον ἰσχυρόν.... 25 ἐγώ εἰμι ἐγώ εἰμι ὁ ἐξαλείφων [מֹחֶה] τὰς ἀνομίας σου.... 44:2 οὕτως λέγει κύριος ὁ θεὸς ὁ ποιήσας σε καὶ ὁ πλάσας σε ἐκ κοιλίας [עֹשֶׂךָ וְיֹצֶרְךָ מִבֶּטֶן]....

43:1 And now thus says the Lord God who made you,[61] Jacob, who formed you, Israel.... 14 Thus says the Lord God who redeemed you, the Holy One of Israel.... 15 I am your holy God who introduced your king, O Israel. 16 Thus says the Lord who gave a path in the sea and a track in mighty water, 17 who brought out chariots and horse and a mighty crowd.... 25 *I am*

---

[59] The two instances that I found are also benedictions, LXX 65:20 ("Blessed be God, who did not stand away from my prayer," εὐλογητὸς ὁ θεός, ὃς οὐκ ἀπέστησεν [אֲשֶׁר לֹא־הֵסִיר] τὴν προσευχήν μου) and LXX 123:6 ("Blessed be the Lord, who did not give us as prey for their teeth," εὐλογητὸς κύριος, ὃς οὐκ ἔδωκεν ἡμᾶς [שֶׁלֹּא נְתָנָנוּ] εἰς θήραν τοῖς ὀδοῦσιν αὐτῶν). Cf. other benedictions, e.g. 1 Kings 1:48 (David: "Blessed be the Lord, the God of Israel, who today gave from my seed one who sits on my throne, and my eyes see him," εὐλογητὸς κύριος ὁ θεὸς Ισραηλ, ὃς ἔδωκεν [אֲשֶׁר נָתַן] σήμερον ἐκ τοῦ σπέρματός μου καθήμενον ἐπὶ τοῦ θρόνου μου, καὶ οἱ ὀφθαλμοί μου βλέπουσιν); 5:21 (Hiram to Solomon: "Blessed be God today, who gave to David a prudent son over this great people," εὐλογητὸς ὁ θεὸς σήμερον, ὃς ἔδωκεν [אֲשֶׁר נָתַן] τῷ Δαυιδ υἱὸν φρόνιμον ἐπὶ τὸν λαὸν τὸν πολὺν τοῦτον); Judith 13:18 (Ozias to Judith: "Blessed are you, daughter ... and blessed be the Lord God, who created the heavens and the earth, who guided you to a head-wound of the leader of your enemies," εὐλογητὴ σύ, θύγατερ ... καὶ εὐλογημένος κύριος ὁ θεός, ὃς ἔκτισεν τοὺς οὐρανοὺς καὶ τὴν γῆν, ὃς κατεύθυνέν σε εἰς τραῦμα κεφαλῆς ἄρχοντος ἐχθρῶν ἡμῶν); 2 Macc 1:17 ("Blessed in every way be our God, who handed over those who committed impiety," κατὰ πάντα εὐλογητὸς ὑμῶν ὁ θεός, ὃς παρέδωκεν τοὺς ἀσεβήσαντας).

[60] Cf. Num 15:41; Lev 20:24, 26 ("I am the Lord your God, who divided you from all the nations.... I am holy, the Lord your God who set you apart from all the nations to be mine," ἐγώ κύριος ὁ θεὸς ὑμῶν, ὃς διώρισα ὑμᾶς [אֲשֶׁר־הִבְדַּלְתִּי אֶתְכֶם] ἀπὸ πάντων τῶν ἐθνῶν.... ἐγώ ἅγιος κύριος ὁ θεὸς ὑμῶν ὁ ἀφορίσας ὑμᾶς [אֲנִי יְהוָה וָאַבְדִּל אֶתְכֶם] ἀπὸ πάντων τῶν ἐθνῶν εἶναι ἐμοί).

[61] Cf. Isa 51:13, "And you forgot the God who made you, who made heaven and founded the earth," καὶ ἐπελάθου θεὸν τὸν ποιήσαντά σε, τὸν ποιήσαντα τὸν οὐρανὸν καὶ θεμελιώσαντα τὴν γῆν [עֹשֶׂךָ נוֹטֶה שָׁמַיִם וְיֹסֵד אָרֶץ].

the one who wipes out your lawlessnesses.... 44:2 Thus says the Lord God who made you and formed you from the womb.....

The prophetic context in which these expanded epithets occur warrants emphasis: they remind their auditors of the great deeds of God in the past while they underscore his tremendous power and continuing concern for Israel in the present. Their formality and gravity summon their hearers to attend carefully to the oracles which follow. The theme of the Exodus pervades mythological expanded epithets in the Septuagint,[62] as one would expect, but sometimes more recent divine activities prompt the creation of new ones:

διὰ τοῦτο ἰδοὺ ἡμέραι ἔρχονται, λέγει κύριος, καὶ οὐκ ἐροῦσιν ἔτι ζῇ κύριος ὁ ἀναγαγὼν [אֲשֶׁר הֶעֱלָה] τοὺς υἱοὺς Ισραηλ ἐκ γῆς Αἰγύπτου, ἀλλὰ ζῇ κύριος ὃς ἀνήγαγεν [אֲשֶׁר הֶעֱלָה] τὸν οἶκον Ισραηλ ἀπὸ γῆς βορρᾶ καὶ ἀπὸ πασῶν τῶν χωρῶν.

Because of this, behold, days are coming, says the Lord, and they will not say any more: "As the Lord who led the children of Israel up from the land of Egypt lives," rather: "As the Lord who led the house of Israel up from a northern land and from all countries lives." (Jer 16:14–15)

This remarkable passage parallels what Paul is doing in his own mythological expanded epithets. God's pending relocation of his people from the four corners of the world will become a divine act of such magnitude that it displaces even the most seminal of his earlier deeds. The God "who led Israel up from Egypt" similarly becomes the God "who raised Jesus from the dead."

---

[62] E.g., 1 Sam 12:6 ("The Lord who made Moses and Aaron, who led our fathers up from Egypt is witness," μάρτυς κύριος ὁ ποιήσας [אֲשֶׁר עָשָׂה] τὸν Μωυσῆν καὶ τὸν Ααρων, ὁ ἀναγαγὼν [וַאֲשֶׁר הֶעֱלָה] τοὺς πατέρας ἡμῶν ἐξ Αἰγύπτου); Baruch 2:11–12 ("And now, O Lord, God of Israel, who brought your people out from the land of Egypt with a mighty hand and with signs and with wonders and with great power and with a raised arm ... we sinned, we were impious, we were unjust," καὶ νῦν, κύριε ὁ θεὸς Ισραηλ, ὃς ἐξήγαγες τὸν λαόν σου ἐκ γῆς Αἰγύπτου ἐν χειρὶ κραταιᾷ καὶ ἐν σημείοις καὶ ἐν τέρασιν καὶ ἐν δυνάμει μεγάλῃ καὶ ἐν βραχίονι ὑψηλῷ ... ἡμάρτομεν ἠσεβήσαμεν ἠδικήσαμεν). Cf. PGM IV.3033–37 (πρὸς δαιμονιαζομένους): "I adjure you who was seen by Osrael in the bright pillar and in the cloud by day, and who rescued his people from Pharaoh and who bore upon Pharaoh the tenfold-plague because he disobeyed," ὁρκίζω σε τὸν ὀπτανθέντα τῷ Ὀσραὴλ ἐν στύλῳ φωτινῷ καὶ νεφέλῃ ἡμερινῇ, καὶ ῥυσάμενον αὐτοῦ τὸν λαὸν ἐκ τοῦ Φαραὼ καὶ ἐπενέγκαντα ἐπὶ Φαραὼ τὴν δεκάπληγον διὰ τὸ παρακούειν αὐτόν. The Israelites refer to their idols similarly in a couple of passages: Exod 32:8 ("They quickly transgressed the way which I commanded them: they made for themselves a calf and they have worshipped it and sacrificed to it and they said, 'These are your gods, O Israel, who led you up from the land of Egypt,'" παρέβησαν ταχὺ ἐκ τῆς ὁδοῦ, ἧς ἐνετειλω αὐτοῖς· ἐποίησαν ἑαυτοῖς μόσχον καὶ προσκεκυνήκασιν αὐτῷ καὶ τεθύκασιν αὐτῷ καὶ εἶπαν· οὗτοι οἱ θεοί σου, Ισραηλ, οἵτινες ἀνεβίβασάν σε [אֲשֶׁר הֶעֱלוּךָ] ἐκ γῆς Αἰγύπτου); 1 Kings 12:28 (Jeroboam introduces his golden calves: "Let your going up to Jerusalem come to an end; behold your gods, O Israel, who led you up from the land of Egypt," ἱκανούσθω ὑμῖν ἀναβαίνειν εἰς Ιερουσαλημ· ἰδοὺ θεοί σου, Ισραηλ, οἱ ἀναγαγόντες σε [אֲשֶׁר הֶעֱלוּךָ] ἐκ γῆς Αἰγύπτου).

4.4 The definition extended (1:3b–4)

In Hellenistic Jewish literature outside of the Septuagint, mythological expanded epithets continue to occur in in God's statements about himself,[63] and in oracles.[64] But in distinction from its rare utilization in the Psalms, one finds it in hymns and prayers as part of a trend toward the conventions of Greek hymns both in structure (invocation, argument, petition) and style. The short prayer of Joseph in *Jos. Asen.* 8:9–11, for example, reads:

9 Κύριε ὁ θεὸς τοῦ πατρός μου Ἰσραὴλ
10 ὁ ὕψιστος ὁ δυνατὸς τοῦ Ἰακὼβ
ὁ ζωοποιήσας τὰ πάντα
καὶ καλέσας ἀπὸ τοῦ σκότους εἰς τὸ φῶς
καὶ ἀπὸ τῆς πλάνης εἰς τὴν ἀλήθειαν
καὶ ἀπὸ τοῦ θανάτου εἰς τὴν ζωήν
σὺ κύριε εὐλόγησον τὴν παρθένον ταύτην
11 καὶ ἀνακαίνισον αὐτὴν τῷ πνεύματί σου
καὶ ἀνάπλασον αὐτὴν τῇ χειρί σου τῇ ⟨κρυφαίᾳ⟩
καὶ ἀναζωοποίησον αὐτὴν τῇ ζωῇ σου
καὶ φαγέτω ἄρτον ζωῆς σου
καὶ πιέτω ποτήριον εὐλογίας σου
καὶ συγκαταρίθμησον αὐτὴν τῷ λαῷ σου
  ὃν ἐξελέξω πρὶν γενέσθαι τὰ πάντα
καὶ εἰσελθέτω εἰς τὴν κατάπαυσίν σου
  ἣν ἡτοίμησας τοῖς ἐκλεκτοῖς σου
καὶ ζησάτω ἐν τῇ αἰωνίῳ ζωῇ σου εἰς τὸν αἰῶνα χρόνον.

---

[63] E.g., *T. Ab.* (rec. A) 8:4–6: "But God said to Michael: 'Depart to my friend Abraham yet once [more], and tell him thus. Thus says your God: why did I leave you behind on earth? I am your God, the one who led you up into the land of your promise; the one who blessed you beyond the sand of the sea and like the stars of the sky; the one who freed Sarah's womb from sterility and generously gave you fruit of the belly in old age, your son Isaac." εἶπεν δὲ ὁ θεὸς τὸν Μιχαήλ· ἄπελθε πρὸς τὸν φίλον μου τὸν Ἀβραὰμ ⟨ἔτι ἅπαξ⟩, καὶ εἰπὲ αὐτὸν οὕτως· τάδε λέγει ὁ θεός σου· τί σε ἐγκατέλειπα ἐπὶ τῆς γῆς; ἐγώ εἰμι ὁ θεός σου ὁ ἀναγαγών σε εἰς τὴν γῆν τῆς ἐπαγγελίας σου· ὁ εὐλογήσας σε ὑπὲρ ἄμμον θαλάσσης καὶ ὡς τοὺς ἀστέρας τοῦ οὐρανοῦ· ὁ διαλύσας μήτραν Σάρρας τῆς στειρώσεως, καὶ χαρισάμενός σοι καρπὸν κοιλίας ἐν γήρει υἱὸν τὸν Ἰσαάκ.

[64] E.g., *Sib. Or.* 3.20–25, "[It is he] who with a word created all things, heaven and sea, | tireless sun and full moon, | shining stars and poweful mother Tethys, | springs and rivers, immortal fire, days, nights, | indeed God himself is the one who molded the tetragrammaton, Adam...," ὃς λόγῳ ἔκτισε πάντα καὶ οὐρανὸν ἠδὲ θάλασσαν | ἠέλιόν τ' ἀκάμαντα σελήνην τε πλήθουσαν | ἄστρα τε λαμπετόωντα, κραταιὰν μητέρα Τηθύν, | πηγὰς καὶ ποταμούς, πῦρ ἄφθιτον, ἤματα, νύκτας, | αὐτὸς δὴ θεός ἐσθ' ὁ πλάσας τετραγράμματον Ἀδάμ.... Cf. 3.11–14: "The one God is monarch, unutterable, who dwells in the aether, | self-generated, an invisible one who himself sees all things, | whom neither hand nor sculptor made, neither from gold | nor from ivory does his image appear by human crafts," εἷς θεός ἐστι μόναρχος ἀθέσφατος αἰθέρι ναίων | αὐτοφυής ἀόρατος ὁρώμενος αὐτὸς ἅπαντα· | ὃν χεὶρ οὐκ ἐποίησε λιθοξόος οὐδ' ἀπὸ χρυσοῦ | τέχνησ' ἀνθρώπου φαίνει τύπος οὐδ' ἐλέφαντος.

9 Lord, the God of my father Israel,
10 the highest, the mighty one of Jacob,
who enlivened all things,
and who called [them] from darkness into light,
and from error into truth,
and from death into life,
Lord bless this maiden [Aseneth],
11 and renew her with your spirit,
and re-mold her with your secret hand,
and re-enliven her with your life,
and let her eat your bread of life,
and drink your cup of blessing,
and number her with your people
 whom you chose before all things came to be,
and let her enter into your rest
which you prepared for your elect,
 and let her live in your eternal life for time eternal.

This prayer divides into invocation (a series of epithets, lines 1–2), argument (the mythological expanded epithets in 3–6), and petition (7–17). That the author means the expanded epithets as the prayer's argument becomes clear from their relationship with the petition: Joseph asks God to apply the power which he exercised in his acts of creation for Aseneth (renew, remold, re-enliven), and then to include her among the children of Israel. Although the prayer has an overtly Hellenic hymnic format, it retains a Septuagintal flavor primarily by its parataxis (the long sentence of many clauses joined with καί). The prayer lacks the feature of parallel couplets throughout, however, but does have triplets in 4–6, 8–10, and 14–17. The *Prayer of Manasseh* (LXX Ode 12) exhibits a similar structure and style,[65] but here the expanded epithets stand in the invocation:

1 Κύριε παντοκράτωρ,
ὁ θεὸς τῶν πατέρων ἡμῶν,
τοῦ Αβρααμ καὶ Ισαακ καὶ Ιακωβ
καὶ τοῦ σπέρματος αὐτῶν τοῦ δικαίου,
2 ὁ ποιήσας τὸν οὐρανὸν καὶ τὴν γῆν σὺν παντὶ τῷ κόσμῳ αὐτῶν,
3 ὁ πεδήσας τὴν θάλασσαν τῷ λόγῳ τοῦ προστάγματός σου,
ὁ κλείσαις τὴν ἄβυσσον καὶ σφραγισάμενος τῷ φοβερῷ καὶ ἐνδόξῳ ὀνόματί σου,
4 ὃν πάντα φρίττει καὶ τρέμει ἀπὸ προσώπου δυνάμεως σου....

1 Lord Almighty,
the God of our fathers,
of Abraham and Isaac and Jacob

---

[65] The text breaks down into invocation (vv. 1–4), argument (vv. 5–10), and petition (vv. 11–15). The point of transition between the first two sections may not seem obvious, but a couple of points support my analysis. V. 4 breaks the sequence of mythological expanded epithets and aids the shift to the author's overview of the circumstances beginning with observations about God's character and his allotment of repentence and forgiveness for sinners. "Manasseh" then confesses his sins that require God's mercy, which he begs in the petition.

and of their righteous seed,
2 who made heaven and earth will all their order,
3 who constrained the sea with the word of your command,
who closed the abyss and sealed it with your fearful and glorious name,
4 whom all things dread and fear from the presentation [lit., "face"] of your power....

The initial epithets identify God through the narrative cycles of the patriarchs, then the expanded epithets unfold his absolute power in the creation and organization of the cosmos.[66] In v. 4 'Manasseh' begins his transition out of the invocation and into the argument with shifts in syntax (from attributive participial phrases to relative clauses) and in theme (from primordial myth to the present universal experience of dread). His point is clear: the God who wields such power for the benefit of humanity has the authority to forgive sins and thus to grant Manasseh's petition to do precisely that. These two samples suggest that the conventions of Greek hymns are beginning to exert some influence, both in the structural features of the prayers, and in the inclusion of mythological expanded epithets in their invocations and arguments alongside shorter epithets. Authors that present characters like Joseph and Manasseh as praying in such a manner furnish implicit evidence of their own (and their communities') petitionary and hymnic practices.

Mythological expanded epithets therefore abbreviate myths by concisely referring to a distinctive part, using συνεκδοχή as the primary method of abbreviation. Expanded epithets in hymns and prayers (indeed *all* epithets when they do not replace a divine name outright) are a form of μακρολογία, especially when they appear in series. Listing the names, attributes and mythical deeds of the gods in prayer constitutes an act of worshipful piety, implying their expectation and enjoyment of such verbal offerings. The mythological expanded epithets achieve this μακρολογία by loading the statements with unstated content which the audience can supply from the mentioned part. Sometimes the selected myths have immediate relevance for the contexts in which they appear. The passages from Homeric *Hymn* 2 *to Demeter* and *Hymn* 4 *to Hermes* discussed above use mythological expanded epithets topically, to introduce the narrative that the hymn will unfold. They may also function as part of the overall persuasive strategy of a hymn or prayer: the myths to which they refer may address a divinity's power or authority which the petition directly invokes,[67] as in the prayer of Joseph for Aseneth. In the legal and prophetic passages of the Bible in which they appear, they establish God's right

---

[66] See also *T. Job* 2:4, Job's question in response to viewing the activities of a pagan shrine near his home: "Is this the God who made heaven and earth and the sea and us ourselves? How indeed will I know?" ἄρα οὗτός ἐστιν ὁ θεὸς ὁ ποιήσας τὸν οὐρανὸν καὶ τὴν γῆν καὶ τὴν θάλασσαν καὶ ἡμᾶς αὐτούς; ἄρα πῶς γνώσομαι;

[67] Cf. Race, "Rhetoric and Form in Greek Hymns," 10: "When there is a petition at the end of a hymn, it must of course be consonant with the god's powers as established in the body of the hymn, and follow naturally from the goodwill established between the god and man."

to issue commands or recall his past benevolences in order to underscore his continuing concern for Israel. Mythological expanded epithets in both Greco-Roman and Hellenistic Jewish sources thus refer to the past but speak to the present and future – to the *kind* of god who did something, and thus would do, or will do, or is doing something similar. They only work properly, however, if one's auditor already knows the myth or will shortly hear it for the first time. If one's addressee is only the god (as in private petitions and many magic spells), this presents less of a concern. But in formal, publically performed hymns or any other context they would be incomprehensible without their auditors' knowledge of the fuller account. The same principle applies to the use of the pattern in oracles: the declaration "thus says the Lord who made heaven and earth," or "who led you up from the land of Egypt," would impart little authority in the absence of an awareness of the creation and Exodus myths.

When used outside of hymnic or poetic contexts, Aristotle says that epithets generally "transform the ordinary and render the style exotic" (ἐξελάττει γὰρ τὸ εἰωθός, καὶ ξενικὴν ποιεῖ τὴν λέξιν).[68] He warns, however, that "those who are speaking poetically cause absurdity and frigidity by their lack of decorum, and obscurity because of their prolixity; for whenever one overloads somebody who knows [already what is being discussed], one dissolves the clarity by overshadowing it" (διὸ ποιητικῶς λέγοντες τῇ ἀπρεπείᾳ τὸ γελοῖον καὶ τὸ ψυχρὸν ἐποιοῦσι, καὶ τὸ ἀσαφὲς διὰ τὴν ἀδολεσχίαν· ὅταν γὰρ γιγνώσκοντι ἐπεμβάλλῃ, διαλύει τὸ σάφες τῷ ἐπισκοτεῖν). Epithets thus elevate the style though their association with poetry. When applied to gods, such epithets in prose would likewise evoke hymnic poetry, resulting in a comparable stylistic heightening. They work so well for this purpose that using them too much can diminish the clarity of what one is saying. Aristotle's advice not to "overload the one who knows" correlates with Menander Rhetor's theoretical remarks in connection with mythological prose hymns:

γυμνοὶ δὲ οἱ μῦθοι τιθέμενοι σφόδρα λυποῦσι καὶ ἐνοχλοῦσι τὰς ἀκοάς. δεῖ τοίνυν ὅτι βραχυτάτοις ἀπαλλάττεσθαι. παραμυθίας οὖν προσακτέον καὶ πρὸς συντομίαν καὶ πρὸς ἡδονήν, πρῶτον μὲν μὴ ἀπ' εὐθείας πάντα εἰσάγειν, ἀλλὰ τὰ μὲν παραλείπειν λέγοντα, τὰ δὲ συγχωρεῖν, τὰ δὲ κατὰ συμπλοκὴν εἰσάγειν, τὰ δὲ προσποιεῖσθαι ἐξηγεῖσθαι, τὰ δὲ μὴ πιστεύειν μηδὲ ἀπιστεῖν. καὶ ὅλως οὐκ ἀπορήσεις μεθόδων, ἕν γε τοῦτο θεώρημα σώζων, ὡς διατριβὴ ἀπρόσφορος. ἡ δὲ ἑρμηνεία, ὅπερ καὶ περὶ τῆς διατριβῆς ἔφαμεν, ἐπὶ ἐλάττονος ἐξουσίας γινέσθω, σώζουσα μὲν τὸν ἐπιδεικτικὸν κόσμον, πολὺ δὲ τοῦ διθυράμβου ἀποβεβηκυῖα. γίγνοιτο δ' ⟨ἂν⟩ τοιαύτη, εἰ τῷ Ἰσοκράτους θεωρήματι χρησόμεθα, καὶ τὸ κάλλος καὶ τὴν σεμνότητα μὴ ἀπὸ τῶν ὀνομάτων μᾶλλον [ἢ] τῆς ἀρχαιότητος ἢ τοῦ μεγέθους θηρώμεθα, ⟨ἀλλ'⟩ ἀπὸ τῆς ἁρμονίας καὶ τῶν σχημάτων.

Myths, if set out naked, very much grieve and annoy the ears. Accordingly one must be done with them as briefly as possible. One therefore needs to furnish consolations both for the purpose of conciseness and for the purpose of enjoyment: first not to bring forward all [parts of the narrative] straightaway, rather when speaking to omit some things, to concede others, to

---

[68] See Excursus 1 above for a fuller quotation of this and the following passage.

introduce some with an intertwining [of several points], to pretend to narrate others, and neither to trust nor mistrust others. But on the whole you will not be at a loss for methods if you keep this one rule in mind, that a full exposition is unsuitable. And, as we said about full exposition, let the style be in the vicinity of lesser excess, retaining epideictic adornment on the one hand, but remaining very far from the dithyramb on the other. Now such a style should occur, if we employ the rule of Isocrates: let us seek after both beauty and dignity not more in archaic or grandiose words, but in intonation and rhetorical figures. (*Epid.* 1.339)

Shorthand references to known mythological narratives with the figure of συνεκδοχή would certainly be one method of adhering to Menander's advice. The motive for issuing his cautionary words about keeping the recitations of myths brief and to the point in oratorical contexts seems sufficiently evident: the proper medium for full recitation of myths is poetry. Doing so in prose clashes with the expectations of one's audience, causing the annoyance to the "ears" (αἱ ἀκοαί). The combination of the perspectives of Aristotle and Menander reveals that mythological expanded epithets (and, by extension, expanded epithets generally) function as extremely abbreviated hymns.

4.4.3 Mythological expanded epithets in the letters of Paul

Having now completed the first stage of my argument, I now turn to the second, an examination of mythological expanded epithets in the letters of Paul, which most often elaborate the death and resurrection of Christ and the soteriological consequences of those events.[69] He deftly takes advantage of the συνεκδοχή which is characteristic of the form, and of the hymnic and prophetic resonances that it carries with it. He relays the outlines of the narrative to which his mythological expanded epithets refer in 1 Cor 15:3–8; another fragment very likely appears in 1 Cor 11:23–26, an account of the institution of the Lord's Supper. Both passages are extremely compressed – almost as much as any of Paul's expanded epithets – and clearly assume greater knowl-

---

[69] Paul also uses expanded epithets that do not abbreviate narratives but instead summarize the attributes or actions of God in other ways: his protection from testing (1 Cor 10:13, πιστὸς δὲ ὁ θεός, ὃς οὐκ ἐάσει ὑμᾶς πειρασθῆναι ὑπὲρ ὃ δύνασθε ἀλλὰ ποιήσει σὺν τῷ πειρασμῷ καὶ τὴν ἔκβασιν τοῦ δύνασθαι ὑπενεγκεῖν), and his roles as the one who acquits (1 Cor 1:8, Christ, ὃς καὶ βεβαιώσει ὑμᾶς ἕως τέλους ἀνεγκλήτους ἐν τῇ ἡμέρᾳ τοῦ κυρίου ἡμῶν Ἰησοῦ [Χριστοῦ]), who calls (1 Cor 1:9, πιστὸς ὁ θεὸς δι' οὗ ἐκλήθητε εἰς κοινωνίαν τοῦ υἱοῦ αὐτοῦ Ἰησοῦ Χριστοῦ τοῦ κυρίου ἡμῶν), who consoles (2 Cor 1:3–4, εὐλογητὸς ὁ θεὸς καὶ πατὴρ τοῦ κυρίου ἡμῶν Ἰησοῦ Χριστοῦ, ὁ πατὴρ τῶν οἰκτιρμῶν καὶ θεὸς πάσης παρακλήσεως, ὁ παρακαλῶν ἡμᾶς ἐπὶ πάσῃ τῇ θλίψει ἡμῶν εἰς τὸ δύνασθαι ἡμᾶς παρακαλεῖν τοὺς ἐν πάσῃ θλίψει διὰ τῆς παρακλήσεως ἧς παρακαλούμεθα αὐτοὶ ὑπὸ τοῦ θεοῦ, cf. the benediction formulations at Rom 1:25, 9:5; 2 Cor 11:31), who raises the dead and rescues from death (2 Cor 1:9–10, ἵνα μὴ πεποιθότες ὦμεν ἐφ' ἑαυτοῖς ἀλλ' ἐπὶ τῷ θεῷ τῷ ἐγείροντι τοὺς νεκρούς· ὃς ἐκ τηλικούτου θανάτου ἐρρύσατο ἡμᾶς καὶ ῥύσεται, εἰς ὃν ἠλπίκαμεν [ὅτι] καὶ ἔτι ῥύσεται), and who leads in triumph (2 Cor 2:14, τῷ δὲ θεῷ χάρις τῷ πάντοτε θριαμβεύοντι ἡμᾶς ἐν τῷ Χριστῷ καὶ τὴν ὀσμὴν τῆς γνώσεως αὐτοῦ φανεροῦντι δι' ἡμῶν ἐν παντὶ τόπῳ).

edge of the events mentioned.[70] The gospel of Paul and his communities includes a passion account that narrates the death, burial, and resurrection of Christ, and that explains how these events fulfill certain passages of scripture (κατὰ τὰς γραφάς, 1 Cor 15:3-4; cf. ἐν γραφαῖς ἁγίαις, Rom 1:2) and how they benefit believers (τὸ σῶμα τὸ ὑπὲρ ὑμῶν, 1 Cor 11:24; ὑπὲρ τῶν ἁμαρτιῶν, 15:3). It may also contain some data regarding Jesus' lineage and birth, although this cannot be definitively established.[71] It clearly predates Paul's evangelistic labors (παρέλαβον, παρέδωκεν, 1 Cor 11:23, 15:3). It is thus 'traditional,' regardless of whether the wording in 1 Cor 11:23-26 and 15:3-8 come from formulas. He can presuppose that the Romans know it in essentially the same form as he does. It is one of the strands that bind Christian communities together across the Mediterranean basin, and is a 'myth' in the sense that is a foundational narrative around which the cult of Christ congregates and builds its distinctive rituals.

The hymnic dimension of the mythological expanded epithet stands out most obviously when Paul uses it to praise God or Christ. Prescripts and thanksgiving sections offer ideal contexts for such praise. Two instances of the form adorn the prescript of Galatians, (1:1-5) where he refers to "God the Father, who raised him [Jesus] from the dead" (διὰ ... θεοῦ πατρὸς τοῦ ἐγείραντος αὐτὸν ἐκ νεκρῶν), and then to "the Lord Jesus Christ, who gave himself on behalf of our sins" (ἀπὸ ... κυρίου Ἰησοῦ Χριστοῦ, τοῦ δόντος ἑαυτὸν ὑπὲρ τῶν ἁμαρτιῶν). 1 Thess 1:9-10 has two coordinated expanded epithets referring to the one "whom he [God] raised from the dead, Jesus who rescues us from the coming wrath" (ὃν ἤγειρεν ἐκ [τῶν] νεκρῶν, Ἰησοῦν τὸν ῥυόμενον ἡμᾶς ἐκ τῆς ὀργῆς τῆς ἐρχομένης). The two-part statement – the first dealing with the past and the second the future – closes the letter's introductory sections soaringly while foreshadowing the eschatological themes of chapters 4 and 5. Paul also constructs expanded epithets in his conclusions of sections of his argument in Romans. In 4:24-25 he effects a transition from Abraham's πίστις to the power of πίστις to bring about "peace with God" in chapter 5:

4:22 διὸ [καὶ] «ἐλογίσθη αὐτῷ εἰς δικαιοσύνην». 23 οὐκ ἐγράφη δὲ δι' αὐτὸν μόνον ὅτι ἐλογίσθη αὐτῷ 24 ἀλλὰ καὶ δι' ἡμᾶς, οἷς μέλλει λογίζεσθαι, τοῖς πιστεύουσιν ἐπὶ τὸν ἐγείραντα Ἰησοῦν τὸν κύριον ἡμῶν ἐκ νεκρῶν, 25 ὃς παρεδόθη διὰ τὰ παραπτώματα ἡμῶν καὶ ἠγέρθη διὰ τὴν δικαίωσιν ἡμῶν.

4:22 Therefore also "it was reckoned to him [Abraham] as righteousness." 23 But it was not written on account of him alone that "it was reckoned to him," 24 but also on account of us for whom it is about to be reckoned, for those who believe *in the one who raised Jesus our Lord from the dead,* 25 *who was handed over on account of our transgressions and was raised on account of our acquittal.*

---

[70] See n. 17 above.
[71] I discuss this possibility further below.

4.4 The definition extended (1:3b–4)

As in 1 Thess 1:9–10, we have a bipartite statement with both a relative clause and an attributive participial phrase. Paul is building a logical bridge from Abraham's faith in God to deliver on his promises, to "our" faith in God who acted through Jesus, then to the immediate benefit of this faith, the cessation of the adversarial relationship of God and humanity (5:1, δικαιωθέντες οὖν ἐκ πίστεως εἰρήνην ἔχομεν πρὸς τὸν θεόν). Similarly Paul closes his argument in chapters 5–8 by deploying the form repeatedly:

8:31 Τί οὖν ἐροῦμεν πρὸς ταῦτα; εἰ ὁ θεὸς ὑπὲρ ἡμῶν, τίς καθ' ἡμῶν; 32 ὅς γε τοῦ ἰδίου υἱοῦ οὐκ ἐφείσατο ἀλλὰ ὑπὲρ ἡμῶν πάντων παρέδωκεν αὐτόν, πῶς οὐχὶ καὶ σὺν αὐτῷ τὰ πάντα ἡμῖν χαρίσεται; 33 τίς ἐγκαλέσει κατὰ ἐκλεκτῶν θεοῦ; θεὸς ὁ δικαιῶν· 34 τίς ὁ κατακρινῶν; Χριστὸς [Ἰησοῦς] ὁ ἀποθανών, μᾶλλον δὲ ἐγερθείς, ὃς καί ἐστιν ἐν δεξιᾷ τοῦ θεοῦ, ὃς καὶ ἐντυγχάνει ὑπὲρ ἡμῶν.

8:31 What, therefore, shall we say regarding these matters? If God is for us, who is against us? 32 How will he, *who did not spare his own Son but handed him over on behalf of us all*, also not give all things to us with him? 33 Who will issue the indictment against God's elect? God, the one who justifies. 34 Who is the one who will condemn? Christ Jesus *who died, and more who was raised, who also is at the right hand of God, who also intercedes on our behalf.*

The remaining verses of chapter 8 build toward a crescendo of praise of the God from whom nothing can or will "separate us" (δυνήσεται ἡμᾶς χωρίσαι). In v. 34 Paul again juxtaposes participial phrases and relative clauses, the former to underscore the past events (but note ὁ δικαιῶν and ὁ κατακρινῶν) and the latter the present status of Jesus. Thematically the mythological expanded epithets in the above passages appropriate the narrative of the gospel via συνεκδοχή with consistent emphasis upon Christ's death and resurrection, and the soteriological significance of these events. Paul uses them primarily to praise God and Christ, tapping directly into the form's home within hymns and prayers. They also noticeably elevate the stylistic tone of the passages in which they appear.

The prophetic dimension of mythological expanded epithets becomes prominent when Paul uses the form argumentatively; the compressed narrative can function as evidence, while the form itself underscores Paul's apostolic (*qua* prophetic) authority. The instances cited above from the prescript of Galatians not only praise God, but reinforce Paul's subsequent claim in 1:6–9 that there is no gospel but his by evoking its content through συνεκδοχή. Galatians offers a couple of other illuminating samples. In 1:15, Paul refers to God, "who set me apart from my mother's womb and called me through his grace" (ὁ ἀφορίσας με ἐκ κοιλίας μητρός μου καὶ καλέσας διὰ τῆς χάριτος αὐτοῦ), an unmistakable allusion to Jer 1:5.[72] Evidently his readers know this

---

[72] God says to Jeremiah: πρὸ τοῦ με πλάσαι σε ἐν κοιλίᾳ ἐπίσταμαί σε καὶ πρὸ τοῦ σε ἐξελθεῖν ἐκ μήτρας ἡγίακά σε, προφήτην εἰς ἔθνη τέθεικά σε. Cf. Isa 44:2. See further Betz, *Galatians*, 69–70; Martyn, *Galatians*, 155–57.

part of Paul's story, but the form maps Paul's own call onto that of God's summoning of his prophets. God chose him to be his agent, his special emissary to the Gentiles, prior to his birth. In 2:20, a mythological expanded epithet helps him to establish the contrast between δικαιοῦσθαι ἐκ πίστεως Χριστοῦ and ἐξ ἔργων νόμου: "But the life that I now live in the flesh I live by faith in the Son of God who loved me and gave himself for me" (ὃ δὲ νῦν ζῶ ἐν σαρκί, ἐν πίστει ζῶ τῇ τοῦ υἱοῦ τοῦ θεοῦ τοῦ ἀγαπήσαντός με καὶ παραδόντος ἑαυτὸν ὑπὲρ ἐμοῦ). The object of faith, the Son of God, is further captured by evocation of what he achieved on "my" behalf.

In his mythological expanded epithets, Paul leaves details about the account to which he synecdochically refers obscured, and he speaks of the soteriological implications in the briefest possible manner. An ancient non-Christian who encountered Paul's abbreviations of the gospel in his expanded epithets would recognize their form, but would probably lack the ability to understand their content without further exposition (why it would be important that Christ died and was raised, or how these events would remove the consequences of the transgressions committed by others). Paul adroitly capitalizes upon the ability of συνεκδοχή in mythological expanded epithets to summon to mind the entirety of τὸ εὐαγγέλιον while retaining a tight focus on the elements specifically mentioned, resulting in rhetorically powerful blends of μακρολογία and βραχυλογία.

I identified earlier four problem that my theory needs to resolve: (1) the syntactical and stylistic regularities that exist between Rom 1:3b–4 and other predicative statements attached to God or Christ; (2) the differences between these statements that make them unique formulations in their contexts; (3) the regularities in topics and the similiarities in methods of setting these topics forth; and (4) the nature of the sources that underpin the statements. The mythological expanded epithet provides a ready explanation for both the syntactical and stylistic similarities and the differences between vv. 3b–4 and other 'pre-Pauline' passages. They are similar because they draw upon a form that consistently uses relative clauses and participles in order to elaborate concisely a myth associated with a divinity through συνεκδοχή. They are different because Paul composes them himself for each unique context in which they appear. They have common topics because of their consistent source: a soteriologically interpreted account of the death and resurrection of Christ that is a central component of τὸ εὐαγγέλιον. Did early Christians formulate their hymns and prayers using expanded epithets of the type seen in Greek hymns? If Paul's facility with them gives any indication, it seems very probable that they did.[73] However, the hymnic association of the form does not mean that

---

[73] For example, the 'hymns' in Philippians and Colossians both begin with relative clauses (Phil 2:6, Col 1:15), the former narrating Christ's decision to "empty himself" (ἐκένωσεν, 2:7).

any instance of it in Paul's writings must have originally come from a hymn. By the same token, the prophetic association of the form does not make any instance of it an oracle. The mythological expanded epithet is adaptable to numerous settings and purposes, even as it retains the texture of the kinds of literature in which it normally appears.

4.4.4 Analysis of 1:3b–4

Paul's two-part mythological expanded epithet in Rom 1:3b–4 stands out boldly from other instances of the form in his letters, both in the topics that he raises and in the sophistication of the tactics of brevity that he employs. It, like many others, mentions Christ's resurrection. But the accent falls primarily upon his birth and appointment on the one hand, and his flesh and spirit on the other: these two pairs represent the points at which God's pre-proclamation and promise in the scriptures intersect with comprehensive fulfillments in the Son. Messianically interpreted oracles link with narratives captured via συνεκδοχή, resulting in a succinct statement of the οἷόν τ' ἔστι of the gospel that has a dense saturation of unstated content. It folds the entirety of the life of Christ – his story and his nature – into τὸ εὐαγγέλιον θεοῦ.[74] Paul's method of encapsulation utilizes two antitheses in conjunction with the συνεκδοχή which is characteristic of the mythological expanded epithet. Verifying these points is my present goal.

It will prove helpful to set forth at the outset the major interpretive questions, which derive in no small measure from Paul's strategies of συντομία ἐκ τῆς λέξεως and ἐκ τῶν πραγμάτων. First, how strongly contrasted are the terms which Paul places in antithetical relation to one another? Each verse contains two principal antithetical elements, the first in the attributive participles, and the second in the prepositional phrases κατὰ σάρκα and κατὰ πνεῦμα ἁγιωσύνης. The latter antithesis does not seem to align with Paul's normal usages of σάρξ and πνεῦμα, especially when they follow the preposition κατά, and herein lies the problem.[75] He declares in Galatians 5: "walk by the Spirit and

---

[74] The commentaries debate whether the genitive here is subjective, objective or of origin. I view it as a genitive of possession, paralleling Paul's expression τὸ εὐαγγέλιόν μου (Rom 2:16; n.b. Gal 1:11, τὸ εὐαγγέλιον τὸ εὐαγγελισθὲν ὑπ' ἐμοῦ: this statement resembles 1:1–2, εὐαγγέλιον θεοῦ, ὃ προεπηγγείλατο). Cf. Cranfield (*Romans* 1.55, 57), who perceives the genitive θεοῦ as definitional. I include θεοῦ as part of the definiendum since the definition states the meaning of "God's gospel" in terms of what God did in pre-proclamation and fulfillment.

[75] For a thorough history of scholarship on the meaning of σάρξ in the corpus Paulinum up to 1971, see Jewett, *Paul's Anthropological Terms*, 49–95.

you will not at all complete the desire of the flesh,"[76] and in Romans 8 he constructs a virtual contrast between "living according to the flesh" and "according to the spirit."[77] He says in 1 Corinthians 15 that the flesh passes away at death, but a new spiritual body will rise.[78] Other contexts reveal that he can use κατὰ σάρκα neutrally, notably when physical heredity or relationship is in view, although a corresponding κατὰ πνεῦμα does not appear.[79] Flesh and spirit can also occur together to refer to the whole of the human self.[80] A sensible interpretive move would be to accept the most common Pauline usage, which strongly contrasts (negative) "flesh" and (positive) "spirit," as what he means here as well. James D. G. Dunn, for example, declares that "Paul does not and would not understand κατὰ σάρκα in a neutral sense."[81] Responding to those who, in his view, put the meanings of σάρξ into discrete "pigeonholes," Dunn sketches its "spectrum" of meaning.[82] He concludes that, although the negative senses of σάρξ may not be present all the time, they nonetheless stand in the background: "... it must be judged highly probable that for Paul κατὰ σάρκα in Rom 1:3 carries its normal note of deprecation," and it "stands

---

[76] Gal 5:16–18: λέγω δέ, πνεύματι περιπατεῖτε καὶ ἐπιθυμίαν σαρκὸς οὐ μὴ τελέσητε. ἡ γὰρ σὰρξ ἐπιθυμεῖ κατὰ τοῦ πνεύματος, τὸ δὲ πνεῦμα κατὰ τῆς σαρκός, ταῦτα γὰρ ἀλλήλοις ἀντίκειται, ἵνα μὴ ἃ ἐὰν θέλητε ταῦτα ποιῆτε. εἰ δὲ πνεύματι ἄγεσθε, οὐκ ἐστὲ ὑπὸ νόμον.

[77] Rom 8:12–14: ἄρα οὖν, ἀδελφοί, ὀφειλέται ἐσμέν οὐ τῇ σαρκὶ τοῦ κατὰ σάρκα ζῆν, εἰ γὰρ κατὰ σάρκα ζῆτε, μέλλετε ἀποθνῄσκειν· εἰ δὲ πνεύματι τὰς πράξεις τοῦ σώματος θανατοῦτε, ζήσεσθε. ὅσοι γὰρ πνεύματι θεοῦ ἄγονται, οὗτοι υἱοὶ θεοῦ εἰσιν.

[78] 1 Cor 15:35–50, esp. v. 44 (σπείρεται σῶμα ψυχικόν, ἐγείρεται σῶμα πνευματικόν), and v. 50 (τοῦτο δέ φημι, ἀδελφοί, ὅτι σὰρξ καὶ αἷμα βασιλείαν θεοῦ κληρονομῆσαι οὐ δύναται οὐδὲ ἡ φθορὰ τὴν ἀφθαρσίαν κληρονομεῖ).

[79] Rom 9:4–5: οἵτινές εἰσιν Ἰσραηλῖται, ὧν ἡ υἱοθεσία καὶ ἡ δόξα καὶ αἱ διαθῆκαι καὶ ἡ νομοθεσία καὶ ἡ λατρεία καὶ αἱ ἐπαγγελίαι ὧν οἱ πατέρες καὶ ἐξ ὧν ὁ Χριστὸς τὸ κατὰ σάρκα, ὁ ὢν ἐπὶ πάντων θεὸς εὐλογητὸς εἰς τοὺς αἰῶνας, ἀμήν. Cf. also 9:3: ὑπὲρ τῶν ἀδελφῶν μου τῶν συγγενῶν μου κατὰ σάρκα. Jewett (*Paul's Anthropological Terms*, 160–63) argues that these occurrences are negative, in anticipation of Paul's application of σάρξ in 9:6–13.

[80] See, e.g., 2 Cor 7:1 (although this may be an interpolated passage): ταύτας οὖν ἔχοντες τὰς ἐπαγγελίας, ἀγαπητοί, καθαρίσωμεν ἑαυτοὺς ἀπὸ παντὸς μολυσμοῦ σαρκὸς καὶ πνεύματος, ἐπιτελοῦντες ἁγιωσύνην ἐν φόβῳ θεοῦ. For σῶμα and πνεῦμα with similar force, see 1 Cor 5:3 (ἐγὼ ... ἀπὼν τῷ σώματι παρὼν δὲ τῷ πνεύματι; cf. v. 5: παραδοῦναι τὸν τοιοῦτον τῷ Σατανᾷ εἰς ὄλεθρον τῆς σαρκός, ἵνα τὸ πνεῦμα σωθῇ ἐν τῇ ἡμέρᾳ τοῦ κυρίου) and 7:34 (καὶ ἡ γυνὴ ἡ ἄγαμος καὶ ἡ παρθένος μεριμνᾷ τὰ τοῦ κυρίου, ἵνα ᾖ ἁγία καὶ τῷ σώματι καὶ τῷ πνεύματι). BDAG 832–36, s.v. πνεῦμα, 3a, notes several instances of coordinated σάρξ and πνεῦμα in the letters of Ignatius, who perhaps is adopting Paul's diction.

[81] "Jesus – Flesh and Spirit," 130–35.

[82] The spectrum includes: (a) a "neutral usage" without a negative connotation; (b) the sense of physical weakness or corruptibility; (c) a broader sense of physical weakness through a contrast to a "superior realm, mode of being, or pattern of conduct"; (d) a "mainly negative" connotation of *merely* human relationships and attitudes (so Rom 4:1, 9:3, 5 according to Dunn); and (e) a meaning sharply antithetical to πνεῦμα, signifying kinds of people or conduct. These appear with supporting arguments in "Jesus – Flesh and Spirit," 130–35.

4.4 The definition extended (1:3b–4) 125

in open antithesis with κατὰ πνεῦμα and so could hardly lack a pejorative significance in Paul's mind."[83] Dunn continues, "[Jesus] was merely son of David and no more – Messiah indeed, but a disappointing, ineffective, irrelevant Messiah, whether judged in terms of Jewish expectations or in terms of the Gentile Christian mission."[84] Does the context of Rom 1:3b–4 justify reading κατὰ σάρκα in such a negative manner?

The ancient rhetorical sources furnish a useful theoretical framework for sharpening the question. Aristotle's remarks on the antithetical organization of clauses in periodic style are especially pertinent:

τῆς δὲ ἐν κώλοις λέξεως ἡ μὲν διῃρημένη ἐστὶν ἡ δὲ ἀντικειμένη, διῃρημένη μέν, οἷον «πολλάκις ἐθαύμασα τῶν τὰς πανηγύρεις συναγαγόντων καὶ τοὺς γυμνικοὺς ἀγῶνας καταστησάντων», ἀντικειμένη δὲ ἐν ᾗ ἑκατέρῳ τῷ κώλῳ ἢ πρὸς ἐναντίῳ ἐναντίον σύγκειται ἢ ταὐτὸ ἐπέζευκται τοῖς ἐναντίοις, οἷον «ἀμφοτέρους δ᾽ ὤνησαν, καὶ τοὺς ὑπομείναντας καὶ τοὺς ἀκολουθήσαντας· τοῖς μὲν γὰρ πλείω τῆς οἴκοι προσεκτήσαντο, τοῖς δ᾽ ἱκανὴν τὴν οἴκοι κατέλιπον»· ἐναντία ὑπομονὴ ἀκολούθησις, ἱκανὸν πλεῖον.

In clauses, [the types of periodic] style are the divided and the opposed: divided, such as "I often marveled at the ones who brought together the festivals and who set up the gymnastic competitions"; and opposed, in which, for each clause, either one is juxtaposed with its opposite, or the same clause has been yoked to opposites, such as "But they benefited both those who remained and those who followed, for to the latter's advantage they acquired more land than was at home, and to the former's advantage they left behind sufficient land at home." 'Remaining' and "following," "sufficient" and "more" are opposites. (*Rhet.* 3.9.7, 1409b–1410a)[85]

---

[83] "Jesus – Flesh and Spirit," 135.

[84] "Jesus – Flesh and Spirit," 142.

[85] After many more examples, Aristotle concludes in 3.9.9: "Such, then, is antithesis," ἀντίθεσις μὲν οὖν τὸ τοιοῦτόν ἐστιν. Cf. Demetrius, *Eloc.* 22–23: "Periods also happen from opposed clauses, but opposed either in the subjects, for example, 'sailing through the land, but marching through the sea,' or in both the wording and the subjects, as the same period has here. There are also kinds of clauses which form their opposition according to the words only, for example, as the one who set Helen alongside Heracles [Isocrates, *Helen* 17] says: '[Zeus] made his life to be painful and very dangerous, but he ordained her nature to be admired by all and a cause of strife.' For article is opposed to article, conjunction to conjunction, like to like, and other things in the same way: 'he ordained' to 'he made,' 'admired by all' to 'painful,' 'a cause of strife' to 'very dangerous,' and on the whole the correspondence is one-to-one, like with like." γίνονται δὲ καὶ ἐξ ἀντικειμένων κώλων περίοδοι, ἀντικειμένων δὲ ἤτοι τοῖς πράγμασιν, οἷον «πλέων μὲν διὰ τῆς ἠπείρου, πεζεύων δὲ διὰ τῆς θαλάσσης», ἢ ἀμφοτέροις, τῇ τε λέξει καὶ τοῖς πράγμασιν, ὥσπερ ἡ αὐτὴ περίοδος ὧδε ἔχει. κατὰ δὲ τὰ ὀνόματα μόνον ἀντικείμενα κῶλα τοιάδε ἐστίν, οἷον ὡς ὁ τὴν Ἑλένην παραβαλὼν τῷ Ἡρακλεῖ φησιν, ὅτι «τοῦ μὲν ἐπίπονον καὶ πολυκίνδυνον τὸν βίον ἐποίησεν, τῆς δὲ περίβλεπτον καὶ περιμάχητον τὴν φύσιν κατέστησεν». ἀντίκειται γὰρ καὶ ἄθρον ἄθρῳ, καὶ σύνδεσμος συνδέσμῳ, ὅμοια ὁμοίοις, καὶ τἆλλα δὲ κατὰ τὸν αὐτὸν τρόπον, τῷ μὲν «ἐποίησεν» τὸ «κατέστησεν», τῷ δὲ «ἐπίπονον» τὸ «περίβλεπτον», τῷ δὲ «πολυκίνδυνον» τὸ «περιμάχητον», καὶ ὅλως ἓν πρὸς ἕν, ὅμοιον παρ᾽ ὅμοιον, ἡ ἀνταπόδοσις. Several later authors approach ἀντίθεσις as a rhetorical figure, e.g., [Cicero], *Rhet. Her.* 4.15.21; Quintilian, *Inst.* 9.3.81–86; [Plutarch], *De Hom.* 2.173.

The divided style (ἡ διῃρημένη λέξις) thus splits a class into two sub-classes (τε–καί), while the opposed style (ἡ ἀντικειμένη λέξις) draws a contrast between each term (μέν–δέ). The syntax in Aristotle's examples is also illuminating. The first joins two attributive participial phrases with a single article that together serve as objects of the verb ἐθαύμασα (τῶν τὰς πανηγύρεις συναγαγόντων καὶ τοὺς γυμνικοὺς ἀγῶνας καταστησάντων). His second does something similar in its first part (ἀμφοτέρους δ' ὤνησαν, καὶ τοὺς ὑπομείναντας καὶ τοὺς ἀκολουθήσαντας), supported subsequently by two contrasted main clauses with μέν and δέ (τοῖς μὲν γὰρ πλείω τῆς οἴκοι προσεκτήσαντο, τοῖς δὲ ἱκανὴν τὴν οἴκοι κατέλιπον). The syntactical flexibility offered by attributive participial phrases makes them highly suitable for both kinds of ἀντίθεσις. So then, which type of ἀντίθεσις does Paul use to design his mythological expanded epithet in 1:3b–4? Is he using the divided style to describe inclusively the Son at the points of his birth κατὰ σάρκα and of his appointment κατὰ πνεῦμα ἁγιωσύνης, or does he draw these points into opposition, in order to deprecate one and elevate the other?

Second, what precisely is Paul talking about when he refers to σάρξ and πνεῦμα? The former may appear straightforwardly to refer to the Son's own flesh, which emerged at birth, grew to adulthood and ultimately died. However, its antithesis, πνεῦμα ἁγιωσύνης, is not so clear, since it seems like an obvious alternative locution for πνεῦμα ἅγιον, God's Holy Spirit, given that a noun with a genitive of description can mimic the Hebrew construct state.[86] So whose spirit is in view here, that of Jesus,[87] or of God?[88] This question in-

---

[86] See BDF 91–92, § 165; GKC 414–19, § 128, esp. 2 p.

[87] So Sanday and Headlam, Romans, 7, 9 ("the human πνεῦμα ... distinguished however from that of ordinary humanity by an exceptional and transcendent Holiness"); Otto Procksch, TDNT 1.114–115, s.v. ἁγιωσύνη. See also Lietzmann, an die Römer, 25, who notes on the one hand: "πνεῦμα ἁγιωσύνης ist hier für πνεῦμα ἅγιον ohne Bedeutungsunterschied ... gewählt, um κατὰ σάρκα – κατὰ πνεῦμα rhetorisch schärfer gegeneinanderzustellen: κατὰ πνεῦμα ἅγιον wäre stumpfer. Das Asyndeton markiert hier wie oft den Gegensatz noch stärker als μὲν – δὲ...." On the other hand, he writes: "σάρξ und πνεῦμα bilden hier nicht schlechthin den paulinischen, metaphysisch-ethischen Gegensatz, sondern bezeichnen formell in at. Weise Leib und Seele, wobei freilich das πνεῦμα durch den Zusatz ἁγιωσύνης als das Göttliche charakterisiert wird: der 'paulinische' Gegensatz müßte lauten κατὰ σάρκα ἁμαρτίας, was doch hier (anders Rom 8 3) nicht in der Gedankenbahn des Pls liegt."

[88] So Barrett, Romans, 19; Hahn, Christological Titles, 249; Schneider, "Κατὰ Πνεῦμα Ἁγιωσύνης," 380–81; Käsemann, Romans, 11; Cranfield, Romans, 1.63–64; Dunn, "Jesus – Flesh and Spirit," 143 and Romans, 1.16; Fitzmyer, Romans, 230 (in his list of arguments for the formulaic origin of Rom 1:3–4, but cf. 236, where the phrase "describes something which is intrinsic to Christ as of the resurrection"); Moo, Romans, 49–50; Wilckens, an die Römer, 57; Schmithals, Römerbrief, 49. Note esp. Scott, Adoption, 233: "... Paul regularly uses a qualitative gentitive with a noun in a way that recalls the Hebrew construct state: for example: πνεῦμα ἅγιον can also be called τὸ πνεῦμα τῆς ζωῆς (Rom. 8:2), πνεῦμα υἱοθεσίας (8:15), and

4.4 The definition extended (1:3b–4) 127

cludes another: does ἁγιωσύνης signify a quality of πνεῦμα (making it a genitive of description, "spirit of holiness"), or is it a *nomen actionis* ("spirit of sanctification," i.e., the spirit that sanctifies)? The problem grows worse because of the ambiguity of the preposition κατά. Scholars have put forward several proposals, some of which are lexically impossible (for example, Eduard Schweizer's rendering, "in the sphere of")[89] or unlikely (James Scott's rendering, "because of").[90] Consultation of the lexicon of Liddell, Scott and Jones produces three contextually viable candidates: (1) "of fitness or conformity, *in accordance with*"; (2) *"in relation to, concerning"*; (3) "periphrastically, with abstract Subst." (i.e., in a fleshly manner, in a spirit-of-holiness manner).[91] Which, then, does Paul have in mind?

πνεῦμα τῆς πίστεως (2 Cor. 4:13). The same Paul who can alternate between σῶμα τοῦ θανάτου (Rom. 7:24) and θνητὸν σῶμα (Rom. 6:12; 8:11) can undoubtedly alternate between πνεῦμα ἁγιωσύνης and πνεῦμα ἅγιον."

[89] Schweizer, "Röm. 1, 3f.," 569: "Die Gemeinde, die sie [i.e., die Formel] gebildet hat, hat einerseits die offizielle jüdische Messiasvorstellung gekannt, die den irdischen Davididen erwarten hat, anderseits die Erhöhungschristologie, nach der die Einsetzung Jesu zum Gottessohn-König erst an Ostern erfolgt ist. Es lag in der Sache begründet, daß der erste innerhalb der irdischen, das zweite innerhalb der himmlischen Existenz zu denken war. Mit dem Schema der beiden Sphären, das die irdische Davidsohnschaft auch deutlich als verläufige, erste Stufe kennzeichnet, hat Gemeinde beides verbunden." (Cf. Jewett, *Romans*, 105–6.) Schweizer's proposal reveals an interpretive pitfall associated with treating vv. 3–4 as a free-standing formula, namely a tendency to ignore the clues present in the immediate context. V. 2 supplies the relevant information for narrowing the options of what Paul intends σάρξ and πνεῦμα to signify. The assertion of Christ's comprehensive fulfillment of the promises governs the contrast of flesh and spirit here, suggesting that the terms have a more limited scope than Schweizer's heavenly or earthly "Sphären": the promises address Christ's σάρξ, fulfilled by his mortal descent from David, and his πνεῦμα ἁγιωσύνης, fulfilled by his appointment as Son of God in power, as I shall argue below. Vv. 2–4 therefore underscore not the relationship of Christ to the mortal and divine spheres of existence (nor, for that matter, the relationship of Christ to God or the Spirit in an ontological sense), but the relationship of Christ to God's promises.

[90] See BDAG 512–13, s.v. κατά 5.a.δ: "Oft. the norm is at the same time the reason, so that *in accordance with* and *because of* are merged." Scott (*Adoption*, 242–43) seems to have this meaning in mind when he cites "BAGD, s.v. κατά, p. 407" as an "instrumental" use of the preposition, with 1 Cor 12:8 as support: "… κατὰ πνεῦμα is used in synonymous parallelism with an instrumental διὰ τοῦ πνεύματος construed with a passive verb." I disagree. The text in question reads: ᾧ μὲν γὰρ διὰ τοῦ πνεύματος δίδοται λόγος σοφίας, ἄλλῳ δὲ λόγος γνώσεως κατὰ τὸ αὐτὸ πνεῦμα, "for to one person a word of wisdom is given through the Spirit, but to another a word of knowledge in accordance with the same Spirit." The person doing the giving in this scenario is θεός (v. 6) or κύριος (v. 5) *through* the Spirit (as a conduit; cf. Smyth 371 § 1678, διά as "intermediate agency"). The second half of v. 8 shifts the emphasis to *accordance* (note also αὐτό), so the two prepositional phrases are not syntactically parallel.

[91] LSJ 883, s.v.: I.1 "of motion *downwards*"; 2. "with or without signif. of motion, *on, over, throughout* a space"; 3. *"opposite, over, against"*; II.1 *"distributively,* of a whole divided into parts"; 2. "of Time, καθ' ἡμέραν … day *by* day"; 3. "of Numbers, *by* so many *at a time*"; III.1 "of direction *towards* an object or purpose"; 2. "of pursuit … simply κ. τινά, *after*

128 Chapter 4: The First Definition of the Gospel (1:2–4)

The third problem pertains to the meaning of the participle τοῦ ὁρισθέντος. Interpreters through the centuries have wrestled with the theological ramifications of ὁρίζειν here, because it implies an adoptionist christology. Some Old Latin manuscripts, the Vulgate and many Western Fathers overcome the difficulty through emendation, reading *qui praedestinatus* (= τοῦ προορισθέντος).[92] Other ancient interpreters spin τοῦ ὁρισθέντος this way or that to minimize conflict with their trinitarian orthodoxy.[93] Paul naturally knows nothing of this problem, since even if he has a conception of a pre-existent Christ, one cannot accurately characterize his christology as trinitarian in a Nicene or Chalcedo-

---

him"; 3. "Geom. in adverbial phrases"; IV.1 "of fitness or conformity, *in accordance with*"; 2. "*in relation to, concerning*"; 3. "in comparison, *corresponding with, after the fashion of*"; V. "*by the favour of* a god, etc."; VI. "of round numbers ... *nearly, about*"; VII.1 "of Time, *during* or *in the course of* a period"; 2. "*about*, κ. τὸν αὐτὸν τοῦτον χρόνον"; 3. "καθ' ἔτος, *this year*"; VIII. "periphrastically with abstract Subst., κατ' ἡσυχίην, κ. τάχος = ἡσύχως, ταχέως."

[92] These texts convert the participles into relative clauses: *qui factus est ex semine David secundum carnem, qui praedestinatus est Filius Dei in virtute secundum Spiritum sanctificationis ex resurrectione mortuorum....* For the MS data, see Tischendorf, *Novum Testamentum Graece*, ad loc; note esp. Origen's text-critical comments at *Comm. Rom.* 1.7 (5), and cf. Ehrman, *Orthodox Corruption*, 71–72.

[93] A common patristic method is to read τοῦ ὁρισθέντος as "to be shown" or "revealed." E.g., Apollinaris of Laodicea (*PKGK* 57): "Therefore after he was born the Son of Man 'according to the flesh' in the likeness of our own birth, according to the Spirit and power *he was displayed as the Son of God* in [his] second birth from the dead, in order that we, by becoming like him, might also become children of God by acquiring adoption in the redemption of the body, as the Apostle himself said." γενόμενος τοίνυν «κατὰ σάρκα» ἐν ὁμοιώματι τῆς ἡμετέρας γενέσεως υἱὸς ἀνθρώπου, κατὰ τὸ πνεῦμα καὶ τὴν δύναμιν υἱὸς ἀναδείκνυται θεοῦ ἐν τῇ δευτέρᾳ γενέσει τῇ ἐκ νεκρῶν, πρὸς τὸ καὶ ἡμᾶς ὁμοιουμένους αὐτῷ υἱοὺς γενέσθαι θεοῦ, τὴν υἱοθεσίαν κομισαμένους ἐν τῇ ἀπολυτρώσει τοῦ σώματος, ὡς αὐτὸς ὁ ἀπόστολος ἔφη. Origen, *Comm. Rom.* fr. 5: "Therefore [Paul] says that he was set apart by God in order to evangelize all 'concerning his Son' Jesus Christ, who 'has been born from the seed of David according to the flesh, but was appointed to be Son of God,' i.e., he was confirmed as being this, *especially and all the more he was revealed* by rising up from the dead to immortality by the power of his Holy Spirit. For, it says, 'he was killed by flesh, but made alive by Spirit,' and 'he was crucified from weakness, but he lives from God's power'" [1 Pet 3:18; 2 Cor 13:4]. φησὶ τοίνυν ὅτι ἀφωρίσθη ἀπὸ θεοῦ εἰς τὸ εὐαγγελίζεσθαι πάντας «περὶ τοῦ υἱοῦ αὐτοῦ» Ἰησοῦ Χριστοῦ ὃς «ἐκ σπέρματος μὲν Δαυὶδ γέγονε κατὰ σάρκα, υἱὸς δὲ ὡρίσθη εἶναι θεοῦ» τουτέστιν ἐκυρώθη τοῦτο ὤν, μάλιστα καὶ πλέον ἐφανερώθη τῇ δυνάμει τοῦ ἁγίου πνεύματος αὐτοῦ πρὸς ἀθανασίαν ἐκ νεκρῶν ἀναστάς· «ἐθανατώθη μὲν» γάρ, φησί, «σάρκι, ἐζωοποιήθη δὲ πνεύματι», καὶ «ἐσταυρώθη ἐξ ἀσθενείας, ἀλλὰ ζῇ ἐκ δυνάμεως θεοῦ». John Chrysostom, *Hom. Rom.* 1.7, 432d: "What then does 'who was designated' mean? *Who was shown, who was displayed,* who was judged, who was confessed by the verdict and vote of all, from the prophets, from his incredible birth according to the flesh, from the power which is in signs, from the Spirit through whom he gave sanctification, from the resurrection through which he utterly dissolved the despotism of death." τί οὖν ἐστιν, «ὁρισθέντος»; τοῦ δειχθέντος, ἀποφανθέντος, κριθέντος, ὁμολογηθέντος παρὰ τῆς ἁπάντων γνώμης καὶ ψήφου, ἀπὸ τῶν προφητῶν, ἀπὸ τῆς παραδόξου γεννήσεως τῆς κατὰ σάρκα, ἀπὸ τῆς δυνάμεως τῆς ἐν τοῖς σημείοις, ἀπὸ τοῦ πνεύματος, δι' οὗ τὸν ἁγιασμὸν ἔδωκεν, ἀπὸ τῆς ἀναστάσεως, δι' ἧς τοῦ θανάτου τὴν τυραννίδα κατέλυσε.

4.4 The definition extended (1:3b–4) 129

nian sense. Some modern interpreters solve the problem by making it vanish with scholarly sleight of hand – the category of 'pre-Pauline traditional formula' – although disagreements about the best way to translate the term persist. Proposals include "appoint,"[94] "designate,"[95] "declare,"[96] and "show to be."[97]

In summary, the major questions are: (1) How does Paul structure his ἀντίθεσις, and how strongly contrasted are its terms? (2) In the pairing of flesh and spirit, what is the meaning of the latter, and what is the force of the preposition κατά? And, (3) in the pairing of τοῦ γενομένου and τοῦ ὁρισθέντος, what is the meaning of the latter? In addition to these three, we have a couple of minor questions: (1) Which syntactical element does ἐκ σπέρματος Δαυίδ have as its parallel?[98] And, (2) how do ἐν δυνάμει and ἐξ ἀναστάσεως νεκρῶν construe with the other elements of v. 4? Both the minor and major problems can find viable solutions through an analysis of vv. 3b–4 which simultaneously recognizes their role within Paul's statement of the gospel's essence, their conformity to the pattern of the mythological expanded epithet, their utilization of συνεκδοχαί of narratives which is typical of this form, and the inclusive nature of the ἀντιθέσεις that Paul constructs. He designs vv. 3b–4 to explain how the gospel fulfills God's pre-proclamation/promise through the prophets

---

[94] So Cranfield (*Romans*, 1.61), adding "constitute" and "install." Also Dodd, *Romans*, 3 ("install"); Barrett, *Romans*, 18–19 ("appoint"); Käsemann, *Romans*, 11–12 ("appoint"); Fitzmyer, *Romans*, 234–35 ("established"); Moo, *Romans*, 47–48; Jewett, *Romans*, 95; K. L. Schmidt, "ὁρίζω," etc., *TDNT* 452–3 ("appoint," "institute"; n.b. the literature cited at 452 n. 1). See LSJ 1250–51, s.v. III, "ordain, determine, lay down." Cf. *PGL* 973, s.v. 3, "appoint, ordain," citing Ignatius, *Eph.* 3.2: ἐπίσκοποι οἱ κατὰ τὰ πέρατα ὁρισθέντες ἐν Ἰησοῦ Χριστοῦ γνώμῃ εἰσίν.

[95] So Sanday and Headlam, *Romans*, 7–8. This is the translation that I prefer, building upon the meaning of the verb as "to define" (see below).

[96] Such is how BDAG (723, 2b) translates Rom 1:4.

[97] See n. 93 above. This rendering has little support among recent interpreters. Cranfield rightly points out: "No clear example, either earlier than, or contemporary with, the NT, of its use in the sense 'declare' or 'show to be' has been adduced. This being so, it is probably right to conclude that the support for this interpretation afforded by various Greek Fathers is due to a doctrinal consideration rather than to their superior knowledge of Greek." LSJ does not list "declare" or "show to be" in its entry at 1250–51, s.v., nor does *PGL* 973, s.v.

[98] Jewett ("Redaction and Use," passim; cf. Schlier, *Römerbrief*, 24) assumes without argument that ἐκ σπέρματος Δαυίδ and ἐξ ἀναστάσεως νεκρῶν are parallel both in the original formula and in subsequent redactional stages; cf. idem, *Romans*, 104–6. See also Schneider, "Κατὰ Πνεῦμα Ἁγιωσύνης," 361–62, 364–65, who adduces the ellision of υἱοῦ ἀνθρώπου in v. 3 as an analogue to υἱοῦ θεοῦ, permitting a clearer parallelism between the two ἐκ-phrases. Schmithals (*Römerbrief*, 49) merges the two options by arguing that ἐκ σπέρματος Δαυίδ has *two* parallels, initially υἱοῦ θεοῦ and then – adding an extra measure of emphasis to this point of comparison – ἐξ ἀναστάσεως νεκρῶν. Many commentators perceive ἐκ σπέρματος Δαυίδ and υἱοῦ θεοῦ as parallels, e.g., Fitzmyer, *Romans*, 229–30; Wilckens, *an die Römer*, 1.56; Moo, *Romans*, 45; Fridrichsen, *Apostle and His Message*, 10; Michel, *an die Römer*, 30.

in the holy scriptures. (Incidentally, this objective places a limitation on the relative completeness of the christology that Paul expresses. A full articulation of his views on christology is not his goal.)

Paul sets out in vv. 3b–4 a two-part mythological expanded epithet, with two attributive participial phrases depending on a single noun, and with no conjunction between them. Within each part are two distinct antithetical pairs.

περὶ τοῦ υἱοῦ αὐτοῦ
    τοῦ γενομένου ἐκ σπέρματος Δαυὶδ κατὰ σάρκα,
    τοῦ ὁρισθέντος υἱοῦ θεοῦ ἐν δυνάμει κατὰ πνεῦμα ἁγιωσύνης ἐξ ἀναστάσεως νεκρῶν,
    Ἰησοῦ Χριστοῦ τοῦ κυρίου ἡμῶν....

The length of the second phrase pulls the latter half of the mythological expanded epithet out of balance with the former, and helps to build to the crescendo of the Son's name and titles, Ἰησοῦ Χριστοῦ τοῦ κυρίου ἡμῶν. The first ἀντίθεσις of the participles and their implied (ἐκ σπέρματος Δαυὶδ = υἱοῦ Δαυίδ) or stated (υἱοῦ θεοῦ) predicates effectively governs the other because of the syntax. It constitutes a *temporal* ἀντίθεσις, addressing the Son's origin (ἀρχή) in his birth, and end (τέλος) in his appointment. The second is an *anthropological* ἀντίθεσις, expressed in κατὰ σάρκα and κατὰ πνεῦμα ἁγιωσύνης. Paul thus divides the Son along these two axes, joining origin with flesh and end with spirit. The two axes capture the whole of the Son through his parts – an instance of Aristotle's divided style, in other words, that artfully deploys συνεκδοχαί of his history and nature as a human being.[99] Paul reverses the συνεκδοχή of the whole of scripture for the parts that pre-proclaim the gospel in v. 2, by shifting to a συνεκδοχή of the parts of Jesus for the whole with the same inclusive intent. The two attributive participles effectively act as a pair of bookends for the entire myth of Christ, a compositional decision that resembles what one finds in the opening lines of the Homeric *Hymn 2 to Demeter*, in its reference to Persephone "whom Hades seized" and "whom loud-thundering, wide-eyed Zeus gave away."[100] Both Paul and the author of this hymn encapsulate an entire myth by stating its outer limits. Paul thereby cre-

---

[99] Cf. another instance of the divided style that emphasizes both sequence and inclusiveness at Rom 1:16, παντὶ τῷ πιστεύοντι, Ἰουδαίῳ τε πρῶτον καὶ Ἕλληνι; cf. 2:7–8. Paul uses the opposed style in 2 Cor 2:15–16: ὅτι Χριστοῦ εὐωδία ἐσμὲν τῷ θεῷ ἐν τοῖς σῳζομένοις καὶ ἐν τοῖς ἀπολλυμένοις, οἷς μὲν ὀσμὴ ἐκ θανάτου εἰς θάνατον, οἷς δὲ ὀσμὴ ἐκ ζωῆς εἰς ζωήν.

[100] The *Mithras Liturgy* has a fascinating parallel reference to ἀρχή and τέλος in one of its ἐγώ εἰμι declarations, at [PGM IV] 644–50: "I, *nn.* son of *nn.*, am a man, who was born from the mortal womb of *nn.* and from seed-like ichor and who, since this man was reborn today by your agency, became immortal from so many myriads in this hour in accordance with the will of the surpassingly good god," ἄνθρωπος ἐγὼ ὁ δ(ε)ῖ(να) τῆς δ(ε)ῖ(να), γενόμενος ἐκ θνητῆς ὑστέρας τῆς δεῖνα καὶ ἰχῶρος σπερματικοῦ καί, σήμερον τούτου ὑπό σου με⟨τα⟩γεννηθέντος, ἐκ τοσούτων μυριάδων ἀπαθανατισθεὶς ἐν ταύτῃ τῇ ὥρᾳ κατὰ δόκησιν θ(εο)ῦ ὑπερβάλλοντος ἀγαθοῦ. For detailed discussion of this passage, see Betz, *Mithras Liturgy*, 170–73.

ates a temporal gap that his audience can fill from their own knowledge of the fuller narrative indicated by εὐαγγέλιον.[101] With this basic architecture in place, I shall now examine in greater detail the temporal axis, and then the anthropological.

Paul appropriately describes the ἀρχή of Christ in terms of his birth.[102] As I emphasized above, this statement and the one that follows in v. 4 speak to the ways that τὸ εὐαγγέλιον θεοῦ is ὃ προεπηγγείλατο διὰ τῶν προφητῶν αὐτοῦ ἐν ταῖς γραφαῖς ἁγίαις. Paul does not elaborate which scriptures he has in mind,[103] but instead treats them as aggregated oracles which collectively have

---

[101] How extensive such knowledge was – in other words, how much interest in and information about the life and ministry of Jesus they may have had beyond a passion account – will remain a matter of speculation. Paul makes little explicit use of such narratives in his letters, strongly implying that many of the types of stories that later become included in the canonical Gospels were not yet available.

[102] On γίνομαι meaning "to be born," see LSJ 349, s.v. γίγνομαι I.1; BDAG 196–97, s.v. 1 (citing Rom 1:3). Moo (*Romans*, 46) has doubts, however: "This clause assumes the preexistence of the Son. How specifically Paul may allude to the incarnation depends on the meaning to be given to the word *genomenon*, 'has come.' Although it is not the usual word for 'give birth,' it can sometimes take this meaning, and some argue for it here. But this probably reads too much into the verb. Perhaps Paul uses the more general term to suggest that more than simple 'birth' was entailed in the 'becoming' of the Son; a change in existence also took place." (Cf. also Cranfield, *Romans*, 1.59: "though γίνεσθαι is certainly sometimes used with reference to birth ..., it is not the ordinary word to denote it"; Fee, *Pauline Christology*, 242–43: the two κατά phrases refer to the humiliation and exaltation of the pre-existent Son). In response, I dispute the assertion that v. 3 presupposes Christ's pre-existence; no part of vv. 3b–4 addresses this subject at all, and the "change in existence" happens in v. 4, not v. 3. One does not need to import the doctrine of pre-existence in order to make sense of the text. Also, γίνομαι can mean "be born," not "give birth to," as Moo translates; and in light of its broad attestation with this meaning, one can confidently say it is in fact a "usual word" for this.

[103] We encounter at this point a crucial limitation of συνεκδοχή as a method of textual citation. Given that Paul does not explicitly cite or linguistically allude to particular passages of scripture, how should one use the passages that we *can* surmise to support the messianic propositions (that the Christ will be son of David and Son of God) in order to interpet Rom 1:2–4? A similar problem afflicts situations where Paul quotes or alludes to the scriptures more or less explicitly: how much of the context of the passage which he quotes or to which he alludes does he mean his abbreviated reference to bring along with it? These questions matter, because the phenomenon of συνεκδοχή is relevant to the interpretive strategy of intertextuality, as utilized by Hays (*Echoes of Scripture*) and others (e.g., for Romans generally, Grieb, *Story of Romans*, Wagner, *Heralds of the Good News*; and for Rom 1:2–4, Whitsett, "Son of God, Seed of David"). At times Paul indeed deploys συνεκδοχή of passages of scripture, using the unstated context of the passages he quotes in his argument and requiring his readers to supply this context for themselves (e.g., Romans 4). But at other times he can display indifference to contextual meaning (or, perhaps better, what *we* would regard as contextual meaning), as in the catenae of oracles that he lifts from their original settings and recontextualizes among one another, e.g., Rom 3:10–18, or in his allegorical interpretation of Abraham's two sons and their mothers in Gal 4:21–31. This situation calls for a clear statement of methodological principle. Συνεκδοχή enables Paul to summon large portions of scripture, but it does not follow that he utilizes all that he implicitly brings along with his abbrevi-

the force of propositions: the Messiah will be the *son of David* and the *Son of God*. Events – transmitted to Paul and his readers in the form of narratives, however rudimentary they may have been – have actualized these propositions. Each element of v. 3b addresses the Messiah as son of David, compressing complex ideas into its sparse diction: γενομένου, the fact of his birth and the special circumstances surrounding it; ἐκ σπέρματος Δαυίδ, his royal lineage; and κατὰ σάρκα, the aspect of his self to which the previous two elements pertain. The second element furthermore evokes the implied predicate for γενομένου: υἱοῦ Δαυίδ. Paul is not avoiding (much less deprecating or rejecting) this christological title, but is instead reinforcing the temporal ἀντίθεσις. Jesus has roots that stretch back through dozens of generations to David and the promises that he received. The form of v. 3b as a mythological expanded epithet may suggest that Paul condenses an actual nativity account, comparable to those of Greco-Roman gods and heroes. For example, to call Athena Διὸς τέκος does more than state a fact,[104] it summons to mind the unique events surrounding her birth: she is the one "whom wise Zeus himself bore from his noble head" (τὴν αὐτὸς ἐγείνατο μητίετα Ζεὺς | σεμνῆς ἐκ κεφαλῆς).[105] Paul's assertion that Jesus fulfills the messianically interpreted oracles neither precludes nor requires a detailed nativity narrative. It does call for a demonstration, however, raising the possibility that Paul is compressing a genealogy similar to Matt 1:1–17 and Luke 3:23–38. The aim of a genealogy distributed among early Christians would presumably be apologetic, to 'prove' that Jesus meets the criterion of Davidic lineage.[106] A potential source was available in the person of James, the brother of Jesus, who was evidently still active in Jerusalem at this time. Assessment of the probability of a nativity narrative underpinning v. 3 depends in part on a hint that Paul gives in Gal 4:4, where he describes Jesus as γενόμενος ἐκ γυναικός, γενόμενος ὑπὸ νόμον. How much do Paul and the Galatian Christians know about this γυνή? Is Paul merely underscoring Jesus' humanity, or is he alluding to an account that elaborates his

---

ated citation (or allusion, or echo). One must therefore pay close attention to how much of the context he actively uses in his arguments. Such determinations must occur on a case-by-case basis. In Rom 1:2–4, the oracles stand completely in the background in order to emphasize their unitary message. As much as we might want Paul to be more discursive about the exegetical foundations and internal logic of the christology that he expresses, he perceives no need to do so. Cf. Sanders, *Paul, the Law, and the Jewish People*, 21–22: "It is a fairly common view that one should interpret what the proof-texts say in order to discover what Paul means. I think that what Paul says in his own words is the clue to what he took the proof-texts to mean."

[104] Homeric *Hymn* 28 *to Athena* 17. Cf. *Orph. Hymn* 32.1, Παλλὰς μουνογενή⟨ς⟩ μεγάλου Διὸς ἔκγονε σεμνή.

[105] Homeric *Hymn* 28 *to Athena* 4–5. Cf. Hesiod, *Theog.* 886–900, 924–26.

[106] On the Davidic Messiah, see Collins, *Scepter*, 49–73, ch. 3, "A Shoot from the Stump of Jesse," and cf. ibid., 154–72, ch. 7, "The Messiah as Son of God." See also the literature cited by Cranfield, *Romans*, 1.58.

origin as the child of a Jewish woman?[107] Also, if Matthew and Luke fashion their nativity accounts based upon earlier versions that had both stories and genealogies, would the genealogy (potentially) available to Paul likewise have also had an elementary nativity story? These questions are unfortunately not susceptible to satisfactory answers.

The τέλος of any normal human being's life, and the obvious correlate of birth, is death. The second half of the two-part mythological expanded epithet in v. 4 presents the τέλος of Christ differently, however. After he died, God raised him and gave him a unique τέλος: eternal life as his Son. An enthronement myth, like the possibility of a nativity narrative in v. 3, could perhaps underpin this expanded epithet,[108] but the συνεκδοχή of his death and resurrection (ἐξ ἀναστάσεως νεκρῶν) serves as a sufficient narrative basis in combination with the supposition that God raised him for a purpose, to make him something other than he was.[109] His τέλος thus becomes a new ἀρχή.

At this point, we encounter the third major interpretive problem that I outlined above, the meaning of ὁρισθέντος. The first datum to consider pertains to whether we have here an instance of 'compound simplex iteration': "the iteration of a compound verb in a succeeding clause or sentence by the simple verb alone, but with the semantic force of the compound."[110] The translation of Rom 1:1–4 would then be: "Paul ... set apart for the gospel ... concerning his Son ... *who was set apart* as Son of God in power...." Ἀφωρισμένος in v. 1 functions as part of Paul's effort to cast himself in prophetic terms, as one specially designated εἰς εὐαγγέλιον θεοῦ. If ὁρισθέντος carries the same meaning, it draws a parallel between Paul and Christ, but with distinct predicates (ἀπόστολος and υἱὸς θεοῦ). Furthermore, if Paul wants to imply in v. 1 what he plainly states in Gal 1:15, i.e., ἀφωρισμένος ἐκ κοιλίας μητρός μου, the Latin textual tradition possibly stands on a firm semantic foundation in its rendering of ὁρισθέντος as *qui praedestinatus*: v. 4 expresses what God intended for ὁ γενόμενος ἐκ σπέρματος Δαυίδ from the very beginning.[111]

---

[107] Cf. Hays, *Faith of Jesus Christ*, 95–102 for his analysis of Gal 4:3–6 as a narrative.

[108] Cf. Käsemann, *Romans*, 11–12: "The one described in earthly terms as the messianic king is destined for appointment and enthronement as the Son of God and thus follows a course which is divided into two stages by the Resurrection...."

[109] Homeric *Hymn 2 to Demeter* again furnishes a meaningful parallel: at the end of the myth, Persephone experiences a permanent, irrevocable change by the pronouncement of Zeus. She becomes Hades' legal wife and queen of the underworld.

[110] Watkins, "Indo-European Construction," 115, with further documentation and support by Renehan, *Greek Textual Criticism*, 77–85, and idem, *Studies in Greek Texts*, 11–27. Watkins adds that scholars who have studied this phenomenon "universally, and quite correctly, attribute this feature to genuine popular speech; in no wise can it be considered by origin a purely literary phenomenon" (117). I thank Prof. David Martinez for calling my attention to this syntactical phenomenon.

[111] I am not, however, suggesting that the text presupposes a pre-existent Christ (cf. my remarks in n. 102 above). Contrast Schmidt, "ὁρίζω," etc., *TDNT* 5.453: "But behind the dis-

The notion of Jesus being "appointed" or "designated" by God seems to have currency in multiple strands of early Christianity, a point which weighs against the supposition of compound simplex iteration in v. 4. The author of Acts views this "appointment" as pertaining to the specific task of executing divine judgment, as in 10:42: "This man is the one designated by God as judge of the living and the dead" (οὗτός ἐστιν ὁ ὡρισμένος ὑπὸ τοῦ θεοῦ κριτὴς ζώντων καὶ νεκρῶν).[112] Acts 17:31 adds other elements which we find in Paul's definitions of the gospel in Romans 1: "Because he fixed the day on which he is about to judge the universe with justice by a man whom he designated, furnishing proof to all by raising him from the dead" (καθότι ἔστησεν ἡμέραν ἐν ᾗ μέλλει κρίνειν τὴν οἰκουμένην ἐν δικαιοσύνῃ ἐν ἀνδρὶ ᾧ ὥρισεν, πίστιν παρασχὼν πᾶσιν ἀναστήσας αὐτὸν ἐκ νεκρῶν). The occurrence of ὁρίζειν in 17:31 hearkens back to an earlier statement in which 'Paul' describes God's benevolent acts of creation (17:26–27): "He made from one man every human nation to dwell upon every surface of the earth, appointing the determined times and the boundaries of their habitation, to seek God" (ἐποίησέν τε ἐξ ἑνὸς πᾶν ἔθνος ἀνθρώπων κατοικεῖν ἐπὶ παντὸς προσώπου τῆς γῆς, ὁρίσας προστεταγμένους καιροὺς καὶ τὰς ὁροθεσίας τῆς κατοικίας αὐτῶν ζητεῖν τὸν θεόν). The God who "appointed" seasons and boundaries has now "appointed" an executor of his judgment on the day which he has "set." In contrast, the only hint of the eschatological trial in Rom 1:2–4 occurs in the phrase ἐξ ἀναστάσεως νεκρῶν. Paul delays explicit discussion of this topic until his second definition (σωτηρία, δικαιοσύνη θεοῦ and eternal ζωή). The passages from Acts differ enough from Rom 1:2–4 to confirm that Luke is not directly depending on Paul, but they are close enough to show that they are dipping from the same well of ideas. Therefore, it seems unlikely that ὁρισθέντος simply duplicates the sense of ἀφωρισμένος in v. 1. The repetition of the stem remains important, however, since with it Paul implies a close relationship between God's "appointment" of the Son and the "setting apart" of his apostle to the Gentiles.

The following prepositional phrase, ἐν δυνάμει, offers decisive assistance regarding the meaning of τοῦ ὁρισθέντος. This phrase can construe with the

---

pute [on the meaning of ὁρίζειν] there is an important point, for in the christological passages adduced, Ac. 10:42 and 17:31 as well as R. 1:4, the appointment of Jesus (Christ) as what He is to be must be equated with what He already is from the very beginning of the world, from all eternity in God's decree. It is no accident that προορισθέντος is attested at R. 1:4 as a pertinent interpretation of ὁρισθέντος, that the ὡρισμένη βουλή and πρόγνωσις are mentioned together at Ac. 2:23, and that we find the reading προτεταγμένους for προστεταγμένους (καιρούς) at Ac. 17:26. The reference is always to the predestination of the Christ event by God."

[112] Cf. Rom 2:16, ἐν ἡμέρᾳ ὅτε κρίνει ὁ θεὸς τὰ κρυπτὰ τῶν ἀνθρώπων κατὰ τὸ εὐαγγέλιόν μου διὰ Χριστοῦ Ἰησοῦ.

participle, expressing how God "appoints" or "designates" Jesus as Son,[113] or with the predicate, "Son of God in the level of power he possesses."[114] Given the sequence of phrases, the latter may initially seem more likely, but Paul means both through the figure of ἀπὸ κοινοῦ. Insofar as it expresses the manner of God's ὁρίζειν, it clarifies the sense of this difficult verb. God exercises his *power to define*, to call something by a name, to specify its attributes and functions, and to make these specifications real.[115] This action is much stronger than the translation "to appoint" or "to designate" conveys. Rom 1:4 contains no obvious allusions to Genesis 1, but Paul appears to be drawing upon a conception of God as the one who organizes the cosmos from chaos by fiat. At the same time, Paul portrays him as sharing this power with his Son, effectively linking the first definition of the gospel with the second. The power that God exercises to define and the power that Jesus wields as the Son now have the gospel as their agent: it is the δύναμις θεοῦ εἰς σωτηρίαν παντὶ τῷ πιστεύοντι (1:16).

The temporal ἀντίθεσις of the Son's ἀρχή in terms of his birth as David's descendant, and his τέλος in terms of his definition by God as his own Son with whom he shares his δύναμις, therefore gathers between the two elements the full narrative of the Son, from start to finish. The ἀρχή and τέλος represent the most important fulfillments of God's pre-proclamation of the gospel, but, insofar as they function as bookends, they enclose other mythic episodes along with their points of contact with other oracles and fulfillments. In short, Paul's careful use of temporal ἀντίθεσις in his mythological expanded epithet enables him to compress the whole of the gospel *qua* narrative into his first definition of the gospel through the evocation of unstated content.

If one accepts that the temporal ἀντίθεσις is inclusive (in Aristotle's terms, divided and not opposed), the likelihood that the anthropological elements of κατὰ σάρκα and κατὰ πνεῦμα ἁγιωσύνης are behaving similarly significantly

---

[113] So Jewett, *Romans*, 107 (adding that Paul's addition of the phrase "counters the adoptionism of the original confession by asserting that Christ was appointed by the 'power' of God prior to the resurrection").

[114] So Käsemann, *Romans*, 12; Cranfield, *Romans*, 1.62; Fitzmyer, *Romans*, 235; Moo, *Romans*, 48–49. There is also a third option, which Origen entertains (*Comm. Rom* fr. 5): "Some attach 'power' to the Holy Spirit, and they read thus: 'in power according to Spirit' as in the passage 'Jesus from Nazareth, how God anointed him with the Holy Spirit and power' [Acts 10:38], this is with the powerful Spirit; and in the letter to the Thessalonians, 'our gospel did not happen among you in word alone, but both in power and in the Holy Spirit'" [1 Thess 1:5]. τινὲς δὲ τὸ «δυνάμει» τῷ ἁγίῳ πνεύματι ἐπισυνάπτουσι καὶ οὕτως ἀναγινώσκουσιν· «ἐν δυνάμει κατὰ πνεῦμα» ὡς ἐν τῷ «Ἰησοῦν τὸν ἀπὸ Ναζαρέθ, ὡς ἔχρισεν αὐτὸν ὁ θεὸς πνεύματι ἁγίῳ καὶ δυνάμει» τουτέστι τῷ δυνατῷ πνεύματι, καὶ ἐν τῇ πρὸς Θεσσαλονικεῖς «τὸ εὐαγγέλιον ἡμῶν οὐκ ἐγενήθη ἐν ὑμῖν ἐν λόγῳ μόνον ἀλλὰ καὶ ἐν δυνάμει καὶ ἐν πνεύματι ἁγίῳ».

[115] Cf. the reading of Tertullian at *Adv. Prax.* 27: *Qui factus est, inquit, ex semine David – hic erit homo et filius hominis; qui definitus est filius dei secundum spiritum – hic erit deus, et sermo dei filius.*

increases. The recognition of this likelihood matters, because some scholars (particularly Dunn) overstress the opposition of flesh and spirit. The fleshly birth of the Son in Paul's presentation is something good, even *essential* to the gospel: God pre-proclaims in the scriptures the birth of his Son from the Davidic line; Jesus was indeed born a son of David, a fleshly creature; therefore, Jesus is also God's Son, and the gospel pre-proclaimed by God and the gospel presently proclaimed by Paul are identical. No pejorative sense appears to accompany σάρξ in the present context, beyond its labeling of the constituent element of the Son that makes him mortal, and thus susceptible to the normal human flaws of weakness, injury and death. To borrow some language from the theory on ancient definition, σάρξ is a particularity (ἴδιον) of all mortal creatures.[116] Without his birth κατὰ σάρκα, the Son's τέλος would not be possible. He could not die on behalf of his fellow humans, rise, and thereby save them, leaving another pre-proclamation unfulfilled (Hab 2:4, via Rom 1:17). The second of the options for rendering κατά that I mentioned above therefore seems optimal: he was born from the seed of David "according to the flesh," in the sense of "in relation to his flesh."[117] The qualities that accompany this human condition of being σαρκινός enable the story to move toward its inevitable conclusion. In this manner, Paul limits τοῦ γενομένου ἐκ σπέρματος Δαυὶδ to Jesus' σάρξ, and τοῦ ὁρισθέντος υἱοῦ θεοῦ to his πνεῦμα. The problem arises from the fact that, although one can easily comprehend what it means for Jesus to be born from the seed of David in relation to his flesh, it is difficult to understand what being designated Son of God in relation to his spirit might mean. The solution is that the πνεῦμα is the part of him that continues to exist in his exalted state, the main ingredient of his resurrected body. The eternal endurance of his πνεῦμα ἁγιωσύνης is yet another one of the ways that he fulfills what God pre-proclaimed. The prepositional phrase ἐξ ἀναστάσεως νεκρῶν, in addition to reinforcing the συνεκδοχή of the narrative of Christ's death and resurrection in conjunction with the temporal ἀντίθεσις, further supports the anthropological ἀντίθεσις by explaining how he obtained this new spiritual body. Ἔλλειψις of the pronoun αὐτοῦ opens a third possible application for the phrase,[118] the general "resurrection of the dead" at the end of the aeon, foreshadowing Paul's definition of the gospel as δύναμις θεοῦ εἰς σωτηρίαν (1:16). These conclusions cohere well with what Paul says in 1 Corinthians 15 about the relationship of Christ's resurrection and that of his believers (15:12–22), and especially about the post-resurrection body (15:35–49): it is a

---

[116] Cf. 1 Cor 15:35–41, esp. 39: οὐ πᾶσα σὰρξ ἡ αὐτὴ σάρξ ἀλλὰ ἄλλη μὲν ἀνθρώπων, ἄλλη δὲ σὰρξ κτηνῶν, ἄλλη δὲ σὰρξ πτηνῶν, ἄλλη δὲ ἰχθύων.

[117] So BDAG 512–13, s.v. κατά 6, citing in addition Rom 4:1; 9:3, 5, as well as 7:22 (κατὰ τὸν ἔσω ἄνθρωπον).

[118] Cf. n. 32 above. The idea here is that Christ's resurrection and spiritual body anticipate the future transformation of his believers at the eschaton (cf. Dunn, *Romans*, 1.15–16).

σῶμα ἐπουράνιον, a σῶμα πνευματικόν. He cannot assume that his addressees know about or would accept his proposal regarding the nature of the body after resurrection, and he does not discuss it in his letter to the Romans.[119] They may have ideas of their own that involve the restoration or transformation of the σάρξ.[120] Vv. 3b–4 notably would not preclude such ideas, although they primarily reflect Paul's own point of view.

Only one other instance of πνεῦμα ἁγιωσύνης (aside from ancient quotations of Rom 1:4 and a Jewish amulet) occurs,[121] in the concluding portions of

---

[119] Paul produces his solution in response to the assertion of some Corinthians ὅτι ἀνάστασις νεκρῶν οὐκ ἔστιν. One may thus infer that he had not hitherto found it necessary to entertain the question, and that it had not yet occurred to other early Christians that there was any problem at all.

[120] 3 Corinthians, a pseudepigraphon of the second century, expresses the former view; see Calhoun, "The Resurrection of the Flesh in 3 Corinthians."

[121] I confirmed this with a search of the TLG database. (Cf. *Odes Sol.* 19:4; Charlesworth renders the Syriac "Holy Spirit," while Lattke [*Odes of Solomon*, 268] has "Spirit of holiness.") The amulet is a "Phylactery of Moses" (Kotansky, *Greek Magical Amulets*, § 32, text and translation at pp. 129–30), dating ii–iii C.E. on paleographical grounds, and inscribed on a copper tablet. Kotansky observes regarding its purpose (ibid., 134): "No doubt the production and preservation of the 'Moses Phylactery' belonged in the hands of special Jewish groups working mystical theurgy and initiation...." It "is no ordinary protective amulet, but an initiate's privileged 'membership card' which he (or she) was to carry throughout life and hand down only to fellow-initiates. It derives its authority from the fact that it is the very phylactery that Moses was given and used in his encounters with the divine." The locution πνεῦμα ἁγιωσύνης occurs in the opening lines: "A phylactery which Moses used when protecting himself [as he entered] into the Holy of Holies; when bringing himself into the glory of the Physicist [i.e., God]. The spirit of holiness was withdrawing, and after these things it [he?] was returning." [φυλα]κτήριον ᾧ [Μωσ]ῆς ἐχρᾶ[το] ἐν τῷ | [φυλά]ξε αὐτὸν εἰς τὰ ἅγια τῶν ἁγίων· | ἐ[ν] τῷ ἀγαγεῖν αὐτὸν εἰς τὴν δόξαν | φυσικοῦ. ἀνεχώρει [τ]ὸ ἁγιωσύν[νης πν]- | [ε]ῦμα· καὶ μετὰ ταῦτα μετέστρεφεν. (Following Kotansky, I take φυλάξε to mean φυλάξαι [itacism], and φυσικοῦ to refer to God; see his comments 135, 137. In contrast to him, I am reading αὐτόν, not αὑτόν.) Kotansky interprets these opening lines as extremely abbreviated *historiolae*, which "supply a mythical paradigm for the desired magical action" (so Faraone, "Mystodokos," 299, n. 6). Lines 8–9, which take up the introductory formulations again after giving some instructions, indeed concisely refer to a narrative ("A phylactery of Moses when he went up to Mount Seilamonai [?] to receive an amulet," φυλακτήριον Μωσέως ὅτε ἀνέβαινεν | τῷ ὄρει Σειλαμωναι λα[β]εῖν κάστυ). The imperfect tense of ἀνεχώρει and μετέστρεφεν leads me to doubt whether the same is the case in lines 1–5. Exodus presents Moses entering the central portions of the tabernacle on several occasions, and lines 3–4 may constitute a redundancy that results from the parallelism. The amulet claims to give protection from a μάγος, κατάδεσμος, and πνεῦμα πονηρόν, and one is to bear it "purely," καθαρείως (ll. 30–36 add several other threats, probably extending the spell's original apotropaic functions). How then does the spell envision this working? Kotansky evidently believes that since it protects Moses from the power of God, it will certainly work on the lesser threats of minor magicians; the spell cites five discrete episodes, Kotansky argues, to underscore its lasting protective power. I too believe that it is advertising its apotropaic endurance, but I understand the logic differently. Moses needed protection from curses and evil spirits, since he could not bring these with him into the divine presence, as ll. 4–5 explain: "the spirit of holiness was

the *Testament of Levi*. Interpreters occasionally cite this passage to show that πνεῦμα ἁγιωσύνης equates with πνεῦμα ἅγιον,[122] but closer examination reveals that such is not the case. The text describes a "new priest" that God will raise up, "to whom all the words of the Lord will be revealed" (ᾧ πάντες οἱ λόγοι κυρίου ἀποκαλυφθήσονται):

18:6 οἱ οὐρανοὶ ἀνοιγήσονται, καὶ ἐκ τοῦ ναοῦ τῆς δόξης ἥξει ἐπ' αὐτὸν ἁγίασμα μετὰ φωνῆς πατρικῆς ὡς ἀπὸ Ἀβραὰμ πατρὸς Ἰσαάκ. 7 καὶ δόξα ὑψίστου ἐπ' αὐτὸν ῥηθήσεται, καὶ πνεῦμα συνέσεως καὶ ἁγιασμοῦ καταπαύσει ἐπ' αὐτὸν ἐν τῷ ὕδατι. 8 αὐτὸς δώσει τὴν μεγαλωσύνην κυρίου τοῖς υἱοῖς αὐτοῦ ἐν ἀληθείᾳ εἰς τὸν αἰῶνα· καὶ οὐκ ἔσται διαδοχὴ αὐτῷ εἰς γενεὰς καὶ γενεὰς ἕως τοῦ αἰῶνος. 9 καὶ ἐπὶ τῆς ἱερωσύνης αὐτοῦ τὰ ἔθνη πληθυνθήσονται ἐν γνώσει ἐπὶ τῆς γῆς

---

withdrawing, and *after these things* (i.e., after the performance of the rituals to create the amulet) it was returning." Τὸ ἁγιωσύνης πνεῦμα could then either be a circumlocution for God (like δόξα φυσικοῦ), or a reference to Moses' own ritual purity. If Kotansky is correct in his belief that the amulet originates among Jewish theurgists, the latter makes better sense: it keeps the taint of curses and the influences of noxious spirits away in order to facilitate its bearer's own mystical encounters with the divine.

[122] E.g., Käsemann, *Romans*, 11. Some also contextualize Rom 1:3b–4 among two other putative quotations of confessional formulas, 1 Pet 3:18 and 2 Tim 3:16, in order to the make the point that πνεῦμα ἁγιωσύνης *must* refer to God's Holy Spirit (e.g., Schweizer, "Röm 1, 3 f.," 569–70). The two passages run as follows. 1 Pet 3:18, ὅτι καὶ Χριστὸς ἅπαξ περὶ ἁμαρτιῶν ἔπαθεν, δίκαιος ὑπὲρ ἀδίκων, ἵνα ὑμᾶς προσαγάγῃ τῷ θεῷ θανατωθεὶς μὲν σαρκὶ ζωοποιηθεὶς δὲ πνεύματι. 1 Tim 3:16, ὃς ἐφανερώθη ἐν σαρκί, ἐδικαιώθη ἐν πνεύματι, ὤφθη ἀγγέλοις, ἐκηρύχθη ἐν ἔθνεσιν, ἐπιστεύθη ἐν κόσμῳ, ἀνελήμφθη ἐν δόξῃ. If we grant for the purposes of argument that 1 Pet 3:18 and 1 Tim 3:16 really are quotations of formulas, two questions immediately arise. (1) What thematic similarities exist between the passages which might justify treating them as texts which have each other as a primary context? (2) Do these passages use σάρξ and πνεῦμα in an unambiguous way, such that our certainty of their meanings in these passages can resolve the ambiguity in Rom 1:3b–4? Regarding the first question, the main thematic commonality between all three passages is simply that they address aspects of the identity of Christ. When one looks at the details, the passages diverge significantly: 1 Pet 3:18 emphasizes Christ's substitutionary death and its purpose ("in order that he might lead you to God by having died ... by having been made alive..."). 1 Tim 3:16 meanwhile does not directly mention Christ's death at all, and takes up some peculiar topics like his appearance to angels (messengers?) and his proclamation among the Gentiles. As for the second question, 1 Pet 3:18 has two parallel adverbial passive participles with dative modifiers. One can construe these datives two ways, as *means* identifying who did the killing and making alive ("having been killed by flesh," i.e., the people responsible for Jesus' execution, and "having been made alive by the Spirit"), or as *respect* ("having been killed in [his] flesh" and "having been made alive in [his] spirit"). 1 Tim 3:16 exhibits a similar ambiguity: ἐν σαρκί and ἐν πνεύματι could express means with the passive verbs ("he was revealed by flesh [i.e., people who carry the message], he was vindicated by the Spirit [i.e., by the activity of the Spirit in the community]"), or the preposition ἐν could have a force similar to the dative of respect: "who was revealed *in* [his] flesh, was vindicated *in* [his] spirit." One may, of course, resolve these ambiguities by viewing σάρξ–πνεῦμα contrasts as only loosely parallel (killed *in* flesh // made alive *by* the Spirit; revealed *in* flesh // vindicated *by* the Spirit). But the existence of multiple viable interpretations of these phrases places the utility of 1 Pet 3:18 and 1 Tim 3:16 for explaining Rom 1:3–4 on precarious ground.

4.4 The definition extended (1:3b–4)

καὶ φωτισθήσονται διὰ χάριτος κυρίου· ὁ δὲ Ἰσραὴλ ἐλαττωθήσεται ἐν ἀγνωσίᾳ καὶ σκοτισθήσεται ἐν πένθει· ἐπὶ τῆς ἱερωσύνης αὐτοῦ ἐκλείψει πᾶσα ἁμαρτία καὶ οἱ ἄνομοι καταπαύσουσιν εἰς κακά· οἱ δὲ δίκαιοι καταπαύσουσιν ἐν αὐτῷ. 10 καίγε αὐτὸς ἀνοίξει τὰς θύρας τοῦ παραδείσου, καὶ στήσει τὴν ἀπειλοῦσαν ῥομφαίαν κατὰ τοῦ Ἀδάμ, 11 καὶ δώσει τοῖς ἁγίοις φαγεῖν ἐκ τοῦ ξύλου τῆς ζωῆς, καὶ πνεῦμα ἁγιωσύνης ἔσται ἐπ᾽ αὐτοῖς. 12 καὶ ὁ Βελιὰρ δεθήσεται ὑπ᾽ αὐτοῦ, καὶ δώσει ἐξουσίαν τοῖς τέκνοις αὐτοῦ τοῦ πατεῖν ἐπὶ τὰ πονηρὰ πνεύματα.

18:6 The heavens will be opened, and from the temple of glory holiness [ἁγίασμα] will come upon him with the ancestral voice as [if] from Abraham, the father of Isaac. 7 And the glory of the Most High will be pronounced on him,[123] and a spirit of understanding and of sanctification [πνεῦμα συνέσεως καὶ ἁγιασμοῦ] will rest on him in the water. 8 He will give the greatness of the Lord to his children in truth forever; and there will not be a succession [of the priesthood] for him for generations and generations forever. 9 And during his priesthood the Gentiles will be multiplied in knowledge on the earth and will be enlightened through the grace of the Lord, but Israel will be diminished in ignorance and benighted in grief. During his priesthood all sin will cease, and the lawless will put an end to their evil deeds [καταπαύσουσιν εἰς κακά], but the just will rest in him [καταπαύσουσιν ἐν αὐτῷ]. 10 And indeed he will open the gates of paradise, and will halt the sword that threatens Adam, 11 and he will allow the holy ones to eat from the tree of life, *and a spirit of holiness will be on them* [πνεῦμα ἁγιωσύνης ἔσται ἐπ᾽ αὐτοῖς]. 12 And Beliar will be bound by them, and he will give authority to his children to trample over evil spirits [τὰ πονηρὰ πνεύματα].

A Christian redactor has obviously tampered with this passage; one notices specifically the contextually irrelevant phrase ἐν τῷ ὕδατι in v. 7,[124] and v. 9 seems to summarize ideas similar to those that Paul puts forward in Romans 9–11, especially the μυστήριον that he discloses in 11:25–32. The redactor understands πνεῦμα συνέσεως καὶ ἁγιασμοῦ in v. 7 to mean τὸ πνεῦμα ὡς περιστερὰν καταβαῖνον εἰς αὐτόν, as in Mark 1:10, Matt 3:16 and Luke 3:22.[125] The messianic priest in contrast receives ἁγίασμα from the temple (18:6). It becomes a quality of *his* πνεῦμα that he possesses and can give to the πνεύματα of other people – hence the distinction between the πνεῦμα ἁγιασμοῦ in v. 3 and the πνεῦμα ἁγιωσύνης of the ἅγιοι in v. 11, which empowers them τοῦ πατεῖν ἐπὶ τὰ πονηρὰ πνεύματα. This πνεῦμα ἁγιωσύνης in v. 11 thus seems closer to the idiom that Paul himself uses in 1 Cor 4:21, τί θέλετε; ἐν ῥάβδῳ ἔλθω πρὸς ὑμᾶς ἢ ἐν ἀγάπῃ πνεύματί τε πραΰτητος;[126] He gives no indication

---

[123] H. C. Kee (*OTP* 795) in his translation evidently takes ῥηθήσεται as a form of ῥήγνυμι. It seems rather to be the future passive of ἐρῶ. LSJ (695, s.v.) lists the first aorist passive as ἐρρήθην and the future passive as ῥηθήσομαι. For ῥήγνυμι/ῥήσσω (ibid. 1568–69), we have ἐρράγην, later ἐρρήχθην, and ῥαγήσομαι.

[124] So also Kee (*OTP* 795, note c).

[125] The text as cited is from Mark. Matt 3:16: καὶ εἶδεν [τὸ] πνεῦμα [τοῦ] θεοῦ καταβαῖνον ὡσεὶ περιστερὰν [καὶ] ἐρχόμενον ἐπ᾽ αὐτόν. Luke 3:22: καὶ καταβῆναι τὸ πνεῦμα τὸ ἅγιον σωματικῷ εἴδει ὡς περιστερὰν ἐπ᾽ αὐτόν. Note also the opening of the heavens and the heavenly voice in the context of these passages and in *T. Levi* 18:6.

[126] See, e.g., Conzelmann, *1 Corinthians*, 93: "πνεῦμα here is not the Holy Spirit, but is used, as is good Jewish practice, in a formal sense," citing Dan LXX 3:39 (ἀλλ᾽ ἐν ψυχῇ συν-

anywhere in his letters that he is aware of the *Testament of Levi*. His mention of the πνεῦμα of Christ and what we find in *T. Levi* 18:6–12 are thus independent attestations of an idea that has its roots in Second Temple Judaism. The author of the *Testament of Levi*, like Paul in Rom 1:3b–4, is drawing upon messianically interpreted oracles; both authors perceive the special πνεῦμα of their Messiahs to fulfill God's prophetic promises.

The context of the prescript of Romans does not supply sufficient information to decide between taking ἁγιωσύνης as a genitive of description or as a *nomen actionis*. Paul probably wants both meanings operative. He certainly would regard Jesus' πνεῦμα as ἅγιον. He also regards sanctification as a primary benefit of Jesus' death and resurrection, and of baptism, hence his description of his addressees as ἅγιοι. The theme of sanctification is muted in Romans, appearing at only a few points,[127] and one might view this as a basis for rejecting the interpretation of ἁγιωσύνη along this line. Paul focuses in his argument on the second definition, however, so such a rejection would be unwarranted. Double-meaning and exploitable ambiguity will furthermore characterize his second definition in 1:16–17. The noun therefore does two things at once: it characterizes the πνεῦμα of Jesus as holy, and as capable of dispensing holiness on others. The author of *T. Levi* 18:6–12 approaches the πνεῦμα of the New Priest similarly.

Reading the anthropological ἀντίθεσις as inclusive – as meant not to oppose the specified elements of the Son's story and nature, but to function like pairs of tongs with which Paul picks up the entirety of the Son and inserts him into the first definition of the gospel – therefore helps to resolve the interpretive problems surrounding κατὰ σάρκα and κατὰ πνεῦμα ἁγιωσύνης. The temporal and anthropological ἀντιθέσεις are mutually supportive: the τέλος of the

---

τετριμμένῃ καὶ πνεύματι τετραπεινωμένῳ προσδεχθείημεν). He also refers to 1QS III.8, which has interesting plays on the "spirit" of God, the community, and the individual (text and trans. per García Martínez/Tigchelaar 1.74–75): "For it is by the spirit of the true counsel of God [ברוח עצת אמת אל] that are atoned the paths of man, all his iniquities, so that he can look at the light of life. And it is by the holy spirit of the community [וברוח קדושה ליחד], in its truth, that he is cleansed of all his iniquities. And by the spirit of uprightness and of humility [וברוח יושר ו{ה}ענו] his sin is atoned." (Cf. further I QS IV.2–8, also mentioned by Conzelmann.) See also Deut 34:9 (καὶ Ἰησοῦς υἱὸς Ναυν ἐνεπλήσθη πνεύματος συνέσεως [רוּחַ חָכְמָה], ἐπέθηκεν γὰρ Μωυσῆς τὰς χεῖρας αὐτοῦ ἐπ' αὐτόν); and Isa 19:14, of the Egyptians (κύριος γὰρ ἐκέρασεν αὐτοῖς πνεῦμα πλανήσεως [רוּחַ עִוְעִים], and cf. the references to "spirits" at 19:3). One may see in these examples a certain fluidity in how πνεῦμα with a genitive dependent can be something imparted by Moses' ritual of the laying-on of hands, or "poured out" by God, and yet remain a quality of the persons of whom the passages speak. Cf. also Rom 1:9.

[127] Aside from references to the "saints," the topic of sanctification occurs at 6:19 (παραστήσατε τὰ μέλη ὑμῶν δοῦλα τῇ δικαιοσύνῃ εἰς ἁγιασμόν), 6:22 (νυνὶ δὲ ἐλευθερωθέντες ἀπὸ τῆς ἁμαρτίας δουλωθέντες δὲ τῷ θεῷ ἔχετε τὸν καρπὸν ὑμῶν εἰς ἁγιασμόν) and 15:16 (ἵνα γένηται ἡ προσφορὰ τῶν ἐθνῶν εὐπρόσδεκτος, ἡγιασμένη ἐν πνεύματι ἁγίῳ). Note also that the law and the command are "holy" at 7:12, as are the ἀπαρχή, φύραμα, ῥίζα and κλάδοι at 11:16.

Son requires his birth κατὰ σάρκα, and the ἀρχή points inevitably toward his appointment and resurrection κατὰ πνεῦμα ἁγιωσύνης. The gospel brings God's pre-proclamation of it to fruition in precisely these two areas, among many others that Paul encloses between them. The apostle deploys the συνεκδοχή of narrative which is characteristic of mythological expanded epithets in order to construct a pair of brackets, such that vv. 3b and 4 not only contain instances of the figure, but also act together as a super-συνεκδοχή. Unfortunately, the extent of the narratives to which Paul concisely refers (the Son's birth, elevation to the status of υἱὸς θεοῦ, and any episodes between) remain occluded for us within vv. 3b–4. He counts on his addressees in Rome to fill out what he leaves unstated, and thus to complete the definition from their own knowledge, as in the case of the oracles that the narratives bring to fulfillment (v. 2).

4.5 Conclusion

Paul assembles his first definition of the gospel's essence with a complex array of tools. He operates foremost under the umbrella of the ancient theory regarding definition. Rom 1:2–4 serves a stipulative goal: he places it in the prescript, presents it as uncontroversial, and draws extensively upon assumptions shared between himself and his Roman Christian addressees. The essence of the gospel exists in the dynamic between God's pre-proclamation and promise in the scriptures, and the manifold fulfillments in the born, resurrected, and exalted Son. The statement also conforms to the instruction that definitions should be brief: it economizes the wording through the omission of anything superfluous, including articles, conjunctions and pronouns which might make the style more smooth or the meaning more clear. The brevity of vv. 2–4 stands in sharp contrast to the μακρολογία in the rest of the prescript and the 'thanksgiving' which follows in vv. 8–15. Paul also draws upon a wealth of 'traditional material,' not through quotation but through evocation. This is additionally his method of offering a relatively complete definition, insofar as he relies upon his readers to furnish what he leaves unstated. In the basic definition (v. 2), he utilizes συνεκδοχή of the whole of scripture in order to gather specific prophetic oracles known to himself and his audience, and thereby to assert the unitary testimony of the scriptures regarding the gospel and the Son. Paul constructs vv. 3–4 by using the mythological expanded epithet, which has ample precedents in both Greco-Roman and Hellenstic Jewish religious literature. His appropriation of it here carries dual resonances, since he addresses converts from pagan polytheism who have some familiarity with the Jewish scriptures. The verses praise the Son on the one hand, and on the other they secure a stamp of prophetic authority that perfectly befits the basic definition in v. 2 and Paul's description of himself as ἀφωρισμένος εἰς εὐαγγέλιον θεοῦ in v. 1. In addition to making promises regarding the Son's story, the oracles also address his identity, an element which Paul inserts with the anthropological ἀντίθεσις of flesh and spirit. Paul weaves all of these together very tightly with a careful application of συνεκδοχή as a means of summoning to mind more than he specifically mentions. The combination of this figure with ἀντίθεσις enables each participial phrase to enclose between them the whole myth of Christ, in an intensification of the normal function of συνεκδοχή within the mythological expanded epithet.

If Paul's addressees recognize that he designs vv. 2–4 as a definition of the gospel, they would probably notice that he has spoken only allusively of its function, in the references to δύναμις, ἁγιωσύνη and ἀνάστασις νεκρῶν. He thus invites their expectation of a second definition that complements the first, even as he previews the strategies of brevity that he will wield therein. He has therefore laid a firm conceptual foundation upon which to build his argument that the gospel is God's power resulting in salvation for everyone who believes.

Chapter 5

The Second Definition of the Gospel (1:16–17)

5.1 Introduction

Paul's first definition of the gospel in Rom 1:2–4 declares its essence (οἷόν τ' ἔστι) by uniting messianically interpreted oracles (a συνεκδοχή of the whole of scripture for its parts) with their fulfillment in the Son (a συνεκδοχή of his parts – origin and end, flesh and spirit – for the whole). Paul's second definition in 1:16–17 builds upon the first by unfolding the gospel's function (ἣν ἔχει δύναμιν). As in the previous chapter, I aim to explain how Paul composes vv. 16–17 with strategies of brevity that enable him to compress the full scope of the gospel's function into two short verses.

Even more than vv. 2–4, vv. 16–17 have the look and feel of a definition. V. 16 has a predicative statement (δύναμις γὰρ θεοῦ ἐστιν), and v. 17 is an abbreviated proof, as indicated by γάρ. Both parts immediately strike the reader as extraordinarily dense in both style and content, in contrast to the μακρολογία in the prescript (aside from vv. 2–4) and the "thanksgiving." The definition includes terms which occur earlier in chapter 1 (δύναμις, πίστις), and introduces others for the first time (δικαιοσύνη θεοῦ, σωτηρία). The verses are interpretable in their context, but they have multiple ambiguities that invite the exposition which follows in the remainder of Romans: in this manner they simultaneously play the roles of ὅρος and of πρόθεσις. Paul first unfolds the function of the gospel in extremely brief compass, then returns to it at various points in Romans to unfold the definition further with recombinations and elaborations of its component terms. Although it might initially seem counterintuitive, vv. 16–17 do not require immediate and complete comprehension by the audience. Paul's definition needs only to obtain their provisional endorsement with an expectation of subsequent exposition. The definition as a whole and its component parts thus have initial layers of meaning that derive from the surrounding context, and numerous other meanings that lie latent within them. In this chapter, I work through vv. 16–17 piece by piece. First, I briefly analyze the second part of the προοίμιον of Romans, the 'thanksgiving' section in 1:8–15 (5.2) in order to obtain a firm grasp of the relevant context. Second, I analyze the basic definition in v. 16, οὐ γὰρ ἐπαισχύνομαι τὸ εὐαγγέλιον, δύναμις γὰρ θεοῦ ἐστιν εἰς σωτηρίαν παντὶ τῷ πιστεύοντι, Ἰουδαίῳ τε πρῶτον καὶ Ἕλληνι (5.3). Third, I examine the abbreviated proof that Paul appends to the basic definition in v. 17, δικαιοσύνη γὰρ θεοῦ ἐν αὐτῷ ἀποκαλύπτεται ἐκ πίστεως εἰς πίστιν, καθὼς γέγραπται, «ὁ δὲ δίκαιος ἐκ πίστεως ζήσεται» (5.4). In the conclusion (5.5), I consider the logic of how the abbreviated proof supports the basic definition, and address the question of how vv. 2–4 and 16–17 operate in tandem.

5.2 'Thanksgiving': the introduction continued (1:8–15)

According to the ancient rhetorical theorists, the aim of a προοίμιον is to obtain favor, attention and receptivity from one's audience.[1] Paul clearly designs his letter's expression of gratitude, in tandem with the prescript, in order to achieve these goals.[2] Vv. 8–15 have two main structural elements: (1) the εὐχαριστῶ formula in v. 8 (πρῶτον μὲν εὐχαριστῶ τῷ θεῷ μου διὰ Ἰησοῦ Χριστοῦ περὶ πάντων ὑμῶν) with a dependent clause explaining why he is thankful (ὅτι ἡ πίστις ὑμῶν καταγγέλλεται ἐν ὅλῳ τῷ κόσμῳ); and (2) the announcement of his desire to visit his addressees in vv. 9–15. Significantly, he does not declare his *plans* to come to Rome (as he will do in chapter 15), only his longstanding *desire* and frustrated *intention*. The second element divides into four parts: (1) the statement of his desire to visit them as something about which he has repeatedly prayed (vv. 9–10); (2) the specification of the first reason for his desire in terms of mutual benefit (vv. 11–12); (3) the specification of the second reason in terms of his obligation to preach (vv. 13–14); and (4) a brief transitional summary (v. 15). The 'thanksgiving' also blends μακρολογία in style and βραχυλογία in content. Regarding the latter, Paul neither belabors his ad-

---

[1] See § 3.3.2 above.

[2] In his structural outline of Romans 1, Jewett ("Following the Argument of Romans," 272; idem, *Romans*, 117–18, 127–34) separates the *exordium* in 1:1–12 from the *narratio* in 1:13–15. It seems that he has overlooked the clear parallelism between vv. 11 and 13, i.e., Paul's statements of his desire to visit (… εἴ πως … εὐοδωθήσομαι … ἐλθεῖν πρὸς ὑμᾶς, ἐπιποθῶ γὰρ ἰδεῖν ὑμᾶς *par*. οὐ θέλω δὲ ὑμᾶς ἀγνοεῖν, ἀδελφοί, ὅτι πολλάκις προεθέμην ἐλθεῖν πρὸς ὑμᾶς) followed by purpose clauses (ἵνα τι μεταδῶ χάρισμα ὑμῖν πνευματικὸν εἰς τὸ στηριχθῆναι ὑμᾶς *par*. ἵνα τινὰ καρπὸν σχῶ καὶ ἐν ὑμῖν). The parallels do not necessarily force the conclusion that vv. 11–15 belong together, but in view of the brevity of his narrative remarks in vv. 13–15 and their close thematic association with the previous verses, it seems better to perceive them as part of the 'thanksgiving.' Also, Schubert (*Form and Function*, 31) notes that vv. 11–13 "constitute formally and functionally an integral part of the thanksgiving, for we have seen that the discussion of intimate personal topics enters more or less into all thanksgivings, not by accident, but according to a definite structural pattern." For other rhetorical analyses of 1:1–15, see Wuellner, "Paul's Rhetoric of Argumentation," 133–36; Kennedy, *New Testament Interpretation*, 153–54; Hellholm, "Amplificatio in the Macro-Structure of Romans," 137.

miration and affection to the point of tediousness, nor reveals the full scope of his objectives for writing. The passage is indeed notable for what he does *not* say, since he will in chapter 15 solicit not only his addressees' prayers but also their financial support for missionary endeavors further west.[3] But even as he carefully limits the πράγματα that he raises in the 'thanksgiving,' he dresses it with a rich λέξις, through superfluous or redundant prepositional phrases (διὰ Ἰησοῦ Χριστοῦ, v. 8; ἐπὶ τῶν προσευχῶν δεόμενος, v. 10; ὑμῖν τοῖς ἐν Ῥώμῃ, v. 15), adverbs (πάντοτε and εἴ πως ἤδη ποτέ, v. 10), and qualifications (v. 12 *in toto*; καὶ ἐκωλύθην ἀχρὶ τοῦ δεῦρο, v. 13). Paul thus continues the expansive style of the prescript in order to balance a friendly with a formal tone.

Overall, Paul portrays himself and his addressees as partners, joined by a shared purpose.[4] He calibrates his self-disclosures to build his ἦθος as an effective evangelist with a track-record of success among the "rest of the Gentiles."[5] He almost seems apologetic, as if the Roman Christians would fault him for having not yet visited them at the capital.[6] His method of asserting their bond with one another involves the combination of friendly expressions of admiration with praise of their πίστις. He has already used this word in 1:5, ὑπακοὴ πίστεως, referring to the acceptance of the proclamation.[7] In 1:8 he draws upon another meaning of πίστις in order to commend his addressees' exhibition of a quintessential Roman virtue, *fides*,[8] which "is proclaimed in

---

[3] Paul requests financial support in 15:22–24, and prayers in 15:30–32.

[4] Cf. the first person plural ἐλάβομεν in v. 5.

[5] Contra Kennedy, *New Testament Interpretation*, 152: "It is interesting that [Paul] does not make an effort at the outset to establish his personal ethos, perhaps by a narrative of his conversion."

[6] So also Williams, "'Righteousness of God,'" 251. Cf. Käsemann (*Romans*, 18–19), who states that Paul "has increasing difficulty in formulating precisely the reasons for his projected journey and his expectations." He concludes that "Paul feels very insecure in relation to the unmet recipients of his letter and is thus forced into an apologetic defensive. He obviously fears the mistrust and the suspicions of both his person and his work which are circulating in Rome...." I agree that Paul is to a large degree contending with his own reputation in 1:8–15, but words like "insecurity" and "apologetic defensive" seem too strong.

[7] The "obedience of faith" is the objective of proclaiming the gospel, and clearly refers here to the acceptance of the proclamation by those who hear it. I thus generally concur with Bultmann (*Theology*, 1.89) that "acceptance of the message is called πίστις... or πιστεύειν" (but cf. his discussion of other meanings at 1.82–92, and in Paul specifically, 1.314–30, and see further n. 9 below), and with Käsemann (*Romans*, 15) that "the obedience of faith means acceptance of the message of salvation." Πίστεως therefore functions as a genitive of apposition or description: "obedience, in other words, faith" (see Smyth 317–18, §§ 1320–22; BDF 92, § 167). For other instances of ὑπακοή and ὑπακούειν in Romans in an evangelistic context, see 10:16, 15:18; cf. 6:17–18.

[8] Liebeschuetz (*Continuity and Change*, 175–76; cf. 51–52) writes: "the virtue of *Fides* had always been held in high esteem at Rome. Indeed it was, in a sense, the keystone of Roman morality." He proposes that this esteem is in part the origin of the cult of Fides, whose

the whole world."⁹ He later invokes πίστις in connection with his reasons for wanting to visit, since it provides the means for mutual encouragement (συμπαρακληθῆναι ἐν ὑμῖν διὰ τῆς ἐν ἀλλήλοις πίστεως ὑμῶν τε καὶ ἐμοῦ, v. 12). *Fides* also drives him to fulfill his own duty (*officium*), another distinctly Roman concern. The common rendering of ὀφειλέτης εἰμί as "I am a debtor" obscures these points.¹⁰ The phrase here means "I am obligated" with an ellipsed

---

foundation Livy (1.21.4) and Dionysius of Halicarnassus (*Ant. rom.* 2.75.3) attribute to Numa (see further Beard, North and Price, *Religions of Rome*, 2.34–35, quoting Cicero, *Nat. d.* 2.60–62; on Numa's reorganization of Roman religion, see Betz, "Credibility and Credulity," 201–4). Roman coins bore her image, symbols and name (Daphne E. M. Nash, *LIMC* 4/1.133–37), and she had a temple on the Capitoline since the third century B.C.E. (*OCD* 595; *BNP* 5.414–15). She also appears in magical contexts with other divinities, e.g. PGM XII.228, "I am Pistis who was found to be in humanity" (ἐγὼ ἡ Πίστις εἰς ἀνθρώπους εὑρεθεῖα); see BDAG 818–19, s.v. πίστις 2, for other instances. (For a full discussion of the worship of virtues in Roman religion, see Fears, "Cult of Virtues." Cf. also Georgi, *Theocracy*, 43, and nn. 32–33, arguing that πίστις as an abstract noun is a "savior figure," citing parallels to its appearances in Gnostic texts.) Whether the virtue gave rise to the cult or vice versa, the two were no doubt mutually supportive, and the cult unambiguously reveals the importance of the virtue of *fides* to the Romans. Cicero's *De officiis* illustrates further the prominence of both *fides* and *officium* in Roman ethics. In 1.4–5 he subordinates the entirety of life's moral decisions to duty, and *fides* to duty appears as a characteristic of some of Rome's most famous heroes, e.g., Regulus (3.111). See moreover 1.23, *fundamentum autem est iustitiae fides*; 1.39–40 and 3.107–8, on the importance of maintaining one's *fides* even toward enemies; and 3.104, on oaths sworn to *iustitia* and *fides*. Cf. Epictetus, *Diatr.* 2.4.1, "The human has come into existence for fidelity, and the one who overturns this overturns the particularity of the human" (ὁ ἄνθρωπος πρὸς πίστιν γέγονεν καὶ τοῦτο ὁ ἀνατρέπων ἀνατρέπει τὸ ἴδιον τοῦ ἀνθρώπου); πίστις also makes Epictetus' short-list of virtues on several occasions (e.g., *Diatr.* 3.14.13, 3.23.18, 4.9.17–18).

⁹ I therefore disagree with Bultmann that Paul's conception of faith-as-obedience prevents it from becoming a "state of soul," a "διάθεσις (propensity, disposition), or an ἀρετή (virtue, excellence)" (*Theology*, 1.316); see in addition Bultmann's article on πιστεύω, etc. in *TDNT* 6.174–228, esp. 204 ("[πίστις] can mean both 'faithfulness' and 'trust,' though it is seldom used in the former sense"), 208 ("πίστις [in Paul] is not faithfulness; it is the faith to which one should be faithful"), and 217–22 (regarding Paul's use of πίστις, omitting any possibility that it refers to a virtue). Cf. 1 Corinthians 13, an encomiastic section on ἀγάπη which climaxes in v. 13 (νυνὶ δὲ μένει πίστις, ἐλπίς, ἀγάπη, τὰ τρία ταῦτα· μείζων δὲ τούτων ἡ ἀγάπη); and Gal 5:22, where πίστις appears among other virtues as ὁ καρπὸς τοῦ πνεύματος (see also Betz, *Galatians*, 286–89). The thanksgiving section of 1 Thessalonians mentions the πίστις of the letter's recipients, at 1:2–3 (εὐχαριστοῦμεν τῷ θεῷ ... μνημονεύοντες ὑμῶν τοῦ ἔργου τῆς πίστεως καὶ τοῦ κόπου τῆς ἀγάπης καὶ τῆς ὑπομονῆς τῆς ἐλπίδος τοῦ κυρίου ἡμῶν Ἰησοῦ Χριστοῦ); and at 1:8 (ἀφ' ὑμῶν γὰρ ἐξήχηται ὁ λόγος τοῦ κυρίου οὐ μόνον ἐν τῇ Μακεδονίᾳ καὶ ἐν τῇ Ἀχαΐᾳ, ἀλλ' ἐν παντὶ τόπῳ ἡ πίστις ὑμῶν ἡ πρὸς τὸν θεὸν ἐξελήλυθεν). Note that in the latter passage Paul uses πρός with πίστις ("your fidelity toward God"), not the other more typical ways of saying "faith in" (i.e., εἰς, ἐπί, ἐν or the objective genitive). Cf. Sanday and Headlam, *Romans*, 19–20, 33–34; Käsemann, *Romans*, 17 ("In [v. 8] πίστις does not mean coming to faith but the state of faith").

¹⁰ E.g., NRSV; Fitzmyer, *Romans*, 250 (but he includes "obligation of his apostolate" as a second meaning); Dunn, *Romans*, 1.27 (but cf. his comments at 33).

infinitive complement,[11] εὐαγγελίσασθαι.[12] Paul has a duty to preach to Greeks and barbarians, to the wise and the foolish,[13] and *therefore* he wants to come to Rome to continue to fulfill his obligation as the gospel's messenger.[14] He thus stresses the πίστις of his audience of Roman Christians and of himself, his own deep commitment to his special duties as apostle, in order to portray himself and them as the best exemplars of Roman virtue.[15]

5.3 The basic definition (1:16)

Paul's second definition of the gospel divides into three main parts, the transition in v. 16a, the basic definition which is the predicative statement in v. 16b, and an abbreviated proof in v. 17.

I. 1:16a, the bridge from the προοίμιον: οὐ γὰρ ἐπαισχύνομαι τὸ εὐαγγέλιον.
II. 1:16b, the basic definition, given as an explanation of 1:16a.
   A. Conjunction, main verb and predicate: δύναμις γὰρ θεοῦ ἐστιν.
   B. Prepositional phrase of purpose/result: εἰς σωτηρίαν.
   C. Dative of advantage: παντὶ τῷ πιστεύοντι.
   D. Expansion of II.C: Ἰουδαίῳ τε πρῶτον καὶ Ἕλληνι.
III. 1:17, the abbreviated proof.
   A. Conjunction and nominative: δικαιοσύνη γὰρ θεοῦ.
   B. Prepositional phrase of agency/means: ἐν αὐτῷ = ἐν εὐαγγελίῳ.
   C. Main verb: ἀποκαλύπτεται.
   D. Prepositional phrase of source: ἐκ πίστεως.
   E. Prepositional phrase of destination: εἰς πίστιν.
   F. Proof-text (Hab 2:4).

---

[11] See, for instance, Gal 5:3 (ὀφειλέτης ἐστὶν ὅλον τὸν νόμον ποιῆσαι); cf. Rom 8:12 (ὀφειλέται ἐσμὲν οὐ τῇ σαρκὶ τοῦ κατὰ σάρκα ζῆν), 15:27 (εὐδόκησαν γάρ καὶ ὀφειλέται εἰσὶν αὐτῶν· εἰ γὰρ τοῖς πνευματικοῖς αὐτῶν ἐκοινώνησαν τὰ ἔθνη, ὀφείλουσιν καὶ ἐν τοῖς σαρκικοῖς λειτουργῆσαι αὐτοῖς), and the entries s.v. ὀφειλέτης and ὀφείλω in BDAG (742–43) and LSJ (1227). Roman philosophers generally use *officium* to translate τὸ καθῆκον, "that which is appropriate"; see, e.g., Long, *Hellenistic Philosophy*, 188–89 (on the ambiguities of *officium* and τὸ καθῆκον), and 213–16 (on the terms' usage in Panaetius' and Cicero's ethics). Cf. Rom 1:28, παρέδωκεν αὐτοὺς ὁ θεὸς εἰς ἀδόκιμον νοῦν, ποιεῖν τὰ μὴ καθήκοντα, and Lietzmann, *an die Römer*, 34–35.

[12] Note also that this infinitive complements τὸ πρόθυμον in v. 15b.

[13] I discuss the phrases Ἕλλησίν τε καὶ βαρβάροις and σοφοῖς τε καὶ ἀνοήτοις below in connection with Ἰουδαίῳ τε πρῶτον καὶ Ἕλληνι in v. 16.

[14] Käsemann (*Romans*, 20) is sensitive to this point: "... it does not denote a general duty ... but the special apostolic obligation." Lietzmann (*an die Römer*, 29) writes: "ὀφειλέτης εἰμι heißt bei Pls einfach 'ich bin schuldig, ich muß ..., ohne Betonung des bildlichen Charakters der Redensart (also nicht 'ich bin Schuldner')." Cf. Barrett, *Romans*, 26; Dodd, *Romans*, 6 ("I owe a duty"); Stuhlmacher, *Romans*, 27–28; Jewett, *Romans*, 132; Schlier, *Römerbrief*, 41.

[15] Cf. the illuminating discussion of Paul's appropriation of *pax* and *iustitia* – key words in the ideology of Roman imperial dominance – by Haacker, *Theology*, 116–24.

1. Quotation formula: καθὼς γέγραπται.
2. Quotation: ὁ δὲ δίκαιος ἐκ πίστεως ζήσεται.

The main exegetical debates pertain to the meanings of δικαιοσύνη θεοῦ, ἐκ πίστεως εἰς πίστιν, and ἐκ πίστεως in the quotation of Hab 2:4. These problems will occupy us in the next sub-section (5.4).

Paul accomplishes a transition from the προοίμιον to his definition and πρόθεσις with the declaration, οὐ γὰρ ἐπαισχύνομαι τὸ εὐαγγέλιον. In order to discern why he does this, it may be helpful to regard the three causal conjunctions (γάρ, at I, II.A, and III.A) as answering a series of questions that arise from what Paul says about himself in the prescript and thanksgiving. He has asserted his apostolic obligation to preach to everyone, οὕτως τὸ κατ' ἐμὲ πρόθυμον καὶ ὑμῖν τοῖς ἐν Ῥώμῃ εὐαγγελίσασθαι (1:15). Why? Because, he answers, "I am not ashamed of the gospel." And why not? Because "it is God's power for salvation for everyone who believes, for both the Jew first and the Greek." And how can it be that? Because "in it God's justice is revealed from faith to faith." The definition therefore looks backward to the προοίμιον, elaborating Paul's desire to visit his addressees and to preach at Rome. The προοίμιον indeed supplies the context necessary for the determination of the definition's meaning *in situ*. The transitional statement represents an instance of the rhetorical figure λιτότης, "understatement."[16] It clearly has greater force than "I am proud," but it is difficult to determine what might prompt feelings of shame given what Paul has said so far.[17] Οὐκ ἐπαισχύνομαι might convey the degree to which his *fides* to his *officium* overrides all other concerns. He may also allude to the controversy that surrounds him, the criticism of his

---

[16] So also Vorster, "Strategies of Persuasion," 157–58; Keck, *Romans*, 50. The term λιτότης is a label of convenience adopted for a phenomenon that has several names in the ancient theoretical literature (Lausberg, *Handbook*, 268–69, §§ 586–88). Zonaeus (*Fig.* 2.22, *RG* 3.169–70) defines it straightforwardly: "Ἀντεναντίωσις is whenever we, wishing to say one thing, disclose it through its opposite, for example: 'I became perhaps not more despicable than most people,'" ἀντεναντίωσίς ἐστιν, ὅταν εἰπεῖν βουλόμενοι διὰ τοῦ ἐναντίου δηλώσωμεν, οἷον «ἴσως οὐ τῶν πολλῶν ἐγενόμην φαυλότερος». See also [Cicero], *Rhet. Her.* 9.38.50 (*deminutio*); Quintilian, *Inst.* 10.1.12 (treating the figure as a type of periphrasis); Alexander Rhetor, *Fig.* 2.23 (*RG* 3.37–38, ἀντεναντίωσις); Tryphoˡ, *Trop.* 2.15 (ἀντίφρασις).

[17] Cf. Wedderburn's thesis (*Reasons for Romans*, 104) that Paul responds to the charge that he *should* be ashamed of his gospel. Vorster ("Strategies of Persuasion," 157–58) also perceives the λιτότης as calculated to address the possibility "of the good news being tainted with shame." On this point, cf. 1 Cor 1:18–25. The description of οὐκ ἐπαισχύνομαι as a "confessional formula" (e.g., Käsemann, *Romans*, 22) diminishes the force of the λιτότης, and for this reason merits rejection. The idea of shame, whether attached to any actual emotions on Paul's part or not, evokes any pressure that would impede his efforts to proclaim the gospel and thereby to fulfill his duty as apostle. Therefore, he argues implicitly, any feelings of shame in supporting him and his mission should vanish in his addressees' own loyalty to the gospel.

apostolate, and previous efforts to interfere with his work.[18] The extension of a warm welcome to Paul by the Roman Christians may entail the appearance of taking sides in a conflict from which they would prefer to remain aloof. Embarassment on Paul's part would be a reasonable emotional reaction to this potentially uncomfortable situation; with οὐκ ἐπαισχύνομαι he pre-emptively sets it aside.

5.3.1 Divine power and salvation

The only major term that the two definitions of the gospel in Romans 1 have in common – aside from the definiendum and θεός – is δύναμις. The figure of ἀπὸ κοινοῦ in v. 4 permits ἐν δυνάμει to construe both with the participle τοῦ ὁρισθέντος and its predicate υἱοῦ θεοῦ. God both exercises his power to define and he shares his power with the Son. Paul has thus already firmly attached divine power to εὐαγγέλιον. His second definition moves δύναμις to the position of primary predicate, to the place where a definition commonly states the *kind* or *class* to which the definiendum belongs, prior to the addition of its differentiating attributes and functions. For example, love is a "dominating desire" (ἡ κρατήσασα ... ἐπιθυμία ... ἔρως ἐκλήθη);[19] knowledge is an "apprehension" (εἶναι δὲ τὴν ἐπιστήμην κατάληψιν);[20] several definitions of ὅρος and ὑπογραφή describe them initially as "statements" (λόγοι);[21] furthermore, God is an "immortal organism" (θεὸν δ᾽ εἶναι ζῷον ἀθάνατον).[22] The prepositional phrases which follow δύναμις θεοῦ in v. 16 identify the special function of εὐαγγέλιον within its class.[23] The placement of εὐαγγέλιον into the class of δυνάμεις θεοῦ imparts to it a quasi-divine status, comparable to the hypostases of ἁμαρτία and θάνατος in Rom 5:12–21. These latter forces have their origin in the transgression of Adam, which has empowered and released them as malevolent agents in the cosmos. God has likewise empowered and released the

---

[18] Cf. Rom 3:8, and esp. 15:31, where Paul solicits his addressees' prayers ἵνα ῥυσθῶ ἀπὸ τῶν ἀπειθούντων ἐν τῇ Ἰουδαίᾳ καὶ ἡ διακονία μου ἡ εἰς Ἰερουσαλὴμ εὐπρόσδεκτος τοῖς ἁγίοις γένηται. By "efforts to interfere with his previous work," I am referring to the occasion of his letter to the Galatians, where οἱ ταράσσοντες ὑμᾶς καὶ θέλοντες μεταστρέψαι τὸ εὐαγγέλιον τοῦ Χριστοῦ (1:7) have evidently come into the churches which he founded. Cf. Stuhlmacher, *Romans*, 28.

[19] Plato, *Phaedr.* 238b–c, see ch. 2, p. 13 above.

[20] Stobaeus, *Anth.* 2.73.16–74.3 = Long/Sedley 41H; see ch. 2, pp. 18–19, n. 19 above.

[21] See ch. 2, p. 18, nn. 17, 18 above.

[22] Diogenes Laertius 7.147 = Long/Sedley 54A; see ch. 2, p. 21, n. 27 above.

[23] Paul refers to this class as a whole in Rom 1:20 as one of God's ἀόρατα perceptible in nature: τὰ γὰρ ἀόρατα αὐτοῦ ἀπὸ κτίσεως κόσμου τοῖς ποιήμασιν νοούμενα καθορᾶται, ἥ τε ἀΐδιος αὐτοῦ δύναμις καὶ θειότης, εἰς τὸ εἶναι αὐτοὺς ἀναπολογήτους. Cf. also 1 Cor 1:23–24, ἡμεῖς δὲ κηρύσσομεν Χριστὸν ἐσταυρωμένον, Ἰουδαίοις μὲν σκάνδαλον, ἔθνεσιν δὲ μωρίαν, αὐτοῖς δὲ τοῖς κλητοῖς, Ἰουδαίοις τε καὶ Ἕλλησιν, Χριστὸν θεοῦ δύναμιν καὶ θεοῦ σοφίαν.

gospel as an agent of σωτηρία.²⁴ Looking back on the first definition through the second, we can now see that Paul identifies the origin of the gospel *qua* δύναμις θεοῦ as the resurrection and appointment of the Son.

The phrase εἰς σωτηρίαν specifies the first particularity (τὸ ἴδιον) of the gospel's function in terms of its purpose and result (εἰς can signify both). Recalling a principle that I outlined at the beginning of chapter 4, the component terms of a definition will often carry the broadest semantic ranges allowable in the context, since this enables an author to compress greater content within the definition. Σωτηρία retains its general meanings of "salvation," "safety" and "deliverance." For the gospel to have this goal and result, a threat of some kind must exist. The combination of σωτηρία with δικαιοσύνη θεοῦ in v. 17 and ὀργὴ θεοῦ in v. 18 identifies the threat as one of legal jeopardy at the eschatological trial. The gospel's primary functionality according to the second definition therefore lies in the area of *forensic eschatology*, with σωτηρία signifying acquittal at the divine trial, and ὀργή condemnation. Paul's forensic usage of these terms conforms with similar usages in the Greco-Roman and Hellenistic Jewish sources. In the opening sections of the *Ars Rhetorica*, Aristotle says that previous *artes rhetoricae* focus upon the stimulation of ὀργή and other emotions in the jurors.²⁵ Werner Foerster's article on σῴζειν in the *Theological Dictionary of the New Testament* identifies two passages, one from Xenophon and the other from Andocides, in which σωτηρία means "deliverance from a guilty verdict at trial."²⁶ Xenophon (*Hell.* 5.4.25–26) tells of a Spartan governor who stands in danger of prosecution for attempting to incite a war with Athens. He has some support from well-positioned friends, who "were disposed to acquit him" (ἀπολυτικῶς αὐτοῦ εἶχον), but as an extra

---

[24] Betz ("Christianity as Religion," 215) summarizes: "In Paul's interpretation, therefore, the expression 'power of God' means more than that God *has* power. Rather, God *is* power and exercises it in creation and in human history. The conduit of this power is 'the gospel' (τὸ εὐαγγέλιον).... The proclamation of the gospel, therefore, is now merely a speech event, but the speech event in this instance is a 'demonstration of spirit and power' (ἀπόδειξις πνεύματος καὶ δυνάμεως [1 Cor 2:4]). If God himself is the power, it is also the energy that drives human history 'toward salvation' (εἰς σωτηρίαν [Rom 1:16])."

[25] *Rhet.* 1.1.3–6, 1354a: "Indeed those nowadays who put together 'Arts' on orations have furnished us with nothing, so to speak; a [mere] part of it, for the proofs are the only thing that qualifies as 'art,' and the other things are supplementary. But they say nothing about enthymemes, which are the body of the proof, and they mostly busy themselves dealing with things outside the subject. For prejudice, pity, anger, and such emotions are not about the subject, but [directed] to the juror." νῦν μὲν οὖν οἱ τὰς τέχνας τῶν λόγων συντιθέντες οὐδὲν ὡς εἰπεῖν πεπορίκασιν αὐτῆς μόριον (αἱ γὰρ πίστεις ἔντεχνόν εἰσι μόνον, τὰ δ' ἄλλα προσθῆκαι), οἱ δὲ περὶ μὲν ἐνθυμημάτων οὐδὲν λέγουσιν, ὅπερ ἐστὶ σῶμα τῆς πίστεως, περὶ δὲ τῶν ἔξω τοῦ πράγματος τὰ πλεῖστα πραγματεύονται· διαβολὴ γὰρ καὶ ἔλεος καὶ ὀργὴ καὶ τὰ τοιαῦτα πάθη τῆς ψυχῆς οὐ περὶ πράγματός ἐστιν, ἀλλὰ πρὸς τὸν δικάστην.

[26] Foerster, "σῴζω," etc., *TDNT* 7.966.

measure of security he urges his son to intercede with a friend who is enamoured with the boy's good looks: "It is possible for you, my son, to save your father by begging Archidamus to make Agesilaus favorable to me in the trial" (ἔξεστί σοι, ὦ υἱέ, σῶσαι τὸν πατέρα, δεηθέντι Ἀρχιδάμου εὐμένη Ἀγισίλαον ἐμοὶ εἰς τὴν κρίσιν παρασχεῖν). The son complies: "And he began to beg him to become his father's savior" (καὶ ἐδεῖτο σωτῆρα αὐτῷ τοῦ πατρὸς γενέσθαι). Foerster also cites Andocides, *Myst.* 31, which contrasts the jurors' capacity to "take vengence on those who commit impiety" and to "save those who do nothing unjust" (ἵνα τιμωρήσητε μὲν τοὺς ἀσεβοῦντας, σώζητε δὲ τοὺς μηδὲν ἀδικοῦντας). The previous paragraph (*Myst.* 30) holds greater relevance, however, since Andocides there uses ὀργίζεσθαι and σώζειν in conjunction with a guilty verdict and acquittal respectively.[27] As for the HB and LXX, Foerster remarks:

> Deliverance may also come through the the resolving of a legal difficulty. Job, confident in God, looks forward to victory in his litigation, Job 13:16. It is said of Tola the judge in Ju. 10:1 that he should deliver Israel, while elsewhere the expression is שפט, "to judge," "to secure the rights." But ישע and שפט are not co-extensive, since the ref. of the former is not to securing justice but to a work of liberation from legal oppression. Thus the personal intervention of the king is sought when legal statutes strictly demand condemnation (2 S. 14:4) or cannot be applied in the tangle of relations (2 K. 6:26). Hence saving intervention can be an alternative to litigation, Ju. 6:31.[28]

Paul, too, gives ample evidence of forensic usages of ὀργή and σωτηρία. In Rom 2:5–11, he sketches the scenario of the eschatological trial, and invokes the principle of impartiality in the execution of divine justice:

5 κατὰ δὲ τὴν σκληρότητά σου καὶ ἀμετανόητον καρδίαν θησαυρίζεις σεαυτῷ ὀργὴν ἐν ἡμέρᾳ ὀργῆς καὶ ἀποκαλύψεως δικαιοκρισίας τοῦ θεοῦ 6 ὃς «ἀποδώσει ἑκάστῳ κατὰ τὰ ἔργα αὐτοῦ»· 7 τοῖς μὲν καθ' ὑπομονὴν ἔργου ἀγαθοῦ δόξαν καὶ τιμὴν καὶ ἀφθαρσίαν ζητοῦσιν ζωὴν αἰώνιον, 8 τοῖς δὲ ἐξ ἐριθείας καὶ ἀπειθοῦσι τῇ ἀληθείᾳ πειθομένοις δὲ τῇ ἀδικίᾳ ὀργὴ καὶ θυμός. 9 θλῖψις καὶ στενοχωρία ἐπὶ πᾶσαν ψυχὴν ἀνθρώπου τοῦ κατεργαζομένου τὸ κακόν, Ἰουδαίου τε πρῶτον καὶ Ἕλληνος· 10 δόξα δὲ καὶ τιμὴ καὶ εἰρήνη παντὶ τῷ ἐργαζομένῳ τὸ ἀγαθόν, Ἰουδαίῳ τε πρῶτον καὶ Ἕλληνι· 11 οὐ γάρ ἐστιν προσωπολημψία παρὰ τῷ θεῷ.

---

[27] After referring to his opponents' citation of precedent in the punishment of other impieties, he says: "For I prosecute a much greater matter than these, and because of this very matter I say that it is necessary that those people perish, because they committed impieties, but that I be saved, because I committed no crime. Otherwise it would be terrible if you were angry with me for the crimes of others, and [if] you will show regard to this slander against me, although you know that it is uttered by my enemies, as better than the truth." Ἐγὼ γὰρ πολὺ μᾶλλον ἐκείνων κατηγορῶ, καὶ δι' αὐτὸ τοῦτό φημι δεῖν ἐκείνους μὲν ἀπολέσθαι, ὅτι ἠσέβησαν, ἐμὲ δὲ σῴζεσθαι, ὅτι οὐδὲν ἡμάρτηκα. ἢ δεινόν γ' ἂν εἴη, εἰ ἐμοὶ ὀργίζοισθε ἐπὶ τοῖς ἑτέρων ἁμαρτήμασι, καὶ τὴν εἰς ἐμὲ διαβολὴν εἰδότες ὅτι ὑπὸ τῶν ἐχθρῶν τῶν ἐμῶν λέγεται, κρείττω τῆς ἀληθείας ἡγήσεσθε. Other illuminating instances of σωτηρία in forensic speeches appear in Lysias, e.g., *Or.* 1.5, 12.24, 12.43 (n.b. ὀργή in 12.42), 19.53–54.

[28] *TDNT* 7.974.

5 But, in accord with your hardness and your unrepentant heart, you store up for yourself wrath on the day of wrath and of the revelation of the just judgment of God, 6 who "will repay to each according to his works" (Prov 24:12, Ps 62:13): eternal life for those who seek glory and honor and immortality in accord with the endurance of good deed; 8 but wrath and anger for those who from contentiousness are disobedient to the truth but are obedient to injustice. 9 Affliction and distress [will be] upon every soul of a person who produces evil, for both the Jew first and the Greek; 10 but glory and honor and peace for everyone who produces good, for both the Jew first and the Greek. 11 For there is no favoritism before God.

Passages such as this one illustrate the danger from which the gospel "saves," even as it confirms that ὀργή means God's determination of guilty verdicts and provision of just penalties. Rom 5:8–9 meanwhile confirms that σωτηρία signifies deliverance from this (universal) guilty verdict:

8 συνίστησιν δὲ τὴν ἑαυτοῦ ἀγάπην εἰς ἡμᾶς ὁ θεός, ὅτι ἔτι ἁμαρτωλῶν ὄντων ἡμῶν Χριστὸς ὑπὲρ ἡμῶν ἀπέθανεν. 9 πολλῷ οὖν μᾶλλον δικαιωθέντες νῦν ἐν τῷ αἵματι αὐτοῦ σωθησόμεθα δι' αὐτοῦ ἀπὸ τῆς ὀργῆς.

8 But God demonstrates his own love to us, because while we were still sinners Christ died on our behalf. 9 Therefore how much more, now after having been justified by his blood, will we be saved through it [or, "him"] from the wrath.

Σωθησόμεθα ἀπὸ τῆς ὀργῆς sets forth the alternate verdicts of acquittal and condemnation in a trial that stands in the future. Paul can speak of this forensic eschatology in a much more compressed way, for example in 1 Thess 1:10 (Ἰησοῦν τὸν ῥυόμενον ἡμᾶς ἐκ τῆς ὀργῆς τῆς ἐρχομένης) and 5:9 (ὅτι οὐκ ἔθετο ἡμᾶς ὁ θεὸς εἰς ὀργὴν ἀλλὰ εἰς περιποίησιν σωτηρίας διὰ τοῦ κυρίου ἡμῶν Ἰησοῦ Χριστοῦ). The precise legal logic by which the gospel converts ὀργή to σωτηρία shall not presently detain us. But another dimension of δύναμις θεοῦ εἰς σωτηρίαν has now emerged: the gospel functions as God's *ability to save* at the eschatological trial, which, prior to the gospel's release into the cosmos, was unavailable even to him.

5.3.2 Faith and universalism

The remaining phrases of v. 16 connect the gospel to faith and to universalism, two themes that factor prominently into the letter as a whole.[29] Paul has up to this point utilized πίστις in two ways. In 1:5 he refers to his reception of "grace and apostleship for the obedience of faith among all the Gentiles" (ἐλάβομεν χάριν καὶ ἀποστολὴν εἰς ὑπακοὴν πίστεως ἐν πᾶσιν τοῖς ἔθνεσιν). Paul is speaking here of acceptance of the gospel, faith at the cognitive and emotional levels (belief and trust). Then, in vv. 8–15, πίστις shifts to fidelity, a reason to praise his addressees in order to acquire their good will, and a

---

[29] Nanos (*Mystery of Romans*) is particularly sensitive to the theme of universalism in Romans; note esp. his overview of the theme at 189–92, wherein he closely aligns the unity and singularity of God (3:29) with it as a central component of Paul's argument throughout.

method of presenting himself as a Roman among his fellows. These meanings remain fully active in 1:16–17: the gospel demands of its adherents cognitive endorsement (belief), emotional reliance (trust), and fidelity (action consistent with belief and trust). All three aspects unite to activate the benefits of the gospel as a δύναμις θεοῦ εἰς σωτηρίαν.

Paul stresses the universality of the gospel twice, with παντί in παντὶ τῷ πιστεύοντι and with the phrase Ἰουδαίῳ τε πρῶτον καὶ Ἕλληνι. The latter represents a sophisticated instance of brevity in style and content: through the combination of the conjunctions τε and καί with the adverb πρῶτον, he simultaneously conveys inclusivity and sequence. Πρῶτον can furthermore fit into the sentence in two ways. It can belong with the participle τῷ πιστεύοντι: "the gospel is God's power for everyone, both for the Jew who believes first and the Greek [who believes thereafter]."[30] Paul thereby acknowledges that Jews were the first to receive and believe the promises from the mouths of the prophets and in the scriptures, and they were the first to accept the gospel of Christ and proclaim it to the Gentiles. He also foreshadows his argument regarding Abraham's πίστις in Romans 4, his effort in chapters 9–11 to reckon with the problem of the Jews who reject the gospel, and his exhortation to the Gentiles in 11:13–24. Πρῶτον can secondly construe with σωτηρίαν, referring to the sequence of the docket at the divine trial: the Jew will receive rewards (and punishments) *first*. The exact phrase "both the Jew first and the Greek" will reappear in 2:9–10 to make this very point. The context offers no definitive criteria for deciding between the construal of πρῶτον with τῷ πιστεύοντι or with σωτηρίαν. Most likely it construes with both, and, like ἐν δυνάμει in 1:4, is an instance of ἀπὸ κοινοῦ.

Paul has already laid a foundation for his assertion of the universal scope of the gospel in 1:5 (πᾶσιν τοῖς ἔθνεσιν) and 14 (Ἕλλησίν τε καὶ βαρβάροις, σοφοῖς τε καὶ ἀνοήτοις ὀφειλέτης εἰμί). The phrase 'Greeks and barbarians' is a common periphrasis for 'all peoples,' in other words, 'we the civilized Greeks and the undifferentiated mass of all other peoples.'[31] The bigotry of the locution would not escape the detection of anyone in the category of βάρβαροι.[32]

---

[30] Several patristic interpreters read the phrase in this manner; see § 5.4.2 below.

[31] This phrase, according to Hans Windisch (*TDNT* 1.547, s.v. βάρβαρος), "does not merely denote the totality of all peoples; it also brings out the distinction.... οἱ βάρβαροι are the other peoples who are different in nature, poor in culture or even uncultured, whom the Greeks hold at arm's length, and over whom they are destined to rule...."

[32] The commentaries generally overlook how strange it would be for Paul to refer indirectly to his *Roman* readers as *Greeks* (e.g., Fitzmyer, *Romans*, 256–57), especially if he means "Gentiles." Romans do not ordinarily call themselves Greeks (cf., however, Cicero, *Resp.* 1.37.58; [Dio Chrysostom], *Or.* 37.25–27), even when they frankly admit their debts to Greek culture. Roman authors occasionally betray a scornful attitude, e.g., the report of Marcus Cato's statements to his son at Pliny, *Nat.* 29.7.14. For a (probably exaggerated) summary of negative Greek attitudes toward the Romans, see Dionysius of Halicarnassus, *Ant. rom.*

The second phrase σοφοῖς τε καὶ ἀνοήτοις immediately prompts the question: to which categories does he suppose the Roman Christians (and do they suppose themselves) to belong? Although they certainly speak Greek, suggesting (but not proving) their origin in immigrant stock, Paul takes pains to portray them as *Romans*, even the *real* Romans who best exemplify their trademark values.[33] In a manner consistent with this aim, v. 15 characterizes them as

---

1.4.2–3 (see also Rawson, "Romans," esp. 4–5; Momigliano, *Alien Wisdom*, 10–11). Jewett (*Romans*, 140) has a different theory: "I suggest that he felt it was politically wise in several contexts to avoid the use of the pejorative term 'Gentiles' in referring to the groups currently dominating the Christian movement at Rome. ... The Greek churches experience salvation in their own right, not as second-class non-Jews, which the epithet 'Gentiles' would have implied." This reading runs into the problem of the appearance of ἔθνη in vv. 5–6: ἐν πᾶσιν τοῖς ἔθνεσιν ... ἐν οἷς ἐστε καὶ ὑμεῖς κλητοὶ Ἰησοῦ Χριστοῦ. I recognize that the singular ἔθνος is not used to refer to a single Gentile, and for this reason Ἕλλην may in Paul's usage serve as the single representative of the class ἔθνη; such seems to be the case, for example, in Gal 3:26 (on which see n. 39 below). But in Galatians he addresses grecophone residents of Asia Minor, who would most likely regard themselves as "Greeks" whether they descended from Gallic stock or not (so also Betz, *Galatians*, 2: "Nothing in Paul's letter points to the Celtic origin of the Galatians"), and regardless of whether Greeks from further west would agree with their self-identification. Cf. also Paul's usage of Ἕλληνες καὶ Ἰουδαῖοι in 1 Cor 1:22–24, a letter addressed to Christian readers of *Roman* Corinth.

[33] Cf. Pliny the Elder, *Nat.* 18.41–43, discussing a Greek freedman farmer who was accused of magic because he persistently earned a better harvest than his more prestigious neighbors; at the trial, he produces his slaves, his tools, and his cattle as the "evil spells" he performed to obtain his harvest. Graf (*Magic in the Ancient World*, 64) observes: "Cresimus presents himself as a more industrious farmer than the others. He knew how to prove that he, too, the former eastern slave, had those virtues of which the Romans were so proud, and that he had more of them than the others had. Hence, a new gap opens, thus reversing once again the social relation between the freedman and the rich citizens; it is the former slave from the east who appears to be a truly perfect Roman."

It is naturally impossible to determine the degree to which the Christians at Rome identify themselves as Romans (unless, of course, they are in fact citizens), particularly if they migrated there from Greek-speaking areas of the empire. My point is simply this: Paul projects an image of his readers, who through their embrace of πίστις embody a cardinal Roman virtue; this in turn evokes a set of Roman attitudes toward themselves and other proudly distinguished groups, i.e., Jews and Greeks. Cf. Aelius Aristides, *Or.* 25.63: "You great people measured the city [Rome] greatly, and for this reason you made it a marvel not arrogantly, so as to give a share of it to no one from other cities, but you sought the fullness worthy of it, and you made being 'Roman' not the name of a city but of a certain common people; and this people was not one among all others, but one in contradistinction to all the rest. For you do not now divide the peoples into Greeks and barbarians ... but you split them into Romans and non-Romans." μεγάλοι μεγάλως ἐμετρήσατε τὴν πόλιν, καὶ οὐκ ἀποσεμνυνάμενοι τούτῳ θαυμαστὴν ἐποιήσατε, τῷ μηδένι τῶν ἄλλων αὐτῆς μεταδιδόναι, ἀλλὰ τὸ πλήρωμα αὐτῆς ἄξιον ἐζητήσατε, καὶ τὸ Ῥωμαῖον εἶναι ἐποιήσατε οὐ πόλεως, ἀλλὰ γένους ὄνομα κοινοῦ τινος, καὶ τούτου οὐχ ἑνὸς τῶν πάντων, ἀλλ' ἀντιρρόπου πᾶσι τοῖς λοιποῖς. οὐ γὰρ εἰς Ἕλληνας καὶ βαρβάρους διαιρεῖται νῦν τὰ γένη ... ἀλλ' εἰς Ῥωμαίους τε καὶ οὐ Ῥωμαίους ἀντιδιείλετε.

'wise barbarians,'[34] a notion that surfaces early in connection with the Scythian Anacharsis,[35] one of the Seven Sages, and is evident in the widespread admiration of the Babylonians,[36] Egyptians,[37] and eventually the Romans.[38] We should also take careful note that Paul does *not* have an obligation to preach to Jews (Gal 2:6–8), a fact to which he alludes in 1:5 and which his addressees surely know. The phrase Ἰουδαίῳ τε πρῶτον καὶ Ἕλληνι does not simply equate with the syntactically similar phrases in v. 14. The gospel offers its benefits to Jew and Gentile on the same basis, yet the division still remains. Paul experiences it daily in his separate apostolate to the 'uncircumcision.' The pairing of the Jew and the Greek here intensifies the universalism of the definition, since with it Paul refers not only to his own work but that of his apostolic colleagues who direct their efforts toward evangelizing Jews. Also, the Greek of v. 16 is not merely a συνεκδοχή for the Gentiles (τὰ ἔθνη). Instead

---

[34] Cf. Betz, "Paul between Judaism and Hellenism," 249: "The reason that Paul wrote to the Romans was that they belonged to the βάρβαροι (Rom 1:14)." See also idem, "The Gospel and the Wisdom of the Barbarians," esp. 88–90; Lovejoy and Boas, *Primitivism*, ch. 11, "The Noble Savage in Antiquity." For discussions of the early Christian development of the concept of wise barbarians, see Waszink, "Some Observations"; Stroumsa, "Philosophy of the Barbarians."

[35] On Anacharsis, see Herodotus 4.76–77; Diogenes Laertius 1.101–5; Kindstrand, *Anacharsis*, esp. 17–18 on "wise barbarians" and 23–26 on "idealization of barbarians." Cf. the pseudepigraphic *Ep.* 2, Ἀνάχαρσις Σόλωνι, which begins: "Greeks are wise men, yet in no way wiser than barbarians. For the gods did not take away from barbarians the know-how to recognize the good." Ἕλληνες σοφοὶ ἄνδρες, οὐδέν γε σοφώτεροι βαρβάρων. τὸ γὰρ ἐπίστασθαι καλὸν εἰδέναι οὐκ ἀφείλοντο θεοὶ βαρβάρων. It is worth noting in this context how Lucian appropriates Anacharsis' sojourn to Greece to learn wisdom in connection with his own arrival in Athens (*Scyth.* 9): "So I say that I myself too am experiencing something similar to Anacharsis...; for he also was a barbarian, and you would in no way say that we Syrians are worse than Scythians," φημὶ δὴ ὅμοιόν τι καὶ αὐτὸς παθεῖν τῷ Ἀναχάρσιδι...· βάρβαρος μὲν γὰρ κἀκεῖνος καὶ οὐδέν τι φαίης ἂν Σύρους ἡμᾶς φαυλοτέρους εἶναι τῶν Σκυθῶν. Lucian's self-presentation is probably playful, but any bite to the irony would require a real expectation that his audience would regard him – as a Syrian and in spite of his mastery of Greek – as a barbarian.

[36] See, e.g., Diogenes Laertius 1.6–9. For discussion of the alleged study of some Greek philosophers with μάγοι and Χαλδαῖοι, see G. Delling, "μάγος," *TDNT* 4.356–57. On the fusion of Babylonian motifs with Middle and Neo-Platonism in the *Chaldean Oracles*, see the introduction of Majercik, *Chaldean Oracles*, 1–46, and Johnston, *Hekate Soteira*, ch. 6 on "Theurgy and Magic," 76–91.

[37] See, e.g., Diogenes Laertius 1.10–11. On the admiration of Egyptian wisdom as partially responsible for the Hermetica, see Fowden, *Egyptian Hermes*, 13–44.

[38] See, e.g., Plutarch's description of Numa, an early king of Rome (*Num.* 3.7): "His character was well-tempered by nature toward every virtue. Still more he tamed himself through education, perserverence and philosophy, banishing not only the reviled passions from his soul, but also the violence and the arrogance which is well-regarded among the barbarians," φύσει δ' εἰς πᾶσαν ἀρετὴν εὖ κεκραμένος τὸ ἦθος, ἔτι μᾶλλον αὐτὸν ἐξημέρωσε διὰ παιδείας καὶ κακοπαθείας καὶ φιλοσοφίας, οὐ μόνον τὰ λοιδορούμενα πάθη τῆς ψυχῆς, ἀλλὰ καὶ τὴν εὐδοκιμοῦσαν ἐν τοῖς βαρβάροις βίαν καὶ πλεονεξίαν ἐκποδὼν ποιησάμενος.

the phrase as a whole is a συνεκδοχή, not just for the two classes mentioned but for every single person within and between them – hence the singular forms. The Greek stands apart from the undifferentiated barbarians; likewise the Jew from the undifferentiated Gentiles. Paul selects two self-consciously separate groups, positioning them at either end of the full spectrum of humankind: the Jew, the Greek, and everyone in between (including the Romans). The gospel summons all with the same imperative: believe. Insofar as every person must stand alone before the divine tribunal,[39] every person must have the opportunity to accept or reject the σωτηρία which the gospel offers.

5.4 Abbreviated proof (1:17)

The abbreviated proof in v. 17 explains how the gospel can do what the basic definition claims: δικαιοσύνη γὰρ θεοῦ ἐν αὐτῷ ἀποκαλύπτεται ἐκ πίστεως εἰς πίστιν. Paul supports this statement further with an adapted quotation of Hab 2:4: καθὼς γέγραπται, ὁ δὲ δίκαιος ἐκ πίστεως ζήσεται. Several very difficult questions arise from v. 17, which again derive primarily from the brevity of Paul's style and his deliberate maximization of the semantic ranges of the proof's component terms. (1) What does δικαιοσύνη θεοῦ mean? (2) What does ἐκ πίστεως εἰς πίστιν mean, and how do the two prepositional phrases function in the sentence? (3) Why does Paul adjust Hab 2:4, and how is ἐκ πίστεως functioning? And, most importantly, (4) how does the gospel's revelation of δικαιοσύνη θεοῦ logically cause it to become δύναμις θεοῦ εἰς σωτηρίαν? I address the fourth question in the conclusion (§ 5.5).

---

[39] Cf. Rom 14:10, πάντες γὰρ παραστησόμεθα τῷ βήματι τοῦ θεοῦ. A difficult tension underlies Paul's shift to the singular and the attending emphasis upon a person's sole appearance before the divine tribunal, namely that between the class ('Jew,' 'Greek,' 'Roman,' 'Gentile') and the individual representative of the class (cf. Käsemann, *Romans*, 22: "Universalism and the most radical individuation are here two sides of the same coin"). Paul regards the election of the Gentiles *en masse* as a primary consequence of Jesus' death and resurrection. But this does not diminish the need for each person to accept the benefits of this election, i.e. πιστεύειν. The tension is also evident in Gal 3:26–28, which has alternations between singular and plural forms: πάντες γὰρ υἱοὶ θεοῦ ἐστε διὰ τῆς πίστεως ἐν Χριστῷ Ἰησοῦ· ὅσοι γὰρ εἰς Χριστὸν ἐβαπτίσθητε, Χριστὸν ἐνεδύσασθε. οὐκ ἔνι Ἰουδαῖος οὐδὲ Ἕλλην, οὐκ ἔνι δοῦλος οὐδὲ ἐλεύθερος, οὐκ ἔνι ἄρσεν καὶ θῆλυ· πάντες γὰρ ὑμεῖς εἷς ἐστε ἐν Χριστῷ Ἰησοῦ. Paul here identifies three pairs of classes, while the singular forms underscore the labels borne by each person within πάντες ὑμεῖς. God's adoption of the Galatian Christians welds them into a new unity, forming (as it were) a new class with its own individual representatives. Cf. Engberg-Pedersen (*Paul and the Stoics*, 13), who admits that it is "quite appropriate to warn against 'individualistic' reading of Paul," and yet "it is false not to allow that Paul is in fact doing philosophy about the self (the 'I') and its relation to God, Christ, the world and others to exactly the same extent as a similar philosophy (of self and others) was being done in antiquity by the philosophers who make up the ancient ethical tradition."

5.4.1 Δικαιοσύνη θεοῦ as divine justice

The meaning of δικαιοσύνη θεοῦ in Rom 1:17 and the other passages in which it appears (3:5, 21–26; 10:3; 2 Cor 5:21) is one of the most persistent debates in the entire field of early Christian studies, as is well known and widely acknowledged.[40] Many scholars today argue that it means "God's righteousness" or "uprightness," as exemplified primarily in his actions to save his people (and, through the gospel, Gentiles), and in his fidelity to the promises that he makes to the Israelites (i.e., his covenant with them).[41] This argument relies upon manifold instances of צדקה and צדק (which the LXX typically renders as δικαιοσύνη) that occur in the HB with that meaning, particularly when it appears alongside other divine attributes: חסד (kindness), אמונה and אמת (fidelity), and טוב (goodness).[42] Paul himself closely aligns God's δικαιοσύνη with his πίστις in Rom 3:1–8. Another group of scholars, who have no less a champion for their position than Rudolf Bultmann, interpret δικαιοσύνη θεοῦ to mean "justification from God," with the genitive expressing source and δικαιοσύνη the result of God's action of acquittal (δικαιοῦσθαι) both ahead of and at

---

[40] For helpful summaries of the positions, see Fitzmyer, *Romans*, 257–63; Käsemann, *Romans*, 25–30; Sanday and Headlam, *Romans*, 28–39; Ziesler, *Meaning of Righteousness*, 1–14; Manfred E. Brauch, "Perspectives on 'God's Righteousness' in Recent German Discussion," in Sanders, *Paul and Palestinian Judaism*, 523–42. The debate received a fresh dose of vigor in response to the "New Perspective on Paul," i.e., Sanders' arguments regarding "covenantal nomism" and the studies by Dunn and others that build upon them. See, e.g., Stuhlmacher, *Revisiting Paul's Doctrine of Justification*; VanLandingham, *Judgment and Justification*. In the discussion which follows, I intend my references to the secondary literature to be illustrative, not exhaustive.

[41] Fitzmyer (*Romans*, 257, cf. 106), e.g., writes: "Paul uses *dikaiosunê theou* in the sense in which God's uprightness is spoken in postexilic writings in the OT, even though the specific phrase never occurs in the LXX. It is the quality whereby God actively acquits his sinful people, manifesting toward them his power and gracious activity in a just judgment." Also Stuhlmacher, "Apostle Paul's View of Righteousness," 78 ("the embodiment of the saving action of God in Christ which creates new life for believers as they face the judgment"); idem, *Revisiting Paul's Doctrine of Justification*, 18–19; Ziesler, *Meaning of Righteousness*, 17–46, esp. 40, with rich citation of the secondary literature; Williams, "Righteousness of God," passim (see n. 49 below); Moo, *Romans*, 75; Du Toit, "Forensic Metaphors in Romans," 236.

[42] Advocates of this position often assert that God's righteousness is a "relational," not a "static" or an "absolute" quality, e.g., Fitzmyer, *Romans*, 257; Wedderburn, *Reasons for Romans*, 117–20; Dunn, *Romans*, 1.40–41; idem, "Justice of God," 15–21; cf. Barr, *Semantics*, 10–12. It is unclear to me why scholars feel the need to stress this point. No attribute of any person – human or divine – simply exists apart from contexts in which it expresses itself. Action and attribute remain logically separable, but the latter can only become tangibly understood through the former. The covenant – the set of agreements with the Israelites into which he voluntarily entered – represents one such context of action, but certainly not the only one advanced by the authors of the HB.

the eschatological trial.[43] Paul supports this interpretation with his statement in Phil 3:9, καὶ εὑρεθῶ ἐν αὐτῷ, μὴ ἔχων ἐμὴν δικαιοσύνην τὴν ἐκ νόμου ἀλλὰ τὴν διὰ πίστεως Χριστοῦ, τὴν ἐκ θεοῦ δικαιοσύνην ἐπὶ τῇ πίστει. Insofar as δικαιοσύνη is a divine predicate, it speaks less to what God *is* than what he *does*. Finally, Ernst Käsemann reads δικαιοσύνη θεοῦ as speaking "of the God who brings back the fallen world into the sphere of his legitimate claim"; it thus simultaneously captures divine power and gift.[44] The difficulties that attend interpretation of δικαιοσύνη θεοῦ stem partly from its obvious centrality to the argument of Romans and to Pauline theology, and partly from the facts that Paul does not define and deploy it as a technical term, and that he uses it variously.[45] One cannot simply pin down its meaning in one passage and generalize that meaning to all other instances. Paul perceives the polyvalence of δικαιοσύνη θεοῦ, like that of πίστις and πιστεύειν, as advantageous to his argument in Romans.

There is another lexically valid possibility,[46] one which can accommodate all of the meanings briefly discussed above as well as some others, and which fits very well with the theme of forensic eschatology in Rom 1:16–17: God's justice.[47] This concept is broad enough to encompass the overlapping covenantal, forensic eschatological, and royal-cosmic contexts in which the HB and LXX refer to God's צדק(ה)/δικαιοσύνη. On one side of the coin are his full conformity to the terms of the covenant into which he entered with the Israelites,

---

[43] See, e.g., Bultmann, *Theology*, 1.270–87; Dunn, *Romans*, 1.41; Cranfield, *Romans*, 1.98–99; cf. the criticism of such interpretations by Käsemann, *Romans*, 27. For a vigorous disputation of this view, with a wholesale rejection of a connection between Paul's concept of justification and the eschatological trial, see VanLandingham, *Judgment and Justification*, 242–332.

[44] Käsemann, *Romans*, 29; idem, "'The Righteousness of God' in Paul"; Stuhlmacher, *Romans*, 29–32.

[45] Cf. Schnelle's discussion of it as a "multidimensional concept" (*Apostle Paul*, 318–21), a "universal-forensic concept" on the one hand, and a "concept expressing transfer and participation" on the other (320).

[46] See BDAG 247, s.v. 1a–b; LSJ 429, s.v., I–II, cf. ibid. 430, s.v. δίκη.

[47] So, e.g., Betz ("Christianity as Religion," 217, n. 39): "God's 'wrath' (ὀργή) is his reaction consistent with his 'righteousness' (δικαιοσύνη). The harsh punishment corresponds to the fundamental character of the human offense against God." Also, Keck, *Romans*, 58; Wedderburn, *Reasons for Romans*, 119; Kensky, *Trying Man, Trying God*, 185–86, esp. n. 7. Koester, in his article on "Paul's Proclamation of God's Justice for the Nations," seems to use "righteousness" and "justice" when predicated to God interchangeably. Some scholars of the HB connect צדק(ה) to the "world order" established and maintained by God, especially when paired with משפט, e.g., J. J. Scullion, "Righteousness [OT]," *ABD* 5.724–36, esp. 727–31; cf. Johnson, "צָדַק, [etc.]," *TDOT* 12.247–48. Scullion describes the pairing as a hendiadys (727), later adding: "*ṣedeq-ṣĕdāqâ* and *mišpāṭ* are the foundation of Yahweh's throne.... His rule is proper order and he sustains it through his throne (i.e., the king)" (731). This all seems well to me, as long as the forensic resonances of צדק(ה) and משפט do not vanish into "world order" in contexts where God is petitioned or acts as royal judge.

his defense of the oppressed, his pronouncements of the verdict "just" and the provision of proper rewards in his capacity as judge, and in his recognition of human (ethical) δικαιοσύνη. On the other side are his demand that those with whom he has made a covenant observe its terms, his vengeance against the oppressor, his pronouncement of the verdict "guilty" and the provision of suitable penalties, and in his recognition of human ἀδικία. When the Israelites cry out to God in their suffering at the hands of their cruel oppressors, salvation and justice naturally become closely aligned – hence the association of the two concepts noted by scholars. One may readily detect, however, a strong reluctance on the part of interpreters of Paul to take the possibility that δικαιοσύνη θεοῦ signifies divine justice, with both positive and negative aspects, into consideration, even when they recognize Paul's interest in theodicy in Romans.[48] Some interpreters of the HB share this reluctance.[49] We should not

---

[48] See, e.g., Fitzmyer, *Romans*, 258. After discussing the Old Latin and Vulgate translations of δικαιοσύνη θεοῦ as *iustitia dei*, he writes: "But 'justice of God,' though defensible as a translation in itself, has often been understood as God's distributive or retributive justice and sometimes as a quality contrasted with God's mercy, specifically his punitive or vindictive justice. Although this sense has been used in the interpretation of Romans, it is far from what Paul means by *dikaiosynē theou*." Stowers (*Rereading of Romans*, 195–98) is sensitive to the forensic dimension of δικαιοσύνη θεοῦ, and he rightly characterizes the first part of Romans as a "defense of God's justice, a theodicy" (197). At the same time, he denies that the term refers to "strict justice," rather to "quite specifically a redeeming merciful justice" (196). See also Du Toit, "Forensic Metaphors in Romans," 236: whenever δικαιοσύνη appears, "it has forensic connotations"; however, "I have no doubt that Paul derived his understanding of δικαιοσύνη from his Jewish heritage, where משפט, צדקה and צדק indicate Jahwe's covenant mercy and goodness." Moo (*Romans*, 75) both invokes and restricts the forensic implications of δικαιοσύνη: "To use the imagery of the law court, from which righteousness language is derived, we can picture God's righteousness as the act or decision *by which the judge declares innocent a defendant*: an activity of the judge, but an activity that is a declaration of status – an act that results in, and indeed includes within in, a gift. In this sense, the term 'righteousness' in this phrase can be understood to be substantival equivalent of the verb 'justify'" (emphasis added). On the basis of parallels from Qumran, Dahl ("Doctrine of Justification," 99) writes: "What the Qumran texts really prove is that the Old Testament idea of God's righteousness was alive in Judaism at the time of the New Testament ...; God's *ṣĕdaḳa* is not a revenging or distributive justice but the saving righteousness he shows in his treatment of his chosen ones."

[49] Twentieth century "theologies of the Old Testament" generally support the idea that צדק(ה) mainly relates to God's conduct within the covenant while denying or minimizing any connection with distributive justice, e.g., Eichrodt, *Theology of the Old Testament*, 1.239–49; von Rad, *Old Testament Theology*, 1.370–83; and Preuss, *Old Testament Theology*, 1.171–79. E. R. Achtemeier provides a succinct summary of this position (*IDB* 4.80, s.v. "Righteousness of God"). She starts with some "negative definitions": "it is not behavior in accordance with an ethical, legal, psychological or religious norm"; nor "conduct which is dictated by either human or divine nature"; nor "equivalent to giving every man his due." She continues: "Rather, righteousness is in the OT the fulfillment of the demands of a relationship, whether the relationship be with men or God. Each man is set within a multitude of relationships.... And each of these relationships brings with it specific demands, the fulfillment of which con-

move too quickly to banish divine justice from the discussion, regardless how disagreeable it may appear at first glance.

The primary contextual factors that should impact understanding of δικαιοσύνη θεοῦ are the eschatological trial and God's role within it as an absolutely impartial judge. Paul says it best in Rom 2:11, οὐ γάρ ἐστιν προσωπολημψία παρὰ τῷ θεῷ. The concept of God's impartiality has rich antecedents in the HB and Second Temple Jewish literature,[50] beginning with his declaration of his own attributes in Exod 34:6–7 and Deut 32:4, which emphasize both his mercy and his punishment without resolving the tension between the two.[51]

---

stitutes righteousness. ... Further, there is no norm of righeousness outside the relationship itself." Williams ("Righteousness of God") directly applies such perspectives to the interpretation of Rom 1:17. He identifies several Hebrew words – חסד, אמונה, אמת and טוב – which appear in parallelism with צדקה in the Psalms, and he notes the association of righteousness and salvation in Second Isaiah. Williams endorses the idea that δικαιοσύνη is an attribute, a "quality of the divine being, a readiness on God's part to help and save his creatures" (262), although with an important caveat: "As we have seen, the 'righteousness of Yahweh' is, for Second Isaiah, virtually synonymous with Yahweh's salvation. Paul's language in Rom 1:16–17, however, precludes our defining 'righteousness of God' as salvation because Paul says quite exactly that the *gospel* is God's power *for* (leading to) salvation because by it the righteousness of God is being revealed. Nevertheless, I think we must acknowledge that for anyone familiar with the book of Isaiah – Paul and, presumably, the Roman Christians – the phrase *dikaiosunê theou* at Rom 1:17 would likely bring to mind ideas of deliverance or salvation" (ibid.). Further down he concludes: "Although on the basis of Rom 1:16–17, we cannot say exactly what Paul 'means' by *dikaiosunê theou*, I think we can say that he intends for this phrase to bring to mind that aspect of God's nature which we might point to with such additional expressions as God's steadfast adherence to what is right and fitting, his constancy, his trustworthiness and his readiness to save" (ibid., 263). Williams ignores the forensic dimension of צדקה in his analysis, except for a very brief dismissal in his survey of data from the Psalms: "Occasionally Yahweh's righteousness parallels his *mišpāṭîm*, his judgments (36:7, 72:1, cf. 103:6: Yahweh does *ṣidqôt* and *mišpāṭîm* for those who are for those who are oppressed); but more frequently the parallel is Yahweh's *ḥesed*, his *'ĕmûnāh*, his *'ĕmet* or his *ṭûb*," ibid., 260.

[50] In addition to the literature that I discuss below, see esp. Bassler, *Divine Impartiality*, and eadem, "Divine Impartiality in Paul's Letter to the Romans"; Kensky, *Trying Man, Trying God*, 13–61.

[51] In Exod 34:6–7, God has summoned Moses to the summit of Mt. Sinai with fresh tablets to replace the broken ones (my translations are from the Hebrew unless otherwise noted). God says of himself: "The Lord is a compassionate and gracious God, slow in anger, great in kindness and fidelity, observing kindness for thousands, removing guilt, transgression and sin – but he will surely not acquit, visiting the guilt of the fathers on [their] sons, and the sons of [their] sons, on the third and fourth [generations]." HB:

יְהוָה אֵל רַחוּם וְחַנּוּן אֶרֶךְ אַפַּיִם וְרַב־חֶסֶד וֶאֱמֶת: נֹצֵר חֶסֶד לָאֲלָפִים נֹשֵׂא עָוֹן וָפֶשַׁע וְחַטָּאָה וְנַקֵּה לֹא יְנַקֶּה פֹּקֵד עֲוֹן אָבוֹת עַל־בָּנִים וְעַל־בְּנֵי בָנִים עַל־שִׁלֵּשִׁים וְעַל־רִבֵּעִים:

LXX: Κύριος ὁ θεὸς οἰκτίρμων καὶ ἐλεήμων, μακρόθυμος καὶ πολυέλεος καὶ ἀληθινὸς καὶ δικαιοσύνην διατηρῶν καὶ ποιῶν ἔλεος εἰς χιλιάδας, ἀφαιρῶν ἀνομίας καὶ ἀδικίας καὶ ἁμαρτίας, καὶ οὐ καθαριεῖ τὸν ἔνοχον ἐπάγων ἀνομίας πατέρων ἐπὶ τέκνα καὶ ἐπὶ τέκνα τέκνων ἐπὶ τρίτην καὶ τετάρτην γενεάν. The text of Deut 32:4 reads: "[He is] the Rock, his work is perfect, since all

Insofar as the sources present him as a judge of all nations with the right to reward and revenge, his righteousness transcends his conduct within the covenant with the Israelites.[52] At a more mundane level, (ה)צדק regularly appears in contexts discussing forensic justice among humans.[53] This justice

---

his ways are justice; he is a God of fidelity, without injustice, righteous and straight-dealing." HB:

הַצּוּר תָּמִים פָּעֳלוֹ כִּי כָל־דְּרָכָיו מִשְׁפָּט אֵל אֱמוּנָה וְאֵין עָוֶל צַדִּיק וְיָשָׁר הוּא׃

LXX: θεός, ἀληθινὰ τὰ ἔργα αὐτοῦ, καὶ πᾶσαι αἱ ὁδοὶ αὐτοῦ κρίσεις· θεὸς πιστός, καὶ οὐκ ἔστιν ἀδικία, δίκαιος καὶ ὅσιος κύριος. Both of these passages combine terms like "kindness" and "fidelity" with terms which plainly have forensic resonances. In Exod 34:6–7, God declares that he consistently exhibits mercy and fidelity in his dealings. חסד shows up twice, וְרַב־חֶסֶד and נֹצֵר חֶסֶד. The two expressions seem largely equivalent, although the LXX translates the first with πολυέλεος and the second with δικαιοσύνην διατηρῶν καὶ ποιῶν ἔλεος. The latter perhaps depends on a different Hebrew text, since, based on πολυέλεος, one would expect διατηρῶν ἔλεος. The presence of δικαιοσύνη in the translation might however point forward to God's assurance that his generosity does not omit the punishment of transgressions; later generations must live with the consequences of previously committed sins. Deut 32:45 also mentions fidelity (אֵל אֱמוּנָה, θεὸς πιστός) alongside righteous judgment (מִשְׁפָּט, κρίσεις), the absence of injustice (וְאֵין עָוֶל, οὐκ ἔστιν ἀδικία), and the adjectives righteous and straight-dealing (צַדִּיק וְיָשָׁר, δίκαιος καὶ ὅσιος). The forensic terminology in these two passages do not address God's behavior in a concrete circumstance of litigation, but they do provide a sense of how terms like justice, righteousness, mercy and punishment can sit alongside one another in a more-or-less unresolved tension, and without deprivation of the forensic senses that some of them carry.

[52] Amos offers an informative case study of this very point. In chapters 1 and 2, the text talks of the "transgressions" (פִּשְׁעֵי, LXX ἀσέβειαι) of Damascus, of Gaza, of Tyre, of Edom, of the Ammonites, and of Moab. What covenant does God have with these peoples, such that he has the right to indict them for their "transgressions"? The text *presupposes* this right, in order to construct the dramatic turning-of-the-tables in 2:6, the indictment of the Israelites, who will *not* be spared *in spite of* his long relationship with them. God's right to visit punishment on all has its foundation in his sustenance of the cosmos (5:8–9, and note משפט and צדקה in v. 7). At one point (5:21–24) Amos avers that the Israelites' responsibility to treat each other justly actually supercedes their covenantal obligations. God rejects their sacrifices and songs, HB:

וְיִגַּל כַּמַּיִם מִשְׁפָּט וּצְדָקָה כְּנַחַל אֵיתָן

LXX: καὶ κυλισθήσεται ὡς ὕδωρ κρίμα καὶ δικαιοσύνη ὡς χειμάρρους ἄβατος (cf. 4:4–5). Amos seems to argue that the Israelites' offenses against justice have risen to the point that he can no longer protect them from the consequences of their actions. Also note that God accuses Damascus, etc. for how they treated their neighboring peoples, presumably in war, but he threatens the Israelites for internal predation, for the way they treat each other.

[53] The Torah establishes some basic parameters for judges, for example Exod 23:6–9: "You will not bend the judgment of your poor in his trial. You will abstain from the word of falsehood, and you will not slay the innocent and the just, because I will not justify the criminal [LXX: and you will not justify the wrongdoer on account of bribes]. You will not take a bribe, because the bribe will blind the clear-eyed and will twist the words [or, cases] of the just. And you will not oppress the alien; you know the life of the alien, because you were aliens in the land of Egypt." HB:

לֹא תַטֶּה מִשְׁפַּט אֶבְיֹנְךָ בְּרִיבוֹ׃ מִדְּבַר־שֶׁקֶר תִּרְחָק וְנָקִי וְצַדִּיק אַל־תַּהֲרֹג כִּי לֹא־אַצְדִּיק רָשָׁע׃ וְשֹׁחַד לֹא תִקָּח כִּי הַשֹּׁחַד יְעַוֵּר פִּקְחִים וִיסַלֵּף דִּבְרֵי צַדִּיקִים׃
וְגֵר לֹא תִלְחָץ וְאַתֶּם יְדַעְתֶּם אֶת־נֶפֶשׁ הַגֵּר כִּי־גֵרִים הֱיִיתֶם בְּאֶרֶץ מִצְרָיִם׃

pertains especially to impartiality in the adjudication of trials by the king or his appointed magistrates.[54] Israel's greatest kings, David and Solomon, merit

---

LXX: οὐ διαστρέψεις κρίμα πένητος ἐν κρίσει αὐτοῦ. ἀπὸ παντὸς ῥήματος ἀδίκου ἀποστήσῃ· ἀθῷον καὶ δίκαιον οὐκ ἀποκτενεῖς καὶ οὐ δικαιώσεις τὸν ἀσεβῆ ἕνεκεν δώρων. καὶ δῶρα οὐ λήμψῃ· τὰ γὰρ δῶρα ἐκτυφλοῖ ὀφθαλμοὺς βλεπόντων καὶ λυμαίνεται ῥήματα δίκαια. καὶ προσήλυτον οὐ θλίψετε· ὑμεῖς γὰρ οἴδατε τὴν ψυχὴν τοῦ προσηλύτου· αὐτοὶ γὰρ προσήλυτοι ἦτε ἐν γῇ Αἰγύπτῳ. The key word in this text's heading is מִשְׁפָּט (κρίμα), and it entertains a few reasons why the miscarriage of justice might occur: false testimony, murder, bribes, and bigotry against resident aliens. Lev 19:15 operates at a more abstract level: "You will not cause injustice in judgment; you will not show partiality toward the poor and you will not show honor to the great; you will judge your fellows with justice." HB:

לֹא־תַעֲשׂוּ עָוֶל בַּמִּשְׁפָּט לֹא־תִשָּׂא פְנֵי־דָל וְלֹא תֶהְדַּר פְּנֵי גָדוֹל בְּצֶדֶק תִּשְׁפֹּט עֲמִיתֶךָ׃

LXX: οὐ ποιήσετε ἄδικον ἐν κρίσει· οὐ λήμψῃ πρόσωπον πτωχοῦ οὐδὲ θαυμάσεις πρόσωπον δυνάστου, ἐν δικαιοσύνῃ κρινεῖς τὸν πλησίον σου. Δικαιοσύνη (צֶדֶק) here pertains unambiguously to justice in the rendering of verdicts (בַּמִּשְׁפָּט, ἐν κρίσει). The only miscarriage which the text considers relates to favoritism on the basis of wealth, a point which has illuminating implications for those passages in the Psalms where the petitioners describe themselves as poor, weak, and in need of defense from the powerful. Other passages in the Torah address fairness in judgment, reworking aspects of the above themes: Lev 24:22 (δικαίωσις μία [מִשְׁפַּט אֶחָד] ἔσται τῷ προσηλύτῳ καὶ τῷ ἐγχωρίῳ); Num 15:16 (νόμος εἷς ἔσται καὶ δικαίωμα ἓν [תּוֹרָה אַחַת וּמִשְׁפָּט אֶחָד] ἔσται ὑμῖν καὶ τῷ προσηλύτῳ τῷ προσκειμένῳ ἐν ὑμῖν); Deut 1:16–17 (διακούετε ἀνὰ μέσον τῶν ἀδελφῶν ὑμῶν καὶ κρίνατε δικαίως [וּשְׁפַטְתֶּם צֶדֶק] ἀνὰ μέσον ἀνδρὸς καὶ ἀνὰ μέσον ἀδελφοῦ καὶ ἀνὰ μέσον προσηλύτου αὐτοῦ. οὐκ ἐπιγνώσῃ πρόσωπον ἐν κρίσει [בַּמִּשְׁפָּט], κατὰ τὸν μικρὸν καὶ κατὰ τὸν μέγαν κρινεῖς, οὐ μὴ ὑποστείλῃ πρόσωπον ἀνθρώπου, ὅτι ἡ κρίσις τοῦ θεοῦ ἐστιν [כִּי הַמִּשְׁפָּט לֵאלֹהִים הוּא]); and especially Deut 16:18–20 (κριτὰς καὶ γραμματοεισαγωγεῖς καταστήσεις σεαυτῷ ἐν πάσαις ταῖς πόλεσίν σου ... καὶ κρινοῦσιν τὸν λαὸν κρίσιν δικαίαν [וְשָׁפְטוּ אֶת־הָעָם מִשְׁפַּט־צֶדֶק]. οὐκ ἐκκλινοῦσιν κρίσιν, οὐκ ἐπιγνώσονται πρόσωπον οὐδὲ λήμψονται δῶρον· τὰ γὰρ δῶρα ἐκτυφλοῖ ὀφθαλμοὺς σοφῶν καὶ ἐξαίρει λόγους δικαίων. δικαίως τὸ δίκαιον διώξῃ [צֶדֶק צֶדֶק תִּרְדֹּף]...). Interestingly, the Torah appropriates forensic justice as part of Israel's contractual obligations, but the abstract concept of justice is assumed: the forbidding of the perversion of justice makes it clear that God perceives such actions as infractions of their covenant, but their fundamental *wrongness* is presupposed.

[54] The responsibility of kings to handle trials and to ensure the integrity of legal processes in their realms is hardly unique to ancient Israel. Regarding the royal judiciary in the ancient Near East, Roth (*Law Collections*, 4–5, cf. 23) remarks: "Throughout Mesopotamian history, the concern of the king with justice and the legal process is emphasized in royal inscriptions, royal epithets, iconographic representations, and literary allusions. Whether or not the king was always himself an active participant in the administration of the legal system, he was always its guardian, for the application of justice was the highest trust given by the gods to a legitimate king." The prologues and epilogues of the monumentally published 'codes' indicate that kings viewed their enactments of justice as being among their greatest achievements, so they preserved for posterity a record of the principles and parameters of their verdicts in abstract terms. Their publication also ensures that the king continues to render justice even after he dies. See further Bottéro, "'Code' of Ḫammurabi," and West on the transmission of some of these ideas into the Greek epic milieu in *East Face of Helicon*, 126 (re divine wrath), 132–37 (re kingship, cf. 14–19). Cf. Ando's observation regarding the emperor's position in the imperial justice system (*Imperial Ideology*, 46–47): "Emperors drew on this special relationship between themselves and each of their subjects not only when they guaranteed on their own authority the fair review of any appeal from below, but in particular when they ex-

praise for their exemplary fairness in rendering verdicts.[55] Various passages in the Hebrew Bible present God as the high king both of Israel and of the cosmos,[56] so it comes as no surprise that his own royal governance likewise includes a judicial role that parallels that of earthly kings. When the authors of the Psalms approach God for deliverance, especially in instances where David is the alleged petitioner, they appeal to him as the judge of last resort for those who cannot acquire justice through any other means; the king must go to his own king, God, in order to obtain fair adjudication. The hymnic petitions in such cases offer insight into the format and content of the more ordinary pleadings which the king would hear on a regular basis: claims of the petitioner's defenselessness, weakness, and poverty;[57] vivid descriptions of the

---

plicitly reminded the provincial populations that local imperial officials could be held accountable for their actions. Ironically, imperial ideology therefore guaranteed the fairness of its administration ... by appeal to the singular, even superhuman status of its highest offical."

[55] For example, 2 Sam 8:15 (par. 1 Chron 18:14) singles out David's justice, his מִשְׁפָּט וּצְדָקָה (κρίμα καὶ δικαιοσύνην), as the definitive characteristic of his reign. In the famous story of his petition for wisdom in 1 Kings 3:5–9 (par. 2 Chron 1:8–10), Solomon begins by briefly recounting the nature of God's relationship with David (חסד [ἔλεος] on God's end, and אמת, צדקה, and ישרה [ἀλήθεια, δικαιοσύνη, and εὐθύτης] on David's), and by noting his own inexperience. He then asks for discernment in v. 9: "And will you give to your servant a listening heart to judge your people, to understand [the difference] between good and evil, for who will be able to judge this heavy people of yours?" HB:

וְנָתַתָּ לְעַבְדְּךָ לֵב שֹׁמֵעַ לִשְׁפֹּט אֶת־עַמְּךָ לְהָבִין בֵּין־טוֹב לְרָע כִּי מִי יוּכַל לִשְׁפֹּט אֶת־עַמְּךָ הַכָּבֵד הַזֶּה:

LXX: καὶ δώσεις τῷ δούλῳ σου καρδίαν ἀκούειν καὶ διακρίνειν τὸν λαόν σου ἐν δικαιοσύνῃ τοῦ συνίειν ἀνὰ μέσον ἀγαθοῦ καὶ κακοῦ· ὅτι τίς δυνήσεται κρίνειν τὸν λαόν σου τὸν βαρὺν τοῦτον; Solomon requests precisely that quality which makes a good king, both in his own understanding and God's: a keen ability to sort out right and wrong in deciding cases (לִשְׁפֹּט, διακρίνειν). The LXX moreover reads an additional phrase, ἐν δικαιοσύνῃ, with διακρίνειν; whether צדקה was present in the translators' Hebrew base or whether they added it for clarity, the text closely associates forensic justice with the performance of one of a king's primary duties. Solomon's justice is also the subject of Psalm 72 (LXX 71), specifically as it pertains to the fortunes of the kingdom. Vv. 1–4 focus on deliverance (יוֹשִׁיעַ, σώσει) of the poor from oppression; the protection of the poor from the powerful seems to fall under the royal judicial aegis. Salvation of the poor means "crushing" (וִידַכֵּא, ταπεινώσει) the oppressor: the deliverance of some involves the violent punishment of others, and the royal judge causes both events to happen. One might feel tempted to perceive the "crushing" as a metaphor (as the LXX evidently does), but other psalms which plead for God's salvation request violent retributions against the ones who are afflicting them. The dual nature of the single event of rendering a verdict presents further problems for a purely positive portrayal of divine righteousness: to *save* one is to *condemn* and even *punish* the other. Cf., for instance, Dodd's remarks (*Bible and the Greeks*, 47): "The Hebrew conception of the function of a judge tends to be not so much to apply with strict impartiality an abstract principle of justice, but rather to come to the assistance of the injured person, and vindicate him." On the contrary, the assistance envisoned by passages that appeal to God as judge often involves returning the injury back upon the person who unjustly afflicts the petitioner.

[56] See Preuss, *Old Testament Theology*, 1.152–59, for references and discussion.

[57] E.g., Pss 3:2–3; 22:7–11, 15–16; 31:10–11; 69:2–4.

malicious cruelty of the oppressors,[58] and of the insult to the king/God implied by their actions,[59] since they believe they can get away with their injustices; expressions of trust in the king/God, that he always supports the just cause of powerless victims;[60] and graphic proposals for appropriate punishments.[61] Invocations of God's צדק(ה) and משפט have a natural place in this thematic universe.[62] Although one may reasonably assert the inseparability of

---

[58] E.g., Pss 7:3; 10:7–9; 17:8–12; 22:13–14, 17–19; 35:11–12, 15–16, 20–21; 57:5–7; 69:5–6, 21–22; 109:2–5; 143:3–4.

[59] E.g., Pss 10:3–6; 59:7–8; 65:3–7; 73:4–12; 94:4–7.

[60] E.g., Pss 3:4–7; 7:10–17; 10:17–18; 11:4–7; 22:23–25; 27:1–6, 13–14; 56:4–5, 9–12; 69:7–19; 140:7–9, 13–14.

[61] E.g. Pss 10:15; 17:13–14; 28:4–5; 35:4–8, 26; 59:12–16; 63:10–11; 69:23–30; 140:10–12. Note esp. 109:8–19, a detailed list of the opponent's proposals for punishments against the petitioner, underscoring the agonistic character of this motif.

[62] Psalm 5 gathers up many of the previously mentioned themes in its thirteen short verses. This text exhibits a high degree of adaptability to various kinds of petitionary situations, such that it could be a template which one could tailor according to a variety of predicaments, as long as other humans are the source of one's difficulties. Another curious facet of this psalm is its broad (and probably accidental) adherence to a structural pattern which is typical of Greek hymns: an "invocation" and appeal to listen (vv. 2–4); an "argument" which points to the relevant attributes of God, the petitioner, and his oppenents (vv. 5–8); and a "petition" (vv. 9–11). The psalm concludes with an additional section (vv. 12–13) which points out to God the benefits of granting the petition. Although the psalm does not directly invoke God as a judge, it projects the scenario of a courtroom, with the litigants standing before the throne where the king is seated. In the invocation, the petitioner begs his king and God (מַלְכִּי וֵאלֹהָי) to hearken to his appeal, which he submits early and often: "in the morning I set out [my case] to you" (בֹּקֶר אֶעֱרָךְ־לְךָ, τὸ πρωὶ παραστήσομαί σοι). The verb עָרַךְ broadly means "to arrange" a wide variety of things: sacrifices, table-settings, battle plans, and so forth. Profs. Brown, Driver and Briggs recommend that here the verb means "to arrange words," but the following section of their entry refers to setting forth a legal case (BDB 789, s.v. עָרַךְ 1f–g, and cf. NRSV; Dahood, *Psalms*, 1.30); the cry of the petitioner in this psalm might thus constitute a complaint in a litigation (פָּלַל, "to pray," has a forensic meaning as well; see BDB 813, s.v., and the entries regarding the nouns פָּלִיל [judge, umpire] and פְּלִילָה [office of judge] which follow). The argument next appeals to God's character, in particular his intolerance of evil and the persons who perpetrate it (boasters, troublemakers, liars, murderers and the treacherous). The petitioner praises the fairness of God, while alluding at the same time to the bad character of his opponents. His own character, meanwhile, is unimpeachable: he appears at the temple "by the greatness of your mercy" (בְּרֹב חַסְדְּךָ) and bows down "in fear of you" (בְּיִרְאָתֶךָ). This remark certainly speaks to his piety, but we should bear in mind that that temple housed the ark, where God sat enthroned between the cherubim. God's throne in the temple would be the analogue to the king's in his palace as the place where cases are tried and decided. V. 8 therefore recapitulates v. 4: he presents his case in the temple before God's throne, but with a clean conscience and a posture of humility, unlike those criminals whom God cannot abide (vv. 6–7). Two petitions next appear in vv. 9–11. The first uses the metaphor of guidance down a difficult road. The enemies are the ones who obstruct the path and endanger the traveller, so the petitioner begs that God clear the way בְּצִדְקָתֶךָ (ἐν τῇ δικαιοσύνῃ σου). The petitioner pauses a moment to point an accusing finger at his enemies as if they were present with him: the right is not in *his* mouth, *their* inner selves are utter ruin, and so forth. V. 10 also focuses on the enemies' organs of speech, their mouths, minds, throats, and

God's righteous attribute and his righteous action, the petitioners in these psalms do actually separate them, insofar as they pray for action on the basis of the attribute. The apocalyptic eschatologes that emerge in some branches of Second Temple Judaism – with direct and pervasive influence on the eschatologies of early Christians – sharpens interest in divine forensic justice, since it predicts a trial at the end of the aeon wherein God's role as supreme judge of the cosmos has its ultimate manifestation.[63] Again, his right to judge stems not from a special relationship or contract with the Israelites, but from his creation of the world and his kingship over it.

One must also take into consideration the impact of the decision by the translators of the LXX to render (ה)צדק with δικαιοσύνη, particularly when predicated to God. Paul's Gentile readers would have encountered the concept of divine justice through their religious practices and ideas prior to conversion. It was indeed a topic of intense concern in Greek and Roman religious and philosphical literature going all the way back to Hesiod,[64] who describes

---

tongues. The issue here is what they are *saying* to the judge, because they are mixing false testimony with flattery. The petitioner then frames his second petition: declare them guilty (הַאֲשִׁימֵם, κρῖνον αὐτούς), cause their conspiracy to fail, and cast them out. The final two verses appeal to public recognition of the king's verdict, since others who stand in a situation parallel to the petitioner can depend on his protection, "because you bless the righteous" (כִּי־אַתָּה תְּבָרֵךְ צַדִּיק, ὅτι σὺ εὐλογήσεις δίκαιον). Supporting his petition will thus enhance God's well-deserved reputation of just rule. God's righteousness makes an appearance only once in this psalm (v. 9) as part of a metaphor which is not specifically forensic, so one might be tempted to understand it as simply equivalent to "salvation," a poetic redundancy, as it were: "guide me, Adonai, by your salvation on account of my enemies." Salvation from enemies is exactly what the author is requesting in both petitions, but the second shows that God grants it by rejecting the case of the opponents and punishing them. The meaning of צדקה and צדיק in Psalm 5 must be viewed in this light. The former refers to the divine quality which supports the right and condemns the wrong, and the latter to the litigant who is in the right, both objectively (he did no wrong and deserves no punishment) and declaratively (God determines the facts and pronounces the correct verdict). Finally, Psalm 5 conspicuously lacks any appeal to a special covenant either with Israel or with the individual petitioner, nor does it not call upon any laws encoded within the covenant that would compel the desired verdict. The petitioner throws himself upon God's mercy, on the voluntary enactment of his attribute of justice in order to rectify gross injustices committed by the petitioner's tormentors.

[63] See, e.g., *1 En.* 1:7–9, 90:20–29, 100:1–13; *4 Ezra* 7:26–44, esp. 33–35; *Sib. Or.* 2:214–20; Rev 20:11–15; *Ascen. Is.* 4:18; cf. *Jub.* 5:12–19.

[64] Lloyd-Jones (*Justice of Zeus*, chs. 1–2) traces this interest even further back to Homeric theology. In Zeus' case, δίκη ("meaning both justice and the preservation of the established order") is one of his special spheres of authority, and violations of it (particularly of oaths, hospitality and the rights of suppliants) offend the τιμή which is due to him from humans and other divinities. Lloyd-Jones remarks: "It must be admitted that the concepts of Zeus as the protector of oaths and as the champion of strangers, hosts and guests are present in the *Iliad*, and I have argued that they are not easily separated from the concept of Zeus as the protector of justice which Hesiod in the *Works and Days* so explicitly put forward" (18). On the post-mortem tribunal in Homer, see Kensky, *Trying Man, Trying God*, 68–80.

the goddess Δίκη as Zeus' constant attendant,[65] and admonishing his addressee (νήπιε Πέρση) in *Works and Days* repeatedly with calls to heed her ways.[66] Cleanthes petitions Zeus to "rescue human beings from their destructive ignorance" (ἀνθρώπους ῥύου ⟨σύ γ'⟩ ἀπειροσύνης ἀπὸ λυγρῆς) and "grant that they obtain the insight on which you rely when governing everything with justice" (δὸς δὲ κυρῆσαι γνώμης ᾗ πίσυνος σὺ δίκης μέτα πάντα κυβερνᾷς).[67] Plutarch's *De superstitione* ridicules the irrational fear of divine vengeance in its arguments that superstition and atheism are equally harmful.[68] The curse tablets (*defixiones*) petition the chthonic gods in order to rectify unfair advantages at court, in business, in love, and at the games.[69] The Isis aretalogies portray her as the one who taught justice to humankind.[70] Overall, the gods in general, and Zeus in particular,[71] were thought to play the role of guarantors of justice in the cosmos. This notion could just as easily generate emotions of fear (especially in times of inexplicable hardship) as of comfort.[72] One of early Christianity's methods of attracting converts from Greco-Roman polytheism may have involved its ability to apply therapy to worries about divine retribution. The gospel's revelation of divine justice as both ὀργή and σωτηρία

---

[65] This description occurs in a section (*Op.* 248–273) addressed to kings, assuring them that their abuses of power and perversions of justice are directly reported to Zeus, who sees and understands all (πάντα ἰδὼν Διὸς ὀφθαλμὸς καὶ πάντα νοήσας, 267).

[66] E.g., *Op.* 27–41, 213–247, 274–292.

[67] Cleanthes, *Hymn to Zeus* lines 33, 34–35, quoted per the text and translation of Thom, *Cleanthes' Hymn to Zeus*, 39, 41, and note esp. Thom's comments at 155–56.

[68] See *Superst.* 166d–167a, esp. on post-mortem punishments; 170d–f.

[69] On the competitive nature of the *defixiones*, see Faraone, "Agonistic Context," and Gager, *Curse Tablets and Binding Spells*. Note also Versnel, "Beyond Cursing" (on "the appeal to justice in judicial prayers"); Faraone, *Ancient Greek Love Magic*, esp. ch. 2; and Pulleyn, *Prayer in Greek Religion*, 70–95 (on the association of curses and justice, and the relation of both to prayer).

[70] See ch. 4, p. 112, n. 58 above for references and discussion.

[71] Burkert, *Greek Religion*, 130: "Justice of Zeus, *Dios dika*; but this is not to say that Zeus is just, *dikaios*; only someone who respects the ordinances in a dispute with an equal can be called just; Zeus stands above all disputes. He gives now good, now evil; often no one knows why; but the very fact that a planning father holds power in his hands makes justice among men possible." Theon's προγυμνάσματα furnish an excellent illustration of the general interest in divine justice in his model of a hypothetical θέσις (*Prog.* 11, *RG* 2.126–27), especially his statements that "God, since he is just, would not allow the ones worshipping him to be without providence," δίκαιος ὢν ὁ θεὸς οὐκ ἂν ἀπρονοήτους περιεώρα τοὺς σεβομένους αὐτόν, and that "if the providence of the gods does not exist, neither is justice able to take shape, nor piety, nor good oaths...," εἰ γὰρ οὐκ ἔστι θεῶν πρόνοια, οὔτε δικαιοσύνη δύναται συνίστασθαι οὔτε εὐσέβεια οὔτε εὐορκία....

[72] See esp. Kensky, *Trying God, Trying Man*, 63–118, a survey of Greco-Roman accounts of post-mortem courtroom scenes, emphasizing human anxiety regarding miscarriages of divine justice.

5.4 Abbreviated proof (1:17)

makes sense in this context: an object of terror has now become a source of consolation and celebration.[73]

Paul himself provides the strongest indications that δικαιοσύνη θεοῦ in Rom 1:17 addresses divine forensic justice, God's responsibility to condemn and his capacity to save through the gospel at the eschatological trial. 1:18 exhibits significant parallels to 1:17, with the same finite verb in the same form (ἀποκαλύπτεται), and prepositions expressing the source and destination of the revelation (ἐκ/ἀπό and εἰς/ἐπί). Scholars occasionally position δικαιοσύνη and ὀργή as opposites by reading γάρ in v. 18 as adversative.[74] This suggestion is unlikely, given that it follows two causal instances of γάρ.[75] The parallel structure between the verses signals two things: (1) that Paul is beginning the first stage of his argument, the elucidation of δικαιοσύνη θεοῦ as a comprehensive and inescapable threat; and (2) that v. 18 functions as the πρόθεσις of this phase of his argument (1:18–3:20), which he designs to establish comprehensive human culpability.[76] Those who indulge vice "deserve death" (1:32, ἄξιοι θανάτου εἰσιν). God will repay all according to what they do (2:6, ὃς ἀποδώσει ἑκάστῳ κατὰ τὰ ἔργα αὐτοῦ, citing Prov 24:12 and Psalm 62:13), a point that Paul elaborates at length (2:7–10) and concludes with a declaration of God's absolute impartiality (2:11). Law – whether encoded explicitly in the Torah or implicitly in the cosmos – supplies the standards of judgment (2:12–29).[77] God is in no way unjust in applying his "wrath," even if human injustice causes the exhibition of his justice (3:5, εἰ δὲ ἡ ἀδικία ἡμῶν θεοῦ δικαιοσύνην συνίστησιν, τί ἐροῦμεν; μὴ ἄδικος ὁ θεὸς ὁ ἐπιφέρων τὴν ὀργήν;). Other parts of Romans, too, emphasize divine forensic justice. The soaring

---

[73] Cf. Haacker, *Theology*, 119 on "peace with God" in Rom 5:1, a phrase which "has no parallels in the imperial propaganda." "But it does answer a deep concern of traditional Roman religion. While Greek philosophy increasingly repudiated the idea that gods are subject to moods and that men must fear their wrath, the concern for peace with the gods (*pax deorum* or *pax deum*) was a vital issue for conservative Romans."

[74] So, e.g., Käsemann, *Romans*, 35; Dodd, *Romans*, 18–19; Fitzmyer, *Romans*, 277; Dunn, *Romans*, 1.54.

[75] So also Roetzel, *Judgement in the Community*, 79–80, but cf. his handling of (ה)קדצ (δικαιοσύνη) at 16–17 (on the literary prophets), 32–37 (on apocalyptic texts; cf. 37–38 on wrath). On causal γάρ, see BDAG, 189 s.v., § 1; Smyth 639, § 2810. If Paul were to want v. 18 to be read adversatively to v. 17, he would probably use a different conjunction (δέ or ἀλλά).

[76] Note especially the summaries at 3:9 (προῃτιασάμεθα γὰρ Ἰουδαίους τε καὶ Ἕλληνας πάντας ὑφ' ἁμαρτίαν εἶναι) and 23 (πάντες γὰρ ἥμαρτον καὶ ὑστεροῦνται τῆς δόξης τοῦ θεοῦ) which compress the conclusions of Rom 1:18–3:20.

[77] Cf. Käsemann's remark on 2:2 (*Romans*, 55): if Paul follows the Jewish presupposition as expressed by some Rabbinic passages, "κατὰ ἀλήθειαν indicates the norm of judgment. There is no important change of sense if the expression is taken in Greek fashion to refer to the objective facts...."

conclusion of chapter 8 features a very concise description of the divine tribunal, mentioning both positive and negative aspects of justice:

8:33 τίς ἐγκαλέσει κατὰ ἐκλεκτῶν θεοῦ; θεὸς ὁ δικαιῶν· 34 τίς ὁ κατακρινῶν; Χριστὸς ['Ιησοῦς] ὁ ἀποθανών, μᾶλλον δὲ ἐγερθείς, ὃς καί ἐστιν ἐν δεξιᾷ τοῦ θεοῦ, ὃς καὶ ἐντυγχάνει ὑπὲρ ἡμῶν.

33 Who will issue the indictment against God's elect? God, the one who justifies. 34 Who is the one who condemns? Christ [Jesus] who died, and more who was raised, who also is at the right hand of God, who also intercedes on our behalf.

Paul is clearly unpacking δικαιοσύνη θεοῦ with these passages and many others, in order to elaborate the principles which underpin its punitive and rewarding manifestations. God's nature demands that he be δίκαιος; his mercy leads him to devise a way to deflect the penalty and to acquit, "in order that he may be just and one who justifies a person from faith in Jesus" (εἰς τὸ εἶναι αὐτὸν δίκαιον καὶ δικαιοῦντα τὸν ἐκ πίστεως 'Ιησοῦ, 3:26).[78]

In sum, δικαιοσύνη θεοῦ in 1:17 carries several resonances under the umbrella of divine rectitude: God's roles as creator, sustainer, high king and supreme judge of the cosmos; his capacity as judge to justify and save, as well as to condemn and punish; his conformity to the agreements that he makes; and his reliability in following through with what he promises. The last two aspects Paul enfolds within the first definition of the gospel (1:2), but he does not there directly attach it to δικαιοσύνη. The second definition brings forward God's role as eschatological judge, without diminishing the ideas of mercy and fidelity to his covenants that δικαιοσύνη θεοῦ brings along with it. The second definition also captures God's ability to justify and declare righteous. Romans prominently features a soteriology of justification, with passive forms of δικαιοῦν occurring at crucial points in his argument.[79] Paul certainly wants his definition to address human justification (δικαιοσύνη θεοῦ = "justification from God"). God's justice includes his power to justify, but is not restricted to it. It also includes his power, indeed his responsibility in some cases, to condemn.[80] Like Paul's versatile use of πίστις, δικαιοσύνη θεοῦ partakes of numerous possible meanings simultaneously as part of his strategy of investing his definition with the richest possible content.

---

[78] Kensky (*Trying Man, Trying God*, 192) phrases Paul's idea here perfectly: "Paul goes so far in this passage to suggest that God put forth Christ Jesus *as his own theodicy*, to demonstrate and provide evidence of his own justice/righteousness."

[79] Rom 3:24, 28; 4:2; 5:1, 9; 6:7.

[80] Cf. the extremely cogent observation of Käsemann (*Romans*, 56–57): "The doctrines of justification and judgment are inseparably linked in Paul..., because the concern in both is the creator's right as Lord of creation as this works itself out in the creature. ... A doctrine of justification which avoids the concept of judgment loses its character as proclamation of the lordship of God and loses therewith the only basis for the humanization of mankind. A concept of judgment which does not receive its meaning from the doctrine of justification leaves no more room for the assurance of salvation."

5.4.2 Ἔλλειψις in ἐκ πίστεως εἰς πίστιν

The two prepositional phrases ἐκ πίστεως εἰς πίστιν pose an enigma comparable in difficulty to that of δικαιοσύνη θεοῦ. Modern interpreters generally fall into three camps in how they handle it. (1) Some treat the phrase as an emphatic "by faith," "as a matter of faith from beginning to end."[81] (2) Others give more weight to the prepositions. Joseph Fitzmyer, for example, proposes two solutions, that the phrase refers to the transition from a less mature to a more mature state of faith,[82] or that ἐκ is instrumental and εἰς is purposive.[83]

---

[81] Barrett, *Romans*, 30–31; Dodd, *Romans*, 13–14; Nygren, *Romans*, 78–79; Althaus, *an die Römer*, 13–14; Murray, *Romans*, 1.31–32; Moo, *Romans*, 75–76; Stuhlmacher, *Romans*, 29; Lohse, *an die Römer*, 78. Cf. also NIV, "by faith from first to last"; NEB, "that starts in faith and ends in faith"; NAB, "which begins and ends in faith." Cranfield (*Romans*, 1.100) after listing various proposals, remarks: "[I]t is an emphatic equivalent of ἐκ πίστεως, the εἰς πίστιν having much the same effect as the 'sola' of 'sola fide'...." Käsemann (*Romans*, 31) offers this cautious assessment: "On the basis of its position the expression can hardly belong to the subject, and on the basis of the subject matter it cannot belong to the verb.... Logically then, it is related only loosely to the preceding statement. ... The revelation of God's righteousness, because it is bound to the gospel, takes place only in the sphere of faith."

[82] Fitzmyer, *Romans*, 263. Cf. Sanday and Headlam, *Romans*, 28, and Lietzmann, *an die Römer*, 31. This notion of the maturation of faith appears also in the commentaries of the Reformers, e.g., Luther, *Vorlesung über den Römerbrief*, 1.42–45; Melanchthon, *Commentary on Romans*, 70; and Calvin, *Calvin's Commentaries*, 28. Cf. also Theodoret's second interpretation of Rom 1:17 (PG 82.57, 60; I discuss the first in n. 99 below): "For the one who believes in the Lord Christ and who receives the grace of all-holy baptism, and who claims for himself the gift of adoption, is led step by step through these things to believe in the good things to come: the resurrection from the dead, I mean, and eternal life, and the kingdom of the heavens." ὁ γὰρ τῷ Δεσπότῃ πιστεύων Χριστῷ, καὶ τοῦ παναγίου βαπτίσματος τὴν χάριν ὑποδεχόμενος, καὶ τὸ τῆς υἱοθεσίας κομιζόμενος χάρισμα, ποδηγεῖται διὰ τούτων εἰς τὸ πιστεῦσαι τοῖς μέλλουσιν ἀγαθοῖς· τῇ ἐκ νεκρῶν ἀναστάσει, φημί, καὶ τῇ αἰωνίῳ ζωῇ, καὶ τῇ βασιλείᾳ τῶν οὐρανῶν. The phrase ἐκ πίστεως εἰς πίστιν therefore refers to the maturation of belief in the teachings of the church. Theodoret characterizes this as a succession of baby-steps, the acceptance of only as much as one can until one is able to accept things which might be more difficult to believe. This progression not only pertains to movement from faith in the prophets to the faith of the gospel, but to additional movement within the latter. The first πίστις (in Christ) directs itself toward the rite of baptism (looking ahead to Rom 6:1–11, especially 6:8–9) and the claim of adoption by God (8:14–15). Having faith in the resurrection (again, Rom 6:1–11), eternal life, and the kingdom of heaven grow from the former "faith." The comments of Gennadius of Constantinople (v C.E.) likewise identify resurrection as faith's object: "But how does he save? 'For the righteousness of God is revealed in it from faith to faith.' Through 'righteousness' he is saying sinlessness; through 'of God' he is saying from divine grace; through 'it is revealed' he is saying that at the proper time, on the day of resurrection, this righteousness will be made known; through 'from faith' he is saying 'not from works of the law' [Rom 3:20] but having faith in the resurrection of Christ; through 'to faith' he is saying having faith not regarding only his resurrection, but regarding their own resurrection which comes from his, as ones who will be resurrected." σώζει δὲ πῶς; «δικαιοσύνη γὰρ θεοῦ ἐν αὐτῷ ἀποκαλύπτεται ἐκ πίστεως εἰς πίστιν.» διὰ μὲν τοῦ «δικαιοσύνη» τὴν ἀναμαρτησίαν φησίν, διὰ δὲ τοῦ «θεοῦ» τὸ ἐκ χάριτος θείας, διὰ δὲ τοῦ «ἀποκαλύπτεται» τὸ κατὰ καιρὸν ἐν τῇ τῆς ἀνα-

Chapter 5: The Second Definition of the Gospel (1:16–17)

The handful of Pauline passages which have combinations of prepositions with forms of the same word appear to lend support to the idea that the phrase refers to the intensification or maturation of faith.[84] (3) Finally, Karl Barth interprets the phrase to mean "from God's faithfulness to human faith."[85] James Dunn takes up Barth's idea,[86] and it has received even more attention in the context of the debate regarding πίστις Χριστοῦ.[87] Douglas Campbell and

---

στάσεως ἡμέρᾳ ταύτην γνωσθήσεσθαι, διὰ δὲ τοῦ «ἐκ πίστεως» τὸ «οὐκ ἐξ ἔργων νόμου» ἀλλὰ τὸ πιστεῦσαι τῇ ἀναστάσει τοῦ Χριστοῦ, διὰ δὲ τοῦ «εἰς πίστιν» τὸ μὴ περὶ ἐκείνου μόνου ἀλλ' ἐξ ἐκείνου καὶ περὶ ἑαυτῶν ὡς ἀναστησομένων πιστεῦσαι (*PKGK* 355). Gennadius' notion that belief in the resurrection of Christ precedes belief in the resurrection of Christians may, like Theodoret's interpretation, depend upon Rom 6:1–11, where Paul draws a line from Christ's resurrection to that of Christians through baptism, especially in 6:4–5. Other passages of the Pauline corpus link faith and resurrection, for instance 1 Cor 15:12–19 and 1 Thess 4:14. Cf. also Frede, *Neuer Paulustext*, 2.23–24, § 16; Photius (ix C.E.), at *PKGK* 475.

[83] "[T]his reading would be in line with the development of 3:21–22. 'Through faith' would express the means by which a person comes to salvation; 'for faith' would express the purpose of the divine plan..." (Fitzmyer, *Romans*, 263); Fitzmyer then points out that both of his interpretations yield the same result, that "salvation is a matter of faith from start to finish, whole and entire." Cf. Schlatter, *Romans*, 23–24; Williams, "'Righteousness of God,'" 256 ("on the basis of faith, faith ... being the goal"); Keck, *Romans*, 52–53; and the NRSV, "through faith and for faith." Note also Fridrichsen ("Aus Glauben zu Glauben," 54), who initially identifies the phrase along the lines of the first group as "einen lose angehängten, fast selbständigen, rhetorisch-pleonastischen Ausdruck und nicht um eine wirkliche Bewegung oder sachliche Differenzierung, sondern nur um die emphatische Feststellung, dass die Gottesgerechtigkeit ausschliesslich mit Glauben zu tun hat." He later observes on the basis of Rom 11:36 and 1 Cor 8:6: "... *von ihm* und *durch ihn* und *zu ihm* ist das All. In allen seinen Teilen und auf jeder Stufe ist das All von Gott total abhängig. Er ist Ursprung und Teil. Zweifellos ist es dieses rhetorische Schema, das auch Röm. 1,17 zu Grunde liegt. Im dortigen Zusammenhange wird das ἐκ nicht so sehr den Ursprung bezeichnen als vielmehr Grund und Wesen, und εἰς mehr die immer erneute Wiederholung als das Ziel." Zeller (*Brief an die Römer*, 44) writes: "Mit einem Pleonasmus ... unterstreicht Paulus, daß sie nur aufgrund von Glauben und für Glaubende (vgl. 3,22) erreichbar ist."

[84] 2 Cor 2:15–16, ἐκ θανάτου εἰς θάνατον, ἐκ ζωῆς εἰς ζωήν; 2 Cor 3:18, ἀπὸ δόξης εἰς δόξαν; cf. Rom 4:18, παρ' ἐλπίδα ἐπ' ἐλπίδι. Fitzmyer (*Romans*, 263) also mentions Ps 84:8 (πορεύσονται ἐκ δυνάμεως εἰς δύναμιν, ὀφθήσεται ὁ θεὸς τῶν θεῶν ἐν Σιών). Käsemann (*Romans*, 31) cites Jer 9:2 (ἐκ κακῶν εἰς κακά) and 2 Cor 4:17 (καθ' ὑπερβολὴν εἰς ὑπερβολήν). For a fuller discussion of such prepositional series, see the recent study by Quarles, "From Faith to Faith."

[85] Barth, *Epistle to the Romans*, 41; "from God's faithfulness to human faith" is my summary, not a quotation. See also the remarks of Manson, "Romans," 942, and Gaston, *Paul and the Torah*, 118–19.

[86] Dunn, *Romans*, 1.43–44.

[87] See, e.g., Hays, "Πίστις and Pauline Christology," 272–94, esp. 278–79: "God's πίστις is his covenant-faithfulness (cf. 3:3), which endures and overcomes all human unfaithfulness. When Paul affirms that the righteousness of God is reavealed ἐκ πίστεως, he is pointing to the source of the revelation. The phrase 'from faith for faith' then becomes a rhetorically effective slogan to summarize the gospel method of a salvation that originates in God's power and is received by the beneficiaries of that power."

Stanley K. Stowers argue along similar lines that ἐκ πίστεως refers to Christ's faithfulness.[88] These interpreters who follow Barth collapse two exegetical steps into one: first, they recognize that the phrase requires additional wording in order to make sense in its context; second, based on their broader understandings of the letter, they have added the missing language in the form of genitive dependents on each instance of πίστις. This third group recognizes that ἔλλειψις is occurring in ἐκ πίστεως εἰς πίστιν, although none calls the figure by name or brings the ancient theory into the discussion.

The ambiguities which drive the exegetical disagreements are partly lexicographical (what does πίστις mean here, and how does it relate to πιστεύειν in the previous verse?), and partly syntactical (how do the two prepositional phrases construe with the other elements of the sentence?). In order to arrive at solutions, we need yet again to reckon with the likelihood that Paul actually wants the phrase to carry plural nuances. He lets πίστις stand undefined. This fact does not make it impossible to determine which of the word's possible meanings he has primarily in mind in v. 17, but we must remain aware of the ambiguity that will serve his purposes later. A second preliminary factor is that Paul is uses two rhetorical figures at once, ἀναδίπλωσις ("doubling") and ἔλλειψις. According to Demetrius, the former figure elevates the forcefulness of an utterance while retaining charm.[89] The supporters of the first option above are thus partially correct, since Paul doubles πίστις in order to underscore its importance. And, in agreement with the supporters of the

---

[88] Campbell, "Romans 1:17," 281: "The eschatological saving righteousness of God is being revealed in the gospel by means of faithfulness (namely, the faithfulness of Christ), with the goal of faithfulness (in the Christian)." Stowers (*Rereading of Romans*, 202) understands εἰς πίστιν to imply "movement into a state, into faithfulness"; "This makes sense if the key question is not the believer's faith but Jesus Christ's faithfulness in which the believer shares. The *eis pistin* parallels the phrase 'to be baptized into Christ' (Rom 6:3; Gal 3:27)." Morna Hooker endorses a similar interpretation (though in passing) in her essay "Πίστις Χριστοῦ," 339–40.

[89] *Eloc.* 140: "The charms from figures are clear and greatest in Sappho, such as from ἀναδίπλωσις where a bride says to Virginity: 'Virginity, Virginity, where do you go after leaving me?' But [Virginity] answers her with the same figure: 'I will no longer return to you—I will no longer return!' For a greater charm is exhibited than if it was said once and without the figure. And indeed ἀναδίπλωσις seems rather to have been invented for forcefulness, but it utilizes the most forceful [words] in a charming manner." αἱ δὲ ἀπὸ τῶν σχημάτων χάριτες δῆλαί εἰσιν καὶ πλεῖσται παρὰ Σαπφοῖ, οἷον ἐκ τῆς ἀναδιπλώσεως, ὅπου νύμφη πρὸς τὴν παρθενίαν φησί, «παρθενία, παρθενία, ποῖ με λιποῦσα οἴχῃ;» ἡ δὲ ἀποκρίνεται πρὸς αὐτὴν τῷ αὐτῷ σχήματι, «οὐκέτι ἥξω πρὸς σέ, οὐκέτι ἥξω»· πλείων γὰρ χάρις ἐμφαίνεται, ἢ εἴπερ ἅπαξ ἐλέχθη καὶ ἄνευ τοῦ σχήματος. καίτοι ἡ ἀναδίπλωσις πρὸς δεινότητας μᾶλλον δοκεῖ εὑρῆσθαι, ἡ δὲ καὶ τοῖς δεινοτάτοις καταχρῆται ἐπιχαρίτως. On this figure see also Alexander Rhetor, *Fig.* 2.2 (*RG* 3.29); Phoebammon, *Fig.* 1.3 (*RG* 3.46–47); [Cicero], *Rhet. Her.* 4.28.38 on *conduplicatio*; and Quintilian, *Inst.* 9.3.28 on *adiectio*. Sometimes the theorists, both ancient and modern, use ἐπανάληψις for rhetorical repetition of any kind, while restricting ἀναδίπλωσις to the repetition of language at the end of one clause and the beginning of another.

third option, ἐκ πίστεως εἰς πίστιν also lacks language which would render the meaning clear. I shall therefore argue that Paul suppresses wording that he intends his readers to supply, yielding multiple interpretive possibilities of which he will take full advantage in his subsequent argument.

But how can one demonstrate the *lack* of language in an utterance? Proving such a thing on strict exegetical grounds borders on impossible, so I call upon Paul's ancient interpreters for assistance. Both Greek and Latin patristic readers engage Paul from within a shared rhetorical culture. They stand in a well-informed position to recognize when his style exhibits rhetorical figures and tropes.[90] They do not all unpack the ἔλλειψις in the same manner, and some solutions are more plausible than others. But when so many of them (al-

---

[90] Note, for example, Origen's application of the rhetorical figures ὑπέρβατον (*ypebatum*) and ἔλλειψις (*elocutionis defectio*) to rearrange the clauses in Rom 1:13–15: "'For I do not want you to be ignorant, brothers, that I often intended to come to you, and I was prevented until now, in order that I might have some fruit among you, just as also among the other nations, Greeks and barbarians, wise and foolish, I am a debtor; therefore, with regard to what is [the case] in me, I am keen to preach also to you who are in Rome' (1:13–15). There is indeed *yperbatum* in this passage; there is also *defectio* of wording. But we are able to restore the *yperbatum* in this way: 'For I do not want you to be ignorant, brothers, that I often intended to come to you in order that I might have some fruit among you just as also among the other nations, Greeks and barbarians, wise and foolish; and I was prevented until now.' The *defectio* of wording will be filled out in this way: in the place where he says 'also among other nations, Greeks and barbarians, wise and foolish,' 'to whom' appears to be lacking, so that [the words] which follow should be read thus: 'to whom I am a debtor,' and the sequence should be read thus: 'just as I have fruit among the other nations, Greeks and barbarians, wise and foolish, to whom I am a debtor....'" «*Nolo autem uos ignorare fratres quia saepe proposui uenire ad uos et prohibitus sum usque adhuc ut aliquem fructum habeam et in uobis sicut et in ceteris gentibus Graecis ac barbaris sapientibus et insipientibus debitor sum; ita quod in me est promtus sum et uobis qui Romae estis euangelizare.*» *Est quidem et yperbatum in hoc loco; est et elocutionis defectio. Sed yperbatum hoc modo possumus reddere:* «*nolo autem uos ignorare fratres quia saepe proposui uenire ad uos ut aliquem fructum habeam et in uobis sicut et in ceteris gentibus Graecis ac barbaris sepientibus et insipientibus, et prohibitus sum usque adhuc*». *Defectio uero elocutionis hoc modo adimplebitur. In eo ubi dicit:* «*et in ceteris gentibus Graecis et barbaris sapientibus et insipientibus*»; *uidetur deesse:* «*quibus*»; *ut ea quae sequuntur sic legantur:* «*quibus debitor sum*»; *et sit talis consequentia:* «*sicut fructum habeo in ceteris gentibus Graecis et barbaris sapientibus et insipientibus quibus debitor sum*» ... (*Comm. Rom.* 1.15 [13]). Origen thus believes that Paul has pulled the phrase *et prohibitus sum usque adhuc* forward from the place in the syntax where it properly belongs (in his opinion) – at the end of the sentence, where Origin "restores" (*reddere*) it. My translation of Origen's quotation of the transition between vv. 13 and 14 reflects the *defectio elocutionis* that he identifies. He does not understand "among other nations" (*in ceteris gentibus*) to conclude a sentence. He instead takes the phrase "Greeks and barbarians, wise and foolish" (*Graecis ac barbaris sepientibus et insipientibus*, agreeing with *gentibus* in case and number) to continue the sentence with a pleonastic specification of which *gentes* Paul has in mind. This reading demands the relative pronoun *quibus* for *debitor sum*, which Origen likewise "restores."

though by no means all)[91] perceive the absence of necessary wording in v. 17 and interpret accordingly, they supply strong indirect evidence of Paul's own compositional methods. They reveal this perception in two ways, either the addition of genitive dependents on each occurrence of the term πίστις or its Latin translation, *fides*,[92] or in the explication of each πίστις with forms of πιστεύειν (*credere*) with expressed objects – or both. As the ancient rhetorical theorists advise, some of these authors look to the immediate context to expand the ἔλλειψις, while others look further afield in Romans, in the corpus Paulinum, or elsewhere in the New Testament.

The most popular patristic interpretation takes the phrase παντὶ τῷ πιστεύοντι, Ἰουδαίῳ τε πρῶτον καὶ Ἕλληνι in v. 16 as its point of departure: the "faith of the Jew" and the "faith of the Greek."[93] Tertullian, appropriating vv. 16–17 to argue for the continuity of Israelite religion and Christianity, draws upon Paul's discussion of law and gospel in Romans 1–3: "Without a doubt [Paul] imputes both the law and salvation to a just God, not a good one ..., who transfers from the faith of the law to the faith of the gospel – surely his own law and his own gospel" (*sine dubio et evangelium et salutem iusto deo deputat, non bono ..., transferenti ex fide legis in fidem evangelii, suae utique legis et sui evangelii*).[94] He thus initially restores *legis* and *evangelii* to each

---

[91] John of Damascus (vii–viii C.E.) (*In. Rom.* ad loc., PG 95.448), for example, writes regarding 1:17a: "The one who becomes righteous, he says, will live not only throughout the life which is past but that which is about to be," ὁ γενόμενος, φησίν, δίκαιος, οὐ κατὰ τὸν παρόντα μόνον βίον, ἀλλὰ τὸν μέλλοντα ζήσεται.

[92] One might wonder why the comments of authors who use Latin translations would bear upon the meaning of the Greek phrase. First, their texts of vv. 16–17 render the Greek fairly literally (though sometimes differently from one another). Second, the Greek and Roman rhetorical traditions had thoroughly cross-pollenated one another well before the time of Cicero, as should be abundantly clear from chapters 2 and 3 above. Finally, Latin- and Greek-speaking Christian communities hardly existed in total isolation from one another. Origen's Greek commentary on Romans enjoyed a Latin readership in Rufinus' translation, and Tertullian's interpretation of 1:17 closely resembles that of Origen and Clement of Alexandria. See Souter, *Earliest Latin Commentaries*, regarding the points of contact between the Latin commentaries and their Greek predecessors and contemporaries, esp. 65–66 on Ambrosiaster and 107–25 on Jerome.

[93] Cf. the very brief comments of Pelagius (iv–v), *In Rom.* 1.17: "'From faith to faith,' or: because the Jew is justified from faith and the Gentile in faith; and for this reason he would be able [to use] ['from' and] 'in,' so that he might avoid the fault of tautology." «*Ex fide in fidem.*» Siue: *quod ex fide iustificatur Iudaeus et in fide gentilis posuerit, et ideo* [«*ex*» *et*] «*in*», *ut tautologiae uitium declinaret.*

[94] *Adv. Marc.* 5.13.2: "But we have shown often already that God is proclaimed by the apostle as judge; and, in his role as judge, as avenger; and, in his role as avenger, as creator. Therefore even here, when he says, 'For I am not ashamed of the gospel, for it is God's power for salvation for every one who believes, Jew and Greek, since God's justice is revealed in it from faith to faith,' without a doubt he imputes both the gospel and salvation to a just God, not a good one (if I were to speak according to the distinction of the heretic), who transfers from the faith of the law to the faith of the gospel – surely his [God's] own law and his own

fides, and adds another item that he apparently thinks Paul to have ellipsed, the verb *transferre*, which he probably understands to be implied in *salus*.[95]

Excursus. Clement of Alexandria also refers to a transference from faith to faith in passing in his essay *The Rich Man's Salvation*. He does not in this text exegete Rom 1:17 directly (his remarks primarily address the devout yet wealthy man who approaches Jesus in Mark 10:17–22 to ask what he must do in order to inherit eternal life), but his appropriation of the phrase reveals an understanding which bears a close resemblance to Tertullian's. The first part of *Quis div.* 8 lays out a σύγκρισις of Moses and Christ: "Therefore he [Jesus] recommends to the one who will live the true life to know him first whom 'no one knows except the Son and the one to whom he reveals him' (Matt 11:27). Then [he is] to learn the greatness of the savior next to that one [i.e., God] and the newness of grace, because indeed, according to the apostle, 'the law was given through Moses, grace and truth through Jesus Christ' (John 1:17). And the things given through a faithful slave are not equal to things given as gifts by a legitimate son. If at any rate the law of Moses were sufficient to supply eternal life, then the savior himself appears, and suffers on our account by running through the human course from birth until the sign [i.e., the cross], in vain. In vain too does the man who has done all the legal commands 'from youth' ask immortality from another on bended knee. ... But nonetheless this sort of person has been correctly convinced that he on the one hand lacks nothing that pertains to righteousness, but that he on the other hand is entirely lacking in life. Therefore he asks it from the only one who is able to give it. And he on the one hand carries boldness toward the law, but on the other he petitions the Son of God. He is transferred 'from faith to faith.' Like someone tossing precariously and anchoring dangerously in the law, he sails for refuge to the savior." τοῦτον οὖν πρῶτον ἐπιγνῶναι τῷ ζησομένῳ τὴν ὄντως ζωὴν παρακελεύεται, ὃν «οὐδεὶς ἐπιγινώσκει εἰ μὴ ὁ υἱὸς καὶ ᾧ ἂν ὁ υἱὸς ἀποκαλύψῃ»· ἔπειτα τὸ μέγεθος τοῦ σωτῆρος μετ' ἐκεῖνον καὶ τὴν καινότητα τῆς χάριτος μαθεῖν, ὅτι δὴ κατὰ τὸν ἀπόστολον «ὁ νόμος διὰ Μωσέως ἐδόθη, ἡ χάρις καὶ ἡ ἀλήθεια διὰ Ἰησοῦ Χριστοῦ»· καὶ οὐκ ἴσα τὰ διὰ δούλου πιστοῦ διδόμενα τοῖς ὑπὸ [τοῦ] υἱοῦ γνησίου δωρουμένοις. εἰ γοῦν ἱκανὸς ἦν ὁ Μωσέως νόμος ζωὴν αἰώ-

---

gospel." *Sed et iudicem deum ab apostolo circumferri saepe iam ostendimus et in iudice ultorem et creatorem in ultore. Itaque et hic, cum dicit, «Non enim me pudet evangelii, virtus enim dei est in salutem omni credenti, Iudaeo et Graeco, quia iustitia dei in eo revelatur ex fide in fidem», sine dubio et evangelium et salutem iusto deo deputat, non bono, ut ita dixerim secundum haeretici distinctionem, transferenti ex fide legis in fidem evangelii, suae utique legis et sui evangelii.*

[95] Tertullian uses the language of Marcion's favorite apostle against him, and in this passage the term *iustitia* provides the requisite leverage. A *just* God gives the law and punishment, and the gospel and salvation: this is evidently Tertullian's interpretation of *in salutem omni credenti, Iudaeo et Graeco* in v. 16 together with *iustitia dei* in v. 17. The meanings of the genitives *legis* and *evangelii* are unclear, however. They could be objective genitives, faith *in* the law and *in* the gospel. Or he might mean them as genitives as description, belief or faithfulness within the context of the law or the gospel: the law-faith of Jews and the gospel-faith of Gentiles, in other words. Another possibility in the category of genitive of description is the faith written about in the law and the faith written about the gospel. Unfortunately Tertullian gives us no obvious means of confirming any one of these options, although I consider the first more probable than the others. He goes on in the last clause cited above to add additional possessive adjectives, *suae legis et sui evangelii*, God's law and gospel, thereby emphasizing the divine author of both. For Tertullian, this seals the case that God is *iustus*: Marcion's separation of the creator-God of the Jews and the good and loving God of the gospel finds no support in this passage of Romans, through Paul's linkage of divine *iustitia*, salvation, Jew and Greek, and the transferrence from faith to faith.

νιον παρασχεῖν, μάτην μὲν ὁ σωτὴρ αὐτὸς παραγίνεται καὶ πάσχει δι' ἡμᾶς ἀπὸ γενέσεως μέχρι τοῦ σημείου τὴν ἀνθρωπότητα διατρέχων, μάτην δὲ ὁ πάσας πεποιηκὼς «ἐκ νεότητος» τὰς νομίμους ἐντολὰς παρὰ ἄλλου αἰτεῖ γονυπετῶν ἀθανασίαν. ... ἀλλ' ὅμως οὗτος ὁ τοιοῦτος ἀκριβῶς πέπεισται, διότι αὐτῷ πρὸς μὲν δικαιοσύνην οὐδὲν ἐνδεῖ, ζωῆς δὲ ὅλως προσδεῖ· διὸ αὐτὴν αἰτεῖ παρὰ τοῦ δοῦναι μόνου δυναμένου· καὶ πρὸς μὲν τὸν νόμον ἄγει παρρησίαν, τοῦ θεοῦ δὲ τὸν υἱὸν ἱκετεύει. «ἐκ πίστεως εἰς πίστιν» μετατάσσεται· ὡς σφαλερῶς ἐν νόμῳ σαλεύων καὶ ἐπικινδύνως ναυλοχῶν εἰς τὸν σωτῆρα μεθορμίζεται. Clement here synthesizes several passages of scripture to explain Jesus' recommendation to the wealthy man who asks him in Mark 10:17, τί ποιήσω ἵνα ζωὴν αἰώνιον κληρονομήσω; The second passage, John 1:17, introduces the σύγκρισις proper: ὁ νόμος διὰ Μωσέως ἐδόθη, ἡ χάρις καὶ ἡ ἀλήθεια διὰ Ἰησοῦ Χριστοῦ. On one side stand Moses and what he delivers as a "faithful servant," but whose law does not supply eternal life even for ὁ πάσας πεποιηκὼς «ἐκ νεότητος» τὰς νομίμους ἐντολάς. On the other side stands a legitimate Son who has brought about exactly what Moses' commands could not. (Interestingly, Clement here uses a logic that E. P. Sanders attributes to Paul, namely that εἰ γοῦν ἱκανὸς ἦν ὁ Μωσέως νόμος ζωὴν αἰώνιον παρασχεῖν, μάτην μὲν ὁ σωτὴρ αὐτὸς παραγίνεται καὶ πάσχει δι' ἡμᾶς. This conditional statement resembles Sanders' argument that Paul reasons "from solution to plight," i.e., "the conclusion that all the world – both Jew and Greek – equally stands in need of a saviour *springs from* the prior conviction that God had provided such a saviour. If he did so, it follows that such a saviour *must* have been needed, and then only consequently that all other possible ways of salvation are wrong.")[96] The wealthy man finds himself caught between these two: carrying παρρησία toward the law but petitioning the Son. At this point Rom 1:17 enters the picture to reinforce the σύγκρισις further: «ἐκ πίστεως εἰς πίστιν» μετατάσσεται· ὡς σφαλερῶς ἐν νόμῳ σαλεύων καὶ ἐπικινδύνως ναυλοχῶν εἰς τὸν σωτῆρα μεθορμίζεται. Clement's application of Rom 1:17 to his comparison assumes an interpretation of ἐκ πίστεως εἰς πίστιν along the lines of ἐκ πίστεως Μωσέως (or νόμου) εἰς πίστιν Χριστοῦ. The way that he invokes the notion of transference (μετατάσσειν) implies that the transfer takes place when the man in the story realizes that the law cannot supply eternal life, and then, on the basis of that realization, addresses his petition to Jesus. The nautical metaphor which concludes the above quotation drives this point home: faith in the law at best provides only precarious anchorage, while faith in Christ provides the safe harbor of eternal life. Clement's interpretation here seems generally consistent with that of Tertullian, although his contrast of Moses the faithful slave and Jesus the legitimate son expresses the objects of faith as persons in addition to the texts associated with them. See also his remarks at *Strom.* 2.6.29.2–3: "'But the righteous will live from faith,' the faith which is according to the covenant and the commands, since these – two in name and time, having been given by divine plan according to even so great a progress, although being one in power, on the one hand the Old [Testament] and on the other the New [Testament] – are furnished through the Son from the one God. Wherefore the apostle also says in the letter to the Romans: 'For God's righteousness is revealed in it from faith to faith,' teaching the one salvation which has been perfected from prophecy to the gospel through one and the same Lord." «ὁ δὲ δίκαιος ἐκ πίστεως ζήσεται», τῆς κατὰ τὴν διαθήκην καὶ τὰς ἐντολάς, ἐπειδὴ δύο αὗται ὀνόματι καὶ χρόνῳ καθ' ἡλικίαν καὶ προκοπὴν οἰκονομικῶς δεδομέναι, δυνάμει μία οὖσαι, ἡ μὲν παλαιά, ἡ δὲ καινή, διὰ υἱοῦ παρ' ἑνὸς θεοῦ χορηγοῦνται. ᾗ καὶ ὁ ἀπόστολος ἐν τῇ πρὸς Ῥωμαίους ἐπιστολῇ λέγει· «δικαιοσύνη γὰρ θεοῦ ἐν αὐτῷ ἀποκαλύπτεται ἐκ πίστεως εἰς πίστιν», τὴν μίαν τὴν ἐκ προφητείας εἰς εὐαγγέλιον τετελειωμένην δι' ἑνὸς καὶ τοῦ αὐτοῦ κυρίου διδάσκων σωτηρίαν. His use of the passage has a different spin, however, at *Strom.* 5.1.2.3–6. He quotes Rom 1:11–12, then 1:17, and interprets as follows: "Therefore the apostle appears to declare a twofold faith – rather one, which

---

[96] *Paul and Palestinian Judaism*, 443; see also his section "The solution as proceeding the problem," 442–47, and cf. Gal 3:21.

additionally admits growth and perfection. For on the one hand the common faith underlies [the old] like a foundation ... but on the other hand the selectively built-up faith is perfected for the believer, and the faith which results from instruction and from reason [λόγος] is completed with it in order to accomplish the commands." φαίνεται οὖν ὁ ἀπόστολος δίττην καταγγέλλων πίστιν, μᾶλλον δὲ μίαν, αὔξησιν καὶ τελείωσιν ἐπιδεχομένην· ἡ μὲν γὰρ κοινὴ πίστις καθάπερ θεμέλιος ὑπόκειται ... ἡ δὲ ἐξαίρετος ἐποικοδομουμένη συντελειοῦται τῷ πιστῷ καὶ συναπαρτίζεται αὐτῇ ἡ ἐκ μαθήσεως περιγινομένη καὶ τοῦ λόγου τὰς ἐντολὰς ἐπιτελεῖν.

Tertullian thus uses both the immediate and the wider context to unpack *ex fide in fidem*. Origen intepret similarly. In a Greek fragment of his commentary on Romans, he avers:

«ἀποκαλύπτεται» δὲ ἡ «τοῦ θεοῦ δικαιοσύνη» τοῖς «ἐκ πίστεως» παλαιοτέρας «εἰς» νέαν ἥκουσι· πιστεῦσαι γὰρ ἀεὶ Μωϋσεῖ ἵνα τις πιστεύσει καὶ τῷ Χριστῷ, καὶ ὁ πιστεύων τῷ Χριστῷ μὴ πιστεύων τοῖς προφήταις οὐκ ὀρθῶς πιστεύει οὐδὲ λέγεται οὗτος κυρίως πιστεύειν. τὸ δὲ «ὁ δίκαιος ἐκ πίστεως ζήσεται» διδάσκει, ὅτι εἴ τις δίκαιος μὲν ᾖ, πίστιν δὲ μὴ ἔχει, ἢ πιστεύει μέν, μὴ ᾖ δὲ δίκαιος, οὐκ ἂν σωθείη.

But "the righteousness of God is revealed" to those who have come "from" an older "faith to" a new faith; for the act of belief in Moses always happened in order that someone may believe also in Christ. And the one who believes in Christ while not believing in the prophets does not believe correctly, nor is that person said to believe properly. But the statement "the righteous will live from faith" teaches that if someone is righteous but does not have faith, or believes but is not righteous, he would not be saved. (*Comm. Rom.* fr. 12 Staab)

Origen initially qualifies each instance of πίστις in Rom 1:17 with adjectives: τοῖς ἐκ πίστεως παλαιοτέρας εἰς νέαν ἥκουσι. He then further interprets the phrase with forms of πιστεύειν with dative objects (πιστεῦσαι Μωϋσεῖ, πιστεύει Χριστῷ, πιστεύων προφήταις) to elaborate further the nature of both the "older" and the "new" faith. The explication of εἰς πίστεως with a clause introduced by ἵνα indicates that εἰς signifies more than the destination of a revelation from the "older faith," rather it additionally expresses purpose here.[97] The Latin translation of Origen's commentary by Rufinus also includes a notion of 'transferrence,' but speaks of a "faith of the Old Testament" and a "new faith of the gospel."[98] The interpretations of Tertullian and Origen stand

---

[97] On ἵνα with the future indicative to express purpose, see BDAG 475, s.v. 1b.

[98] *Comm. Rom.* 1.15 (13): "For I was never ashamed to proclaim the gospel to any nation, because God's power is in it for salvation for everyone who believes, for the Jew first and the Greek; because in the gospel God's righteousness, which was previously concealed, having been hidden in the law, is revealed. It is revealed, however, in those who come from the faith of the Old Testament to the new faith of the gospel, just as was announced in the prophet that the 'righteous person,' even if hitherto he is in the law, by believing in God and his servant Moses, 'lives from faith.' And when he comes to the gospel, he is steered from the faith of the law to the faith of Christ, and thus advances from faith to faith." *Numquam enim apud ullam gentem erubui praedicare euangelium, quia uirtus Dei est in eo ad salutem omni credenti, Iudaeo primum et Graeco; quia in euangelio iustitia Dei reuelatur quae obtecta prius uelebatur in lege. Reuelatur autem in his qui ex fide ueteris testamenti ad fidem nouam euangelii ueniunt; sicut et in profeta praedictum est: quia iustus etiamsi adhuc in lege sit Deo credens*

on firm exegetical ground: they solve the ambiguity of ἐκ πίστεως εἰς πίστιν with πιστεύειν and the coordination of Jew and Greek in the previous verse. They take the "transfer" from one faith to another as a facet of σωτηρία, and add the objects of faith (the law, Moses, the prophets and the Old Testament on one side, and the gospel, Christ and the New Testament on the other) from elsewhere in Romans.[99]

---

et famulo Mosi ex fide uiuit; et cum ad euangelium uenit ex fide legis in fidem Christi dirigitur et ita ex fide in fidem proficit. Note also the expansions at *Comm. Rom.* 1.18 (15): "'For the righteousness of God is revealed in it from faith to faith.' The righteousness of God is revealed in the gospel through this, that in terms of salvation nobody is excepted, whether a Jew or a Greek or a barbarian may come. For the savior says to all equally: 'Come to me, all who labor and are oppressed' [Matt 11:28]. Regarding 'faith to faith,' moreover, we spoke also above already, that even the earlier people, who had believed God and his slave Moses, were in faith, from which faith they now pass over to the faith of the gospel. Moreover because it says from the testimony of Habakkuk the prophet that 'a righteous person lives from my faith,' either he who is in the law [is meant], that he must likewise believe in the Gospels, or he who is in the Gospels [is meant], that he must likewise believe in the law and the prophets. For one without the other does not have completeness of life." «*Iustitia enim Dei in eo reuelatur ex fide in fidem.*» *Iustitia Dei in euangelio reuelatur per id quod ad salutem nullus excipitur siue Iudaeus siue Graecus siue barbarus ueniat. Omnibus enim aeque saluator dicit: «uenite ad me omnes qui laboratis et onerati estis». De fide autem in fidem iam et superius diximus quia et prior populus in fide erat qui crediderat Deo et Mosi famulo eius, ex qua fide nunc ad fidem euangelii transit. Quod autem dicit ex testimonio Ambacum profetae, quia «iustus ex fide mea uiuit»; siue is qui in lege est ut etiam euangeliis credat siue is qui in euangeliis est ut etiam legi credat et profetis. Alterum enim sine altero integritatem non habet uitae.*

[99] Other representatives of this interpretation include the following. Apollinaris of Laodicea (iv C.E., *PKGK* 58) writes: "And he [Christ] was freely giving the life [that comes] through faith instead of the righteousness through works, which is neither sincere nor life-giving. And the prophet has said 'from faith to faith': 'For if you had believed Moses,' [Jesus] says, 'you would have believed me' (John 5:46)." Καὶ ἀντὶ τῆς δι' ἔργων οὐκ εἰλικρινοῦς οὐδὲ ζωοποιοῦ δικαιοσύνης τὴν διὰ πίστεως ζωὴν χαριζόμενος ἦν. καὶ ὁ προφήτης εἴρηκεν· «ἐκ πίστεως εἰς πίστιν». «εἰ γὰρ ἐπιστεύετε», φησί, «Μωϋσεῖ, ἐπιστεύετε ἂν ἐμοί». He thus interprets the dual use of πίστις in Rom 1:17 with the dual use of πιστεύειν in John 5:46: the objects of ἐπιστεύετε in the latter passage become the implied genitive dependants in the former. Note also the remarks of an anonymous Latin commentator: "The first 'faith' in the law was to believe in God [or: the first faith was to believe God in the law]; the second 'faith' is to believe in Christ, his only-begotten Son. That is: to be 'from faith to faith' is to come 'from' law 'to' gospel, and to uphold both the New Testament and the Old Testament, God the Father and Christ." *Prima «fides» in lege erat deum credere, secunda «fides» est Christum credere unigenitum filium eius, id est esse «ex fide in fidem», «ex» lege «in» evangelium venire, et novum et vetus testamentum tenere deum patrem et Christum* (Frede, *Ein neuer Paulustext*, 2.23, § 15A). Acacius of Caesarea (iv C.E.; *PKGK* 53) offers a somewhat different interpretation based on the faith of law and gospel: "[Paul] says 'the righteousness of God is revealed in him,' namely, [in] the one who believes. The foregoing, 'the righteousness of God is revealed,' says that there is repayment for those who did excellent things, just as also in the case of their opposites likewise 'it is revealed' with respect to 'wrath.' 'From faith to faith.' For the Jew, [this means] from faith in a set law to [the faith] which is through Christ; but for the Greek, [this means] from faith in natural law to the same faith [as for the Jew] in Jesus

Three other major interpreters – John Chrysostom, Ambrosiaster and Augustine – also offer illuminating readings of ἐκ πίστεως εἰς πίστιν. John, whose analysis I handle at length elsewhere,[100] classifies the phrase as a

Christ." «δικαιοσύνη θεοῦ», φησίν, «ἐν αὐτῷ ἀκοκαλύπτεται» δηλονότι τῷ πιστεύοντι. τοιοῦτον λέγει τὸ ἀποκαλύπτεται δικαιοσύνη θεοῦ ⟨οἷον⟩ τὴν ἄμειψιν τῶν τὰ σπουδαῖα πραξάντων, ὥσπερ καὶ ἐπὶ τῶν ἐναντίων «τὴν ὀργὴν» ὁμοίως ἀποκαλύπτεται. «ἐκ πίστεως εἰς πίστιν», τῷ μὲν Ἰουδαίῳ ἐκ τῆς τοῦ θεοῦ νόμου πίστεως εἰς τὴν διὰ Χριστοῦ, τῷ δὲ Ἕλληνι ἐκ τῆς τοῦ φυσικοῦ εἰς τὴν αὐτὴν Ἰησοῦ Χριστοῦ πίστιν. Acacius, no doubt under the influence of Rom 1:19–20 and 2:12–16, adds natural law into the mix, since Moses' law addresses Jews and not Gentiles: the Jews move ἐκ τῆς τοῦ θεοῦ νόμου πίστεως εἰς τὴν διὰ Χριστοῦ, while the Gentiles move ἐκ τῆς τοῦ φυσικοῦ εἰς τὴν αὐτὴν Ἰησοῦ Χριστοῦ πίστιν. Note also Theodoret's first interpretation of Rom 1:17 (*Interp. Rom.* 1.17, PG 82.57): "'For the righteousness of God is revealed in it from faith to faith.' It is not revealed to all, but to the ones who have the eyes of faith. And the divine apostle teaches us that God from the beginning managed [matters] thus with us in mind, and that he foretold these things through the prophets, and before the prophets he had the plan concerning these things hidden in himself. ... And here, therefore, he did not say "righteousness is given" but "it is revealed." For [the righteousness] which has been hidden of old becomes manifest to those who believe. He says "from faith to faith," for it is necessary to believe the prophets, and through those to be led step by step to the faith of the gospel. «δικαιοσύνη γὰρ θεοῦ ἐν αὐτῷ ἀποκαλύπτεται, ἐκ πίστεως εἰς πίστιν.» οὐ πᾶσιν ἀποκαλύπτεται, ἀλλὰ τοῖς ἔχουσι τοὺς τῆς πίστεως ὀφθαλμούς. διδάσκει δὲ ἡμᾶς ὁ θεῖος Ἀπόστολος, ὡς ἄνωθεν ὁ θεὸς οὕτω καθ' ἡμᾶς ᾠκονόμησε, καὶ ταῦτα διὰ τῶν προφητῶν προέθεσπισε, καὶ πρὸ τῶν προφητῶν, τὴν περὶ τούτων εἶχε βουλὴν ἐν αὐτῷ κεκρυμμένην. ... καὶ ἐνταῦθα τοίνυν οὐκ εἶπε δίδοται δικαιοσύνη, ἀλλ' «ἀποκαλύπτεται». ἡ γὰρ πάλαι κεκρυμμένη δήλη γίνεται τοῖς πιστεύουσιν. «ἐκ πίστεως εἰς πίστιν», φησι. δεῖ γὰρ πιστεῦσαι τοῖς προφήταις, καὶ δι' ἐκείνων εἰς τὴν τοῦ Εὐαγγελίου πίστιν ποδηγηθῆναι.

[100] Calhoun, "John Chrysostom on ἐκ πίστεως εἰς πίστιν." I summarize John's interpretation of 1:16–17 as follows (143–44): "We have now found that Chrysostom makes four discrete interpretive moves in his complex homiletical exposition of v. 17 and the phrase ἐκ πίστεως εἰς πίστιν. (1) God dispenses his σωτηρία and δικαιοσύνη to humanity through the mechanism of faith, or, as John phrases it, ἓν μόνον εἰσφέρων οἴκοθεν, τὸ πιστεῦσαι. He also connects ἐκ πίστεως εἰς πίστιν not with ἀποκαλύπτεται but with δικαιοσύνη θεοῦ. (2) He takes the mysterious phrase as a βραχὺ ῥῆμα designed by Paul to capture a vast array of possible Old Testament narratives, investing the prepositions ἐκ and εἰς with the sense of the extremes of moral character: from the faith of the patriarch at one end of the ethical spectrum to the faith of the prostitute at the other. The phrase thus further supports μόνον τὸ πιστεῦσαι: it does not matter whether one enjoys the rectitude of Abraham or labors under the degeneracy of Rahab, faith *and nothing else* empowers heroism and produces salvation. John moreover hypothesizes that Paul uses this βραχὺ ῥῆμα to overcome the initial skepticism which might greet his claim that divine righteousness could become available even to the immoral merely διὰ πίστεως. (3) John then shifts away from the pairing of Rahab and Abraham as παραδείγματα designed to verify a point in Paul's argument, to exhortation of his own audience, featuring Rahab as a παράδειγμα of the consequences of Christian faith. He brings her forward as a model whose acceptance of an apparent absurdity resulted in her salvation from the destruction of Jericho. Chrysostom also conjures up a couple of negative παραδείγματα: the people of Jericho who perished in their ἀπιστία, and the heretics whose penchant for more knowledge than is necessary or desireable will lead to a similar fate. (4) The introduction of the heretics and the δόγματα of the church facilitate John's application of Rom 1:17 to his

βραχὺ ῥῆμα, and determines it to be the first of two scriptural proofs designed to rectify the "implausibility" of the notion that God would dispense his righteousness to the worst sort of people merely on the basis of faith.

καὶ πρῶτον μὲν βραχεῖ ῥήματι πέλαγος ἱστοριῶν ἀχανὲς τῷ δυναμένῳ βλέπειν ἀναπετάννυσιν. εἰπὼν γὰρ «ἐκ πίστεως εἰς πίστιν» παρέπεμψε τὸν ἀκροατὴν ἐπὶ τὰς οἰκονομίας τοῦ θεοῦ τὰς ἐν τῇ παλαιᾷ γενομένας οὕτως, ἃς Ἑβραίοις ἐπιστέλλων μετὰ πολλῆς ἐξηγεῖται τῆς σοφίας, καὶ τοὺς δικαίους καὶ τοὺς ἁμαρτωλοὺς οὕτω δικαιωθέντας δεικνὺς καὶ τότε· διὸ καὶ τῆς πόρνης καὶ τοῦ Ἀβραὰμ ἐμνημόνευσεν. ἔπειτα δὲ ἐνταῦθα αἰνιξάμενος αὐτὸ μόνον· καὶ γὰρ ἐφ' ἕτερον ἔτρεχε θεώρημα κατεπεῖγον· ἀπὸ τῶν προφητῶν πάλιν πιστοῦται τὸν λόγον, τὸν Ἀμβακοὺμ εἰς μέσον παράγων βοῶντα καὶ λέγοντα, ὅτι οὐδὲ ἕνι ἄλλως ζῆν τὸν μέλλοντα ζήσεσθαι, ἀλλ' ἢ διὰ πίστεως. «ὁ γὰρ δίκαιος», φησίν, «ἐκ πίστεως ζήσεται», περὶ τῆς μελλούσης λέγων ζωῆς. ἐπειδὴ γὰρ ἅπερ ὁ θεὸς χαρίζεται, πάντα ὑπερβαίνει λογισμόν, εἰκότως πίστεως ἡμῖν δεῖ. «ὁ δὲ κατοιόμενος καὶ καταφρονητὴς ἀνὴρ ἀλαζών, οὐδὲν οὐ μὴ περάνῃ.»

And, initially by means of a brief expression [βραχεῖ ῥήματι], he unfolds a vast sea of stories for the one who is able to perceive [them]. For by saying "from faith to faith" he referred the reader to God's providential plans[101] that happened in this way in the Old [Testament], which, when he sent [his letter] to the Hebrews, he expounded with much wisdom, demonstrating also then that both the righteous and sinners were justified in this way. Therefore he called to mind both the prostitute [Rahab] and Abraham. But then, at this point, after only hinting at this – for he was running on to another urgent subject – he again confirms [his] argument from the prophets, bringing Habakkuk to the center, who cries out and says: for the one who is going to live in the future, it is not possible to live in any other way but through faith. For "the righteous one," he says, "will live from faith," speaking about the life to come. For since that which God freely gives surpasses all reasoning, there is reasonably a need on our part for faith. "But the conceited and condescending, pretentious man will never bring anything at all to completion" [Hab 2:5]. (*Hom. Rom.* 2.6, 446a–b, PG 60.409)

John thus regards ἐκ πίστεως εἰς πίστιν as an instance of συνεκδοχή: it compresses "a vast sea of stories" (πέλαγος ἱστοριῶν ἀχανές) from the Old Testament, and it cross-references the anaphoric catalogue in Hebrews 11 through the verbal link of πίστις.[102] John determines that this move by Paul demonstrates that "both the righteous and sinners were justified in this way" (καὶ

---

support of the cause of orthodoxy. He thereby steers his audience away from the vain pursuit of heavenly γνῶσις and toward πίστις."

[101] Calhoun, "John Chrysostom on ἐκ πίστεως εἰς πίστιν," 136, n. 20: "Οἰκονομία is little difficult to translate here; 'providential plans' seems to capture best the sense of God's salvific activity in the Old Testament as it pertains to the πίστις of his chosen instruments (see BDAG 697–98 s.v., §§ 2.a–c, 'arrangement, order, plan'; LSJ 1204 s.v., § I.6, 'plan, dispensation'; cf. also Otto Michel, 'οἰκονομία,' *TDNT* 5.151–52). The term begins to acquire a broader range of meanings in the writings of the church fathers, where it can refer to dispensations of divine grace, not only in the operation of the sacraments, but also more generally (see *PGL* 940–43 s.v., § C)."

[102] John accepts Hebrews as Pauline in agreement with Eastern tradition at his time. For futher discussion of ancient and modern theories regarding the authorship of Hebrews and its eventual inclusion in the corpus Paulinum, see Attridge, *Epistle to the Hebrews*, 1–6; Rothschild, *Hebrews as Pseudepigraphon*, chs. 2 and 3.

τοὺς δικαίους καὶ τοὺς ἁμαρτωλοὺς οὕτω δικαιωθέντας δεικνύς), insofar as it "calls to mind" (μνημονεύειν) Rahab and Abraham. At this point ἔλλειψις comes into play, since he implicitly expands the phrase as ἐκ πίστεως τῆς πορνῆς εἰς πίστιν τοῦ Ἀβραάμ, with the prepositions expressing a sense of extremes: from the prostitute at one end of the moral spectrum to the patriarch at the other. From a contemporary standpoint, John's exegesis seems flimsier than that of Tertullian and Origen, if for no other reason than the impossibility that Paul could want his readers to connect ἐκ πίστεως εἰς πίστιν to Hebrews 11. But in viewing the phrase as a proof paralleling the quotation of Hab 2:4, and as addressing the meaning of δικαιοσύνη θεοῦ, John takes his cues from the immediate context.

Ambrosiaster[103] understands Paul's declaration that he is not ashamed of the gospel because it is God's power to mean that the Romans had been heeding non-apostolic, heretical preachers who could not perform miraculous signs to verify their message, such as the real apostles (including Paul) could.[104] His interpretation of the phrase "for the Jew first, and the Greek" includes a short account of the history of the term "Jew," which he ties to the name of the hero Judas Maccabeus. Ambrosiaster then says:

Quamvis {ergo} praeponat Iudaeum causa patrum, tamen similiter etiam ipsum indigere dicit dono evangelii Christi. Si ergo et Iudaeus non iustificatur nisi per fidem Christi Iesu, quid opus est esse sub lege?

{Therefore,} although he puts the Jew first on account of their ancestors, he still in like manner says that this very person also needs the gift of the gospel of Christ. Therefore if even the Jew is not justified except through faith in Christ Jesus, what need is there to be under the law? (*Rom.* 1.16.4)

This remark looks forward to Paul's argument as it will unfold in Romans 2–3. In the light of these comments, one might expect Ambrosiaster to interpret *fides Christi Iesu* to mean human belief in Christ, but he does not. He defines "faith" further in his comments on v. 17:

«*Iustitia enim dei in eo revelatur ex fide in fidem.*» *Hoc dicit, quia in illo {qui credit}, sive Iudaeus sit sive Graecus, iustitia dei revelatur. Ostenditur enim in eo veritas et iustitia dei, dum credit et profitetur. Iustitia est dei, quia quod promisit, dedit. Ideo credens hoc esse se*

---

[103] I use the text of Vogels, *Ambrosiastri qui dicitur commentarius in epistulas Paulinas*. There are apparently three recensions of Ambrosiaster's commentaries, which Vogels groups into αβ (verso) and γ (recto). In what follows, I quote from the αβ version; the γ version for this part of the commentary has a fuller text with some passages omitted by the other two recensions. I cite the Latin text with Vogels' critical symbols.

[104] *Rom.* 1.16.1–2: "Therefore it is God's power [shown through miracles] which invites to faith and gives salvation to everyone who believes, at the same time that it forgives sins and justifies, so that the one who has been marked by the mystery of the cross may not be able to be detained by a second death," *virtus igitur dei est, quae invitat ad fidem et dat salutem omni credenti, dum peccata donat et iustificat, ut a secunda morte detineri non possit signatus mysterio crucis.*

consecutum quod promiserat deus per profetas suos, iustum deum probat et testis est iustitiae eius.

"For the righteousness of God is revealed in him from faith to faith." He is saying this, because the righteousness of God is revealed in the one {who believes}, whether Jew or Greek.[105] For the truth and righteousness of God is shown in him, at the same time that he believes and declares.[106] The righteousness is God's, because what he promised, he gave. For this reason, the one who believes that he has acquired what God promised through his prophets demonstrates that God is righteous, and he is a witness of his [God's] righteousness. (*Rom.* 1.17.1–2)

Ambrosiaster thus defines *fides* as the belief that God has fulfilled what he promised through the prophets. It might then seem probable that he will next explain the meaning of *ex fide in fidem* with a theory of transference from faith in the law and the prophets to faith in Christ. Instead he stays on the subject of God's promises:

«*Ex fide in fidem.*» *quid aliud est* «*ex fide in fidem*», *nisi quia fides dei est in eo, quod de se repromisit, et fides hominis qui credit promittenti, ut ex fide dei promittentis in fidem hominis credentis dei iustitia reveletur? in credente enim iustus deus apparet; in eo autem qui non credit, iniustus videtur. negat enim veracem deum, qui non credit dedisse deum, quod promisit. hoc contra Iudaeos loquitur, qui negant hunc esse Christum quem promisit {deus}.*

"From faith to faith." What else is "from faith to faith" to mean if not that the faith of God in that which he promised concerning himself, and the faith of the human who believes the one who promises, so that God's righteousness is revealed from the faith of the God who promises to the faith of the human who believes [*ex fide dei promittentis in fidem credentis*]? For God appears to be righteous in the one who believes. In the one who does not believe, however, he seems to be unrighteous. For the one who does not believe that God gave what he promised denies that God is true. This is said against the Jews, who deny that Christ is the one whom {God} promised. (*Rom.* 1.17.2–3)

Ambrosiaster seems to have invented the interpretation which Karl Barth reintroduced into the modern discussion, that ἐκ πίστεως εἰς πίστιν means "from God's faith[fulness] to human faith[fulness]."[107] Ambrosiaster perhaps builds this interpretation on his Latin version's use of different stems in translating

---

[105] At this point, recension γ has a long variant: "He says 'righteousness of God,' because he freely justifies the impious through faith without works of the law, just as he says elsewhere: 'In order that I might be found in him, as one who does not have my own righteousness which is from the law, but one which is from faith, which is a righteousness from God in faith' (Phil 3:9). He says that this very righteousness is revealed in the gospel, as long as he gives a human faith through which he may be justified." *Iustitiam dei dicit, quia gratis iustificat inpium per fidem sine operibus legis, sicut alibi dicit:* «*ut inveniar in illo non habens meam iustitiam quae ex lege est, sed illam, quae ex fide est, quae ex deo est iustitia in fide*», *ipsam iustitiam dicit revelari in evangelio, dum donat homini fidem, per quam iustificetur.* This addition differs substantially from the interpretation in the text of αβ, since it takes *in eo* to mean "in the gospel" as opposed to "in him," i.e., in the believer, and since it understands *iustitia dei* to mean "righteousness from God" as opposed to his fidelity to keep his promises.

[106] Cf. Rom 10:8–13.

[107] Barth does not mention Ambrosiaster in this comments on 1:17 (*Epistle to the Romans*, 41).

πιστεύειν with *credere* and πίστις with *fides*. Although he understands both *fides* and *credere* to pertain to "faith" as "belief" in his comments on v. 16,[108] for v. 17 he shifts the focus of *fides* from human belief (which remains linked with *credere*) to divine fidelity and human trust:[109] God faithfully keeps his promises on the one hand (*ex fide dei promittentis*), and on the other the human shows fidelity and trust (*fides*) in God by believing (*credere*) that he has kept his promises in the past and will do so in the future (*in fide hominis credentis*).[110] This all coheres very well with Paul's arguments in Romans 4 regarding Abraham's trust (πίστις) in God's promise (ἐπαγγελία). Ambrosiaster says nothing of transference from one covenant to another, but rather connects *ex fide in fidem* with *revelatur*, as the second half of the above quotation elaborates: one's belief that God is righteous hinges on whether one believes that he follows through with his promises. Ambrosiaster also looks back to Rom 1:2–4, where promise and fulfillment play a prominent role. He thus registers an awareness of a close relationship between vv. 2–4 and 16–17, insofar as he uses the former to explain the ambiguity of *ex fide in fidem* in the latter.

Augustine also offers an interpretation in his essay *De spiritu et littera*,[111] wherein he argues from Romans that the human ability to behave righteously

---

[108] See *OLD* 698, s.v. *fides*, § 12a; 456, s.v. *credo*, §§ 4–5 for these meanings.

[109] Re *fides* as fidelity, see *OLD*, 698, s.v., § 6; as trust, § 12b. The *OLD* entries for *fides* and *credo* carry many of the same connotations as πίστις and πιστεύειν respectively, so these words are aptly flexible translations of Paul's diction.

[110] This trust would also extend to God's apostles and their message, a point which Ambrosiaster makes in connection with non-apostolic preachers in his comments on 1:16: "This refers, in a word, to those [preachers] from whom they [the Romans] had accepted not-right faith," *hoc dicto illos tangit, a quibus acceperant non rectam fidem* (*Rom.* 1.16.1).

[111] Another interpretation appears in *Quaest. ev.* 2.39.1, utilizing a strategy that resembles Clement's: Augustine invokes Rom 1:17 to explain Luke 17:5, where the disciples ask Christ to increase their faith (*Domine, auge nobis fidem*). Augustine argues that they are asking not for a faith in words regarding what it unseen, but a "faith in [real] things" (*fides rerum*), "since that which is in the future is believed not by words but by things which are themselves present" (*quando non uerbis sed rebus ipsis praesentibus creditur, quod futurum est*). He then goes on to cite Rom 1:17 alongside 2 Cor 3:18, which has a similar prepositional series (ἀπὸ n. εἰς n., *de n. in n.*): "'But we, as we gaze with revealed countenance upon the glory of the Lord, are transformed into the same image from glory to glory, as from the Spirit of the Lord.' For just as here one passes from glory to glory, thus also there [in Rom 1:17 one passes] from faith to faith; clearly from the glory of the gospel (by which those who believe are now illuminated) to the glory of the immutable and manifest truth itself (which those who were then changed fully enjoy); thus from faith in words (by which we now believe what we have not yet seen), to faith in things (by which, in eternity, we will obtain that which we now believe)." «*Nos autem reuelata facie gloriam domini speculantes, in eandem imaginem tranformamur de gloria in gloriam, tamquam a domini spiritu.*» *Sicut enim hic ait de gloria in gloriam, ita et ibi ex fide in fidem, de gloria scilicet euangelii, quo nunc credentes inluminantur, in gloriam ipsius incommutabilis et manifestae ueritatis, qua tunc commutati perfruentur, ita ex fide uerborum, quibus nunc credimus quod nondum uidemus, in fidem rerum, qua in aeternum quod nunc credimus obtinebimus*. Augustine perceives *ex fide in fidem* to signify the progression of faith, *ex fide uerborum in fidem rerum*, expanding the phrase with

5.4 Abbreviated proof (1:17)

is itself a gift from God through the Holy Spirit, without which the moral commands of the NT would become a "letter which kills." In section 18, he reflects upon *pietas*, worshipful gratitude, as the proper human response to the divine gift, since it would not be right to attribute to oneself the origin of something which one has received from someone else. Augustine returns to Romans to verify this point.

Unde idem apostolus in eadem epistola, in qua uehemens defensor est gratiae, cum se dixisset esse Graecis ac barbaris, sapientibus et insipientibus debitorem et ideo quod ad ipsum pertineret, promptum esse et his qui Romae essent euangelizare: «non enim confundor» inquit, «de euangelio; uirtus enim dei est in salutem omni credenti, Iudaeo primum et Graeco, iustitia enim dei in eo reuelatur ex fide in fidem, sicut scriptum est: iustus autem ex fide uiuit».

For this reason, the same apostle in the same letter in which he is a staunch defender of grace (after he said he was a debtor to Greeks and also barbarians, to the wise and to the unlearned, and that thus, as far as he is concerned, he is ready even to preach the gospel to those who are in Rome) says: "For I am not ashamed of the gospel; for it is God's power resulting in salvation for everyone who believes, for the Jew first and the Greek. For God's righteousness is revealed in it from faith to faith, just as it is written: 'But the righteous will live from faith.'" (*Spir. et Litt.* 18 [11])

Augustine's analysis then unfolds in two stages, the first pertaining to *iustitia dei* and the second to *fides*. Regarding the former, he says:

Haec est iustitia dei, quae in testamento uetere uelata in nouo reuelatur; quae ideo iustitia dei dicitur, quod inpertiendo eam iustos facit, sicut «domini est salus», qua saluos facit.

This is the righteousness of God which, after being concealed in the Old Testament, is revealed in the New, [and] which therefore is called the righteousness of God because, when he imparts it, it causes people to be righteous, just as "it is the Lord's salvation" (Ps 3:9) which causes people to be saved.

Augustine here raises the topic of the Old and New Testaments in connection with these verses, although he does not attach them to *ex fide in fidem* in the way that Tertullian and Origen do. Instead the Testaments pertain to how *iustitia dei reuelatur*: since Paul says that the gospel "reveals" God's righteousness, Augustine reasons that prior to that point it must have been "concealed" in the OT. He is moreover sensitive to the multiple senses of *iustitia*: on the one hand it is a divine attribute, but on the other it is a divine posses-

---

the addition of genitives. The "words" and "things" in question he takes from his expansion of a similar ἔλλειψις in 2 Cor 3:18: *de gloria euangelii in gloriam ipsius incommutabilis et manifestae ueritas*. He thus takes Rom 1:17 as one of three mutually illuminating instances of ἔλλειψις (one in Luke's writings and two in Paul's). His reasoning seems to run something like this: Luke 17:5 links with Rom 1:17 via *fides*, while Rom 1:17 links with 2 Cor 3:18 via the notion of "from" (*ex/de*) and "to" (*in*) in both; this series of linkages permits him to use these texts to solve the interpretive mysteries presented by each. He uses a kind of canonical exegesis in combination with the stylistic key of ἔλλειψις. The meaning of the individual texts in their contexts takes a back seat to the light they shed on one another once he has brought them together.

sion, since it is his to dispense to humanity to make them righteous. Where then does faith fit into all this?

> *Et haec est fides, ex qua et in quam reuelatur, ex fide scilicet annuntiantium in fidem oboedientium. qua fide Iesu Christi, id est quam nobis contulit Christus, credimus ex deo nobis esse pleniusque futurum esse quod iuste uiuimus. unde illi ea pietate, qua solus colendus est, gratias agimus.*

And this is the faith, from which and to which it [i.e., righteousness] is revealed – clearly from the faith of those who preach to the faith of those who obey [*ex fide scilicet annuntiantium in fidem oboedientium*]. In this way by the faith of Jesus Christ – that is, the faith which Christ granted to us – we believe that the life which we live righteously is ours from God, and will be so more fully [in the future]. For this reason we give thanks by means of that piety with which he alone is to be revered.

Augustine interprets the revelation as occurring from the faith of one group to that of another. God's righteousness is the subject of proclamation, and so the person who preaches (*ex fide annuntiantium*) transmits it to the person who responds favorably (*in fidem oboedientium*). Augustine's reference to "obedience" in this context hearkens back to Rom 1:5, where Paul refers to his reception of "grace" and a "mission for the obedience of faith among all the Gentiles" (ἐλάβομεν χάριν καὶ ἀποστολὴν εἰς ὑπακοὴν πίστεως ἐν πᾶσιν τοῖς ἔθνεσιν). In a manner similar to his explanation of *iustitia dei* as something which is simultaneously attributed to, possessed by, and granted by God, Augustine also declares *fides Iesu Christi* to be *quam nobis contulit Christus*, a statement that is tantalizingly obscure. He appears to be playing with the various ways one can take *fides Iesu Christi* here, since it could be possessive or subjective (in which case *quam nobis contulit Christus* restates *fides Iesu Christi* as the faith which is his to give), or objective (in which case *quam nobis contulit Christus* corrects *fides Iesu Christi* to make the point that even one's own faith has its origin in Christ's grace). In spite of this ambiguity, however, he clearly understands the phrase *ex fide in fidem* to pertain to evangelism, identifying the sources and recipients of the proclamation as the ellided elements.

The patristic authors surveyed above determine that ἐκ πίστεως εἰς πίστιν (*ex fide in fidem*) omits wording required in order for the phrase to make sense. They thus take the phrase as an instance of ἔλλειψις, and expand it by supplying the appropriate language, either the addition of adjectives or genitive nouns to each πίστις (*fides*) on the one hand, or the unpacking of each "faith" with forms of the verb πιστεύειν (*credere*) with expressed objects on the other. The forms of πιστεύειν (*credere*) with objects possess the force of πίστις (*fides*) with objective genitives. In other words, when these commentators regard "from faith to faith" to mean "from believing (in) x to believing (in) y," they are, for all intents and purposes, adding objective genitives to Paul's original phrase. The rhetorical theorists' definitions of ἔλλειψις refer to the omission of language with the audience can supply for themselves from the context. It comes as no surprise, then, that some patristic interpreters search nearby Rom 1:17 for solutions. The interpretations of Tertullian and Origen work with the connection of Jew and Greek with πιστεύειν in 1:16. Paul must, they reason, be referring to Jewish πίστις (faith in the the law, the Old Testament, Moses and the prophets) and Gentile or Christian πίστις (faith in the gospel, the New Testament, the apostles and Christ). They see the phrase as furthermore foreshadowing Paul's handling of the law in Romans 2–3 as something valuable yet insufficient without the gospel. This exegetical conclusion does not undermine the continuity of Israel and the church, however: the need for the Christian to believe in the law and the prophets does not diminish, just as the Jews must "be transferred" or "be led" to belief in Christ. Augustine's interpretation in *De spiritu et littera*, too, looks to the neighboring context, in particular Paul's emphasis on evangelism in 1:1–15. He reads the phrase as a further expression of Paul's missionary goals, reinforcing his declaration of a desire to preach in Rome and his assertion that the gospel affects salvation by its proclamation and acceptance.

Others pay less attention to the immediate context, and instead expand the ἔλλειψις with elements of Paul's later argument. Ambrosiaster's references to human trust in God's fidelity look ahead to language and themes from Romans 4 (Abraham's πίστις and God's ἐπαγγελία). John Chrysostom, meanwhile, looks into the broader corpus Paulinum to explain ἐκ πίστεως εἰς πίστιν, concluding that Paul compresses in these four short words the entirety of Hebrews 11, if not many more of the "vast sea of stories" omitted from that passage. One should not, however, suppose that John posits this reading through a neglect of the context, since he takes the quotation of Hab 2:4 in Rom 1:17 as his cue. He reasons that if the quotation confirms the plausibility of the statement that all can become righteous by faith, then the mysterious phrase ἐκ πίστεως εἰς πίστιν must do so as well.

If these patristic interpreters are correct in their determination of ἔλλειψις in ἐκ πίστεως εἰς πίστιν, we should do as Paul's audience of Roman Christians would do and gather the relevant data from the context toward a logical expansion. (1) The phrase occurs in a definition, wherein the primary method of συντομία ἐκ τῶν πραγμάτων so far has been the maximization of polyvalence. (2) A valid interpretation will not neglect the force of each preposition. Since δικαιοσύνη θεοῦ refers to a divine attribute, ἐκ πίστεως εἰς πίστιν most plausibly construes with the verb ἀποκαλύπτεται, expressing the *source* and *destination* of the revelation. (3) Πίστις in v. 17 obviously connects with παντὶ τῷ πιστεύοντι in v. 16. On the one hand, πιστεύειν here refers to responsive faith (belief and trust). Paul also designs the phrase Ἰουδαίῳ τε πρῶτον καὶ Ἕλληνι as a συνεκδοχή meant simultaneously to include all of humanity yet to retain a focus on single believers, while conveying the notion of sequence and progression. On the other hand, πίστις carries the sense of "fidelity to one's duty," specifically "to preach," in vv. 8–15. This meaning remains important given the coordination of πίστεις that occurs in v. 12, συμπαρακληθῆναι ἐν ὑμῖν διὰ τῆς ἐν ἀλλήλοις πίστεως ὑμῶν τε καὶ ἐμοῦ. Paul means these πίστεις literally: the quality of fidelity that he and his addressees share will become a mutual source of encouragement when they finally meet face to face. Each πίστις (ὑμῶν τε καὶ ἐμοῦ) also represents more instances of συνεκδοχή. "Faith" is a part standing in for the whole of the persons who possess it. And, finally, (4) πίστις links the themes of evangelism and forensic eschatology. Regarding the latter, faith is the *from which* and *to which* the gospel reveals divine justice. Regarding the former, vv. 16–17 in their immediate context explain why Paul wants so urgently to come to Rome to preach. Faith as belief is the *purpose* of evangelism (1:5, εἰς ὑπακοὴν πίστεως), while faith as fidelity is its *motive* (1:11–13).

With these factors in mind, Augustine's proposal, *ex fide annuntiantium in fidem oboedientium* (ἐκ πίστεως τοῦ εὐαγγελιζομένου εἰς πίστιν ὑπακούοντος) begins to show promise. The ἔλλειψις of the "one who preaches" and the "one who obeys" explains the logic of vv. 16–17. Why is Paul not ashamed of the gospel? Because it is God's power for salvation for everyone who believes. Why? Because it reveals God's justice from person to person, from believer to believer.[112] The chain of transmission indeed extends from the *fidelity* of those who proclaim to the *new responsive faith* of those who accept the proclamation, who in turn continue the cycle. The gospel requires messengers – not only ἀπόστολοι, who have a specific commission, but also people like the Roman Christians, whom Paul presents as his partners. In this manner, Paul unites the multiple senses of πίστις within the definition. The decision to leave the genitives of possession which expand ἐκ πίστεως εἰς πίστιν unstated provides him with a great deal of flexibility. Tertullian, Origen and the others who expand it with Ἰουδαίου and Ἕλληνος indeed identify one other such expansion which the subsequent argument in Romans directly supports (for example, from the faith of Abraham to the faith of his children in chapter 4). Paul will also detach ἐκ πίστεως from εἰς πίστιν and connect it with δικαιοσύνη in its verbal form (for example, 5:1, δικαιωθέντες οὖν ἐκ πίστεως εἰρήνην ἔχομεν πρὸς τὸν θεὸν διὰ τοῦ κυρίου ἡμῶν Ἰησοῦ Χριστοῦ). Furthermore, he has said nothing yet regarding the object of πίστις, which he will later express genitively (for example, 3:21–22, νυνὶ δὲ χωρὶς νόμου δικαιοσύνη θεοῦ πεφανέρωται μαρτυρουμένη ὑπὸ τοῦ νόμου καὶ τῶν προφητῶν, δικαιοσύνη δὲ θεοῦ διὰ πίστεως Ἰησοῦ Χριστοῦ εἰς πάντας τοὺς πιστεύοντας). These moves represent Paul's exegesis of his definition, in order to bring forward meanings which presently lie latent within it. The evangelistic expansion of ἐκ πίστεως εἰς πί-

---

[112] Cf. Jewett, *Romans*, 144: "... it is most likely that the progression in this verse refers to missionary expansion of the gospel, which relies on the contagion of faith."

στιν therefore best fits the immediate context of vv. 16–17, as the place where Paul's definition starts and will ultimately end (in 15:14–33).

5.4.3 The quotation of Hab 2:4

The problems inherent in the quotation of Hab 2:4 relate on the one hand to Paul's source, and on the other to what he does with it. (1) What is the form of the text which he quotes? (2) If he changes it, why? (3) Does ἐκ πίστεως construe with the nominative ὁ δίκαιος or with the verb ζήσεται? (4) How much of the quotation's context does he want to bring along with it?

The problem of the text of Hab 2:4 as Paul encounters it in his LXX is convoluted and not susceptible to definitive resolution. The disjunction between the texts of the LXX and the MT in this verse is just one of several that occur throughout Hab 2:1–5.[113] The differences may derive from the translators' use of a different Hebrew base, or it may result from obscurities in the text which the translators or subsequent copyists attempt to repair.[114] The MT of Hab 2:4b

---

[113] On this question, see esp. the study by Fitzmyer, "Habakkuk 2:3–4."
[114] In Hab 2:2, the MT reads

כְּתוֹב חָזוֹן וּבָאֵר עַל־הַלֻּחוֹת לְמַעַן יָרוּץ קוֹרֵא בוֹ

which the LXX renders γράψον ὅρασιν καὶ σαφῶς ἐπὶ πυξίον, ὅπως διώκῃ ὁ ἀναγινώσκων αὐτά. The meaning of the final clause is ambiguous. Does it mean "so that the reader may run through it easily" (so BDB 930, s.v. , "fig. of reading smoothly"), or "so that a runner may read it" (so NRSV)? The LXX appears to opt for the former, "so that the one reading them may press on." In v. 3, the LXX seems confused, switching abruptly from the feminine ὅρασις to a masculine pronoun and participle, διότι ἔτι ὅρασις εἰς καιρὸν καὶ ἀνατελεῖ εἰς πέρας καὶ οὐκ εἰς κενόν· ἐὰν ὑστερήσῃ, ὑπόμεινον αὐτόν, ὅτι ἐρχόμενος ἥξει καὶ οὐ μὴ χρονίσῃ. חָזוֹן ("vision") is masculine:

כִּי עוֹד חָזוֹן לַמּוֹעֵד וְיָפֵחַ לַקֵּץ וְלֹא יְכַזֵּב אִם־יִתְמַהְמָהּ חַכֵּה־לוֹ כִּי־בֹא יָבֹא לֹא יְאַחֵר

"For there is still a vision for the appointed time, and a witness for the end, and it will not lie; if it tarries, wait for it, for it will surely come, it will not delay." The masculine verbal and pronominal forms in the second half of the verse clearly have חָזוֹן as their antecedent, but the LXX gives the impression that there has been a change in topic to a *person* (cf. v. 4) upon whom Habakkuk should wait. This verse may also have an instance of a different texual base, וְיָפֵחַ לַקֵּץ. Following Fitzmyer ("Habakkuk 2:3–4; cf. KB 139, s.v. יפח), I take this to mean "witness"; BDB 806, s.v. פוח, meanwhile takes it to mean "the vision panteth toward the end" (Hiphil imperfect), i.e., "hastens." BHS recommends an emendation, (וְ)יִפְרַח, the Qal imperfect of פרח, "to bud, sprout, shoot" (BDB 827): this is perhaps the text which the LXX renders as ἀνατελεῖ εἰς πέρας. In the first half of v. 4, the MT has:

הִנֵּה עֻפְּלָה לֹא־יָשְׁרָה נַפְשׁוֹ בּוֹ

"Behold, his life within him was swollen and was not upright"; the LXX completely changes the sense of the verse: ἐὰν ὑποστείληται, οὐκ εὐδοκεῖ ἡ ψυχή μου ἐν αὐτῷ. This change perhaps both from a different Hebrew text and from an effort to clarify its ambiguity (e.g., the feminine form of עֻפְּלָה, which I resolve by understanding נַפְשׁוֹ as its subject). Finally, we have the first part of v. 5:

וְאַף כִּי־הַיַּיִן בּוֹגֵד גֶּבֶר יָהִיר וְלֹא יִנְוֶה

reads: וְצַדִּיק בֶּאֱמוּנָתוֹ יִחְיֶה, "but the righteous one by his fidelity will live." This "righteous one" contrasts with the person whose "life within him was swollen and was not upright" in 2:4a (עֻפְּלָה לֹא־יָשְׁרָה נַפְשׁוֹ בּוֹ) and the "proud man" in 2:5 (גֶּבֶר יָהִיר). Unfortunately the text of Hab 2:4a in the Qumran Habakkuk pesher is missing, but the interpretation indicates that it too reads באמונתו,[115] fixing the third person singular pronominal suffix to around Paul's day. The more authoritative MSS of the LXX meanwhile have ὁ δὲ δίκαιος ἐκ πίστεώς μου ζήσεται.[116] Ἐκ πίστεώς μου has an analogue in how the LXX handles 2:4a, ἐὰν ὑποστείληται, οὐκ εὐδοκεῖ ἡ ψυχή μου ἐν αὐτῷ. Wherever μου comes from – a lost Hebrew version, the efforts of ancient translators to clarify obscurities, or scribal emendation or error – either it or αὐτοῦ most likely stood in the text of Habakkuk known to Paul.

If this conclusion is correct, Paul deliberately omits the genitive pronoun both in Rom 1:17 and in Gal 3:11, ὅτι δὲ ἐν νόμῳ οὐδεὶς δικαιοῦται παρὰ τῷ θεῷ δῆλον, ὅτι «ὁ δίκαιος ἐκ πίστεως ζήσεται» (with no reported textual variation).[117] The omission alters the meaning of the passage significantly, since it increases the ambiguity – a desirable result from Paul's point of view. In the MT, בֶּאֱמוּנָתוֹ, and, in the LXX, ἐκ πίστεώς μου both construe with their verbs, and both clearly refer to *fidelity*, whether of God or of the righteous person. The retention of μου would thus narrow the meaning of πίστις and interfere with the quotation's utility within the definition, which has already taken advantage of the polyvalence of πίστις. Paul most probably selects Hab 2:4 be-

---

"And indeed wine is deceitful, a man is proud, but he will not endure"; the LXX renders these three separate clauses as a single one: ὁ δὲ κατοινωμένος καὶ καταφρονητὴς ἀνὴρ ἀλάζων οὐδὲν μὴ περάνῃ.

[115] 1QpHab VII.17–VIII.3: "Its intepretation concerns all observing the Law in the House of Judah, whom God will free from the house of judgment on account of their toil and of their loyalty to the Teacher of Righteousness,"

פשרו על כול עושי התורה בבית יהודה אשר יצילם אל מבית המשפט בעבור עמלם ואמנתם במורה הצדק

(text and trans. per García Martínez/Tigchelaar 1.16–17).

[116] The major witnesses supporting the text as given here are א, B, Q, W*; in support of ὁ δὲ δίκαιός μου ἐκ πίστεως ζήσεται are A, 49, 407 and several witnesses of the Lyciancian recension (36, 46, 86, 711); W^c and 106 lack μου. (This data per Ziegler and my own examination of facsimile editions of א and B.) Cf. Aquila (ἐν πίστει αὐτοῦ) and Symmachus (τῇ ἑαυτοῦ πίστει), both conforming to the MT. The testimony of Heb 10:38 supports δίκαιός μου (NA²⁷, following 𝔓⁴⁶, א, A, H*, 33 and 1739), although not unequivocally. Other MSS omit μου (𝔓¹³, D², H^c, I, Ψ, 1881, 𝔐), but this probably reflects efforts to bring the quotation into line with Rom 1:17 and Gal 3:11 (so also Metzger, *Textual Commentary*, 601). Only D* and a few others read πίστεώς μου. In Rom 1:17, one MS (C*) restores μου after πίστεως.

[117] Contra Käsemann, (*Romans*, 31), who argues that "we have here an exposition of the original text which understands באמונתו in terms of the situation in the Christian community," and that "[h]e took it over from the Jewish-Christian mission, which found in Hab 2:4 a prophecy of salvation by faith in the Messiah just as Qumran found salvation in commitment to the Teacher of Righteousness."

cause it unites three of his definition's main themes: justice (ὁ δίκαιος), faith (ἐκ πίστεως), and forensic eschatology (ζήσεται). Contextually ἐκ πίστεως best construes with ζήσεται;[118] but the ambiguity will allow Paul to join it to ὁ δίκαιος in his subsequent exposition.[119] The quotation further reinforces the focus of the definition on the positive aspect of divine justice, the power of God to bestow salvation through the proclamation and acceptance of the gospel.

The final question relates to how much of the context of Hab 2:4 Paul wishes to import into his definition. The quotation of part of a passage in order to evoke the whole would be a reasonable application of συνεκδοχή. It does not appear, however, that Paul intends συνεκδοχή of some larger portion of Habakkuk.[120] The immediate context of Hab 2:4 offers little of relevance to Rom 1:16–17 – neither the "vision" (2:2, γράψον ὅρασιν καὶ σαφῶς ἐπὶ πυξίον), nor the "drunkard and despiser, the pretensious man" (2:5, ὁ δὲ κατοινωμένος καὶ καταφρονητὴς ἀνὴρ ἀλάζων οὐδὲν μὴ περάνῃ) whom the text places in contrast to the righteous. Some read ὁ δίκαιος as the Messiah, parallel to ὁ ἐρχόμενος in 2:3,[121] but this interpretation runs into the problem that Christ is present in this definition only within the definiendum (Rom 1:2–4), because Paul is here defining the gospel's *function*. Also, if ὁ δίκαιος refers to Christ, it is difficult to ascertain how the quotation verifies 1:16–17a.[122] Paul rather surgically extracts the portion of 2:4 that he needs, recontextualizes it within

---

[118] So also Dodd, *Romans*, 14–15; Fitzmyer, *Romans*, 265; Jewett, *Romans*, 146; and many others. The opposing viewpoint remains popular, however: Käsemann, *Romans*, 32; Cranfield, *Romans*, 1.102; Moo, *Romans*, 76–79; Sanders, *Paul and Palestinian Judaism*, 484. Cf. Betz, *Galatians*, 146–47 and Hays, *Faith of Jesus Christ*, 133–34, on the quotation in Gal 3:11.

[119] Cf. Dunn, *Romans*, 1.45: "In the tradition of Jewish exegesis Paul would not necessarily want to narrow the meaning to *exclude* other meanings self-evident in the text forms used elsewhere, so much as to *extend* and broaden the meaning to include the sense he was most concerned to bring out. ... In this case the fuller meaning would include the possibility of taking the ἐκ πίστεως with both ὁ δίκαιος and ζήσεται...." See also ibid., 48–49, cf. Hays, *Faith of Jesus Christ*, 140–41; Barrett, *Romans*, 31 ("[M]an (if righteous at all) is righteous by faith; he also lives by faith").

[120] For efforts to read portions of the context of Hab 2:4 into Rom 1:16–17, see Watts, "For I Am Not Ashamed," Hays, *Echoes of Scripture*, 39–41.

[121] See, e.g., Campbell, "Romans 1:17," 282–84; Hays, "Apocalyptic Hermeneutics," 137–40, and cf. ibid., 140–42 and idem, *Faith of Jesus Christ*, 134–38 re Gal 3:11. Demonstrating that ὁ δίκαιος for some Christians (and perhaps some contemporary Jews) was a messianic title does not constitute proof that Paul (or anyone else) reads the word as referring to Jesus in Hab 2:4. The evidence adduced by Hays ("Apocalyptic Hermeneutics," 124–25) from Acts 7:51–53 is thin, and ὁ δίκαιος in Heb 10:37–38 could just as easily refer to the person benefited by the arrival of ὁ ἐρχόμενος. Finally, Paul has a rich palette of christological titles, but ὁ δίκαιος does not appear to be one of them, if his failure to use it unambiguously in this manner elsewhere is any indication.

[122] That is, unless the first half of ἐκ πίστεως εἰς πίστιν refers to Christ's fidelity, which is equally difficult to prove from the immediate context.

his definition, and leaves the rest behind. The oracle, as he presents it, is complete and self-contained.[123] But, although the quotation does not bring along its immediate context, it may work similarly to the συνεκδοχή of the whole of scripture for its parts in the first definition (Rom 1:2, ὃ προεπηγγείλατο διὰ τῶν προφητῶν αὐτοῦ ἐν γραφαῖς ἁγίαις). Hab 2:4 establishes a relationship between faith, justice and salvation, motivating its inclusion in Rom 1:17. In addition to this point, one may also note that the topic of scripture begins the first definition and concludes the second, forming a neat symmetry. The quotation may thus loosely mirror the συνεκδοχή in v. 2, furnishing a part of the whole body of oracles that address the gospel's revelatory and soteriological functions. Furthermore, since the quotation comprises a portion of an abbreviated proof, it signals to his audience that his argument will rely foremost on evidence supplied by the scriptures.

5.5 Conclusion

It may prove helpful in drawing this chapter to a close to organize my findings into major and minor conclusions. First among the former is that analysis of 1:16–17 as a definition the gospel's function clarifies its internal structure (a basic definition and an abbreviated proof) as well as a number of obscurities within it. Chief among these is why such obscurities are there at all: Paul puts them there deliberately in order to provide himself with the flexibility to reorganize the definition's component parts to bring forward meanings latent within them in subsequent parts of Romans. Already in the prescript and 'thanksgiving' Paul uses πίστις to refer both to fidelity, as part of his praise of the Romans and the presentation of his ἦθος, and to responsive faith, as the

---

[123] Paul's approach resembles that of 1QpHab for this portion of the text: each line represents a distinct oracle, with its own interpretation. For example, "the one who reads" in 2:2 refers to "the Teacher of Righteousness, to whom God has made known all the mysteries of the words of his servants, the prophets,"

פשרו על מורה הצדק אשר הודיעו אל את כול רזי דברי עבדיו הנבאים

(VII.4–5). 2:3a means that "the final age will be extended and go beyond all that the prophets say, because the mysteries of God are wonderful,"

פשרו אשר יארוך הקץ האחרון ויתר על כול אשר דברו הנביאים כיא רזי אל להפלה

(VII.7–8). The assurance that the vision will surely come in 2:3b pertains to "the men of truth, those who observe the Law, whose hands will not desert the service of truth when the final age is extended beyond them,"

פשרו על אנשי האמת עושי התורה אשר לוא ירפו ידיהם מעבודת האמת בהמשך עליהם הקץ האחרון

(VII.10–12). I quote the interpretation of 2:4 in n. 115 above. And 2:5–6 is about "the Wicked Priest, who was called loyal at the start of his office,"

פשרו על הכוהן הרשע אשר נקרא על שם האמת בתחלת עומדו

(VIII.8–9). (Texts and translations per García Martínez/Tigchelaar 1.16–17.) The theme of eschatology and the experiences of the community hold these interpretations together, but each oracle has its own individual contribution to make.

objective of his mission, εἰς ὑπακοὴν πίστεως. Another major conclusion is the disclosure of several strategies of brevity other than the maximization of the ambiguities inherent in his definition's terms, namely the rhetorical figures of ἀπὸ κοινοῦ with the multiple construals of πρῶτον in v. 16 and of ἐκ πίστεως in the quotation of Hab 2:4, συνεκδοχή with the phrase Ἰουδαίῳ τε πρῶτον καὶ Ἕλληνι, and ἔλλειψις with ἐκ πίστεως εἰς πίστιν. I have also argued that δικαιοσύνη θεοῦ means divine justice, including his royal-judicial role at the eschatological trial as well as his reliability in fulfilling his promises (1:2). Both of these facets are manifest in the gospel's ability to effect justification, to make acquittal at the eschatological trial possible without compromising the integrity of divine justice.

Turning now to the minor conclusions, I have shown here and in the previous chapter how rhetorical figures as an aspect of style are more than mere dressing; they can be – and, in the case of figures of brevity, usually are – integral to the meanings of the utterances in which they appear, at the levels both of composition and interpretation. Second, patristic readers of Paul sometimes offer extremely useful exegesis, particularly when one can correlate their interpretive methods with ancient rhetorical theory. I directed attention particularly to evidence that they interpret ἐκ πίστεως εἰς πίστιν as an instance of ἔλλειψις; on this point they are correct, and Augustine's proposed expansion, "from the faith of those who preach to the faith of those who obey," hits the mark perfectly.

My analysis also clarifies the internal logic of the second definition, and it helps to reorient our thinking about how it operates as the πρόθεσις of the letter. It flows directly from Paul's statements in 1:8–15, specifically those which he offers about himself as a means of impressing his ἦθος upon his addressees in Rome. Paul does the same thing in vv. 2–4, which elaborates his special status as one ἀφωρισμένος εἰς εὐαγγέλιον θεοῦ. He positions his second definition in relation to vv. 8–15 as an explanation of his πρόθυμον καὶ ὑμῖν τοῖς ἐν Ῥώμῃ εὐαγγελίσασθαι. The gospel overrides all other concerns for him. It is no mere message about or story of a god's isolated intrusion into human affairs, as a superficial reading of the first definition might (wrongly) lead one to conclude. The gospel itself – its content, its proclamation and its acceptance – constitute an ongoing divine intervention aimed at saving humanity from eschatological condemnation and restoring peace with God. It is not sufficient to speak of justification, or God's righteousness, or faith as the theme of Romans. The theme of Romans is *the gospel* as *God's power at work in the cosmos*. Both the abbreviated proof in v. 17 and the proofs which follow in the letter serve the purpose of demonstrating the veracity of the basic definition, that is, the way that the gospel unites divine power, forensic eschatology, faith and universalism. The "I" in οὐκ ἐπαισχύνομαι must not slip out of focus, however. Paul unites himself and this new divine power. He does so again in

v. 17. The gospel is God's power *because* it reveals God's justice through a chain of transmission moving "from faith to faith," from the fidelity of people like Paul toward the generation of new responsive faith. The gospel *needs* Paul, and the other apostles, and the Roman Christians, in order to fulfill God's objectives in releasing it into the world.

Chapter 6

Paul's Exegesis of His Definitions in Romans

6.1 Introduction

At several points in Romans, Paul explicitly returns to his definitions of the gospel in order to unfold them further, to recombine their component terms into new sequences, to bring forward meanings that are latent within them, and to refocus his audience's attention on the proposition that he sets out to prove. The second definition receives greater emphasis than the first, and naturally so, since it serves as the πρόθεσις of the letter. Paul's procedure at points resembles the "exegesis of the terms" that Dio Chrysostom implements in *Or.* 14 on slavery and freedom, and *Or.* 76 on custom. In the former, Dio posits a definition of ἐλευθερία, destroys it by playing its component parts against one another, and rebuilds a new definition out of its remains. In the latter, the oration opens with a series of expansions of his definition of τὸ ἔθος, presented in reverse order.[1]

My goal in the present chapter is not to give a full account of 'the rhetoric of Romans,' with precise determinations of the point(s) to be adjudicated, the γένος of the letter, or its τάξις. These questions, vitally important as they are, stand far beyond the scope of this study, and it would require hundreds of additional pages to justify any answers that I might put forward. Instead, I pursue a much more limited objective, to show that portions of the argument exegete his definitions of the gospel. I argued in the previous chapter that the second definition unites several themes in its declaration of the gospel's function: divine power, forensic eschatology (salvation and divine justice), faith, evangelism, and universalism. In Rom 2:1–11, which I have already discussed in connection with σωτηρία and δικαιοσύνη θεοῦ,[2] Paul unfolds the relationship of divine justice and universalism in order to establish the comprehensive condemnation of humanity before the eschatological tribunal. I have selected three passages that further illustrate Paul's elaboration and recombination of the terms of his definitions, and his deft manipulation of the ambiguities within them. The first, 3:1–8, raises the question of the integrity of God's

---

[1] See §§ 2.4.2, 2.4.3.
[2] See §§ 5.3.1, 5.4.1.

δικαιοσύνη in relation to both his own and human πίστις (fidelity) (6.2). The second, 3:21–31, recapitulates 1:16–17 with substantial expansions of each of the themes in 1:16–17 and of the logic of how the gospel can function as a δύναμις θεοῦ εἰς σωτηρίαν παντὶ τῷ πιστεύοντι (6.3). In connection with 3:21–31, I consider whether and how συνεκδοχή may be operating in the disputed phrase πίστις Ἰησοῦ Χριστοῦ (6.4). The third, 9:1–10:21, brings the second definition into conversation with the first in order to pose hard questions about God's promises to the Israelites, and to build upon the discussion in 3:1–8 (6.5). Each of the three passages has numerous interpretive problems that scholars have debated; I direct my very brief treatments primarily to how these arguments appropriate and extend Paul's definitions of the gospel.

6.2 Romans 3:1–8

Paul designs 1:18–3:20 to establish universal human guilt before the divine tribunal (3:9, 19–20). How exactly he does this at the level of his logic remains a difficult and debated question – one which I shall not entertain here.[3] I have already touched upon how in 2:1–11 Paul addresses the impartial nature of divine δικαιοσύνη, which in the context of the eschatological trial will manifest itself as σωτηρία and ὀργή, and will extend over every human, Ἰου-

---

[3] The main problem relates to Paul's arguments about νόμος, which have prompted accusations of logical inconsistency. See esp. Sanders, *Paul, the Law, and the Jewish People*, 29–36, 123–32, 144–48; also, Räisänen, *Paul and the Law*, passim ("contradictions and tensions have to be *accepted* as *constant* features of Paul's theology of the law," 10–11). Watson (*Paul, Judaism, and the Gentiles*, esp. chs. 6–7) interprets Romans 1–3 as a foundational component of Paul's argument that Jewish Christians should "abandon all the remaining ties that bind them to the Jewish community, which they once sought and failed to reform, and to join with his own followers in a new shared identity as 'Christians'" (216). Some scholars (e.g., Gager, *Reinventing Paul*) argue that his break with his Jewish heritage and his criticism of the Torah have been badly overstated, in large part because of an uncritical anachronism: the misapplication of the terms 'Christianity' and 'Christian,' which properly belong to a much later form of the 'Jesus movement' that was using Paul's letters to distinguish itself from its parents, the Judaisms of the Greco-Roman world. The anachronism contributes to the evaluation of his statements about the Torah as inconsistent. I agree with Sanders that Paul is viewing the law through the lens of the gospel (see now Sanders' incisive article, "God Gave the Law to Condemn"). Paul's statements about it are unique for this very reason. He neither claims nor implies that his fellow Jews would agree with him regarding its soteriological insufficiency or condemnatory function at the eschatological trial. He regards the law, from his post-gospel point of view, as a prisoner of sinister cosmic agents that have perverted whatever good intention God had in giving it. In a way, Paul's second definition of the gospel as revealing God's justice also discloses his perception that the gospel reveals *God's* perspective on the limitations and failures of his own law. He gave it as an act of love and grace; instead it forces his δικαιοσύνη into a posture of ὀργή. The gospel overturns this situation, and makes it possible for his promises to come to full fruition.

δαῖός τε πρῶτον καὶ Ἕλλην. He thus deals foremost in this passage with the themes of forensic eschatology and universalism. He retains a focus on these themes in 3:1–8, while reintroducing πίστις into the mix.

In the foregoing context, Paul relativizes circumcision from two angles: adherence to the law's commands (2:25–27), and the place where authentic circumcision occurs (the heart, not the flesh, 2:28–29).[4] He does not want to trivialize circumcision of the flesh, however, since it remains a sign of the special relationship that Jews enjoy with God.

3:1 τί οὖν τὸ περισσὸν τοῦ Ἰουδαίου ἢ τίς ἡ ὠφέλεια τῆς περιτομῆς; 2 πολὺ κατὰ πάντα τρόπον. πρῶτον μὲν [γὰρ] ὅτι ἐπιστεύθησαν τὰ λόγια τοῦ θεοῦ. 3 τί γάρ; εἰ ἠπίστησάν τινες, μὴ ἡ ἀπιστία αὐτῶν τὴν πίστιν τοῦ θεοῦ καταργήσει; 4 μὴ γένοιτο.

1 What then is the advantage of the Jew? Or what is the benefit of circumcision? 2 Much in every respect. First there is the fact that they were entrusted with the oracles of God. 3 So what? If some were unfaithful, their infidelity will not cancel the fidelity of God, will it? 4 Of course not!

The questions in vv. 1 and 3,[5] and the answers in vv. 2 and 4, address the definitive particularity of the Jewish people as chosen by God. Paul brings forward some meanings of πίστις and πιστεύειν here which he has not yet directly used in Romans. God *entrusted*, this is to say, *he put his trust in* (ἐπιστεύθησαν, πίστις τοῦ θεοῦ) the Israelites and the circumcision that marks their particularity. "Some," however, have been unfaithful (ἠπίστησαν, ἀπιστία αὐτῶν). How did "some" do this? An answer based on the immediate context would be: by failing to observe the law (2:17–27), or by failing to circumcize the heart as well as the flesh (2:28–29). And yet, we have a future tense verb, καταργήσει, correlating with what we find in 2:27 (καὶ κρινεῖ ἡ ἐκ φύσεως ἀκροβυστία τὸν νόμον τελοῦσα σὲ τὸν διὰ γράμματος καὶ περιτομῆς παραβάτην νόμου), and suggesting that Paul still has the eschatological trial in view.[6]

---

[4] In 2:25–29, Paul additionally alludes to part of the eschatological judicial procedure, which evidently not only involves assessment on the basis of law, but also comparative evaluation, as he says in v. 27 (καὶ κρινεῖ ἡ ἐκ φύσεως ἀκροβυστία τὸν νόμον τελοῦσα σὲ τὸν διὰ γράμματος καὶ περιτομῆς παραβάτην νόμου). The gist here is not that ἡ ἐκ φύσεως ἀκροβυστία will do the judging, rather that its attainments dramatically underscore "your" failure.

[5] On the question of whom Paul presents as asking these questions in the diatribe (a Jew? a Jewish Christian?), the most important answer is Paul himself. It does not seem necessary to analyze the passage into a dialogue with distinct characters (see, e.g., Stowers, *Rereading of Romans*, 165–75; Jewett, *Romans*, 241). Paul raises the questions because they legitimately arise from what he has said so far, and he uses them to move his argument toward its conclusion that all will justly stand condemned at the eschatological trial. He designs this passage in part to close off any apotropaic appeal to God's promises to the Israelites.

[6] Käsemann (*Romans*, 80) says that, although "καταργεῖν is a common and specifically Pauline term which usually means 'destroy' in an eschatological sense," the future here is logical: "[w]hen calling accompanies God's promise, human unfaithfulness cannot nullify God's faithfulness." I agree that Paul is expressing a principle, and thus that the future is to a

Πίστις τοῦ θεοῦ refers not only back to his investment of the Israelites with τὰ λόγια, but also forward to his conduct at the trial. The unstated premise is a forensic-eschatological understanding of God's promise to save his people. And herein lies the problem: his fidelity and his justice appear to conflict. Paul must bring these two divine attributes into line.

Interestingly, Paul does not offer a substantive solution. He instead argues that pitting these attributes against each other at all constitutes a dangerously impious absurdity. First, he renders explicit the apparent conflict of fidelity and justice with a quotation of Ps 50:6, and then sharpens the questions further:

3:4 γινέσθω δὲ ὁ θεὸς ἀληθής, πᾶς δὲ ἄνθρωπος ψεύστης, καθὼς γέγραπται, «ὅπως ἂν δικαιωθῇς ἐν τοῖς λόγοις σου καὶ νικήσεις ἐν τῷ κρίνεσθαί σε». 5 εἰ δὲ ἡ ἀδικία ἡμῶν θεοῦ δικαιοσύνην συνίστησιν, τί ἐροῦμεν; μὴ ἄδικος ὁ θεὸς ὁ ἐπιφέρων τὴν ὀργήν; κατὰ ἄνθρωπον λέγω. 6 μὴ γένοιτο· ἐπεὶ πῶς κρινεῖ ὁ θεὸς τὸν κόσμον; 7 εἰ δὲ ἡ ἀλήθεια τοῦ θεοῦ ἐν τῷ ἐμῷ ψεύσματι ἐπερίσσευσεν εἰς τὴν δόξαν αὐτοῦ, τί ἔτι κἀγὼ ὡς ἁμαρτωλὸς κρίνομαι; 8 καὶ μὴ καθὼς βλασφημούμεθα καὶ καθώς φασίν τινες ἡμᾶς λέγειν ὅτι ποιήσωμεν τὰ κακά, ἵνα ἔλθῃ τὰ ἀγαθά; ὧν τὸ κρίμα ἔνδικόν ἐστιν.

3:4 But let God be true, and every human false,[7] just as it has been written: "So that you would be justified in your words, and you will prevail when you are judged." 5 But if our injustice demonstrates the justice of God, what will we say? The God who brings his wrath to bear is not unjust, is he? (I am speaking in a human manner.)[8] 6 Of course not! How then will God judge the cosmos? 7 But if the truth of God abounded in my falsehood resulting in *his* glory, why am *I* still judged as a sinner? 8 And [we should not say] – as we are slandered and as some say that we say – "let us do evil in order that the good may result," should we? Their [guilty] verdict is deserved.

Questioning God's fidelity is tantamount to questioning his justice, to asking things that only a fool would ask – a fool intent upon recklessly transgressing a proper human posture toward God.[9] No sane person would invite condemnation by insulting the justice of the judge; by analogy, no sane person would

---

certain extent logical, but the substantive context in which God's πίστις (like his δικαιοσύνη) will be tested and affirmed – in other words, where he will or will not do what he promises – is the eschatological trial. As Käsemann himself says on the following page, God's πίστις "manifests itself eschatologically and the struggle for it is the content, center, and meaning of world history."

[7] Regarding the adjectival usage of ψευστής, see LSJ 2021, s.v. 2.

[8] The remark κατὰ ἄνθρωπον λέγω probably means something like "I am speaking from a human perspective." The analogy would be a statement like: "*According to Paul*, the judgment of such persons is deserved," which is to say, *from Paul's perspective* (LSJ 883, s.v. κατά IV.1, "in quotations"). Cf. Gal 3:15.

[9] Paul will use this tactic again in 9:19–23 and 10:6–7, on which see below. He also escalates the tactic considerably in 14:1–15:6, his exhortation to the "strong" (οἱ δυνατοί), with explicit criticism of the legitimacy of "judging" (κρίνειν) somebody else's οἰκέτης or one's own ἀδελφός. To do so constitutes arrogation of an authority that belongs only to God (14:10, πάντες γὰρ παραστησόμεθα τῷ βήματι τοῦ θεοῦ).

accuse God of infidelity. And one should certainly not indulge in doing τὰ κακά according to the idiotic logic that Paul presses to its conclusion.[10] We might describe his strategy here as argumentation by deflection (why would anyone want to ask these questions at all?), in order to establish the general principle that no human action can compromise the integrity of a divine attribute. Once Paul has made this point, he lets it stand so that he may return to it from a different angle later in his letter.

The second definition of the gospel operates broadly as a foundation for Paul's arguments in 3:1–8, and he is clearly reorganizing its component elements. Πίστις appears for the first time since 1:16–17, but as an attribute of God, not of humans. Paul extends the meaning of δικαιοσύνη ἐκ πίστεως here, working out the general validity of the relationship of these two concepts at the divine level prior to reintroducing them at a human level (δικαιοῦσθαι ἐκ πίστεως). In other words, God's πίστις and his δικαιοσύνη logically belong together and are mutually supportive; therefore, so too are human πίστις and δικαιοσύνη. The ambiguity of these words in his definition permits him to make both moves. Also, the verb ἐπιστεύθησαν introduces the idea of faith as "trust," specifically God's trust, which has a corresponding human fidelity to what he entrusts to them. Conversely, humans trust God to show fidelity to what he promises them; this idea is present in the presupposed idea of God's promise to save his people. Paul restricts his comments on the matter to ἀπιστία, which has its tangible manifestation in the failure to adhere to the law. But the theme of forensic eschatology allows for another interpretation: "unfaith," the refusal of "some" to accept the gospel.[11] This meaning presently remains latent, but it will move to the front when Paul later wrestles at greater length with the problem of the relationship between God's fidelity to his promises to Israel and his justice as revealed in the gospel.

6.3 Romans 3:21–31

Of the three passages surveyed in this chapter, 3:21–31 most directly exegetes all of the themes of the second definition, unfolding them both in relation to Paul's negative argument in 1:18–3:20 and in relation to the positive, merciful manifestation of God's justice. He takes two propositions as proven from the foregoing argument: (1) that all people, Jews and Gentiles, will stand con-

---

[10] "There can be little doubt that we have here objections actually raised against Paul.... He himself complains now that ideas which he regarded as blasphemous were being urged as necessary deductions from his message" (Käsemann, *Romans*, 84).

[11] Jewett (*Romans*, 244–45; cf. Cranfield, *Romans*, 1.180) argues that "unfaith" is the primary meaning of ἀπιστία in 3:3. Others see both meanings in play, e.g. Fitzmyer, *Romans*, 327; Dunn, *Romans*, 1.131–32; Moo, *Romans*, 183–85.

demned before the divine tribunal; and (2) that knowledge of or boasting in ὁ νόμος furnishes no defense, because it is the instrument of comprehensive condemnation. The passage has three main structural elements: (1) a recapitulation of 1:17 (3:21–22a); (2) a recapitulation of 1:16 with extensive expansions (3:22b–26); and (3) a recapitulation of 1:18–3:20 in light of 3:21–26 (3:27–31). Paul's elaboration of his definition in this pericope still remains very dense in both its style and content.[12]

The recapitulation of 1:17 in 3:21–22a exhibits some significant shifts in language and emphasis: "But now, apart from the law, God's justice has been made manifest, although it is attested by the law and the prophets; but God's justice [has been made manifest] through faith in Jesus Christ to all who believe" (νυνὶ δὲ χωρὶς νόμου δικαιοσύνη θεοῦ πεφανέρωται μαρτυρουμένη ὑπὸ τοῦ νόμου καὶ τῶν προφητῶν, δικαιοσύνη δὲ θεοῦ διὰ πίστεως Ἰησοῦ Χριστοῦ εἰς πάντας τοὺς πιστεύοντας). The first thing to note is the perfect passive verb πεφανέρωται, which parallels ἀποκαλύπτεται in 1:17.[13] The two passages also feature δικαιοσύνη θεοῦ in the nominative, as well as two prepositional phrases with forms of πίστις (πιστεύειν). Τὸ εὐαγγέλιον is thus very likely the implied agent of the revelation in 3:21, as in 1:17. Second, the mention of the testimony of the law and the prophets inserts a major element of the first definition, God's pre-proclamation of the gospel "by the prophets in the holy scriptures."[14] Their testimony regarding δικαιοσύνη θεοῦ indeed continues in the present time, hence the tense of the participle μαρτυρουμένη.[15] Third, v. 22a

---

[12] Campbell (*Rhetoric of Righteousness*, 70–101; cf. the analysis of Jewett, *Romans*, 271, who accepts some of Campbell's conclusions) offers an interesting rhetorical analysis of 3:21–26 with which I interact below.

[13] One should not overstate the significance of the changes in tense and stem between 1:17 (ἀποκαλύπτεται) and 3:21 (πεφανέρωται), in order to draw a contrast between "the currently preached gospel" and "the ongoing import of a completed event in the past, here the Christ event" (Keck, *Romans*, 104). The former effectively includes the latter, in the proclamation and acceptance of the narrative of what God has achieved in Christ.

[14] Cf. τὰ λόγια τοῦ θεοῦ, 3:2.

[15] Campbell (*Rhetoric of Righteousness*, 83–86) analyzes v. 21 as an ἀντίθεσις, with χωρὶς νόμου and μαρτυρουμένη ὑπὸ τοῦ νόμου καὶ τῶν προφητῶν as opposed elements. The ἀντίθεσις here may be logical, but it does not seem to be syntactical (i.e., the two divided or opposed elements are not performing parallel syntactical roles in their clauses; both are, in fact, standing within the same clause, cf. ch. 4, pp. 125–26 above). Campbell's description of it as "not particularly elegant" (83) raises the question of whether it is occurring here at all. It seems to me that the two phrases are performing distinct functions. The full revelation of God's justice happens apart from the law, i.e., in the gospel, the narrative components of which Paul will go on to summarize. Χωρὶς νόμου abruptly sweeps the law from the table in the dramatic turn from his explication of the threat against humanity to that of its solution. Μαρτυρουμένη seems to be concessive, "although it is attested in the law and the prophets." Paul wants to retain the law's testimonial activity, and for that reason he reappropriates it as an element of his first definition (γραφαὶ ἅγιαι). Such would be the extent of the logical antithesis, i.e., that between the law's condemnatory and revelatory functions.

borrows its finite verb from v. 21 (via ἔλλειψις), "the justice of God *has been made manifest* through faith in Jesus Christ to all those who believe."[16] Vv. 21-22a simultaneously underscore the testimonial activity of the law and prophets on the one hand, and the revelatory activity of the gospel on the other. The two prepositional phrases (διὰ πίστεως Ἰησοῦ Χριστοῦ εἰς πάντας τοὺς πιστεύοντας) in v. 22a thus (like ἐκ πίστεως εἰς πίστις in 1:17) construe with the ellipsed verb. The first phrase expresses the medium ("through faith") as opposed to the source ("from faith"). The second repeats the stem (ἀναδίπλωσις), but shifts to the verbal form in a manner that recalls παντὶ τῷ πιστεύοντι in 1:16. The ἔλλειψις of the verb in v. 22a is strategic: it allows the prepositional phrases to construe also with δικαιοσύνη θεοῦ (ἀπὸ κοινοῦ), marking a transition to God's action of acquittal: the gospel reveals God's δικαιοσύνη as justification through faith (δικαιοῦσθαι διὰ πίστεως) a topic which will arise later in the pericope.

The recapitulation of 1:16 in 3:22b-26 begins with universalism, but it quickly ventures into the definition's other themes. "For there is no distinction," Paul declares, "for all sinned and fall short of God's glory" (οὐ γάρ ἐστιν διαστολή, πάντες γὰρ ἥμαρτον καὶ ὑστεροῦνται τῆς δόξης τοῦ θεοῦ), compressing his argument in 1:18-3:20. Comprehensive human culpability calls for a comprehensive solution: "... although they are justified freely, by his grace, through the redemption which is [available] in Christ Jesus" (δικαιούμενοι δωρεὰν τῇ αὐτοῦ χάριτι διὰ τῆς ἀπολυτρώσεως τῆς ἐν Χριστῷ Ἰησοῦ).[17]

---

[16] So also Jewett (*Romans*, 268; cf. Barrett, *Romans*, 72-73; Bryan, *Preface to Romans*, 102-3) in his translation of the passage, but he strangely makes little use of the restoration of the ellipsed verb in his interpretive remarks on v. 22a (but cf. 278). The perfect tense draws attention to the death and resurrection of Christ (= the gospel) as a singular event with continuing reverberations.

[17] Many scholars regard all or part of vv. 24-26 as having originally been a pre-Pauline formula (e.g., Käsemann, *Romans*, 95-101; Stuhlmacher, "Recent Exegesis"; Fitzmyer, *Romans*, 342-43; Jewett, *Romans*, 269-71; for a history of the scholarship, see Campbell, *Rhetoric of Righteousness*, 37-45) for some of the same reasons that I criticize in chapter 4 above (§ 4.4.1), primarily a concentration of terms and ideas otherwise unattested in Paul's letters, the syntactically odd δικαιούμενοι, and a relative clause that is an expanded epithet. As in the case of 1:3-4, I perceive Paul to have appropriated traditional themes and christological ideas, but to have composed the sentence himself; cf. Campbell, *Rhetoric of Righteousness*, 45-57, and Wright, "Romans," *NIB* 10.466-67, 472, who agree. On the debated meaning of ἀπολύτρωσις here, Campbell (*Rhetoric of Righteousness*, 102-7) gives a helpful summary of the positions and history of the scholarship. I incline toward a broad understanding of it as "deliverance" (LSJ 208, s.v. II; BDAG 117, s.v. 2; on the commercial overtones, i.e. "redemption," see esp. Finlan, *Background and Contents*, 163-92), with a meaning similar to σωτηρία, the word which Paul generally prefers. The context gives the word eschatological content (i.e., deliverance from condemnation). And yet, Paul will later unpack it in terms of deliverance from enslavement to sin (e.g., 6:14, and esp. 7:14, ἐγὼ δὲ σάρκινός εἰμι πεπραμένος ὑπὸ τὴν ἁμαρτίαν). This enslavement is not metaphorical for Paul: it accurately de-

Paul introduces the concept of ἀπολύτρωσις to explain how δικαιοῦσθαι can occur, then shifts in vv. 25–26 to cultic motifs.

3:25 ὃν προέθετο ὁ θεὸς ἱλαστήριον διὰ [τῆς] πίστεως ἐν τῷ αὐτοῦ αἵματι εἰς ἔνδειξιν τῆς δικαιοσύνης αὐτοῦ διὰ τὴν πάρεσιν τῶν προγεγονότων ἁμαρτημάτων 26 ἐν τῇ ἀνοχῇ τοῦ θεοῦ, πρὸς τὴν ἔνδειξιν τῆς δικαιοσύνης αὐτοῦ ἐν τῷ νῦν καιρῷ, εἰς τὸ εἶναι αὐτὸν δίκαιον καὶ δικαιοῦντα τὸν ἐκ πίστεως Ἰησοῦ.

3:25 ... whom he put forward [intended] as a propitiation through faith in his blood, for the demonstration of his justice because of the remittance of previously committed sins 26 in the forbearance of God, for a demonstration of his justice in the present time, so that he may [both] be just and the one who justifies a person on the basis of faith in Christ.

Syntactically, these verses are a long relative clause with four strings of prepositional phrases that exegete 1:16, δύναμις θεοῦ εἰς σωτηρίαν παντὶ τῷ πιστεύοντι:

ὃν προέθετο ὁ θεὸς ἱλαστήριον
(1) διὰ [τῆς] πίστεως ἐν τῷ αὐτοῦ αἵματι,
(2) εἰς ἔνδειξιν τῆς δικαιοσύνης αὐτοῦ διὰ τὴν πάρεσιν τῶν προγεγονότων ἁμαρτημάτων ἐν τῇ ἀνοχῇ τοῦ θεοῦ,
(3) πρὸς τὴν ἔνδειξιν τῆς δικαιοσύνης αὐτοῦ ἐν τῷ νῦν καιρῷ,
(4) εἰς τὸ εἶναι αὐτὸν δίκαιον καὶ δικαιοῦντα τὸν ἐκ πίστεως Ἰησοῦ.

Paul is unfolding the logic of δικαιοῦσθαι as the conversion of wrath to salvation, from guilty verdicts to acquittals. We may regard vv. 25–26 as a very complex expanded epithet incorporating both συνεκδοχαί of mythological narratives (ὃν προέθετο ὁ θεὸς ἱλαστήριον, ἐν τῷ αἵματι) and statements regarding God's character (δικαιοσύνη, ἀνοχή). The cultic imagery (ἱλαστήριον, αἷμα) reinforces this perception. Rhetorically, the first, second, and third conclude with a phrase beginning with ἐν (ἐν τῷ αὐτοῦ αἵματι, ἐν τῇ ἀνοχῇ τοῦ θεοῦ, ἐν τῷ νῦν καιρῷ), and the theme of πίστις forms an inclusio around the whole series (διὰ [τῆς] πίστεως, ἐκ πίστεως Ἰησοῦ).[18] Each string has a pair of prepositional phrases, except the second, which places two divine attributes (δικαιοσύνη, ἀνοχή) on either side of the cause of their present activity (διὰ τὴν πάρε-

---

scribes humanity's involuntary submission to the powerful control of an evil cosmic force bent upon destruction.

[18] Again, my analysis differs from that of Campbell's (*Rhetoric of Righteousness*, 86–95). He perceives v. 23b through τῇ αὐτοῦ χάριτι as an instance of παρένθεσις, a rhetorical aside (an indisputable occurrence of the figure is in 3:5). Paul would then resume the sentence with διὰ τῆς ἀπολυτρώσεως. Within this structure, he reads the three prepositional phrases beginning with διά as instances of ἐπαναφορά, wherein the same word leads a series of clauses. This produces a tidy breakdown of the sentence structure into alternating διά-phrases that restate or reinforce one another (see ibid., 116–18). Vv. 22b–24a, insofar as they contribute significantly to Paul's unpacking of the theme of universalism from v. 16 (cf. εἰς πάντας τοὺς πιστεύοντας), play an integral role in the passage, reducing the likelihood that they constitute a parenthetical aside.

σιν τῶν προγεγονότων ἁμαρτημάτων). Logically, the entire series deals with God's purposes (προέθετο). The first completes the thought of the relative clause: God put Jesus forward and intended him as a propitiation *through faith in his blood.*[19] Paul highlights the one aspect of the narrative about Christ that speaks most directly to his nature as a sacrificial gift,[20] that believers rely specifically on his death as that which averts divine wrath and restores harmony between themselves and God. The second addresses God's purpose of demonstrating his justice in its manifestation as ἀνοχή:[21] Christ as ἱλαστήριον enables

---

[19] Although most interpreters disagree (e.g., Dodd, *Romans*, 56; Barrett, *Romans*, 78; Moo, *Romans*, 236–37; Keck, *Romans*, 110; those who perceive Paul to be quoting a formula often regard διὰ πίστεως as an editorial intrusion by him, e.g., Jewett, *Romans*, 287–88; Fitzmyer, *Romans*, 97–98), I understand ἐν τῷ αὐτοῦ αἵματι as the object of πίστις. I argue below that in the phrase πίστις Ἰησοῦ Χριστοῦ the objective genitive serves as a συνεκδοχή of the narrative of the gospel. Two passages that expand this phrase emphasize the propitiatory character of Christ's death (Rom 4:25, διὰ τὰ παραπτώματα ἡμῶν; 1 Cor 15:3, ὑπὲρ τῶν ἁμαρτιῶν ἡμῶν). The locution ἱλαστήριον διὰ τῆς πίστεως ἐν τῷ αὐτοῦ αἵματι brings forward precisely the same concept in a much more graphic and direct manner.

[20] The commentaries debate the precise meaning of ἱλαστήριον, which could be an adjective (agreeing with ὅν, so Sanday and Headlam, *Romans*, 87–88) or a noun. If it is the latter, it can mean "appeasement, propitiation" (cf. Vulgate, *quem proposuit Deus propitiationem per fidem in sanguine ipsius*), "expiation," or, more specifically, "the place of expiation" referring to the "mercy seat" and its role in the rites of the Day of Atonement (see Campbell, *Rhetoric of Righteousness*, 107–13 for a history of the scholarship; also Finlan, *Background and Contents*, 124–40). Fitzmyer (*Romans*, 349–50) rejects the first as lacking support from parallel usage in the LXX (cf. Dodd, *Bible and the Greeks*, 82–95). He also notes that the verb ἱλάσκεσθαι often means "appeasing angry gods in classical and hellenistic Greek literature" (see LSJ 828, s.v. 1 for examples, and cf. 2, "to conciliate" people; also BDAG 473–74, s.v. 1). The idea of appeasement is contextually suitable, however. Paul has just finished explaining that divine justice stands in a posture of wrath toward all humanity. Christ's absorption of the penalty appeases God's ὀργή (cf. Moo, *Romans*, 235–36). Ἱλαστήριον retains its cultic overtones from both Jewish and Greco-Roman religion. It simultaneously evokes the Day of Atonement and the expiation obtained by its rites (Lev 16:1–34; cf. Dunn, *Romans*, 1.171–72), and pagan rites designed to conciliate angry gods (cf. Finlan, *Background and Contents*, 156–57, who correctly points to the synecdochic character of ἱλαστήριον). This notion creates an apparent problem: the gods are ordinarily the *object* of appeasement. To some it seems implausible that Paul would say that God is appeasing his own wrath (e.g., Barrett, *Romans*, 77). Paul's logic depends on the inescapability of the wrath by any means available to humans, i.e., the law and God's covenant with the Israelites (3:1–8). God would thus need to provide such a means, and indeed he has done so in the gospel. The repugnance of human sacrifice (both ancient and modern) has colored the debate, and makes this reading seem unacceptably barbaric. One must keep in mind what Paul says in 1:32 regarding τὸ δικαίωμα τοῦ θεοῦ (ὅτι οἱ τὰ τοιαῦτα πράσσοντες ἄξιοι θανάτου εἰσίν), which he reinforces in 5:9 (δικαιωθέντες νῦν ἐν τῷ αἵματι αὐτοῦ σωθησόμεθα δι' αὐτοῦ ἀπὸ τῆς ὀργῆς), 6:23 (τὰ γὰρ ὀψώνια τῆς ἁμαρτίας θάνατος) and 8:1–11 (esp. v. 4, ἵνα τὸ δικαίωμα τοῦ νόμου πληρωθῇ ἐν ἡμῖν): somebody has to die, and God arranges a situation wherein the necessary death occurs.

[21] I interpret ἀνοχή as an attribute here, like δικαιοσύνη, meaning God's attitude of clemency or restraint which urges him to devise the solution for humanity that Paul outlines in 3:21–26 (cf. BDAG 86, s.v. 3). Cf. Rom 2:4, where Paul coordinates the word with μα-

him to disregard the sins which people have previously committed. The third emphasizes that this proof of his justice is happening *right now* in the gospel. The last shifts the syntax to a purpose/result clause with εἰς and the articular infinitive, and is the climax of the series. Paul thus explains how the gospel can be a δύναμις θεοῦ εἰς σωτηρίαν παντὶ τῷ πιστεύοντι: the sacrifice settles the penalty, such that he can acquit the wrongdoers at the eschatological trial without violating his justice.

Finally, Paul in the third section (3:27–31) merges his argument in 1:18–3:20 with his expansions of 1:16–17 toward an exposition of the legal logic of justification. The return to diatribe supports this integration stylistically. The theme of "boasting" (καύχησις, 2:17–23) serves as a point of entry for Paul's assertion of a νόμος πίστεως, in contrast to a νόμος ἔργων: "Where, then, is boasting? It was excluded. Through what sort of law? That of works? No, rather through the law of faith." (ποῦ οὖν ἡ καύχησις; ἐξεκλείσθη. διὰ ποίου νόμου; τῶν ἔργων; οὐχί, ἀλλὰ διὰ νόμου πίστεως). He then furnishes an explanation of νόμος πίστεως in v. 28: "For we reckon a person to be justified apart from works of law" (λογιζόμεθα γὰρ δικαιοῦσθαι πίστει ἄνθρωπον χωρὶς ἔργων νόμου).[22] Next, he reinforces the centrality of πίστις after a dialogical appeal to

---

κροθυμία and χρηστότης. A TLG search reveals that it is not very well attested outside of Christian literature. The entry in LSJ (148, s.v.) reveals that it most often refers to armistice, the cessation of battle. The concept of "forbearance" derives from the related verb ἀνέχεσθαι (LSJ 136, s.v. C.II; *TDNT* 1.359–60, s.v. ἀνέχω), "to bear with patience." Paul's usage of the word in 2:4 alongside other attributes would seem to justify a similar reading of it here; John Chrysostom thinks so, at any rate (*Hom. Rom.* 7, 486B, PG 60.445): οὐδὲ γὰρ ἂν ἔχοιτε εἰπεῖν, φησίν, ὅτι οὐκ ἀπελαύσατε πολλῆς ἀνοχῆς καὶ χρηστότητος, and cf. the similar nouns in the next sentence: τὸ δέ, «ἐν τῷ νῦν καιρῷ», τὴν πολλὴν δεικνύντος ἐστὶ δύναμιν καὶ φιλανθρωπίαν.

[22] The meaning of ἔργα νόμου is another vigorously contested question. Dunn has published extensively on this issue (see, e.g., "Works of the Law"; "Yet Once More"; "Noch einmal"). He argues, I think persuasively, that ἔργα νόμου often refer to boundary-markers between Jews and Gentiles: circumcision, dietary regulations, Sabbath observance, etc. These ἔργα "characterize the whole mindset of 'covenantal nomism' – that is, the conviction that status within the covenant (= righteousness) is maintained by doing what the law requires ('works of the law')" ("Yet Once More," 214). The boundary markers furthermore reinforce the cohesion of the community, and support the performance of other, more broadly construed, ἔργα νόμου. Paul argues, therefore, that Gentiles do not need to embrace the law or its "works" (*qua* boundary markers) – i.e., to become Jews – in order to experience the benefits of the Christ-event. This is all well, as long as we keep what Paul is doing in Rom 1:18–3:20 in focus. He initially raises the topic of ἔργα as *standards of judgment* at the eschatological trial (2:6–11), as the basis for the distribution of rewards and punishments. This move injects into the discussion a prominent motif in the literature of Second Temple Judaism, judgment according to works (see esp. Gathercole, *Where is Boasting*, chs. 1–2). In 3:20, Paul is again referring to the basis upon which "all flesh will *not* be justified" (ἐξ ἔργων νόμου οὐ δικαιωθήσεται πᾶσα σάρξ): "works of law" can thus *in principle* include the deeds *both* of Gentiles (2:12–16) and Jews (2:17–24). Insofar as circumcision is a most significant ἔργον, as it were a

universalism in vv. 29–30: "Or is God only [the God] of the Jews? Is he not also [the God] of the Gentiles? Yes, also of the Gentiles, if indeed 'God is one,' who will justify circumcision from faith and uncircumcision through faith." (ἢ Ἰουδαίων ὁ θεὸς μόνον; οὐχὶ καὶ ἐθνῶν; ναὶ καὶ ἐθνῶν, εἴπερ εἷς ὁ θεός ὃς δικαιώσει περιτομὴν ἐκ πίστεως καὶ ἀκροβυστίαν διὰ τῆς πίστεως.) The ἀναδίπλωσις of πίστις here performs the figure's normal function of italicizing the repeated element: faith alone is God's mechanism of justification for both circumcision and uncircumcision. It is difficult, however, to discern why Paul uses different prepositions, which must have virtually equivalent meanings in this context ("from" and "through" = "on the basis of"). They may subtly evoke 1:17 (ἐκ πίστεως) and 3:22 (διὰ τῆς πίστεως), and thereby summon the necessity of evangelism (the revelation of divine justice) in order to stimulate justifying πίστις. Paul concludes in v. 31 with a declaration that may seem self-contradictory: "Do we therefore cancel the law through faith? Of course not, we rather affirm the law." (νόμον οὖν καταργοῦμεν διὰ τῆς πίστεως; μὴ γένοιτο· ἀλλὰ νόμον ἱστάνομεν.) In order to comprehend what he means, we must first recognize that the law – both revealed and natural – needs to remain in full force as an instrument of comprehensive condemnation. The gospel does not repeal the law, it supplements it with a means of acquittal that upholds – and, at least until the eschaton, is the supreme manifestation of – divine justice. This observation helps to explain what "boasting" means: it refers broadly to the Jews' pride in their distinctive heritage and special covenant with God,[23] and it also refers more narrowly to one's posture at the eschatological trial in the assertion of sufficient obedience to the law (the possibility of which Paul admits in principle but denies in fact), or of favoritism from God which derives from his promises to the Israelites.[24] Paul can thus pit πί-

---

συνεκδοχή of obedience to all of the Torah's demands (again, as standards of judgment), it too is not sufficient and will furnish no protection from divine wrath. Paul thus appropriates ἔργα νόμου both universally (πᾶσα σάρξ) and particularly (as boundary-markers). The idea in 3:19a, that the law is speaking to those "in the law," also has a doubled reference: τοῖς ἐν τῷ νόμῳ obviously refers to Jews, but it must also include Gentiles, otherwise the purpose clause in v. 19b makes no sense. Those "in the law" are in its power, subject to condemnation, from which no ἔργα of any kind can provide an escape. Gaston (*Paul and the Torah*, 100–6) proposes an interesting alternative to reading ἔργα νόμου as deeds prescribed by the Torah, i.e., that it means the Torah's *effects*, as Paul uses τὸ ἔργον τοῦ νόμου in 2:15. This reading helps to explain 3:20b, since one of the effects of the Torah is ἐπίγνωσις ἁμαρτίας. One cannot, however, eliminate human deeds from the picture, because of 2:6 and 4:4.

[23] Paul unpacks this pride further in 2:17–20 and 9:1–4.

[24] On the latter, cf. Sanders' interpretation of 10:4 (τὴν ἰδίαν [δικαιοσύνην] ζητοῦντες): "'Their own righteousness,' in other words, means 'that righteousness which the Jews alone are privileged to obtain,' rather than 'self-righteousness which consists in individuals' presenting their merits as a claim upon God'" (*Paul, the Law, and the Jewish People*, 38). This interpretation collides with 10:5 and the quotation of Lev 18:5. While the references to "boasting" and "zeal" reinforce the general validity of Sanders' thesis, Paul seems to stress

στις against καύχησις, the latter referring to reliance upon oneself (including one's heritage) and the former to reliance upon Christ at the trial.

Therefore, in 3:21–31 Paul expands his second definition of the gospel substantially, outlining the logic underpinning his assertion that the gospel is δύναμις θεοῦ εἰς σωτηρίαν activated by faith toward the provision of acquittals at the eschatological trial. This can occur because of the ἀπολύτρωσις available through Christ. Paul's exegesis of his definition here moves from the punitive manifestation of δικαιοσύνη θεοῦ to the rewarding and redemptive. In this connection Paul attaches πίστις to it, and the meaning of "justice of God" *qua* "justification from God" begins to emerge.

6.4 'The faithfulness of Jesus Christ' (3:22, 26)?

A vigorously contested exegetical question arises in connection with 3:21–31, which further relates directly to Paul's usage of συνεκδοχή to capture the whole of the gospel's narrative by reference to its parts: the meaning of πίστις Ἰησοῦ Χριστοῦ in 3:22 and πίστις Ἰησοῦ in 3:26. A substantial number of scholars now contend, building upon Richard B. Hays' influential study of Galatians, *The Faith of Jesus Christ* (1983, ²2002), that these phrases refer to Christ's own faithfulness,[25] and that they function as shorthand references to the narrative of his death and resurrection.[26] This interpretation thus approaches πίστις Ἰησοῦ Χριστοῦ as an instance of συνεκδοχή (Hays prefers "metonymy")[27] with πίστις referring to Christ's fidelity to the mission given to

---

that the law cannot – and, most importantly, *will* not – fufill the hopes which his fellow Jews place in it. At the trial, law becomes an instrument of condemnation, and (whether one "boasts" in one's observance of it or not, or whether one hopes to "earn" salvation with "works," or one regards them as signs of "getting in and staying in") it inevitably results in guilty verdicts for all, Jew and Greek. (Cf. ibid., 45: "Those who have the righteousness that comes by observing the law ... do not have the righteousness of God – that is, true righteousness.") Gathercole (*Where is Boasting*, passim, esp. 197–215) establishes the relationship of boasting and obedience in the HB and Second Temple Jewish sources, and he argues compellingly that boasting in obedience is precisely what Paul is criticizing in Romans 2–3.

[25] Scholars had made similar arguments prior to Hays' study; for a history of the scholarship, see idem, *Faith of Jesus Christ*, 142–48.

[26] These two points are contentions of Hays' study that emerge from his demonstration of a "narrative substructure" of Paul's argumentation (see his ch. 1, esp. 21–31). In subsequent debate, however, the second has largely fallen out of view.

[27] See, e.g., *Faith of Jesus Christ*, xxx–xxxi. Trypho^II (*Trop*. 9) defines it thus: "Metonymy is part of an utterance which is fittingly put in the place of another, but which indicates that other thing according to what is related to it," μετωνυμία ἐστὶ μέρος λόγου ἐφ' ἑτέρου μὲν τινος κυρίως κείμενον, ἕτερον δὲ σημαῖνον κατὰ τὸ οἰκεῖον. See also Quintilian, *Inst*. 8.6.23 (noting the trope's similarity with συνεκδοχή); [Plutarch], *De Hom*. 2.23; Trypho^I, *Trop*. 6 (*RG* 3.195); Anonymous, *Trop*. 5 (*RG* 3.209); Cocondrius, *Trop*. 7 (*RG* 3.233–34). The illustrations often point to the names of gods replacing their domains of authority, e.g., Hephaes-

him by God. Hays is certainly correct to point out the compact nature of the phrase and its connection with narratives. The proposal has proven attractive, however, for several reasons that are not, strictly speaking, exegetical:[28] it brings Paul's writings into closer alignment with the canonical Gospels, since Jesus' fidelity can in principle include narratives about him prior to his death;[29] it stresses divine grace over human action;[30] it reinforces the perception of Paul's theology as grounded in a salvation-historical narrative;[31] and it further weakens the dominance of "traditional Protestant" (Lutheran) methods of reading Paul.[32] I have argued in chapter 5 that Paul takes full advantage of the ambiguities inherent in all of the terms of his second definition of the gospel – including πίστις, which already in Romans 1 refers to Paul's and the Roman Christians' fidelity to their duties (1:8, 12–15), to the faith that embraces the proclaimed gospel (1:5, 16), and to both at the same time (ἐκ πίστεως εἰς πίστιν, 1:17). The immediate contexts of none of these passages suggest that Paul has Christ's own πίστις in mind. So, how might συνεκδοχή be operating in the phrase? Is it possible to decide definitively between the objective interpretation of the genitive (faith *in* Jesus Christ) and the subjective interpretation (the faith *of* Jesus Christ) in this passage? I shall consider the second question first.

---

tus = fire, Demeter = harvest, Dionysius = wine, etc. Hays does not engage the ancient theory on μετωνυμία, but uses the term in a modern literary critical fashion. I regard συνεκδοχή as a category that better describes what Hays is talking about, i.e., that Jesus' fidelity (one part of his character) stands in for the tangible manifestations of his fidelity (the narrative of his death, burial, and resurrection) and its soteriological consequences.

[28] Cf. Hooker, "Πίστις Χριστοῦ," 324: "Indeed, from one point of view, one can almost say that if Paul does not use this idea [i.e., the faithfulness of Christ], he ought to!"

[29] See, e.g., Hays, *Faith of Jesus Christ*, 218–20.

[30] See, e.g., Johnson, "Romans 3:21–26," 78–79. Hays (*Faith of Jesus Christ*, 120) expresses concern that the "traditional" reading "has always carried the risk of turning faith into another kind of work, a human achievement." The resolution of the apparent tension between divine grace and human faith seems to be the primary benefit of reading Χριστοῦ as a subjective genitive, especially when it extends to instances of ἐκ/διὰ πίστεως (without an expressed genitive) with soteriological applications (e.g., Rom 5:1). It shifts all aspects of justification and salvation away from any human action and into the column of divine grace.

[31] See, e.g., Grieb, *Story of Romans*, xxi–xxiv, 35–42.

[32] Campbell, e.g., describes the "traditional anthropocentric reading" of 1:17 as "directed to the generic individual" and as something which "comes naturally to a good Protestant," and which has a distinct "Cartesian" cast ("Romans 1:17," 271–72). Note also his description of a quotation from Dunn as "positively Reformationist" ("Romans 1:17," 266, n. 6), and cf. idem, *Rhetoric of Righteousness*, 60–61. Somehow, in the late twentieth century, 'Lutheran' became and remains for some a term of invective, referring to a theological sickness that urgently needs to be purged from scholarship on Paul (see esp. Watson, *Paul, Judaism, and the Gentiles*, 27–50), instead of (more reasonably) a recognizable limitation of earlier scholarship stemming from unexamined presuppositions.

At the level of syntax, nouns of emotion or cognition frequently express their objects with the genitive.[33] Ancient authors regularly use πίστις with the objective genitive in a number of senses:[34] "belief in,"[35] "trust" or "confidence in,"[36] "proof of,"[37] and "guarantee" or "pledge of."[38] The use of the objective

---

[33] See Smyth 319, § 1331: "The Objective Genitive is passive in sense, and is very common with substantives denoting a frame of mind or an emotion." Cf. also BDF 90, § 163, citing Rom 10:2 (ζῆλος θεοῦ), also 2:7 (ὑπομονὴ ἔργου ἀγαθοῦ). Other examples include Rom 3:18 (quoting LXX Ps 35:2, οὐκ ἔστιν φόβος θεοῦ ἀπέναντι τῶν ὀφθαλμῶν αὐτῶν); 2 Cor 5:11 (εἰδότες οὖν τὸν φόβον τοῦ κυρίου ἀνθρώπους πείθομεν, θεῷ δὲ πεφανερώμεθα), 7:1 (ἐπιτελοῦντες ἁγιωσύνην ἐν φόβῳ θεοῦ); Gal 5:5 (ἡμεῖς γὰρ πνεύματι ἐκ πίστεως ἐλπίδα δικαιοσύνης ἀπεκδεχόμεθα, and cf. 1:14, περισσοτέρως ζηλωτὴς ὑπάρχων τῶν πατρικῶν μου παραδόσεων); Phil 1:25 (καὶ τοῦτο πεποιθὼς οἶδα ὅτι μενῶ καὶ παραμενῶ πᾶσιν ὑμῖν εἰς τὴν ὑμῶν προκοπὴν καὶ χαρὰν τῆς πίστεως); 2:1–2 (εἴ τις οὖν παράκλησις ἐν Χριστῷ, εἴ τι παραμύθιον ἀγάπης, εἴ τις κοινωνία πνεύματος, εἴ τις σπλάγχνα καὶ οἰκτιρμοί, πληρώσατέ μου τὴν χαράν); 1 Thess 1:3 (μνημονεύοντες ὑμῶν τοῦ ἔργου τῆς πίστεως καὶ τοῦ κόπου τῆς ἀγάπης καὶ τῆς ὑπομονῆς τῆς ἐλπίδος τοῦ κυρίου ἡμῶν Ἰησοῦ Χριστοῦ); 5:8 (ἡμεῖς δὲ ἡμέρας ὄντες νήφωμεν ἐνδυσάμενοι θώρακα πίστεως καὶ ἀγάπης καὶ περικεφαλαίαν ἐλπίδα σωτηρίας); Phlm 6 (ὅπως ἡ κοινωνία τῆς πίστεώς σου ἐνεργὴς γένηται ἐν ἐπιγνώσει παντὸς ἀγαθοῦ τοῦ ἐν ἡμῖν εἰς Χριστόν). See also Dunn, "Once More, πίστις Χριστοῦ," 251–52.

[34] In addition to the data cited below, see Matlock, "Detheologizing the πίστις Χριστοῦ Debate," esp. 9, nn. 22–23, and 19, n. 59.

[35] E.g., Cassius Dio, *Hist. Rom.* 1.6.3, referring to Numa: "For, since he doubted well the majority of people – because, on the one hand, they regard something of the same nature and kindred to them as if it is nothing better than themselves, and, on the other hand, by their belief in the divine they worship the invisible and the different as higher – he consecrated a certain precinct to the Muses...," ἐπειδὴ γὰρ εὖ ἠπίστατο τοὺς πολλοὺς τῶν ἀνθρώπων τὸ μὲν ὁμοφυές σφισι καὶ σύννομον ἐν ὀλιγωρίᾳ ὡς μηδὲν βέλτιον ἑαυτῶν ὂν ποιουμένους, τὸ δὲ ἀφανὲς καὶ ἀλλοῖον ὡς καὶ κρεῖσσον πίστει τοῦ θείου θεραπεύοντας, χωρίον τέ τι ταῖς Μούσαις ἱέρωσεν..... Note also, Philo, *Migr.* 171: "... just as has happened to countless sophists, who supposed wisdom to be the persuasive contrivance of arguments, but not the truest belief in real things," καθάπερ μυρίοις συνέβη τῶν σοφιστῶν, οἵτινες ᾠήθησαν σοφίαν πιθανὴν εἶναι λόγων εὕρεσιν, ἀλλ' οὐ πραγμάτων ἀληθεστάτην πίστιν; also *Mos.* 1.90, "Moses begins to perform wonders which were taught of before, thinking he would convert the witnesses from disbelief which hinders to belief in what is being said," δεικνύειν ἄρχεται Μωυσῆς ἃ προὐδιδάχθη τέρατα, νομίσας τοὺς θεασομένους ἐκ τῆς ἐπεχούσης ἀπιστίας εἰς πίστιν τῶν λεγομένων μεταβαλεῖν. See also Jewett, *Romans*, 279, nn. 94–96 for further literature.

[36] E.g., Plato, *Phaedr.* 275a, regarding writing: "For it will cause forgetfulness in the souls of those who learned it by their inattention to memory, inasmuch as, because of their trust in writing, they remember things from outside, by alien replicas, not by themselves, from within," τοῦτο γὰρ τῶν μαθόντων λήθην μὲν ἐν ψυχαῖς παρέξει μνήμης ἀμελετησίᾳ, ἅτε διὰ πίστιν γραφῆς ἔξωθεν ὑπ' ἀλλοτρίων τύπων, οὐκ ἔνδοθεν αὐτοὺς ὑφ' αὑτῶν ἀναμιμνῃσκομένους; Plutarch, *Brut.* 29.4: "And confidence in his character was greatly accruing, toward good will and reputation for him," καὶ μέγιστον ὑπῆρχεν αὐτῷ πρὸς εὔνοιαν καὶ δόξαν ἡ τῆς προαιρέσεως πίστις; Cassius Dio, *Hist. Rom.* 36.7.3, regarding Lucullus' assault of the Mesopotamian city of Nisibis: "And thus he demolished a certain part of the trench (for the barbarians earlier broke down the bridges) ... and, after crossing it the rest of the way, he took [the town] immediately, since the inner ring [of fortifications] was not very strong because of [their] confidence in those which had been previously erected outside of it," καὶ οὕτω τῆς τε τάφρου μέρος

genitive with πίστις evokes the subjective as well, and vice versa, for example: God's fidelity (to his promises) in 3:1–8; Abraham's trust (in God) in chapter 4; and, potentially, ("our") faith in Christ in 3:21–31.[39] In short, nothing about normal Greek syntax prevents πίστις Χριστοῦ from meaning "faith in Christ" any more or less than "faith(fulness) of Christ." They are equally available options to someone encountering the phrase for the first time in a text.[40]

Therefore, we must rely on the context. The phrase εἰς πάντας τοὺς πιστεύοντας in v. 22a provides a strong clue as to whose faith is in view, although supporters of the subjective interpretation have raised two objections to reading the verbal and nominal instances of the πιστ- stem in light of each other. First, Luke Timothy Johnson (among others) argues that, if διὰ πίστεως Ἰησοῦ Χριστοῦ refers to human faith, εἰς πάντας τοὺς πιστεύοντας would be redundant, so the former must therefore have a different referent.[41] Setting aside the

---

τι (τὰς γὰρ γεφύρας οἱ βάρβαροι προκατέρρηξαν) συνέχωσεν ..., καὶ διαβὰς αὐτὴν τὰ μὲν ἄλλα, οὐ πάνυ ἰσχυροῦ τοῦ ἔνδον κύκλου πίστει τῶν ἔξωθεν αὐτοῦ προβεβλημένων ὄντος, εὐθὺς εἷλε.

[37] This usage is very common in the philosophical sources, e.g., Epictetus, *Diatr.* 1.28.3, asking rhetorically, "What is the proof of this?" τίς τούτου πίστις; Also, Philo, *Virt.* 34: "And the sacred books contain the clearest proof of what was said [above]," τῶν δὲ λεχθέντων σαφεστάτην πίστιν αἱ ἱεραὶ βίβλοι περιέχουσιν.

[38] E.g., Xenophon, *Hell.* 3.4.5: when Agesilaus expresses some concern that Tissaphernes will break truce while he is away, the latter replies, "But it is possible for you to receive a guarantee of these things, with no deception whatsoever – if you do them [too] – that we will harm nothing of your governance during the truce," ἀλλ᾿ ἔξεστιν, ἔφη, σοὶ τούτων πίστιν λαβεῖν ἦ μὴν ἀδόλως ... σοῦ πράττοντος ταῦτα ἡμᾶς μηδὲν τῆς σῆς ἀρχῆς ἀδικήσειν ἐν ταῖς σπονδαῖς. Also, Josephus, *B.J.* 6.346, the message of Titus to besieged Jerusalem: "When I was near the temple, I again intentionally forgot the laws of war, and was urging you to spare your own holy places and to save the shrine for yourselves, giving a licence of departure and a pledge of safety," τοῦ ἱεροῦ πλησίον γενόμενος πάλιν ἑκὼν ἐξελαθόμην τῶν τοῦ πολέμου νόμων, φείσασθαι δὲ παρεκάλουν τῶν ἰδίων ὑμᾶς ἁγίων καὶ σῶσαι τὸν ναὸν ἑαυτοῖς, διδοὺς ἄδειάν τ᾿ ἐξόδου καὶ πίστιν σωτηρίας.

[39] On this point, see esp. Downing, "Ambiguity, Ancient Semantics, and Faith," 150–160.

[40] Contra Hays, *Faith of Jesus Christ*, 147: "Faith *in* Jesus Christ is not the most natural translation of πίστις Ἰησοῦ Χριστοῦ."

[41] "Romans 3:21–26," 79: "Why should Paul add *eis pantas tous pisteuontas*, if he has just said, 'through faith in Jesus Christ'? The added note of 'all' (*pantas*) lends some specificity, it is true, but not enough to make this added phrases necessary. On the other hand, a subjective reading makes the two phrases distinct. Now, with the righteousness of God being revealed *through the faith of Jesus*, the emphasis on God's gift is maintained." Johnson goes on to adduce ἐκ πίστεως εἰς πίστιν in 1:17 as a parallel. See also Hooker, "Πίστις Χριστοῦ," 322; Hays, *Faith of Jesus Christ*, 158 ("a ponderous redundancy"), and cf. 142 regarding Gal 3:22; Wright, "Romans," *NIB* 10.470. Campbell (*Rhetoric of Righteousness*, 62–63) avers that if Ἰησοῦ Χριστοῦ is an objective genitive, "the construction is clumsy. The needless repetition is doubly unusual in that the surrounding text is compact and carefully crafted.... This oscillation between prosaic brevity and verbose repetition is an embarrassment for the objec-

facts that Paul is capable of using πλεονασμός and that the repetition of the stem is an instance of ἀναδίπλωσις (cf. 3:30), Johnson apparently overlooks the ἔλλειψις of πεφανέρωται in v. 22a: the justice of God *has been made manifest* διὰ πίστεως Ἰησοῦ Χριστοῦ εἰς πάντας τοὺς πιστεύοντας. These prepositional phrases express the *medium* of revelation and its *destination* (in a manner similar to ἐκ πίστεως εἰς πίστιν in 1:17, expressing source and destination). In their construal with δικαιοσύνη θεοῦ, they distinguish the phenomenon of πίστις and the people who exhibit it:[42] δικαιοσύνη as "justification" has a method (διὰ πίστεως) and intended recipients (εἰς τοὺς πιστεύοντας).[43] As in 1:17, πίστις captures the numerous ways Paul has hitherto used it: the faith that embraces the gospel; the fidelity of those that proclaim it; and God's own fidelity which Paul links with his δικαιοσύνη in 3:1–8. Once again, Paul is taking advantage of the ambiguities in terminology and syntax. Second, Douglas A. Campbell, responding to Brian Dodd's article criticizing the subjective interpretation,[44] rejects any "transfer of sense from the verb to the noun," which he characterizes as "a critical assumption of the traditional reading" and as "the basic axiom for this paradigm."[45] He continues:

In fact such is the embeddedness of the axiom that many traditionalists assume in their discussions that only one semanitic motif is being dealt with.... Dodd himself illustrates this

---

tive genitive reading." Campbell's statement clashes with his correct observation (ibid., 82) that Paul is aiming here for a grand style, for which μακρολογία is typical, and figures like ἀναδίπλωσις and πλεονασμός are useful. Such "redundancies" are not at all embarrassing to Paul or to supporters of the objective interpretation, nor is their combination with methods of brevity, since the latter enables him to pack his generous use of language with dense content. The prescript of Romans offers an ideal example of the juxtaposition of methods of brevity and a grand style, as I argue in chapter 4 above.

[42] Cf. Gal 3:21–22: εἰ γὰρ ἐδόθη νόμος ὁ δυνάμενος ζῳοποιῆσαι, ὄντως ἐκ νόμου ἂν ἦν ἡ δικαιοσύνη· ἀλλὰ συνέκλεισεν ἡ γραφὴ τὰ πάντα ὑπὸ ἁμαρτίαν, ἵνα ἡ ἐπαγγελία ἐκ πίστεως Ἰησοῦ Χριστοῦ δοθῇ τοῖς πιστεύουσιν. In the protasis of v. 21, we read: "if a law which is able to make alive were given"; and in the apodosis: "justification would be from law." V. 22 then reverses the logical sequence, i.e., scripture "imprisoned all things under sin in order that the promise may be given." The phrase ἐκ πίστεως Ἰησοῦ Χριστοῦ belongs with ἐπαγγελία, i.e., "the promise [which is able to make alive] from faith in Jesus Christ" (via ἔλλειψις), or, more simply, "the promise [which is, or, which comes] from faith in Jesus Christ." Here, as in Rom 3:22, Paul distinguishes the phenomenon of faith in Christ, which has direct bearing upon God's soteriological methods, and the persons who benefit by their exhibition of it (τοῖς πιστεύουσιν).

[43] My arguments regarding the dual construal of the prepositional phrases (initially with the ellipsed πεφανέρωται, secondarily with δικαιοσύνη) solve two problems that Campbell notes, that of "causality" ("the believers' faith functions as both means and goal") and the objective reading's supposed failure to "complete the sense of the passage" (*Rhetoric of Righteousness*, 63).

[44] "Romans 1:17."

[45] "False Presuppositions," 715.

well, speaking repeatedly of "the term πιστ-" (passim), a lexical nonsense but nicely indicative of the traditionalist's monovalent basic assumption.[46]

In opposition to such "traditionalists," "christological advocates[47] detect a seam ... in Paul between the noun and the verb," and "they hold that the transfer of this meaning associated with the verb to substantives based on the same stem *is deeply problematic.*"[48] I agree that approaching πίστις as "monovalent" is interpretively unacceptable. Nonetheless, Campbell's rigid separation of πίστις and πιστεύειν does not seem justified. The reason that we can have a debate between taking Ἰησοῦ Χριστοῦ as subjective or as objective is the verbal idea in the noun upon which it depends. The proximity of πίστις and πιστεύειν in 3:22 are part of Paul's strategy of unpacking his second definition with interchanges between nominal and verbal forms. He means, in other words, for adjacent instances of the stem to be mutually illuminating, as a method not of limiting their potential contextual meanings but of broadening them, especially in a recapitulation that paves the way toward a discussion of Abraham's trust in God's promises that further unpacks the logic behind the association of πίστις and God's reckoning of someone εἰς δικαιοσύνην (4:3, 9). Abraham thus serves as a model not of Christ's faith but that of his followers, "to whom [righteousness] is about to be reckoned, to those who trust in the one who raised Jesus our Lord from the dead" (οἷς μέλλει λογίζεσθαι, τοῖς πιστεύουσιν ἐπὶ τὸν ἐγείραντα Ἰησοῦν τὸν κύριον ἡμῶν ἐκ νεκρῶν, 4:24). Even with Paul's maximization of the meanings of πίστις and πιστεύειν in Romans, however, the fidelity of Christ remains difficult to extract persuasively from the argumentative context of Rom 3:22 and 26.

Paul's gospel certainly has a narrative of Christ's death and resurrection as a central component. His definition of its essence in Rom 1:2–4 includes compressions of this narrative within two mythological expanded epithets, as I have shown. Συνεκδοχή helps him to condense the narrative in many other contexts as well. For example, at several points in his letters, Paul appears to expand the components of πίστις Ἰησοῦ Χριστοῦ:

Rom 4:23–25, οὐκ ἐγράφη δὲ δι' αὐτὸν μόνον ὅτι ἐλογίσθη αὐτῷ ἀλλὰ καὶ δι' ἡμᾶς, οἷς μέλλει λογίζεσθαι, τοῖς πιστεύουσιν ἐπὶ τὸν ἐγείραντα Ἰησοῦν τὸν κύριον ἡμῶν ἐκ νεκρῶν, ὃς παρεδόθη διὰ τὰ παραπτώματα ἡμῶν καὶ ἠγέρθη διὰ τὴν δικαίωσιν ἡμῶν.
Rom 10:9, ὅτι ἐὰν ὁμολογήσῃς ἐν τῷ στόματί σου κύριον Ἰησοῦν καὶ πιστεύσῃς ἐν τῇ καρδίᾳ σου ὅτι ὁ θεὸς αὐτὸν ἤγειρεν ἐκ νεκρῶν, σωθήσῃ.
1 Cor 15:3–4, 11, παρέδωκα γὰρ ὑμῖν ἐν πρώτοις, ὃ καὶ παρέλαβον, ὅτι Χριστὸς ἀπέθανεν ὑπὲρ τῶν ἁμαρτιῶν ἡμῶν κατὰ τὰς γραφὰς καὶ ὅτι ἐτάφη καὶ ὅτι ἐγήγερται τῇ ἡμέρᾳ τῇ τρίτῃ κατὰ τὰς γραφάς.... εἴτε οὖν ἐγὼ εἴτε ἐκεῖνοι, οὕτως κηρύσσομεν καὶ οὕτως ἐπιστεύσατε.

---

[46] Ibid.
[47] Campbell is referring with this phrase to himself and fellow supporters of the subjective genitive.
[48] Ibid., emphasis original.

1 Thess 4:14, εἰ γὰρ πιστεύομεν ὅτι Ἰησοῦς ἀπέθανεν καὶ ἀνέστη, οὕτως καὶ ὁ θεὸς τοὺς κοιμηθέντας διὰ τοῦ Ἰησοῦ ἄξει σὺν αὐτῷ.

We have here forms of πιστεύειν in the first and second person (τοῖς πιστεύουσιν [with ἡμᾶς as antecedent], πιστεύσῃς, ἐπιστεύσατε, πιστεύομεν). These obviously refer to the πίστις of Christians, not of Christ. The objects of this πίστις are expressed in ὅτι-clauses (Rom 10:9, 1 Thess 4:14), a prepositional phrase (Rom 4:24), and a main clause that Paul gathers up and inserts into another statement with οὕτως (1 Cor 15:11). In every case, he mentions Christ's resurrection, and the soteriological benefits of this event stand nearby in the contexts. The phrase πίστις Ἰησοῦ Χριστοῦ would be a logical and stylistically suitable compaction of these instances of πιστεύειν with summaries of the narrative about Christ. It furthermore permits Christ himself, as the one who sits at God's right hand, able to intercede for those who put their trust in him (Rom 1:4, 8:34), to serve as the object of πίστις. The narrative which Paul compresses in Ἰησοῦ Χριστοῦ pertains not only to what he *did* but what he *is doing* and *will do*. Συνεκδοχή is occurring in πίστις as well: it summons the narrative of each believer, how she or he came to hear about and accept the proclamation. It points to the precise cusp of the re-encounter of human and divine in the gospel, and the cessation of hostility between the two (Rom 5:1). It also points backward in time to models of πίστις, such as Abraham, whom Paul will shortly introduce into the discussion. Paul can even use πίστις as a συνεκδοχή of the gospel when he wants to emphasize its human dimension, as in Gal 1:23–24: "They were hearing only that 'our former persecutor is now *preaching the faith* which he was formerly destroying,' and they were praising God because of me" (μόνον δὲ ἀκούοντες ἦσαν ὅτι ὁ διώκων ἡμᾶς ποτε νῦν εὐαγγελίζεται τὴν πίστιν ἥν ποτε ἐπόρθει, καὶ ἐδόξαζον ἐν ἐμοὶ τὸν θεόν).[49] He does not, however, describe Christ as πιστός, or his heroic deeds and trust in God as πιστεύειν.[50] In the case of his letter to the Galatians, one might sup-

---

[49] Cf. also Gal 3:23–24: πρὸ τοῦ δὲ ἐλθεῖν τὴν πίστιν ὑπὸ νόμον ἐφρουρούμεθα συγκλειόμενοι εἰς τὴν μέλλουσαν πίστιν ἀποκαλυφθῆναι, ὥστε ὁ νόμος παιδαγωγὸς ἡμῶν γέγονεν εἰς Χριστόν, ἵνα ἐκ πίστεως δικαιωθῶμεν.

[50] Others have made similar points, e.g., Dunn, *Romans*, 1.166; Fitzmyer, *Romans*, 345. At a couple of points, Paul discusses Christ's obedience (Rom 5:19, Phil 2:8); he also closely associates faith and obedience in Rom 1:5. These are not adequate warrants for a subjective interpretation of πίστις Χριστοῦ (contra Hays, *Faith of Jesus Christ*, 152; Johnson, "Romans 3:21–26," 85–87). In Rom 1:5, Paul clearly means human faith (ἐν πᾶσιν τοῖς ἔθνεσιν), and in Rom 5:19 and Phil 2:8 faith is nowhere to be found in their contexts such that one can reasonably infer that Christ's obedience constitutes his πίστις. Campbell ("2 Corinthians 4:13") argues that in 2 Cor 4:13 Paul offers an instance where Christ is "the directly implicit subject" of πιστεύειν: ἔχοντες δὲ τὸ αὐτὸ πνεῦμα τῆς πίστεως κατὰ τὸ γεγραμμένον, «ἐπίστευσα, διὸ ἐλάλησα», καὶ ἡμεῖς πιστεύομεν, διὸ καὶ λαλοῦμεν. Campbell builds his case primarily around (1) a strongly participatory interpretation of τὸ αὐτὸ πνεῦμα, taking it to refer to the Holy

6.4 'The faithfulness of Jesus Christ' (3:22, 26)? 211

pose that Paul handed over to his readers a conception of the gospel *qua* Christ's fidelity, such that he can deploy the phrase and assume their comprehension of it. In the case of his letter to the Romans, which he addresses to a community he did not found, the members of his audience would presumably need to have such a conception from some other source in order for them to recognize the 'real' meaning of the phrase, and thus to override the soteriological and revelatory applications of human πιστεύειν in the context – in other words, to interfere with their reading of adjacent instances of the πιστ-stem in light of each other.[51] Patristic authors take this very step when they convert ἐκ πίστεως εἰς πίστιν to "from believing in *x* to believing in *y*" in their interpretations of 1:17.[52]

In sum, (1) Greek syntax equally supports both the subjective and objective interpretations of Ἰησοῦ Χριστοῦ with a noun like πίστις; (2) as in 1:16–17, πίστις appears alongside a form of πιστεύειν in 3:22, and the latter is con-

---

Spirit and not to a disposition of belief or trust (BDAG 833, s.v. 3.c), which the context suggests; and (2) a christological interpretation of LXX Ps 115, which he unnecessarily reads back into 2 Corinthians 4 (ibid., 343–48). He provides no evidence that early Christians interpret this psalm messianically, i.e., as if Christ is speaking it in the first person. The psalm's easy submission to such analysis (in Campbell's view, at any rate; 347) does not prove that Paul or other early Christians read in the same manner. Paul, with the quotation, claims the same attitude of fidelity in hardship that the psalmist professes. He takes the passage as an inspiration for "our" πιστεύειν and λαλεῖν. If he understands the psalm as oracular, it predicts not the attitude of Christ but of his followers, who must wait for the full realization of their hope, which Paul expresses as a matter of knowledge in v. 14: εἰδότες ὅτι ὁ ἐγείρας τὸν κύριον Ἰησοῦν καὶ ἡμᾶς σὺν Ἰησοῦ ἐγερεῖ καὶ παραστήσει σὺν ὑμῖν.

[51] My point applies as well to ἐκ πίστεως in 1:17, which some (see ch. 5, n. 88) read as "from the faithfulness of Christ." Campbell, for example, dichotomizes the cosmic and human dimensions of the gospel ("Romans 1:17," 272–73) as a method of making his case. In his "cosmic eschatological reading," he says: "Here God's eschatological saving righteousness functions dynamically ..., breaking into a chaotic or rebellious order from above but, crucially for Paul, here definitively in the Christ-event. The primary relationship by this reading is therefore that between God and the gospel in the context of the cosmos, not between the gospel and the individual (or nation)." He next correctly points out that ἐν αὐτῷ expresses agency with ἀποκαλύπτεται, and that "the eschaton is being realized in the context of the gospel." If the cosmic scope of the gospel is accepted, he reasons, "then an interpretation of ἐκ πίστεως in terms of anthropocentric faith is utterly impossible," since "[t]o make the eschatological disclosure of God's saving power conditional upon the believer's faith would be to press the role of anthropocentric faith rather too far.... It would be to make the coming of the eschaton dependent on individual faith, and this is theologically (and practically [!]) ludicrous." Campbell implicitly recognizes that ἔλλειψις is occurring in ἐκ πίστεως. According to the ancient theoretical sources on this figure, the reader should be able to infer the omitted element(s) from the context. Therefore, Campbell needs to show *from the context* how Paul cues his readers that they should understand him to have omitted Χριστοῦ, and that they should ignore παντὶ τῷ πιστεύοντι in 1:16 and πίστις in 1:5, 8 and 12 in figuring out what ἐκ πίστεως εἰς πίστιν is doing in its clause.

[52] See § 5.4.2 above.

textually relevant for discerning the meaning of the former; and (3) Paul gives several expansions of πίστις Ἰησοῦ Χριστοῦ that strongly support the objective reading. Συνεκδοχή indeed occurs in both elements of the phrase. The genitive stands in for the narrative of Christ's death and resurrection as well as for his exalted status and for the divine power that he wields as risen Son. Πίστις stands in for the circumstances that surround the believer's and community's initial and continuing encounter with the gospel. I thus conclude that the objective interpretation best captures what Paul means by the phrase on syntactical, contextual and rhetorical theoretical grounds.

6.5 Romans 9:1–10:21

To a much greater degree than in chapters 5–8,[53] Paul in chapters 9–11 explicitly returns to and builds upon his second definition of the gospel, and he also

---

[53] At a few points in 5:1–8:39, Paul returns to his second definition and its expansions in 3:21–31 with recapitulations that orient them to his arguments in their contexts. 5:6–11, for example, takes up the theme of intercessory sacrifice from 3:24–25, δικαιωθέντες νῦν ἐν τῷ αἵματι αὐτοῦ σωθησόμεθα δι' αὐτοῦ ἀπὸ τῆς ὀργῆς, which means "we" are καυχώμενοι ἐν τῷ θεῷ διὰ τοῦ κυρίου ἡμῶν Ἰησοῦ Χριστοῦ (5:9, 11). The themes of forensic eschatology and divine justice move to the front here, while faith and universalism take a back seat. 8:31–39 includes a snapshot of the eschatological trial: God is ὃς ἐγκαλέσει and ὁ δικαιῶν, and Christ ὁ κατακρινῶν and ὃς καὶ ἐντυγχάνει ὑπὲρ ἡμῶν. In both 5:6–9 and 8:31–39 Paul unites narrative elements and ideas buried within the συνεκδοχαί of 1:2–4 with the themes of 1:16–17. The passage from chapter 8 in particular specifies what being "appointed Son of God in power" means in terms of the forensic roles of Christ at the eschaton. If an enthronement myth lies behind 1:4, it may elaborate these duties as belonging solely to ὁ ἀποθανών, μᾶλλον δὲ ἐγερθείς, ὃς καί ἐστιν ἐν δεξιᾷ τοῦ θεοῦ (8:34). Also, in chapters 5–8 Paul turns to the subject of ethics, which he regards as a vital consequence of acceptance of the gospel and baptism, since the reception of the Spirit empowers ethical behavior. Paul will later call this phenomenon ἡ ἀνακαίνωσις τοῦ νοός (12:2), the reversal of an event narrated in 1:28, παρέδωκεν αὐτοὺς ὁ θεὸς εἰς ἀδόκιμον νοῦν. Ethical behavior flows not from obedience to the law's command but from the resuscitation of humanity's broken faculty of ethical reasoning. Paul significantly does not at this point place ethics entirely under the heading of human δικαιοσύνη. The word appears alongside other forensic terms in 8:1–11 (κατάκριμα, 8:1; νόμος τοῦ πνεύματος τῆς ζωῆς and νόμος τῆς ἁμαρτίας καὶ τοῦ θανάτου, 8:2; δικαίωμα, 8:4). Δικαιοσύνη moves most boldly into the territory of human ethical righteousness in 6:12–23, wherein Paul posits a transfer of cosmic affiliation, brought about by baptism, from the dominance of one set of forces to that of another. On one side stand ἁμαρτία, θάνατος and ἀδικία; on the other, θεός, χάρις and δικαιοσύνη. The ethical dimension is clearest in v. 13 (ὅπλα ἀδικίας, δικαιοσύνης). Paul's presentation of these terms as antithetical personified forces in this context overshadows his other applications of them elsewhere, although the latter do not entirely recede from view. This observation is especially true for δικαιοσύνη, which furthermore retains its forensic dimension, as v. 16 in particular illustrates (οὐκ οἴδατε ὅτι ᾧ παριστάνετε ἑαυτοὺς δούλους εἰς ὑπακοήν, δοῦλοί ἐστε ᾧ ὑπακούετε, ἤτοι ἁμαρτίας εἰς θάνατον ἢ ὑπακοῆς εἰς δικαιοσύνην; cf. 1:32, 6:7–8, 21 and esp. 23). Even when Paul treats such concepts as "sin," "death," "grace" and "justice"

appropriates aspects of his first definition as well. Up to this point Paul has (1) established comprehensive human culpability (1:18–3:20); (2) shown how the gospel is the solution to this problem, with verifications from Abraham and from a comparison of Adam and Christ (3:21–5:21); and (3) explained the benefits of the gospel in eschatological and ethical terms (6:1–8:39). Evidently Paul sees only one other major problem that requires solution: if the gospel is everything that he claims, why have the vast majority of Jews not embraced it? And how can God maintain his justice in condemning the Israelites who reject the gospel, given the promises he had previously made to their ancestors? As Paul's expressions of grief clearly indicate (9:1–2, 10:1), he wrestles with a subject of intense concern for himself, his audience in Rome, and other early Christians. His goal is consolation. They may all take solace in knowing that God's justice will work inexorably toward its full resolution. His strategy mainly involves a redefinition of Israel in light of his definitions of the gospel, his foregoing argument, and several oracles which he brings forward to speak to the questions under consideration.

The first definition of the gospel aids Paul in his transition from chapter 8 to the new topic of chapters 9–11, in particular his description of it as ὃ προεπηγγείλατο διὰ τῶν προφητῶν αὐτοῦ ἐν γραφαῖς ἁγίαις (1:2). Paul lays out God's promises with short summaries of Israel's previous interactions with God (9:4–5): his kin are the ones "who are Israelites; to whom belong the adoption, the glory, the covenants, the legislation, the cult, and the promises; to whom belong the ancestors, from whom Christ also [descended] according to the flesh" (οἵτινές εἰσιν Ἰσραηλῖται, ὧν ἡ υἱοθεσία καὶ ἡ δόξα καὶ αἱ διαθῆκαι καὶ ἡ νομοθεσία καὶ ἡ λατρεία καὶ αἱ ἐπαγγελίαι, ὧν οἱ πατέρες καὶ ἐξ ὧν ὁ Χριστὸς τὸ κατὰ σάρκα). This last phrase picks up portions of the mythological expanded epithet in 1:3 (τοῦ γενομένου ... κατὰ σάρκα), and with them Paul neatly frames the problem in general terms, since Christ and the gospel about him constitute for early Christians the fulfillment of the purpose behind Israel's reception of the honors listed. Paul then leaps directly to his subproposition in v. 6, which has two parts, the basic thesis (οὐχ οἷον δὲ ὅτι ἐκπέπτωκεν ὁ λόγος τοῦ θεοῦ) and an abbreviated proof (οὐ γὰρ πάντες οἱ ἐξ Ἰσραὴλ οὗτοι Ἰσραήλ).[54] In the following paragraphs he will redefine "Israel" in terms of a remnant in order to explain how "the word of God has not failed." He first supports the premise that "not all from Israel are Israel" with the examples of the birth of Isaac (and the implied rejection of Ishmael) and the selection of Jacob over Esau (9:7–13). The second proof introduces a concept of

---

as personified abstractions or real agents at work in the cosmos, he can simultaneously speak of them in terms of their functions and consequences.

[54] Keck (*Romans*, 229), Wright ("Romans," *NIB* 10.635), and Jewett (*Romans*, 572–73) also recognize v. 6a to convey the thesis statement.

central importance to Paul's argument, specifically ἡ κατ' ἐκλογὴν πρόθεσις: God has an objective in his election of these individuals.

This "purpose according to election" brings along with it the problem of theodicy which Paul has already briefly addressed in 3:1–8: "What then will we say? There is not injustice with God, is there? Of course not." (τί οὖν ἐροῦμεν; μὴ ἀδικία παρὰ τῷ θεῷ; μὴ γένοιτο, 9:14). Paul reaffirms the principle of election by quoting a passage (Exod 33:19) wherein God declares his absolute right to show mercy on whomever he wishes. He then quotes "scripture" speaking to Pharaoh, declaring that God has selected him "so that I may show my power in you, and so that my name may be proclaimed in all the earth" (ὅπως ἐνδείξωμαι ἐν σοὶ τὴν δύναμίν μου καὶ ὅπως διαγγελῇ τὸ ὄνομά μου ἐν πάσῃ τῇ γῇ, 9:17, Exod 9:16). Paul has now laid a foundation for his contention that election – both as "mercy" and as "hardening" – happens for a purpose, and not capriciously.[55] But how is this *fair*? "Therefore you will say to me, why then does he still find fault? For who has resisted his will?" (Ἐρεῖς μοι οὖν, τί [οὖν] ἔτι μέμφεται; τῷ γὰρ βουλήματι αὐτοῦ τίς ἀνθέστηκεν; 9:19) Paul's response – unsatisfactory as it may seem[56] – turns these questions back upon the one who asks them: is it *fair* for any human to interrogate his or her creator or the purpose for which he or she is created? God has the right to use people however he wants, and the purpose that Paul entertains resembles that put forward to Pharaoh, "to demonstrate his wrath and to make known his might" (ἐνδείξασθαι τὴν ὀργὴν καὶ γνωρίσαι τὸ δυνατὸν αὐτοῦ, 9:22). Election in this case serves the aim of demonstrating God's justice (as wrath) and power.

In the discussion so far, divine justice overshadows the other themes of the second definition, especially faith and evangelism. And, as the initial counterpart to universalism, Paul has focused on the particularity of God's relationship with Israel. He broadens the picture to explain the inclusion of the Gentiles and the division of Israel into the remnant and the "hardened" in 9:24–10:21. After stating the premise upon which he will proceed in 9:24 (οὓς καὶ ἐκάλεσεν ἡμᾶς οὐ μόνον ἐξ Ἰουδαίων ἀλλὰ καὶ ἐξ ἐθνῶν), he again leads with scriptures in order to confirm that the gospel's enclosure of Gentiles and an Israelite remnant is a matter of prophecy, of what God has promised. Paul next in 9:30–33 reveals God's method of separating the remnant from the

---

[55] The verb θέλει in his summary statement, ἄρα οὖν ὃν θέλει ἐλεεῖ, ὃν δὲ θέλει σκληρύνει (9:18), captures both of Paul's points in the two passages cited: God can show mercy on whomever he "wishes," and he has a clear goal in mind, an "intention."

[56] Dodd (*Romans*, 158–59) perceives a serious error on Paul's part here: "Paul has driven himself into a position in which he has to deny that God's freedom of action is limited ... by moral considerations. 'Has the potter no right over the clay?' It is a well-worn illustration. But the trouble is that a man is not a pot; he *will* ask, 'Why did you make me like this?' and he will not be bludgeoned into silence. It is the weakest point in the whole epistle." Cf. the response by Barrett (*Romans*, 188–89).

"hardened": he uses the law to set a trap.[57] The "hardened" put their trust in the law as a means of access to δικαιοσύνη,[58] and are scandalized by the gospel's offer of it to the Gentiles ἐκ πίστεως.[59] Paul seems aware of just how disagreeable this notion of a trap would be. He assures his readers that he relentlessly petitions God ὑπὲρ αὐτῶν εἰς σωτηρίαν while confronting his fellow Jews with their harmful zeal οὐ κατ' ἐπίγνωσιν (10:1–2), since it leads them to refuse to submit to divine justice (10:3). Paul then avers: τέλος γὰρ νόμου Χριστὸς εἰς δικαιοσύνην παντὶ τῷ πιστεύοντι (10:4).[60] Given that he has been discussing God's purposes, τέλος probably means "goal" here.[61] The law, which,

---

[57] Cf. E. E. Johnson, "Romans 9–11," 227: "If God consistently calls impartially and also keeps faith with Israel, then why have the Gentiles reached the finish line and left Israel in the dust? The answer is that God rigged the racecourse."

[58] Cf. Hooker ("Christ: The 'End of the Law,'" 128), who aptly observes: "Paul's accusation, then, is not simply that Israel did not attain righteousness, but that she pursued the wrong goal, which meant inevitably that she misunderstood the role of the law." She says later: "The contrast is not between *law* and faith, but between two principles set out *in* the law – 'works' (v. 20) and 'faith' (vv. 21–2)" (ibid.). Nonetheless, Gathercole (*Where is Boasting*, 226–30) correctly stresses that Paul is attacking more than Israel's pursuit of a wrong goal, but rather the entire logic of obedience to the Torah as a means of eschatological vindication: "Israel's error was to expect God's righteousness as a result of their obedience rather than simply to believe the promise" (228); and, "However, as soon as the Torah is seen as primarily directing the reader to faith in the one God ... as the means to justification irrespective of what works are performed, then the pattern works → justification → boasting is abandoned. We are left only with the pattern faith → justification" (230).

[59] Cranfield (*Romans*, 2.504–5) describes 9:30–33 as a "definition in summary form" of "the nature of Israel's obedience and the nature of the Gentiles' obedience," which Paul "proceeds to expand, develop, and clarify" in chapter 10. I disagree with this description. From a formal standpoint, 9:30–33 does not declare the essence and function of "obedience" (or of anything else), nor do any predicative statements ("obedience is..." or "does...") occur. The passage instead addresses what the Jews were and the Gentiles were not pursuing, and why the former failed. Cf. my remarks on 10:4 in nn. 60 and 62 below.

[60] 10:4 recalls 1:16 in some interesting ways. The two sentences have remarkably similar structures, i.e., "for [the gospel] is God's power resulting in salvation for everyone who believes," and, "for Christ is the law's goal resulting in justification for everyone who believes." The second statement meaningfully explicates the first, when the implications of the gospel relative to the function and purpose of the law (cf. 9:33) are in view.

[61] I need to underscore "probably" in this sentence, because the meaning of τέλος is impossible to establish definitively (for summaries of the positions, see Cranfield, *Romans*, 2.516–19). A firm choice between "goal" and "end" (in the sense of termination) has a wide-ranging impact upon one's perception of the role of law in Paul's argument in Romans and his theology as a whole (see esp. Räisänen, *Paul and the Law*, 53–56). As I have suggested above, Paul needs to retain a condemnatory function of the law; if he means in 10:4 something similar to what he says in 8:1 (οὐδὲν ἄρα νῦν κατάκριμα τοῖς ἐν Χριστῷ Ἰησοῦ), the law's ability to condemn has come to an end εἰς δικαιοσύνην παντὶ τῷ πιστεύοντι (which I perceive as expressing result or purpose, contra Sanders, *Paul, the Law, and the Jewish People*, 39). His statements in v. 3 and the questions in vv. 5–8 would thus regard human δικαιοσύνη as the pronounced verdict of δίκαιος at the eschatological trial. Paul's ethics do not directly rely upon the commands but upon "fulfillment" (another possible translation of τέλος, see LSJ

as he argues in chapter 2 and 3, functions as an instrument of comprehensive condemnation, has the appearance and deeds of Christ (i.e., the gospel) as its ultimate objective, since the benefits of these events (principally in this context the reception of δικαιοσύνη) extend to both Jews and Gentiles. 10:4 also speaks to the nature of the trap, as Paul's subsequent exposition reveals. Ἡ δικαιοσύνη ἡ ἐκ νόμου relies upon doing what the law prescribes in order to "live," while ἡ ἐκ πίστεως δικαιοσύνη adopts a posture of submission (such is what Paul designs the quoted questions in 10:6–8 to signify) to God's purpose and of refusal to encroach upon that which is properly God's domain of authority.[62]

Paul thus elaborates his second definition of the gospel toward confirmation of his thesis that "the word of God has not failed": we have the universalism that he introduces in 9:24; the activity of divine justice in its capacity to make humans just by faith; the salvation at the eschatological trial that some obtain by their submission to God; and most importantly the power that God exercises over the whole situation, expressed as ἡ κατ' ἐκλογὴν πρόθεσις. In 10:9–13, however, Paul actually merges his two definitions of the gospel into a unified statement that addresses both the essence and the function of τὸ ῥῆμα τῆς πίστεως ὃ κηρύσσομεν,

9 ὅτι ἐὰν ὁμολογήσῃς ἐν τῷ στόματί σου κύριον Ἰησοῦν καὶ πιστεύσῃς ἐν τῇ καρδίᾳ σου ὅτι ὁ θεὸς αὐτὸν ἤγειρεν ἐκ νεκρῶν, σωθήσῃ· 10 καρδίᾳ γὰρ πιστεύεται εἰς δικαιοσύνην, στόματι δὲ ὁμολογεῖται εἰς σωτηρίαν. 11 λέγει γὰρ ἡ γραφή, πᾶς «ὁ πιστεύων ἐπ' αὐτῷ οὐ καταισχυνθήσεται». 12 οὐ γάρ ἐστιν διαστολὴ Ἰουδαίου τε καὶ Ἕλληνος, ὁ γὰρ αὐτὸς κύριος πάντων, πλουτῶν εἰς πάντας τοὺς ἐπικαλουμένους αὐτόν· 13 «πᾶς» γὰρ «ὃς ἂν ἐπικαλέσηται τὸ ὄνομα κυρίου σωθήσεται».

9 ... that if you confess with your mouth that Jesus is Lord, and you believe with your heart that God raised him from the dead, you will be saved. 10 For it is believed with the heart re-

---

1772, s.v., I.1, "consummation") of the law (which does not mean the same thing as "keeping" or "doing"!) through the Spirit and its "fruit" (i.e., virtue, Gal 5:19–24), or upon the spiritual resuscitation of the broken faculty of ethical reasoning (Rom 12:1–2, ἡ ἀνακαίνωσις τοῦ νοός) – so the purview of the law comes to an end here as well. Thus, while I incline toward reading τέλος as "goal" for the reasons stated in the text above, I can still readily produce support for "end," and I conclude that he wants both meanings on the table, not because he could not make up his mind (Räisänen, *Paul and the Law*, 53), but because this move permits him to make two contextually relevant points with a single sentence (so also Barrett, *Romans*, 197–98).

[62] Cf. 9:19–25. I would classify 10:4 as "quasi-definitional," since (1) it is a predicative statement of what Christ (= εὐαγγέλιον) is (τέλος νόμου) and what he does (εἰς δικαιοσύνην παντὶ τῷ πιστεύοντι); (2) it is very succinct, insofar as each element compresses Paul's foregoing arguments and following exposition; (3) it is not, however, as complete as 1:2–4 or 16–17; in other words, Paul does not seem to want to define Christ *in toto*, but to define him relative to νόμος as its τέλος; (4) the following passage unpacks the concepts within the statement very carefully, in order to build toward a definition in 10:9–12 of the gospel, which merges his earlier definitions.

sulting in justification, and it is confessed with the mouth resulting in salvation. 11 For scripture says: everyone "who believes in him will not be put to shame" (Isa 28:16). 12 For there is no distinction of the Jew and the Greek, for he is the same Lord of all, who enriches all those who call on him. 13 For "everyone, whoever calls on the name of the Lord, will be saved" (Joel 3:5).

The merged definition echoes the structure of 1:16–17, with a basic definition (10:9) followed by abbreviated proofs (10:10–13). From 1:2–4, we have the condensed narrative of God raising Jesus from the dead, and three instance of promises (or, pre-proclamations) in the holy scriptures (including v. 8); from 1:16–17, we have πίστις and πιστεύειν, σωτηρία, δικαιοσύνη, and universalism. He again defines essence in terms of narrative and Jesus' current status (κύριος Ἰησοῦς, ὁ θεὸς αὐτὸν ἤγειρεν ἐκ νεκρῶν), and function in terms of salvation as acquittal at the eschatological trial (σωθήσῃ, σωτηρία, and human δικαιοσύνη). Paul then returns to the theme of evangelism under which he subsumes his merged definition in v. 8 (τὸ ῥῆμα τῆς πίστεως ὃ κηρύσσομεν). He has saved it for last to give it special emphasis:

14 Πῶς οὖν ἐπικαλέσωνται εἰς ὃν οὐκ ἐπίστευσαν; πῶς δὲ πιστεύσωσιν οὗ οὐκ ἤκουσαν; πῶς δὲ ἀκούσωσιν χωρὶς κηρύσσοντος; 15 πῶς δὲ κηρύξωσιν ἐὰν μὴ ἀποσταλῶσιν; καθὼς γέγραπται, «ὡς ὡραῖοι οἱ πόδες τῶν εὐαγγελιζομένων [τὰ] ἀγαθά».

14 How then will they call on one in whom they have not believed? And how might they believe that which they have not heard? And how might they hear apart from someone who proclaims? 15 And how might they proclaim unless they are sent? Just as it has been written, "How beautiful are the feet of those who announce good tidings."

This remarkable passage draws all of the strands of his definitions of the gospel, as well as his previous expansions and utilizations of them, into a new unity here in the heart of his argument that the "hardening" of the Israelites conforms to God's purpose. The climactic chain of questions in vv. 14–15 may initially seem irrelevant to the immediate context, but they speak to a point that Paul perceives as crucial: that the problem here derives not from whether the Israelites have *heard* (ἀκοή) the message but whether they *heeded* (ὑπακοεῖν) it and embraced (πιστεύειν) it. Again, Paul summons the prophets to verify his claims: Isa 53:1 to link faith and hearing (κύριε, τίς ἐπίστευσεν τῇ ἀκοῇ ἡμῶν;); Ps 18:15 to confirm that the message has made its way εἰς τὰ πέρατα τῆς οἰκουμένης; and Deut 32:21 and Isa 65:1–2 to show that gospel's rejection by the Jews was anticipated, as was its acceptance by the Gentiles.

In his recapitulation, expansion and merger of his definitions in 10:9–15, Paul also speaks indirectly to one of his objectives in writing to Rome, namely his solicitation of support for his mission to one of the 'ends of the universe,' Spain. He intends to go not to his fellow Jews, but to the Gentiles who reside there. Vv. 14–15 in particular address the logic behind his request that his addressees *send* him to *preach* so that others may *hear* and *believe* and *call upon* the name of the Lord for salvation.

6.6 Conclusion

Paul, in 3:1–8, 21–31, and 9:1–10:21, reappropriates the component elements of his definitions of the gospel in Romans 1 in order explicate them further and to take advantage of the ambiguities that he deliberately places within them. His handling of the second definition reveals that he regards it as positing a nexus between a group of themes: divine power, forensic eschatology, faith, evangelism, and universalism. He works out the validity of the relationships between individual themes in his exposition, producing recombinations that bring forward latent implications of both definitions. 1:16–17 thus serves as a facilitator of subsidiary arguments (for example, that divine πίστις and δικαιοσύνη are not inconsistent; or, that the word of God has not failed), which in turn confirm the basic thesis, that the gospel is God's power resulting in salvation for everyone who believes. The strategies of brevity that Paul uses in his definitions also continue to feature prominently in his exegeses, most notably in 3:21–31. Therefore, we may characterize Paul's argument in Romans as definitional, at least in part.

Chapter 7

Conclusion

This study has now taken us through the ancient sources on definition (ὅρος) and brevity (βραχυλογία, συντομία, βραχύτης) in order to apply them to the interpretation of Paul's definitions of the gospel in Rom 1:2–4 and 16–17. I have shown that philosophical and rhetorical definitions share important features, namely brevity and a stipulative function, although rhetorical definitions do not generally pursue scientific accuracy or full coextension with the definiendum by the location of it on a taxonomic map of related phenomena. Both strive to "unfold" the definiendum (ἐξάπλωσις) clearly and credibly, to capture its essence and function in a nutshell. We have also seen how definitions can operate in the process of εὕρεσις in forensic contests as one of the στάσεις; how they can play a supporting role in deliberation by articulating the concepts buried within a question, or how they can become the central question of a deliberation; and how they can function as προθέσεις in encomia of the gods or of abstractions. The investigation of brevity has revealed its prominence in the ancient rhetorical curriculum, and has exposed several tactics of "unfolding" the definiendum concisely, including those which Paul wields to great effect in his definitions of the gospel. With συνεκδοχή he asserts the unitary testimony of the prophets and scriptures regarding the coming Son of God, while summoning to mind specific oracles known to himself and his addressees. Συνεκδοχή permits him also to press the entirety of the Son into the first definition with two ἀντιθέσεις, the temporal (ἀρχή and τέλος) and anthropological (σάρξ and πνεῦμα), which act as bookends, creating a gap that his audience can fill with their own knowledge. This figure is also characteristic of the form that he adopts in structuring vv. 3–4, the mythological expanded epithet. Paul similarly presses the entirety of humanity into his second definition with the ἀντίθεσις of two exclusive cultural groups (Jew and Gentile) that encloses all other groups between them. Ἔλλειψις of conjunctions, pronouns and definite articles in vv. 2–4 give the passage a dense character that sets these verses apart from the μακρολογία of the prescript and "thanksgiving." In ἐκ πίστεως εἰς πίστιν the figure enables Paul to invest v. 17 with multiple layers of meaning through the suppression of genitive dependents for each πίστις. Ἀπὸ κοινοῦ allows ἐν δυνάμει in v. 4 to construe with both τοῦ ὁρισθέντος and υἱοῦ θεοῦ, and πρῶτον in v. 16 with both τῷ πιστεύοντι (the Jew who believes first) and Ἰουδαίῳ (the Jew's priority εἰς σωτηρίαν). And, most importantly, Paul's definitions take full advantage of the ambiguities inherent in the terms included within them. In the case of πίστις and πιστεύειν, he uses the stem once to refer to acceptance of the gospel (ὑπακοὴ πίστεως, 1:5) and twice to refer to fidelity (1:8, 12). Πίστις in vv. 16–17 partakes of both of these meanings. He furthermore leaves δύναμις, σωτηρία and δικαιοσύνη θεοῦ undefined. The confluence of these terms along with ὀργὴ θεοῦ in v. 18 makes it sufficiently clear that God unleashes the gospel as an instrument of his justice in the context of the looming eschatological trial, although Paul does not remove other resonances from view. The two definitions act together in conformity with the common instruction that a definition should declare the essence and function of the definiendum. Paul sets forth the former as part of his credentials as an apostle: the gospel is nothing less than the most important promise given by God, that which pertains to his Son. Paul thus indirectly praises himself by praising the gospel which he received a commission to proclaim. The latter he deploys as the πρόθεσις of his letter. In a similar manner it explains why he urgently wants to come to Rome, and why he is not ashamed of the gospel. At points in his argument, he returns to his definitional πρόθεσις and his earlier definition of the gospel's essence. He reorganizes their component terms into new logical sequences. He also maximizes the semantic ranges of the terms and takes full advantage of syntactical ambiguities. He relies upon his addressees to furnish unstated content from their own knowledge and experiences of the gospel. He deftly unpacks them toward a rich exploration of their implications.

Once it has been shown that Paul utilizes methods of brevity in 1:2–4 and 16–17 in order to economize the language and to evoke a wealth of implied content, we should be on the lookout for similar condensations of wording and content elsewhere in his writings. When confronted with a statement that seems impenetrably dense, the questions which have proven helpful in the present study can supply additional assistance. What might Paul want his audience to supply from the context in order to complete the sense? Are words or phrases playing multiple syntactical roles? Might Paul be loading the statement with implied content with συνεκδοχή? If the ambiguity derives from the meaning of one or more words, could Paul want the multiple meanings of these words active in the statement? This final question when applied to 1:16–17 brought forward Paul's maximization of the semantic ranges of πίστις and δικαιοσύνη as a primary feature of both the composition of his definition and his exegesis of it in his argument. Even terms so central to his thought and to the proclamation of his gospel do not have fixed, singular meanings for him.

The analysis of 1:2–4 and 16–17 as definitions furthermore raises the question of where else Paul might construct and deploy definitions or use definitional argument. For example, he begins his argument in 1 Corinthians

15 by expanding τὸ εὐαγγέλιον with a series of relative clauses which seem to behave like ὑπογραφαί that summon to mind the Corinthian Christians' prior and present empirical experiences of it,[1] followed by an extremely brief recitation of its narrative content.[2] The latter does not have the form of a definition, but in Paul's argument it certainly has the function of one. The gospel *is* the confirmed death, burial and resurrection of Christ on behalf of our sins according to the scriptures; we preached it, and you believed it. The reality of resurrection is thus established. Therefore, the claim by some in Corinth, ὅτι ἀνάστασις νεκρῶν οὐκ ἔστιν (15:12), is unsustainable and absurd. The summary of the gospel thus functions as a conceptual anchor that Paul constructs in order to defeat a proposition; he subsequently uses it to establish the relationship between the particular event of Christ's resurrection and the general event of the resurrection of Christians at the eschaton. Definitional argument also does not require fully articulated statements of essense and function, as we saw in Romans 9. It can proceed on the basis of assumptions (Israelites are the children of Abraham), simple counter-statements (Israelites are not the children of flesh but the children of promise), and undefined concepts ("remnant").

My study also confirms that Paul thoroughly engages ancient rhetorical theory and popular philosophy in a way that is more than fleeting. In fact, he uses both from the very inception of Romans, since the decision to use definitional argument would happen during the first stage of composition (εὕρεσις), and his definitions conform to the philosophical axiom that ὅρος should state the essence and function of the definiendum. This engagement is clear also in his λέξις, since he taps the wealth of rhetorical resources to achieve the brevity necessary for definition. Since his definitions of the gospel frame the προοίμιον, with the second playing the role of a πρόθεσις, and since the argument either assumes these definitions or expands their elements further, we may frame the questions regarding the purpose(s) and rhetorical/epistolary γένος of Romans with greater clarity. What is Paul asking his readers to decide? Is the point to be adjudicated (τὸ κρινόμενον) somewhere in the second definition, or does it lie elsewhere, such that Paul crafts 1:16–17 and its confirmation in order to achieve some other goal? And what is the relationship of the πρόθεσις to its proof? Is Paul demonstrating *that* the gospel is God's power resulting in salvation for everyone who believes, or *how*? Would his audience

---

[1] 15:1–2: γνωρίζω δὲ ὑμῖν, ἀδελφοί, τὸ εὐαγγέλιον ὃ εὐηγγελισάμην ὑμῖν, ὃ καὶ παρελάβετε, ἐν ᾧ καὶ ἑστήκατε δι' οὗ καὶ σῴζεσθε, τίνι λόγῳ εὐηγγελισάμην ὑμῖν εἰ κατέχετε, ἐκτὸς εἰ μὴ εἰκῇ ἐπιστεύσατε.

[2] 15:3–5: παρέδωκα γὰρ ὑμῖν ἐν πρώτοις, ὃ καὶ παρέλαβον, ὅτι Χριστὸς ἀπέθανεν ὑπὲρ τῶν ἁμαρτιῶν ἡμῶν κατὰ τὰς γραφάς καὶ ὅτι ἐτάφη καὶ ὅτι ἐγήγερται τῇ ἡμέρᾳ τῇ τρίτῃ κατὰ τὰς γραφάς καὶ ὅτι ὤφθη Κηφᾷ εἶτα τοῖς δώδεκα. Paul continues with further appearances which confirm Christ's resurrection.

of Roman Christians regard part or all of his definitions of the gospel as controversial, or does the controversy lie elsewhere, for example, in Paul himself or in the reputation of his teachings about the gospel's implications? What precisely is he convincing them to think and to do, and how do his definitions and confirmations help him to achieve these objectives?

Returning now at the end to the topic with which I began in chapter 1, the historical Paul furnishes in Romans an answer to the what-if that Luke poses in Acts 17. Paul does not address an audience of philosophers, but he closely conforms to philosophical and rhetorical instruction on definitions in his sophisticated statements of the essence and function of the gospel. He achieves whatever level of completeness that he attempts through evocation and strategic ambiguity. With his coordinated definitions he signals to his audience that his letter will demand careful attention, intense intellectual engagement, and a thorough knowledge of the scriptures. This decision perfectly befits the seriousness of what he sets out to show, that the gospel deserves praise, and that he merits their support in his proclamation of it in new territories.

Bibliography

Ancient sources: abbreviations and editions

All "LCL" volumes are Cambridge, MA: Harvard University Press or New York: Putnam's Sons; "OCT" volumes are Oxford: Oxford University Press; "Teubner" volumes are Leipzig: Teubner, Stuttgart: Teubner, or München: K. G. Saur; "Budé" volumes are Paris: Les Belles Lettres. For the reader's convenience, I also give volumes of English translations (ET) where available if they are not already part of the cited edition.

Classical sources

Corpora

Ancient Epistolary Theorists (*AET*). Abraham J. Malherbe, ed. and trans., *Ancient Epistolary Theorists* (SBLSBS 19; Atlanta: Scholars Press, 1988).
Furley/Bremer. William D. Furley and Jan Maarten Bremer, eds. and trans., *Greek Hymns: Selected Cult Songs from the Archaic to the Hellenistic Period* (2 vols.; STAC 9–10; Tübingen: Mohr Siebeck, 2001).
Isis Aretalogies. Maria Totti, ed., *Ausgewählte Texte der Isis- und Sarapis-Religion* (Subsidia Epigraphica 12; Hildesheim: Georg Olms, 1985).
Kirk/Raven. G. S. Kirk, J. E. Raven and M. Schofield, eds. and trans., *The Presocratic Philosophers: A Critical History with a Selection of Texts* (2nd ed.; Cambridge: Cambridge University Press, 1983).
Long/Sedley. Anthony A. Long and David N. Sedley, eds. and trans., *The Hellenistic Philosophers* (2 vols.; Cambridge: Cambridge University Press, 1987).
Orphic Hymns (*Orph. Hymn*). Apostolos N. Athanassakis, trans., *The Orphic Hymns: Text, Translation and Notes* (SBLTT 12; Atlanta: Scholars Press, 1977).
Papyri Graecae Magicae (PGM). Karl Preisendanz and Albert Henrichs, eds. and trans., *Papyri Graecae Magicae: Die Griechischen Zauberpapyri* (2 vols; 2nd ed.; Teubner, 1973–74). ET Hans Dieter Betz, ed., *The Greek Magical Papyri in Translation, Including the Demotic Spells* (2nd ed.; Chicago: University of Chicago Press, 1992).
Rhetores Graeci (*RG*). L. Spengel and C. Hammer, eds., *Rhetores Graeci Vol. I* (Teubner, 1894), L. Spengel, ed., *Rhetores Graeci Vol. II* (Teubner, 1853), and idem, ed., *Rhetores Graeci Vol. III* (Teubner, 1853).
Rhetores Graeci (*RG*-W). Christian Walz, ed., *Rhetores Graeci* (9 vols.; Stuttgart and Tübingen: J. G. Cottae, 1832–36).
Rhetores Latini Minores (*RLM*). Carolus Halm, ed., *Rhetores Latini Minores* (Teubner, 1863).
Stoicorum Veterum Fragmenta (*SVF*). Hans F. A. von Arnim, ed., *Stoicorum Veterum Fragmenta* (4 vols.; Teubner, 1903–1924).
Suda. Ada Adler, ed., *Suidae lexicon* (5 vols.; Teubner, 1928–30; repr. 1971).

Individual authors

Aelius Aristides, *Orationes* (*Or.*). F. W. Lenz and C. A. Behr, eds., *P. Aelii Aristides opera quae exstant opera omnia*, vol. 1, *Orationes I–XVI complectens* (Leiden: Brill, 1976–80). Bruno Keil, ed., *Aelii Aristides Smyrnaei quae supersunt omnia*, vol. 2, *Orationes XVII–LIII* (rev. ed.; Berlin: Weidmann, 1958). ET C. A. Behr, trans., *P. Aelius Aristides: The Complete Works* (2 vols.; Leiden: Brill, 1981, 1986).

[Aelius Aristides], *Ars rhetorica* (*Rhet.*) Michel Patillon, ed. and trans., *Pseudo-Aelius Aristide, Ars Rhétorique* (2 vols.; Budé, 2002). ET of book 1: George A. Kennedy, trans., *Later Greek Rhetoric Fascicle I* (self-published, 2000), 75–107. ET of book 2: Ian Rutherford, *Canons of Style in the Antonine Age:* Idea-*Theory in its Literary Context* (Oxford: Clarendon, 1998), 124–53.

Aelius Herodian, *De soloecismo et barbarismo* (*Soloec.*). Augustus Nauck, ed., *Lexicon Vindobonese* (St. Petersburg: Eggers; Leipzig: Voss, 1867; repr. Hildesheim: Olms, 1969).

Alexander of Aphrodisias, *In Aristotelis Topicorum* (*In. Ar. Top.*). Maximillian Wallies, ed., *Alexandri Aphrodisi in Aristotelis topicorum libros octo commentaria* (Commentaria in Aristotelem Graeca 2; Berlin: Georg Reimer, 1891).

Alexander Rhetor, Περὶ τῶν τῆς διανοίας καὶ τῆς λέξεως σχημάτων (*Fig.*). *RG* 3.9–40.

[Anacharsis], *Epistulae* (*Ep.*). Abraham J. Malherbe, ed., *The Cynic Epistles: A Study Edition* (SBLSBS 12; Missoula: Scholars Press, 1977), 35–51, trans. Anne M. McGuire.

Andocides, *De mysteriis* (*Myst.*). Douglas MacDowell, ed., *Andokides: On the Mysteries* (Oxford: Clarendon, 1962). ET K. J. Maidment and J. O. Burtt, trans., *Minor Attic Orators* (2 vols.; LCL, 1941, 1954), 1.325–451.

Anonymous, *Carmen de figuris vel schematibus* (*Carm. Fig.*). *RLM* 63–70.

Anonymous, Περὶ ποιητικῶν τρόπων (*Trop.*). *RG* 3.207–14.

Anonymous, Περὶ σχημάτων (*Fig.*). *RG* 3.171–73.

Anonymous, Προλεγόμενα τῆς ῥητορικῆς (*Proleg.*). *RG*-W 6.33–44.

Anonymous Seguerianus, Τέχνη τοῦ πολιτικοῦ λόγου (*Rhet.*). Marvin R. Dilts and George A. Kennedy, eds. and trans., *Two Greek Rhetorical Treatises from the Roman Empire: Introduction, Text and Translation of the Arts of Rhetoric Attributed to Anonymous Seguerianus and to Apsines of Gadara* (MnemSup 168; Leiden: Brill, 1997), 1–73.

Antiphon, *Tetralogy* (*Tetr.*). Fridericus Blass and Theodorus Thalheim, eds., *Antiphontis orationes et fragmenta* (Teubner, 1914). ET K. J. Maidment, trans., *Minor Attic Orators* (2 vols.; LCL, 1941), 1.34–145.

Aphthonius, *Progymnasmata* (*Prog.*). *RG* 2.21–56. ET George A. Kennedy, trans., *Progymnasmata: Greek Textbooks of Prose Composition and Rhetoric* (SBLWGRW 10; Atlanta: Society of Biblical Literature, 2003), 89–127.

Apsines, *Ars rhetorica* (*Rhet.*). Dilts and Kennedy, *Two Greek Rhetorical Treatises*, 75–239.

Aquila Romanus, *De figuris sententiarum et elocutionis* (*Fig.*). *RLM* 21–37.

Aristotle, *Analytica posteriora* (*An. post.*). W. D. Ross, ed., *Aristotle's Prior and Posterior Analytics: A Revised Text with Introduction and Commentary* (Oxford: Clarendon, 1949). ET Hugh Tredennick, trans., *Aristotle: Posterior Analytics* (LCL, 1960), 2–261.

—, *Ars rhetorica* (*Rhet.*). W. D. Ross, ed., *Aristotelis ars rhetorica* (OCT, 1959). ET John Henry Freese, trans., *Aristotle: The "Art" of Rhetoric* (LCL, 1926).

—, Ἀθηναίων πολιτεία (*Ath. pol.*). Hans Oppermann, *Aristotelis Ἀθηναίων πολιτεία* (Teubner, 1961). ET H. Rackham, trans., *Aristotle: The Athenian Constitution* (LCL, 1952), 2–188.

—, Fragments (fr.). Valentinius Rose, ed., *Aristotelis qui ferebantur librorum fragmenta* (Teubner, 1966).

—, *Metaphysica* (*Metaph.*). W. D. Ross, ed., *Aristotle's Metaphysics: A Revised Text with Introduction and Commentary* (2 vols.; Oxford: Clarendon, 1958). ET Hugh Tredennick, trans., *Aristotle: The Metaphysics* (2 vols.; LCL, 1933–35).

—, *Topica* (*Top*.). W. D. Ross, ed., *Aristotelis topica et sophistici elenchi* (OCT, 1958). ET E. S. Forster, trans., *Aristotle: Topics* (LCL, 1960), 263–739.
[Aristotle], *Rhetorica ad Alexandrum* (*Rhet. Alex.*). Manfred Fuhrmann, ed., *Anaximenes: Ars rhetorica vulgo fertur Aristotelis ad Alexandrum* (Teubner, 2000). ET H. Rackham, trans., *Aristotle: Rhetorica ad Alexandrum* (LCL, 1957), 257–449.
Cicero, *Brutus* (*Brut.*). E. Malcovati, ed., *M. Tullius Cicero: Brutus* (Teubner, 1965). ET G. L. Hendrickson, trans., *Cicero: Brutus* (rev. ed.; LCL, 1962), 18–293.
—, *De finibus bonorum et malorum* (*Fin.*). L. D. Reynolds, ed., *M. Tulli Ciceronis de finibus bonorum et malorum* (OCT, 1998). ET H. Rackham, trans., *Cicero: De finibus bonorum et malorum* (2nd ed.; LCL, 1931).
—, *De inventione* (*Inv.*). E. Stroebel, ed., *M. Tulli Ciceronis scripta quae manserunt omnia*, Fasc. 2.: *Rhetorici libri duo qui vocantur de inventione* (Teubner, 1965). ET H. M. Hubbell, trans., *Cicero: De inventione* (LCL, 1949), 2–346.
—, *De natura deorum* (*Nat. d.*). W. Ax, ed., *M. Tulli Ciceroni scripta quae manserunt omnia*, Fasc. 45, *De natura deorum* (Teubner, 1949). ET H. Rackham, trans., *Cicero: De natura deorum* (LCL, 1933), 2–387.
—, *De officiis* (*Off.*). C. Atzert, ed., *M. Tulli Ciceroni scripta quae manserunt omnia*, Fasc. 48, *De officiis* (Teubner, 1958), 1–160. ET Walter Miller, trans., *Cicero: De officiis* (LCL, 1913).
—, *De oratore* (*De or.*). K. Kumaniecki, ed., *M. Tullius Cicero: De oratore* (Teubner, 1969). ET E. W. Sutton and H. Rackham, trans., *Cicero: De oratore Books I–II* (LCL, 1942); H. Rackham, trans., *Cicero: De oratore Book III* (LCL, 1942), 2–185.
—, *De partitione oratoria* (*Part. or.*). A. S. Wilkins, ed., *M. Tulli Ciceronis rhetorica* (2 vols.; OCT, 1903), vol. 2. ET H. Rackham, trans., *Cicero: De partitione oratoria* (LCL, 1942), 310–421.
—, *De respublica* (*Resp.*). K. Ziegler, ed., *M. Tulli Ciceroni scripta quae manserunt omnia*, Fasc. 39, *De re publica* (Teubner, 1949). ET Clinton Walker Keyes, trans., *Cicero: De re publica* (LCL, 1928), 2–285.
—, *Orator ad M. Brutum* (*Or.*). Wilkins, *M. Tulli Ciceronis rhetorica*, vol. 2. ET H. M. Hubbel, trans., *Cicero: Orator* (rev. ed.; LCL, 1962), 306–509.
—, *Topica* (*Top.*). Wilkens, *M. Tulli Ciceronis rhetorica*, vol. 2. ET H. M. Hubbell, trans., *Cicero: Topica* (LCL, 1949), 377–459.
[Cicero], *Rhetorica ad Herennium* (*Rhet. Her.*). Frederick Marx and Winfred Trillitzsch, eds., *M. Tulli Ciceronis: Incerti auctoris de ratione dicendi ad C. Herennium* (Teubner, 1963). ET Henry Caplan, trans., *[Cicero]: Rhetorica ad Herennium* (LCL, 1954).
Cleanthes, *Hymn to Zeus*. Johan C. Thom, ed. and trans., *Cleanthes' Hymn to Zeus: Text, Translation, and Commentary* (STAC 33; Tübingen: Mohr Siebeck, 2005).
Cocondrius, Περὶ τρόπων (*Trop.*). *RG* 3.230–43.
Demetrius, *De elocutione* (*Eloc.*). Doreen C. Innes, ed. and trans., *Demetrius: On Style* (LCL, 1995).
[Demetrius], Τύποι ἐπιστολικοί (*Typ.*). *AET* 30–41.
Demosthenes, *Oratio 9 Philippica 3* (*3 Philipp.*). M. R. Dilts, ed., *Demosthenis orationes* (3 vols.; OCT, 2002–8), 100–20. ET J. H. Vince, trans., *Demosthenes I: Philippics* (LCL, 1926), 222–65.
—, *Oratio 18 de corona* (*Cor.*). Dilts, *Demosthenis orationes*, 1.209–318. ET C. A. Vince and J. H. Vince, trans., *Demosthenes II: De corona* (LCL, 1926), 3–229.
—, *Oratio 19 de falsa legatione* (*Fals. leg.*). Dilts, *Demosthenis orationes*, 2.1–112. ET C. A. Vincea and J. H. Vince, trans., *Demosthenes II: De falsa legatione* (LCL, 1926), 232–473.
—, *Oratio 20 adversus Leptinem* (*Lept.*). Dilts, *Demosthenis orationes*, 2.113–63. ET J. H. Vince, trans., *Demosthenes I: Against Leptines* (LCL, 1926), 487–603.

—, *Oratio 23 in Aristocratem* (*Aristocr.*). Dilts, *Demosthenis Orationes*, 2.263–330. ET J. H. Vince, trans., *Demosthenes III: Against Aristocrates* (LCL, 1935), 212–367.

Dio Chrysostom, *Orationes* (*Or.*) Guy D. Budé, ed., *Dionis Chrysostomi Orationes* (2 vols.; Teubner, 1916–19). ET J. W. Cohoon and H. Lamar Crosby, trans., *Dio Chrysostom* (5 vols.; LCL, 1932–51).

Diodorus Siculus. Fr. Vogel, C. Th. Fischer and L. Dindorf, eds., *Diodori bibliotheca historica* (6 vols.; repr. Teubner, 1964–70). C. H. Oldfather, trans., *Diodorus Siculus: The Library of History* (12 vols.; LCL, 1933–67).

Diogenes Laertius. Miroslav Marcovich, ed., *Diogenis Laertii vitae philosophorum* (3 vols.; Teubner, 1999–2002). ET R. D. Hicks, trans., *Diogenes Laertius: Lives of the Eminent Philosophers* (2 vols.; LCL, 1972).

Dionysius of Halicarnassus, *Antiquitates romanae* (*Ant. rom.*). C. Jacoby, ed., *Dionysii Halicarnasei antiquitatem Romanarum quae supersunt* (4 vols.; repr. Teubner, 1967). ET Earnest Cary, trans., *Dionysius of Halicarnassus: The Roman Antiquities* (7 vols.; LCL, 1937–50).

—, *De compositione verborum* (*Comp.*). H. Usener and L. Radermacher, eds., *Dionysius Halicarnaseus: Quae exstant* (2 vols. [5 and 6 of above, s.v. *Ant. rom.*]; Teubner, 1965), 2.3–43.

—, *De Demosthene* (*Dem.*). Usener and Radermacher, *Dionysius Halicarnaseus*, 1.127–254. ET Stephen Usher, trans., *Dionysius of Halicarnassus: Critical Essays* (2 vols.; LCL, 1974, 1985), 1.232–455.

—, *De Isaeo* (*Is.*). Usener and Radermacher, *Dionysius Halicarnaseus*, 1.93–124. ET Usher, *Dionysius of Halicarnassus*, 1.170–231.

—, *De Isocrate* (*Isoc.*). Usener and Radermacher, *Dionysius Halicarnaseus*, 1.54–92. ET Usher, *Dionysius of Halicarnassus*, 1.100–69.

—, *De Lysia* (*Lys.*). Usener and Radermacher, *Dionysius Halicarnaseus*, 1.8–53. ET Usher, *Dionysius of Halicarnassus*, 1.16–99.

—, *De Thucydide* (*Thuc.*). Usener and Radermacher, *Dionysius Halicarnaseus*, 1.323–418. ET Usher, *Dionysius of Halicarnassus*, 1.456–633.

—, *Epistula ad Pompeium Geminum* (*Pomp.*). Usener and Radermacher, *Dionysius Halicarnaseus*, 2.221–48. ET Usher, *Dionysius of Halicarnassus*, 2.349–99.

Epictetus, *Dissertationes* (*Diatr.*). Henricus Schenkl, ed., *Epicteti dissertationes ab Arriani digestae* (Teubner, 1965). ET W. A. Oldfather, trans., *Epictetus: The Discourses as Recorded by Arrian; Fragments; Encheiridion* (2 vols.; LCL, 1925–28).

Epicurus, *Ad Herodotum epistula prima de rerum natura* (*Herod.*). Hermann Usener, ed., *Epicurea* (Sammlung Wissenschaftlicher Commentare; Teubner, 1966), 1–32. ET Cyril Bailey, ed. and trans., *Epicurus: Extant Remains* (Oxford: Clarendon, 1926), 18–55.

—, *Ad Menoeceum epistula tertia moralis* (*Menoec.*). Usener, *Epicurea*, 57–66. ET Bailey, *Epicurus*, 82–93.

Galen, *De differentia pulsuum* (*Diff. puls.*), book 4. C. G. Kühn, ed., *Claudii Galeni opera omnia* (20 vols.; repr. Hildesheim: Georg Olms, 2001), 8.695–765.

—, *Definitiones medicae* (*Def. med.*). Kühn, *Claudii Galeni opera omnia*, 19.346–462.

[Galen], *De historia philosophica* (*Hist. Phil.*). Kühn, *Claudii Galeni opera omnia*, 19.222–345.

Georgius Choeroboscus, Περὶ τρόπων ποιητικῶν (*Trop.*). RG 3.244–56.

Hermogenes, Περὶ ἰδεῶν (*Id.*). Hugo Rabe, ed., *Hermogenis opera* (repr. Teubner, 1985), 213–413. ET Cecil W. Wooten, trans., *Hermogenes' On Types of Style* (Chapel Hill: University of North Carolina Press, 1987).

—, Περὶ στάσεως (*Stas.*). Rabe, *Hermogenis opera*, 28–92. ET Malcolm Heath, *Hermogenes, On Issues: Strategies of Argument in Later Greek Rhetoric* (Oxford: Clarendon Press, 1995).

[Hermogenes], *Progymnasmata* (*Prog.*). Rabe, *Hermogenis opera*, 73–88. ET Kennedy, *Progymnasmata*, 73–88.
Hesiod, Fragments (fr.). R. Merkelbach and Martin L. West, eds., *Fragmenta Hesiodea* (Oxford: Clarendon Press, 1967).
—, *Opera et dies* (*Op.*). Martin L. West, ed., *Hesiod: Works and Days* (Oxford: Clarendon, 1978). ET Glenn W. Most, ed. and trans., *Hesiod: Works and Days* (LCL, 2006), 86–153.
—, *Theogonia* (*Theog.*). Martin L. West, ed., *Hesiod: Theogony* (Oxford: Clarendon, 1966). ET Glenn W. Most, ed. and trans., *Hesiod: Theogony* (LCL, 2006), 2–85.
Homer, *Hymns*. Martin L. West, ed. and trans., *Homeric Hymns* (LCL, 2003).
Isocrates, *De pace*. Basilius G. Mandilaras, ed., *Isocrates: Opera omnia* (3 vols.; Teubner, 2003), 2.192–233. ET George Norlin and Larne van Hook, trans., *Isocrates* (3 vols.; LCL, 1928–45), 2.2–97.
—, *Nicocles* (*Nic.*). Mandilaras, *Isocrates*, 2.28–45. ET Norlin and van Hook, *Isocrates*, 1.38–113.
Julius Victor, *Ars rhetorica* (*Rhet.*). R. Giomini and M. S. Celentano, eds., *C. Iulii Victoris ars rhetorica* (Teubner, 1980). (I retain the paragraph divisions of *RLM* 373–448 and give the pages in *AET* 62–65 [Jerome Neyrey, trans.].)
Lesbonax, Περὶ σχημάτων (*Fig.*). David L. Blank, ed., *Lesbonax:* Περὶ σχημάτων (Sammlung griechischer und lateinischer Grammatiker 7; Berlin: de Gruyter, 1988), 129–216.
[Libanius], Ἐπιστολιμαῖοι χαρακτῆρες (*Epist.*). *AET* 66–81.
Longinus, *Ars rhetorica*, Fragments (*Rhet.*, fr.). Michel Patillon and Luc Brisson, eds. and trans., *Longin: Fragments, Art Rhétorique* (Budé, 2001), 143–234.
Lucian, *De morte Pererini* (*Peregr.*). M. D. MacLeod, *Lucian: Opera* (4 vols.; OCT, 1972–87), 3.188–205. ET A. M. Harmon, trans., *Lucian V* (LCL, 1936), 2–51.
—, *Quomodo historia conscribenda sit* (*Hist. cons.*). MacLeod, *Lucian*, 3.287–319. ET K. Kilburn, trans., *Lucian VI* (LCL, 1959), 2–73.
—, *Scytha* (*Scyth.*). MacLeod, *Lucian*, 3.379–91. ET Kilburn, *Lucian VI*, 240–57.
Menander Rhetor, Γενεθλίων διαίρεσις τῶν ἐπιδεικτικῶν (*Epid.*). D. A. Russell and N. G. Wilson, eds. and trans., *Menander Rhetor* (Oxford: Clarendon, 1981).
Mithras Liturgy (*Mith. lit.*) = PGM IV.475–820. Hans Dieter Betz, ed. and trans., *The "Mithras Liturgy": Text, Translation and Commentary* (STAC 18; Tübingen: Mohr Siebeck, 2003).
Mithridates, *Letter*. Luigi Torraca, ed. and trans., *Marco Giunio Bruto: Epistole Greche* (Collana di Studi Greci; Naples: Liberia Scientifica Editrice, 1959), 5–6. ET Robert Matthew Calhoun, "The *Letter* of Mithridates: A Neglected Item of Ancient Epistolary Theory," in *Pseudepigraphie und Verfassersfiktion in frühchristilichen Briefen* (eds. Jörg Frey, Jens Herzer, Martina Janssen, and Clare K. Rothschild; WUNT 246; Tübingen: Mohr Siebeck, 2009), 295–330.
Nicolaus, *Progymnasmata* (*Prog.*). Joseph Felten, ed., *Nicolai Progymnasmata* (Teubner, 1913). ET Kennedy, *Progymnasmata*, 129–72.
Philostratus, *De epistulis* (*Epist.*). *AET* 42–43.
—. *Vita Apollonii* (*Vit. Apoll.*). C. L. Kayser, ed., *Flavii Philostrati opera* (2 vols.; Teubner, 1870–71; repr. Hildesheim: Georg Olms, 1964), 1.1–344. ET Christopher P. Jones, ed. and trans., *Philostratus: The Life of Apollonius of Tyana* (2 vols.; LCL, 2005).
—. *Vitae sophistarum* (*Vit. soph.*). Kayser, ed., *Flavii Philostrati opera*, 2.1–127. ET Wilmer Cave Wright, trans., *Philostratus: The Lives of the Sophists* (LCL, 1922), 2–315.
Phoebammon, Περὶ σχημάτων ῥητορικῶν (*Fig.*). *RG* 3.43–56.
Plato, *Euthyphro* (*Euthyphr.*). John Burnet, ed., *Platonis opera* (5 vols.; OCT, 1906–24), 1.2–16. ET Harold North Fowler, trans., *Plato: Euthyphro* (LCL, 1914), 3–59.

—, *Gorgias* (*Gorg.*). E. H. Dodds, ed., *Plato: Gorgias: A Revised Text with Introduction and Commentary* (Oxford: Clarendon, 1959). ET W. R. Lamb, trans., *Plato: Gorgias* (LCL, 1925), 249–533.

--, *Phaedrus* (*Phaedr.*). Burnet, *Platonis opera*, 2.227–79. ET Harold North Fowler, trans., *Plato: Phaedrus* (LCL, 1914), 407–579.

—, *Protagoras* (*Prot.*). Burnet, *Platonis opera*, 3.309–62. W. R. M. Lamb, trans., *Plato: Protagoras* (LCL, 1924), 86–257.

—, *Sophista* (*Soph.*). Burnet, *Platonis opera*, 1.216–69. ET Harold North Fowler, trans., *Plato: Sophist* (LCL, 1921), 261–459.

—, *Symposium* (*Symp.*). Burnet, *Platonis opera*, 2.172–223. ET W. R. M. Lamb, trans. *Plato: Symposium* (LCL, 1925), 74–245.

Plutarch, *Brutus* (*Brut.*). K. Ziegler, ed., *Plutarchi vitae parallelae* (vol. 2.1; Teubner, 1960), 135–83. ET Bernadotte Perrin, trans., *Plutarch's Lives VI: Dion and Brutus* (LCL, 1918), 126–247.

—, *De garrulitae* (*Garr.*). M. Pohlenz and W. Sieveking, eds., *Plutarchi moralia* (vol. 3; Teubner, 1972), 279–311. ET W. C. Helmbold, trans., *Plutarch's Moralia VI* (LCL, 1939), 395–467.

—, *Lycurgus* (*Lyc.*) Ziegler, *Plutarchi vitae parallelae* (vol. 3.2; Teubner, 1973), 1–48. ET Bernadotte Perrin, trans., *Plutarch's Lives I: Lycurgus and Numa* (LCL, 1914), 204–303.

—, *Numa*. Cl. Lindskog and K. Zieger, eds., *Plutarchi vitae parallelae* (vol. 3.2), 49–85. ET Perrin, *Plutarch's Lives I*, 306–83.

—, *Phocion* (*Phoc.*). Ziegler, *Plutarchi vitae parallelae* (vol. 2.1), 1–31. ET Bernadotte Perrin, trans., *Plutarch's Lives VIII* (LCL, 1919), 144–233.

—, *De pythiae oraculis* (*Pyth. orac.*). Pohlenz and Sieveking, *Plutarchi Moralia* (vol. 3), 25–59. ET F. C. Babbitt, *Plutarch's Moralia V* (LCL, 1936), 256–345.

—, *De superstitione* (*Superst.*). Hans Gärtner, ed., *Plutarchi Moralia* (vol. 1; Teubner, 1993), 338–54. ET F. C. Babbitt, *Plutarch's Moralia II* (LCL, 1928), 452–95.

[Plutarch], *Apophthegmata laconica*. W. Nachstädt, W. Sieveking and J. B. Titchener, eds., *Plutarchi Moralia* (vol. 2; Teubner, 1971), 110–224. ET F. C. Babbitt, trans., *Plutarch's Moralia III* (LCL, 1931), 240–469.

—, *De Homero* (*De Hom.*). J. F. Kindstrand, ed., *[Plutarchi] de Homero* (Teubner, 1990). ET J. J. Keaney and Robert Lamberton, eds. and trans., *[Plutarch]: Essay on the Life and Poetry of Homer* (APAACS 40; Atlanta: Scholars Press, 1996).

—, *Regum et imperatorum apophthegmata* (*Reg. imp. apoph.*). Nachstädt, Sieveking and Titchener, *Plutarchi Moralia* (vol. 2), 1–109. ET Babbitt, *Plutarch's Moralia III*, 3–53.

Quintilian, *Institutio oratoria* (*Inst.*). Donald A. Russell, ed. and trans., *Quintilian: The Orator's Education* (5 vols.; LCL, 2001).

Rufus, *Ars rhetorica* (*Rhet.*). Michel Patillon, ed. and trans., *Rufus: Art Rhétorique* (Budé, 2001), 236–84.

Rutilius Lupus, *De figuris sententiarum et elocutionis* (*Fig.*). Edward Brooks, Jr., ed., *P. Rutilii Lupi de figuris sententiarum et elocutionis: Edited with Prolegomena and Commentary* (MnemSup 11; Leiden: Brill, 1970).

Sextus Empiricus, *Adversus mathematicos* (*Math.*). Hermann Mutschmann, ed., *Sexti Empirici opera* (vol. 2; Teubner, 1914), and J. Mau, ed., *Sexti Empirici opera* (vol. 3; Teubner, 1954). ET R. G. Bury, *Sextus Empiricus* (4 vols; LCL, 1933–49), vols. 2–4.

—, *Pyrrhoniae hypotyposes* (*Pyr.*). Hermann Mutschmann, ed., *Sexti Empirici opera* (vol. 1; Teubner, 1912). ET Bury, *Sextus Empiricus*, vol. 1.

Stobaeus, *Anthologium* (*Anth.*). Curtis Wachsmuth and Otto Hense, eds., *Ioannis Stobaei anthologium* (5 vols; Berlin: Weidmann, 1958).

Theon, *Progymnasmata* (*Prog.*). Michel Patillon and Giancarlo Bolognesi, eds. and trans., *Aelius Théon: Progymnasmata* (Budé, 1997). (I use this edition's reconstructed sequence of exercises, as well as citing *RG* pp.) ET Kennedy, *Progymnasmata*, 1–72.

Tiberius Rhetor, Περὶ τῶν παρὰ Δημοσθένει σχημάτων (*Fig.*). Guilelmus Ballaira, ed., *Tiberius de figuris Demosthenis* (Rome: Edizioni dell'Ateneo, 1968).
Trypho[I], Περὶ τρόπων (*Trop.*). *RG* 3.191–206.
Trypho[II], Περὶ τρόπων (*Trop.*). Martin L. West, ed., "Tryphon *De Tropis*," *CQ* 15 n.s. (1965): 230–48. (This article replaces the text of "Gregory of Corinth," *RG* 3.215–26.)
Varro, *De lingua latina* (*De ling. lat.*). Georgius Goetz and Fridericus Scholl, eds., *M. Terenti Varronis de lingua latina* (Teubner, 1910). ET Roland G. Kent, trans., *Varro: On the Latin Language* (2 vols.; LCL, 1938).
Xenophon, *Anabasis* (*Anab.*). C. Hude and J. Peters, eds., *Xenophontis Expeditio Cyri, Anabasis* (rev. ed.; Teubner, 1972). ET Carleton C. Brownson and John Dillery, trans., *Xenophon: Anabasis* (rev. ed.; LCL, 1998).
—, *Hellenica* (*Hell.*). Carolus Hude, ed., *Xenophontis historia graeca* (Teubner, 1934). ET Carleton L. Brownson, trans., *Xenophon: Hellenica* (2 vols.; LCL, 1918–21).
Zonaeus, Περὶ σχημάτων τῶν κατὰ λόγον (*Fig.*). *RG* 3.161–70.

Jewish, early Christian and patristic sources

Corpora

Apostolic Fathers. Andreas Lindemann and Henning Paulsen, eds. and trans., *Die Apostolischen Väter: Griechisch-deutsche Parallelausgabe* (Tübingen: Mohr Siebeck, 1992). ET Bart D. Ehrman, ed. and trans., *The Apostolic Fathers* (2 vols.; LCL, 2003).
Dead Sea Scrolls (García Martinez/Tigchelaar). Florentino García Martínez and Eibert J. C. Tigchelaar, eds. and trans., *The Dead Sea Scrolls: Study Edition* (2 vols.; Leiden: Brill; Grand Rapids: Eerdmans, 1997–98).
Hebrew Bible (HB, BHS). A. Alt, O. Eißfeldt, P. Kahle, R. Kittel, K. Elliger, W. Rudolph et al., eds., *Biblia Hebraica Stuttgartensia* (5th ed.; Stuttgart: Deutsche Bibelgesellschaft, 1997).
New Testament (NT, NA[27]). Barbara Aland, Kurt Aland, Johannes Karavidopoulos, Carlo M. Martini and Bruce M. Metzger, eds., *Novum Testamentum Graece* (27th ed. rev.; Stuttgart: Deutsche Bibelgesellschaft, 1997).
Patrologia Graeca (PG). J.-P. Migne and Theodorus Hopfner, eds., *Patrologiae Cursus Completus: Series Graeca* (162 vols.; Paris: Librairie Orientaliste Paul Geuthner, 1928–1945).
Old Testament Pseudepigrapha (*OTP*). James H. Charlesworth, ed., *Old Testament Pseudepigrapha* (2 vols.; New York: Doubleday, 1983, 1985).
Pauluskommentare aus der griechieschen Kirche (*PKGK*). Karl Staab, ed., *Pauluskommentare aus der griechischen Kirche aus Katenenhandschriften gesammelt und herausgegeben* (NTAbh 15; Münster: Aschendorff, 1933).
Septuagint (LXX). Alfred Rahlfs, ed., *Septuaginta* (2 vols.; Stuttgart: Deutsche Bibelgesellschaft, 1979).
Vulgate. Bonifatio Fischer, Iohanne Gribomont, H. F. D. Sparks, W. Theile and Robertus Weber, *Biblia Sacra Iuxta Vulgatum Versionem* (3rd ed.; Stuttgart: Deutsche Bibelgesellschaft, 1983).

Individual authors and texts

Acacius of Caesarea, fragments. *PKGK* 53–56, cited by pp.
Ambrosiaster, *In epistulam ad Romanos* (*Rom.*). Heinrich Joseph Vogels, ed., *Abrosiastri qui dicitur commentarius in epistulas Paulinas* (3 vols.; CSEL 81.1–3; Vindobonae: Heolder-Pichler-Tempsky, 1966–69).

Anonymous commentator on Romans. Josef Frede, ed., *Ein neuer Paulustext und Kommentar* (2 vols.; VL 8; Freiburg: Herder, 1973–74).
Apollinarus of Laeodicea, fragments. *PKGK* 57–82, cited by pp.
Augustine, *Quaestiones evangeliorum* (*Quaest. ev.*). Almut Mutzenbecher, ed., *Sancti Aurelii Augustini: Quaestiones evangeliorum cum appendice quaestionem XVI in Matthaeum* (CCSL 44b; Turnhout: Brepols, 1980).
—. *De spiritu et littera* (*Spir. et litt.*). Carol F. Urba and Joseph Zycha, eds., *Sancti Aurelii Augustini: De peccatorum meritis et remissione*, etc. (CSEL 60; Vindobonae: Tempsky; Leipzig: Freytag, 1913), 154–229.
Clement of Alexandria, *Quis dives salvetur* (*Quis. div.*). G. W. Butterworth, trans. *Clement of Alexandria: The Exhortation to the Greeks, The Rich Man's Salvation, To the Newly Baptized* (LCL, 1919), 270–367.
Gennadius of Constantinople, fragments. *PKGK* 352–418, cited by pp.
Gregory of Nazianzus, *Epistula* 51 (*Ep.* 51). *AET* 58–61.
John Chrysostom, *Homiliae in epistulam ad Romanos* (*Hom. Rom.*). Frederick Field, ed., *Sancti patris nostris Joannis Chrysostomi Archepiscopi Constantinopolitani in Divi Pauli epistolam ad Romanos Homiliae XXXIII* (Oxford: J. H. Parker, 1849). ET Philip Schaff, ed., *A Select Library of the Nicene and Post-Nicene Fathers of the Christian Church*, First Series, vol. 21, *Saint Chrysostom: Homilies on the Acts of the Apostles and the Epistle to the Romans* (repr. Edinburgh: T&T Clark; Grand Rapids: Eerdmans, 1997), 333–564.
Joseph and Asenath (*Jos. Asen.*). Christoph Burchard, ed., *Joseph und Aeseneth* (PVTG 5; Leiden: Brill, 2003). ET C. Burchard, trans., *OTP* 2.177–247.
Odes of Solomon (*Odes Sol.*). ET J. H. Charlesworth, trans., *OTP* 2.725-71.
Origen, *Commentarii in Romanos* (*Comm. Rom.*). Catherine P. Hammond Bammel, ed., *Der Römerbriefkommentar des Origenes: Kritische Ausgabe der Übersetzung Rufins* (3 vols.; VL 16; Freiburg: Herder, 1990, 1997–98). Also: Karl Staab, "Neue Fragmente aus dem Kommentar des Origenes zum Römerbrief," *BZ* 18 (1929): 72–82. ET Thomas P. Schenk, *Origen: Commentary on the Epistle to the Romans* (2 vols.; Fathers of the Church 103–4; Washington, D.C.: Catholic University of America Press, 2001–2).
Pelagius, *In Romanos* (*Rom.*). J. Armitage Robinson, editor. *Texts and Studies Volume 9: Pelagius's Expositions of the Thirteen Epistles of St. Paul* (3 vols.; Cambridge: Cambridge University Press, 1922–31), 2.6–126.
Photius, *Epistulae* (*Ep.*). B. Laourdas and L. G. Westerink, eds., *Photii Patriarchae Constantinopolitani epistulae et amphilochia* (6 vols; Leipzig: Teubner, 1983–87), 2.106–7.
Sibylline Oracles (*Sib. Or.*). Johannes Geffcken, *Die Oracula Sibyllina* (GCS; Leipzig: J. C. Henrichs, 1902).
Tertullian, *Adversus Marcionem* (*Adv. Marc.*). Ernest Evans, ed. and trans., *Adversus Marcionem Books 4 and 5* (Oxford: Clarendon Press, 1972).
—, *Adversus Praxean* (*Adv. Prax.*). Ernest Evans, ed. and trans., *Tertullian's Treatise against Praxeas* (London: SPCK, 1948).
Testament of Abraham (*T. Ab.*). Francis Schmidt, ed. and trans., *Le Testament grec d'Abraham: Introduction, édition critique des deux recensions grecques, traduction* (TSAJ 11; Tübingen: Mohr Siebeck, 1986). ET E. P. Sanders, trans., *OTP* 1.871–902.
Testament of Job (*T. Job*). S. P. Brock, ed., *Testamentum Iobi* (PVTG 2; Leiden: Brill, 1967), 1–59. ET R. P. Spittler, *OTP* 1.829–68.
Testament of Levi (*T. Lev.*). Marius de Jonge, editor. *Testamenta XII Patriarcharum, Edited according to Cambridge University Library MS Ff I.24 fol. 203a–262b, with Short Notes* (PVTG 1.1; Leiden: Brill, 1964). ET H. C. Kee, trans., *OTP* 1.788–95.
Theodoret, *Interpretatio epistolae ad Romanos* (*Interp. Rom.*). PG 82.43–226.

Modern works consulted and cited

Ackerman, H. C. and J.-R. Gisler, eds., *Lexicon iconographicum mythologiae classicae* (9 vols.; Zürich: Artemis, 1981–99).
Aichele, George, Peter Miscall and Richard Walsh, "An Elephant in the Room: Historical-Critical and Postmodern Interpretations of the Bible," *JBL* 128 (2009): 383–404.
Alexander, Loveday, *The Preface to Luke's Gospel: Literary Convention and Social Context in Luke 1.1–4 and Acts 1.1* (SNTSMS 78; Cambridge: Cambridge University Press, 1993).
Algra, Keimpe, Jonathan Barnes, Jaap Mansfeld and Malcolm Schofield, eds., *The Cambridge History of Hellenistic Philosophy* (Cambridge: Cambridge University Press, 1999).
Althaus, Paul, *Der Brief an die Römer* (NTD 6; 9th edition; Göttingen: Vandenhoecht & Ruprecht, 1959).
Anderson, R. Dean, Jr., *Ancient Rhetorical Theory and Paul* (CBET 18; rev. ed.; Leuven: Peeters, 1998).
—, *Glossary of Greek Rhetorical Terms* (CBET 24; Leuven: Peeters, 2000).
Ando, Clifford, *Imperial Ideology and Provincial Loyalty in the Roman Empire* (Classics and Contemporary Thought 6; Berkeley: University of California Press, 2000).
Asher, Jeffrey A., *Polarity and Change in 1 Corinthians 15* (HUT 42; Tübingen: Mohr Siebeck, 2000).
Asmis, Elizabeth, *Epicurus' Scientific Method* (Cornell Studies in Classical Philology 42; Ithaca: Cornell University Press, 1984).
Attridge, Harold W., *The Epistle to the Hebrews: A Commentary on the Epistle to the Hebrews* (Hermeneia; Philadelphia: Fortress, 1989).
Aune, David E., *The New Testament in Its Literary Environment* (LEC 8; Philadelphia: Westminster, 1987).
—, "Romans as a *Logos Protreptikos*," in Donfried, *Romans Debate*, 278–96.
—, "Romans as a *Logos Protreptikos* in the Context of Ancient Religious and Philosophical Propaganda," in *Paulus und das Antike Judentum: Tübingen-Durham Symposium in Gendenken an den 50. Todestag Adolf Schlatters* (eds. Martin Hengel and Ulrich Hechel; WUNT 58; Tübingen: Mohr Siebeck, 1991), 91–124.
—, *Westminster Dictionary of New Testament and Early Christian Literature and Rhetoric* (Louisville: Westminster/John Knox, 2003).
—, Torrey Seland, and Jarl Henning Ulrichsen, eds., *Neotestamentica et Philonica: Studies in Honor of Peder Borgen* (NovTSup 106; Leiden: Brill, 2003).
Balch, David L., Everett Ferguson and Wayne Meeks, eds., *Greeks, Romans, and Christians: Essays in Honor of Abraham J. Malherbe* (Minneapolis: Fortress, 1990).
di Baradino, A., *Encyclopedia of the Early Church* (trans. A. Walford; 2 vols.; New York: Oxford University Press, 1992).
Barr, James, *The Semantics of Biblical Language* (Oxford: Oxford University Press, 1961; repr. London: SCM; Philadelphia: Trinity Press International, 1983).
Barrett, C. K., *A Commentary on the Epistle to the Romans* (New York: Harper & Row, 1957).
Barth, Karl, *The Epistle to the Romans* (trans. Edwyn C. Hoskyns; Oxford: Oxford University Press, 1933).
Barth, Markus, "Traditions in Ephesians," *NTS* 30 (1984): 3–25.
Bassler, Jouette, "Divine Impartiality in Paul's Letter to the Romans," *NovT* 26 (1984): 43–58.
—, *Divine Impartiality: Paul and a Theological Axiom* (SBLDS 59; Chico: Scholars Press, 1982).

Bauer, W., F. W. Danker, W. F. Arndt, and F. W. Gingrich, *Greek-English Lexicon of the New Testament and Other Early Christian Literature* (3rd ed.; Chicago: University of Chicago Press, 1999).
Bayer, Greg, "Classification and Explanation in Aristotle's Theory of Definition," *Journal of the History of Philosophy* 36.4 (1998): 487–505.
Beard, Mary, John North and Simon Price, *Religions of Rome* (2 vols.; Cambridge: Cambridge University Press, 1998).
Becker, Jürgen, *Paul: Apostle to the Gentiles*, (trans. O. C. Dean; Louisville: Westminster/John Knox, 1993).
Benson, Hugh H., "Priority of Definition and the Socratic Elenchus," *Oxford Studies in Ancient Philosophy* 8 (1990): 19–65.
Berger, Klaus, *Formgeschichte des Neuen Testaments* (Heidelberg: Quelle & Meyer, 1984).
Betz, Hans Dieter, *Antike und Christentum: Gesammelte Aufsätze IV* (Tübingen: Mohr Siebeck, 1998).
—, "Christianity as Religion: Paul's Attempt at Definition in Romans," in idem, *Paulinische Studien*, 206–39.
—, "Credibility and Credulity in Plutarch's Life of Numa Pompilius," in idem, *Paulinische Theologie*, 191–207.
—, "The Foundation of Christian Ethics according to Romans 12:1–2," in *Witness and Existence: Essays in Honor of Schubert M. Ogden* (eds. Philip E. Devenish and George L. Goodwin; Chicago: University of Chicago Press, 1989), 55–72.
—, "Fragments from a Catabasis Ritual in a Greek Magical Papyrus," in idem, *Hellenismus und Urchristentum*, 147–155.
—, *Galatians: A Commentary on Paul's Letter to the Churches of Galatia* (Hermeneia; Philadelphia: Fortress, 1979).
—, "The Gospel and the Wisdom of the Barbarians: The Corinthians' Question behind Their Question," in idem, *Paulinische Theologie*, 87–97.
—, *Hellenismus und Urchristentum: Gesammelte Aufsätze I* (Tübingen: Mohr Siebeck, 1990).
—, "In Defense of the Spirit: Paul's Letter to the Galatians as a Document of Early Christian Apologetics," in idem, *Paulinische Studien*, 98–109.
—, "The Literary Composition and Function of Paul's Letter to the Galatians," in idem, *Paulinische Studien*, 63–97.
—, "Magic and Mystery in the Greek Magical Papyri," in idem, *Hellenismus und Urchristentum*, 209–29.
—, *The "Mithras Liturgy": Text, Translation and Commentary* (STAC 18; Tübingen: Mohr Siebeck, 2003).
—, "Paul between Judaism and Hellenism: Creating a Space for Christianity," in idem, *Antike und Christentum*, 244–66.
—, *Paulinische Studien: Gesammelte Aufsätze III* (Tübingen: Mohr Siebeck, 1994).
—, *Paulinische Theologie und Religionsgeschichte: Gesammelte Aufsätze V* (Tübingen: Mohr Siebeck, 2009).
—, "The Problem of Rhetoric and Theology according to the Apostle Paul," in idem, *Paulinische Studien*, 126–62.
—, "2 Cor 6:14–7:1: An Anti-Pauline Fragment?" in idem, *Paulinische Studien*, 21–45.
—, *2 Corinthians 8 and 9: A Commentary on Two Administrative Letters of the Apostle Paul* (Hermeneia; Philadelphia: Fortress, 1985).
Blass, F., A. Debrunner, and R. W. Funk, *A Greek Grammar of the New Testament and Other Early Christian Literature* (Chicago: University of Chicago Press, 1961).
Bonner, S. F., *Education in Ancient Rome: From the Elder Cato to the Younger Pliny* (Berkeley: University of California Press, 1977).

—, *The Literary Treatises of Dionysius of Halicarnassus: A Study in the Development of Critical Method* (Cambridge Classical Studies 5; Cambridge: Cambridge University Press, 1939).
Booth, Alan D., "Elementary and Secondary Education in the Roman Empire," *Florilegium* 1 (1979): 1–14.
—, "The Schooling of Slaves in First-Century Rome," *TAPA* 109 (1979): 11–19.
Bornkamm, Günther, "The Letter to the Romans a Paul's Last Will and Testament," in Donfried, *Romans Debate*, 16–28.
—, "Lord's Supper and Church in Paul," in idem, *Early Christian Experience* (trans. Paul L. Hammer; London: SCM Press, 1969), 123–60.
—. *Paul* (trans. D. M. G. Stalker; New York: Harper & Row, 1971).
Bousset, Wilhelm, *Kyrios Christos* (trans. John F. Steely; Nashville: Abingdon, 1970).
Bottéro, Jean, "The 'Code' of Hammurabi," in idem, *Mesopotamia: Writing, Reasoning and the Gods* (trans. Z. Bahrani and M. van de Mieroop; Chicago: University of Chicago Press, 1992), 156–84.
Brauch, Manfred T., "Perspectives on 'God's Righteousness' in Recent German Discussion," in Sanders, *Paul and Palestinian Judaism*, 523–42.
Bremer, J. M., "Greek Hymns," in *Faith, Hope and Worship* (ed. H. S. Versnel; SGGR 2; Leiden: Brill, 1981), 192–215.
Brown, Francis, S. R. Driver, and Charles Briggs, *Hebrew and English Lexicon of the Old Testament* (Oxford: Clarendon, 1951).
Brown, Lesley, "Definition and Division in Plato's *Sophist*," in Charles, *Definition in Greek Philosophy*, 151–71.
Bruce, F. F., "The Romans Debate – Continued," in Donfried, *Romans Debate*, 175–94.
Bryan, Christopher, *A Preface to Romans: Notes on the Epistle and Its Literary and Cultural Setting* (Oxford: Oxford University Press, 2000).
Bultmann, Rudolf, *Theology of the New Testament* (trans. Kendrick Grobel; 2 vols.; London: SCM Press, 1952).
Burgess, Theodore C., *Epideictic Literature* (Chicago: University of Chicago, 1902).
Burkert, Walter, *Ancient Mystery Cults* (Cambridge: Harvard University Press, 1987).
—, *Greek Religion* (trans. John Raffan; Cambridge: Harvard University Press, 1985).
Buttrick, G. A., ed., *Interpreter's Dictionary of the Bible* (4 vols.; Nashville: Abingdon, 1962).
Calhoun, Robert Matthew, "John Chrysostom on ἐκ πίστεως εἰς πίστιν in Rom. 1:17: A Reply to Charles L. Quarles," *NovT* 48 (2006): 131–46.
—, "The Resurrection of the Flesh in *3 Corinthians*," in *Christian Body, Christian Self* (eds. Clare K. Rothschild and Trevor W. Thompson; Tübingen: Mohr Siebeck, 2011), 235–57.
Calvin, John, *Calvin's Commentaries: The Epistles of Paul the Apostle to the Romans and to the Thessalonians* (trans. Ross Mackenzie; Grand Rapids: Eerdmans, 1961).
Campbell, Douglas A., "False Presuppositions in the πίστις Χριστοῦ Debate: A Response to Brian Dodd," *JBL* 116 (1997): 713–19.
—, *The Rhetoric of Righteousness in Romans 3.21–26* (JSNTSup 65; Sheffield: JSOT Press, 1992).
—, "Romans 1:17 – A *Crux Interpretum* for the πίστις Χριστοῦ Debate," *JBL* 113 (1994): 265–85.
—, "2 Corinthians 4:13: Evidence in Paul That Christ Believes," *JBL* 128 (2009): 337–56.
Cancik, Hubert and Helmut Schneider, eds., *Der Neue Pauly: Enzyklopädie der Antike* (16 vols.; Stuttgart: J. B. Metzler, 1996–2003). Also: *Brill's New Pauly: Encyclopedia of the Ancient World* (eds. of ET Christine F. Salazar and David E. Orton; 6 + vols.; Leiden: Brill, 2002–).
Charles, David, "Definition and Explanation in the *Posterior Analytics* and *Metaphysics*," in idem, *Definition in Greek Philosophy*, 286–328.

—, ed., *Definition in Greek Philosophy* (Oxford, New York: Oxford University Press, 2010).
—, "The Paradox of the *Meno* and Aristotle's Attempts to Resolve It," in idem, *Definition in Greek Philosophy*, 115–150.
Chiba, Kei, "Aristotle on Essence and Defining-Phrase in His Dialectic," in Charles, *Definition in Greek Philosophy*, 203–251.
Classen, Carl Joachim, *Rhetorical Criticism and the New Testament* (WUNT 128; Tübingen: Mohr Siebeck, 2000).
—, "St. Paul's Epistles and Ancient Greek and Roman Rhetoric," in Porter and Olbricht, *Rhetoric and the New Testament*, 265–91.
Cohen, S. Marc, "Socrates on the Definition of Piety: *Euthyphro* 10A–11B," *Journal of the History of Philosophy* 9 (1971): 1–13.
Cohen, Shaye J. D., *From the Maccabees to the Mishna* (LEC 7; Philadelphia: Westminster, 1987).
Collins, Adela Yarbro and Margaret M. Mitchell, eds., *Antiquity and Humanity: Essays on Ancient Religion and Philosophy Presented to Hans Dieter Betz on His 70th Birthday* (Tübingen: Mohr Siebeck, 2001).
Collins, John J., *The Scepter and the Star: The Messiahs of the Dead Sea Scrolls and Other Ancient Literature* (AB Reference Library; New York: Doubleday, 1995).
Conzelmann, Hans, *1 Corinthians: A Commentary on the First Epistle to the Corinthians* (Hermeneia; trans. J. W. Leitch; G. W. MacRae, ed.; Philadelphia: Fortress, 1975).
Cranfield, C. E. B., *A Critical and Exegetical Commentary on the Epistle to the Romans* (ICC; corr. ed.; 2 vols; Edinburgh: T & T Clark, 1980–81).
Crivelli, Paolo, "The Stoics on Definition," in Charles, *Definition in Greek Philosophy*, 359–423.
Cullmann, Oscar, *The Christology of the New Testament* (trans. S. C. Guthrie and C. A. M. Hall; London: SCM Press, 1959).
—, *The Earliest Christian Confessions* (trans. J. K. S. Reid; London: Lutterworth, 1949).
Dahl, Nils Alstrup, "The Doctrine of Justification: Its Social Function and Implications," in idem, *Studies in Paul: Theology for the Early Christian Mission* (Minneapolis: Augsburg, 1977), 95–120.
—, "Form-Critical Observations on Early Christian Preaching," in idem, *Jesus in the Preaching of the Early Church* (Minneapolis: Augsburg, 1976), 30–36.
Dahood, Mitchell, *Psalms* (3 vols.; AB; Garden City, NY: Doubleday, 1970).
Dee, James H., ed., *Epitheta Deorum apud Homerum: The Epithetic Phrases for the Homeric Gods: A Repertory of the Descriptive Expressions for the Divinities in the* Iliad *and the* Odyssey (rev. ed.; Hildesheim: Olms – Weidmann, 2001).
Delling, Gerhard, *Worship in the New Testament* (trans. Percy Scott; Philadelphia: Westminster, 1962).
Deslauriers, Marguerite, "Plato and Aristotle on Definition and Division," *Ancient Philosophy* 10 (1990): 203–19.
Dihle, Albrecht, *A History of Greek Literature: From Homer to the Hellenistic Period* (trans. Clare Krojzl; London: Routledge, 1994).
Dodd, Brian, "Romans 1:17 – A *Crux Interpretum* for the πίστις Χριστοῦ Debate?" *JBL* 114 (1995): 470–73.
Dodd, C. H., *The Apostolic Preaching and Its Developments* (London: Hodder & Stoughton, 1936).
—, *The Bible and the Greeks* (London: Hodder & Stoughton, 1935).
—, *The Epistle of Paul to the Romans* (MNTC; New York: Harper & Bros., 1932).
Donfried, Karl P., "False Presuppositions in the Study of Romans," in idem, *The Romans Debate*, 102–25 (with a response by Karris, 125–27).
—, ed., *The Romans Debate* (rev. ed.; Peabody, MA: Hendrickson, 1991).
—, "A Short Note on Romans 16," in idem, *The Romans Debate*, 44–52.

Downing, F. Gerald, "Ambiguity, Ancient Semantics, and Faith," *NTS* 56 (2009): 139–62.
Duff, Paul Brooks, "Metaphor, Motif, and Meaning: The Rhetorical Strategy behind the Image 'Led in Triumph' in 2 Corinthians 2:14," *CBQ* 53 (1991): 79–92.
Dunn, James D. G., *Christ and the Spirit: Collected Essays of James D. G. Dunn, Volume 1: Christology* (Grand Rapids: Eerdmans, 1998).
—, *Christology in the Making* (2nd ed.; London: SCM Press, 1989).
—, "Jesus – Flesh and Spirit: An Exposition of Rom 1:3–4," in idem, *Christ and the Spirit*, 126–53.
—, "The Justice of God: A Renewed Perspective on Justification by Faith," *JTS* 43 (1992): 1–22.
—, *The New Perspective of Paul* (rev. ed.; Grand Rapids: Eerdmans, 2005).
—, "Noch einmal 'Works of the Law,'" in idem, *New Perspective*, 413–20.
—, *Romans* (WBC 38a–b; 2 vols.; Dallas: Word Books, 1988).
—, "Works of the Law and the Curse of the Law," in idem, *New Perspective*, 121–40.
—, "Yet Once More – 'The Works of the Law,'" in idem, *New Perspective*, 213–26.
Egan, Rory B., "Lexical Evidence on Two Pauline Passages," *NovT* 19 (1977): 34–62.
Ehrmann, Bart, *The Orthodox Corruption of Scripture: The Effect of Early Christological Controversies on the Text of the New Testament* (Oxford: Oxford University Press, 1993).
Eichrodt, Walther, *Theology of the Old Testament* (2 vols.; trans. J. A. Baker; OTL; Philadelphia: Westminster, 1961–67).
Elliott, Neil, *The Rhetoric of Romans: Argumentative Constraint and Strategy, and Paul's Dialogue with Judaism* (JSNTSup 45; Sheffield: JSOT Press, 1990).
Engberg-Pedersen, Troels, *Paul and the Stoics* (Louisville: Westminster/John Knox, 2000).
Faraone, Christopher A., "The Agonistic Context of Early Greek Binding Spells," in idem and Obbink, *Magika Hiera*, 3–32.
—, *Ancient Greek Love Magic* (Cambridge: Harvard University Press, 1999).
—, "The Mystodokos and the Dark-Eyed Maidens: Multicultural Influences on a Late-Hellenistic Incantation," in *Ancient Magic and Ritual Power* (eds. Marvin Meyer and Paul Mirecki; Leiden: Brill, 1995), 297–333.
— and Dirk Obbink, eds., *Magika Hiera: Ancient Greek Magic and Religion* (Oxford: Oxford University Press, 1991).
Fears, J. Rufus, "The Cult of Virtues and Roman Imperial Ideology," *ANRW* II.17.2.827–948.
Fee, Gordon D., *Pauline Christianity: An Exegetical-Theological Study* (Peabody: Hendrickson, 2007).
Ferejohn, Michael T., "Definition and the Two Stages of Aristotelian Demonstration,," *Review of Metaphysics* 36 (1982): 375–95.
Finlan, Stephen, *The Background and Content of Paul's Cultic Atonement Metaphors* (SBL Academica Biblica 19; Leiden: Brill, 2004).
Fitzmyer, Joseph, "Habakkuk 2:3–4 and the New Testament," in idem, *To Advance the Gospel: New Testament Studies* (2nd ed.; BRS; Grand Rapids: Eerdmans, 1981), 236–46.
—, *Romans: A New Translation with Introduction and Commentary* (AB 33; New York: Doubleday, 1993).
Foley, Helene P., ed., *The Homeric Hymn to Demeter: Translation, Commentary, and Interpretive Essays* (Princeton: Princeton University Press, 1993).
Forbes, Clarence H., "The Education and Training of Slaves in Antiquity," *TAPA* 86 (19575): 321–60.
Fortenbaugh, William W. and David C. Mirhady, eds., *Peripatetic Rhetoric after Aristotle* (Rutgers University Studies in Classical Humanities 6; New Brunswick & London: Transaction Publishers, 1994).
Fowden, Garth. *The Egyptian Hermes: A Historical Approach to the Late Pagan Mind* (Princeton: Princeton University Press, 1986).

Freedman, David Noel, et al., eds., *The Anchor Bible Dictionary* (6 vols.; New York: Doubleday, 1992).
Fridrichsen, Anton, "Aus Glauben zu Glauben, Röm. 1,17," *Coniectanea Neotestamentica* 12 (1948): 54.
—, *The Apostle Paul and His Message* (UUA 1947.3; Uppsala: A.-B. Lundequistaka, 1947).
Funk, Robert W., "The Apostolic Parousia: Form and Significance," in *Christian History and Interpretation: Studies Presented to John Knox* (eds. W. R. Farmer, C. F. D. Moule, and R. K. Niebuhr; Cambridge: Cambridge University Press, 1967), 249–68.
—, *Language, Hermeneutic, Word of God* (New York: Harper & Row, 1966).
Gager, John G., *Curse Tablets and Binding Spells from the Ancient World* (Oxford: Oxford University Press, 1992).
—, *Reinventing Paul* (Oxford: Oxford University Press, 2000).
Gaines, Robert N, "Qualities of Rhetorical Expression in Philodemus," *TAPA* 112 (1982): 71–81.
Gamble, Harry, Jr., *The Textual History of the Letter to the Romans* (SD 42; Grand Rapids: Eerdmans, 1977).
Gaston, Lloyd, *Paul and the Torah* (Vancouver: University of British Columbia Press, 1987).
Gathercole, Simon J., *Where is Boasting? Early Jewish Soteriology and Paul's Response in Romans 1–5* (Grand Rapids: Eerdmans, 2002).
Georgi, Dieter, *Theocracy in Paul's Praxis and Theology* (trans. David E. Green; Minneapolis: Fortress, 1991).
Gesenius, Wilhelm, *Hebrew Grammar* (eds. E. Kautzsch and A. E. Cowley; 2nd English ed.; Oxford: Clarendon, 1910).
Gill, Mary Louise, "Division and Definition in Plato's *Sophist* and *Statesman*," in Charles, *Definition in Greek Philosophy*, 172–99.
Given, Mark D., *Paul's True Rhetoric: Ambiguity, Cunning, and Deception in Greece and Rome.* (ESIC 7; Harrisburg, PA: Trinity Press International, 2001).
Glare, P. G. W., ed., *Oxford Latin Dictionary* (Oxford: Oxford University Press, 1982).
Goldstein, Jonathan, "Jewish Acceptance and Rejection of Hellenism," in volume 2 of *Jewish and Christian Self-Definition* (ed. E. P. Sanders; 3 vols.; Philadelphia: Fortress, 1980–83), 64–87.
Gordley, Matthew E., *The Colossian Hymn in Context: An Exegesis in Light of Jewish and Greco-Roman Hymnic and Epistolary Conventions* (WUNT 2.228; Tübingen: Mohr Siebeck, 2007).
Graf, Fritz, *Greek Mythology: An Introduction* (trans. Thomas Merier; Baltimore: John Hopkins University Press, 1993).
—, *Magic in the Ancient World* (trans. Franklin Philip; Cambridge: Harvard University Press, 1997).
—, "Prayer in Magic and Ritual," in Faraone and Obbink, *Magika Hiera*, 188–213.
Greenough, J. B., A. A. Howard, G. L. Kittredge and B. L. Dodge, *Allen and Greenough's New Latin Grammar* (rev. by Anne Maloney; Newburyport, MA: Focus, 2001).
Grieb, A. Katherine, *The Story of Romans: A Narrative Defense of God's Righteousness* (Louisville: Westminster John Knox, 2002).
Guerra, Anthony J., *Romans and the Apologetic Tradition: The Purpose, Genre and Audience of Paul's Letter* (SNTSMS 81; Cambridge: Cambridge University Press, 1995).
Haacker, Klaus, *The Theology of Paul's Letter to the Romans* (New Testament Theology; Cambridge: Cambridge University Press, 2003).
Hahn, Ferdinand, *The Titles of Jesus in Christology* (trans. H. Knight and G. Ogg; New York and Cleveland: World Publishing, 1969).
Hall, Robert G., "Historical Inference and Rhetorical Effect: Another Look at Galatians 1 and 2," in *Persuasive Artistry: Studies in New Testament Rhetoric in Honor of George A. Kennedy* (ed. Duane Watson; JSNTSup 50; Sheffield: JSOT Press, 1991), 308–20.

Halm, Carolus, ed., *Rhetores Latini Minores* (Leipzig: Teubner, 1863).
Hankinson, R. J., "Philosophy of Science," in *The Cambridge Companion to Aristotle* (ed. Jonathan Barnes; Cambridge: Cambridge University Press, 1995), 109–39.
Harris, William V., *Ancient Literacy* (Cambridge, MA: Harvard University Press, 1989).
Hatch, W. H. P., "On the Relationship of Codex Augiensis and Codex Boernerianus of the Pauline Epistles," *HSCP* 60 (1951): 187–99.
Hays, Richard B., "Apocalyptic Hermeneutics: Habakkuk Proclaims 'the Righteous One,'" in idem, *The Conversion of Imagination: Paul as Interpreter of Israel's Scripture* (Grand Rapids: Eerdmans, 2005), 119–42.
—, *Echoes of Scripture in the Letters of Paul* (New Haven: Yale University Press, 1989).
—, *The Faith of Jesus Christ: The Narrative Substructure of Galatians 3:1–4:11* (2nd ed.; BRS; Grand Rapids: Eerdmans, 2002).
—, "Πίστις and Pauline Christology: What Is at Stake?" in idem, *Faith of Jesus Christ*, 272–97.
Heath, Malcolm, *Hermogenes, On Issues: Strategies of Argument in Later Greek Rhetoric* (Oxford: Clarendon, 1995).
—, *Menander: A Rhetor in Context* (Oxford: Oxford University Press, 2004).
—, "Pseudo-Dionysius Art of Rhetoric 8–11: Figured Speech, Declamation, and Criticism," *AJP* 124 (2003): 81–105.
—, "The Substructure of *Stasis*-Theory from Hermagoras to Hermogenes," *CQ* 44 (1994): 114–29.
Hellholm, David, "Amplificatio in the Macro-Structure of Romans," in Porter and Olbricht, *Rhetoric and the New Testament*, 123–51.
—, "The Impact of the Situational Contexts for Paul's Use of Baptismal Traditions in His Letters," in Aune, Seland and Ulrichsen, *Neotestamentica et Philonica*, 147–75.
Hendrickson, G. L., "Ancient Reading," *CJ* 25 (1929–30): 186–96.
—, "The Origin and Meaning of Ancient Characters of Style," *AJP* 26 (1909): 249–70.
—, "The Peripatetic Mean of Style and the Three Stylistic Characters," *AJP* 25 (1904): 125–46.
Hengel, Martin, *Judaism and Hellenism: Studies in Their Encounter in Palestine during the Early Hellenistic Period* (trans. John Bowden; 2 vols.; Minneapolis: Fortress, 1974).
—, with Roland Deines, *The Pre-Christian Paul* (London: SCM; Philadelphia: Trinity Press International, 1991).
—, *The Son of God* (trans. John Bowden; Philadelphia: Fortress, 1976).
— and Anna Maria Schwemer, *Paul between Damascus and Antioch: The Unknown Years* (trans. John Bowden; Louisville: Westminster/John Knox, 1997).
Hock, Ronald F., "Paul and Greco-Roman Education," in Sampley, *Paul and the Greco-Roman World*, 198–227.
— and Edward N. O'Neil, eds. and trans., *The Chreia in Ancient Rhetoric* (2 vols.; SBLTT 27 and SBLWGRW 2; Atlanta: Scholars Press and Society of Biblical Literature, 1986, 2002).
Hooker, Morna, "Christ: The 'End' of the Law," in Aune, Seland and Ulrichsen, *Neotestamentica et Philonica*, 126–46.
—, "Πίστις Χριστοῦ," *NTS* 35 (1989): 321–42.
Hornblower, Simon and Anthony Spawforth, eds., *The Oxford Classical Dictionary* (3rd ed.; Oxford: Oxford University Press, 1996).
Hurtado, Larry W., *Lord Jesus Christ* (Grand Rapids: Eerdmans, 2003).
Jeremias, Joachim, *The Eucharistic Words of Jesus* (trans. Norman Perrin; New York: Charles Scribner's Sons, 1966).
Jervell, Jacob, "The Letter to Jerusalem," in Donfried, *Romans Debate*, 53–64.
Jervis, L. Ann, *The Purpose of Romans: A Comparative Letter Structure Investigation* (JSNTSup 55; Sheffield: JSOT Press, 1991).

Jewett, Robert, "Following the Argument of Romans," in Donfried, *Romans Debate*, 265–77.
—, *Paul's Anthropological Terms: A Study of Their Use in Conflict Settings* (Arbeiten zur Geschichte des antiken Judentums und Urchristentum 10; Leiden: Brill, 1971).
—, "The Redaction and Use of an Early Christian Confession in Romans 1:3–4," in *The Living Text: Essays in Honor of Ernest W. Saunders* (eds. Dennis E. Groh and Robert Jewett; Lanham and New York: University Press of America, 1985), 99–122.
—, *Romans: A Commentary* (asst. Roy D. Kotansky; ed. Eldon Jay Epp; Hermeneia; Minneapolis: Fortress, 2007).
—, "Romans as an Ambassadorial Letter," *Interpretation* 36 (1982): 5–20.
Johnson, E. Elizabeth, "Romans 9–11: The Faithfulness and Impartiality of God," in *Pauline Theology Volume 3: Romans* (eds. David M. Hay and E. Elizabeth Johnson; SBL Symposium Series 23; Atlanta: Society of Biblical Literature, 2002), 211–39.
Johnson, Luke Timothy, "Rom 3:21–26 and the Faith of Jesus," *CBQ* 44 (1982): 77–90.
—, "Taciturnity and True Religion: James 1:26–27," in Balch et al., *Greeks, Romans and Christians*, 329–39.
Johnston, Sarah Iles, *Hecate Soteira: A Study of Hekate's Roles in the Chaldean Oracles and Related Literature* (APAACS 21; Atlanta: Scholars Press, 1990).
de Jonge, Marinus, *Christology in Context* (Philadelphia: Westminster, 1988).
—. "Jesus, Son of David, Son of God," in *Intertextuality in Biblical Writings: Essays in Honor of Bas van Iersal*, (ed. S. Draisma; Kampen: J. H. Kok, 1989), 95–104.
Judge, Edwin A., "St. Paul and Classicism," *JAC* 15 (1992): 19–36.
Judson, Lindsay, "Carried Away in the *Euthyphro*," in Charles, *Definition in Greek Philosophy*, 31–61.
Karris, Robert J., "Romans 14:1–15:13 and the Occasion of Romans," in Donfried, *Romans Debate*, 65–84.
Käsemann, Ernst, *Commentary on Romans* (ed. and trans. Geoffrey W. Bromiley; Grand Rapids: Eerdmans, 1980).
Kaster, Robert A., *Guardians of Language: The Grammarian and Society in Late Antiquity* (The Transformation of the Classical Heritage 11; Berkeley: University of California Press, 1988).
—, "Notes on 'Primary' and 'Secondary' Schools in Late Antiquity," *TAPA* 113 (1983): 323–46.
Keck, Leander, *Romans* (ANTC; Nashville: Abingdon, 2005).
Kennedy, George A., *A New History of Classical Rhetoric* (Princeton: Princeton University Press, 1994).
—, *New Testament Interpretation through Rhetorical Criticism* (Chapel Hill: University of North Carolina Press, 1984).
Kensky, Meira Ziva, *Trying Man, Trying God: The Divine Courtroom in Early Jewish and Christian Literature* (WUNT 2.289; Tübingen: Mohr Siebeck, 2010).
Kern, Philip H., *Rhetoric and Galatians: Assessing an Approach to Paul's Epistle* (SNTSMS 101; Cambridge: Cambridge University Press, 1998).
Kindstrand, Jan Frederick, *Anacharsis: The Legend and the Apophthegmata* (Acta Universitatis Upsaliensis, Studia Graeca Upsaliensia 16; Uppsala: Almqvist & Wiksell, 1981).
Kittel, G. and G. Friedrich, eds., *Theological Dictionary of the New Testament* (trans. G. W. Bromiley; 10 vols.; Grand Rapids: Eerdmans, 1964–76).
Klauck, Hans Josef, *Die antike Briefliteratur und das Neue Testament: Ein Lehr- und Arbeitsbuch* (Paderborn, etc.: Ferdinand Schöningh, 1998); idem, with Daniel P. Bailey, *Ancient Letters and the New Testament: A Guide to Context and Exegesis* (Waco, Tex.: Baylor University Press, 2006).
Klein, Günther, "Paul's Purpose in Writing the Epistle to the Romans," in Donfried, *Romans Debate*, 29–43.

Knox, John, *Chapters in a Life of Paul* (rev. Douglas R. A. Hare; Macon, GA: Mercer University Press, 1987).
Koester, Helmut, *Introduction to the New Testament* (2nd ed.; 2 vols.; New York & Berlin: Walter de Gruyter, 1995).
—, "Paul's Proclamation of God's Justice for the Nations," in idem, *Paul and His World: Interpreting the New Testament in Its Context* (Minneapolis: Fortress, 2007), 3–14.
Koehler, Ludwig and Walter Baumgartner, *The Hebrew and Aramaic Lexicon of the Old Testament* (5 vols.; rev. Walter Baumgartner and Johann Jakob Stamm; Leiden: Brill, 1994–2000).
Koskenniemi, Heikki, *Studien zur Idee und Phraseologie des griechischen Briefes bis 400 n. Chr.*, (Suomalainen Tiedeakatemian Toimituksia Annales Academiae Scientiarum Fennicae ser. B 102.2; Helsinki: Suomalainen Tiedeakatemia, 1956).
Kotansky, Roy, *Greek Magical Amulets: The Inscribed Gold, Silver, Copper and Bronze Lamellae, Part 1, Texts of Known Provenance* (Papyrologica Coloniensia 22.1; Opladen: Westdeutscher Verlag, 1994).
Kramer, Werner, *Christ, Lord, Son of God* (trans. Brian Hardy; SBT 50; Naperville, IL: Allenson, 1966).
Kümmel, Werner Georg, *Introduction to the New Testament* (rev. ed.; trans. Howard Clark Kee; Nashville: Abingdon, 1975).
Lampe, G. W. H., ed., *Patristic Greek Lexicon* (Oxford: Oxford University Press, 1968).
Lampe, Peter, *From Paul to Valentinus: Christians at Rome in the First Two Christian Centuries* (trans. Michael Steinhauser; ed. Michael D. Johnson; Minneapolis: Fortress, 2003).
—, "The Roman Christians of Romans 16," in Donfried, *Romans Debate*, 216–30.
Lattke, Michael, *The Odes of Solomon: A Commentary* (Hermeneia; trans. Marianne Ehrhardt; ed. Harold W. Attridge; Minneapolis: Fortress, 2009).
Lausberg, Heinrich, *Handbook of Literary Rhetoric: A Foundation for Literary Study* (eds. David E. Orton and R. Dean Anderson, Jr.; trans. Matthew T. Bliss, Annemiek Jansen and David E. Orton; Leiden: Brill, 1998).
Le Blond, J. M., "Aristotle on Definition," in *Articles on Aristotle*, vol. 3, *Metaphysics* (eds. Jonathan Barnes, Malcolm Schofield and Richard Sorabji; London: Duckworth, 1979), 63–79.
Levine, Lee I., *The Ancient Synagogue: The First Thousand Years* (New Haven: Yale University Press, 2000).
Lichtheim, Miriam, *Ancient Egyptian Literature* (3 vols.; Berkeley: University of California Press, 1973, 1976, 1980).
Liddell, H. G., R. Scott, and H. S. Jones, *A Greek-English Lexicon* (9th ed.; with rev. supp.; Oxford: Oxford University Press, 1996).
Liebeschuetz, J. H. W. G., *Continuity and Change in Roman Religion* (Oxford: Clarendon Press, 1979).
Lietzmann, Hans, *Einführung in die Textgeschichte der Paulusbriefe; An die Römer* (HNT 8; 4th ed.; Tübingen: Mohr Siebeck, 1933).
Linnemann, Eta, "Tradition und Interpretation in Röm 1,3 f.," *EvT* 31 (1971): 264–75.
Lloyd-Jones, Hugh, *The Justice of Zeus* (2nd ed.; Berkeley: University of California Press, 1983).
Lohse, Eduard, *Der Brief an die Römer* (KEKNT 15; Göttingen: Vandenhoeck & Ruprecht, 2003).
Long, Anthony A., *Hellenistic Philosophy: Stoics, Epicureans, Sceptics* (2nd ed.; Berkeley: University of California Press, 1986).
Longenecker, Richard, *Galatians* (WBC 41; Dallas: Word Books, 1990).
—, *Paul: Apostle of Liberty* (New York: Harper & Row, 1964).

Lovejoy, Arthur O. and George Boas, *Primitivism and Related Ideas in Antiquity* (A Documentary History of Primitivism and Related Ideas 1; Baltimore: The Johns Hopkins University Press, 1935).

Luther, Martin, *Vorlesung über den Römerbrief, 1515/1516* (2 vols.; Darmstadt: Wissenschaftliche Buchgesellschaft, 1960).

Mack, Burton, *Rhetoric and the New Testament* (GBS; Minneapolis: Fortress, 1990).

Majercik, Ruth, ed. and trans., *The Chaldean Oracles: Text, Translation and Commentary* (SGRR 5; Leiden: Brill, 1989).

Malherbe, Abraham J., "Hellenistic Moralists and the New Testament," *ANRW* II.26.1:267–33.

—, *The Letters to the Thessalonians: A New Translation with Introduction and Commentary* (AB; New York: Doubleday, 2000).

—, "'Seneca' on Paul as Letter Writer," in *The Future of Early Christianity: Essays in Honor of Helmut Koester* (ed. Birger A. Pearson; Minneapolis: Fortress, 1991), 216–30.

Manson, T. W., "Romans," in *Peake's Commentary on the Bible* (eds. Matthew Black and H. H. Rowley; repr. Berkeshire, England: Van Nostrand Reinhold, 1982), 940–53.

—, "St. Paul's Letter to the Romans – and Others," in Donfried, *Romans Debate*, 3–15.

Marrou, H. I., *A History of Education in Antiquity* (trans. George Lamb; New York: Sheed & Ward, 1956).

Martin, Dale B., *The Corinthian Body* (New Haven: Yale University Press, 1995).

Martin, Ralph P., *Carmen Christi: Philippians ii. 5–11 in Recent Interpretation and in the Setting of Early Christian Worship* (SNTSMS 4; Cambridge: Cambridge University Press, 1967).

Martyn, J. Louis, *Galatians: A New Translation with Introduction and Commentary* (AB; New York: Doubleday, 1998).

Marxsen, W, *Introduction to the New Testament: An Approach to Its Problems* (trans. G. Buswell; Oxford: Basil Blackwell, 1968).

Matlock, R. Barry, "Detheologizing the πίστις Χριστοῦ Debate: Cautionary Remarks from a Lexical Semantic Perspective," *NovT* 42 (2000): 1–23.

McDonald, J. I. H., "Was Romans XVI a Separate Letter?" *NTS* 16 (1969–70): 369–72.

McGuire, Martin R. P., "Letters and Letter Carriers in Christian Antiquity," *CW* 53 (1960): 148–53, 184–85, 199–200.

Melanchthon, Philip, *Commentary on Romans* (Fred Kramer, trans.; St. Louis: Concordia, 1992).

Metzger, Bruce M.. *A Textual Commentary on the Greek New Testament* (2nd ed.; Stuttgart: Deutsche Bibelgesellschaft, 1994).

Michel, Otto, *Der Brief an die Römer* (KEK; Göttingen: Vandenhoeck & Ruprecht, 1955).

Migne, J.-P., ed., *Patrologiae cursus completus: Series graeca* (162 vols.; Paris: Migne, 1857–86).

Minear, Paul S., *The Obedience of Faith: The Purposes of Paul in the Epistle to the Romans* (SBT 2nd ser. 19; Naperville, IL: Alec R. Allenson, 1971).

Mitchell, Margaret M, "The Corinthian Correspondence and the Birth of Pauline Hermeneutics," in *Paul and the Corinthians: Studies on a Community in Conflict, Essays in Honor of Margaret Thrall* (eds. Trevor J. Burke and J. Keith Elliott; NovTSup 109; Leiden: Brill, 2003), 17–53.

—, *The Heavenly Trumpet: John Chrysostom and the Art of Pauline Interpretation* (HUT 40; Tübingen: Mohr Siebeck, 2000; repr. Louisville: Westminster John Knox, 2002).

—, "New Testament Envoys in the Context of Greco-Roman Diplomatic and Epistolary Conventions: The Example of Timothy and Titus," *JBL* 111 (1992): 641–662.

—, *Paul and the Rhetoric of Reconciliation: An Exegetical Investigation of the Language and Composition of 1 Corinthians* (HUT 28; Tübingen: Mohr Siebeck, 1991; repr. Louisville: Westminster/John Knox, 1992).

—, "Reading Rhetoric with Patristic Exegetes: John Chrysostom on Galatians," in Collins and Mitchell, *Antiquity and Humanity*, 333–56.

—, Review of R. Dean Anderson, Jr., *Ancient Rhetorical Theory and Paul*, *CBQ* 60 (1998): 356–58.

—, "Rhetorical and New Literary Criticism," in *The Oxford Handbook of Biblical Studies* (eds. J. W. Rogerson and Judith M Lieu; Oxford: Oxford University Press, 2006).

—, "Rhetorical Shorthand in Pauline Argumentation: The Functions of 'the Gospel' in the Corinthian Correspondence," in *Gospel in Paul: Studies on Corinthians, Galatians and Romans for Richard N. Longenecker* (eds. L. Ann Jervis and Peter Richardson; JSNTSup 108; Sheffield: Sheffield Academic Press, 1994), 63–88.

Modrak, Deborah, "Nominal Definition in Aristotle," in Charles, *Definition in Greek Philosophy*, 252–85.

Mohler, S. L., "Slave Education in the Roman Empire," *TAPA* 71 (1940): 262–80.

Momigliano, Arnaldo, *Alien Wisdom: The Limits of Hellenization* (Cambridge: Cambridge University Press, 1975).

Moo, Douglas, *The Epistle to the Romans* (NICNT; Grand Rapids: Eerdmans, 1996).

Morgan, Teresa, *Literate Education in the Hellenistic and Roman Worlds* (CCS; Cambridge: Cambridge University Press, 1998).

Mullins, Terence Y., "Petition as a Literary Form," *NovT* 5 (1962): 46–53.

Munck, Johannes, *Paul and the Salvation of Mankind* (trans. Frank Clarke; London: SCM, 1959).

Murphy-O'Connor, Jerome, *Paul: A Critical Life* (Oxford: Clarendon Press, 1996).

—, *Paul the Letter-Writer: His World, His Options, His Skills* (Collegeville, MN: Liturgical Press, 1995).

Murray, John, *The Epistle to the Romans* (NICNT; 2 vols.; Grand Rapids: Eerdmans, 1959, 1965).

Nanos, Mark, *The Mystery of Romans: The Jewish Context of Paul's Letter* (Minneapolis: Fortress, 1996).

Nagy, Gregory, "Ellipsis in Homer," in *Written Voices, Spoken Signs* (eds. Egbert Bakker and Ahuvia Kahane; Cambridge, MA: Harvard Univerrsity Press, 1997), 167–89, 253–57.

Neufeld, Verson H., *The Earliest Christian Confessions* (NTTS 5; Leiden: Brill; Grand Rapids: Eerdmans, 1963).

Nygren, Anders, *Commentary on Romans* (Philadelphia: Fortress, 1949).

O'Neill, J. C., *Paul's Letter to the Romans* (Baltimore, etc.: Penguin, 1975).

Pestman, P. W., *The New Papyrological Primer* (2nd ed.; Leiden: Brill, 1994).

Politis, Vasilis, "Explanation and Essence in Plato's *Phaedo*," in Charles, *Definition in Greek Philosophy*, 62–114.

Polythress, Vern S., "Is Romans 1^{3-4} a *Pauline* Confession After All?" *ExpTim* 87 (1976): 180–83.

Porter, Stanley E., "Ancient Rhetorical Analysis and Discourse Analysis of the Pauline Corpus," in idem and Thomas H. Olbricht, eds., *The Rhetorical Analysis of Scripture: Essays from the 1995 London Conference* (JSNTSup 146; Sheffield: Sheffield Academic Press, 1997), 249–74.

—, ed., *Handbook of Classical Rhetoric in the Hellenistic Period 300 B.C. – A.D. 400* (Leiden: Brill, 1997).

—, "The Theoretical Justification for Application of Rhetorical Categories to Pauline Epistolary Literature," in idem and Olbricht, *Rhetoric and the New Testament*, 100–22.

— and Thomas H. Olbricht, eds., *Rhetoric and the New Testament: Essays from the 1992 Heidelberg Conference* (JSNTSup 90; Sheffield: JSOT Press, 1993).

Poster, Carol, "The Economy of Writing in Graeco-Roman Antiquity," in *Rhetorical Argumentation in Biblical Texts: Essays from the Lund 2000 Conference* (eds. Anders Erik-

son, Thomas H. Olbricht and Walter Überlacker; ESIC 8; Harrisburg: Trinity Press International, 2002), 112–24.
Preuss, Horst Dietrich, *Old Testament Theology* (2 vols.; OTL; trans. Leo G. Perdue; Louisville: Westminster John Knox, 1995–96).
Pulleyn, Simon, "The Power of Names in Classical Greek Religion," *CQ* n.s. 44 (1994): 17–25.
—, *Prayer in Greek Religion* (Oxford Classical Monographs; Oxford: Clarendon, 1997).
Quarles, Charles L., "From Faith to Faith: A Fresh Examination of the Prepositional Series in Romans 1:17," *NovT* 45 (2003): 1–21.
Räisänen, Heikki, *Paul and the Law* (WUNT 29; Tübingen: Mohr Siebeck, 1983; repr. Philadelphia: Fortress, 1986).
von Rad, Gerhard, *Old Testament Theology* (2 vols.; trans. D. M. G. Stalker; Edinburgh: Oliver & Boyd, 1962, 1965).
Race, William H., "Aspects of Rhetoric and Form in Greek Hymns," *GRBS* 23 (1982): 5–14.
—, "How Greek Poems Begin," *Yale Classical Studies* 29 (1992): 13–38.
—, *Style and Rhetoric in Pindar's Odes* (American Classical Studies 24; Atlanta: Scholars Press, 1990).
Rawson, Elizabeth, "The Romans," in *Perceptions of the Ancient Greeks* (ed. Kenneth J. Dover; Oxford: Blackwell, 1992), 1–28.
Reed, Jeffrey T., "The Epistle," in Porter, *Handbook of Classical Rhetoric*, 171–93.
—, "Using Ancient Rhetorical Categories to Interpret Paul's Letters: A Question of Genre," in Porter and Olbricht, *Rhetoric and the New Testament*, 292–324.
Reinhardt, Alexander, *Der Codex Boernerianus der Briefe des Apostels Paulus* (Leipzig: Hiersemann, 1909).
Renehan, Robert, *Greek Textual Criticism: A Reader* (Loeb Classical Monographs; Cambridge, MA: Harvard University Press, 1969).
—, *Studies in Greek Texts* (Hypomnemata 43; Göttingen: Vandenhoeck & Ruprecht, 1976).
Richards, E. Randolph, *Paul and First-Century Letter Writing* (Downers Grove, IL: InterVarsity, 2004).
Roetzel, Calvin J., *Judgement in the Community: A Study of the Relationship between Eschatology and Ecclesiology in Paul* (Leiden: Brill, 1971).
Roth, Martha T., *Law Collections from Mesopotamia and Asia Minor* (2nd ed.; SBLWAW 6; Atlanta: Scholars Press, 1997).
Rothschild, Clare K., *Hebrews as Pseudepigraphon: The History and Significance of the Pauline Attribution of Hebrews* (WUNT 235; Tübingen: Mohr Siebeck, 2009).
Rowe, Galen O., "Style," in Porter, *Handbook of Classical Rhetoric*, 121–57.
Russell, Donald A., *Criticism in Antiquity* (2nd ed.; London: Gerald Duckworth & Co., 1995).
—, *Greek Declamation* (Cambridge: Cambridge University Press, 1983).
Rutherford, Ian, *Canons of Style in the Antonine Age:* Idea-*Theory in Its Literary Context* (Oxford Classical Monographs; Oxford: Clarendon, 1998).
Sampley, J. Paul, ed., *Paul in the Greco-Roman World: A Handbook* (Harrisburg: Trinity Press International, 2003).
Sanday, William and Arthur C. Headlam, *A Critical and Exegetical Commentary on the Epistle to the Romans* (5th ed.; ICC; Edinburgh: T & T Clark, 1902).
Sanders, E. P., "God Gave the Law to Condemn: Providence in Paul and Josephus," in *The Impartial God: Essays in Biblical Studies in Honor of Jouette M. Bassler* (eds. Calvin J. Roetzel and Robert L. Foster; New Testament Monographs 22; Sheffield: Sheffield Phoenix Press, 2007), 78–97.
—, *Paul* (Oxford: Oxford University Press, 1991).
—, *Paul and Palestinian Judaism: A Comparison of Patterns of Religion* (Philadelphia: Fortress, 1977).
—, *Paul, the Law, and the Jewish People* (Philadelphia: Fortress, 1983).

Sanders, Jack T., "The Transition from Opening Epistolary Thanksgiving to Body in the Letters of the Pauline Corpus," *JBL* 81 (1962): 348–62.
Schenkeveld, Dirk Marie, *Studies in Demetrius On Style* (Amsterdam: Adolf M. Hakkert, 1964).
Schlatter, Adolf, *Romans: The Righteousness of God* (trans. S. S. Schutzmann; Peabody, MA: Hendrickson, 1995).
Schlier, Heinrich, *Der Römerbrief* (HTKNT 6; Freiburg: Herder, 1977).
Schmithals, Walter, "The Pre-Pauline Traditions in 1 Corinthians 15:20–28," *Perspectives in Religious Studies* 20 (2006): 357–80.
—, *Der Römerbrief: Ein Kommentar* (Güttersloh: Gerd Mohn, 1988).
Schneider, Bernadin, "Κατὰ Πνεῦμα Ἁγιωσύνης (Romans 1,4)," *Biblica* 48 (1967): 359–87.
Schnelle, Udo, *Apostle Paul: His Life and Theology* (trans. M. Eugene Boring: Grand Rapids: Baker, 2003).
Schubert, Paul, *Form and Function of the Pauline Thanksgivings* (Beihefte zur Zeitschrift für die neutestamentliche Wissenschaft 20; Berlin: Alfred Töpelmann, 1939).
Schütz, John Howard, *Paul and the Anatomy of Apostolic Authority* (NTL; Louisville: Westminster John Knox, 2007).
Schweizer, Eduard, "Röm 1, 3f. und der Gegensatz von Fleisch und Geist vor und bei Paulus," *EvT* 15 (1955): 563–71.
Scott, James M., *Adoption as Sons of God: An Exegetical Investigation of the Background of* υἱοθεσία *in the Pauline Corpus* (WUNT 2.48; Tübingen: Mohr Siebeck, 1992).
Scrivner, Frederick Henry, *An Exact Transcript of Codex Augiensis* (Cambridge: Deighton, Bell & Co., 1859).
Slingerland, H. Dixon, *Claudian Policymaking and the Early Imperial Repression of Judaism at Rome* (South Florida Studies in the History of Judaism 160; Atlanta: Scholars Press, 1997).
Smyth, Herbert Weir, *Greek Grammar* (rev. Gordon M. Messing; Cambridge, MA: Harvard University Press, 1920).
Solmsen, Friedrich, "The Artistotelian Tradition in Ancient Rhetoric," *AJP* 62 (1941): 35–50, 169–90.
Souter, Alexander, *Earliest Latin Commentaries on the Epistles of St. Paul* (Oxford: Clarendon, 1927; repr. London: Sandpiper, 1999).
Stauffer, Ethelbert, *New Testament Theology* (trans. John Marsh; London: SCM Press, 1955).
Stirewalt, M. Luther, *Studies in Ancient Greek Epistolography* (SBLRBS 27; Atlanta: Scholars Press, 1993).
Stowers, Stanley K., *Letter Writing in Greco-Roman Antiquity* (LEC 5; Philadelphia: Westminster, 1986).
—, *A Rereading of Romans: Justice, Jews and Gentiles* (New Haven: Yale University Press, 1994).
—, "Social Typification and the Classification of Ancient Letters," in *The Social World of Formative Christianity and Judaism: Essays in Tribute to Howard Clark Kee* (eds. Jacob Neusner, Peder Borgen, Ernest S. Frerichs and Richard Horsley; Philadelphia: Fortress, 1988), 78–90.
Strecker, Georg, *Theology of the New Testament* (ed. William Horn; trans. M. Eugene Boring; Berlin: de Gruyter; Louisville: Westminster/John Knox, 2000).
Stroumsa, Guy G., "Philosophy of the Barbarians: On Early Christian Ethnological Representations," in *Geschichte – Tradition – Reflexion: Festschrift für Martin Hengel zum 70. Geburtstag* (eds. Hubert Cancik, Hermann Lichtenberger and Peter Schäfer; 3 vols.; Tübingen: Mohr Siebeck, 1996), 2.339–68.
Stuhlmacher, Peter, "The Apostle Paul's View of Righteousness," in idem, *Reconciliation*, 68–93.

—, *Paul's Letter to the Romans: A Commentary* (trans. Scott J. Hafemann; Louisville: Westminster/John Knox, 1994).
— "Recent Exegesis on Romans 3:24–26," in idem, *Reconciliation*, 94–109.
—, *Reconciliation, Law and Righteousness: Essays in Biblical Theology* (Philadelphia: Fortress, 1986).
—, *Revisiting Paul's Doctrine of Justification: A Challenge to the New Perspective* (Downers Grove, IL: InterVarsity, 2001).
Temporini, Hildegaard, Wolfgang Haase, and Joseph Vogt, eds., *Aufstieg und Niedergang der römischen Welt: Geschichte und Kultur Roms im Spiegel der neueren Forschung* (Berlin: de Gruyter, 1972–).
Thrall, Margaret, *A Critical and Exegetical Commentary on the Second Letter to the Corinthians* (2 vols.; ICC; Edinburgh: T & T Clark, 1994, 2000).
Tischendorf, Constantine von, *Novum Testamentum Graece* (8th ed.; 2 vols.; repr. Graz: Akademische Druck-u. Verlagsanstalt, 1965).
du Toit, Andrie B., "Forensic Metaphors in Romans and Their Soteriological Significance," in *Salvation in the New Testament: Perspectives on Soteriology* (ed. Jan G. van der Watt; NovTSup 121; Leiden: Brill, 2005), 213–46.
Torraca, L., ed. and trans., *Marco Giunio Bruto: Epistole Greche* (Collana di Studi Greci 31; Naples: Liberia Scientifica Editrice, 1959).
van Unnik, Willem C., *First Century A.D. Literary Culture and Early Christian Literature* (ed. W. Wuellner; Berkeley: Center for Hermeneutical Studies in Hellenistic and Modern Culture, 1975).
VanLandingham, Chris, *Judgment and Justification in Early Judaism and the Apostle Paul* (Peabody, MA: Hendrickson, 2006).
Versnel, H. S., "Beyond Cursing: The Appeal to Justice in Judicial Prayers," in Faraone and Obbink, *Magika Hiera*, 60–106.
—, *Inconsistencies in Greek and Roman Religion* (2 vols.; SGRR 6; Leiden: Brill, 1990–93).
Vivante, *The Epithets of Homer: A Study in Poetic Values* (New Haven: Yale University Press, 1982).
Vorster, Johannes N., "Strategies of Persuasion in Romans 1.16–17," in Porter and Olbricht, *Rhetoric and the New Testament*, 152–70.
Wagner, J. Ross, *Heralds of the Good News* (NovTSup 101; Leiden: Brill, 2002).
Walker, William O., Jr., *Interpolations in the Pauline Letters* (JSNTSup 213; Sheffield: Sheffield Academic Press, 2001).
Waszink, J. H., "Some Observations on the Appreciation of 'the Philosophy of the Barbarians' in Early Christian Literature," in *Mélanges Offerts à Mademoiselle Christine Mohrmann* (eds. L. J. Engels, H. W. F. M. Hoppenbrouwers and A. J. Vermeulen; Utrecht: Spectrum Editeurs, 1963), 41–56.
Watkins, Calvert, "An Indo-European Construction in Greek and Latin," *HSCP* 71 (1966): 115–19.
Watson, Duane, "Paul's Rhetorical Strategy in 1 Corinthians 15," in Porter and Olbricht, *Rhetoric and the New Testament*, 231–49.
Watson, Francis, *Paul, Judaism, and the Gentiles: Beyond the New Perspective* (rev. ed.; Grand Rapids: Eerdmans, 2007).
—, "The Two Roman Congregations: Romans 14:1–15:13," in Donfried, *Romans Debate*, 203–15.
Watts, Rikki E., "'For I Am Not Ashamed of the Gospel': Romans 1:16–17 and Habakkuk 2:4," in *Romans and the People of God: Essays in Honor of Gordon D. Fee on the Occasion of His 65th Birthday* (eds. Sven K. Soderhund and N. T. Wright; Grand Rapids: Eerdmans, 1999), 3–25.
Wedderburn, A. J. M., "The Problem of the Denial of the Resurrection in I Corinthians XV," *NovT* 23 (1981): 229–41.

—, "The Purpose and Occasion of Romans Again," in Donfried, *The Romans Debate*, 195–202.

—, *The Reasons for Romans* (Edinburgh: T & T Clark, 1991).

Weiss, Johannes, *Das Urchristentum* (ed. Rudolf Knopf; Göttingen: Vandenhoeck & Ruprecht, 1917); idem, *Earliest Christianity: A History of the Period A.D. 30–150* (ed. and trans. Frederick Clifton Grant; 2 vols.; New York: Harper & Bros., 1959).

Wengst, Klaus, *Christologische Formeln und Lieder des Urchristentums* (SNT 7; Güttersloh: Gerd Mohn, 1972).

West, Martin, *The East Face of Helicon: West Asiatic Elements in Greek Poetry and Myth* (Oxford: Clarendon, 1997).

—, "Tryphon *De Tropis*," *CQ* n.s. 15 (1965): 230–48.

White, John Lee, "New Testament Epistolary Literature in the Framework of Ancient Epistolography," *ANRW* II.25.2:1730–56.

Whitsett, Christopher G., "Son of God, Seed of David: Paul's Messianic Exegesis in Romans 2:3–4" [sic; properly 1:3–4], *JBL* 119 (2000): 661–81.

Wiefel, Wolfgang, "The Jewish Community in Ancient Rome and the Origins of Roman Christianity," in Donfried, *Romans Debate*, 85–102.

Wilckens, Ulrich, *Die Brief an die Römer* (3 vol.; EKKNT 6; Neukirchen-Vluyn: Neukirchener Verlag, 1978–83).

Williams, Sam K., "The 'Righteousness of God' in Romans," *JBL* 99 (1980): 241–90.

Wilson, Todd A., "'Under Law' in Galatians: A Pauline Theological Abbreviation," *JTS* 56 (2005): 362–92.

Wooten, Cecil W., "Dionysius of Halicarnassus and Hermogenes on the Style of Demosthenes," *AJP* 110 (1989): 576–88.

—, "The Peripatetic Tradition in the Literary Essays of Dionysius of Halicarnassus," in Fortenbaugh and Mirhady, *Peripatetic Rhetoric after Aristotle*, 121–30.

Wright, N. T., "Romans," in *The New Interpreter's Bible* (12 vols.; eds. Leander E. Keck, et al.; Nashville: Abingdon, 1994–2004), 10.395–770.

Wuellner, Wilhelm, "Paul's Rhetoric of Argumentation in Romans," in Donfried, *Romans Debate*, 128–46.

Wyk Cronjé, Jacobus van, *Dionysius of Halicarnassus:* De Demosthene*: A Critical Appraisal of the* Status Quaestionis (Spudasmata 39; Zürich: Georg Olms, 1986).

Zeller, Dieter, *Der Brief an die Römer* (Regensburg: Friedrich Pustet, 1985).

Ziesler, J. A., *The Meaning of Righteousness in Paul: A Linguistic and Theological Enquiry,* (SNTSMS 20; Cambridge: Cambridge University Press, 1972).

Index of Ancient Sources

Hebrew Bible and Septuagint

Genesis
1   135

Exodus
9:16   214
20:2   113
23:6–9   161–62
32:8   114
33:19   214
34:6–7   160–61

Leviticus
16:1–34   201
18:5   203
19:15   162
20:24   113
20:26   113
24:22   162

Numbers
15:16   162
15:41   113

Deuteronomy
1:16–17   162
5:6   113
16:18–20   162
32:4   160–61
32:21   217
32:45   161
34:9   140

Judges
6:31   151
10:1   151

1 Samuel
12:6   114

2 Samuel
7:12–14   101
8:15   163
14:14   151

1 Kings
1:48   113
3:5–9   163
5:21   113
12:28   114

2 Kings
6:26   151

1 Chronicles
18:14   163

2 Chronicles
1:8–10   163

Isaiah
11:10   101
19:3   140
19:14   140
28:16   216–17
43:1   113–14
43:14–17   113–14
43:25   113–14
44:2   121
51:13   113
53:1   217
65:1–2   217

Jeremiah
1:5   121
9:2   170
16:14–15   114

Joel
3:5	216–17

Amos
1–2	161
2:6	161
4:4–5	161
5:7–9	161
5:21–24	161

Habakkuk
2:2–5	187–88
2:2	189, 190
2:3	189, 190
2:4	136, 148, 156, 179–80, 185, 187–90, 191
2:5–6	190
2:5	179–80, 189

Daniel
3:39 (LXX)	140–41

Psalms (LXX)
2:7	103
3:2–3	163
3:4–7	164
3:9	183
5	164–65
7:3	164
7:10–17	164
10:3–9	164
10:15	164
10:17–18	164
11:4–7	164
17:8–14	164
18:15	217
22:7–11	163
22:13–14	164
22:15–16	163
22:17–19	164
22:23–25	164
27:1–6	164
27:13–14	164
28:4–5	164
31:10–11	163
35:2	206
35:4–8	164
35:11–12	164
35:15–16	164
35:20–21	164
35:26	164
36:7	160
50:6	196
56:4–5	164
56:9–12	164
57:5–7	164
59:7–8	164
59:12–16	164
62:13	152, 167
63:10–11	164
65:3–7	164
66:20 (65:20)	113
69:2–30	163–64
72:1–4	163
72:1	160
73:4–12	164
84:8 (83:8)	170
94:4–7	164
103:6	160
109:2–5	164
109:8–19	164
116 (115)	211
124:6 (123:6)	113
140:7–14	164
143:3–4	164

Proverbs
24:12	152, 167

Job
13:16	151

Baruch
2:11–12	114

Judith
13:18	113

Prayer of Manasseh
1–4	116–17

2 Maccabees
1:17	113

Old Testament Pseudepigrapha

Ascension of Isaiah
4:18   165

1 Enoch
1:7–9   165
90:20–29   165
100:1–13   165

4 Ezra
7:26–44   165

Joseph and Aseneth
8:9–11   115–16

Jubilees
5:12–19   165

Odes of Solomon
19:4   137

Sibylline Oracles
2.214–20   165
3.11–14   115
3.20–25   115

Testament of Abraham
8:4–6   115

Testament of Job
2:4   117

Testament of Levi
18:6–12   138–40

Dead Sea Scrolls

1QpHab
VII.4–5   190
VII.7–12   190
VII.17–VIII.3   188

1QS
III.8   140
IV.2–8   140

New Testament

Matthew
1:1–17   132
1:1   101
3:16   139
11:27   174–75
11:28   177
22:41–46   101

Mark
1:10   139
10:17–22   174–75
12:35–37   101

Luke
1:32   101
3:22   139
3:23–28   132
17:5   182–83
20:41–44   101

John
1:17   174
5:46   177
6:63   99
7:42   101

Acts
2:23   134
7:51–53   189
8:37   94
10:38   135
10:42   134
13:23   101
13:33   103
17:16–33   1–2, 222
17:26–27   134
17:31   134
20:17–30   6

Romans

1–3	173, 194	2:17–20	203
1:1–3:19	104	3:1–8	157, 193–97, 201, 207, 214, 218
1:1–15	185	3:2	198
1:1–7	87–90, 99, 104	3:5	98, 157, 167, 200
1:1	98	3:8	3, 149
1:2–4	passim	3:9	167, 194
1:5–6	7, 154	3:10–18	131
1:5	145, 152, 153, 155, 184, 186, 205, 210, 211, 220	3:18	206
		3:19–20	194
		3:19	203
1:7	98	3:20	169
1:8–15	89–90, 141, 143–47, 152–53, 185–86, 191	3:21–5:21	213
		3:21–31	194, 197–212, 218
		3:21–26	157
1:8	205, 211, 220	3:21–22	186
1:9	140	3:21	98
1:11–13	186	3:22	170
1:11–12	175–76	3:23	167
1:12–15	205	3:24–25	212
1:12	186, 211, 220	3:24	168
1:13–15	172	3:26	168
1:13	7	3:28	168
1:14	153–56	3:29	152
1:16–17	passim	4	3, 131, 153, 182, 185, 186, 207
1:18–3:20	167, 194, 199, 202, 213	4:1	100, 124
1:18	99, 167, 220	4:2	168
1:19–20	178	4:3	209
1:20	149	4:4	203
1:25	119	4:9	209
1:28	147, 212	4:17	98
1:32	167, 201, 212	4:18	170
2–3	3, 185, 204, 216	4:22–25	120–21
2:1–11	193, 194	4:23–25	209–10
2:2	167	4:24–25	97
2:3	98	4:24	209
2:4	201	4:25	201
2:5–11	151–52	5:1–8:39	212
2:6–24	202	5:1	121, 167, 168, 186, 205, 210
2:6	167, 203		
2:7–11	160, 167	5:6–11	212
2:7–8	130	5:8–9	152
2:7	206	5:9	168, 201
2:9–10	153	5:12–21	149
2:12–29	167	5:19	210
2:12–16	178	6:1–8:39	213
2:15	203	6:1–11	92, 169–70
2:16–25	104	6:3	171
2:16	123, 134	6:4–5	170
2:17–29	195	6:7–8	212
2:17–23	202	6:7	168

6:8–9	169	11:36	170
6:12–13	212	12:1–2	4, 216
6:12	127	12:2	212
6:14	199	14–15	3
6:17–18	145	14:1–15:6	196
6:19	140	14:10	156, 196
6:21	212	15	144–45
6:22	140	15:12	101
6:23	201, 212	15:14–33	6, 90, 144, 187
7:1	7	15:14	6
7:5–6	100	15:16	140
7:12	140	15:18–19	3
7:14	199	15:18	145
7:24	127	15:22–24	145
8:1–11	201, 212	15:27	100, 147
8:1	215	15:30–32	145
8:2	100, 126	15:31	149
8:3–4	100	15:33	94
8:3	99, 126	16	6–7
8:11	97, 127	16:17–20	6
8:12–14	124	16:20	94
8:12	147		
8:14–15	169	*1 Corinthians*	
8:15–16	96	1:1–9	98
8:15	100, 126	1:8–9	119
8:31–39	212	1:18–2:5	2
8:31–34	121	1:18–25	148
8:33–34	168	1:18	83
8:34	98, 210	1:22–24	154
9–11	139, 153, 212	1:23–24	149
9:1–10:21	194, 212–18	2:2	101
9:1–4	203	2:4	150
9:3	100, 124	2:6	98–99
9:4–5	124	3:8–16	104
9:5	100, 119	3:10	99
9:6–13	124	4:21	100, 139–40
9:19–23	163, 196	5:3	124
10:2	206	5:5	124
10:3	157	6:7–14	104
10:5	203	7:34	124
10:6–7	196	8–9	3
10:8–13	181	8:6	96, 170
10:9–10	96	10:13	119
10:9	209–10	11:23–26	94–95, 102–3, 119–20
10:16	145		
11:1–2	175	11:23	82
11:1	101	12:3	96
11:13–24	153	12:5–6	127
11:13	7	12:8	127
11:14	100	13:13	146
11:16	140	15	2, 220–21
11:25–32	139	15:1–11	79

15:1–5	221	1:15	99, 121, 133
15:1–4	104	1:23–24	210
15:3–8	94–95, 119–20	1:23	99
15:3–4	209–10	2:6–8	155
15:3	82, 201	2:6	99
15:10	99	2:8–9	99
15:11	209–10	2:12	99
15:12–22	136	2:15–21	3
15:12–19	100, 170	2:16	84
15:12	221	2:20	122
15:35–49	124, 136	3:1–5	84
15:35–41	136	3:6–18	3
15:39	100–1	3:10	84
15:50	124	3:11	188, 189
16:23–24	94	3:15	196
		3:16	101
2 Corinthians		3:17	98
1:1–9	98	3:20	96
1:3–4	119	3:21–22	208
1:9–10	119	3:21	175
1:19	99	3:22	207
2:14	119	3:23–4:7	84
2:15–16	130, 170	3:23–39	35
3:13	93	3:23–24	210
3:18	170, 182–83	3:26–28	156
4:4	132	3:26	154
4:13–14	210	3:27	171
4:13	127	4:3–6	133
4:17	170	4:3–5	102
5:11	206	4:3	35
5:16	101	4:4	132–33
5:16–17	102–3	4:6	96
5:21	157	4:21–5:1	84
7:1	124, 206	4:21–31	131
11:2	101	5:3	147
11:31	119	5:5	206
13:4	128	5:16–18	123–24
13:13	93–94	5:18	84
		5:19–24	216
Galatians		5:22	146
1:1–17	3	6:18	94
1:1–5	120		
1:1	97	*Ephesians*	
1:3–4	98	4:4–6	96
1:6–9	121	5:14	95
1:7	149		
1:10–2:14	99	*Philippians*	
1:11–2:21	81	1:1	89
1:11–17	3	1:2	98
1:11	99, 123	1:21–22	101
1:14	206	1:25	206
1:15–16	91	2:1–2	206

2:5–11	103	5:8	206
2:6–7	122	5:9	152
2:8	210	5:28	94
3:9	158, 181		
4:23	94	*1 Timothy*	
		2:5–6	96
Colossians		3:16	95, 138
1:15	122		
		2 Timothy	
1 Thessalonians		2:8	101
1:2–3	146		
1:3	206	*Philemon*	
1:5	135	6	206
1:8	146		
1:9–10	120–21	*Hebrews*	
1:9	98	10:37–38	189
1:10	97, 152	10:38	188
2:12	98	11	179–80, 185
2:14	98		
3:13	100	*1 Peter*	
4:3–4	100	3:18	128, 138
4:5	98		
4:7	100	*Revelation*	
4:8	98	20:11–15	165
4:14	100, 170, 210		
4:16	100		

Ancient Authors

Acacius of Caesarea
Comm. Rom. (*PKGK*)
53   177–78

Aelius Aristides
Or.
25.63   154
43.7   37
45.15   37

[*Rhet.*]
1.1   44
1.136–37   48
2.98   78

Aelius Herodian
[*Fig.*]
RG 3.94   79

Soloec.
308   44

Alexander of Aphrodisias
In. Arist. Top.
42.27–43.2   18

Alexander Rhetor
Fig.
1.16   68
1.17   69
2.2   171
2.12   69
2.13   72
2.17   80
2.23   148

Ambrosiaster
Rom.
1.16.1–2   180
1.16.1   182
1.16.4   180
1.17.1–2   180–81
1.17.2–3   181

Anacharsis
[*Ep.*]
2   155

Anaxagoras
Kirk/Raven 362–64,
§ 476   10

Anaximenes
Kirk/Raven 144,
§§ 140–41   10

Andocides
Myst.
30–31   151

Anonymous
Comm. Rom. (Frede)
2.23–24   170
2.23   177

Anonymous
In Plat. Theat.
22.39–47   21

Anonymous
Proleg.
RG-W 6.36   44

Anonymous
Trop.
5   204
7   78
12   73

Anonymous Seguerianus
Rhet.
9   52
10–11   54
21   51
26–36   51
63   50
69–78   69
113–31   51
161–66   53

Antiphon
Tetr.
3.2.5   26

Aphthonius
Prog.
2   50

Apollinaris of Laodicea
Comm. Rom. (*PKGK*)
57   128
58   177

Aquila Romanus
Fig.
46   74–75

Aristotle
An. post.
2.10 (93b29–94a14)   16

Ath. pol.
57.3   25

Metaph.
7.14.12–13
  (1013a17–23)   16

Rhet.
1.1.3–6 (1354a)   150
1.2.1 (1355b)   22
1.3.5 (1358b)   30
1.5.5 (1360b)   23
1.9.2 (1366a)   33
1.13.9–10
  (1373b–74a)   25–26
2.21.8 (1395a)   61
2.24.3 (1401b)   77
2.24.7 (1401b)   77
2.24.29 (1401b–2a)   77
3.2.1–5 (1404b)   43
3.2.14 (1405b)   106–7
3.3.3 (1406a)   107, 118
3.5.1–6 (1407a–b)   43
3.6 (1407b–8a)   43
3.6.1 (1407b)   41, 64
3.7.1–5 (1408a)   43
3.7.6–7 (1408a)   43
3.8 (1408b–9a)   43
3.9.7 (1409b–10a)   125–26
3.9.9 (1410a)   125
3.11.6 (1412a)   61
3.12.1–3 (1413b)   42
3.12.6 (1414a)   42–43
3.13.1 (1414a)   34, 51
3.13.4 (1414b)   51–52
3.14.6 (1415a)   52
3.14.8 (1415b)   54

Index of Ancient Sources

3.16 (1416b-17b)	51	*Inv.*	
3.16.4 (1416b–17a)	49	1.10	26, 27
		1.12	27
[*Rhet. Alex.*]		1.14	27
4.8–9 (1427a)	26	1.20	52
22.5 (1434b)	64–65	1.23	52
29.1–2 (1436a–b)	52, 54	1.26	53
30.4–5 (1438a)	49–50	1.28	50
30.8 (1438a)	51, 65	2.12	25
35.1–4 (1440b)	52	2.52–56	28–29
36.1–16 (1441b–42a)	52		
		Nat. d.	
Top.		2.60–62	146
1.4–5 (101b–102b)	16		
		Off.	
Athanasius		1.4–5	146
[*De def.*]		1.23	146
3	18, 20	1.39–40	146
		3.104	146
Augustine		3.107–8	146
Quaest. ev.		3.111	146
2.39.1	182–83		
		Or.	
Spir. et litt.		79	43
18 (11)	183–84	113	19
		115–17	17–19
Brutus			
Ep.		*Part. or.*	
1	58	19	44
19	59	31–32	50
25	58		
55	59	*Resp.*	
69	58	1.37.58	153
Cassius Dio		[*Rhet. Her.*]	
Hist. Rom.		1.11.19	27
1.6.3	206	1.13	50
36.7.3	206	1.18.14	50
		2.12.17	29
Cicero		3.2.3	30
Brut.		4.15.21	125
50	44	4.25.35	24–25
		4.28.38	171
De or.		4.33.44–45	76, 78
2.80	50	4.53.67	70
2.83	44, 50	4.54.67	68
2.107	29	4.54.68	70
3.202	69	9.38.50	148
Fin.		*Top.*	
1.22	20	83	19
		93–94	25

255

Cleanthes
Hymn to Zeus
1–2   108–9
33–35   166

Clement of Alexandria
Quis div.
8   174–75

Strom.
2.6.29.2–3   175
5.1.2.3–6   175–76

Cocondrius
Trop.
7   204
12   78
27   74

Demetrius
Eloc.
7–9   59–63
22–23   125
137   60
140   171
223–35   55, 58
224–25   55
228   47, 55
229   56, 57
230   56, 58
231   55
233–34   58
235   56
241–43   61–62

Demosthenes
Aristocr.
74–75   25

Cor.
1   74
174   74
243   72, 74

Ep.
1.1   74

Fals. leg.
65   74
136   72

Lept.
158   25

Mid.
74–75   80

3 Philip.
27   69

Dio Chrysostom
Or.
14   30–33, 193
18.11   46
[37.25–27]   153
75.1–2   34
75.9   34
76   34–36, 193

Diodorus Siculus
9.26.3   62

Diogenes of Apollonia
Kirk/Raven 434,
 § 596   10
Kirk/Raven 442–43,
 § 603   10

Diogenes Laertius
1.6–9   155
1.10–11   155
1.101–5   155
7.16–18   43
7.41–42   16–17
7.59   43–44
7.60   18, 19
7.137–38   23
7.147   21, 149
10.33   21

Dionysius of Halicarnassus
Ant. rom.
1.4.2–3   153–54
2.75.3   146

Dem.
7   13
23   15
58   47

Is.
3   46

Index of Ancient Sources

Isoc.			Gregory of Nazianzus	
2–3	46		*Ep.* 51	
11	46		2	57
Lys.			Hermogenes	
4–5	46		*Id.*	
17	53		2.1	46
24	54			
			[*Inv.*]	
Pomp.			3.14	26
3.17–20	45			
			[*Prog.*]	
Thuc.			1.13–15	67
22	45		2	50
23	45		10.49	51
Epictetus			*Stas.*	
Diatr.			37	26
1.22.9–10	22		59–65	26
1.28.3	207			
2.4.1	146		Herodotus	
3.6.8	23		4.76–77	155
3.14.13	146			
3.23.18	146		Hesiod	
4.1.1	30		fr.	
4.9.17–18	146		3.10	108
Epicurus			*Op.*	
Herod.			1–2	108
37–38	20–21		8	108
			27–41	166
Menoec.			213–92	166
123	21			
			Theog.	
Eusebius of Emesa			1–4	108
PKGK 46	88		886–900	132
			924–26	132
Galen				
Def. med.			Homer	
Kühn 19.349	19		*Hymn 2 to Demeter*	
			1–3	110, 117, 130, 133
Diff. puls.				
Kühn 8.708–9	19		*Hymn 3 to Apollo*	
			334–36	108
[*Hist. phil.*]				
Kühn 19.236–37	18		*Hymn 4 to Hermes*	
			13–16	110, 117
Gennadius of Constantinople				
PKGK 355	169–70		*Hymn 28 to Athena*	
			4–5 17	132
Georgius Choeroboscus				
Trop.				
15	73			

Index of Ancient Sources

Il.
1.15–16	79
1.135–36	73
1.429	74
8.19	23
8.43	77
8.489–91	73
9.531	74
10.194–200	73
18.20-21	70–71
21.602	74

Od.
6.115–17	70–71
12.172	77

Ignatius
Eph.
3.2	129

Irenaeus
Adv. haer.
3.8.8	94

Isocrates
De pace
18	29–30

Helen
17	125

Nic.
9	30

John Chrysostom
Hom. Rom.
1.7 (432d)	128
2.6 (446a–b)	179–80
7 (486b)	207

John of Damascus
In Rom.
1.17	173

Josephus
B.J.
6.346	207

Julius Victor
Rhet.
27	56

Lesbonax
Fig.
31B	79

Libanius
[*Epist.*]
49–50	57

Livy
1.21.4	146

Longinus
Rhet.
fr. 48.124–25	52
fr. 48.132	52
fr. 48.141–47	53–54

Lucian
Hist. conscr.
58	57

Scyth.
9	155

Lysias
Or.
1.5	151
12.24	151
12.42–43	151
19.53–54	151

Menander Rhetor
Epid.
1.332	33
1.333	36
1.334	36
1.339	118–19

Mithridates
Letter   57–59, 61

Nicolaus
Prog.
2	50
10	57

Olympiodorus
In Plat. Gorg.
12.1	19

Origen			Plato		
Comm. Rom.			*Euthyphr.*		
1.4 (2)	87		3e–4e	27	
1.7 (5)	128				
1.15 (13)	172, 176–77		*Gorg.*		
1.18 (15)	177		449b–d	40	
fr. 5	128, 135		461d–e	40	
fr. 12	176		465e	40	
			519e	40	
Pelagius					
In Rom.			*Phaedr.*		
1.17	173		227c	10	
			230e–234c	10, 33	
Philo of Alexandria			234e	42	
Migr.			237a–241d	10–14	
171	206		238b–c	149	
			245c–46a	15	
Mos.			265d–e	12	
1.90	206		267a–b	40–41	
			275a	206	
Virt.					
34	207		*Prot.*		
			333c–335c	40	
Philolaus			334e	40	
Kirk/Raven 346,			343b	63	
§ 451	10				
			Soph.		
Philostratus			218b–c	14	
Epist.			221a–b	14–15	
AET 42	57		223b	15	
			224c–e	15	
Vit. Apoll.			231b	15	
4.33	46		247d–e	15	
			253d–e	12	
Vit. soph.					
16.503	46		*Symp.*		
20.514	46		180b	36	
			186a–b	36–37	
Phoebammon			194e–97e	36–38	
Fig.					
prologue	67		Pliny the Elder		
1.2	68–69, 79		*Nat.*		
1.3	171		29.7.14	153	
2	72		18.41–43	154	
2.1	68, 69–70				
			Plutarch		
Photius			*Brut.*		
Comm. Rom.			2.5–8	56, 58	
PKGK 475	170		29.4	206	
Ep. 206			[*De Hom.*]		
10–16	58		2.9	72–73	

2.15	67	8.3.50	77
2.18	23	8.6.1–3	67
2.22	78	8.6.19–22	76–77
2.23	204	8.6.23	204
2.24	107	8.6.43	107
2.37	72	9.1.1–21	67
2.39	72, 75	9.2.54–57	68
2.173	125	9.3.28	171
		9.3.50	70
Garr.		9.3.58–59	76
17 (510e-11d)	63	9.3.64	76
		9.3.81–86	125
Lyc.		9.3.99	70
19.1–5	41–42	9.4.19	56
20.6	62–63	10.1.12	148
		10.1.107	58
Num.			
3.7	155	Rufus	
		Rhet.	
Phoc.		17	50
5.1–6	61–62		
		Rutilius Lupus	
Pyth. orac.		*Fig.*	
29 (408e–9a)	63	2.8	71
[*Reg. imp. apophth.*]		Sextus Empiricus	
16 (193d)	41–42	*Math.*	
		2.7	19
Superst.			
165b	22–23	*Pyr.*	
166d–67a	166	2.207	20
170d–f	166	2.212	18
Quintilian		Stobaeus	
Inst.		*Anth.*	
1.5.1	44	2.67.11–12	19–20
3.5.5–9	26	2.73.16–74.3	18–19, 149
3.6	26	2.88.8–90.6	17
3.6.56–57	26, 27	3.35.9	41
3.6.60–61	27		
3.6.81–82	25	Tertullian	
3.7.6	33	*Adv. Marc.*	
3.7.7–9	37	5.13.2	173–74
3.7.26–28	33		
3.7.28	25	*Adv. Prax.*	
3.8.1	30	27	135
4.1.34–35	54		
4.1.62	53	Theodoret	
4.2.4–8	52	*In Rom.*	
4.2.31–33	49	1.17	169, 178
4.2.40	66		
4.2.48–50	66		

Theon		Trypho[II]	
Prog.		*Trop.*	
3	67	7	78
4	66–67	9	204
5	50–51, 65–66	13	73
10	57		
11	166	Varro	
12	77	*Ling. lat.*	
		10.75	31
Thucydides			
1.21.1–4	57	Virgil	
		Aen.	
Tiberius Rhetor		11.142	77
Fig.			
10	68	*Ecl.*	
37	80	3.8–9	76
40	69		
42	73–74	Xenophon	
		Anab.	
Trypho[I]		3.1.31	60
Trop.			
1.13	73	*Hell.*	
2.8	70–71	3.4.5	207
2.9	63, 71	5.4.25–26	150–51
2.15	148		
2.17	106	Zonaeus	
6	204	*Fig.*	
7	77–78	2.10	72
		2.14	79–80
		2.19	69
		2.22	148

Corpora

AET		§ 2.6.2	108
6–7	57	§ 4.5	108
21–29	55		
42	57–58	Kirk/Raven	
58	57	144 (§§ 140–41)	10
62	56	346 (§ 451)	10
72	57	362–64 (§ 476)	10
		434 (§ 596)	10
Isis aretalogies		442–43 (§ 603)	10
Totti 1a	112		
		Long/Sedley	
Furley/Bremer		17C	20
§ 1.1	108	17E	21
§ 2.3	108	19F	21
§ 2.6.1	108	23B	21

26H	19–20	2.103–4	67
31A	16	2.129	77
31E	19	2.126–27	166
32C	18	3.22	68, 69
32E	18	3.23–33	69
40T	22	3.29	171
41H	18–19, 149	3.33	72
42A	19	3.35	80
44F	23	3.37–38	148
54A	21, 149	3.44	67
65A	17	3.45–46	68–69
		3.46	72, 79
Orph. Hymn		3.46–47	171
25	109	3.50	68, 69
32.1	132	3.62	68
		3.76	80
PG		3.77–78	69
28.533	18, 20	3.78–79	73–74
60.409	179–80	3.94	79
60.445	202	3.167	72
82.57	169, 178	3.168	79–80
82.60	169	3.169	69
95.448	173	3.169–70	148
		3.195–96	77
PGM		3.195	204
I.30–32	111	3.198	73
IV.185–87	112	3.202	70–71
IV.644–50	130	3.204	106
IV.987-97	111	3.209–10	78
IV.1146–58	111	3.209	204
IV.3033–37	114	3.211	73
XII.228	146	3.233–34	204
Hymn 2.2–4	110–11	3.242	74
		3.252	73
PKGK			
46	88	*RG*-W	
53	177–78	6.36	44
57	128		
58	177	*RLM*	
355	169–70	37	74–75
475	170		
		Suda	
RG		561	59
2.4	50		
2.22	50	*SVF*	
2.75	67	2.226	18
2.79	50	2.227	19
2.83	50–51, 65	2.229	19
2.84–86	66		
2.96	67		

Index of Modern Authors

Achtemeier, E. R. 159–60
Aichele, George 7
Alexander, Loveday 39
Althaus, Paul 169
Anderson, R. Dean 4, 7, 8, 71
Ando, Clifford 162–63
Asher, Jeffrey A. 2
Asmis, Elizabeth 20–21
Attridge, Harold W. 179
Aune, David E. 50, 51, 76

Barr, James 157
Barrett, C. K. 85, 90, 91, 93, 97, 103–4, 126, 129, 147, 169, 189, 199, 201, 214, 216
Bassler, Jouette 160
Barth, Karl 170–71, 181
Barth, Marcus 93, 95
Bayer, Greg 16
Beard, Mary 146
Benson, Hugh H. 10
Betz, Hans Dieter 4, 7, 39, 81, 97, 102, 111, 121, 130, 146, 150, 154, 155, 158, 189
Boas, George 155
Bonner, S. F. 42, 45, 50
Bornkamm, Günther 4, 91, 94
Bottéro, Jean 162
Bousset, Wilhelm 94, 96
Brauch, Manfred E. 157
Bremer, Jan Maarten 106, 109, 110
Brown, Lesley 15
Bryan, Christopher 199
Bultmann, Rudolf 91, 93, 103, 145, 146, 157–58
Burgess, Theodore C. 33–34
Burkert, Walter 166

Calhoun, Robert Matthew 57, 137, 178–79
Calvin, John 169

Campbell, Douglas A. 7, 170–71, 189, 198, 199, 200, 201, 205, 207–11
Charles, David 9, 16
Charlesworth, James H. 137
Chiba, Kei 16
Cohen, S. Marc 27
Collins, John J. 132
Conzelmann, Hans 94, 139–40
Cranfield, C. E. B. 7, 85, 87, 90, 92, 104, 123, 126, 129, 131, 132, 135, 158, 169, 189, 197, 215
Crivelli, Paolo 17
Cullmann, Oscar 93–94, 96

Dahl, Nils 93, 159
Dahood, Mitchell 164
Dee, James H. 106
Delling, Gerhard 92, 155
Descartes, René 205
Deslaurier, Marguerite 16
Dihle, Albrecht 110
Dilts, Marvin R. 50
Dodd, Brian 208
Dodd, C. H. 85, 90, 91, 95, 103, 129, 147, 163, 167, 169, 189, 201, 214
Donfried, Karl P. 7
Downing, F. Gerald 86, 207
Dunn, James D. G. 6, 91, 100, 104, 124–25, 126, 136, 146, 157, 158, 167, 170, 189, 197, 201, 202, 206, 210

Ehrmann, Bart 128
Eichrodt, Walther 159
Engberg-Pedersen, Troels 7, 156

Faraone, Christopher A. 137, 166
Fears, J. Rufus 146
Fee, Gordon D. 4, 131
Ferejohn, Michael T. 16
Finlan, Stephen 199, 201

Fitzmyer, Joseph 6, 87, 90, 91, 93, 97, 126, 129, 146, 153, 157, 159, 167, 169, 170, 187, 189, 197, 199, 201, 210
Foerster, Werner 150–51
Foley, Helene P. 110
Fowden, Garth 155
Fridrichsen, Anton 92, 129, 170
Friedrich, Gerhard 90
Furley, William D. 106, 109, 110

Gager, John G. 166, 194
Gaines, Robert N. 44
Gamble, Harry 7
García Martínez, Florentino 140, 188, 189, 190
Gaston, Lloyd 170, 203
Gathercole, Simon J. 202, 204, 215
Georgi, Dieter 146
Gill, Mary Louise 15
Gordley, Matthew E. 109, 112
Graf, Fritz 109, 111–12, 154
Grieb, A. Katherine 131, 205
Guerra, Anthony J. 7, 96

Haacker, Klaus 147, 167
Hahn, Ferdinand 93, 104, 126
Hatch, W. H. P. 104
Hays, Richard B. 86, 109, 131, 133, 170, 189, 204–5, 207, 210
Headlam, Arthur C. 126, 129, 146, 157, 169, 201
Heath, Malcolm 26, 27
Hellholm, David 94, 144
Hendrickson, G. L. 42, 55
Hengel, Martin 91
Henrichs, Albert 110
Hock, Ronald F. 39, 67
Hooker, Morna 171, 205, 207, 215
Hornblower, Simon 106
Hunter, A. M. 92
Hurtado, Larry W. 91

Innes, Doreen C. 48

Jeremias, Joachim 94
Jervell, Jacob 7
Jervis, L. Ann 85, 87, 88
Jewett, Robert 4, 6, 7, 87, 90, 91, 92–106, 123, 124, 127, 129, 135, 144, 147, 154, 186, 189, 195, 197, 198, 199, 201, 206, 213
Johnson, B. 158

Johnson, E. E. 215
Johnson, Luke Timothy 39, 86, 205, 207, 210
Johnston, Sarah Iles 155
de Jonge, Marius 91, 93
Judson, Lindsay 27

Käsemann, Ernst 85, 90, 91, 97, 99, 103, 126, 129, 133, 135, 138, 145, 146, 147, 148, 156, 157, 158, 167, 168, 169, 188, 189, 195–96, 197, 199
Keck, Leander 88, 148, 158, 170, 198, 201, 213
Kee, H. C. 139
Kennedy, George A. 26, 43, 44, 48, 50, 52, 67, 144
Kensky, Meira Ziva 158, 160, 165, 166, 168
Kindstrand, Jan Frederick 155
Klein, Günther 89
Koester, Helmut 7, 158
Kotansky, Roy 137
Kramer, Werner 93, 95, 96, 97, 102, 103
Kumaniecki, K. 69
Kümmel, W. G. 6

Lampe, Peter 7
Lattke, Michael 137
Lausberg, Heinrich 51, 70, 71, 76, 80, 148
Lennox, James G. 16
Liebeschuetz, J. H. W. G. 145–46
Lietzmann, Hans 126, 147, 169
Linnemann, Eta 91
Lloyd-Jones, Hugh 165
Lohr, Winrich A. 103
Lohse, Eduard 90, 91, 169
Long, Anthony A. 16–24, 147, 149
Lovejoy, Arthur O. 155
Luther, Martin 169, 205

Majercik, Ruth 155
Malanchthon, Philip 169
Malherbe, Abraham J. 57, 97
Manson, T. W. 6–7, 170
Marrou, H. I. 50
Martin, Ralph P. 95
Martin, Dale B. 2
Martin, Troy 7
Martinez, David 133
Martyn, J. Louis 97, 121
Matlock, R. Barry 206

Metzger, Bruce M. 94, 188
Michel, Otto 129, 179
Minear, Paul S. 7
Miscall, Peter 7
Mitchell, Margaret M. 7-8, 30, 39, 78-79, 82-83, 106
Modrak, Deborah 16
Momigliano, Arnaldo 154
Moo, Douglas 88, 90, 92, 97, 103, 126, 129, 131, 157, 159, 169, 189, 197, 201
Munck, Johannes 7
Murray, John 169

Nagy, Gregory 71
Nanos, Mark 7, 152
Nash, Daphne E. M. 146
Neufeld, Verson H. 93, 94, 96
North, John 146
Nygren, Anders 169

O'Neil, Edward N. 39, 67
O'Neill, J. C. 6, 104

Polythress, Vern S. 92, 94, 98, 101, 103
Porter, Stanley 8
Preisendanz, Karl 110
Preuss, Horst Dietrich 159, 163
Price, Simon 146
Procksch, Otto 126
Pulleyn, Simon 106, 111, 166

Quarles, Charles L. 170

Race, William H. 109-10, 111, 117
von Rad, Gerhard 159
Räisänen, Heikki 194, 215, 216
Raven, J. E. 10
Rawson, Elizabeth 154
Reinhardt, Alexander 104
Renehan, Robert 133
Richards, E. Randolph 93
Roetzel, Calvin J. 167
Rose, H. J. 106
Rose, Valentius 56
Roth, Martha 162
Rothschild, Clare K. 179
Rowe, Galen O. 71
Russell, Donald A. 26, 42, 45, 46, 48, 55, 64, 67, 68
Rutherford, Ian 46

Sanday, William 126, 129, 146, 157, 169, 201
Sanders, E. P. 86, 132, 157, 175, 189, 194, 203-4, 215
Schlatter, Adolf 170
Schlier, Heinrich 85, 90, 91, 129, 147
Schmidt, K. L. 129
Schmithals, Walther 6, 102, 126, 129
Schneider, Bernadin 91, 126, 129
Schnelle, Udo 158
Schniewind, Julius 90
Schubert, Paul 144
Schütz, John Howard 104
Schweizer, Eduard 91, 127, 138
Scott, James M. 92, 101, 102, 103, 104, 126-27
Scrivner, Frederick Henry 104
Scullion, J. J. 158
Sedley, David N. 16-24, 149
Simonetti, M. 103
Smyth, Herbert Weir 71, 72, 75, 76, 96, 127, 145, 262
Solmsen, Friedrich 42
Souter, Alexander 173
Stauffer, Ethelbert 93, 95, 99, 104
Stowers, Stanley K. 92, 159, 170-71, 195
Strecker, Georg 91, 93, 94, 103
Stroumsa, Guy G. 155
Stuhlmacher, Peter 3, 4, 85, 147, 157, 158, 169, 199

Thom, Johan 166
Tigchelaar, Eibert J. C. 140, 188, 189, 190
Tischendorf, Constantin von 128
du Toit, Andrie B. 157, 159
Torraca, L. 59
Totti, Maria 112

VanLandingham, Chris 157, 158
Versnel, H. S. 96, 166
Vogels, Heinrich Joseph 180
Vorster, Johannes N. 148

Wagner, J. Ross 131
Walker, William O. 6
Walsh, Richard 7
Waszink, J. H. 155
Watkins, Calvert 133
Watson, Francis 7, 194, 205
Watts, Rikki E. 189

Wedderburn, A. J. M. 7, 91, 148, 157, 158
Weiss, Johannes 91
Wengst, Klaus 93, 102
West, Martin 68, 162
Whitsett, Christopher G. 101, 103, 131
Wickham, Lionel R. 103
Wilckens, Ulrich 90, 91, 126, 129
Williams, Sam K. 145, 157, 160, 170
Windisch, Hans 153

Wilson, Todd A. 82–84
Wooten, Cecil W. 47
Wright, N. T. 199, 207, 213
Wuellner, Wilhelm 144
van Wyk Cronjé, Jacobus 42

Zeller, Dieter 170
Ziegler, Joseph 188
Ziesler, J. A. 157

Index of Subjects

Allegory (ἀλληγορία) 61
Apophthegm (ἀπόφθεγμα) 42, 56, 58, 62–63, 71
Arrangement (τάξις) 49–55
– introduction (προοίμιον) 3, 11, 30, 34, 38, 49, 51–55, 143–49, 221
– thesis (πρόθεσις) 3, 10, 34, 38, 49, 51–53, 143–92, 213, 220–21
– narrative (διήγησις, διήγημα) 48–51, 65–66, 69, 70–71, 80–81, 143
– proof (πίστις) 24, 34, 51, 143–44, 156–90
– conclusion (ἐπίλογος) 51–52

Barbarian (βάρβαρος) 147, 153–56, 183, 206–7
Benediction 113, 119
Boasting (καύχησις) 202–4, 215
Brevity (βραχυλογία, βραχύτης, συντομία) *passim*
– as a figure *s.v.* figure
– compression (συστρέφειν) 54, 66–67
– division into language (λέξις) and content (γνώμη, πράγματα) 47–48, 51, 65–67, 80–81, 123
– impression of wisdom 60–63
– in letters 55–59, 60–62
– in narrative *s.v.* style
– in virtue-theory *s.v.* style
– Sophistic instruction 40–41, 48, 66
– Spartan taciturnity 41–42, 48, 60–63

Canon (κανών)
– of stylistic exemplars 44–47
– 'rules' 54
Chreia (χρεία) *s.v.* progymnasma
Christology 4
– adoptionist 100, 103, 128
– 'primitive' 4, 91–92, 94–95, 100–3
– trinitarian 93–94, 128–29

Circumcision 195, 202–3
Covenant 157–69, 175, 201, 203, 213
Covenantal nomism 202–3
Cross (σταυρός) 83–84, 101, 180
Cult
– civic 110–13, 145–46, 201, 206
– Jewish 201, 212
– mystery 1, 110

Definition (ὅρος) *passim*
– as a rhetorical figure 24–25
– as a στάσις 27–29
– completeness 18–19, 219
– conciseness 5, 18–19, 31, 219
– division (διαίρεσις) 11–12, 15, 33
– ἐξάπλωσις 17–20, 29, 31, 38, 86, 219
– exegesis of the terms 31–36, 193–218
– formal features 22–23
– outline (ὑπογραφή, ὑποτύπωσις) 16, 19–22, 221
– particularity (ἴδιον) 16, 18, 86, 136, 150
– securing agreement (ὁμολογία) 11, 17, 19, 22, 29, 38
– specific definitions and outlines
– – art (τέχνη) 19
– – atheism (ἀθεότης) 22
– – avarice (*avaritia*) 24
– – bad luck (ἀτυχία) 26
– – being (τὸ ὄν, οὐσία) 15
– – common sense (ὁ κοινὸς νοῦς) 23
– – custom (ἔθος) 34–36, 193
– – definition (ὅρος) 11, 15–16, 20, 24–25, 149
– – education (τὸ παιδεύεσθαι)
– – error (ἄγνοια) 26
– – fisherman's art (ἀσπαλιευτική) 14–15
– – fortitude (*fortitudo*) 24–25
– – freedom (ἐλευθερία) 30–33, 193

– – frugality (*diligentia*) 24
– – god (θεός) 21, 37, 149
– – happiness (εὐδαιμονία) 23
– – immortal (ἀθανατόν) 15
– – injury (*iniuria*) 24
– – king (ὁ βασιλεύων) 30
– – knowledge (ἐπιστήμη) 18–19, 149
– – law (νόμος) 34–36
– – lèse-majesté (*maiestas*) 28–29
– – love (ἔρως) 13, 21, 36–38, 149
– – outline (ὑπογραφή, ὑποτύπωσις) 19–21
– – preconception (πρόληψις) 21
– – pursuit (ἐπιτήδευμα) 19–20
– – rhetoric (ῥητορική) 22
– – sophist (σοφιστής) 15
– – soul (ψυχή) 15
– – sovereignty (*maiestas*) 24
– – superstition (δεισιδαιμονία) 22
– – temerity (*temeritas*) 24–25
– – world (κόσμος) 23
– taxonomy 11–15, 33, 219
– theory
– – Aristotle 15–16
– – Epicurus 19–22
– – Plato 10–15
– – presocratics 10
– – rhetoricians 17–19
– – Stoics 16–24
Delphic court 25
Delphic maxims 60–61, 63
Duty 145–47

Education
– General rhetorical 2, 42–67
– Athenian 40–41
– Spartan 41–42
Epicureanism 1–2, 19–22, 44
Epithet (ἐπίθετον)
– simple 106–9, 118–19
– expanded 107–9, 119
– mythological expanded 5, 91, 105–42, 209, 213
– ἀντονομασία *s.v.* figure
Ethics 212, 215–16
– virtue (ἀρετή) 12–14, 19–20, 41–43, 145–47, 154–55
Faith (πίστις) 86–89, 97, 120–22, 144–48, 152–58, 169–87, 189, 190–212, 216–17, 219–20

– 'faith of Christ' (πίστις Χριστοῦ) 86, 170–71, 204–12
– Roman cult of *Fides* 145–46
Figure (σχῆμα) and Trope (τροπή, τρόπος) 59, 67–80
– ἀναδίπλωσις 59, 171, 199, 203, 208
– ἀντίθεσις *s.v.* style
– ἀντονομασία 106–7
– ἀπὸ κοινοῦ 4–5, 39, 69, 79–80, 84, 86, 135, 149, 153, 191, 219
– ἀποσιώπησις 68–69, 70, 71, 76
– ἀσύνδετον 68–69, 130
– βραχυλογία, βραχύτης, συντομία 67–71, 75, 82–84
– ἔλλειψις 4–6, 39, 69, 71–75, 76–78, 84–86, 95–96, 136–37, 169–87, 191, 199, 208, 219
– ἔμφασις 69, 71, 72, 74
– ἐπανάληψις 171
– ἐπαναφορά 200
– ἐπιμονή 69
– ἐπιτροχασμός 69
– ζεῦγμα 68–69, 79–80
– κατάχρησις 23
– λιτότης 148
– μεταφορά 82
– μετωνυμία 204–5
– ὅρος *s.v.* definition
– παρένθεσις 200
– παρονομασία 40
– πλεονασμός 42, 72, 90, 95, 208
– σύγκρισις 34–36, 174
– συναθροισμός 69
– συνεκδοχή 4–5, 39, 69, 76–79, 82–84, 86, 90–91, 107–23, 124, 155–56, 179–80, 185–86, 189, 191, 200–5, 209–10, 212, 219–20
– ὑπέρβατον 172
– χιασμός 34–35, 95
Flesh (σάρξ) 5, 88, 91, 96, 99–100, 123–27, 129, 132, 136–38, 219
Forensic eschatology 150–52, 158–69, 189, 193–96, 212
– eschatological trial 1–2, 121, 134, 150–52, 156–69, 194–95, 197–98, 202–4, 217
– forbearance (ἀνοχή) 200–2
– Justice, righteousness (δικαιοσύνη, δίκη)

Index of Subjects

– – divine 86, 134, 143–44, 147–48, 156–69, 173–85, 189, 191–97, 200–4, 208, 212, 215, 220
– – human 86, 147, 156–69, 178, 182–84, 197–204, 208, 212, 215–17
– redemption 199–202
– salvation (σωτηρία) 134, 143–44, 149–52, 156, 159, 173–85, 193–94, 199–202, 212, 220
– wrath (ὀργή) 97, 120, 150–52, 167, 194–202, 212, 214, 220
Form-criticism 93–95

Genre (γένος)
– deliberative 24–25, 27–34, 38, 42, 46
– epideictic 24–25, 28, 33–38, 42
– forensic 24–29, 33–34, 38 42, 56, 58
Grace (χάρις) 88–89, 99, 169, 205, 212

Historical criticism 7
Hymn, prayer 5, 36–38, 96–97, 106–13, 115–119, 122–23
– tripartite structure 109–10, 115–17
Hypostasis 149–50

Intertextuality 101, 103, 131–32, 189–90
Invention (εὕρεσις) 3, 24–29, 221–22
– point to be adjudicated (τὸ κρινόμενον) 28–29, 193, 221–22
– *stasis*-theory (στάσις) 26–29, 219

Judicial procedure
– Babylonian 162
– Greek 25
– Israelite 161–65
– Roman 162–63

Law (νόμος) 34–36, 82–84, 102, 140, 160–63, 167, 173–78, 180–81, 185, 194–97, 198–99, 201, 212, 215–16
– natural 203
– 'works of law' (ἔργα νόμου) 84, 122, 202–4, 215
Letter (ἐπιστολή) 47, 55–59, 80
Love (ἔρως) 10–15, 30

Piety (εὐσέβεια) 1–2, 14, 22, 196–97
Polysemy 5–6, 65, 84, 86, 90, 150, 153, 158, 168, 171–72, 185–90, 205, 208–9, 215–16, 220
Popular philosophy 9–10, 22, 29–33, 38

'Postmodernism' 7
'Pre-Pauline formula' 5, 87, 91–106, 129, 138, 199–201
Progymnasma (προγύμνασμα) 50–51, 65–67
– γνώμη 63
– διήγημα, διήγησις 50–51, 65–66
– μῦθος 66–67
– χρεία 39, 67
Prolixity (μακρολογία) 40–42, 64–67, 88–89, 117–18, 122, 141, 144–45, 208, 219

Revelation 144, 147–48, 173–85, 198–99, 203
Rhetorical theory, modern 7–8
Ritual
– Christian
– – baptism 92–94, 169–70
– – eucharist 92–95, 119–20
– Jewish
– – day of atonement 201
– 'magic'
– – amulet 137–38
– – *defixio* 166
– – *historiola* 137–38
– – *magus* (μάγος) 155
– – 'spells' 110–11, 114, 118, 130, 146, 154
– – *voces magicae* 111
– relation to myth 109
Romans (letter) *passim*
– audience 3, 6–7, 144–49, 165–67, 211, 221–22
– date 6
– genre 7–8, 193, 221–22
– occasion 3, 141–45, 148–49, 217
– structure 7–8, 193, *also s.v.* arrangement
– unity 6

Shame 148–49
Slavery (δουλεία) 30–33, 60–62, 87–88, 102, 174–75, 177
Spirit (πνεῦμα) 88, 91, 96, 99–100, 123–27, 129, 136–40, 187, 210–12, 219
Stoicism 1–2, 16–24, 43–44, 67
Style (λέξις) *passim*
– antithesis (ἀντίθεσις) 91, 95–96, 99–100, 123–26, 129–42, 198, 219
– charm (χάρις) 59

- characterization (ἦθος) 58–59, 67, 145–47, 190–91
- clause (κῶλον) 60–61
- compound simplex iteration 133–34
- forcefulness (δεινότης) 59, 60–61
- imitation (μίμησις) 44, 55, 57–58
- period (περίοδος) 56–57
- phrase (κόμμα) 61
- types (Demetrius) 55–56, 59–60
- virtue-theory 40, 42–51, 65, 67, 70
- – in narrative (διήγησις) 49–51
- – two-tiered system (Dionysius) 44–47
- – clarity (σαφήνεια) 42–47, 49–50, 56–57
- – conciseness (συντομία) 43–47, 49–50
- – correctness (Ἑλληνισμός) 43–47
- – ornament (κατασκευή) 43–47
- – plausibility (πιθανότης) 46, 47, 49–50
- – propriety (πρέπον) 43–47, 55–56, 58, 65

Symbol (σύμβολον) 61

Textual criticism 6–7, 94, 104, 128, 133–34, 187–88

Universalism 152–56, 193, 199–200, 202–3, 212, 214, 216–17

Wissenschaftliche Untersuchungen zum Neuen Testament
Alphabetical Index of the First and Second Series

Ådna, Jostein: Jesu Stellung zum Tempel. 2000. Vol. II/119.

Ådna, Jostein (Ed.): The Formation of the Early Church. 2005. Vol. 183.

- and *Kvalbein, Hans* (Ed.): The Mission of the Early Church to Jews and Gentiles. 2000. Vol. 127.

Ahearne-Kroll, Stephen P., Paul A. Holloway, and *James A. Kelhoffer* (Ed.): Women and Gender in Ancient Religions. 2010. Vol. 263.

Aland, Barbara: Was ist Gnosis? 2009. Vol. 239.

Alexeev, Anatoly A., Christos Karakolis and *Ulrich Luz* (Ed.): Einheit der Kirche im Neuen Testament. Dritte europäische orthodox-westliche Exegetenkonferenz in Sankt Petersburg, 24.–31. August 2005. 2008. Vol. 218.

Alkier, Stefan: Wunder und Wirklichkeit in den Briefen des Apostels Paulus. 2001. Vol. 134.

Allen, David M.: Deuteronomy and Exhortation in Hebrews. 2008. Vol. II/238.

Anderson, Charles A.: Philo of Alexandria's Views of the Physical World. 2011. Vol. II/309.

Anderson, Paul N.: The Christology of the Fourth Gospel. 1996. Vol. II/78.

Appold, Mark L.: The Oneness Motif in the Fourth Gospel. 1976. Vol. II/1.

Arnold, Clinton E.: The Colossian Syncretism. 1995. Vol. II/77.

Ascough, Richard S.: Paul's Macedonian Associations. 2003. Vol. II/161.

Asiedu-Peprah, Martin: Johannine Sabbath Conflicts As Juridical Controversy. 2001. Vol. II/132.

Attridge, Harold W.: Essays on John and Hebrews. 2010. Bd. 264.

- see *Zangenberg, Jürgen.*

Aune, David E.: Apocalypticism, Prophecy and Magic in Early Christianity. 2006. Vol. 199.

Avemarie, Friedrich: Die Tauferzählungen der Apostelgeschichte. 2002. Vol. 139.

Avemarie, Friedrich and *Hermann Lichtenberger* (Ed.): Auferstehung – Ressurection. 2001. Vol. 135.

- Bund und Tora. 1996. Vol. 92.

Baarlink, Heinrich: Verkündigtes Heil. 2004. Vol. 168.

Bachmann, Michael: Sünder oder Übertreter. 1992. Vol. 59.

Bachmann, Michael (Ed.): Lutherische und Neue Paulusperspektive. 2005. Vol. 182.

Back, Frances: Verwandlung durch Offenbarung bei Paulus. 2002. Vol. II/153.

Backhaus, Knut: Der sprechende Gott. 2009. Vol. 240.

Baker, William R.: Personal Speech-Ethics in the Epistle of James. 1995. Vol. II/68.

Bakke, Odd Magne: 'Concord and Peace'. 2001. Vol. II/143.

Balch, David L.: Roman Domestic Art and Early House Churches. 2008. Vol. 228.

Baldwin, Matthew C.: Whose *Acts of Peter*? 2005. Vol. II/196.

Balla, Peter: Challenges to New Testament Theology. 1997. Vol. II/95.

- The Child-Parent Relationship in the New Testament and its Environment. 2003. Vol. 155.

Baltes, Guido: Hebräisches Evangelium und synoptische Überlieferung. 2011. Bd. II/312.

Bammel, Ernst: Judaica. Vol. I 1986. Vol. 37.

- Vol. II 1997. Vol. 91.

Barclay, John M.G.: Pauline Churches and Diaspora Jews. 2011. Vol. 275.

Barreto, Eric D.: Ethnic Negotiations. 2010. Vol. II/294.

Barrier, Jeremy W.: The Acts of Paul and Thecla. 2009. Vol. II/270.

Barton, Stephen C.: see *Stuckenbruck, Loren T.*

Bash, Anthony: Ambassadors for Christ. 1997. Vol. II/92.

Bauckham, Richard: The Jewish World around the New Testament. Collected Essays Volume I. 2008. Vol. 233.

Bauer, Thomas Johann: Paulus und die kaiserzeitliche Epistolographie. 2011. Vol. 276.

Bauernfeind, Otto: Kommentar und Studien zur Apostelgeschichte. 1980. Vol. 22.

Baum, Armin Daniel: Pseudepigraphie und literarische Fälschung im frühen Christentum. 2001. Vol. II/138.

Bayer, Hans Friedrich: Jesus' Predictions of Vindication and Resurrection. 1986. Vol. II/20.

Becker, Eve-Marie: Das Markus-Evangelium im Rahmen antiker Historiographie. 2006. Vol. 194.

Becker, Eve-Marie and *Peter Pilhofer* (Ed.): Biographie und Persönlichkeit des Paulus. 2005. Vol. 187.

- and *Anders Runesson* (Ed.): Mark and Matthew I. 2011. *Vol. 271.*
Becker, Michael: Wunder und Wundertäter im frührabbinischen Judentum. 2002. *Vol. II/144.*
Becker, Michael and *Markus Öhler* (Ed.): Apokalyptik als Herausforderung neutestamentlicher Theologie. 2006. *Vol. II/214.*
Bell, Richard H.: Deliver Us from Evil. 2007. *Vol. 216.*
- The Irrevocable Call of God. 2005. *Vol. 184.*
- No One Seeks for God. 1998. *Vol. 106.*
- Provoked to Jealousy. 1994. *Vol. II/63.*
Bennema, Cornelis: The Power of Saving Wisdom. 2002. *Vol. II/148.*
Bergman, Jan: see *Kieffer, René*
Bergmeier, Roland: Das Gesetz im Römerbrief und andere Studien zum Neuen Testament. 2000. *Vol. 121.*
Bernett, Monika: Der Kaiserkult in Judäa unter den Herodiern und Römern. 2007. *Vol. 203.*
Betho, Benjamin: see *Clivaz, Claire.*
Betz, Otto: Jesus, der Messias Israels. 1987. *Vol. 42.*
- Jesus, der Herr der Kirche. 1990. *Vol. 52.*
Beyschlag, Karlmann: Simon Magus und die christliche Gnosis. 1974. *Vol. 16.*
Bieringer, Reimund: see *Koester, Craig.*
Bittner, Wolfgang J.: Jesu Zeichen im Johannesevangelium. 1987. *Vol. II/26.*
Bjerkelund, Carl J.: Tauta Egeneto. 1987. *Vol. 40.*
Blackburn, Barry Lee: Theios Aner and the Markan Miracle Traditions. 1991. *Vol. II/40.*
Blackwell, Ben C.: Christosis. 2011. *Vol. II/314.*
Blanton IV, Thomas R.: Constructing a New Covenant. 2007. *Vol. II/233.*
Bock, Darrell L.: Blasphemy and Exaltation in Judaism and the Final Examination of Jesus. 1998. *Vol. II/106.*
- and *Robert L. Webb* (Ed.): Key Events in the Life of the Historical Jesus. 2009. *Vol. 247.*
Bockmuehl, Markus: The Remembered Peter. 2010. *Vol. 262.*
- Revelation and Mystery in Ancient Judaism and Pauline Christianity. 1990. *Vol. II/36.*
Bøe, Sverre: Cross-Bearing in Luke. 2010. *Vol. II/278.*
- Gog and Magog. 2001. *Vol. II/135.*
Böhlig, Alexander: Gnosis und Synkretismus. Vol. 1 1989. *Vol. 47* – Vol. 2 1989. *Vol. 48.*
Böhm, Martina: Samarien und die Samaritai bei Lukas. 1999. *Vol. II/111.*
Börstinghaus, Jens: Sturmfahrt und Schiffbruch. 2010. *Vol. II/274.*
Böttrich, Christfried: Weltweisheit – Menschheitsethik – Urkult. 1992. *Vol. II/50.*

- and *Herzer, Jens* (Ed.): Josephus und das Neue Testament. 2007. *Vol. 209.*
Bolyki, János: Jesu Tischgemeinschaften. 1997. *Vol. II/96.*
Bosman, Philip: Conscience in Philo and Paul. 2003. *Vol. II/166.*
Bovon, François: New Testament and Christian Apocrypha. 2009. *Vol. 237.*
- Studies in Early Christianity. 2003. *Vol. 161.*
Brändl, Martin: Der Agon bei Paulus. 2006. *Vol. II/222.*
Braun, Heike: Geschichte des Gottesvolkes und christliche Identität. 2010. *Vol. II/279.*
Breytenbach, Cilliers: see *Frey, Jörg.*
Broadhead, Edwin K.: Jewish Ways of Following Jesus Redrawing the Religious Map of Antiquity. 2010. *Vol. 266.*
Brocke, Christoph vom: Thessaloniki – Stadt des Kassander und Gemeinde des Paulus. 2001. *Vol. II/125.*
Brunson, Andrew: Psalm 118 in the Gospel of John. 2003. *Vol. II/158.*
Büchli, Jörg: Der Poimandres – ein paganisiertes Evangelium. 1987. *Vol. II/27.*
Bühner, Jan A.: Der Gesandte und sein Weg im 4. Evangelium. 1977. *Vol. II/2.*
Burchard, Christoph: Untersuchungen zu Joseph und Aseneth. 1965. *Vol. 8.*
- Studien zur Theologie, Sprache und Umwelt des Neuen Testaments. Ed. by D. Sänger. 1998. *Vol. 107.*
Burnett, Richard: Karl Barth's Theological Exegesis. 2001. *Vol. II/145.*
Byron, John: Slavery Metaphors in Early Judaism and Pauline Christianity. 2003. *Vol. II/162.*
Byrskog, Samuel: Story as History – History as Story. 2000. *Vol. 123.*
Calhoun, Robert M.: Paul's Definitions of the Gospel in Romans 1. 2011. *Vol. II/316.*
Cancik, Hubert (Ed.): Markus-Philologie. 1984. *Vol. 33.*
Capes, David B.: Old Testament Yaweh Texts in Paul's Christology. 1992. *Vol. II/47.*
Caragounis, Chrys C.: The Development of Greek and the New Testament. 2004. *Vol. 167.*
- The Son of Man. 1986. *Vol. 38.*
- see *Fridrichsen, Anton.*
Carleton Paget, James: The Epistle of Barnabas. 1994. *Vol. II/64.*
- Jews, Christians and Jewish Christians in Antiquity. 2010. *Vol. 251.*
Carson, D.A., O'Brien, Peter T. and *Mark Seifrid* (Ed.): Justification and Variegated Nomism.
  Vol. 1: The Complexities of Second Temple Judaism. 2001. *Vol. II/140.*

Vol. 2: The Paradoxes of Paul. 2004. *Vol. II/181.*
Caulley, Thomas Scott and *Hermann Lichtenberger* (Ed.): Die Septuaginta und das frühe Christentum – The Septuagint and Christian Origins. 2011. *Vol. 277.*
– see *Lichtenberger, Hermann.*
Chae, Young Sam: Jesus as the Eschatological Davidic Shepherd. 2006. *Vol. II/216.*
Chapman, David W.: Ancient Jewish and Christian Perceptions of Crucifixion. 2008. *Vol. II/244.*
Chester, Andrew: Messiah and Exaltation. 2007. *Vol. 207.*
Chibici-Revneanu, Nicole: Die Herrlichkeit des Verherrlichten. 2007. *Vol. II/231.*
Ciampa, Roy E.: The Presence and Function of Scripture in Galatians 1 and 2. 1998. *Vol. II/102.*
Classen, Carl Joachim: Rhetorical Criticsm of the New Testament. 2000. *Vol. 128.*
Claußen, Carsten (Ed.): see *Frey, Jörg.*
Clivaz, Claire, Andreas Dettwiler, Luc Devillers, Enrico Norelli with *Benjamin Bertho* (Ed.): Infancy Gospels. 2011. *Vol. 281.*
Colpe, Carsten: Griechen – Byzantiner – Semiten – Muslime. 2008. *Vol. 221.*
– Iranier – Aramäer – Hebräer – Hellenen. 2003. *Vol. 154.*
Cook, John G.: Roman Attitudes Towards the Christians. 2010. *Vol. 261.*
Coote, Robert B. (Ed.): see *Weissenrieder, Annette.*
Coppins, Wayne: The Interpretation of Freedom in the Letters of Paul. 2009. *Vol. II/261.*
Crump, David: Jesus the Intercessor. 1992. *Vol. II/49.*
Dahl, Nils Alstrup: Studies in Ephesians. 2000. *Vol. 131.*
Daise, Michael A.: Feasts in John. 2007. *Vol. II/229.*
Deines, Roland: Die Gerechtigkeit der Tora im Reich des Messias. 2004. *Vol. 177.*
– Jüdische Steingefäße und pharisäische Frömmigkeit. 1993. *Vol. II/52.*
– Die Pharisäer. 1997. *Vol. 101.*
Deines, Roland, Jens Herzer and *Karl-Wilhelm Niebuhr* (Ed.): Neues Testament und hellenistisch-jüdische Alltagskultur. III. Internationales Symposium zum Corpus Judaeo-Hellenisticum Novi Testamenti. 21.–24. Mai 2009 in Leipzig. 2011. *Vol. 274.*
– and *Karl-Wilhelm Niebuhr* (Ed.): Philo und das Neue Testament. 2004. *Vol. 172.*
Dennis, John A.: Jesus' Death and the Gathering of True Israel. 2006. *Vol. 217.*

Dettwiler, Andreas and *Jean Zumstein* (Ed.): Kreuzestheologie im Neuen Testament. 2002. *Vol. 151.*
– see *Clivaz, Claire.*
Devillers, Luc: see *Clivaz, Claire.*
Dickson, John P.: Mission-Commitment in Ancient Judaism and in the Pauline Communities. 2003. *Vol. II/159.*
Dietzfelbinger, Christian: Der Abschied des Kommenden. 1997. *Vol. 95.*
Dimitrov, Ivan Z., James D.G. Dunn, Ulrich Luz and *Karl-Wilhelm Niebuhr* (Ed.): Das Alte Testament als christliche Bibel in orthodoxer und westlicher Sicht. 2004. *Vol. 174.*
Dobbeler, Axel von: Glaube als Teilhabe. 1987. *Vol. II/22.*
Docherty, Susan E.: The Use of the Old Testament in Hebrews. 2009. *Vol. II/260.*
Dochhorn, Jan: Schriftgelehrte Prophetie. 2010. *Vol. 268.*
Downs, David J.: The Offering of the Gentiles. 2008. *Vol. II/248.*
Dryden, J. de Waal: Theology and Ethics in 1 Peter. 2006. *Vol. II/209.*
Dübbers, Michael: Christologie und Existenz im Kolosserbrief. 2005. *Vol. II/191.*
Dunn, James D.G.: The New Perspective on Paul. 2005. *Vol. 185.*
Dunn, James D.G. (Ed.): Jews and Christians. 1992. *Vol. 66.*
– Paul and the Mosaic Law. 1996. *Vol. 89.*
– see *Dimitrov, Ivan Z.*
–, *Hans Klein, Ulrich Luz,* and *Vasile Mihoc* (Ed.): Auslegung der Bibel in orthodoxer und westlicher Perspektive. 2000. *Vol. 130.*
Ebel, Eva: Die Attraktivität früher christlicher Gemeinden. 2004. *Vol. II/178.*
Ebertz, Michael N.: Das Charisma des Gekreuzigten. 1987. *Vol. 45.*
Eckstein, Hans-Joachim: Der Begriff Syneidesis bei Paulus. 1983. *Vol. II/10.*
– Verheißung und Gesetz. 1996. *Vol. 86.*
–, *Christoph Landmesser* and *Hermann Lichtenberger* (Ed.): Eschatologie – Eschatology. The Sixth Durham-Tübingen Research Symposium. 2011. *Vol. 272.*
Ego, Beate: Im Himmel wie auf Erden. 1989. *Vol. II/34.*
Ego, Beate, Armin Lange and *Peter Pilhofer* (Ed.): Gemeinde ohne Tempel – Community without Temple. 1999. *Vol. 118.*
– and *Helmut Merkel* (Ed.): Religiöses Lernen in der biblischen, frühjüdischen und frühchristlichen Überlieferung. 2005. *Vol. 180.*
Eisele, Wilfried: Welcher Thomas? 2010. *Vol. 259.*
Eisen, Ute E.: see *Paulsen, Henning.*

Elledge, C.D.: Life after Death in Early Judaism. 2006. *Vol. II/208.*
Ellis, E. Earle: Prophecy and Hermeneutic in Early Christianity. 1978. *Vol. 18.*
– The Old Testament in Early Christianity. 1991. *Vol. 54.*
Elmer, Ian J.: Paul, Jerusalem and the Judaisers. 2009. *Vol. II/258.*
Endo, Masanobu: Creation and Christology. 2002. *Vol. 149.*
Ennulat, Andreas: Die 'Minor Agreements'. 1994. *Vol. II/62.*
Ensor, Peter W.: Jesus and His 'Works'. 1996. *Vol. II/85.*
Eskola, Timo: Messiah and the Throne. 2001. *Vol. II/142.*
– Theodicy and Predestination in Pauline Soteriology. 1998. *Vol. II/100.*
Farelly, Nicolas: The Disciples in the Fourth Gospel. 2010. *Vol. II/290.*
Fatehi, Mehrdad: The Spirit's Relation to the Risen Lord in Paul. 2000. *Vol. II/128.*
Feldmeier, Reinhard: Die Krisis des Gottessohnes. 1987. *Vol. II/21.*
– Die Christen als Fremde. 1992. *Vol. 64.*
Feldmeier, Reinhard and *Ulrich Heckel* (Ed.): Die Heiden. 1994. *Vol. 70.*
Felsch, Dorit: Die Feste im Johannesevangelium. 2011. *Vol. II/308.*
Finnern, Sönke: Narratologie und biblische Exegese. 2010. *Vol. II/285.*
Fletcher-Louis, Crispin H.T.: Luke-Acts: Angels, Christology and Soteriology. 1997. *Vol. II/94.*
Förster, Niclas: Marcus Magus. 1999. *Vol. 114.*
Forbes, Christopher Brian: Prophecy and Inspired Speech in Early Christianity and its Hellenistic Environment. 1995. *Vol. II/75.*
Fornberg, Tord: see *Fridrichsen, Anton.*
Fossum, Jarl E.: The Name of God and the Angel of the Lord. 1985. *Vol. 36.*
Foster, Paul: Community, Law and Mission in Matthew's Gospel. *Vol. II/177.*
Fotopoulos, John: Food Offered to Idols in Roman Corinth. 2003. *Vol. II/151.*
Frank, Nicole: Der Kolosserbrief im Kontext des paulinischen Erbes. 2009. *Vol. II/271.*
Frenschkowski, Marco: Offenbarung und Epiphanie. Vol. 1 1995. *Vol. II/79 –* Vol. 2 1997. *Vol. II/80.*
Frey, Jörg: Eugen Drewermann und die biblische Exegese. 1995. *Vol. II/71.*
– Die johanneische Eschatologie. Vol. I. 1997. *Vol. 96. –* Vol. II. 1998. *Vol. 110. –* Vol. III. 2000. *Vol. 117.*
Frey, Jörg, Carsten Claußen and *Nadine Kessler* (Ed.): Qumran und die Archäologie. 2011. *Vol. 278.*

– and *Cilliers Breytenbach* (Ed.): Aufgabe und Durchführung einer Theologie des Neuen Testaments. 2007. *Vol. 205.*
– *Jens Herzer, Martina Janßen* and *Clare K. Rothschild* (Ed.): Pseudepigraphie und Verfasserfiktion in frühchristlichen Briefen. 2009. *Vol. 246.*
– *Stefan Krauter* and *Hermann Lichtenberger* (Ed.): Heil und Geschichte. 2009. *Vol. 248.*
– and *Udo Schnelle (Ed.):* Kontexte des Johannesevangeliums. 2004. *Vol. 175.*
– and *Jens Schröter* (Ed.): Deutungen des Todes Jesu im Neuen Testament. 2005. *Vol. 181.*
– Jesus in apokryphen Evangelienüberlieferungen. 2010. *Vol. 254.*
–, *Jan G. van der Watt,* and *Ruben Zimmermann* (Ed.): Imagery in the Gospel of John. 2006. *Vol. 200.*
Freyne, Sean: Galilee and Gospel. 2000. *Vol. 125.*
Fridrichsen, Anton: Exegetical Writings. Edited by C.C. Caragounis and T. Fornberg. 1994. *Vol. 76.*
Gadenz, Pablo T.: Called from the Jews and from the Gentiles. 2009. *Vol. II/267.*
Gäbel, Georg: Die Kulttheologie des Hebräerbriefes. 2006. *Vol. II/212.*
Gäckle, Volker: Die Starken und die Schwachen in Korinth und in Rom. 2005. *Vol. 200.*
Garlington, Don B.: 'The Obedience of Faith'. 1991. *Vol. II/38.*
– Faith, Obedience, and Perseverance. 1994. *Vol. 79.*
Garnet, Paul: Salvation and Atonement in the Qumran Scrolls. 1977. *Vol. II/3.*
Gemünden, Petra von (Ed.): see *Weissenrieder, Annette.*
Gese, Michael: Das Vermächtnis des Apostels. 1997. *Vol. II/99.*
Gheorghita, Radu: The Role of the Septuagint in Hebrews. 2003. *Vol. II/160.*
Gordley, Matthew E.: The Colossian Hymn in Context. 2007. *Vol. II/228.*
– Teaching through Song in Antiquity. 2011. *Vol. II/302.*
Gräbe, Petrus J.: The Power of God in Paul's Letters. 2000, ²2008. *Vol. II/123.*
Gräßer, Erich: Der Alte Bund im Neuen. 1985. *Vol. 35.*
– Forschungen zur Apostelgeschichte. 2001. *Vol. 137.*
Grappe, Christian (Ed.): Le Repas de Dieu / Das Mahl Gottes. 2004. *Vol. 169.*
Gray, Timothy C.: The Temple in the Gospel of Mark. 2008. *Vol. II/242.*
Green, Joel B.: The Death of Jesus. 1988. *Vol. II/33.*

Gregg, Brian Han: The Historical Jesus and the Final Judgment Sayings in Q. 2005. *Vol. II/207.*
Gregory, Andrew: The Reception of Luke and Acts in the Period before Irenaeus. 2003. *Vol. II/169.*
Grindheim, Sigurd: The Crux of Election. 2005. *Vol. II/202.*
Gundry, Robert H.: The Old is Better. 2005. *Vol. 178.*
Gundry Volf, Judith M.: Paul and Perseverance. 1990. *Vol. II/37.*
Häußer, Detlef: Christusbekenntnis und Jesusüberlieferung bei Paulus. 2006. *Vol. 210.*
Hafemann, Scott J.: Suffering and the Spirit. 1986. *Vol. II/19.*
– Paul, Moses, and the History of Israel. 1995. *Vol. 81.*
Hahn, Ferdinand: Studien zum Neuen Testament.
 Vol. I: Grundsatzfragen, Jesusforschung, Evangelien. 2006. *Vol. 191.*
 Vol. II: Bekenntnisbildung und Theologie in urchristlicher Zeit. 2006. *Vol. 192.*
Hahn, Johannes (Ed.): Zerstörungen des Jerusalemer Tempels. 2002. *Vol. 147.*
Hamid-Khani, Saeed: Relevation and Concealment of Christ. 2000. *Vol. II/120.*
Hannah, Darrel D.: Michael and Christ. 1999. *Vol. II/109.*
Hardin, Justin K.: Galatians and the Imperial Cult? 2007. *Vol. II/237.*
Harrison, James R.: Paul and the Imperial Authorities at Thessolanica and Rome. 2011. *Vol. 273.*
– Paul's Language of Grace in Its Graeco-Roman Context. 2003. *Vol. II/172.*
Hartman, Lars: Text-Centered New Testament Studies. Ed. von D. Hellholm. 1997. *Vol. 102.*
Hartog, Paul: Polycarp and the New Testament. 2001. *Vol. II/134.*
Hasselbrook, David S.: Studies in New Testament Lexicography. 2011. *Vol. II/303.*
Hays, Christopher M.: Luke's Wealth Ethics. 2010. *Vol. 275.*
Heckel, Theo K.: Der Innere Mensch. 1993. *Vol. II/53.*
– Vom Evangelium des Markus zum viergestaltigen Evangelium. 1999. *Vol. 120.*
Heckel, Ulrich: Kraft in Schwachheit. 1993. *Vol. II/56.*
– Der Segen im Neuen Testament. 2002. *Vol. 150.*
– see *Feldmeier, Reinhard.*
– see *Hengel, Martin.*
Heemstra, Marius: The Fiscus Judaicus and the Parting of the Ways. 2010. *Vol. II/277.*

Heiligenthal, Roman: Werke als Zeichen. 1983. *Vol. II/9.*
Heininger, Bernhard: Die Inkulturation des Christentums. 2010. *Vol. 255.*
Heliso, Desta: Pistis and the Righteous One. 2007. *Vol. II/235.*
Hellholm, D.: see *Hartman, Lars.*
Hemer, Colin J.: The Book of Acts in the Setting of Hellenistic History. 1989. *Vol. 49.*
Henderson, Timothy P.: The Gospel of Peter and Early Christian Apologetics. 2011. *Vol. II/301.*
Hengel, Martin: Jesus und die Evangelien. Kleine Schriften V. 2007. *Vol. 211.*
– Die johanneische Frage. 1993. *Vol. 67.*
– Judaica et Hellenistica. Kleine Schriften I. 1996. *Vol. 90.*
– Judaica, Hellenistica et Christiana. Kleine Schriften II. 1999. *Vol. 109.*
– Judentum und Hellenismus. 1969, ³1988. *Vol. 10.*
– Paulus und Jakobus. Kleine Schriften III. 2002. *Vol. 141.*
– Studien zur Christologie. Kleine Schriften IV. 2006. *Vol. 201.*
– Studien zum Urchristentum. Kleine Schriften VI. 2008. *Vol. 234.*
– Theologische, historische und biographische Skizzen. Kleine Schriften VII. 2010. *Vol. 253.*
– and *Anna Maria Schwemer:* Paulus zwischen Damaskus und Antiochien. 1998. *Vol. 108.*
– Der messianische Anspruch Jesu und die Anfänge der Christologie. 2001. *Vol. 138.*
– Die vier Evangelien und das eine Evangelium von Jesus Christus. 2008. *Vol. 224.*
Hengel, Martin and *Ulrich Heckel* (Ed.): Paulus und das antike Judentum. 1991. *Vol. 58.*
– and *Hermut Löhr* (Ed.): Schriftauslegung im antiken Judentum und im Urchristentum. 1994. *Vol. 73.*
– and *Anna Maria Schwemer* (Ed.): Königsherrschaft Gottes und himmlischer Kult. 1991. *Vol. 55.*
– Die Septuaginta. 1994. *Vol. 72.*
–, *Siegfried Mittmann* and *Anna Maria Schwemer* (Ed.): La Cité de Dieu / Die Stadt Gottes. 2000. *Vol. 129.*
Hentschel, Anni: Diakonia im Neuen Testament. 2007. *Vol. 226.*
Hernández Jr., Juan: Scribal Habits and Theological Influence in the Apocalypse. 2006. *Vol. II/218.*
Herrenbrück, Fritz: Jesus und die Zöllner. 1990. *Vol. II/41.*
Herzer, Jens: Paulus oder Petrus? 1998. *Vol. 103.*

- see *Böttrich, Christfried.*
- see *Deines, Roland.*
- see *Frey, Jörg.*
- Hill, *Charles E.:* From the Lost Teaching of Polycarp. 2005. *Vol. 186.*
- Hoegen-Rohls, *Christina:* Der nachösterliche Johannes. 1996. *Vol. II/84.*
- Hoffmann, *Matthias Reinhard:* The Destroyer and the Lamb. 2005. *Vol. II/203.*
- Hofius, *Otfried:* Katapausis. 1970. *Vol. 11.*
- Der Vorhang vor dem Thron Gottes. 1972. *Vol. 14.*
- Der Christushymnus Philipper 2,6–11. 1976, ²1991. *Vol. 17.*
- Paulusstudien. 1989, ²1994. *Vol. 51.*
- Neutestamentliche Studien. 2000. *Vol. 132.*
- Paulusstudien II. 2002. *Vol. 143.*
- Exegetische Studien. 2008. *Vol. 223.*
- and *Hans-Christian Kammler:* Johannesstudien. 1996. *Vol. 88.*
- Holloway, *Paul A.:* Coping with Prejudice. 2009. *Vol. 244.*
- see *Ahearne-Kroll, Stephen P.*
- Holmberg, *Bengt* (Ed.): Exploring Early Christian Identity. 2008. *Vol. 226.*
- and *Mikael Winninge* (Ed.): Identity Formation in the New Testament. 2008. *Vol. 227.*
- Holtz, *Traugott:* Geschichte und Theologie des Urchristentums. 1991. *Vol. 57.*
- Hommel, *Hildebrecht:* Sebasmata.
  Vol. 1 1983. *Vol. 31.*
  Vol. 2 1984. *Vol. 32.*
- Horbury, *William:* Herodian Judaism and New Testament Study. 2006. *Vol. 193.*
- Horn, *Friedrich Wilhelm* and *Ruben Zimmermann* (Ed.): Jenseits von Indikativ und Imperativ. Vol. 1. 2009. *Vol. 238.*
- Horst, *Pieter W. van der:* Jews and Christians in Their Graeco-Roman Context. 2006. *Vol. 196.*
- Hultgård, *Anders* and *Stig Norin* (Ed): Le Jour de Dieu / Der Tag Gottes. 2009. *Vol. 245.*
- Hume, *Douglas A.:* The Early Christian Community. 2011. *Vol. II/298.*
- Hvalvik, *Reidar:* The Struggle for Scripture and Covenant. 1996. *Vol. II/82.*
- Jackson, *Ryan:* New Creation in Paul's Letters. 2010. *Vol. II/272.*
- Janßen, *Martina:* see *Frey, Jörg.*
- Jauhiainen, *Marko:* The Use of Zechariah in Revelation. 2005. *Vol. II/199.*
- Jensen, *Morten H.:* Herod Antipas in Galilee. 2006; ²2010. *Vol. II/215.*
- Johns, *Loren L.:* The Lamb Christology of the Apocalypse of John. 2003. *Vol. II/167.*
- Jossa, *Giorgio:* Jews or Christians? 2006. *Vol. 202.*

Joubert, *Stephan:* Paul as Benefactor. 2000. *Vol. II/124.*
Judge, *E. A.:* The First Christians in the Roman World. 2008. *Vol. 229.*
- Jerusalem and Athens. 2010. *Vol. 265.*
Jungbauer, *Harry:* „Ehre Vater und Mutter". 2002. *Vol. II/146.*
Kähler, *Christoph:* Jesu Gleichnisse als Poesie und Therapie. 1995. *Vol. 78.*
Kamlah, *Ehrhard:* Die Form der katalogischen Paränese im Neuen Testament. 1964. *Vol. 7.*
Kammler, *Hans-Christian:* Christologie und Eschatologie. 2000. *Vol. 126.*
- Kreuz und Weisheit. 2003. *Vol. 159.*
- see *Hofius, Otfried.*
Karakolis, *Christos:* see *Alexeev, Anatoly A.*
Karrer, *Martin* und *Wolfgang Kraus* (Ed.): Die Septuaginta – Texte, Kontexte, Lebenswelten. 2008. *Vol. 219.*
- see *Kraus, Wolfgang.*
Kelhoffer, *James A.:* The Diet of John the Baptist. 2005. *Vol. 176.*
- Miracle and Mission. 2000. *Vol. II/112.*
- Persecution, Persuasion and Power. 2010. *Vol. 270.*
- see *Ahearne-Kroll, Stephen P.*
Kelley, *Nicole:* Knowledge and Religious Authority in the Pseudo-Clementines. 2006. *Vol. II/213.*
Kennedy, *Joel:* The Recapitulation of Israel. 2008. *Vol. II/257.*
Kensky, *Meira Z.:* Trying Man, Trying God. 2010. *Vol. II/289.*
Kessler, *Nadine* (Ed.): see *Frey, Jörg.*
Kieffer, *René* and *Jan Bergman* (Ed.): La Main de Dieu / Die Hand Gottes. 1997. *Vol. 94.*
Kierspel, *Lars:* The Jews and the World in the Fourth Gospel. 2006. *Vol. 220.*
Kim, *Seyoon:* The Origin of Paul's Gospel. 1981, ²1984. *Vol. II/4.*
- Paul and the New Perspective. 2002. *Vol. 140.*
- "The 'Son of Man'" as the Son of God. 1983. *Vol. 30.*
Klauck, *Hans-Josef:* Religion und Gesellschaft im frühen Christentum. 2003. *Vol. 152.*
Klein, *Hans, Vasile Mihoc* und *Karl-Wilhelm Niebuhr* (Ed.): Das Gebet im Neuen Testament. Vierte, europäische orthodox-westliche Exegetenkonferenz in Sambata de Sus, 4. – 8. August 2007. 2009. Vol. 249.
- see Dunn, James D.G.
Kleinknecht, *Karl Th.:* Der leidende Gerechtfertigte. 1984, ²1988. *Vol. II/13.*
Klinghardt, *Matthias:* Gesetz und Volk Gottes. 1988. *Vol. II/32.*
Kloppenborg, *John S.:* The Tenants in the Vineyard. 2006, student edition 2010. *Vol. 195.*

Koch, Michael: Drachenkampf und Sonnenfrau. 2004. *Vol. II/184.*
Koch, Stefan: Rechtliche Regelung von Konflikten im frühen Christentum. 2004. *Vol. II/174.*
Köhler, Wolf-Dietrich: Rezeption des Matthäusevangeliums in der Zeit vor Irenäus. 1987. *Vol. II/24.*
Köhn, Andreas: Der Neutestamentler Ernst Lohmeyer. 2004. *Vol. II/180.*
Koester, Craig and *Reimund Bieringer* (Ed.): The Resurrection of Jesus in the Gospel of John. 2008. *Vol. 222.*
Konradt, Matthias: Israel, Kirche und die Völker im Matthäusevangelium. 2007. *Vol. 215.*
Kooten, George H. van: Cosmic Christology in Paul and the Pauline School. 2003. *Vol. II/171.*
– Paul's Anthropology in Context. 2008. *Vol. 232.*
Korn, Manfred: Die Geschichte Jesu in veränderter Zeit. 1993. *Vol. II/51.*
Koskenniemi, Erkki: Apollonios von Tyana in der neutestamentlichen Exegese. 1994. *Vol. II/61.*
– The Old Testament Miracle-Workers in Early Judaism. 2005. *Vol. II/206.*
Kraus, Thomas J.: Sprache, Stil und historischer Ort des zweiten Petrusbriefes. 2001. *Vol. II/136.*
Kraus, Wolfgang: Das Volk Gottes. 1996. *Vol. 85.*
– see *Karrer, Martin.*
– see *Walter, Nikolaus.*
– and *Martin Karrer* (Hrsg.): Die Septuaginta – Texte, Theologien, Einflüsse. 2010. *Bd. 252.*
– and *Karl-Wilhelm Niebuhr* (Ed.): Frühjudentum und Neues Testament im Horizont Biblischer Theologie. 2003. *Vol. 162.*
Krauter, Stefan: Studien zu Röm 13,1–7. 2009. *Vol. 243.*
– see *Frey, Jörg.*
Kreplin, Matthias: Das Selbstverständnis Jesu. 2001. *Vol. II/141.*
Kuhn, Karl G.: Achtzehngebet und Vaterunser und der Reim. 1950. *Vol. 1.*
Kvalbein, Hans: see *Ådna, Jostein.*
Kwon, Yon-Gyong: Eschatology in Galatians. 2004. *Vol. II/183.*
Laansma, Jon: I Will Give You Rest. 1997. *Vol. II/98.*
Labahn, Michael: Offenbarung in Zeichen und Wort. 2000. *Vol. II/117.*
Lambers-Petry, Doris: see *Tomson, Peter J.*
Lampe, Peter: Die stadtrömischen Christen in den ersten beiden Jahrhunderten. 1987, ²1989. *Vol. II/18.*

Landmesser, Christof: Wahrheit als Grundbegriff neutestamentlicher Wissenschaft. 1999. *Vol. 113.*
– Jüngerberufung und Zuwendung zu Gott. 2000. *Vol. 133.*
– see *Eckstein, Hans-Joachim.*
Lange, Armin: see *Ego, Beate.*
Lau, Andrew: Manifest in Flesh. 1996. *Vol. II/86.*
Lawrence, Louise: An Ethnography of the Gospel of Matthew. 2003. *Vol. II/165.*
Lee, Aquila H.I.: From Messiah to Preexistent Son. 2005. *Vol. II/192.*
Lee, Pilchan: The New Jerusalem in the Book of Relevation. 2000. *Vol. II/129.*
Lee, Sang M.: The Cosmic Drama of Salvation. 2010. *Vol. II/276.*
Lee, Simon S.: Jesus' Transfiguration and the Believers' Transformation. 2009. *Vol. II/265.*
Lichtenberger, Hermann: Das Ich Adams und das Ich der Menschheit. 2004. *Vol. 164.*
– see *Avemarie, Friedrich.*
– see *Eckstein, Hans-Joachim.*
– see *Frey, Jörg.*
– and *Thomas Scott Caulley* (Ed.): Die Septuaginta und das frühe Christentum – The Septuagint and Christian Origins. 2011. *Vol. 277.*
Lierman, John: The New Testament Moses. 2004. *Vol. II/173.*
– (Ed.): Challenging Perspectives on the Gospel of John. 2006. *Vol. II/219.*
Lieu, Samuel N.C.: Manichaeism in the Later Roman Empire and Medieval China. ²1992. *Vol. 63.*
Lindemann, Andreas: Die Evangelien und die Apostelgeschichte. 2009. *Vol. 241.*
Lincicum, David: Paul and the Early Jewish Encounter with Deuteronomy. 2010. *Vol. II/284.*
Lindgård, Fredrik: Paul's Line of Thought in 2 Corinthians 4:16–5:10. 2004. *Vol. II/189.*
Livesey, Nina E.: Circumcision as a Malleable Symbol. 2010. *Vol. II/295.*
Loader, William R.G.: Jesus' Attitude Towards the Law. 1997. *Vol. II/97.*
Löhr, Gebhard: Verherrlichung Gottes durch Philosophie. 1997. *Vol. 97.*
Löhr, Hermut: Studien zum frühchristlichen und frühjüdischen Gebet. 2003. *Vol. 160.*
– see *Hengel, Martin.*
Löhr, Winrich Alfried: Basilides und seine Schule. 1995. *Vol. 83.*
Lorenzen, Stefanie: Das paulinische Eikon-Konzept. 2008. *Vol. II/250.*
Luomanen, Petri: Entering the Kingdom of Heaven. 1998. *Vol. II/101.*
Luz, Ulrich: see *Alexeev, Anatoly A.*

- see *Dunn, James D.G.*
Mackay, Ian D.: John's Raltionship with Mark. 2004. *Vol. II/182.*
Mackie, Scott D.: Eschatology and Exhortation in the Epistle to the Hebrews. 2006. *Vol. II/223.*
Magda, Ksenija: Paul's Territoriality and Mission Strategy. 2009. *Vol. II/266.*
Maier, Gerhard: Mensch und freier Wille. 1971. *Vol. 12.*
- Die Johannesoffenbarung und die Kirche. 1981. *Vol. 25.*
Markschies, Christoph: Valentinus Gnosticus? 1992. *Vol. 65.*
Marshall, Jonathan: Jesus, Patrons, and Benefactors. 2009. *Vol. II/259.*
Marshall, Peter: Enmity in Corinth: Social Conventions in Paul's Relations with the Corinthians. 1987. *Vol. II/23.*
Martin, Dale B.: see *Zangenberg, Jürgen.*
Maston, Jason: Divine and Human Agency in Second Temple Judaism and Paul. 2010. *Vol. II/297.*
Mayer, Annemarie: Sprache der Einheit im Epheserbrief und in der Ökumene. 2002. *Vol. II/150.*
Mayordomo, Moisés: Argumentiert Paulus logisch? 2005. *Vol. 188.*
McDonough, Sean M.: YHWH at Patmos: Rev. 1:4 in its Hellenistic and Early Jewish Setting. 1999. *Vol. II/107.*
McDowell, Markus: Prayers of Jewish Women. 2006. *Vol. II/211.*
McGlynn, Moyna: Divine Judgement and Divine Benevolence in the Book of Wisdom. 2001. *Vol. II/139.*
McNamara, Martin: Targum and New Testament. 2011. *Vol. 279.*
Meade, David G.: Pseudonymity and Canon. 1986. *Vol. 39.*
Meadors, Edward P.: Jesus the Messianic Herald of Salvation. 1995. *Vol. II/72.*
Meißner, Stefan: Die Heimholung des Ketzers. 1996. *Vol. II/87.*
Mell, Ulrich: Die „anderen" Winzer. 1994. *Vol. 77.*
- see *Sänger, Dieter.*
Mengel, Berthold: Studien zum Philipperbrief. 1982. *Vol. II/8.*
Merkel, Helmut: Die Widersprüche zwischen den Evangelien. 1971. *Vol. 13.*
- see *Ego, Beate.*
Merklein, Helmut: Studien zu Jesus und Paulus. Vol. 1 1987. *Vol. 43.* - Vol. 2 1998. *Vol. 105.*
Merkt, Andreas: see *Nicklas, Tobias*
Metzdorf, Christina: Die Tempelaktion Jesu. 2003. *Vol. II/168.*

Metzler, Karin: Der griechische Begriff des Verzeihens. 1991. *Vol. II/44.*
Metzner, Rainer: Die Rezeption des Matthäusevangeliums im 1. Petrusbrief. 1995. *Vol. II/74.*
- Das Verständnis der Sünde im Johannesevangelium. 2000. *Vol. 122.*
Mihoc, Vasile: see *Dunn, James D.G.*
- see *Klein, Hans.*
Mineshige, Kiyoshi: Besitzverzicht und Almosen bei Lukas. 2003. *Vol. II/163.*
Mittmann, Siegfried: see *Hengel, Martin.*
Mittmann-Richert, Ulrike: Magnifikat und Benediktus. *1996. Vol. II/90.*
- Der Sühnetod des Gottesknechts. 2008. *Vol. 220.*
Miura, Yuzuru: David in Luke-Acts. 2007. *Vol. II/232.*
Moll, Sebastian: The Arch-Heretic Marcion. 2010. *Vol. 250.*
Morales, Rodrigo J.: The Spirit and the Restorat. 2010. *Vol. 282.*
Mournet, Terence C.: Oral Tradition and Literary Dependency. 2005. *Vol. II/195.*
Mußner, Franz: Jesus von Nazareth im Umfeld Israels und der Urkirche. Ed. von M. Theobald. 1998. *Vol. 111.*
Mutschler, Bernhard: Das Corpus Johanneum bei Irenäus von Lyon. 2005. *Vol. 189.*
- Glaube in den Pastoralbriefen. 2010. *Vol. 256.*
Myers, Susan E.: Spirit Epicleses in the Acts of Thomas. 2010. *Vol. 281.*
Nguyen, V. Henry T.: Christian Identity in Corinth. 2008. *Vol. II/243.*
Nicklas, Tobias, Andreas Merkt und *Joseph Verheyden* (Ed.): Gelitten – Gestorben – Auferstanden. 2010. *Vol. II/273.*
- see *Verheyden, Joseph*
Niebuhr, Karl-Wilhelm: Gesetz and Paränese. 1987. *Vol. II/28.*
- Heidenapostel aus Israel. 1992. *Vol. 62.*
- see *Deines, Roland.*
- see *Dimitrov, Ivan Z.*
- see *Klein, Hans.*
- see *Kraus, Wolfgang.*
Nielsen, Anders E.: "Until it is Fullfilled". 2000. *Vol. II/126.*
Nielsen, Jesper Tang: Die kognitive Dimension des Kreuzes. 2009. *Vol. II/263.*
Nissen, Andreas: Gott und der Nächste im antiken Judentum. 1974. *Vol. 15.*
Noack, Christian: Gottesbewußtsein. 2000. *Vol. II/116.*
Noormann, Rolf: Irenäus als Paulusinterpret. 1994. *Vol. II/66.*
Norelli, Enrico: see *Clivaz, Claire.*
Norin, Stig: see *Hultgård, Anders.*

Novakovic, Lidija: Messiah, the Healer of the Sick. 2003. *Vol. II/170.*
Obermann, Andreas: Die christologische Erfüllung der Schrift im Johannesevangelium. 1996. *Vol. II/83.*
Öhler, Markus: Barnabas. 2003. *Vol. 156.*
– see *Becker, Michael.*
– (Ed.): Aposteldekret und antikes Vereinswesen. 2011. *Vol. 280.*
Okure, Teresa: The Johannine Approach to Mission. 1988. *Vol. II/31.*
Onuki, Takashi: Heil und Erlösung. 2004. *Vol. 165.*
Oropeza, B. J.: Paul and Apostasy. 2000. *Vol. II/115.*
Ostmeyer, Karl-Heinrich: Kommunikation mit Gott und Christus. 2006. *Vol. 197.*
– Taufe und Typos. 2000. *Vol. II/118.*
Pao, David W.: Acts and the Isaianic New Exodus. 2000. *Vol. II/130.*
Park, Eung Chun: The Mission Discourse in Matthew's Interpretation. 1995. *Vol. II/81.*
Park, Joseph S.: Conceptions of Afterlife in Jewish Insriptions. 2000. *Vol. II/121.*
Parsenios, George L.: Rhetoric and Drama in the Johannine Lawsuit Motif. 2010. *Vol. 258.*
Pate, C. Marvin: The Reverse of the Curse. 2000. *Vol. II/114.*
Paulsen, Henning: Studien zur Literatur und Geschichte des frühen Christentums. Ed. von Ute E. Eisen. 1997. *Vol. 99.*
Pearce, Sarah J.K.: The Land of the Body. 2007. *Vol. 208.*
Peres, Imre: Griechische Grabinschriften und neutestamentliche Eschatologie. 2003. *Vol. 157.*
Perry, Peter S.: The Rhetoric of Digressions. 2009. *Vol. II/268.*
Pierce, Chad T.: Spirits and the Proclamation of Christ. 2011. *Vol. II/305.*
Philip, Finny: The Origins of Pauline Pneumatology. 2005. *Vol. II/194.*
Philonenko, Marc (Ed.): Le Trône de Dieu. 1993. *Vol. 69.*
Pilhofer, Peter: Presbyteron Kreitton. 1990. *Vol. II/39.*
– Philippi. Vol. 1 1995. *Vol. 87.* – Vol. 2 ²2009. *Vol. 119.*
– Die frühen Christen und ihre Welt. 2002. *Vol. 145.*
– see *Becker, Eve-Marie.*
– see *Ego, Beate.*
Pitre, Brant: Jesus, the Tribulation, and the End of the Exile. 2005. *Vol. II/204.*
Plümacher, Eckhard: Geschichte und Geschichten. 2004. *Vol. 170.*

Pöhlmann, Wolfgang: Der Verlorene Sohn und das Haus. 1993. *Vol. 68.*
Poirier, John C.: The Tongues of Angels. 2010. *Vol. II/287.*
Pokorný, Petr and *Josef B. Souček:* Bibelauslegung als Theologie. 1997. *Vol. 100.*
– and *Jan Roskovec* (Ed.): Philosophical Hermeneutics and Biblical Exegesis. 2002. *Vol. 153.*
Popkes, Enno Edzard: Das Menschenbild des Thomasevangeliums. 2007. *Vol. 206.*
– Die Theologie der Liebe Gottes in den johanneischen Schriften. 2005. *Vol. II/197.*
Porter, Stanley E.: The Paul of Acts. 1999. *Vol. 115.*
Prieur, Alexander: Die Verkündigung der Gottesherrschaft. 1996. *Vol. II/89.*
Probst, Hermann: Paulus und der Brief. 1991. *Vol. II/45.*
Puig i Tàrrech, Armand: Jesus: An Uncommon Journey. 2010. *Vol. II/288.*
Rabens, Volker: The Holy Spirit and Ethics in Paul. 2010. *Vol. II/283.*
Räisänen, Heikki: Paul and the Law. 1983, ²1987. *Vol. 29.*
Rehkopf, Friedrich: Die lukanische Sonderquelle. 1959. *Vol. 5.*
Rein, Matthias: Die Heilung des Blindgeborenen (Joh 9). 1995. *Vol. II/73.*
Reinmuth, Eckart: Pseudo-Philo und Lukas. 1994. *Vol. 74.*
Reiser, Marius: Bibelkritik und Auslegung der Heiligen Schrift. 2007. *Vol. 217.*
– Syntax und Stil des Markusevangeliums. 1984. *Vol. II/11.*
Reynolds, Benjamin E.: The Apocalyptic Son of Man in the Gospel of John. 2008. *Vol. II/249.*
Rhodes, James N.: The Epistle of Barnabas and the Deuteronomic Tradition. 2004. *Vol. II/188.*
Richards, E. Randolph: The Secretary in the Letters of Paul. 1991. *Vol. II/42.*
Riesner, Rainer: Jesus als Lehrer. 1981, ³1988. *Vol. II/7.*
– Die Frühzeit des Apostels Paulus. 1994. *Vol. 71.*
Rissi, Mathias: Die Theologie des Hebräerbriefs. 1987. *Vol. 41.*
Röcker, Fritz W.: Belial und Katechon. 2009. *Vol. II/262.*
Röhser, Günter: Metaphorik und Personifikation der Sünde. 1987. *Vol. II/25.*
Rose, Christian: Theologie als Erzählung im Markusevangelium. 2007. *Vol. II/236.*
– Die Wolke der Zeugen. 1994. *Vol. II/60.*
Roskovec, Jan: see *Pokorný, Petr.*
Rothschild, Clare K.: Baptist Traditions and Q. 2005. *Vol. 190.*

- Hebrews as Pseudepigraphon. 2009. *Vol. 235.*
- Luke Acts and the Rhetoric of History. 2004. *Vol. II/175.*
- see *Frey, Jörg.*

Rudolph, David J.: A Jew to the Jews. 2011. *Vol. II/304.*

Rüegger, Hans-Ulrich: Verstehen, was Markus erzählt. 2002. *Vol. II/155.*

Rüger, Hans Peter: Die Weisheitsschrift aus der Kairoer Geniza. 1991. *Vol. 53.*

Ruf, Martin G.: Die heiligen Propheten, eure Apostel und ich. 2011. *Vol. II/300.*

Runesson, Anders: see *Becker, Eve-Marie.*

Sänger, Dieter: Antikes Judentum und die Mysterien. 1980. *Vol. II/5.*
- Die Verkündigung des Gekreuzigten und Israel. 1994. *Vol. 75.*
- see *Burchard, Christoph*
- and *Ulrich Mell* (Ed.): Paulus und Johannes. 2006. *Vol. 198.*

Salier, Willis Hedley: The Rhetorical Impact of the Semeia in the Gospel of John. 2004. *Vol. II/186.*

Salzmann, Jörg Christian: Lehren und Ermahnen. 1994. *Vol. II/59.*

Samuelsson, Gunnar: Crucifixion in Antiquity. 2011. *Vol. II/310.*

Sandnes, Karl Olav: Paul – One of the Prophets? 1991. *Vol. II/43.*

Sato, Migaku: Q und Prophetie. 1988. *Vol. II/29.*

Schäfer, Ruth: Paulus bis zum Apostelkonzil. 2004. *Vol. II/179.*

Schaper, Joachim: Eschatology in the Greek Psalter. 1995. *Vol. II/76.*

Schimanowski, Gottfried: Die himmlische Liturgie in der Apokalypse des Johannes. 2002. *Vol. II/154.*
- Weisheit und Messias. 1985. *Vol. II/17.*

Schlichting, Günter: Ein jüdisches Leben Jesu. 1982. *Vol. 24.*

Schließer, Benjamin: Abraham's Faith in Romans 4. 2007. *Vol. II/224.*

Schnabel, Eckhard J.: Law and Wisdom from Ben Sira to Paul. 1985. *Vol. II/16.*

Schnelle, Udo: see *Frey, Jörg.*

Schröter, Jens: Von Jesus zum Neuen Testament. 2007. *Vol. 204.*
- see *Frey, Jörg.*

Schutter, William L.: Hermeneutic and Composition in I Peter. 1989. *Vol. II/30.*

Schwartz, Daniel R.: Studies in the Jewish Background of Christianity. 1992. *Vol. 60.*

Schwemer, Anna Maria: see *Hengel, Martin*

Scott, Ian W.: Implicit Epistemology in the Letters of Paul. 2005. *Vol. II/205.*

Scott, James M.: Adoption as Sons of God. 1992. *Vol. II/48.*

- Paul and the Nations. 1995. *Vol. 84.*

Shi, Wenhua: Paul's Message of the Cross as Body Language. 2008. *Vol. II/254.*

Shum, Shiu-Lun: Paul's Use of Isaiah in Romans. 2002. *Vol. II/156.*

Siegert, Folker: Drei hellenistisch-jüdische Predigten. Teil I 1980. *Vol. 20* – Teil II 1992. *Vol. 61.*
- Nag-Hammadi-Register. 1982. *Vol. 26.*
- Argumentation bei Paulus. 1985. *Vol. 34.*
- Philon von Alexandrien. 1988. *Vol. 46.*

Siggelkow-Berner, Birke: Die jüdischen Feste im Bellum Judaicum des Flavius Josephus. 2011. *Vol. II/306.*

Simon, Marcel: Le christianisme antique et son contexte religieux I/II. 1981. *Vol. 23.*

Smit, Peter-Ben: Fellowship and Food in the Kingdom. 2008. *Vol. II/234.*

Smith, Julien: Christ the Ideal King. 2011. *Vol. II/313.*

Snodgrass, Klyne: The Parable of the Wicked Tenants. 1983. *Vol. 27.*

Söding, Thomas: Das Wort vom Kreuz. 1997. *Vol. 93.*
- see *Thüsing, Wilhelm.*

Sommer, Urs: Die Passionsgeschichte des Markusevangeliums. 1993. *Vol. II/58.*

Sorensen, Eric: Possession and Exorcism in the New Testament and Early Christianity. 2002. *Vol. II/157.*

Souček, Josef B.: see *Pokorný, Petr.*

Southall, David J.: Rediscovering Righteousness in Romans. 2008. *Vol. 240.*

Spangenberg, Volker: Herrlichkeit des Neuen Bundes. 1993. *Vol. II/55.*

Spanje, T.E. van: Inconsistency in Paul? 1999. *Vol. II/110.*

Speyer, Wolfgang: Frühes Christentum im antiken Strahlungsfeld. Vol. I: 1989. *Vol. 50.*
- Vol. II: 1999. *Vol. 116.*
- Vol. III: 2007. *Vol. 213.*

Spittler, Janet E.: Animals in the Apocryphal Acts of the Apostles. 2008. *Vol. II/247.*

Sprinkle, Preston: Law and Life. 2008. *Vol. II/241.*

Stadelmann, Helge: Ben Sira als Schriftgelehrter. 1980. *Vol. II/6.*

Stein, Hans Joachim: Frühchristliche Mahlfeiern. 2008. *Vol. II/255.*

Stenschke, Christoph W.: Luke's Portrait of Gentiles Prior to Their Coming to Faith. *Vol. II/108.*

Stephens, Mark B.: Annihilation or Renewal? 2011. *Vol. II/307.*

Sterck-Degueldre, Jean-Pierre: Eine Frau namens Lydia. 2004. *Vol. II/176.*

Stettler, Christian: Der Kolosserhymnus. 2000. *Vol. II/131.*

- Das letzte Gericht. 2011. *Vol. II/299.*
Stettler, Hanna: Die Christologie der Pastoralbriefe. 1998. *Vol. II/105.*
Stökl Ben Ezra, Daniel: The Impact of Yom Kippur on Early Christianity. 2003. *Vol. 163.*
Strobel, August: Die Stunde der Wahrheit. 1980. *Vol. 21.*
Stroumsa, Guy G.: Barbarian Philosophy. 1999. *Vol. 112.*
Stuckenbruck, Loren T.: Angel Veneration and Christology. 1995. *Vol. II/70.*
-, *Stephen C. Barton* and *Benjamin G. Wold* (Ed.): Memory in the Bible and Antiquity. 2007. *Vol. 212.*
Stuhlmacher, Peter (Ed.): Das Evangelium und die Evangelien. 1983. *Vol. 28.*
- Biblische Theologie und Evangelium. 2002. *Vol. 146.*
Sung, Chong-Hyon: Vergebung der Sünden. 1993. *Vol. II/57.*
Svendsen, Stefan N.: Allegory Transformed. 2009. *Vol. II/269.*
Tajra, Harry W.: The Trial of St. Paul. 1989. *Vol. II/35.*
- The Martyrdom of St.Paul. 1994. *Vol. II/67.*
Tellbe, Mikael: Christ-Believers in Ephesus. 2009. *Vol. 242.*
Theißen, Gerd: Studien zur Soziologie des Urchristentums. 1979, ³1989. *Vol. 19.*
Theobald, Michael: Studien zum Corpus Iohanneum. 2010. *Vol. 267.*
- Studien zum Römerbrief. 2001. *Vol. 136.*
- see *Mußner, Franz.*
Thornton, Claus-Jürgen: Der Zeuge des Zeugen. 1991. *Vol. 56.*
Thüsing, Wilhelm: Studien zur neutestamentlichen Theologie. Ed. von Thomas Söding. 1995. *Vol. 82.*
Thurén, Lauri: Derhethorizing Paul. 2000. *Vol. 124.*
Thyen, Hartwig: Studien zum Corpus Iohanneum. 2007. *Vol. 214.*
Tibbs, Clint: Religious Experience of the Pneuma. 2007. *Vol. II/230.*
Toit, David S. du: Theios Anthropos. 1997. *Vol. II/91.*
Tolmie, D. Francois: Persuading the Galatians. 2005. *Vol. II/190.*
Tomson, Peter J. and *Doris Lambers-Petry* (Ed.): The Image of the Judaeo-Christians in Ancient Jewish and Christian Literature. 2003. *Vol. 158.*
Toney, Carl N.: Paul's Inclusive Ethic. 2008. *Vol. II/252.*
Trebilco, Paul: The Early Christians in Ephesus from Paul to Ignatius. 2004. *Vol. 166.*
Treloar, Geoffrey R.: Lightfoot the Historian. 1998. *Vol. II/103.*

Troftgruben, Troy M.: A Conclusion Unhindered. 2010. *Vol. II/280.*
Tso, Marcus K.M.: Ethics in the Qumran Community. 2010. *Vol. II/292.*
Tsuji, Manabu: Glaube zwischen Vollkommenheit und Verweltlichung. 1997. *Vol. II/93.*
Twelftree, Graham H.: Jesus the Exorcist. 1993. *Vol. II/54.*
Ulrichs, Karl Friedrich: Christusglaube. 2007. *Vol. II/227.*
Urban, Christina: Das Menschenbild nach dem Johannesevangelium. 2001. *Vol. II/137.*
Vahrenhorst, Martin: Kultische Sprache in den Paulusbriefen. 2008. *Vol. 230.*
Vegge, Ivar: 2 Corinthians – a Letter about Reconciliation. 2008. *Vol. II/239.*
Verheyden, Joseph, Korinna Zamfir and *Tobias Nicklas* (Ed.): Prophets and Prophecy in Jewish and Early Christian Literature. 2010. *Vol. II/286.*
- see *Nicklas, Tobias*
Visotzky, Burton L.: Fathers of the World. 1995. *Vol. 80.*
Vollenweider, Samuel: Horizonte neutestamentlicher Christologie. 2002. *Vol. 144.*
Vos, Johan S.: Die Kunst der Argumentation bei Paulus. 2002. *Vol. 149.*
Waaler, Erik: The *Shema* and The First Commandment in First Corinthians. 2008. *Vol. II/253.*
Wagener, Ulrike: Die Ordnung des „Hauses Gottes". 1994. *Vol. II/65.*
Wagner, J. Ross: see *Wilk, Florian.*
Wahlen, Clinton: Jesus and the Impurity of Spirits in the Synoptic Gospels. 2004. *Vol. II/185.*
Walker, Donald D.: Paul's Offer of Leniency (2 Cor 10:1). 2002. *Vol. II/152.*
Walter, Nikolaus: Praeparatio Evangelica. Ed. von Wolfgang Kraus und Florian Wilk. 1997. *Vol. 98.*
Wander, Bernd: Gottesfürchtige und Sympathisanten. 1998. *Vol. 104.*
Wardle, Timothy: The Jerusalem Temple and Early Christian Identity. 2010. *Vol. II/291.*
Wasserman, Emma: The Death of the Soul in Romans 7. 2008. *Vol. 256.*
Waters, Guy: The End of Deuteronomy in the Epistles of Paul. 2006. *Vol. 221.*
Watt, Jan G. van der (Ed.): Eschatology of the New Testament and Some Related Documents. 2011. *Vol. II/315.*
- see *Frey, Jörg*
- see *Zimmermann, Ruben*
Watts, Rikki: Isaiah's New Exodus and Mark. 1997. *Vol. II/88.*
Webb, Robert L.: see *Bock, Darrell L.*

Wedderburn, Alexander J.M.: Baptism and Resurrection. 1987. *Vol. 44.*
– Jesus and the Historians. 2010. *Vol. 269.*
Wegner, Uwe: Der Hauptmann von Kafarnaum. 1985. *Vol. II/14.*
Weiß, Hans-Friedrich: Frühes Christentum und Gnosis. 2008. *Vol. 225.*
Weissenrieder, Annette: Images of Illness in the Gospel of Luke. 2003. Vol. II/164.
–, and *Robert B. Coote* (Ed.): The Interface of Orality and Writing. 2010. *Vol. 260.*
–, *Friederike Wendt* and *Petra von Gemünden* (Ed.): Picturing the New Testament. 2005. *Vol. II/193.*
Welck, Christian: Erzählte ‚Zeichen'. 1994. *Vol. II/69.*
Wendt, Friederike (Ed.): see *Weissenrieder, Annette.*
Wiarda, Timothy: Peter in the Gospels. 2000. *Vol. II/127.*
Wifstrand, Albert: Epochs and Styles. 2005. *Vol. 179.*
Wilk, Florian and *J. Ross Wagner* (Ed.): Between Gospel and Election. 2010. *Vol. 257.*
– see *Walter, Nikolaus.*
Williams, Catrin H.: I am He. 2000. *Vol. II/113.*
Wilson, Todd A.: The Curse of the Law and the Crisis in Galatia. 2007. *Vol. II/225.*
Wilson, Walter T.: Love without Pretense. 1991. *Vol. II/46.*
Winn, Adam: The Purpose of Mark's Gospel. 2008. *Vol. II/245.*
Winninge, Mikael: see *Holmberg, Bengt.*
Wischmeyer, Oda: Von Ben Sira zu Paulus. 2004. *Vol. 173.*
Wisdom, Jeffrey: Blessing for the Nations and the Curse of the Law. 2001. *Vol. II/133.*
Witmer, Stephen E.: Divine Instruction in Early Christianity. 2008. *Vol. II/246.*
Wold, Benjamin G.: Women, Men, and Angels. 2005. *Vol. II/2001.*

Wolter, Michael: Theologie und Ethos im frühen Christentum. 2009. *Vol. 236.*
– see *Stuckenbruck, Loren T.*
Wright, Archie T.: The Origin of Evil Spirits. 2005. *Vol. II/198.*
Wucherpfennig, Ansgar: Heracleon Philologus. 2002. *Vol. 142.*
Yates, John W.: The Spirit and Creation in Paul. 2008. *Vol. II/251.*
Yeung, Maureen: Faith in Jesus and Paul. 2002. *Vol. II/147.*
Young, Stephen E.: Jesus Tradition in the Apostolic Fathers. 2011. *Vol. II/311.*
Zamfir, Corinna: see *Verheyden, Joseph*
Zangenberg, Jürgen, Harold W. Attridge and *Dale B. Martin* (Ed.): Religion, Ethnicity and Identity in Ancient Galilee. 2007. *Vol. 210.*
Zimmermann, Alfred E.: Die urchristlichen Lehrer. 1984, ²1988. *Vol. II/12.*
Zimmermann, Johannes: Messianische Texte aus Qumran. 1998. *Vol. II/104.*
Zimmermann, Ruben: Christologie der Bilder im Johannesevangelium. 2004. *Vol. 171.*
– Geschlechtermetaphorik und Gottesverhältnis. 2001. *Vol. II/122.*
– (Ed.): Hermeneutik der Gleichnisse Jesu. 2008. *Vol. 231.*
– and *Jan G. van der Watt* (Ed.): Moral Language in the New Testament. Vol. II. 2010. *Vol. II/296.*
– see *Frey, Jörg.*
– see *Horn, Friedrich Wilhelm.*
Zugmann, Michael: „Hellenisten" in der Apostelgeschichte. 2009. *Vol. II/264.*
Zumstein, Jean: see *Dettwiler, Andreas*
Zwiep, Arie W.: Christ, the Spirit and the Community of God. 2010. *Vol. II/293.*
– Judas and the Choice of Matthias. 2004. *Vol. II/187.*